THE SONG OF ROLAND

I. Introduction and Commentary

Published in 1978

in commemoration of the

twelfth centenary

of the Battle of Roncevaux

THE SONG OF ROLAND

AN ANALYTICAL EDITION

I. Introduction and Commentary

Gerard J. Brault

THE PENNSYLVANIA STATE UNIVERSITY PRESS

UNIVERSITY PARK AND LONDON

Library of Congress Cataloging in Publication Data

Chanson de Roland. English & Old French.
The Song of Roland.

Bibliography: v. 1.
Contents: v. 1. Introduction and commentary.—
v. 2. Oxford text and English translation.
Includes index.
1. Roland—Romances. I. Brault, Gerard J.
PQ1521.E5B7 1978 841'.1 77-22946

ISBN: 9780271024554

Designed by Glenn Ruby

Printed in the United States of America

Second printing, 1981

UXORI CARISSIMAE

Contents

Volume I. Introduction and Commentary

Volume II. Oxford Text and English Translation

Acknowledgments

It is a pleasure for me to thank those who have assisted me in various ways *set anz tuz pleins.*

I am grateful to my students for listening to my ideas about the *Song of Roland* and for giving me the benefit of their reactions. In the preliminary phase of this project, three of them, John H. D'Espinosa, Joseph M. Hovanyecz, and Phyllis Brooks Stouffer, helped me with bibliography and with the collation of key editions.

I wish to thank the American Philosophical Society for awarding me a grant in 1966 which enabled me to make excellent headway that year. I spent the academic year 1968–69 in Strasbourg, France, as a Guggenheim Fellow and Fulbright-Hays Research Scholar, independently studying mostly Romanesque iconography. The approach in the present work is in a large measure the result of that educational experience. In 1973, thanks to a travel grant from the American Council of Learned Societies and to a supplementary allocation from Penn State's Central Fund for Research, I was able to pursue my study of Romanesque art in Auvergne, Burgundy, and Provence.

During the winter of 1974, Jan Van der Meulen, now Chairman of the Department of Art at Cleveland State University, agreed to teach a course with me entitled "Artist and Poet in the Twelfth Century" as part of the Interdisciplinary Graduate Program in the Humanities sponsored by a grant from the National Endowment for the Humanities. This seminar centered on the *Song of Roland*, and I am indebted to my former colleague for his encouragement on this occasion.

Several other persons helped make these volumes a reality. Richard L. Frautschi, Head of the Department of French, supported my requests for research funds, and Thomas F. Magner, Associate Dean for Research and Graduate Study, acted favorably upon them. Stanley Weintraub, Director of the Institute for the Arts and Humanistic Studies and a force promoting scholarship at Penn State, backed this project at crucial junctures and repeatedly acted in my interests. The manuscript was typed by Mae Smith.

Alice Colby-Hall of Cornell University, Wilbur M. Frohock of

Harvard University, and William Roach of the University of Pennsylvania kindly agreed to look at my typescript critically. Each offered valuable suggestions, and I am grateful for their advice and insights. However, any flaws this work may have are entirely due to me.

Publication of this book was made possible by a grant approved by Stanley F. Paulson, Dean of the College of Liberal Arts. I am pleased to acknowledge his help in financing the cost of this undertaking. I also wish to thank Chris W. Kentera, Director of The Pennsylvania State University Press, for his assistance in this and other respects.

Finally, I should like to express my gratitude to my wife, Jeanne, and to my children, Frank, Anne Marie, and Sue, who rejoiced with me when this book was going well and did much to sustain me when it was not.

Foreword

Feudalism offered solutions to certain problems of daily living, but its values at times came into conflict with the Christian ethos. More than any other work perhaps, the *Song of Roland* exemplifies this deep-seated opposition of the Middle Ages.

Most commentators recognize that this discontinuity plays a prominent part in Turoldus's epic. Nevertheless they have dwelt almost exclusively on human factors, in particular on the clash of interests: Roland against Ganelon, Oliver against Roland, Charlemagne against Ganelon. Also, scholars, even those who maintain that the *Song of Roland* is profoundly Christian, generally consider that there is a dark side to Roland's personality.

The chief contention here is that these interpretations fail to do justice to the poem's religious dimension or misconstrue its techniques of character portrayal. Roland has no fault or flaw and makes no mistake.

Turoldus's conception of the hero may not be to our liking, but to understand it is to gain valuable insight into the mind of the Middle Ages. The poet viewed the world in unrelieved black and white.

* * *

The *Song of Roland* survives in several versions, but it is universally acknowledged as one of the greatest masterpieces of Western literature because of the remarkable text preserved in a manuscript in the Bodleian Library at Oxford.

The serious student usually begins by consulting the editions of Bédier and Jenkins. However, a half century has elapsed since these monumental works first appeared, and numerous contributions since then have increased our knowledge of the poem. Scholars of Old French have, for the most part, remained faithful to the historical and philological concerns in vogue at the turn of the century and have tended to neglect literary analysis. The problems that continue to engross specialists are worthy of renewed investigation, but a large part of the *Song of Roland* is without fresh elucidation. Segre's magisterial edition provides a thorough review of the many technical questions regarding the establishment of the text, but it is not concerned with literary matters.

This edition has two main objectives: It takes into account the many studies that have been published since Bédier and Jenkins, but, above all, it endeavors, for the first time, to provide a systematic literary analysis of the entire poem. The method of analysis utilized here is eclectic, but it may be said to combine thematic criticism with philology, and exegetical interpretation with iconography.

The Introduction is a preliminary discourse, not a summary, but some anticipation of the Commentary is involved. The laisse-by-laisse Commentary is divided into forty-nine analytical units, an arrangement prompted by convenience more than by structural considerations. All translations of the *Song of Roland* involve a certain amount of conjecture and interpretation. Justification for these and for novel renderings is provided either in the Commentary or in the Notes. In Volume II, the Notes to the Manuscript explain the few changes introduced into the text. The Notes to the Oxford Text, English Translation are concerned with variant readings and with the meaning of words and phrases. No glossary or table of proper names is appended because this information is readily available in Bédier's *Commentaires* and in Jenkins's edition.

This book is chiefly intended for medievalists. However, it is hoped that it will also be of use to others who seek a better understanding of the Middle Ages.

Abbreviations and Frequently Cited Works

Bédier	*La Chanson de Roland,* publiée d'après le manuscrit d'Oxford et traduite par J. Bédier. Paris: Piazza, 1921. Glossary and Index of Proper Names by Lucien Foulet (= Foulet, *Glossaire*) in Bédier, *Commentaires.* The "édition définitive" (1937) has often been reissued.
Bédier, *Commentaires*	*La Chanson de Roland commentée* par Joseph Bédier. 1927; rpt. Paris: Piazza, 1968.
Blaise	Blaise, Albert. *Le Vocabulaire latin des principaux thèmes liturgiques.* Turnhout: Brepols, 1966.
Châteauroux	See Mortier.
CL	Classical Latin.
Conrad	*Das Rolandslied des Pfaffen Konrad.* Ed. Carl Wesle. 2d ed. Altdeutsche Textbibliothek 69. Tübingen: Niemeyer, 1967. For Modern French translation, see Mortier.
Curtius	Ernst Robert Curtius. *La Littérature européenne et le moyen âge latin.* 2d ed. Trans. Jean Bréjoux. Paris: Presses Universitaires de France, 1956.
d.	died.
E.	English.
FEW	Wartburg, Walther von. *Französisches etymologisches Wörterbuch.* Basel, Bonn, Leipzig, Tübingen, 1922– . In progress (22 vols; 2d ed. of vol. 1 [1922–28] numbered vols. 24 and 25).
Foulet, *Glossaire*	See Bédier.
Fr.	French.
Ger.	Germanic.

Godefroy	Godefroy, Frédéric. *Dictionnaire de l'ancienne langue française et de tous ses dialectes, du IXe au XVe siècle.* 10 vols. 1881–1902; rpt. Paris: Librairie des sciences et des arts, 1937–38.
Gr.	Greek.
Greimas	Greimas, A. J. *Dictionnaire de l'ancien français jusqu'au milieu du XIVe siècle.* Paris: Larousse, 1969.
Harrison	*The Song of Roland.* Newly translated and with an Introduction by Robert Harrison. Mentor Book. New York and Toronto: New American Library; London: New English Library, 1970.
Heb.	Hebrew.
Horrent	Horrent, Jules. *La Chanson de Roland dans les littératures française et espagnole au moyen âge.* Bibliothèque de la Faculté de philosophie et lettres de l'Université de Liège 120. Paris: Les Belles Lettres, 1951.
Jenkins	*La Chanson de Roland: Oxford Version.* Edition, Notes and Glossary by T. Atkinson Jenkins. Rev. ed. Heath's Modern Language Series. Boston – New York – Chicago – London: Heath, 1929.
Jones	Jones, George Fenwick. *The Ethos of the Song of Roland.* Baltimore: Johns Hopkins Press, 1963.
Lat.	Latin.
Le Gentil	Pierre Le Gentil. *La Chanson de Roland.* Connaissance des lettres 43. Paris: Hatier-Boivin, 1955.
Lejeune and Stiennon	Lejeune, Rita, and Jacques Stiennon. *La Légende de Roland dans l'art du moyen âge.* 2d ed. 2 vols. Brussels: Arcade, 1967.
Lyon	See Mortier.
ME.	Middle English.
Menéndez Pidal	Ramón Menéndez Pidal. *La Chanson de Roland et la tradition épique des Francs.* Trans. Irénée-Marcel Cluzel. 2d ed. Paris: Picard, 1960.

Meredith-Jones	*Historia Karoli Magni et Rotholandi ou Chronique du Pseudo-Turpin.* Textes revus et publiés d'après 49 manuscrits. Ed. C. Meredith-Jones. 1936; rpt. Geneva: Slatkine, 1972.
MFr.	Modern French.
Moignet	*La Chanson de Roland.* Texte original et traduction par Gérard Moignet. Bibliothèque Bordas. Paris: Bordas, 1969.
Mortier	*Les Textes de la Chanson de Roland.* Ed. Raoul Mortier. 10 vols. Paris: La Geste Francor, 1940–44. I. *La Version d'Oxford* (1940). II. *La Version de Venise IV* (1941). III. *La Chronique de Turpin et les Grandes Chroniques de France, Carmen de proditione Guenonis, Ronsasvals* (1941). IV. *Le Manuscrit de Châteauroux* (1943). V. *Le Manuscrit de Venise VII* (1942). VI. *Le Texte de Paris* (1942). VII. *Le Texte de Cambridge* (1943). VIII. *Le Texte de Lyon* (1944). IX. *Les Fragments lorrains* (1943). X. *Le Texte de Conrad.* Trans. Jean Graff (1944).
OE.	Old English.
OFr.	Old French.
OHG.	Old High German.
OPr.	Old Provençal.
Owen	*The Song of Roland: The Oxford Text.* Translated by D. D. R. Owen. Unwin Books Classics 3. London: Unwin, 1972.
Paris	See Mortier.
PL	Migne, Jacques-Paul. *Patrologiae cursus completus . . . Series latina.* 221 vols. Paris: Migne, 1884–91.
Pseudo-Turpin Chronicle	See Meredith-Jones.
Réau	Réau, Louis. *Iconographie de l'art chrétien.* 3 parts in 6 vols. Paris: Presses Universitaires de France, 1955–59.
Ronsasvals	See Mortier.

Rychner	Jean Rychner. *La Chanson de geste: Essai sur l'art épique des jongleurs.* Société de publications romanes et françaises 53. Geneva: Droz; Lille: Giard, 1955.
Samaran	*La Chanson de Roland.* Reproduction phototypique du Manuscrit Digby 23 de la Bodleian Library d'Oxford. Edition avec un avant-propos par le Comte Alexandre de Laborde. Etude historique et paléographique de M. Ch. Samaran. Paris: Société des anciens textes français, 1933.
Segre	*La Chanson de Roland.* Edizione critica a cura di Cesare Segre. Documenti di filologia 16. Milan and Naples: Ricciardi, 1971.
Sp.	Spanish.
The Jerusalem Bible	*The Jerusalem Bible.* Gen. ed. Alexander Jones. Garden City: Doubleday, 1966.
Tobler and Lommatzsch	Tobler, Adolf, and Erhard Lommatzsch. *Altfranzösisches Wörterbuch.* Berlin: Weidmann; Wiesbaden: Steiner, 1925– . In progress (10 vols.).
Venice IV	See Mortier.
Venice VII	See Mortier.
VL	Vulgar Latin
Whitehead	*La Chanson de Roland.* Ed. F. Whitehead. Blackwell's French Texts. 2d ed. 1946; rpt. Oxford: Blackwell, 1965. Often reissued.

I

Introduction

1. The Historical Event

The Song of Roland is an epic poem that recounts the events surrounding the death of Charlemagne's nephew Roland at Roncevaux in the Pyrenees. The Emperor and his men were journeying home after a military campaign in Spain. The disaster actually took place in the year 778, some three centuries before the poem is generally dated.[1]

In 732, twenty-one years after landing on the Spanish Peninsula, the Saracens were decisively stopped at Poitiers by Charles Martel (688?–741), Charlemagne's grandfather.[2] Throughout this Muslim advance, however, Christians in the Asturias, the northwestern corner of Spain, had succeeded in resisting the general onslaught. By the ninth century the Christians had broadened their dominions to encompass a number of adjacent provinces, including Galicia and most of León to the south and east.

Christian reconquest of the northern tier of Spain was greatly facilitated by internal dissention among the Arabs.[3] At the invitation of Suleiman, the Arab governor of Barcelona—and recognizing an opportunity to establish a buffer against the Saracen threat from south of the Pyrenees, and to make converts to Christianity—Charlemagne amassed an army and entered Spain in two main columns in 778. Alerted to a Saxon uprising to the north and forced to lift the siege of Saragossa, Charlemagne took a number of hostages including Suleiman himself, whom he suspected of treachery, and fell back on Pamplona, destroying it and forcing its inhabitants, including many Christians, to flee. As the Franks were making their way back across the Pyrenees, Gascons ambushed the rearguard, killing all its defenders. Loaded down with booty, they escaped into the night. Charlemagne was unable for the moment to avenge this stunning defeat, but he returned several years later and established a zone of Frankish influence in the northern tier of the peninsula known as the Spanish March.

This is the most faithful account of the events of the year 778, which has been pieced together by historians from scattered and often contradictory sources. The best-known narrative of these events is contained in the *Vita Karoli Magni* by Einhard, Charlemagne's biographer (d. 840):

> Cum enim absiduo ac pene continuo cum Saxonibus bello certaretur, dispositis per congrua confiniorum loco praesidiis, Hispaniam quam maximo poterat belli apparatu adgreditur; saltuque Pyrinei superato, omnibus quae adierat oppidis atque castellis in deditionem acceptis, salvo et incolomi exercitu revertitur, praeter quod in ipso Pyrinei jugo Wasconicam perfidiam parumper in redeundo contigit experiri. Nam cum agmine longo, ut loci et angustiarum situs permittebat, porrectus iret exercitus, Wascones in summi montis vertice positis insidiis—est enim locus ex opacitate silvarum, quarum ibi maxima est copia, insidiis ponendis oportunus—extremam inpedimentorum partem et eos qui, novissimi agminis incedentes subsidio, praecedentes tuebantur desuper incursantes in subjectam vallem deiciunt consertoque cum eis proelio usque ad unum omnes interficiunt ac, direptis inpedimentis, noctis beneficio quae jam instabat protecti, summa cum celeritate in diversa disperguntur. Adjuvabat in hoc facto Wascones et levitas armorum et loci in quo res gerebatur situs; econtra Francos et armorum gravitas et loci iniquitas per omnia Wasconibus reddidit inpares. In quo proelio Eggihardus regiae mensae praepositus, Anshelmus comes palatii et Hruodlandus Brittannici limitis praefectus cum aliis conpluribus interficiuntur. Neque hoc factum ad praesens vindicari poterat, quia hostis, re perpetrata, ita dispersus est ut ne fama quidem remaneret ubinam gentium quaeri potuisset.[4]
>
> (While the war against the Saxons is being fought energetically and almost continuously, he [Charlemagne], having stationed troops at strategic places along the borders, attacks Spain with all the forces that he can muster. He crosses the Pyrenees, accepts the surrender of all the towns and fortified places that he encounters along the way, and returns without his army having sustained any losses except that, during the withdrawal, while traversing the Pyrenees, he happened to experience Gascon treachery. While his army was marching in a long column, because of a narrow pass, some Gascons lying in ambush at the top of the mountain—for the thick woods which are very plentiful in that area afford a great opportunity for sneak attacks—swoop down on the last elements of the baggage train

and on the rearguard protecting the main body of the army. They drive them back into the valley, join battle, and massacre every last one of them. Then, having looted the baggage train, they disperse very rapidly in every direction under cover of night which was falling. On this occasion, the Gascons had the advantage of light armament and control of the terrain; the Franks were greatly hindered by their heavy armament and lower position. In this battle were slain Eggihard, the royal seneschal; Anselm, count of the palace; and Roland, prefect of the Breton march, and many others. This reverse could not be avenged immediately because the enemy, having done this deed, dispersed in such a way that no one could even tell in which direction they might have been sought.)

In this account no reason for Charlemagne's invasion of Spain is provided, and the ambush is said to have taken place after he had conquered all the towns and castles in his path on the peninsula.[5] According to Einhard, the defeat was occasioned by Gascon treachery (Wasconicam perfidiam).[6] Duke Lupus of Gascony had earlier submitted to Charlemagne's authority but, breaking his oath, allowed a marauding band of his followers to lead a successful attack against the rearguard.[7] Charlemagne's campaign was motivated by political and religious considerations.[8] The *Annales Mettenses priores*, written shortly after 805, indicate that Charlemagne responded to appeals from the oppressed Christian community in Spain, an assertion confirmed by a letter from Pope Hadrian dated May 778 and reiterated by the Astronomer of Limoges about 840.[9] It has been suggested that Saracens as well as Gascons participated in the ambush.[10]

What is most significant in Einhard's narrative is the amount of space devoted to the disaster, which not only suggests the impact of the defeat on the people of the day, but lists a number of illustrious victims, including *Hruodlandus Brittannici limitis praefectus*, the hero of the *Song of Roland*,[11] and mentions treachery, which will later motivate the action in the poem.[12]

2. *Legend, Poem, and Text*

The myth of Charlemagne (742–814) began to grow during his lifetime, and in the two centuries after his death, numerous anecdotes about him had been circulated and his name intimately associated with the Empire.[13] There are scattered references to the incident in the Pyrenees in medieval annals, and it is safe to assume that by the eleventh century a fairly elaborate legend had developed, perhaps giving rise to more than one work in Latin or French, none of which have survived.[14] The custom of naming brothers Roland and Oliver, which dates from the beginning of the eleventh century, is an important witness to the development of the legend.[15]

There has been considerable speculation concerning the presumed ancestry of chansons de geste in general and of the *Song of Roland* in particular. If the prototype of this epic was Latin, it doubtless circulated in monastic circles in written form, like the saints' lives, which it probably resembled in form and content. On the other hand, a vernacular version, the product of oral composition, may have been part of the repertory of jongleurs, or singers of tales, who traveled about the country at the time.[16] In any event, many scholars are convinced that the so-called Baligant episode—roughly a thousand lines, or about one-fourth of the poem in its present state—was not part of the original material.[17]

Whether inspired by legend or poem, a man of genius, referred to henceforth as Turoldus[18]—the name found in the Oxford manuscript—living in France about 1100,[19] composed the work known today as the *Song of Roland.* The questions as to the precise manner and form in which Turoldus received his material and how much of the poem's style is due to his creativity and skill are much debated. However, the extant French works composed before 1100 are but pale forerunners of this remarkable epic, and the oral literature, the existence of which one can assume and even reconstruct to a certain extent, was doubtless far less complex and sophisticated.

Turoldus's masterpiece is superior to the kind of verse that singers of tales usually composed, but it has many features in common with this oral literature. Jean Rychner links the repetitions in the initial laisses of the *Roland* to the poet's need to have his audience clearly understand Marsile's proposal.[20] On the other hand, he finds only one instance of recapitulation in Turoldus's poem (vv. 2769–2787), a technique which the singer of tales often utilized to refresh his listeners' memory when a new session was beginning or to allow recent arrivals in the audience to catch up on what had already been narrated.[21]

Turoldus was obviously familiar with the formulaic diction used by the jongleurs, and he skillfully fused this procedure with the techniques of written literature taught in the schools. Other authors of his day did the same, if somewhat varying the blend, although the chansons de geste that have survived generally appear to be more the work of clerks than of jongleurs.[22]

The lines between chanson de geste, chronicle, and saint's life are not always easy to discern in Old French literature. Traditional definitions remain valid for the most part; but how does one classify a poem like *Ami et Amile?*[23] The confrontation of, say, the *Song of Roland*, the *Pseudo-Turpin Chronicle*, and the *Rolandslied* (INTRODUCTION, 10), with their varying mixtures of the sacred and the profane, of edifying, historical, and legendary material, tends to negate the concept of genre. The medieval author's habit of citing well-known but often—as in the *Song of Roland*—nonexistent annals or chronicles for authentification complicates the matter even further.[24]

If one is to appreciate the condition of the surviving chansons de geste, it is also important to understand the habits of medieval scribes. Copyists at times reproduced the manuscript before them quite faithfully but at other times altered their transcript, with changes ranging from occasional word substitutions to substantial abridgments and lengthy amplifications or interpolations. Transposition into a different dialect, modernization of language to reflect current usage, and, from the thirteenth century onward, switching from assonance to rhyme and from verse to prose, were common practices. Many years and even centuries sometimes elapsed between the time the original work was composed and a particular manuscript was copied, and there was often more than one intervening transcript. Turoldus's poem was subjected to all of these transformations.

Scholars have established the relationship between the extant manuscripts of the *Roland*[25] and, in general, agree that the copy preserved in the Bodleian Library at Oxford offers the oldest and the best surviving version of the poem. This manuscript, often referred to by its library reference number, Digby 23, is in a twelfth-century hand.[26] In Anglo-Norman dialect, it is believed to reflect rather closely Turoldus's original poem, which was composed sometime earlier.[27]

Efforts to narrow down the date of the poem itself and of the Bodleian copy continue. There are many proposals for dating the work before or after 1100, but no convincing argument has been advanced for dissociating the poem in its present form from the other early French epics it resembles and which were composed about this time: *Chanson de Guillaume*, *Gormont et Isembart*, *Pèlerinage de Charlemagne*.

The copy of the *Roland* in Digby 23 has too many scribal errors to be an original,[28] and a second hand ("the revisor") made some sixty-odd changes in the text. [29] The manuscript seems too small and inelegant in execution to have been a presentation copy for some important personage.[30] Was it, then, as some have proposed, meant to be used by a jongleur?[31] After reviewing all the available evidence in this regard, Charles Samaran was unable to resolve the matter[32] and later efforts have not removed this uncertainty.[33]

A good deal is known about the circumstances under which a chanson de geste was recited,[34] but relatively little effort has been made to visualize how such a performance appeared to a medieval audience. New light on the oral interpretation of the *Song of Roland* is provided below (INTRODUCTION, 20).

To sum up, some jongleurs were also trouvères, or authors, but their compositions probably have not survived. The epics that the jongleurs performed as they traveled about the country may have been of two different types: (1) the popular form, now lost, which was heavily dependent upon the formulas, motifs, themes, and techniques about which Rychner has written, and (2) the more literate, polished, and sophisticated form, which has much in common with the popular form but which bears the hallmark of the clerical tradition. However, there is no incontrovertible proof that the *Roland* or any other chanson de geste was ever sung before an audience in the form preserved in medieval manuscripts.[35] There are limits, therefore, to any claim that can be made about the medieval audience's presumed reaction to any epic passage.

One can only speculate, too, about the manner in which jongleurs transmitted chansons de geste to the clerks who copied and doubtless altered them. Turoldus may have combined the skills of jongleur and clerk, but this does not seem likely.

One thing is certain, however: The *Song of Roland* is the greatest French epic and its appearance was an event of the highest importance in the history of Western literature.

3. *Recent Scholarship on the Song of Roland*

In his presidential address entitled "Les tendances actuelles de la critique et de l'interprétation des chansons de geste" at the Third International Congress of the Société Rencesvals held at Barcelona in 1964, Pierre Le Gentil asserted that a firm grasp of history and philology were indispensable to the study of Old French epics.[36] He did not suggest, however, that these disciplines offered the only valid approaches to the subject. Sociology, he conceded, may lead to stimulating new insights, but it entails grave risks in that it lends itself to "fantaisies dépourvues de fondement et de prudence."[37] As for Freudian analysis, structuralism, and American New Criticism, none could serve any useful purpose in elucidating these epics. Thus Le Gentil remained faithful to a statement of principle made by Gaston Paris in his first public lecture at the Collège de France in 1872. After praising the efforts of earlier scholars, the father of Old French studies said: "Nous comprenons aujourd'hui un peu différemment l'étude du moyen âge. Nous nous attachons moins à l'apprécier et à le faire apprécier qu'à le connaître et à le comprendre. Ce que nous y cherchons avant tout, c'est de l'histoire."[38]

When one contrasts these statements with the growing realization in other fields that history and philology are far from providing the only workable approaches to literary criticism and that scholarship should, as much as possible, relate to other disciplines, one cannot help but find such an attitude narrow and outmoded. Curiously missing here, for that matter, is any view regarding character analysis. Le Gentil's own book on the *Song of Roland* offers a fine model of the genre.[39]

A poem may at times convey meanings which the author never intended.[40] This does not mean that all interpretations are equally illuminating or valid, for any view must ultimately stand the test of common sense and plausibility. The analogy of the news photograph helps us to understand the principle to which we allude and which critics call the intentional fallacy.[41] Many images impressed in our memory because they have captured the essence of a momentous event or period in history were discovered in the developing room, among dozens of other exposures taken at random.[42] The picture's arresting quality and its epochal significance, initially unsuspected, were sensed afterward, and often by others. In similar fashion, a poem's impact on its audience may exceed its author's design.

Modern commentators of course have every right to offer interpretations of medieval works that strike them as valid, but explanations that correspond to and shed new light on medieval modes of thought will always be prized above others. The critic who communicates personal impressions risks being accused of subjectivity. Yet impressions are the very stuff of poetry and, when buttressed by evidence garnered from medieval sources, are unquestionably as valuable as the data collected with philological and historical methods.

A review of the scholarship of the past quarter century concerning the *Song of Roland*—the dozen or so major publications every year, the work of three colloquia on the Romance epic and seven international congresses of the Société Rencesvals—confirms the view that Le Gentil's judgment is shared by a majority of medievalists today.[43] Article after article, paper after paper focuses on a few dozen problems of a historical or philological nature, each purporting to shed light on the *Roland*, but, as if powered by some mysterious force, they almost invariably draw attention away from fundamental questions concerning the *Song of Roland* as literature.

In the preface of his important monograph published in 1955, Jean Rychner observes that scholars have expended much energy speculating on the origin of the epic without first having devoted adequate time to a descriptive study of the epics in the form in which they have actually survived.[44] Characterizing the laisse as the fundamental building block of the epic, Rychner asserts that structural regularity and the arrangement of narrative units determine to a great extent the literary merit of the work as a whole. He notes that the laisse itself consists in the main of stereotyped phrases or formulas, and that in all epics there is a recurrence of themes (royal ingratitude, battles, the death of the hero) and motifs (duels, ritual insults before and after the fight, prayers, laments, weeping, dreams). According to Rychner, the *Song of Roland* is atypical in that it is well-constructed and contains fine psychological, dramatic, or lyrical statements, such as *Rollant est proz e Oliver est sage* and *Bon sunt li cunte e lur paroles haltes*.

Rychner's ideas were not new: other Old French scholars—Rita Lejeune in 1954, Paul Aebischer in 1952, Maurice Wilmotte as early as 1915[45]—had discussed epic formulas, and of course there have been many studies concerning the relationship between the laisses in the *Roland*. Rychner's method and terminology were based on an approach pioneered by Milman Parry as early as 1930 in his analysis of Homeric style, followed by Francis P. Magoun, Jr., in a study of Anglo-Saxon narrative poetry, and by Parry's pupil Albert B. Lord in a book on Serbo-Croatian heroic songs.[46]

On the other hand, Rychner's compelling study was the first systematic application of this approach to Old French epics and should, above all, have stimulated scholars toward more literary analysis. However, it was Rychner's conclusion that created a stir, for it defended the oral origins of the epic.

The fact that the chansons de geste were not read but chanted, the formulaic diction, the mnemonic devices, the fact, too, that other heroic literatures have strikingly similar characteristics, lead to Rychner's conclusion that in all probability there were earlier and shorter songs behind these epics.[47] Having maintained that each rendition of the epic was to a great extent an improvisation, the Swiss scholar even went so far as to state in a bold assertion, which he has since modified, that the earliest manuscript copies that have survived are merely witnesses to this continual evolution.[48]

Virtually every scholar in the field now accepts Rychner's terminology and comparative approach to formulas and motifs, and there have been numerous publications refining his data and using his study as the point of departure for literary analysis.[49] However, a number of Rychner's views have been challenged, and the fact that the surviving chansons de geste are not oral but written literature has been repeatedly stressed.[50]

Although efforts are still made from time to time to link various historical events, personages, and places to incidents, characters, and locales in the *Song of Roland*,[51] the majority of scholars today view the poem as an original creation, reflecting contemporary feudal society and its concerns with a degree of realism[52] but containing few if any topical allusions.[53] The prevailing interpretation of Turoldus's poem is that it glorifies the crusading spirit—Christian militancy wedded to feudal imperatives—and that it centers on the debate between Roland and Oliver.

While there is much controversy as to whether or not the epic preceded Pope Urban II's call to arms at Clermont in 1095 and the capture of Jerusalem in 1099, no one denies that the conflict between Christians and Saracens in the *Song of Roland* reflects crusading zeal and exalts France's heroic mission.[54] A series of expeditions into Spain by Christian forces, notably Franks, constituting a kind of proto-Crusade throughout the eleventh century, has also been adduced to explain this feature of the poem.[55] Charlemagne's earlier Spanish campaigns also lend themselves to epic aggrandizement and provide sufficient basis for the Christian-Saracen conflict found in the *Roland*.

The ethos of Turoldus's epic has been characterized as everything from completely pagan to profoundly Christian. Léon Gautier suggested that the Old French epics exuded "l'esprit germanique dans une forme romane,"[56] a judgment that understandably irritated many of his contemporaries. This view is not unlike that recently propounded by George Fenwick Jones and others, who consider the poem to be the product of a shame culture having nothing to do with Christianity—a guilt culture.[57]

Jones's study offers valuable clarifications of a number of key words in the *Song of Roland* and is characterized by rigorous philology and a strict approach to problems that scholars have tended to dismiss all too airily. However, Jones is reluctant to grant anything but secular and warlike virtues to the eleventh-century French aristocracy. To wage war in the name of the Lamb of God, in the name of Him who proclaimed "Happy the peacemakers," shocks those who have a different concept of Christianity.[58] Yet the Crusaders viewed themselves as devout Christians. The only way to understand this paradox—as well as that of Roland, who risks all in order to win a victory over the Infidel and who goes so far as to sacrifice the elite of Charlemagne's army and his own life in the process—is to recall Abraham's sacrifice (INTRODUCTION, 13, C). For medieval as well as modern exegetes, Abraham's seemingly senseless and barbaric act is the perfect symbol of Faith, that is, of total submission to God's will. Roland's behavior borders on madness, but it is possible to understand and even, in a sense, to share the point of view (without necessarily approving the actions) of a martyr who sacrifices himself for a cause he believes is just.

The poem's curious brand of Christian idealism is a much-debated question. Bédier believed that Turoldus deliberately left unanswered the question of whether Roland or Oliver was right in the famous oliphant scene,[59] but other scholars have argued either for or against Roland's *desmesure*, concluding more often than not that the hero was morally wrong in his initial decision to make a stand at Roncevaux.[60] Offering a corollary to the latter view, some critics have maintained that Roland does indeed commit the sin of pride, but that he repents and is forgiven by God.[61] Le Gentil, for instance, believes that the hero's suffering and self-immolation for a crusading ideal guarantees his redemption.[62] For such scholars the *Song of Roland* is an Epic of Atonement.[63] Others argue that the hero is a scapegoat, expiating Charlemagne's sin (INTRODUCTION, 19, E) or providentially recalling the Emperor to his divinely inspired mission to vanquish the Infidel.[64] But Christ, whose death is often compared to that of the sacrificial animal, was guiltless of course, and it is reasonable to assume that Turoldus would have given the hero or at least the audience to understand the nature of the burden he supposedly bears. The visitation of evil upon the hero is not a sign that he has sinned. Like Job—and Charlemagne[65]—Roland is cast in the role of the Suffering Just.[66]

It was Joseph Bédier who put forth the theory that the Roland-Oliver debate was the key to Turoldus's poem. For the French scholar, the *Song of Roland* was born in that "sacred moment" when the contrast between the two comrades-in-arms was conceived and epitomized in v. 1093: *Rollant est proz e Oliver est sage* ("Roland est preux et Olivier sage").[67] When taken out of context, this line has an aphoristic quality, but it is simplistic and grossly misleading to suggest that it is the gist of Turoldus's poem.

One of the tendencies of late-nineteenth-century critics of medieval French literature was to seek to enhance the reputation of the masterpieces they studied by means of favorable comparisons with works of the Classical period. Thus the term Cornelian was used by Bédier and many scholars thereafter to describe the grandeur of the Roland-Oliver opposition.[68] Jenkins speaks of Roland's "fatal weakness of character," an interpretation stemming from Aristotle's concept of the tragic flaw.[69] These views, such as the notion of the "misunderstood" Ganelon, distort the meaning of the text by introducing totally anachronistic critical concepts and distract the attention from that which is truly original and significant in the *Song of Roland.*

The Roland-Oliver debate is interesting in its own right,[70] but it does not have the importance it has been accorded in discussions of the poem's central meaning. Bédier's view has gained widespread scholarly acceptance and much evidence has been collected in support of this interpretation.

According to Ernst R. Curtius, physical strength and courage (fortitudo) and wisdom (sapientia) were qualities that were often found in two opposing characters in the literature of antiquity. The idea of a contrast between Roland and Oliver would thus be a classical topos.[71] *Fortitudo et sapientia* was not only a literary commonplace but also an ideal of the Roman people. The Roman aristocrat had to demonstrate courage and wisdom, which were considered to be the fundamental virtues of the general and the magistrate.[72] One of the oldest documents of Roman history, the epitaph of Scipio Barbatus, who was consul in 298 B.C., alludes to these two traits: *fortis vir sapiensque.*[73] There are many similar references in Greek and Latin literature and in the works of Roman historians. Isidore of Seville (d. 636), whose works were widely disseminated during the Middle Ages, mentions this concept in his *Etymologiae*: "Heroicum carmen dictum, quod eo virorum fortium res et facta narrantur; nam heroes appellantur viri quasi aerii et caelo digni propter sapientiam et fortitudinem."[74]

However, Leo Spitzer noted that the olive tree is one of the biblical symbols of divine wisdom, and he found support for this identification in Alain de Lille's *Distinctiones* from the second half of the twelfth century.[75] According to Spitzer, Turoldus was thinking of the Scriptural symbol when he named Roland's companion Oliver.[76] The Bible contains numerous passages celebrating either prowess or wisdom but, more often than not, affirms the primacy of wisdom in this regard.[77] There can be no doubt that the courage-and-wisdom theme—whether it stems from classical tradition or biblical thought, or whether it derives from *rhétorique coutumière* (INTRODUCTION, 6)—plays an important role in medieval literature.[78] Finally, Jones has established a connection between *fortitudo et sapientia* and the locution *auxilium et consilium*, which without doubt is the best definition one can offer of feudal obligations,[79] and William Calin regards Durendal as the symbol of prowess and the oliphant as that of wisdom.[80] These conjectures do not all have the same weight, but they do lend support to Bédier's interpretation.

However, not everyone shares Bédier's view on this point. Ramón Menéndez Pidal conceded that "l'opposition entre Olivier et Roland est celui de deux conceptions de la vertu héroïque," but he had reservations with regard to the bearing of the antithesis *fortitudo et sapientia* on the composition of Turoldus's work:

> d'autres passages du poème ne prêtent aucune attention à l'opposition [des mots *proz* et *sage*]: l'adjectif *sage*, *saive*, est appliqué banalement, tout comme à Olivier, à d'autres personnages chrétiens ou païens. Ce cas est le même pour l'adjectif *proz*; nous sommes même surpris de le voir attribuer avec insistance à Olivier, comme un qualificatif habituel. . . . Quant à l'archevêque Turpin, il est à la fois *sages e proz* (v. 3691), groupant les qualités d'Olivier et de Roland réunis, sans apparaître pour autant comme supérieur au héros principal. Il semble donc que le vers mémorable *Rollant est proz e Oliver est sage*

> pâlisse quelque peu, négligé ou ignoré par d'autres passages du poème. Il semble surtout que l'auteur de cette antithèse brillante n'aurait pas dû l'oublier ensuite en composant l'éloge de Turpin.[81]

Matthias Waltz based his analysis on this argument by Menéndez Pidal when he affirmed that critics have erred in stressing the conflict between Roland and Oliver. He correctly pointed out that the description of the hero's death is of far greater significance.[82]

The Roland-Oliver contrast calls for further reservations. Three factors come into play here: (1) the statements made by characters in the poem who give their opinion of Roland and Oliver; (2) the seemingly decisive affirmation in v. 1093; (3) the conclusion we ourselves can draw relative to the behavior of the two companions-in-arms based on other evidence found in the text.[83]

The unfavorable interpretation of Roland's character is based in part on two anecdotes related by Ganelon about his stepson and on words exchanged with Ganelon and, especially, with Oliver.[84] But Ganelon deliberately distorts facts in order to discredit Roland and repeatedly lies in order to avenge himself.[85] The villain's character is complex, but his role is essentially that of a traitor and a liar. Oliver is certainly more favorably disposed toward Roland. On the other hand, he, too, becomes incensed by his companion's behavior, and his statements concerning Roland need to be studied in this light. Oliver is not afraid of death: He simply feels that Roland's reasons for dying are not good enough. In the two oliphant scenes Oliver advances several cogent arguments, but his companion, typical of the martyr, turns a deaf ear to his entreaties and stubbornly insists on fulfilling his destiny.

Oliver maintains that *mesure* (v. 1725) 'reasonableness', that is, *vasselage par sens* (v. 1724) 'heroism tempered with common sense' is better than *estultie* (v. 1725) 'recklessness', but this description of Roland's behavior is that of a man under pressure (Oliver) and not that of the poet judging the same events with impartiality.

Roland's arguments fail to convince Oliver. In the second oliphant scene, Oliver, using a debating technique known to classical rhetoricians as antistrephon,[86] turns the tables on his opponent by reiterating Roland's assertions. Critics have often commented upon the irony of Oliver's procedure and have felt obliged to side with either Roland or his comrade-in-arms in this debate.[87] The poet does not ask us to choose: The two points of view are irreconcilable but, in a sense, defensible.[88]

However, the circular configuration of Oliver's argumentation (COMMENTARY, 18) symbolizes the vanity of worldly wisdom, one of the modalities of the Theme of Sapientia in the *Song of Roland* (INTRODUCTION, II, C). Turpin's intervention in this debate is of capital importance, for the Archbishop speaks plainly and places the Battle of Roncevaux in its proper perspective, elucidating the true significance of the death of the Christians.

If, in order to obtain a true perception of Roland's character, one must beware of Ganelon's lying assertions and understand, too, that the statements made by Oliver are conditioned by point of view, what is one to think now of the celebrated passage where the poet himself gives his own opinion of Roland and Oliver?

In his lament Roland mentions, among other qualities, that Oliver has been a trustworthy adviser:

2207 Ço dit Rollant: "Bels cumpainz Oliver,
Vos fustes filz al duc Reiner
Ki tint la marche del Val de Runers.
Pur hanste freindre e pur escuz peceier,
Pur orgoillos veintre e esmaier
E pur prozdomes tenir e cunseiller
E pur glutun veintre e esmaier,
En nule tere n'ad meillor chevaler!"

But it is above all v. 1093 that has held critics in its sway: *Rollant est proz e Oliver est sage*. This line has been seriously misinterpreted: *proz* here does not mean 'brave' but 'worthy' (COMMENTARY, 14). Thus, rather than standing out in sharp contrast to *sage*, *proz* complements it. Turoldus's point is that Roland and Oliver are equal in chivalric virtue. On a purely human plane the two knights are identical in worth, but Roland by far surpasses his companion by the nature of his aspiration. In short, *fortitudo et sapientia* scholarship hangs together nicely, but it does not come to the heart of the matter. The central meaning of the *Song of Roland* lies elsewhere (INTRODUCTION, II). There is Sapientia in Turoldus's poem, but it is of a different sort (INTRODUCTION, II, C).

The chief purpose of this book is to provide a literary analysis of the *Song of Roland*, but this will inevitably entail religious considerations. The presence of the supernatural in this poem is incontrovertible, and few scholars subscribe to the view that Turoldus's inspiration was exclusively secular. However, studies of the work's moral and spiritual content have thus far centered on the problem of Roland's guilt, a question to which Turoldus simply did not address himself. On the other hand, Christian beliefs and imagery play a far more important role in this epic than is generally suspected.

4. *Turoldus and His World*

In the late eleventh century Western Europe was very different from what it is today.[89] Its diverse peoples were just beginning to emerge from a long era marked by armed invasions and raids from far and near. They had abandoned once-flourishing cities established by the Romans[90] and had retreated from the countryside into isolated, self-sufficient, fortified enclaves. Royal authority was not very strong. Villages had developed in the shadow of castles and a small class of warriors—perhaps one-tenth of one percent of the population—ruled over serfs clustered around them for protection.[91] By now the hierarchical structure of lord and vassal had assumed its definitive form and individuals at all levels of society were bound together by vows of homage and fealty.[92] Whenever the term *chevaler* is used in the *Song of Roland* it refers to a fighting man, distinguished by birth and by ownership of expensive heavy armor, weapons, and a war-horse.[93] Armies of Turoldus's day also included a large number of attendants (serjanz) who assisted the warrior, but usually in a noncombatant role.[94]

Commerce had disappeared for the most part and virtually everyone was engaged in the serious business of subsistence agriculture. The local lord offered protection in return for ownership of all the land, a percentage of the crop and domestic animals, and various services. The baron and his knights spent a good part of their time in martial activities, warring against marauding aggressors or among themselves. Whether in a castle or in a village hut, life was rude and precarious by modern standards, alternating between times of starvation and relative plenty, between grim survival and joyous feasting. Nature and man-made violence were important factors conditioning the daily routine and seasonal cycle of work and rest. Age-old religious and folk beliefs, customs, and traditions also influenced the lives of these profoundly conservative people.

Two major activities could seriously affect an individual's life.

A military expedition or a pilgrimage to a distant land might remove a person for years at a time from familiar surroundings.[95] Powerful dukes and counts often became involved in foreign campaigns (there were numerous expeditions into Italy and Spain, for instance), and permanent resettlement at times ensued, such as that of certain Norman barons and their retinues in Sicily. The most popular pilgrimages were of course to local shrines, but they might also involve a trip to Rome, Santiago de Compostela, or even the Holy Land.[96] Crude itineraries—maps or narrative accounts—provided some assistance to pilgrims who were, by custom, accorded hospitality in monasteries and hostels along the way.[97] Travelers followed ancient routes, but it is misleading to think in terms of specific "pilgrimage roads," a fiction invented by turn-of-the-century scholars.[98] Pilgrims normally traveled in groups, a custom immortalized in Chaucer's *Canterbury Tales*. The services of a guide (OFr. guieor, guior), that is, a person who had presumably traveled the road at least once before, helped pilgrims establish a pace and avoid obvious hazards. Whether embarking on a military adventure abroad or on a distant pilgrimage, individuals knew that travel entailed grave risks. Modern historians estimate that, in the Middle Ages, life expectancy was thirty-five years until the thirteenth century.[99]

Patriotism as we conceive it today was nonexistent in Turoldus's day.[100] National and ethnic stereotypes, extending down to the regional level, were commonplace, as evidenced perhaps in v. 3796 (Icels d'Alverne i sunt li plus curteis). Foreigners and even inhabitants of neighboring lands were commonly viewed with distrust. The poet's use of the recurring expression *dulce France* may be in imitation of classical models.[101] On the other hand, affection and nostalgia for one's homeland and for familiar surroundings are only natural. For Turoldus, to be a *Franc de France* meant one enjoyed special status in Charlemagne's army.

Local political matters at times altered daily living in the eleventh century. A marriage contract negotiated between two noble families (the bride usually had little say in this matter) might bring about a change of administration and improve or worsen the serf's lot dramatically, depending on his new lord's humaneness or greed.[102] The eruption of a feud between barons could spell disaster for everyone concerned.

The sense of belonging to Christianity imparted a much stronger feeling of solidarity than any corresponding national identification, but religion then as now affected individuals' outlook on life and ethical behavior in a variety of ways. The notion of Christian unity and of a certain internationalism[103] was enhanced during the course of the eleventh century by a growing concern over the Saracen peril, a situation precipitated by the appearance of the Turks upon the scene, which sent shock waves throughout Europe and inaugurated a new phase in history.[104] The many disruptions occasioned by the Turkish conquests, among many other factors, culminated in the world-shaking proclamation of the First Crusade at Clermont on 27 November 1095.[105] The *Roland*'s international appeal is evident from the fact that it was translated into several languages.

5. *The Church and the Arts*

The impact of the Church on the Middle Ages is incalculable, for its influence permeated and shaped every activity known to man. In the eleventh century the Catholic hierarchy was associated with every facet of life, imparting counsel and ministering to spiritual needs in the entourage of sovereigns and lords of every degree, as well as among the lowest-ranking serfs. Regular clergy, living under vows in monasteries and various religious establishments, or as recluses, outnumbered knights by perhaps five to one; secular priests and clerks in minor orders (INTRODUCTION, 7) doubtless increased that proportion to ten to one.[106]

A theoretical distinction had long ago[107] been drawn between the powers of Church and State, and the question of investiture was a bone of contention.[108] However, in practice the Church usually succeeded in maintaining its primacy, symbolized notably by the incident at Canossa. In January 1077, Henry IV, King of Germany and the Holy Roman Emperor, stood for three days bareheaded and barefoot in the snow in a castle courtyard until Pope Gregory VII, who was staying there, consented to grant him an audience and absolve him from excommunication. Less than a century later, in 1177, Henry II of England, having quarreled with Thomas Becket on the question of ecclesiastical authority—a dispute resulting in the latter's murder—was forced to perform a humiliating public penance at the Archbishop's shrine.

Abbots and bishops shared in the benefits of the feudal system, holding estates in fief and exercising the right to collect tolls and market dues.[109] On the other hand, sovereigns and even lesser lords commonly held churches in benefice and derived considerable income from their tithes and other revenues, a practice the Church succeeded in limiting in Turoldus's day.[110]

Monks maintained schools and, although the age of the great universities was yet to come, institutions such as those at Chartres, Cluny, Laon, Orleans, Reims, Saint-Benoît-sur-Loire, and Saint-Riquier, to name but the major French establishments,[111] were already regarded as important centers of learning. Lesser schools could be found in areas boasting a few thousand inhabitants or a thriving monastery.[112] Most of the artistic activity of the period can be traced to the monastic orders, which supervised the construction and decoration of abbeys, churches, and related edifices, copied and illuminated Bibles, hymnals, pericopes, and other manuscripts, composed music and simple liturgical dramas,[113] and in general promoted esthetic values.[114]

Monks also produced a wide variety of didactic, exegetical, and theological writings in Latin. Every monastery corresponded regularly with its mother house, reporting on its activities and particular needs. A talent for composing homilies and hymns was highly regarded. However, even greater interest was shown in the writing and reworking of Latin chronicles and hagiographic literature. When they were in a position to do so, monasteries maintained annals and recorded important occurrences in their community life and other events deemed worthy of note. Other sources were consulted when more ambitious narratives were undertaken, the result being so-called universal chronicles. The scope and value of these compilations vary a good deal, some being a mere list of dates and occurrences, while others present biased or fragmentary accounts. To establish a simple historical fact—for instance, the incident in the Pyrenees in 778—one must often sift a bewildering mass of hearsay and contradictory evidence.

W. J. Brandt has classified medieval chronicles according to the particular mode of perception that characterizes them.[115] He finds that chronicles present either an aristocratic or a clerical view of the world and that these perceptions of reality are essentially antagonistic: "The important discontinuity in the value system of the medieval cleric was within the profession itself, between absolutely unreconcilable views of life which were equally cherished and equally believed."[116] The aristocratic ideal, he maintains, was one of worldly values and stances, great admiration being shown for profit and materialistic concerns, whereas the clerical tradition constantly judged people and events according to atemporal norms, and held innocence, purity, and the like in high esteem. The former usually adopted a narrative mode of expression, while the latter depended a good deal more on rhetorical models.[117]

Without perforce disagreeing with this typology, which, like most generalizations, tends to lose some of its luster upon close examination, Paul Archambault has shown that the early chroniclers differ rather significantly from their later counterparts, and that one can also distinguish between "mirror" and "window" chroniclers, the former merely recounting events, the latter endeavoring to grasp their deep significance.[118] Archambault's categorization should be borne in mind in discussions of the meaning of Turoldus's poem.

Clerical activity in the eleventh century was not restricted to chronicling events that impressed contemporaries as being interesting or significant. The production of saints' lives was another major preoccupation. The earliest narratives of this type provide relatively few details and are documentary in style.[119] However, there arose in the Middle Ages a group of writers—known today as hagiographers—who developed a vast corpus of fiction loosely termed saints' lives. With a few exceptions, the typical Latin *passio* was drawn up according to a well-defined plan, but one that betrayed an astonishing lack of imagination:

> Il ne faudrait pourtant point exagérer la fécondité des "trouveurs" hagiographes. Un classement méthodique des thèmes exploités par eux amène à constater que les répétitions du même trait merveilleux sont fréquentes, et que c'est surtout grâce à diverses combinaisons de lieux communs qu'il règne, dans certains groupes de légendes hagiographiques, un semblant de variété. Ce qu'il faut surtout se garder de croire, c'est qu'au point de vue de l'esthétique même, le niveau des créations merveilleuses de l'hagiographie populaire soit, en général, bien élevé. A côté de quelques trouvailles réellement heureuses et de certains motifs ingénieux et intéressants, que de banalités s'y rencontrent, que d'inventions bizarres et souvent extravagantes!
>
> Le cadre de la narration est nettement dessiné. D'abord, une description plus ou moins détaillée de la persécution. Les chrétiens sont partout recherchés; un grand nombre tombe aux mains des soldats, et parmi eux le héros du récit; il est arrêté et jeté en prison. Mené

devant le juge, il confesse sa foi et endure d'affreux supplices. Il meurt, et son tombeau devient le théâtre d'une foule de prodiges.[120]

Certain hagiographic themes and narrative techniques appear in the *Song of Roland*. Saints' lives were read, but others—in the vernacular and in metrical form—were sung by jongleurs, constituting an important contact with the chansons de geste.[121] Turoldus's poem is neither chronicle nor saint's life; it is an epic. Each, however, was composed by clerks and it was inevitable that the first two genres would influence the other.

One cannot discuss the Church and the arts in the eleventh century without mentioning the Cluniac movement.[122] Monasticism, which dates to the dawn of Christianity, was given a decisive impetus with the foundation of the Abbey of Monte Cassino and the institution of the rule of Saint Benedict in A.D. 529. Abbeys began to proliferate throughout Europe, and, in addition to preserving for centuries the classical learning that managed to survive the Fall of the Roman Empire, they steadfastly nurtured the beliefs and exercised the moral authority that generally characterize our concept of the Church in the Middle Ages. In the year 910 the Benedictine abbey of Cluny was founded, inaugurating an unparalleled era of construction and of intellectual and spiritual vitality. About the time the *Song of Roland* was composed, Cluny controlled no fewer than 1,450 different religious establishments housing 10,000 monks throughout Europe.[123] Cluniac monasteries and hostels dotted the countryside and were familiar landmarks encountered by pilgrims and travelers everywhere.[124] "You are the light of the world," wrote Pope Urban II to the monks at Cluny in 1098.[125]

Cluny's impact on monasticism was characterized by a spirit of reform that emphasized asceticism and war on secularism. This new seriousness was reflected in the contemporary strictures of monks and councils against the jongleurs.[126] Recriminations against scandalous personal conduct and licentious performances were part of the condemnation of public amusements and spectacles that originated with the Fathers of the Church. There is evidence, however, that some religious looked with favor upon the singing of saints' lives and epics by the jongleurs, even authorizing performances of the former in church and of the latter in the cloister.[127] This practice and the strongly clerical adaptations known as the *Pseudo-Turpin Chronicle* and the *Rolandslied* (INTRODUCTION, 10) lend considerable support to the view that the *Roland* and other early chansons de geste were considered to have important didactic content.

In the eleventh century the Church strove mightily to inspire Christians to cease their constant warring against one another and upon the unarmed and the helpless. It sought energetically to establish law and order by means of various associations and oaths, notably by instituting the Peace of God, designed to protect certain classes of persons and objects—such as churches, clerics, livestock, and vineyards—and the Truce of God, prohibiting violence on certain days.[128] Although enforced by spiritual penalties and eventually by temporal punishments, these movements were only intermittently successful. "The human race," wrote the contemporary chronicler Raoul Glaber, "was like a dog that returns to its vomit. The promise was made, but it was not fulfilled."[129] The Crusades were to afford the military class with an unprecedented outlet for their warlike energies. Historians and moralists continue to debate whether any true ethical progress was achieved during this era.

The Church transformed what was primitively a pagan dubbing ritual into the knighting ceremony, which assumed its definitive form by the eleventh century and included the blessing of the sword and other Christian observances.[130] The religious also fostered the evolution of what was originally simple class-consciousness into the code of chivalry, whose Christian coloring reached its highest expression in later times, but a number of whose essential elements can already be found in the *Song of Roland*.[131] The moral position of the Church had an important bearing upon such concepts as avarice, pride, right and wrong, and spoils in Turoldus's poem.

6. *Popular Tradition*

Dancing, singing, and storytelling, like ornamental and ritual painting and sculpture, are part of the folklore of all nations, and this tradition is reflected in the *Song of Roland*. Demonology and belief in magic, the marvelous power of the oliphant, the naming of swords and horses, and teratology are among the most obvious forms of popular influence in Turoldus's epic. Councils, cursing, dreams, and oath-taking are frequent motifs in the tales told by people all over the world. Bruce

Rosenberg believes that the image of the betrayed hero dying on a hill as the last survivor is an age-old cliché whose manifestations can be found in the Bible, the *Roland*, and in the myth that developed following Custer's Last Stand.[132]

The authors of the chansons de geste and Old French romances were fond of inserting brief anecdotes in their narratives.[133] These miniature stories—as a rule no more than a few verses long—either concern a notable event in the character's life or the origin of an object to which he is strongly attached. At first glance they seem rather trifling, and for the most part they have been neglected by scholars or regarded as mere digressions or make-rhymes. The following examples drawn from the *Song of Roland* illustrate the genre:

Marsile's mules:
90 Que li tramist li reis de Suatilie.

Margariz's sword:
967 Si la tramist li amiralz de Primes.

Siglorel:
1391 L'encanteür ki ja fut en enfer,
Par artimal l'i cundoist Jupiter.

Valdabron:
1523 Jerusalem prist ja par traïsun,
Si violat le temple Salomon,
Le patriarche ocist devant les funz.

Turpin's war-horse:
1649 Siet el cheval qu'il tolit a Grossaille,
Ço ert uns reis qu'il ocist en Denemarche.

Abisme's shield:
1663 En Val Metas li dunat uns diables,
Si li tramist li amiralz Galafes.

Durendal:
2318 Carles esteit es vals de Moriane,
Quant Deus del cel li mandat par sun agle
Qu'il te dunast a un cunte cataignie:
Dunc la me ceinst li gentilz reis, li magnes.

Charlemagne's horse:
2994 Il le cunquist es guez desuz Marsune,
Sin getat mort Malpalin de Nerbone.

As is evident from the preceding illustrations, anecdotes of this type utilize formulaic diction and spin fantastic yarns, often involving the supernatural. Proper names play an important and affective role in these formulas, and the objects and animals have all been acquired either as a gift or as a battle trophy. Some of these stories within a story seem plausible enough, but they are all fictions designed to place events in an appropriate epic context. Thus the medieval audience grasped full well that Charlemagne's expedition in Spain in 778 and the Muslim peril of the eleventh century were historically authentic, but they felt quite differently about the anecdotes concerning the Emperor's horse or a Saracen's shield. Nevertheless, a skillful author knew how to go about elaborating a story involving heroic exploits and extraordinary events, on the one hand, and historical facts, on the other, so as to blur the line that separates illusion and reality.

Like literary portraits in medieval literature, with which they may usefully be compared, these thumbnail sketches, which can be classified as marginal anecdotes, possibly derive from classical models,[134] but it is better to study them according to their own esthetic. Alice M. Colby has defined the literary portrait in terms that also apply to the anecdote. It is, she says in part, a description that

> may give many different kinds of information about an individual, which affects the listener's interpretation of the work by provoking in him an emotional reaction to the important character being described, and which stands out from the context as a semi-independent, stylistically ornate, well-organized, and completely panegyrical or censorious descriptive unit, much of the content of which is stereotyped. We have shown that this definition is partially supported by material available in the treatises on Latin rhetoric and poetic art which were widely read in the twelfth century or which, in all probability, represent twelfth-century practice, but we have also demonstrated the wisdom of tentatively basing this definition entirely on the empirical evidence to be found in the vernacular literature before seeking support from the Latin theorists. Although most of the Old French poets had in all likelihood studied formal Latin composition, it cannot automatically be assumed that, when writing in the vernacular, they applied all the rules they had learned or made no attempt to develop independent vernacular traditions.[135]

These important principles influenced Turoldus's technique of character portrayal. Marginal anecdotes must be distinguished from what can be referred to as kernel anecdotes. The latter—for instance, the stories which Ganelon and Charlemagne tell about Roland—are of vital importance to the proper interpretation of the poem and, in certain instances, provided the nucleus around which elaborate episodes and even whole epics were later constructed.

One must not confuse rhetoric of the type originally developed by Greek and Latin authors (INTRODUCTION, 7) with forms that appeared in medieval French literature independently of this tradition, albeit often along parallel lines. The latter is *rhétorique coutumière*, a mode of expression that is no less formal and systematic for all its indigenous characteristics than *rhétorique scolaire.*[136] When Turoldus describes Turpin's horse, he is following quite closely a model cited by Isidore of Seville.[137] On the other hand, the brief portraits that the poet gives of certain individuals in the *Song of Roland*, the elaborate parallelism, and the *laisses similaires* technique [138] belong to a rhetorical tradition clearly distinct from that found in the works of Latin grammarians and treatise writers.

Finally, synonymic repetition deserves special mention here.[139] Classical authors—Cicero, notably—joined related expressions for the purpose of adding nuances to their thought. Old French writers paired words that were semantically identical in order to reinforce a single concept. No shading of meaning was intended. As Jones has shown, association is the key to understanding many elusive terms in the *Song of Roland.* The known form elucidates the doubtful expression to which it is joined.[140] On the other hand, one must also have a firm grasp of the ethical possibilities of each member before attempting to arrive at a conclusion as to the meaning intended by the author. Thus Jones is correct in pointing out that *proz e vaillanz* in v. 3186—the epithets concern Oliver—"is practically tautological,"[141] but he errs when he asserts that the usefulness implied in the adjective *proz* (< Late Latin *prodis* < *prode est* < Classical Latin *prodest*, a form of *prodesse* 'to be useful') alludes exclusively to the courage and physical strength of the fighting man; [142] for *proz* refers to all the virtues of the ideal knight, including wisdom (COMMENTARY, 14).

7. *Learned Tradition*

One cannot always distinguish between popular and learned matter in the *Song of Roland*. For instance, knowledge of the Bible, demonology, and proverbs[143] can be both. Many, or perhaps most, of the elements cited above as popular could just as easily be relegated to the category of learned matter. It would be a gross oversimplification, too, to characterize popular influence as coarse, learned as elegant, when the opposite is often the case.

What is a clerk?[144] The Old French word represents Ecclesiastical Latin *clericus* and is ultimately derived from *clerus*, the Latin term for clergy. Clerk is used in a variety of ways in the Middle Ages. It can mean a person who has been to school, a learned man, or simply a man of the church, a clergyman, although there were of course many degrees of association with the Church. In theory it is possible to distinguish between the cleric, whose duties were essentially religious, and the clerk, whose functions were purely secretarial or bureaucratic, but in practice, the clerk often served in both capacities.[145] It is not until the fifteenth century, in fact, that the word clerk becomes specialized in its present-day meaning; that is, a person who has minor administrative duties in an office.[146]

The situation was otherwise, however, in the eleventh century, and if Turoldus was a clerk, it may be assumed that he was in one of the several ranks of the ministry, that is, either in major or in minor orders. Being a clerk implies that Turoldus attended school and was exposed to classical learning, especially rhetoric, and received religious training involving familiarity with the Bible and other works of edification and spirituality. Clerks were often attached to royalty or to the households of noblemen or high-ranking ecclesiastics. Literary patronage at this time did not necessarily entail the explicit commissioning of a poem or other work as the clerk's sole obligation in return for payment of one kind or another. Quite frequently it resembled the sort of sponsorship or support a modern university provides professors—whose chief duty it is to teach—for creative writing or research in the humanities.[147]

How did Turoldus's learning shape his poem? The most important influence was the Bible. This knowledge has been abundantly detailed by Busigny, Jenkins, Dickmann, Faral, and others.[148] To cite but the most obvious borrowings, there are certain proper names—*Canelius*, *Dathan* and *Habirun*,[149] for example—the sun-stopping episode, a reminiscence of the Book of Joshua; the earthquake and storm announcing Roland's death, which are modeled on the Passion of Our Lord; Ganelon as a Judas figure; the role of the angels; and a number of biblical words and expressions.[150]

Fortitudo et sapientia has been accorded far too much significance for the interpretation of the *Roland* (INTRODUCTION, 3). This is not to say, however, that the theme does not play a role in the poem. This and the *ubi sunt* motif, as Charles searches for his nephew's body, are also part of the epic's religious inspiration.[151] A certain amount of material derives from the saints' lives, in particular the manner of depicting the hero's death as martyrdom in imitation of Christ, and the concept of death as a victory.[152] Some of this can be classified as the sort of knowledge with which almost anyone living in the Middle Ages would have been familiar. However, these allusions taken as a whole, together with the archetypes, stereotypes, and other clerical modes of perception discussed below, point to advanced schooling of the traditional sort.

A second type of clerical inspiration results from familiarity with classical authors. Several scholars—Tavernier, Jenkins, and Curtius, in particular—have studied the many situations, techniques, and themes in the *Roland* that may be said to be imitated from the classics.[153] One may mention, for instance, death wishes, foreboding, irony, olive branches as symbols of peace, omens, laments, nature responding to strong human emotion, nostalgia for a "sweet" homeland, and understatement. One of the most characteristic devices in the *Song of Roland* is that of foreshadowing, a device traditionally associated with classical writers.

No specific allusion to a classical author has been ascribed to Turoldus, but many scholars strongly sense that he was exposed to certain masterpieces of Latin literature, the *Aeneid* in particular.[154] Suetonius was also widely read in the Middle Ages and influenced Einhard's *Vita Karoli Magni*, which may in turn have been familiar to our poet.[155] There is a possible allusion in the Gautier de l'Hum episode to Suetonius's account of Augustus's cry "Vare, redde legiones." The passage is missing in Digby 23 but may have been found in the original poem composed by Turoldus.[156] Finally, one of the major themes of the *Song of Roland*, the Struggle, may derive from Prudentius, whose *Psychomachia* exerted a lasting influence on medieval art and literature.[157]

Virtually all the classical borrowings in Turoldus's epic were skillfully adapted to his purpose and are not immediately evident.[158] The poet appears to have consciously tempered his display of learning and to have artfully masked his sources.[159] Not infrequently, the modern scholar accurately perceives the nature of the influence but, being unable to put his finger on the exact source, concludes, as does Maurice Delbouille in his discussion of Ganelon's anecdote about Roland and the apple, that "cela sent l'école."[160] Curtius, Martín de Riquer, and others have listed the rhetorical figures that abound in the *Roland*: amplificatio, antithesis, apostrophe, iteratio, recapitulation, repetition, and so on, characteristics never found in such profusion in popular literature.[161]

The principal reason Latin literature was read and classical rhetoric was studied in the schools was to provide a proper foundation for interpreting the Bible and to prepare the clerk for his religious duties and for such mundane tasks as keeping records or carrying on correspondence. A by-product, doubtless considered incidental by the men of the Middle Ages but of surpassing interest to us today, was the fact that this schooling influenced clerks when they composed literature in the vernacular.

In the final analysis the difference between Turoldus and other authors of chansons de geste is not so much a question of the degree of his familiarity with the techniques of oral composition or of his mastery of clerical skills: It is rather a matter of his superior talent, that is, that spark of genius and devotion to his task which enabled him to use his knowledge and training to great effect.

8. Realism, Idealism, and the Epic Universe

Turoldus did not deliberately set out to transpose Charlemagne's campaign of 778 into contemporary terms or to make propaganda for the First Crusade or for any other similar endeavor. He simply wished to tell of an event that happened some three hundred years earlier. That circumstance, however, had been seriously altered by the passage of time and by the process of myth-building. The story would be further transformed now through the workings of his poetic imagination.

The chansons de geste were sung before aristocratic audiences who enjoyed being entertained in their castles after the evening meal, in their gardens, or while on long horseback journeys.[162] The jongleurs numbered among their many talents juggling, playing various musical instruments, singing, and tumbling, and the performance of chansons de geste was doubtless viewed in that light, that is, as entertainment. Noblemen enjoyed visualizing themselves accomplishing great deeds, striking mighty blows, and achieving the high renown associated with epic heroes.[163]

Jules Horrent points out that aristocratic audiences were sophisticated enough to appreciate esthetic effects and to recognize biblical and literary allusions.[164] This would have been even truer in the case of the clerks who happened to be present on such occasions. The moral and spiritual value of the chansons de geste was also acknowledged, for, as we have seen, authorization to have epics sung in the cloister is known to have been granted.[165] Finally, poems such as the *Song of Roland* were also heard in public squares.[166] Thus while the major figures in Turoldus's poem are aristocrats involved in actions familiar, for the most part, only to members of the privileged class, the epic itself no doubt elicited an enthusiastic response from all levels of medieval society.

The *Song of Roland* is replete with aristocratic situations: Sovereigns and knights deal with problems in characteristic fashion, assuming stances designed to enhance their reputations and relentlessly pursuing their own advantage, profit, and revenge. There is decided realism here as well as in the description of contemporary armor, equitation, feudal relationships, military organization, and the like. However, constant exaggeration and fantasy offer important counterpoint to this reflection of contemporary manners and mores, projecting everything away from the here and now into the universe of the chansons de geste.[167] There are a few conscious archaisms,[168] but epic distantiation is Turoldus's main technique for situating his characters in a realm where realism plays no part.

Of even greater significance for the interpretation of the poem is the fact that Turoldus idealizes and spiritualizes these very same activities. Thus, for example, boasting and refusing help in the face of danger are familiar aristocratic stances, but in the *Roland* they become part of the Theme of Victory associated with the hero, a process which in the present instance is religious in essence.

The metamorphosis of worldly into spiritual achievements and attitudes, and the symbolic process by which a lion becomes the devil, and a tree the Cross, constitute the least understood phenomenon in the *Song of Roland*. Viewing events and utterances in isolation or with clinical detachment, as scholars studying a particular aspect of this epic frequently do, often strips them of their true significance. It is only by situating these activities in the context of the entire work and by allowing oneself to be swept along by the poem's evocative power that one can penetrate Turoldus's overall design.

The myth-making process itself also militates against realism. Given that Roland must die, Christians are in the right, pagans in the wrong, Charles is Emperor, treachery must be punished, and so on, Turoldus is constrained to make his story line conform to these inflexible parameters. On the other hand, he obviously feels free to elaborate the legend, to create new characters and situations, and to make legendary personages behave according to his poetic vision. Thus the majestic character Charlemagne, Defender of the Faith and Ruler over the Christian World, was drawn from tradition, but Turoldus imagined him as an Abraham-Job figure, knowingly yet unhesitatingly sacrificing his nephew and steadfast in his great travail. In the eleventh century royal power was at one of its low points, yet the poet instilled great authority in the Emperor, depicted him as a priest-king, and showed him in almost daily communication with the Deity.

Whether or not consciously, Turoldus utilized archetypes and topoi that are familiar to the literary critic. He makes frequent use of irony and symbols, revealing a constant search on his part for what lies beyond literalness. Individuals are often limned with a striking gesture or are involved in dramatic confrontation, thus manifesting the poet's predilection for visual impact.

9. *Ambiguity and Logic*

Poetry often involves a peculiar ordering of reality and always entails exceptional use of language. In order to achieve certain effects, the author suggests meanings, employing, notably, the metaphorical mode. Allusive speech is inherently ambiguous, yet it conveys emotion and impressions with particular force and appeal. That medieval writers were acutely aware of the relevance of these matters is borne out by Saint Augustine in a famous passage: "No one doubts that things are perceived more readily through similitudes and that what is sought with difficulty is discovered with more pleasure."[169]

In order to reconstruct the interplay of concepts and associations in the *Song of Roland*, one must at times put aside twentieth-century notions of what constitutes logic or common sense (this is notably true in the two oliphant scenes), for what appears bizarre or unorthodox today may not have seemed at all peculiar to the poet's contemporaries.[170] Finally, it must not be assumed that all the workings of Turoldus's imagination were typical for his day and age.

10. Some Exegetical Guideposts

There are indications which suggest that Turoldus was influenced by certain contemporary views regarding literary interpretation.

In medieval Christian thought the chief events of the Old Testament were held to be mere prefigurations or archetypes of those in the New Testament.[171] This tradition dates back to the time of the Apostles. However, these typological patterns often appear forced today. For instance, Samson carrying the gates of Gaza upon his shoulders was said to prefigure Christ carrying his Cross;[172] or associating Eve with the Blessed Virgin seemed perfectly natural.[173] Medieval madonnas, such as the one dated about 1100, preserved at Essen (*Fig. 1*), frequently represent Mary as the New Eve, holding the Infant Jesus on her lap and an apple in her right hand.[174] Through Eve's fault Man was lost, through Mary's intercession he was saved.[175]

Medieval exegetes combed the Scriptures for adumbrations of the Gospel narratives, eventually concluding that all things in Creation were, in a very real sense, metaphors of the Christian experience. By the eleventh century an impressive list of such identifications had been compiled and had found its way into glosses, homilies, and a variety of devotional and didactic literature. So far as interpretation of the Bible is concerned, many exegetes distinguished four levels of meaning: the literal, the allegorical, the tropological (or moral), and the anagogical. The latter view was crystallized in a celebrated rhyming couplet:

Littera gesta docet, quod credas allegoria,
Moralis quid agas, quo tendas anagogia.[176]

The classic illustration was that Jerusalem, in the literal sense, is a city of Palestine; in the allegorical sense, the Church; in the tropological sense, the Christian soul; and in the anagogical sense, Heaven.[177]

A slight modification of this system is to be found in what Hugh of Saint Victor describes as the standard approach to all literature, whether sacred or profane, in the schools of his day. This approach involved exposing the *littera*, or grammatical points, the *sensus*, or surface meaning, then the *sententia*, or doctrinal content, of each text under consideration.[178] A widely attested formulation provides yet another distillation of the process and probably offers the most useful formula for approaching medieval texts in this fashion. Sacred texts were held to consist of a kernel and an outer shell. According to Honorius Augustodunensis: "Nux est Sacra Scriptura, cujus cortex est littera, nucleus vero spiritualis intelligentia."[179]

It would of course be ideal if one were always able to distinguish purely literary devices and meanings from deeper spiritual sense.[180] An effort will be made to do so here whenever possible, but more often than not the line between the two levels of significance cannot be discerned.

From the time of the Church Fathers, pagan literature was read by the exegetically-inclined for its moral precepts as well as for the Christian truths it was believed to mask. Thus Saint Jerome spoke of secular literature as a captive woman whose beauty and eloquence could lead to higher spiritual understanding,[181] while Saint Augustine compared its value to that of the gold and silver ornaments which the Israelites took with them when they fled from Egypt in order to put them to a better use.[182]

It is but one step from such views of the Scriptures and of classical authors to similar interpretations of vernacular literature. D. W. Robertson, Jr., is in the forefront of scholars who have promoted the study of exegetical writings as the key to understanding medieval secular authors.[183] While the "polarities" popularly associated with the Princeton professor need not concern us here,[184] many of his views are applicable to the *Song of Roland*.[185]

The *Song of Roland* has different meanings for different readers, but the possibilities afforded by what has become known as a "medieval reading" should not be overlooked. Symbolism was part and parcel of medieval education at all levels; it had important manifestations in Romanesque art and was utilized in sermons from the pulpit. The recurrence of the ironic mode in Turoldus's poem implies that the audience will be able to distinguish surface from real meanings. Reading more than one meaning into a poem or perceiving a symbolic allusion in a particular passage is not at all the same as applying the fourfold exegetical method. The latter approach is always possible of course, but Turoldus doubtless expected a far less technical mental operation on the part of most individuals in his audience—for instance, grasping the notions referred to below in the sections relating to meaning and structure.

Modern critics use the term allegory in a variety of ways that irritate many Old French specialists who prefer to restrict its meaning to the consistent and elaborate form found, for example, in the *Roman de la Rose*.[186] Yet medieval writers conceived of allegory in a much broader sense, encompassing all figurative speech, and they uncovered symbols in a manner some scholars of today find contradictory, excessive, or incongruous.[187]

The Latin *Pseudo-Turpin Chronicle* and the German *Rolandslied* are important witnesses to the process of medieval interpretation of the *Song of Roland*. The first of these works was strongly influenced by Turoldus's epic and the second is essentially a translation of the French poem.

A. *The Pseudo-Turpin Chronicle*

Opinions vary as to the exact date of the prose work purporting to be by Archbishop Turpin, but it would appear that the earliest surviving version of the Latin chronicle was composed about 1130 by a Frenchman who was familiar with Spain.[188] The following interpretations are noteworthy, for they relate to images, motifs, and themes present in the *Song of Roland* and doubtless were not foreign to Turoldus's intentions.

1. The Flowering Lances. On the eve of Charlemagne's first battle with Aigolandus near Sahagún in the province of León, the Christians plant their lances in the ground. The next morning the lances of those who are destined to die have taken root, are covered with bark, and have sprouted leaves.[189] The miracle is repeated later before the castle of Taillebourg (Charente-Maritime).[190] The image of the flowering lances ultimately stems from Psalms 92:12–13: "So the virtuous flourish like palm trees and grow as tall as the cedars of Lebanon. Planted in the house of Yahweh, they will flourish in the courts of our God."[191] In the *Song of Roland* the hero is associated with a lance or spear[192] on several occasions (vv. 707–708, 1156, Roland raises or brandishes his pennant-tipped lance; v. 720, he is the spear that Ganelon shatters in Charlemagne's first dream);[193] this weapon is merely an extension of the right arm, a symbol of power and strength (Psalms 98:1; 138:8), and a metaphor linking Charles and Roland (vv. 597, 727, 1195).[194] The flowers of Paradise (vv. 1856, 2197, 2898) and the blossoms stained with the blood of the Christian martyrs at Roncevaux (v. 2871) are related to this motif, as is the concept of the French being interred inside a church (COMMENTARY, 18, v. 1750).

2. Dying in Battle Against the Saracens Constitutes Martyrdom and Is a Source of Edification and Joy for All Christians. The miracle of the flowering lances is interpreted in the following terms: "Mira res, magnumque gaudium, magnum animabus proficuum, ingensque corporibus detrimentum! ... In praefata acies fas est intelligi salus certantium Christi."[195] Turoldus refers to Roland and his men as martyrs (vv. 1134, 1922) and their deeds help *sustenir chrestïentet* (v. 1129). The joy of martyrdom is intimately related to Charlemagne's thoughts about the slain Roland and to the terms Joyeuse and Monjoie (COMMENTARY, 28).[196]

3. Arming for Battle Likened to Girding for Spiritual Combat. In what is evidently, to the anonymous chronicler's mind, a logical development, the flowering lances suggest the battle for man's soul:

> Sicut enim Karoli milites pugnatori ante bellum arma sua ad debellandum praeparaverunt, sic et nos arma nostra, id est bonas virtutes, contra vicia pugnaturi praeparare debemus. Quisquis enim vel fidem contra haereticam pravitatem, vel caritatem contra odium, vel largitatem contra avaritiam, vel humilitatem contra superbiam, vel castitatem contra libidinem, vel orationem assiduam contra daemoniacam temptationem, vel paupertatem contra felicitatem, vel perseverantiam contra instabilitatem, vel silentium contra iurgia, vel obedientiam contra carnalem animum ponit, hasta eius florida et victrix in die iudicii Dei erit. O quam felix et florida erit in celesti regno victoris anima qui legitime contra vicia decertavit in terra! Non coronabitur quis nisi qui legitime certaverit.[197]

The metaphor derives from Ephesians 6:10–17.[198] Arming is an epic commonplace,[199] but this does not mean that it is always devoid of the spiritual significance alluded to here. In fact, Christian symbolism is strongly suggested in the riverside encampment episode (Laisses

180–182), where the motif of vigilance appears together with that of weapons. Cf. Ephesians 6:13–18:

> You must rely on God's armour ... So stand your guard, with truth buckled round your waist, and integrity for a breastplate, wearing for shoes on your feet the eagerness to spread the gospel of peace and always carrying the shield of faith so that you can use it to put out the burning arrows of the evil one. And then you must accept salvation from God to be your helmet and receive the word of God from the Spirit to use as a sword. . . . Never get tired of staying awake.

The battle of the virtues and vices, overtones of which are frequently perceived throughout Turoldus's epic, notably in the single combats, was graphically portrayed in the *Psychomachia*, but the oppositions noted in the *Pseudo-Turpin Chronicle* are not those found in Prudentius's poem. The particular alignment here derives either from contemporary tracts or from Romanesque sculpture.[200]

4. Dying in Battle Represents the Obligation to Abandon Vices and to Lead a Moral Life. In another free association the Latin chronicler links the notion of spiritual combat and martyrdom to that of "dying" to vices: "Et sicut Karoli pugnatores pro Christi fide obierunt in bello, sic et nos mori debemus viciis et vivere virtutibus sanctis in mundo, quatinus palmam de triumpho floridam habere mereamur in celesti regno."[201] The comparison is a patristic commonplace[202] stemming from Romans 6:2: "We are dead to sin, so how can we continue to live in it?" Cf. 6:11: "You too must consider yourselves to be dead to sin but alive for God in Christ Jesus."

5. Fleeing from the Enemy Signifies Moral Laxness in Combating Vices. Following a truce, during which Charles attempts to convert Aigolandus in a theological debate, battle is resumed. Twenty, forty, then a hundred Christians slay an equal number of Saracens. However, when a hundred more Christians attack, the enemy destroys them all because they have fled out of fear.

> Hii vero tipum gerunt certantium fidelium Christi. Quia, qui pro Dei fide volunt pugnare, nullo modo debent retro abire. Et sicut illi ideo occiduntur quia retro fugerunt, sic Christi fideles qui debent fortiter contra vicia pugnare, si retro reversi fuerint, in viciis turpiter

> moriuntur. Sed qui bene contra vicia pugnant, hi inimicos, id est daemones qui vicia administrant, leviter occidunt. Non coronabitur quis, inquit apostolus, nisi qui legitime certaverit.[203]

The reference in the last sentence is to 2 Timothy 2:5.[204] In the *Song of Roland* fleeing is an act generally associated with the Saracens, and *Paien s'en fuient* is a first-hemistich formula used in vv. 2162, 2164, 2460, 3625, 3634 (cf. v. 1875). Scholars have read religious meaning in the image of the Saracens running before Roland (v. 1874: Si cum li cerfs s'en vait devant les chiens). It is also worth noting that when Gautier de l'Hum makes his eleventh-hour appearance, he is said to have been forced to flee from the enemy (v. 2043: Voeillet o nun, desuz cez vals s'en fuit). (See COMMENTARY, 21.)

6. Charlemagne's Victory Demonstrates that Christianity Transcends All Other Faiths. There is no Baligant episode in the *Pseudo-Turpin Chronicle*, but the Emperor's struggle against Aigolandus, which precedes Roncevaux in the Latin work, has points in common with this lengthy incident in Turoldus's poem. When Aigolandus is decisively defeated at Pamplona, the chronicler offers this commentary: "Quapropter patet quia lex christiana omnes ritus et leges tocius mundi excellit sua bonitate. Cuncta transcendit, super angelos etiam ascendit."[205] The idea that Christianity is superior to all other religions is central to the meaning of the *Song of Roland* (INTRODUCTION, 11, A). Unwavering faith permeates Turoldus's entire epic. Its major themes gravitate about this ideal and its story line is constructed on the Abraham-Isaac archetype, a symbol of instant and unquestioning acquiescence to divine promptings. One of the most important metaphors in the *Roland* has to do with Ascent (INTRODUCTION, 15, C). The Latin chronicler thinks along the same lines, for he continues the passage in the following fashion:

> O Christiane, si fidem bene tenueris corde, et operibus in quantum poteris adimpleveris, veraciter super angelos cum capite tuo Christo, cuius membrum es, sublimatus eris. Si vis ascendere, firmiter crede; quia omnia possibilia sunt credenti, dicit Dominus.[206]

7. Despoiling Battlefield Victims Viewed as Returning to Sinful Ways. Following Charlemagne's great victory over Aigolandus, about a thousand Christians, coveting gold, silver, and other riches, return to the battlefield. Loaded down with spoils, they are on their way back to camp when the Almaçor of Córdoba and his cohorts ambush and slay them to the last man. According to the chronicler:

> Hii vero tipum gerunt certancium Christi. Quia sicut illi, postquam inimicos suos devicerunt, ad mortuos, cupiditatis causa, redierunt, et interficiuntur ab inimicis, sic fidelis quisque, qui vicia sua devicit, et poenitenciam accepit, ad mortuos, id est ad vicia, iterum redire non debet, ne forte ab inimicis, id est a daemonibus, interficiatur malo fine.[207]

Amplifying his thought and aiming his shafts now at monks who betray their calling, the anonymous author adds:

> Et sicut illi qui ad aliena spolia revertentes praesentem vitam perdiderunt, et necem turpe acceperunt, sic religiosi quique qui seculum dimiserunt, et ad terrena negocia postea inflectuntur, vitam celestem perdunt, et mortem perpetuam amplectuntur.[208]

There is no such episode in the *Song of Roland*, but readers will be struck by the parallel with the Rash Saracen incident in Laisses 178–179. As Roland, eyes closed, solemnly prepares to meet his Maker, a pagan soldier, who until this moment has been feigning death, rushes toward him, hoping to take Durendal away as a trophy. The hero, feeling his sword slip from his grasp, opens his eyes and, summoning up his last reserve of strength, strikes the Saracen a mortal blow with the oliphant. The passage lends itself to various interpretations, one of which readily suggests itself following a reading of the battlefield despoliation scene in the *Pseudo-Turpin*.

8. Ganelon's Betrayal Parallels that of Judas. At bay at Roncevaux, Roland sounds the oliphant. Charlemagne hears its call and wants to rush to his nephew's aid. Ganelon attempts to dissuade the Emperor, suggesting that his stepson blows the horn at the slightest provocation and is probably merely hunting a wild animal in the forest. However, Ganelon is well aware that Roland is dying and his counsel is the height of treachery: "O subdola controversia! O Ganaloni pravum consilium, Iudae proditoris tradicioni comparatum!"[209] The Judas comparison, clearly yet only indirectly alluded to in the French original (e.g., the manner in which Ganelon is introduced in v. 178, betrayal with a kiss, the greed motive including the *denarii* mentioned in v. 1148, and, by inference, the Christlike characterization of Roland, the individual he betrays),[210] is thus spelled out in the *Pseudo-Turpin Chron-*

icle. The Ganelon-Judas connection became a literary commonplace in the Middle Ages.[211]

B. The Rolandslied

Exegetical commentary is also evident in Conrad's German adaptation of the *Song of Roland.* As in the case of the *Pseudo-Turpin Chronicle,* from which it borrowed, considerable controversy swirls around the date of the *Rolandslied,* which appears to have been composed about 1170.[212] Following are some of the observations by Conrad that relate to the matter at hand.

1. Ganelon's Treason again Likened to that of Judas. On the way to Saragossa Blancandrin and Ganelon reach an agreement to kill the hero. In Turoldus's poem the plot is hatched on horseback but in no particular locale (vv. 402–404: Tant chevalcherent Guenes e Blancandrins / Que l'un a l'altre la sue feit plevit / Que il querreient que Rollant fust ocis). Although the preliminary discussion in Conrad takes place in the same fashion, the final details are worked out during a halt under an olive tree (v. 1920: under einem oeleboume), mentioned only in passing at the beginning of the scene in the French original (v. 366: Guenes chevalchet suz une olive halte).[213] The German translator then states that Ganelon imitated "poor" Judas (v. 1925: den armen Iudas er gebildot), who betrayed Christ for thirty pieces of silver.[214] Conrad even suggests that Ganelon's treachery was greater, for whereas Judas sold only his Master, the villain of his poem sold a large number of noble Christians to the Infidel (vv. 1936–1939). Finally, when Ganelon vainly tries to persuade Charles not to answer Roland's oliphant call, Conrad has Naimes characterize the villain as a man in Satan's power and whose behavior has been worse than that of Judas, who betrayed Our Lord (vv. 6102–6104).

2. A Handsome Exterior May Mask an Evil Heart. Ganelon's good looks and impressive physique are detailed by Turoldus in vv. 283–285, immediately after Roland nominates his stepfather for the mission to Saragossa, and again at Aix just as the traitor begins his formal defense (v. 3763). In the latter instance Ganelon's handsomeness is promptly followed by a crucial disclaimer: *S'il fust leials, ben resemblast barun* (v. 3764), a phrase linking him to the evil Saracens (vv. 899, 3164).

Ganelon's attractive features have misled many scholars into believing that Turoldus stood in grudging admiration of the traitor or, for some reason or other, refrained from painting him completely black. Nothing could be further from the truth, as the German version makes abundantly clear. Conrad omits the two descriptions of Ganelon cited above, but he inserts a comparable phrase (v. 1960: Genelun was michel unde lussam) in the council scene on the way to Saragossa. He compares the handsome villain to a tree that is green on the outside but is rotten to the core. This symbol, he explains, represents the man who speaks fine words but has a false heart (vv. 1962–1975). The allusion is doubtless to Christ's warning about false prophets: "You will be able to tell them by their fruits. Can people pick grapes from thorns, or figs from thistles? In the same way, a sound tree produces good fruit but a rotten tree bad fruit."[215]

3. Ganelon Was Inspired by the Devil. In Conrad the discussion between Ganelon and Marsile at Saragossa begins, as in the French version, beneath a pine tree (v. 407: Un faldestoet out suz l'umbre d'un pin; cf. v. 500: Vait s'apuier suz le pin a la tige). However, in Turoldus's poem Marsile and his advisers subsequently withdraw to a garden (v. 501: Enz el verger s'en est alez li reis) where Ganelon is later led before the Saracen king (v. 510: Enz el verger l'en meinet josqu'al rei). No garden is mentioned in the German translation, although movement away from the pine tree is clearly implied at one point (vv. 2176–2178). In the *Rolandslied* the council is chiefly associated with the pine tree and is, in fact, referred to in a style reminiscent of the manner of designating adventures in the romances as *der Pinrat* (v. 2411). Nowhere in the *Song of Roland* does the poet specify that Ganelon was inspired by the devil, although the villain's machinations and sacrilegious oath are clearly diabolical, and Charlemagne's angry reaction to his nomination of Roland to the rearguard (vv. 746–747: Si li ad dit: "Vos estes vifs diables, / El cors vos est entree mortel rage!") is tantamount to such an accusation. Conrad shows no comparable reticence (v. 2365: Den tuuil gab ime den sin) and, having identified the diabolical source of Ganelon's deeds in the Pine Tree episode, likens his words to that of the Accuser (Heb. *satan*) in Psalms 109:6.

4. Companionage is a Holy Bond. As the French heroes prepare for battle, Conrad compares their comradely devotion to one another to the brotherly love binding priests and Levites in Psalm 133 (vv. 3455–

3457). Companionage is frequently alluded to in the French original and, at times, clearly assumes the mystical quality referred to by the German poet.[216]

5. *The Pinabel-Thierry Duel Compared to the Slaying of Goliath.* Pinabel's giant stature as opposed to his adversary's slightness is plainly designed to enhance the magnitude of Thierry's victory. Such an unequal duel also, however, brings to mind the David and Goliath archetype, a connection specifically made by Conrad (vv. 8847–8850).[217]

One must avoid the pitfall of suggesting that, because Conrad or the author of the *Pseudo-Turpin Chronicle* read certain meanings into characters and situations found in the *Song of Roland*, Turoldus necessarily shared these views. One must always distinguish, too, between the artist's work and the meanings that contemporary or later translators and adapters—not to mention modern critics—attach to it.[218] A good example of the gap that exists between theory and practice in the Middle Ages may be seen in the curious views found in heraldic treatises, which are often strikingly at variance with the art practiced by contemporary compilers of blazoned or painted rolls of arms.[219]

Turoldus tends to narrate events and leave their interpretation to his audience, whereas the Latin chronicler and the German translator frequently explain them to us. Their glosses may at times seem destructive of the obscurity or variety of possible interpretations we enjoy wrestling with.[220]

On the other hand, Turoldus had no intention of mystifying his audience. His art is often one of subtle suggestion, but he also wanted his meaning to be understood: *Ki tant ne set ne l'ad prod entendut* (v. 2098). Many renderings in the *Pseudo-Turpin* and the *Rolandslied* ring false and must obviously be ignored. This does not mean, however, that their novel interpretations and commentaries should all be summarily dismissed. There is, after all, a good chance that Conrad and the Latin chronicler were at times more attuned to Turoldus than modern readers can ever hope to be.

11. *The Meaning of the Song of Roland*

In addition to the literal sense conveyed by the story line, there is another dimension in Turoldus's poem. This deeper meaning, which has to do with its moral and spiritual significance, is at times only dimly perceived, yet it is ever-present in this work and is fundamental to its correct interpretation.

A. *Superiority of the Christian Religion*

The essential statement made by Turoldus is that Christianity transcends all other faiths. It is so superior, in fact, as to be in a class by itself, other forms of belief being poor excuses for religion.

B. *Election*[221]

In Turoldus's view God has chosen Charlemagne and the Franks for a special task, that of establishing his rule throughout the world by means of armed conquest or conversion. This election is chiefly embodied in the figure of Charlemagne. Roland fights to defend his *los* and the reputation of his parents, of France, and of Charlemagne. However, at the time the poem was composed, these ideals were frequently synonymous and had deep spiritual significance (COMMENTARY, 13 and 14). In the eleventh century Frenchmen considered themselves to be the Chosen People, the nation selected by God to accomplish his ends, and believed that the Emperor was the *vicarius Christi*.[222] This ideology is manifest in the *De consecratione pontificum et regum*, composed by the Norman Anonymous about 1100:

> The power of the king is the power of God, in that God possesses it by his nature and the king through grace. Thus the king also is God and Christ, but through grace; and everything he does, he does not do simply as a man but as a result of having become God and Christ through grace.[223]

This christological concept explains the bold transposition of the Majestas Domini in the Gospel Book of Otto II at Aachen (*Fig. 2*), executed about 973:

> [L'empereur] est véritablement divinisé en ce sens qu'il trône comme le Sauveur carolingien de Gyulia Fehervar, comme les Sauveurs

ottoniens de Darmstadt et de Heidelberg, originaires de la Reichenau, au sein d'une gloire entourée du tétramorphe. Otton II tient le globe crucigère, tandis que sur sa tête, la Main du Père dépose un diadème. Ce couronnement est un legs carolingien (cf. Sacramentaire de Corbie à Paris, B.N. lat. 1141, 2e moitié du IXe siècle), ainsi que l'assistance des guerriers et des clercs (comme dans le Codex aureus de Saint-Emmeran à Munich Clm. 14000, vers 870). Aussi bien, la célèbre formule "a deo coronatus" est-elle utilisée dès le règne de Charlemagne sur les actes de chancellerie. Cependant les apports de la Basse-Antiquité sont encore plus significatifs à Aix-la-Chapelle: intervention de la Terre, symbole de domination universelle, qui, accroupie, supporte le poids du tabouret impérial—mais surtout "christomimétisme" dont s'accompagne l'apothéose, comme le montre E. Kantorowicz: entrée en vigueur, sur le plan chrétien, d'un principe cher aux derniers empereurs de la Rome païenne, car Otton II est la réplique visible de la Majestas Domini, comme Probus ou Constantin le sont du "Sol Invictus" dont ils s'avèrent les sosies sur certaines de leurs monnaies. Quant au fond d'or, utilisé ici pour la première fois dans l'enluminure occidentale, il provient directement de l'art byzantin posticonoclaste.[224]

C. Sapientia

Christomimeticism leads inevitably to Sapientia. The virtually inexhaustible concept of wisdom in the Middle Ages derives from popular as well as from learned sources.[225] However, a distinction was always drawn between worldly wisdom and Divine Wisdom. The latter was considered to be one of the attributes of God and was identified with Christ. As a corollary, one finds the notion that all worldly wisdom was vanity, whereas the Folly of the Cross was the only true Wisdom. This idea is frequently expressed in the Epistles of Saint Paul. Saint Augustine's views, which dominated all metaphysical speculation on the subject until the end of the eleventh century, are derived from that concept.

A study of the terminology of wisdom in the *Song of Roland* reveals that, with one notable exception,[226] it has nothing to do with Sapientia in the biblical sense but refers instead to things of this world. Most of the time these terms have to do with military decisions—either in a council or before or during a battle—or with diplomacy. Such wisdom was held in high regard during the Middle Ages except, of course, when it pertained to an evil person whose vice transformed it into cunning or guile. Turoldus repeatedly underscores the vanity of such wisdom, represented here by the advice and counsel offered by the majority of the Franks, and by the Saracens.

Nevertheless, the type of Sapientia found in the Bible and in the writings of the Fathers of the Church is very much in evidence in Turoldus's poem. It is apparent in Turpin's revelations concerning the significance of the Battle of Roncevaux, and in Roland's arduous ascent and incarnation of the Folly of the Cross. Above all, it is evident in Charlemagne's perception of the tragedy as it unfolds and in his key role in allowing it to happen.[227]

Wisdom in the *Song of Roland* implies unswerving faith in God, absolute confidence in the inevitability of Christian victory, and total commitment to the view that immediate and spontaneous compliance with divine promptings is the way to personal salvation and to the edification of mankind.

Sapientia is the supreme virtue and, like all such qualities, a gift from God. But it is not easily acquired. The Church Fathers believed that the Liberal Arts could at best provide a beginning of learning. True insight into the meaning of things was to be found in Scripture alone.[228] Turoldus epitomizes Wisdom in his poem by *Monjoie*, which often suggests Joy mixed with Suffering,[229] and *Roncevaux*, where life is viewed as a Vale of Tears, but with Joy at the End of the Journey.[230]

D. *Martyrdom: Imitatio Christi*

Roland's *passio* is the central fact in Turoldus's poem: The hero's suffering and death is an imitation of Christ, and his sacrifice constitutes a new kind of martyrdom.[231]

Anyone endeavoring to justify Roland's behavior has to contend with a number of ambivalent character traits, in particular his boasting (INTRODUCTION, 19, C) and his apparent indifference to the fate of his men at Roncevaux (COMMENTARY, 18). Roland may be a martyr, but his behavior does not coincide with the modern idea of the individual who voluntarily suffers death for his faith.

It is difficult for the modern mind to apprehend the medieval ideal embodied by Roland. However, an illuminating parallel is to be found in the stubborn and imprudent conduct of Thomas Becket, whom the Church has always regarded as one of its most glorious martyrs.[232]

Turoldus created complex characters, but he surely did not mean to highlight the hero's weakness or to portray him as a scapegoat. Roland's unswerving determination to play the role assigned to him and his exemplary death are Christlike and were intended to edify, that is, to instruct and fortify Turoldus's contemporaries. "Mira res, magnumque gaudium, magnum animabus proficuum, ingensque corporibus detrimentum," exclaims the anonymous author of the *Pseudo-Turpin Chronicle* at the death of the Franks, revealing indifference to what is detrimental to the body as he considers with unbounded joy the soul's enormous benefit (INTRODUCTION, 10, A, 2).[233]

The seeming ingenuousness that characterizes the Latin chronicler's solution to the age-old problem of the premature death of just men (quia noluit ut ad propriam patriam amplius redirent, ne forte in aliquibus delictis incurrerent; et enim voluit illis pro laboribus suis coronam celestis regni per passionem impendere)[234] has a basis in Wisdom 4:11 ([The virtuous man] has been carried off so that evil may not warp his understanding or treachery seduce his soul), an answer which, the biblical sage readily admits, leaves many looking on, uncomprehending (4:14).

Roland must die, for "unless a wheat grain falls on the ground and dies, it remains only a single grain, but if it dies, it yields a rich harvest."[235]

The hero's sacrifice gives the poem a mystical dimension that is extended by Durendal, Joyeuse, the oliphant, the landscape, and the rituals associated with the passing of the Franks. Sacredness in the *Roland* is further enhanced by the contrasting effect of Ganelon's sacrilegious oath and Judas-like betrayal, the pagans' demonic presence, and the intrusion of the Rash Saracen at the moment of Roland's death. The dying attitude and position on the field assumed by Roland and the way he arranges the bodies of his slain comrades are important semaphore messages for Charles and his men (COMMENTARY, 21–24, 26, 34). Viewed from a Romanesque perspective, Charles's triumphs over Marsile's and Baligant's forces, Bramimonde's conversion, and Thierry's victory are the fruits of Roland's martyrdom. Miraculous occurrences such as these traditionally follow the saint's *passio*.[236]

E. The Strict Alternative

The *Song of Roland* is not merely a paean to martyrdom; it is also, and above all, life viewed as a series of difficult choices, the correct response requiring one to follow the hard road and to enter by the narrow gate.[237] Roland, like Christ, provokes dissension because of the strict alternative he offers, whether in council (his recommendation with respect to Marsile's proposal) or on the battlefield (the debate with Oliver): "Do not suppose that I have come to bring peace to the earth: it is not peace I have come to bring, but a sword. For I have come to set a man against his father, a daughter against her mother, a daughter-in-law against her mother-in-law. A man's enemies will be those of his own household" (Matthew 10:34–36). At the conclusion of the poem, the prospect before Charles of yet another campaign constitutes a brilliant extension of this agonistic metaphor.[238] Life is a never-ending Roncevaux that must be faced with courage and with faith (INTRODUCTION, 15, A and E).

12. Literature Through Art: Iconographic Formulas[239] *and Transpositions*

Visualizing a scene in the way Turoldus imagined it is not as simple as it may seem. Details provided by the author are sparse, and the association of ideas and images of a poet who lived nine hundred years ago is often very different from our own. Contemporary literary witnesses can be of help in interpreting the *Song of Roland*. Romanesque art also offers insights into the working of Turoldus's poetic imagination.

Looking at a picture as opposed to reading or listening to literature involves a different set of skills—and these should decidedly not be minimized—but in each instance the critical faculty finds itself engaged in similar operations: perceiving the various levels of meaning conveyed by the object before it, understanding how it functions, and appreciating its originality by studying it against the background of the sources and analogues that influenced it.

One also wonders perhaps whether it is legitimate to use religious art to interpret profane works. The didactic content of medieval secular literature is a moot question, but in the *Song of Roland* the line separating this world and the next often simply does not exist. Also, no real obstacle prevented the transfer of artistic models to the literary domain whether the latter was ostensibly religious or secular.

Investigations of the *Song of Roland* in the light of contemporary art have tended to emphasize structure, although formulas and themes, symbolism and typology have also been studied in this respect. In their monumental study of the Roland legend in medieval art, Rita Lejeune and Jacques Stiennon have argued that the iconography of the hero remains remarkably close to the literary texts that have survived.[240] Whether dealing with manuscript illuminations, murals, sculpture, tapestry, or the work of gold and silversmiths, one finds, according to the Belgian scholars, great faithfulness to the written versions of the legend. The Oxford version of the *Song of Roland* will be considered here from exactly the opposite point of view. The impact of Romanesque models on Turoldus's artistic imagination will be studied rather than the relationship of the text to the interpretations of artists and craftsmen who came later.

In two key passages Roland and then Charles invoke God, using the curious expression *veire Paterne* 'true God' (vv. 2384, 3100). *Paterne* here is merely a synonym for God and is said to derive from Ecclesiastical Latin *(imago) paterna,* literally 'image, picture of God the Father'.[241] *Veire Paterne* in this context elicited the following observation from Gaston Paris at the turn of the century:

> On pense à ces colossales images de Dieu le père, à ces 'majestés' en mosaïque, qui remplissent le fond des absides ou les voûtes des coupoles dans les églises byzantines.[242]

When Paris wrote these lines, Romanesque art was little appreciated. It is not surprising, then, that the dean of French medievalists thought of Byzantine mosaics rather than the more obvious Romanesque wall-paintings, for instance the magnificent Christ in majesty at Berzé-la-Ville (*Fig. 3*), which is contemporary with Turoldus's poem.[243] Paris wrote that *he* was reminded of a Majestas Domini. The point that needs to be made is that the *poet* doubtless had this image in mind too.

Romanesque art is extremely conservative and is characterized by the recurrence in time and space of conventional figurations. Once one or two basic forms had evolved to depict the major events of the Bible, they persisted. While these patterns remained frozen, they were used with great economy and flexibility. One depiction is considered suitable for another—to our way of thinking—quite different set of circumstances. Strange metamorphoses are commonplace, particularly in the transference from the religious to the secular domain.[244] From Byzantine times, for example, the shape of the table used in illustrations of the Last Supper and of the Wedding at Cana was often the one found in the window of the narthex at Charlieu (*Fig. 4*), dated about 1140.[245] The table is of the sigma type, a term derived from the archaic Greek letter resembling a C on its side. The sigma table also appears in the Bayeux Tapestry, embroidered sometime before the end of the eleventh century, in a scene depicting Bishop Odo surrounded by William and the chiefs of the expedition shortly after the Normans have landed on English soil[246] (*Fig. 5*).

Two types of transposition may be discerned: An arbitrary or purely formal one, that is, one where the formula is merely a convenient mould into which new meaning is poured, as opposed to the kind in which a little and sometimes a good deal of the meaning of the prototype is carried over. Leaving artistic examples aside for the moment, when Charles, in the *Song of Roland*, is looking for the bodies of the fallen heroes, his lament is based upon the *ubi sunt* refrain.[247] However, the Emperor is not decrying the vanity of worldly endeavors, the traditional use made of this topos; he is, rather, showing great honor to the dead by his royal lament.[248] There is relatively little carry-over here, then. On the other hand, when Roland dies in a manner recalling the Passion, this *imitatio Christi* can hardly be said to be devoid of significance.[249] Often, though, the carry-over is problematical: Does the scene in the Bayeux Tapestry suggest that William and his men are doing God's work on English soil?

In the illustration of the communion of the Franks before the Battle of Roncevaux in the *Rolandslied*, the sketches form a pair (*Figs. 6 and 7*)[250] and are plainly modeled on the Communion of the Apostles formula in Byzantine and Ottonian art. In synoptic fashion—two succeeding scenes shown simultaneously—the two central figures, both of which depict Christ, serve bread then wine to the Twelve[251] (*Fig. 8*). For the German artist Turpin represents Christ, and the Twelve Peers, the Twelve Apostles.

The early-fourteenth-century manuscript known as Venice IV contains two works, a Franco-Italian version of the *Roland* and a copy of the epic known as *Aspremont*, which purports to tell Roland's childhood adventures.[252] There are several historiated initials, one of which (*Fig. 9*) concerns Turoldus's poem. Lejeune and Stiennon note the similarity between this initial and the one that begins *Aspremont* in the same manuscript[253] (*Fig. 10*). The latter shows a Saracen king crowning his son. According to the Belgian scholars, the *Roland* initial illustrates the encounter between Ganelon and Marsile. However, it is hard to imagine that a medieval illuminator would assign such a prominent place to the latter scene to the exclusion of all others in the poem and portray the traitor kneeling with arms crossed.

It seems far more likely that the Venice IV artist was reproducing here a formula associated with the Coronation of the Virgin, notably in Italian painting of the fourteenth century[254] (*Fig. 11*). The kneeling and crossed-armed pose recalls in striking fashion the attitude of humility adopted by Mary. Humility and virginity correspond to the hero's character traits in Turoldus's poem (INTRODUCTION, 19, F).[255] Was the manuscript illuminator, then, visualizing the arrival of Roland's soul before its Maker in a manner slightly different from that found in depictions of Turpin's vision in the *Pseudo-Turpin Chronicle*?[256] (*Fig. 12*) Or is this perhaps an adaptation of another formula representing Abraham's Bosom?[257] (*Fig. 13*) The Abraham archetype figures in the *Song of Roland* (INTRODUCTION, 13, C).[258]

Turoldus appears to have been influenced by a number of iconographic formulas used by contemporary artists to depict scenes in the Old and New Testaments. The author's use of formulaic diction parallels this practice, since at times he employed patterns strictly according to tradition, whereas at other times he adapted them in an original way.

13. Structure[259]

The *Song of Roland* is a very complex work. However, since Bédier, scholars have been in agreement about one thing—that Turoldus's epic is a well-structured poem.

Most commentators consider the work to have four parts. Some assert that the third section, which includes a long battle in the course of which the Emperor routs Baligant's army, was an interpolation by Turoldus, that is, by the individual responsible for the version preserved in the Oxford manuscript.[260] The four divisions are usually given as (1) the betrayal of Ganelon; (2) the death of Roland; (3) the punishment of the Saracens; and (4) the punishment of Ganelon. Rychner's detailed outline shows four subdivisions in the first part (Prélude à Roncevaux), eight in the second (Roncevaux), four in the third (Baligant), and three in the last part (Le Jugement de Ganelon).[261]

The many analyses of the *Roland* that have been published thus far suggest that there is but one story line or plot, and that its various parts are well defined. Closer examination reveals that Turoldus imagined a twofold and parallel structure from beginning to end, and that each episode is so well-integrated into the whole that it loses much of its meaning when considered in isolated fashion.

The word *tableau* should be avoided when referring to individual scenes in the *Roland*, except where a decidedly static or frozen impression is conveyed by the passage. Instead, one should think in terms of interlocked episodes, such as those found in the Durham Life of Saint Cuthbert, c. 1120–30[262] (*Fig. 14*). This strip-composition technique sets off each scene without isolating it, thus preserving the integrity of the narrative and suggesting that the various points of the story are intimately related.[263]

There are many narrative patterns in Turoldus's poem—some are designated below as themes or metaphors—that can be referred to as "structures." For instance, the work may be viewed as focusing on three battles, each interrupted by a verbal clash:

1. Roncevaux—the Roland-Oliver debate has two phases, vv. 1051 ff., 1702 ff.
2. Baligant—Charles's heated exchange with the Emir is recorded in vv. 3589–3600.
3. The Judicial Combat—Pinabel's offer to give quarter is countered by a similar attempt at persuasion by Thierry, vv. 3892–3909.

Or, one may consider the *Roland* in terms of three series of angelic visitations anticipating events at the heart of the poem:

1. Charles dreams of Ganelon's treachery and of the Pinabel-Thierry duel,[264] vv. 717 ff., 725 ff.
2. Charles dreams of the battle against Baligant and of the trial of Ganelon, vv. 2525 ff., 2555 ff.
3. Charles dreams of a new campaign against the Infidel, vv. 3992 ff.[265]

Finally, a seven-day chronology—preceded by an allusion to a seven-year campaign[266] and followed, later,[267] by a trial lasting another day—takes up the major portion of the narrative (COMMENTARY, 9, 29, 30).

However, the following organizing principles have far greater relevance to the structure of the *Song of Roland*.

13. STRUCTURE

A. Parallelism

Scholars have long emphasized the numerous oppositions and parallels in the poem.[268] Roland and Oliver constitute the most often-cited antithesis, but there is also a conscious contrast between Charles and his archrival Baligant, and between the Twelve French Peers and the Twelve Saracen Peers. Bédier seems to have been the first to point out parallelism in the Saracen council in the opening scene and the French gathering, which immediately follows.[269] Roland volunteers his stepfather for the dangerous mission to Saragossa (v. 277: "Ço ert Guenes, mis parastre"); Ganelon, upon his return, designates his stepson for the perilous rearguard (v. 743: "Rollant, cist miens fillastre"). Roland gives Oliver a number of reasons for not sounding the oliphant to call Charles to the rescue; Oliver uses the same arguments against his companion when Roland decides to blow the horn after all. These and many other antithetical characters and situations[270] evince a decided taste for irony and, above all, a marked tendency for dual modes of expression on the part of the poet.

B. The Two Story Lines

Turoldus constructed a twofold narrative, the two plots each hinging on betrayal: the attempt by Marsile to deceive Charlemagne (Plot A) and Ganelon's treason (Plot B).

Plot A	*Plot B*
CHARLES–MARSILE–BALIGANT	ROLAND–GANELON
I. Prologue: The Initial Betrayal; Marsile plots to deceive Charles	
	II. The quarrel between Roland and Ganelon
	III. The Second Betrayal; Ganelon arranges a Saracen ambush
	IV. Death of Roland at Roncevaux

V. The Initial Punishment; Marsile's army is routed by Charles

VI. Amplification: Arrival of Baligant's forces, which are in turn defeated by Charles

VII. The Final Punishment; Ganelon is found guilty and is executed

VIII. Epilogue: Charles must undertake two new campaigns

There are some fourscore separate scenes in the *Song of Roland*, and it is possible to arrive at an outline containing three, four, five, or more parts, but Turoldus's episodes are so closely intertwined that undue concern over the exact number of subdivisions has caused scholars to lose sight of the poem's essentially parallel structure. If one leaves aside chronological considerations, this parallelism becomes even more evident:

Plot A CHARLES–MARSILE–BALIGANT	*Plot B* ROLAND–GANELON
I. Prologue: The Initial Betrayal; Marsile plots to deceive Charles	II. The quarrel between Roland and Ganelon
V. The Initial Punishment; Marsile's army is routed by Charles	III. The Second Betrayal; Ganelon arranges a Saracen ambush

VI. Amplification: Arrival of Baligant's forces, which are in turn defeated by Charles	IV. Death of Roland at Roncevaux
VIII. Epilogue: Charles must undertake two new campaigns	VII. The Final Punishment; Ganelon is found guilty and is executed

It is helpful to think of this bipartite alignment in terms of the narrative technique utilized in certain works of Romanesque art. In the famous bronze doors of the Chapel of Saint Anne in the Cathedral of Hildesheim (*Fig. 15*), cast for Bishop Bernward in 1015, the left-hand panels figure scenes from the Old Testament, the right-hand, episodes from the New Testament.[271] Parallel arrangement of scenes is found in numerous Ottonian and Romanesque gospel books and pericopes. The technique was in even greater vogue in Gothic art, notably in diptychs and triptychs. The reason is quite simple: A side-by-side arrangement lends itself admirably well to typology.

C. The Abraham Archetype

One of the most important typological symbols of the Middle Ages was that of Abraham sacrificing Isaac, considered as a prefiguration of God the Father sacrificing his son Jesus.[272] Abraham did not actually slay his son, for the blade was stayed by an angel sent from On High, whereas Jesus did die on the Cross. For biblical exegetes, however, what mattered was Abraham's gesture. The passage in Genesis reads: "Abraham stretched out his hand and seized the knife to kill his son." And the angel of Yahweh said: "Do not harm him, for now I know you fear God. You have not refused me your son, your only son."[273]

This typology plays a key role in the *Song of Roland*.[274] Like Abraham, Charlemagne is a priest-king. He is associated with great age, is venerated as the father of his people, and is personally summoned by God to accomplish certain acts, one of the most significant of which is the sacrifice of a close relative. For medieval exegetes Abraham was the exemplar of Faith.

Referring back to the twofold structure of Turoldus's poem, one perceives that the Abraham archetype, which dominates Plot A, relates to a Christ figure, Roland, in Plot B, that is, when viewing reality in a Romanesque way.

14. Thematic Unity

The *Song of Roland* is compartmentalized to a certain degree, but major themes provide important links between its various parts and constitute a matter of far greater consequence than the precise number of sections.[275]

A. Good versus Evil

The notion of Good versus Evil assumes myriad forms in Turoldus's poem. In this, the *Song of Roland* mirrors recurring patterns in contemporary iconography. In numerous artistic examples these elemental conflicting forces are further characterized, for instance, as the Battle of the Virtues and Vices, Daniel and the Lion, David and the Bear, Saint George and the Dragon, or Theodoric's Wild Ride.[276] Just as frequently, however, the combat is represented as an anonymous and obscure one, pitting beast against beast, beast against man, or man against man. Bizarre animals and horrifying monsters are at times involved, and man is either victor or victim in these death struggles. This theme recurs so frequently in Romanesque art that in effect, if not in intent, it often loses its original impact and becomes purely ornamental in nature.[277]

The close affinity between the notion of Good versus Evil and the opposition between *dreit* and *tort* and its related modalities in the *Song of Roland* is obvious. Lejeune and Stiennon affirm that the poem suggested popular identifications of these forms and shapes at a very early date.[278] Conflicts between armed knights gave rise to the notion that these religious symbols portrayed incidents in the *Roland*. Early in the twelfth century, at Angoulême, Limoges, and Verona, for instance, the poem would inspire artists to depict certain episodes in the churches they were decorating.[279]

Reversing the procedure, what specific portrayals of the Theme of Good versus Evil in contemporary art may have influenced Turoldus's choice of imagery?

1. Beast versus Man. In Charlemagne's second and third dreams, wild animals and monsters prey upon him and his men. Hapless men being devoured by wild animals appear frequently in Romanesque sculpture and are generally believed to symbolize spiritual death. This motif should not be confused with that of a man being regurgitated by an animal, an image associated with Jonah and the Whale, representing Christ's Resurrection, or that of the bodies on Judgment Day.[280] Before his battle against Baligant, Charlemagne prays God to spare him as he did Jonah and also Daniel in the lions' den (vv. 3101–3102, 3104–3105).[281] The Emperor implores God for physical protection here, but also for the salvation of his soul.

Reversal of the traditional identification of good and evil is suggested in the *Song of Roland* when the French are compared to lions and leopards (vv. 1111, 1888), and when swine and dogs devour the idols of Mohammed, the Saracen deity (v. 2590).

2. Beast versus Beast. The image of dogs chasing a stag is often found in Romanesque churches. Lejeune and Stiennon believe that the stag hunt at Angoulême (*Fig. 16*) is a direct allusion to vv. 1874–1875 in the *Song of Roland.*[282] This iconographic motif is usually interpreted as the wages of sin, which lead man inexorably to Hell, or Christ delivering the repentant sinner from eternal damnation.

Another use of the theme of animals fighting against each other is found in Charles's second dream (vv. 730–733).

3. Man versus Man. Fear of the Saracens developed steadily in the tenth and eleventh centuries, and it is only natural that, beginning with the earliest Romanesque sculpture, the confrontation of armed knights should be an ambivalent motif representing either the struggle between Good and Evil, between Christian and Muslim, or both.[283] Kite-shaped shields are sometimes used to distinguish Christian soldiers from their Saracen counterparts, who bear round bucklers. Lejeune and Stiennon have shown that this formula readily lent itself to representations of the duel between Roland and Ferracutus in the *Pseudo-Turpin.*[284]

4. Light versus Dark. While the reflection of sunlight on armor, shields, and weapons in the *Song of Roland* is obviously a cliché,[285] Helmut A. Hatzfeld and others have suggested that the contrasting play of light and darkness in the poem is also related to traditional symbols of hope and despair.[286] Linking light with hope is a natural association and has a biblical as well as a liturgical basis.[287] Images of light and darkness are prevalent in the baptismal rite and in the Holy Week office of Tenebrae, and pagans in the Middle Ages were thought of in terms of obscurity and murk.[288] In Romanesque miniatures and mural paintings, devils are depicted as dark spirits, God and his angels and saints as shining figures.[289] The alternation of light and dark stones in archivolts, a style doubtless influenced by Byzantine models, is said to symbolize the same opposition.[290] In Turoldus's poem the shadowy valleys and the succession of day and night produce the same effect. The dawning of a new day, as in Laisses 11, 54, 58, and 267, also signals imminent new developments, while shadows and nightfall (vv. 11, 366, 501, 715–716, 993, 3658, and 3991) cloak evil or prelude trouble. After Roland and his men are slain, the sun is miraculously stayed in its path. The prolongation of daylight symbolizes grace thanks to whose illuminating effects Charles sees his duty and gains the strength to accomplish it.[291]

5. *Heaven and Earth.* In the *Song of Roland* angels descend earthward and the souls of the slain French heroes rise to Heaven. The visualization of the journey between this world and the next owes a good deal to portrayals in contemporary art. The conventional attitudes of angelic messengers in Romanesque Annunciation scenes,[292] (*Fig. 17*) and in representations of dreams and visions, link poet and audience in a common conceptual pattern.[293] The manner of showing the soul's departure from the body was even more stylized, and it is fair to assume that Turoldus imagined a tiny figure emerging from Oliver's mouth at the moment of death precisely as it is depicted in the Brindisi mosaic[294] (*Fig. 18*).

The opening laisse of the *Song of Roland* depicts a two-level scene, as it were; the war between Christians and Saracens on earth is reflected in the opposition of deities in heaven. The dichotomy of this representation is strongly reminiscent of Last Judgment depictions on Romanesque tympana, when heaven and earth appear on separate registers.[295] Last Judgment motifs are elsewhere in evidence in Turoldus's poem. The oliphant, whose doleful sound reverberates from hill to hill and toward heaven, recalls the Trump of Doom to such an extent that Judgment Day trumpeters such as the one at Conques have long been identified as Roland figures[296] (*Fig. 19*). In the death scene Heaven and Earth meet when Roland raises the gauntlet, which Gabriel receives (COMMENTARY, 26, n. 10). The hero's soul is borne heavenward by three angels. If contemporary illustrations are any guide, Turoldus imagined the soul being lifted in a kind of long scarf, a cliché derived from stylized depictions of the line separating heaven from earth[297] (*see Fig. 2*).

B. Betrayal

The two main story lines hinge on treachery, a notion even more abhorrent in medieval society, which was structured on the basis of solemn vows of allegiance, than it is today.[298] Symbolically, Ganelon's deed recalls Judas's betrayal of Jesus and triggers a host of other associations, notably Satan's deceitful ways. The Saracens in Turoldus's poem participate in this imagery. They, too, characteristically resort to cunning and ruse to achieve their nefarious ends.[299]

C. Conversion

The Theme of Conversion appears at the outset of Turoldus's epic (Blancandrin suggests that Charles will listen to any proposal if it means that the Saracens will abjure their faith and become Christians) and is ever-present in the form of an option at the conclusion of battles and sieges.[300] However, conversion *par amur* (v. 3674) and *par veire conoissance* (v. 3987) is symbolized by Bramimonde's rejection of pagan idols and by the awakening of a sincere desire on her part for baptism as a result of her hearing the *sermuns e essamples* (v. 3979).[301] The christening, which concludes the poem, holds out the promise of universal conversion and peace, one of the fondest hopes of the Middle Ages.[302]

D. Victory

If betrayal is epitomized in the person of Ganelon and conversion in Bramimonde, conquest in Turoldus's epic centers on Roland. Only when one realizes the full implication of this view can one begin to understand why the author constantly places triumphal words in the hero's mouth.[303] Charlemagne's triumphs and those of the Franks participate in the Theme of Victory, but it is above all Roland's death as a conqueror that constitutes its supreme expression.[304] Dying *cunquerrantment* (v. 2867) was not simply the realization of a heroic *gab* made at Aix (COMMENTARY, 34). Roland was vanquished by death, but he died without fear, certain of having merited an eternal reward. His courage would also inspire the Emperor and the rest of his men. Thus one is led to conclude with the poet that it was because of this that Roland died triumphant (cunquerant, v. 2363) and not for the trivial reason that his face was turned toward the enemy and that he stood a few paces ahead of his companions. But one also cannot fail to see in the victorious death of a holy martyr (v. 1134) a reflection of the Passion of Our Lord, for the Church has always considered it one of its fundamental doctrines that Christ triumphed over death.[305] The saints' lives continually reiterate, in the martyr's death scene, the notion that this death is a victory, in imitation of that of Christ. The following examples prove that this idea was a commonplace:

> Gardat vers le ciel en haut
> "Deu", fait il, "Le rei de glorie,
> Desur tuz avez *victorie* . . ."
> . . . .
> Une voiz li dist aprés:
> "George, vus ne morrez mes!
> Sosfrez volenters la mort,
> La endreit avrez bon cunfort.
> Pur la mort cunquerez vie
> Que mort ne poet tolir mie."[306]

> Od la *victorie* que out conquise
> Od la corune de justise
> Entra en pardurable ben . . .
> . . . .
> E cist pur la gloire conquere . . .[307]

> "Cruel tirant, or pues veer
> Qu'en mon tresor ai bon espeir,
> Sus tes tormenz ai ja *vitoire*,
> La paine que jeo sent m'est gloire
> Quanque tu fais si m'est delit!"
> . . . .

Lorenz dit: "Ne plorer, amis,
Mais teis tei e si t'esjois:
Car la ou vois arai *vitoire* . . ."[308]

De veintre l'anguisse de fu
E ke *victorie* li donast
E par martire coronast.[309]

Kar el ciel avez par *victorie*
Conquis la pardurable glorie.
. . . .
Recevez el ciel la glorie
Od corune de *victorie*.[310]

The description of Roland's death was profoundly influenced by hagiographic tradition (COMMENTARY, 26). It follows that the idea of a victorious death also derives from that source. As in the case of the *ubi sunt* topos mentioned above, we shall probably never know whether the poet was unconsciously influenced by the rhetorical techniques found in the early saints' lives or whether he deliberately sought to innovate by adopting a hagiographic commonplace to his own ends.[311]

15. *Metaphorical Consistency*

One of the least appreciated facets of the *Song of Roland* is the remarkable extension of its meaning and themes in the form of recurring images. Such figurative language could not be understood or appreciated in the same way by everyone in the audience, but, then, could carved capitals or remotely situated sculpture have been grasped—or, for that matter, even *seen*—by every individual viewing a Romanesque church? The fact that the patterns of imagery analyzed here may not have been consciously arrived at by the poet does not mean that they do not exist. Metaphors may be of secondary importance when compared to the poem's central meaning, but they are part and parcel of its structure and themes, and due consideration must be accorded to them. In fact, the success with which the poet organizes imagery around the principal ideas he wishes to impart is one of the surest ways to distinguish a masterpiece from an ordinary poem.

A. *The Struggle*

The desperate fighting, which makes up a good part of the narrative, may be viewed as a reflection of the struggle for man's soul. Prudentius (d. 415) gave this combat its classic form in the Latin poem *Psychomachia*, which made a profound mark on the art, literature, and thought of the Middle Ages.[312] The affinity between Turoldus and Prudentius is particularly great in the many passages of the French poem involving a duel, for the confrontation of virtues and vices dominates the Latin work.[313] In Prudentius Sapientia, which plays an important role in the *Song of Roland* (INTRODUCTION, 11, C), is enthroned following the decisive victory of the virtues. Finally, Saint Paul uses the struggle metaphor to refer to the spiritual war Christians must continually wage against the devil (Ephesians 6:10–13).[314] The unending aspect of this strife is brought out by Charlemagne's dream at the conclusion of the poem (COMMENTARY, 49).

B. *The Road*

One of Bédier's cherished views was that the chansons de geste developed along the so-called pilgrimage roads leading, notably, in France, to Santiago de Compostela.[315] The French scholar defended his thesis brilliantly, but critics now regard it as nothing more than one of several partial explanations of the origins and early development of the Old French epics. However, the importance of the road metaphor in the *Song of Roland* has not been sufficiently underscored.[316] Much of the story takes place on the road, many key incidents (Ganelon's trip to Saragossa, the discovery of the betrayal, the Battle of Roncevaux itself, the army's return to Aix) involve travel or movement, and the poem ends with the prospect of another long voyage. The verb *chevalchier* is used no fewer than fifty times, a graphic indication of the time spent in this activity. In addition, *veie* appears seven times, *chemin* five, and *acheminer*, *pelerin*, *senter*, and *veiage* once each. Such statistics might warrant only passing mention were it not for the fact that earthly life is often compared to a road, a distant journey, a peregrination, a voyage home in the gospels and in the writings of the Fathers of the Church.[317] A late-fifteenth-century manuscript of the *Pseudo-Turpin* has none of the illustrations traditionally associated with this chronicle but epitomizes it instead by showing the haloed figures of Roland and Oliver straddling the road to Compostela.[318] If one recalls, too, the vogue for celestial and earthly journeys and pilgrimages in medieval literature,[319] one begins to appreciate the symbolic meaning Turoldus probably intended giving to this image.

C. *The Ascent*

Even critics who do not as a rule deal with the pattern of symbols in the *Song of Roland* concede metaphoric significance in the hero's arduous climb.[320] Rising or vertical imagery (brandished lances, mountains,[321] trees, [322] the sound of the oliphant, the proffered gauntlet, etc.) characterize the first part of the poem, beginning with the sight of Saragossa *ki est en une muntaigne* (v. 6).[323] The road to Roncevaux is a tragic path followed by all, but especially by the hero, whose distressful upward gazes and pathetic dying gesture emphasize the physical as well as the spiritual nature of his agony and indicate the direction his soul aspires to take on leaving this world.

Painful ascent to or the quest for God is a metaphor ultimately derived from the evangelical notion of the narrow gate and the hard road (INTRODUCTION, II, E),[324] but it is also associated with the Ladder of Virtue, a variation on the *psychomachia* theme.[325] The motif, which appears in art as early as the eleventh century, ultimately derives from a Greek work entitled *Klimax tou paradeisou* (Ladder of Paradise) by the church father John Klimakos (d. c. 600).[326]

The image of arduous ascent is quite evident in the *Song of Roland*, but nothing suggests that the hero gradually overcomes any sinful proclivities or experiences any sort of conversion.[327] In this respect Turoldus's poem differs very significantly from the traditional Ladder of Virtue concept. Finally, and with specific reference to this important distinction, the author of the *Pseudo-Turpin Chronicle* sees in Charlemagne's victory a symbol of the Christian transcending the very angels as he ascends to his reward in Paradise.[328] No suggestion of any victory over self in order to achieve beatific vision is made by the Latin chronicler.

D. *The Two Cities*

The metaphors of road and ascent lead naturally to the notion of city.[329] In his discussion of the important role played by the Saracen capital in the structure of the *Song of Roland*, Le Gentil stresses the Saragossa-Roncevaux opposition:

> C'est à Saragosse que fut ourdie la trahison et c'est de là qu'est partie l'attaque contre Roland. C'est encore à Saragosse que Baligant reçoit l'hommage de Marsile et prend en main la conduite de la guerre. C'est à Saragosse enfin que, Baligant ayant péri, le roi désespéré meurt à son tour, ne laissant à ses sujets d'autre choix que le massacre ou la conversion. Mais c'est à Roncevaux que tout s'est décidé, que tout a pris un sens, d'abord par la mort de Roland, ensuite par le triomphe de Charlemagne. On notera encore, pour ne négliger aucune symétrie, le rôle joué par la reine Bramimonde à l'arrivée de Baligant, puis à l'annonce de sa défaite. On n'oubliera pas davantage le contraste qui, au lendemain de la première bataille, oppose la grave douleur des Francs enterrant leurs morts à Roncevaux et la rage des païens de Saragosse, insultant leurs idoles.[330]

Le Gentil's perceptive observations ring true. However, the road from Saragossa does not end at Roncevaux but continues on to Aix, and the opposition between the pagan capital at one end of the *Song of Roland* and the Christian capital at the other offers a polarity that deserves special note.

The ancient Iberian settlement known as Salduba was occupied about 25 B.C. by the Romans, who transformed it into a flourishing military colony and named it in honor of the then ruling Emperor (Lat. *Caesar Augustus* [with a change of gender] > Modern Sp. *Zaragoza*). After many of its inhabitants were converted to Christianity, the city became the scene of numerous persecutions in the fourth century: *Caesaraugusta studiosa Christo* 'Saragossa, zealous for Christ', wrote Prudentius.[331] Occupied by the Muslims in 713, Saragossa was besieged but never captured by Charlemagne in 778. The Muslim citadel was not among the Emperor's later conquests on the peninsula, nor was it ever part of the so-called Spanish March. In fact, the resounding capture of Saragossa in 1118 is believed by Prosper Boissonnade to have inspired Turoldus to write his poem.[332] Most scholars feel, however, that 1118 is much too late a date for the *Song of Roland*.[333]

Boissonnade argued that Turoldus's description of Saragossa was reasonably accurate and reflected historical reality, but the details he cites in support of this view are anything but convincing (COMMENTARY, 31) and fail totally in v. 6, where it is said that the fortress—in reality a fertile oasis in the middle of an arid plain—*est en une muntaigne*.

Turoldus's Saracen capital, therefore, would appear to be essentially a conventional city of the type frequently encountered in medieval art and literature.[334] However, the mountain stronghold is also a symbol of Pride, and a connection with ancient Babylon is inevitable.[335] William Calin, noting the presence of four bridges guarding the approaches to Babylon in *Huon de Bordeaux*, as well as to Saragossa in the *Song of Roland*, suggests that they are an otherworld motif:

> Christian typology has traditionally associated Babylon with hell and the antichrist, an impression furthered by the *coutume* of the four bridges. Dunostre too is intimately connected with the number *four*. Sebille explains to Huon how he must proceed to confront Orgueilleux: he is to traverse four chambers, the first containing provisions, the second treasure, the third four idols, the fourth the redoubtable master of the keep himself, whose bedstead is adorned with magic birds (singing automatons) at the four corners. Once again we find progressive initiation to an inner sanctum, fraught with danger and consecrated by the number *four* (see *Roland*, vs. 2690).[336]

Strictly speaking, the word *Babilonie* in the *Song of Roland* (v. 2614) and in most other medieval French epics refers to Old Cairo in Egypt, the residence of the Fatimite caliphs. In Turoldus's poem it is the emirate of Marsile's uncle, Baligant.[337] Like many other anthroponyms and toponyms in the *Roland*, it also conjures up biblical associations, for Babylon was then and remains today the archetypal wicked city.

Like Saragossa, Aix (Lat. *Aquaegrani*, Modern German *Aachen*) was at one time an important Roman colony. Turoldus correctly identifies it as Charlemagne's capital. It was also the coronation site of the Holy Roman Emperors throughout the Middle Ages, and many early church councils were held in that city (A.D. 799, 809, 816–17, 836). If Saragossa reminds one of Babylon, Charlemagne's capital city, too, has symbolic overtones. In a chapter on *Aymeri de Narbonne*, Calin states:

> [Narbonne] appears almost miraculously on the crusaders' path, an object of immeasurable strength and beauty. It is not only a challenge to the Frenchmen, a measure of their worth, but an archetypal figure of all cities and communities, reflecting, perhaps, the splendors of the *Civitas Dei*.[338]

Calin makes no allusion to Aix, but one thinks immediately of the capital of the Franks in the *Song of Roland*.[339] Reached after a long journey and an absence of seven long years—one can readily imagine that the joy and relief of the Franks on first sighting the homeland from atop the Pyrenees is repeated when they reach their final destination—Aix is the place where justice is dispensed in an awesome Day of Retribution.

In a very real sense, then, Turoldus's epic is a tale of two cities, the one representing earthly evil, which must be overcome, the other the Heavenly Jerusalem, where the just are rewarded and find repose, where sinners are tried and sent to their eternal damnation. Since peace is not of this world, Charles will be obliged, in the end, to leave Aix to carry on the struggle.

E. Roncevaux

A slight but very significant alteration in toponymy introduced by Turoldus bears out the metaphors comparing the hero's arduous ascent on the way to Calvary. Several documents written in Latin, the earliest dating from the end of the eleventh century, refer to Roncevaux as *Roscida* (or *Roscidae*) *vallis* 'dewy valley',[340] but the original form of this place-name was doubtless closer to *Rozaballes*, found in the contemporary *Nota Emilianense*.[341] Part of this toponym evidently stems from Basque *çabal* or *zabal* 'flat, spread out', which coincides with the fact that Roncevaux is not a valley at all but a plain.[342] For purposes of discussion here, it really matters very little whether Turoldus was aware of the actual physical appearance of the battlefield or merely chanced to visualize it fairly accurately, or whether or not he knew of its association with moisture. The fact is he consistently chose to designate the locale of his hero's agony by the name *Rencesvals* (fifteen times, *Renceval* once), a term that can only mean 'Vale of Thorns'.[343] Such a designation, with its obvious kinship with the Valley of Tears of Psalms 84:6, universally regarded in the Middle Ages as a synonym for the trials of this life,[344] and with the Crown of Thorns, could not fail but suggest a connection with Christ's Passion.[345] It hardly seems necessary to buttress this view with the observation that in Prudentius, the hard road alluded to in the Gospel according to Saint Matthew (INTRODUCTION, II, E) is conceived of as a narrow, rocky path along a ridge with a briar forest,[346] or that, in the Eadwine Psalter (1147–

50), the psalmist is shown among thorns in the illustration accompanying Psalm 32, which describes his suffering as he admits his past transgressions.[347] In the rhymed version of the *Song of Roland*, Charles is able to distinguish the Christian victims at Roncevaux by the white hawthorn bushes that have sprouted from their bodies, a sign of their innocence, while prickly thorns identify the Saracen dead.[348] The dragging of Ganelon over thorns in Conrad (v. 9012), then, is probably less an aping of Saint Hippolytus's martyrdom than condign punishment for Roland's Christlike agony.[349] Thorns are traditionally associated with the rose of martyrdom,[350] which may explain the red flowers mentioned in *Roland*, vv. 2871–2872. Typologically, the thicket in which the ram, sacrificed as a burnt offering by Abraham in place of Isaac, caught its horns was held to prefigure the Crown of Thorns.[351] In 1115, when Saint Bernard established a new Cistercian abbey in a locale referred to as the Vale of Absinth, so-called because of the wormwood that grew in abundance there, he promptly changed its name to Clairvaux (Clara vallis).[352]

16. Landscape

In addition to the road and the two cities, other aspects of the natural and man-made scenery play a major role in the *Song of Roland*.[353]

A. Mountains and Valleys

Beginning at v. 814, one becomes acutely aware that nature is responding to tragic developments in the narrative. The formidable mountains and the dark, terrifying gorges are burnt into the memory of anyone familiar with Turoldus's poem, thanks largely to the refrain *Halt sunt li pui*.[354] These verses are much more than a descriptive element in the rhetorical tradition and transcend the limits of historical and topographical realism. They show that the poet had a genius for transforming a formula into a powerful device that fuses setting and story line and helps to create its distinctive mood.[355] The phrase appears in four crucial passages:

1\. 814 Halt sunt li pui e li val tenebrus,
Les roches bises, les destreiz merveillus.

As the homeland comes into view, the men in Charlemagne's army burst into tears of *pitet* (v. 822), a term in the *Song of Roland* frequently connoting sorrow for a lost friend or relative, or accompanying a formal lament. Here, however, Turoldus makes it clear that *pitet* is largely an expression of nostalgia and longing for loved ones left behind for seven long years, mixed with relief at reaching a place of safety. In the same laisse the Emperor also sheds tears of *pitet* (v. 825). Fearing for his nephew, who commands the exposed rearguard following at a distance, Charles is overcome with anguish and foreboding (v. 823). *Pitet* has a very different connotation, then, in the two passages in question.[356] The towering mountains and the shadowy defiles strike a note of gloom in an otherwise joyous scene.[357] Their brooding presence is evidently felt by Charles alone and increases the anxiety that weighs heavily upon him like the cloak beneath which he vainly attempts to hide his troubled countenance (v. 830).

2\. 1755 Halt sunt li pui e la voiz est mult lunge.

Having finally decided to call his uncle, the hero gives the oliphant a mighty blast.[358] The miracle, which sends the sound of Roland's horn reverberating a full thirty leagues, is underscored by the soaring mountains that seem to draw the warning notes upward to help them reach the Emperor and his men.

3\. 1830 Halt sunt li pui e tenebrus e grant, AOI.
Li val parfunt e les ewes curant.

Charlemagne rides desperately to the rescue but what's the use, Turoldus tells us, they will never reach Roland and his beleaguered men in time. *Ireement* (v. 1834), *curuçus e dolent* (v. 1835), *sei dementer* (v. 1836), *grant irur* (v. 1842), and *irance* (v. 1845) amply characterize the angry frustration felt by the would-be rescuers; *halt*, *grant*, *parfunt*, and *curant* in the refrain suggest the power of the dark (v. 1830: tenebrus) forces allied against them.

4\. 2271 Halt sunt li pui e mult halt les arbres.

About to die, Roland retires within himself and turns his thoughts to God. The vertical imagery of the mountains and trees, accentuated by the repetition of the word *halt*, indicates the strength of his aspiration and suffuses the scene with grace and grandeur, a solemn moment shattered by the intrusion of the Rash Saracen.[359]

All four uses of this refrain produce tension and help to create the atmosphere of awe in the *Song of Roland* (INTRODUCTION, 17). Several formulas and like-sounding phrases relating to daylight or the sun mark the passage of time and, more often than not, announce important developments:[360]

157 Bels fut li vespres e li soleilz fut cler.

1002 Clers fut li jurz e bels fut li soleilz.

1807 Esclargiz est li vespres e li jurz.

2646 Clers est li jurz e li soleilz luisant.

3345 Clers fut li jurz e li soleilz luisanz.

3991 Passet li jurz, la nuit est aserie.

Verses 157 and 2646 seem unrelated when considered from the point of view of form alone. However, the beauty and brightness of the sunlight in the first passage reflect the fact that at this moment Charles is at the zenith of his expectations for Saracen conversion and lasting peace, while in the second instance parallel optimism is manifested by Baligant, the Emperor's archfoe, as he sets out to right the wrong he believes Marsile has suffered.

B. *Meteorological and Seismic Disturbances*

The storms, earthquake, and stopping of the sun are as important as mountains and valleys, so far as the interaction of man and his natural surroundings is concerned in the poem.

Charlemagne's condition for accepting Marsile's offer was the handing over of the Caliph, the latter's uncle, as a hostage (v. 493). Upon his return from Saragossa, Ganelon reports to Charlemagne that, learning of the Saracen king's decision to become a convert, the Caliph fled with 40,000 of his men. No sooner had the Caliph set sail, however, than a violent storm arose, drowning them all. Ganelon's account is a pure fabrication of course, for the Caliph[361] figures in later episodes of the poem, mortally wounding Oliver and being himself slain by Roland's comrade-in-arms. Ironically, Ganelon unwittingly prophesies the watery grave awaiting the remnants of Marsile's forces in Laisse 180. Ganelon's lie succeeds nevertheless in deceiving the Emperor and his men because the storm is viewed as just retribution for daring to oppose God's will and as a sign from above that all will now go well. A tempest representing the power of God subduing the enemies of the Chosen People is of course a biblical image (e.g., Exodus 19:16, Psalm 29),[362] and the parallel between the destruction of Pharaoh's army in the Red Sea (Exodus 14) and Marsile's forces in the Ebro is obvious.

The most specific instance of the pathetic fallacy[363] in the *Song of Roland* occurs in the terrifying storm and earthquake, which, Turoldus explains, is an expression of sorrow over the hero's impending death (v. 1437: Ço est li granz dulors por la mort de Rollant).[364] Like the tempest that is said to have destroyed Marsile's army, the hail and fire storm in Charlemagne's third prophetic dream (Laisse 185) also implies the finger of God. This time, however, divine retribution inexplicably appears to be directed against the Franks.

It is noteworthy, then, that the three storms and the earthquake in the *Song of Roland* are not ordinary tempests but disturbances viewed as supernatural events—identical in this respect with Charlemagne's Joshua-like staying of the sun, a miracle brought about by God's intervention—whether occurring in the inner space of the characters' imagination (Ganelon's lie, Charles's dream) or in the outer world in which they move about (the storm over France). This correspondence recalls the image of the Microcosm (*Fig. 20*) in the chapter of the *Elucidarum* of Honorius Augustodunensis entitled "De hominis formatione; et quomodo sit parvus mundus et ad imaginem Dei."[365] Here the four elements (fire, air, earth, and water) are related to parts of the human body. According to Honorius's anatomy, the breast is the location of miniature storms (breathing and coughing) and of the heart, seat of all consciousness and dispositions of the spirit.[366]

C. Streams

Water, a symbol of life, purification, and regeneration in the New Testament and in Christian liturgy,[367] appears in two passages of the *Song of Roland.* At Roncevaux Turpin takes Roland's oliphant and dies during the merciful act of trying to reach a stream in order to fetch the dying hero a refreshing drink, an image with powerful penitential overtones. In the execution scene at Aix the headlong pulling of the four horses toward the stream amid the field has no clear symbolic significance, although some might fancy it as a grotesque parody of the stag drawn to water, a metaphor of the soul's longing for God.[368]

D. Forests, Gardens, and Trees

Paul Aebischer has suggested that the laurel, olive, pine, and yew trees in the *Song of Roland* are proof of its meridional origin.[369] Others have pointed out that trees, which appear in profusion in the Old French epics, virtually always seem arbitrarily chosen and that there are some curious instances of anatopism, for example, olive trees near Paris, Liège, and in Ponthieu.[370] However, the most influential view has been Curtius's observation that in medieval epics, forests, gardens, and trees—like flowers, gentle breezes, meadows, singing birds, springs, and streams—constitute a *locus amoenus*, that is, an idyllic place with paradisiacal associations.[371] This literary topos dates back to antiquity and was one of the conventions promoted by rhetorical treatises.[372] Gardens are a favorite locale for lovers' trysts in early Provençal poetry.[373] Curtius points out that the laurel beneath which Baligant holds his council (v. 2651) is a conventional tree, a passage in Gautier de Châtillon's *Alexandreis* describing an identical site.[374] Expressions such as *en un (grant) verger*, *enz el verger* (cf. *el grant verger*), *(de)suz un pin*, and *(de)suz une olive* are formulaic.[375]

At first glance the scene in the *Song of Roland* that fits Curtius's idyllic interpretation most readily is the one which finds the Emperor and his nobles gathered *en un grant verger* (vv. 103–107) when Blancandrin and his messengers arrive. Fifteen thousand Franks are said to be disporting themselves in the vicinity (vv. 108–113). As further details are provided by the poet, Charlemagne, it turns out, is actually seated upon a throne *Desuz un pin, delez un eglenter* (v. 114). This tree and bush are usually thought of as growing wild and, consequently, offer some contrast to a garden, which implies cultivation by man (OFr. *vergier*, derived from Lat. *viridiarum* 'tree garden' < *viridis* 'green', is not restricted to the modern meaning 'orchard, planting of fruit trees'; cf. E. *orchard*, an adaptation of Lat. *hortus* 'garden'). The scene is decidedly conventional but the passage is far from tranquil. On the contrary, the atmosphere is laden with fear and eschatological associations (COMMENTARY, 3).

A garden is mentioned again in v. 159—Charles has a tent set up there for the Saracen messengers—and there is every reason to suppose that this grove is the same as the one discussed above (v. 103). Absent now, however, is the Emperor's glowering presence. On the other hand, the garden at Saragossa (vv. 11, 501, 510) is a sinister place: Marsile is lying on a marble slab *suz l'umbre* (v. 11)[376] and shadows surround his throne (v. 407). Shadows are mentioned in only one other passage of Turoldus's poem. In Ganelon's anecdote about Roland, the apple incident finds the Emperor seated *suz l'umbre* (v. 383). The darkness suggests Charles's blindness or perhaps the diabolic aspect of the scene as imagined in Ganelon's perverted brain.[377]

Observing that the olive tree is always associated with Saracens in the *Song of Roland*, and the pine—except in v. 407, which may be an error—with Franks,[378] Karl-Josef Steinmeyer suggests that the pine may be a symbol of Faith.[379] He cites Rabanus Maurus (d. 856): "Pinus est veritas fidei, ut in Isaia: 'Ad te venient abies et buxus et pinus simul' (Isa. LX, 13), quod in Ecclesia sunt et sublimus in contemplatione, et fortis in opere, et virides in fide."[380] That the pine was often confused with the cedar, cypress, fir, juniper, and other trees of the same family is evident from the various translations of the passage cited by Rabanus, which refers to the building of the Temple of Jerusalem.[381] The *Jerusalem Bible* translates: "The glory of Lebanon [i.e., the cedars] will come to you, with cypress and plane and box, to adore the site of my sanctuary."

In Scripture the cedar of Lebanon is a familiar symbol of grandeur and might (seventy mentions, e.g., Psalms 29:3–5: The voice of Yahweh in power! The voice of Yahweh in splendour! The voice of Yahweh shatters the cedars, Yahweh shatters the cedars of Lebanon!),[382] is much more widely attested in exegetical commentaries, and it seems as fitting an association with the Franks as the connection proposed by Steinmeyer. Curtius notes that, according to medieval rhetorical treatises, the cedar and the laurel were suitable for the *stilus gravis*, which treats of warriors.[383] It seems curious, finally, that Conrad, who is conversant with exegetical views, depicts the Saracen king parleying with Ganelon under a pine tree and refers to the council as *der Pinrat* (vv. 2411–2414).[384] It is true, however, that the scene involves a Christian (Ganelon) and that Turoldus shows the traitor leaning against a pine in v. 500.

In the *Song of Roland* trees must be studied in their own context, since they do not have uniform symbolic significance. Thus the pine beneath which Charlemagne holds council connotes strength, whereas the same kind of tree toward which Roland directs his final steps (v. 2357), near which he lies down to die (v. 2375) and is eventually found by Charlemagne (v. 2884), symbolizes the Cross. In these examples the verdant aspect of the tree, with its strong liturgical associations, rather than its shape or botanical classification, probably determined Turoldus's choice.

As for the olive tree, Steinmeyer notes the following exegetical commentary in Rabanus: "Oliva, quilibet hypocrita, ut in Job: 'Quasi oliva projiciens florem suum' (Job XV, 33) quod hypocrita exteriores sanctitatis nitorem habere videtur, nonnunquam amittit."[385] Here again it is important to understand that tree symbolism, in Scripture and in the exegetical interpretations that depend upon it, is very complex.[386] One need only point out, for instance, that many *Roland* specialists subscribe to the view that the name Oliver may have been chosen for its biblical—as well as classical—associations with wisdom.[387] It should also be noted that the olive branches in vv. 72, 80, 93, and 203 are not to be confused with the olive trees in vv. 366, 2571, and 2705.[388] In his first mention of olive branches Turoldus has Marsile explain: "*Ço senefiet pais et humilitet*" (v. 73).[389]

While hypocrisy could fit the fateful conversation between Ganelon and Blancandrin on the way to Saragossa, this interpretation would be clearly forced in the case of Marsile's arrival there after his defeat at the hands of Charles's army (v. 2571) and of Baligant's messengers leaving their mounts under an olive tree also in that city (v. 2705).

The olive tree beneath which Ganelon is riding, having joined the Saracen emissaries and affording both Blancandrin and him an opportunity to speak privately and *par grant saveir* (vv. 366–369), may have been suggested by the image of the Jewish nation, which rejected the Messiah (Romans 11:16–24).[390] On the other hand, Ganelon is a Judas figure and the olive tree leads inevitably to the betrayal of Jesus in the Garden of Olives, a reference that could very well explain v. 366. Judas, who according to tradition, hanged himself in an olive grove,[391] is one of the best-known figures of Despair, an attitude corresponding to that of Marsile in v. 2571 and also, perhaps, in spite of their insolent manner and surface optimism, to that of Baligant's envoys in v. 2705.

Further evidence supporting the Ganelon-Judas-olive tree nexus of associations is to be found in Conrad. In v. 1920 of the German translation, Ganelon's conference with Blancandrin takes place under an olive tree, as in *Roland*, v. 366. Conrad thereupon introduces the

Ganelon-Judas parallel, followed immediately by the green tree/lying exterior analogy (INTRODUCTION, 10, B, 1 and 2).

There are trees in Turoldus's epic that are merely designated by the term *arbre*. The reader is referred to the Commentary for the significance of the trees in vv. 2267, 2874, and 3953, and the forests in v. 714 (bruill), v. 2549 (gualt), and v. 3293 (selve, bois).

E. Flowers, Grass, and Meadows

In three passages (vv. 1856, 2197, and 2898), Heaven is assimilated to a bed of flowers, an image found nowhere in the Bible but which is akin to the meadows of green grass of Psalms 23:2 and its analogues (Ezekiel 34:14; Micah 7:14; John 10:9).[392] Garlands of flowers signifying the paradisiacal state of the martyrs and saints are a widely attested motif in medieval iconography and thought, dating back to the era of the Catacombs.[393] The beauty and fragrance of flowers evoke the joys of the Garden of Eden and of its celestial counterpart. The flowers of Paradise are eternal in sharp contrast with the ephemeral nature of earthly plant and human life, the usual meaning of floral and grass symbolism in the Bible (e.g., Job 14:1–2: Man, born of woman, has a short life. . . . He blossoms, and he withers, like a flower; Isaiah 40:6–7: All flesh is grass and its beauty like the wild flower's. The grass withers, the flower fades; James 1:10: riches last no longer than the flowers in the grass).[394]

In the *Song of Roland* grass and meadows are most frequently associated with quiet repose (vv. 2448, 2486, 2492, 2496, 2521, 2523) or dying, which may be peaceful or violent and involve either Christians or Saracens (vv. 1334, 1375, 1614, 2175, 2236, 2269, 2273, 2358, 2871, 2876). The mentions of grass in the passages concerning death are noticeably more formulaic, involving no fewer than seven instances of the expression *erbe verte* (cf. also vv. 2573: sur la verte herbe, 3389: L'erbe . . . verte).[395] The formula *erbe verte* also appears in contexts with the related notion of blood spattering on the ground (vv. 1614, 3453, 3972; cf. 3925: pred herbut). While hints of ephemerality may at times appear here, particularly in view of the scriptural tradition alluded to above, more often than not Turoldus seems to be simply providing a conventional landscape detail or striving to achieve visual impact with vivid colors. Grass and meadows are also routinely mentioned in scenes involving a council (vv. 671, 2652), a judicial combat (vv. 3873, 3917; cf. v. 2565), and prayer (v. 3097).

F. The Stone and the Four Marble Objects

While the Christological significance of the stone against which Roland vainly tries to smash Durendal is obscured by other aspects of the incident that clamor for our attention, the four marble objects near which the hero dies constitute a man-made landscape feature with unmistakable paradisiacal associations (COMMENTARY, 24).

17. Tone

Roland's stirring words and deeds, his edifying death, and Charlemagne's terrible revenge were not simply viewed as epic events in the modern sense, that is, as larger-than-life happenings one accepts with a willing but patronizing suspension of disbelief. The medieval listener ardently desired the story to be true, and this emotional involvement greatly enhanced the narrative's reality to him.[396] The typical modern reader's insensitivity to the poem's tone is further proof of the emotional discontinuity between the Middle Ages and our time.

Jenkins wrote of the *Song of Roland*'s "exceptional refinement and elevation of tone." Others have noted the poem's martial accents and elegiac passages highlighted by the use of exclamations, laments, swoons, tears, and, no doubt, by that mysterious word AOI.; or have marveled at its atmosphere laden with foreboding, enhanced notably by the haunting refrain *Halt sunt li pui*.[397] However, certain assonances and key words also create mood.

The agreement in quality or timbre of the last stressed vowels in each laisse is exact, not merely approximate.[398] Of the twenty-two different assonances listed by Jenkins, the most frequent patterns are in *ãn/ãin* (forty-five laisses), close *o* (forty-five laisses), and *i* (forty-one laisses): "There may be a tendency toward rhyme, that is, the homophony of the consonant(s) which may follow the last tonic vowel, in the laisses in *-en* and *-an* masculine: the number of words assonating in *-ent* or *-ant* is strikingly large, and later epics will develop this tendency."[399] Jenkins might have pointed out that the latter pattern is often used by Turoldus when he wishes to impart a ringing tone to a speech, as, for example, when Turpin volunteers to go to Saragossa (Laisse 19), Roland declines Charles's offer of more than 20,000 men for the rearguard (Laisse 63), or the hero and his companion debate whether or not to sound the oliphant (Laisses 85, 129). Also in this assonance are the passages providing the memorable portrait of Roland (Laisse 91), announcing his impending demise (Laisse 110), describing his delivery of a prodigious blow (Laisse 122), and showing him assuming a victorious attitude in death (Laisse 174). It is therefore no surprise that the poet uses the same sound pattern in scenes where Ganelon or a Saracen leader rages or speaks out of bravado (Laisses 22, 24, 30, 42, 47, 69, 76).

Probably the most interesting instance of vowel quality producing a desired tonal effect occurs in laisses with assonances in close *o*, almost always in combinations of oral and nasal assonances. Such passages are usually highly emotive: Laisse 66, Charlemagne's army crosses the Pyrenees and sights France; 80, Oliver spies the great pagan army from atop a hill; 106, the exchange between Roland and Oliver apropos of Oliver's broken spear; 111, Turpin addresses the rearguard before the final battle with Marsile; 137, Ganelon is chained and beaten; 162, Roland ranges the bodies of his fallen comrades before Turpin; 166, the hero hears the Archbishop's dying prayers; 178, Naimes calls Charles to duty; 186, the Emperor's fourth dream; 204 and 205, Charlemagne finds Roland's body; 267, Ganelon's trial begins; 273, the traitor makes his desperate defense; 276, Charles's angry reply to the Franks' verdict.

Analysis of the vocabulary of the assonances in close *o* reveals a preponderance of emotion-packed abstract nouns derived from Latin words in *-ōrem* (VL *-or*), notably: *amor*, *baldor*, *brunor*, *color*, *deshonor*, *dolor*, *flambor*, *fremor*, *haör*, *honor*, *iror*, *poör*, *rimor*, *tendror*, *valor*, and *vigor*. Terms such as *adort*, *almaçor*, *anceïssor*, *contor*, *empereor*, *halçor*, *flor*, *Francor*, *jugeor*, *maior*, *meillor*, *oixor*, *paienor*, *peior*, *plusor*, *poigneor*, *seignor*, and *tabor* not only contain the same *-or* sound but also, in these contexts, fall within the same general semantic range. Another group of words in the assonances in question—all adjectives with suffixes stemming from Latin *-ōsus* (VL *-osu*)—provide similar convergence of meaning: *angoissos*, *chevaleros*, *contrarios*, *coroços*, *flambeios*, *glorios*, *herbos*, *merveillos*, *orgoillos*, *poldros*, and *tenebros*.

Perhaps the most important key to perceiving the tone, which everywhere characterizes the *Song of Roland* but is particularly noticeable in the scenes depicting Roland's death and Ganelon's punishment, is to be found in a group of words suggesting awe, that is, wonder tinged with fear, a profound emotion inspired by something essentially mysterious or sacred. One is reminded here of the religious dread imparted by Greek tragedy, although the medieval audience's reaction to Turoldus's poem doubtless involved more admiration mixed with strangeness than terror. The feeling, then, is akin to that alluded to in the Introit of the Mass for the Dedication of a Church ("How awe-inspiring this place is! This is nothing less than a house of God; this is the gate of heaven"), a hymn sung by the assembly at the consecration of the choir of Canterbury Cathedral in 1130. When he heard these words, King Henry I exclaimed: "[This sanctuary] is truly awesome."[400]

Dying abroad (v. 448: en l'estrange cuntree; v. 839: en une estrange marche; v. 2864: en estrange regnet) means much more to Ganelon, Charles, and Roland, respectively, than the inconveniences occasioned by foreign burial or transfer of the remains home. It is clear that dread is associated with the notion of "strange" land. Turpin's reassuring remark in Laisse 132, to the effect that Charles will not fail to give their bodies a proper funeral, specifies that the French heroes are to be transported home and interred in consecrated ground. Their fears in this regard are crystallized by the Archbishop's reference to being devoured by wolves, pigs, and dogs (v. 1751). A similar concern is later voiced by Charlemagne (v. 2436: Que n'i adeist ne beste ne lion). Bédier, reacting against the anatopism of lions in the Pyrenees, believed that the Emperor was alluding to a familiar image of Satan or the devils who prey upon the unwary.[401] This insight illustrates very well that the line separating this world from the next in Turoldus's poem is blurred and that angelical as well as diabolic figures appear frequently in various guises. Being home offered no real protection against demonic visitations, but military campaigns abroad, particularly in pagan lands, entailed vastly greater perils in this respect—witness the satanic characteristics mentioned in Turoldus's descriptions of the Saracens and their places of origin.[402] *Estrange cuntree* implies much more, then, than the innocuous foreignness we tend to associate today with countries other than our own,[403] and there is plainly more than routine anxiety in Oliver's reaction after spying the Saracen foe: "*Granz sunt les oz de cele gent estrange*" (v. 1086).

It is important to distinguish between the strangeness we have been analyzing, which is characterized by an element of religious dread, and the bizarre world of fantasy that the heroes of romance inhabit or visit, notably the Estrange Marche, Estrange Terre, Estranges Deserz, Estranges Isles, and Forest Estrange of Arthurian literature.[404]

At times, however, *estrange* may be tinged with some of the meaning found in the *Roland* as, for example, the Espee as Estranges Renges, which Gawain must seek at the Castle of Montesclaire (*Conte del graal*, v. 4712), later identified as having once belonged to Judas Maccabaeus.[405] With reference to the road metaphor discussed above (INTRODUCTION, 15, A), it is worth noting that this present life was often said by medieval writers to be a place of exile, a wilderness, and, therefore, a strange land.[406]

Two additional uses of *estrange* serve to create mood at particular junctures in the *Song of Roland* and are related to, yet distinct from, the notions mentioned thus far. In Charlemagne's battlefield lament for his dead nephew, the Emperor twice alludes to men coming from far-off lands to learn of Roland's fate (v. 2911: De plusurs regnes vendrunt li hume estrange; v. 2918: Vendrunt li hume, demanderunt noveles). The prophecy suggests the dimensions of the tragedy in space and time and lends a note of solemnity to Charlemagne's elegy. The strange appearance of these unidentified visitors evokes the atmosphere of mystery surrounding the visit of the three "men," that is, Yahweh accompanied by two angels, to Abraham at the Oak of Mamre (Genesis 18). There is on this occasion more than a hint of religious awe in Charlemagne's reaction described as *merveilluses e pesmes* (v. 2919).

Finally, Alda's reply to the announcement of Roland's death ("Cest mot mei est estrange," v. 3717) has long been recognized as peculiarly affecting. There is little doubt that Alda's dramatically sudden demise, linked as it is with her fiancé's death and coming as it does in answer to her fervent prayer, has clear religious overtones. The strangeness to which Alda alludes would appear to have less to do with any hurt she may feel as a result of Charlemagne's offer of a *mult esforcet eschange* for Roland, namely his own son Louis, than with the apartness (Lat. *extra* 'outside' > *extraneus* 'external' > OFr. *estrange*) she already experiences from this life. The Emperor's words, life itself, in fact, no longer have any meaning for her now that the bond that united her to Roland has been severed. The tie, involving affection as well as feudal obligations, parallels that between Roland and Oliver.

In three passages Turoldus puts the word *merveille*, *merveillos*, or *sei merveillier* into the mouths of Saracens to express the grudging admiration they feel for Charlemagne (vv. 370, 537, 550). There is of course more than a little fear involved here, for the legendary Emperor obviously intimidates them. Elsewhere *merveille* and *sei merveillier* are simply emphatic ways of expressing surprise or doubt (vv. 571, 1774, 2877, 3179). In numerous other instances *merveillos* and *merveillosement* underscore Turoldus's desire to make his audience grasp the extraordinary nature of a particular activity or thing (Charles's armies, v. 598; battle, vv. 1320, 1412, 1610, 1620, 2566, 3381, 3420; blows, vv. 1397, 3385; the number of knights, v. 3218), or its terrifying aspect (ravines, v. 815; a river, v. 2466; storms, vv. 1423, 2534; Daniel's danger in the lions' den, v. 3104). It is difficult at times to distinguish between these two meanings, but such uses correspond well to the aggrandizement traditionally associated with the epic genre.

Two other uses of *merveillos* converge once again on the tone of strangeness we find in the *Song of Roland.* In a first series of examples Turoldus seems to be saying that individuals are confounded by a dolorous perspective or spectacle: the Franks at the thought of the threatened Roland (v. 843: E de Rollant merveilluse poür) and upon seeing the carnage at Roncevaux (vv. 2853–2854: Si vunt vedeir le merveillus damage / En Rencesvals, la o fut la bataille), and Charles, announcing his nephew's death to the mysterious visitors at Aix (vv. 2918–2919: Vendrunt li hume, demanderunt noveles./ Jes lur dirrai, merveilluses e pesmes).

The second group suggests a certain exemplariness as well as astonishment. The two punishments, which are key elements in the poem's structure, are involved: The remnants of Marsile's forces are destroyed in the Val Tenebrus (v. 2474: Tuz sunt neiez par merveillus ahan), and Ganelon's death is called for by the Franks with virtually identical phrasing (v. 3963: Que Guenes moerget par merveillus ahan). Finally, v. 1094 also seems to belong in the latter category. Turoldus stresses the identity of worthiness of Roland and Oliver in this, perhaps the most famous, laisse in the entire poem. The sublime courage exhibited by each hero, he says, excites our wonder and esteem, and also serves as an example for us all (Ambedui unt meveillus vasselage).

18. Narrative Devices and Techniques

It has been seen that there is scholarly consensus regarding the skill with which Turoldus structured his poem and that parallelism is its dominant feature. Other studies have further revealed patterns in the *Song of Roland* and have attached varying significance to these designs.

18. NARRATIVE DEVICES AND TECHNIQUES

A. Geometricism

Rychner discovered that certain groups of laisses constitute symmetrical arrangements when considered either as narrative or as lyrical developments.[407] The Swiss scholar illustrates simple narration with a vertical line—each number in this schema represents a laisse—while a series of lyrical or descriptive strophes may be shown by a horizontal line. Sometimes the patterns are suggestive, and they are always geometrical:[408]

79
80
81
82
83 84 85
86
87
88
89
90
91
92

139
140
141
142 143
144
145 146
147 148 149 150

167
168
169
170 171 172
173 174 175

Rychner believes that one can find regular configurations in another regard. If one links up verses where continuity, sometimes even identity, of expression or concept are involved, one can imagine designs such as this:[409]

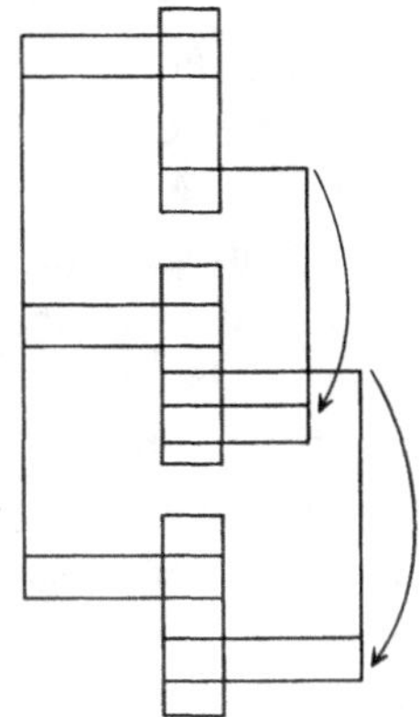

According to Rychner, these subordinate structures were conscious on the part of the poet and were used for mnemonic as well as esthetic purposes. He suggests no symbolism for these patterns and is content with demonstrating that the *Roland* is not only divided into four neat sections, each with a balanced number of subdivisions, but also possesses a rigorously mathematical architectonic at the level of the laisse.

Fern Farnham sees a relationship between Turoldus's epic and the disposition of figures on the tympanum of the abbey church at Moissac[410] (*Fig. 21*). At the center of this sculpture, one of the masterpieces of Romanesque art, one finds Christ in Majesty between symbols of the four evangelists. According to Farnham, the true center of the *Roland* is the death of the hero, and one can compare the two natural events that led up to it to the figures on the left side of the tympanum, considering the two supernatural events connected with the Emperor's revenge to be similar to the personages on the right side. The death of the hero occupies relatively little space in the poem's structure, which Farnham believes to be fivefold, when one considers only the number of laisses affected, but the impact of the scene gives it the dimensions of Christ in the Moissac sculpture.

Although not noticed by Farnham, Hatzfeld had earlier mentioned the same tympanum in connection with the *Roland*, but his commentary was altogether different.[411] Hatzfeld also discussed the tympanum at Vézelay in this connection.[412] But it is his observation that Turoldus's poem has five parts, which has attracted scholarly attention. André de Mandach has observed that Venice VII, a manuscript providing a rhymed rather than an assonanced version of the *Roland*, has only six initials, five of them corresponding exactly with Hatzfeld's partitions: (1) the betrayal of Ganelon; (2) Roland's rearguard action; (3) Charlemagne's victory over Marsile; (4) Baligant's counterattack; (5) Charlemagne's final victory and the punishment of Ganelon; and the sixth setting off the narrative of Alda's death.[413]

By far the most systematic outlines of the *Song of Roland*, however, are those given by Per Nykrog and Eleanor W. Bulatkin. The Danish scholar proposes a fivefold division but holds that each part is made up of several blocks of exactly five hundred verses each.[414] Bulatkin believes a sixty-six pattern of laisses constitutes the original structure of the *Roland*, to which a ninety-one pattern was later added by Turoldus.[415]

Fascinating as all this geometry may be, much of it is altogether in the eye of the beholder. Such views at times require modifications in the numbering of laisses or verses or fail to account for the fact that several verses are assumed to be missing in the Oxford version.

B. Laisses Similaires: Ambulatory Perception

Although not unique to our poem, laisses similaires—repetition of the same idea in a second, third, and even a fourth strophe, often with virtually identical phrasing—are associated with Turoldus, who made effective use of this technique at critical points in his narrative.[416] Laisses similaires constitute striking examples of Turoldus's ability to inject fresh meaning into a reiterated formula. The new strophe is only slightly altered, yet each subtle accretion or original combination adds fresh significance. Eugene Vinaver has detailed the poet's skill in achieving this result in the remarkable series of laisses similaires describing Roland's death.[417]

The technique is the exact opposite of synoptic views found in medieval art. In the latter, two separate actions are typically involved. For instance, Christ distributing communion first under one species, then under the other (INTRODUCTION, 12; and *Fig. 8*), or, in a medallion of the famous Charlemagne window at Chartres, Roland first attempting to break his sword on a stone, then sounding the oliphant[418] (*Fig. 22*). In the *Roland* two or three distinct perceptions of the same action are given in successive laisses, with change of assonance and slight modifications in phrasing only, affording the listener an opportunity to ponder the significance of the situation. In a sense, then, laisses similaires function in the way AOI. does, if the latter signals a pause for reflection.[419] However, AOI. appears to be an exclamation and of course does not have the same effect as a series of laisses.

Jenkins, citing Tavernier, opines that laisses similaires "are a form of repetition which eases the tension in an emotional crisis and imparts a sense of power and achievement, as of one who lingers a while upon an eminence."[420] Laisses similaires actually increase tension and, rather than giving the impression of a halt, definitely produce the effect of forward movement. Ambulatory perception is a more apt designation for the technique. Ambulatory, in this sense, refers to the passageway circling a focal point, such as an altar or throne, for example, the two-story gallery of the late-eighth-century octagonal palace chapel of Charlemagne at Aachen (*Fig. 23*) affording a view in the round of the central feature.[421]

A comparable stereoscopic effect is produced in certain Romanesque Last Judgment tympana with similar repetition of content but in completely different forms. For instance, the Separation of the Chosen from the Damned may be accompanied by the Wise and Foolish Virgins, a reiteration of essentially the same eschatological theme emphasizing, however, the importance of eternal vigilance.[422] Other tympana show a Majestas Domini at the center, surrounded or surmounted by multiple Christ symbols, such as a Lamb of God, a Tree of Life, a Cross, or typological figures such as David or Samson.[423] At Aulnay, for example, the Lamb of God is replicated by a bust of the Savior and the signs of the Zodiac, here interpreted as Christological symbols.[424] Laisses similaires contain no such drastic metamorphoses but they are characterized rather by small additions or alterations. The tympanum at Civray (*Fig. 24*), where Christ in Majesty is repeated two more times in slightly different configurations, offers perhaps the best iconographic parallel with Turoldus's device.[425]

C. Number Symbolism: Bipartite and Tripartite Patterns

Philipp August Becker long ago showed that the laisse structure and other patterns of the *Song of Roland* are often two or threefold and, like many other scholars before and after him, demonstrated quite convincingly that Turoldus availed himself of the unique possibilities for contrast and opposition afforded by these arrangements.[426] Composition based on numbers is one of the favorite techniques of the Middle Ages and is one of the most striking points of contact between art and literature during this period.[427] There is no apparent significance in Turoldus's use of number two or three, or, for that matter, in the recurrence of *quatre*, *cinc*, *set*, *dis*, *duze*, *vint*, *trente*, *quarante*, *cinquante*, *cent*, or *mil*, not to mention their combinations and multiples, verbally and structurally.[428] On the other hand, the author made extensive use of twofold modes of expression (INTRODUCTION, 13, A, B, C). Consequently, symbolism based on one or more numbers is not to be ruled out.[429]

Such associations often strike modern readers as fanciful and quaint, but medieval listeners, in particular those exposed to exegetical learning, found such relationships very meaningful. Thus Twelve Peers doubtless suggested a connection with the Twelve Apostles (one finds this identification in the *Pseudo-Turpin*, for example),[430] and when only Roland, Turpin, and Gautier de l'Hum are left and the three heroes ride forth (vv. 2066–2069), Conrad is reminded of the Holy Trinity (vv. 6581–6583: Dar huben sich do drí, / Ich wan iz also gescriben sí, / Inden drin namen unseres herren).

D. *Framing and Vantage Points*

Scholars have been so intent upon showing that the *Song of Roland* has three, four, or five parts and have expended so much effort trying to identify the precise location of presumed demarcations[431] that they have completely overlooked a structural form that transcends the compartmentalizing in the author's design. Correspondences and echoes of various sorts frequently constitute discernible poles, forming a delicate infrastructure for the poem.

The first and last appearances of Marsile emphasize his calamitous destiny (v. 15: "Oëz, seignurs, quel pecchet nus encumbret"; v. 3646: Morz est de doel, si cum pecchet l'encumbret). A friendly gesture marks Ganelon's arrival and departure at Saragossa (vv. 415, 647), threatening gestures (Marsile-Ganelon, vv. 439–444; Ganelon, vv. 499–500) actually constituting a frame within a frame. The two phases of the debate between Roland and Oliver enclose the first phase of the Battle of Roncevaux, while the hero's speeches in Laisses 79 and 88 set off the first of these disputes. The raising of the Mohammed idol *en la plus halte tur* (v. 853) marks the high point of Saracen hopes; Bramimonde's view of Baligant's routed forces *en sum sa tur* (v. 3636) signals the shattering of any remaining illusions on that score.

It is surely not without significance, finally, in light of the rising metaphors in the *Song of Roland*, that Turoldus chooses to move the narrative literally from elevation to elevation, the story reverberating from peak to peak, as it were, like the sound of the hero's oliphant (v. 3: la tere altaigne; v. 6: une muntaigne; v. 209: desuz Haltilie; v. 708: En sum un tertre; v. 714: par sum les puis; v. 814, etc.: Halt sunt li pui; v. 1017: Oliver est desur un pui; v. 1125: e muntet un lariz; v. 2267: Muntet sur un tertre; v. 2367: Devers Espaigne est en un pui agut). Each height offers a new vantage point from which to view developments, until the hero's final ascent (v. 2396: L'anme del cunte portent en pareïs).

E. Emphasis

Farnham has compared the relative importance assumed by Roland's death in Turoldus's poem to the disproportionate size of the Christ figure in the Moissac tympanum (INTRODUCTION, 18, A and *Fig. 21*). Emphasis is given to certain other events in the *Song of Roland*. Prominence is accorded to the sounding of the oliphant, the duel between Charles and Baligant, and the death of Alda, for instance, by isolating these episodes. This highlighting may be compared to the technique used by the artist of the Bible of San Paolo (*Fig. 25*) in enclosing certain actions within a ciborium, or canopy supported by four columns.[432] The occasional use of sententious phrases (v. 2524: Mult ad apris ki bien conuist ahan; v. 3959: Ki hume traïst sei ocit e altroi) underscores passages with comparable force; and lines such as *Des ore cumencet le plait de Guenelun* (v. 3704) serve less for demarcation than for bringing our minds to bear on what follows.

F. Linking

The discussion thus far has dwelt on formal procedures, that is, arrangements where the outward aspect can be distinguished from and even, to a certain extent, tends to assume as much importance as the content. However, Turoldus orders things in a variety of other ways where no such distinction is apparent.

Linking, referred to by William A. Nitze in his commentary on the *Perlesvaus* as "an elaborate system of cross-reference . . . through which the author integrates his narrative by [connecting] motifs, episodes or incidents, and personages,"[433] is much in evidence in the *Song of Roland.*

Plot A has been shown to be linked to Plot B in a narrative way by the idea that Charles must sacrifice his nephew (the Abraham archetype) and in a typological way by the fact that Abraham's sacrifice of Isaac, viewed as an antecedent of God sacrificing his Son, is reflected in Roland's imitation of Christ's Passion. Other relationships, which help to give Turoldus's poem its remarkable unity, have also been alluded to above.

The linking of characters or situations by means of an identical epithet or turn of phrase has traditionally been considered to be unintentional in so formulaic a genre as the Old French epic.[434] The repetition of hemistichs and even of entire verses has been regarded as similarly inconsequential.[435] Yet at times there can be no doubt that Turoldus uses these procedures consciously and with artistic effect as, for example, in the *parastre-fillastre* word-play (vv. 277, 743), and when Roland and Alda are associated in death by the locution *aler a sa fin* (vv. 2392, 3723).[436] In the next section it will be noted that the poet is particularly adept at exploiting iteration of an image, or of a seemingly formulaic locution, for ironic purposes.

G. *Irony: Antiphrasis, Understatement, Triplication, Inverted Images, Aping*

The procedure by which an author says one thing but means the exact opposite is not totally absent from popular literature, but its subtle use assumes sophistication on the part of the audience and generally points to learned influences.[437] So far as the *Song of Roland* is concerned, the fact that irony plays a key role implies that Turoldus fully expected his audience to distinguish literal from true meanings and, therefore, lends important support to the view that the work also has deeper significance than that found at the level of plot.[438]

Roland's observation "*Sire parastre, mult vos dei aveir cher*" (v. 753) is an excellent example of irony in its simplest form. Oliver's reiteration of his companion's arguments for not sounding the oliphant in the second horn scene (v. 1705 ff.) strikes many critics as being tinged with sarcasm, but the formal aspect of this debate militates against this view. In a different use of irony Baligant tells his messenger to have Marsile put his gauntlet *el destre poign* (v. 2678): Here the audience doubtless reacted in scornful fashion, for it knew that the Saracen king's hand was cut off by Roland while the Emir ignored this fact.[439] A similar situation exists in v. 698 when Charles praises God because Saracen conversion appears to be a distinct possibility, but in actuality the offer is known to be the height of deceit, as the preceding scene made clear.

Understatement, as a technique for adding emphasis, often borders on irony, as when Turoldus states that the embattled hero *ad . . . endreit sei asez que faire* (v. 2123). Ironic understatement in the *Song of Roland* indicates restraint on the part of the speaker and is, consequently, a technique for building tension as, for example, when Ganelon, angry at being nominated to carry Charles's message to Saragossa, threatens his nephew with *un poi de legerie* (v. 300). OFr. *amer* refers at times to feudal ties rather than to personal devotion but, despite Jones's statements to the contrary,[440] Ganelon's observation cannot be understood without specific reference to affection in this instance (see also vv. 323, 494, 1548, 1642). Emotional control is similarly in evidence when, after he has dropped the Emperor's proffered gauntlet, Ganelon observes to the Franks: "*vos en orrez noveles!*" (v. 336). There is comparable repression of true feelings in Oliver's comment after sighting the massed enemy forces: "*De Sarrazins purum bataille aveir*" (v. 1007), an interpretation that explains at least in part the hero's initial reaction to his comrade's accusation that Ganelon has betrayed them: "*Mis parrastre est, ne voeill que mot en suns*" (v. 1027). An additional illustration of ironic understatement can be seen when Roland addresses the Rash Saracen, who is trying to steal his sword: "*Men escïentre, tu n'ies mie des noz!*" (v. 2286).

A more subtle form of irony consists in echoing phrases.[441] When Ganelon finds himself obliged to go to Saragossa, he initially utters a vague threat: "*Einz i frai un poi de legerie, / Que jo n'esclair ceste meie grant ire*" (vv. 300–301). In what is perhaps the longest interval between such repetitions, Turoldus indicates that vengeance in the *Song of Roland* belongs to Charlemagne, not to the traitor. After Ganelon has been tried and executed for his unspeakable crime, the Emperor, says the poet, has been vindicated: *E esclargiez est la sue grant ire* (v. 3989). Poetic justice is apparent in one of the forms of retribution with which Ganelon menaces the Saracen king ("Getet serez sur un malvais sumer," v. 481), a humiliating punishment meted out to the traitor himself

(Sur un sumer l'unt mis a deshonor, v. 1828). Quartering, the awesome penalty inflicted upon Ganelon for his crime at the conclusion of the poem, is also peculiarly appropriate (COMMENTARY, 47).

Trinary composition is one of Turoldus's favorite narrative techniques. This pattern is at times repeated at close intervals, but at others at considerable distance, and takes the form of groupings of verses, laisses, characters, and scenes (INTRODUCTION, 18, C). What seems particularly notable in these arrangements is the prevalence of a pair of compatible items contrasted with a third whose incongruity produces an ironic effect. Thus the parallel deaths of Roland and Alda are offset by Marsile's ignominious end. The points of contact reside in the word *anme* (vv. 2396–2397, 3647, 3721) and, insofar as Roland and Marsile are concerned, in the direction each faces (v. 2360: Turnat sa teste vers la paiene gent; v. 3644: Quant l'ot Marsilie, vers sa pareit se turnet).

Other examples of ironic triplication include Roland's two discussions with Oliver contrasted with Charles's quarrel with Ganelon;[442] the selection of a messenger for the Saragossa mission corresponding to the nomination of a leader for the rearguard as opposed to the designation of Marsile's nephew to the Saracen vanguard; Ganelon's removal of his cloak in vv. 281 and 464, and Charles's ceremonial wiping of Thierry's face with his fur mantle in v. 3940; and the arming of the Franks in Laisses 136 and 214–216, followed by that of the Saracens in Laisse 228.

Two other uses of irony remain to be discussed. Each instance involves conscious modulation of a familiar attitude or scene, usually with sardonic intent.

An inverted image accurately reflects an object but turns it inside out or upside down. Blancandrin's callous abandonment of his own son (v. 149) anticipates in grotesquely distorted fashion Charlemagne's anguish at having to sacrifice his nephew Roland. The Saracens pray to Mohammed, then call on Marsile for help (vv. 1616–1619), exactly the reverse of the procedure recommended by Turpin, who urges the Franks to turn their thoughts away from the Twelve Peers toward God (vv. 1469–1473).[443] Bramimonde's swoon (v. 2825) is matched by her husband's effort to rise from his bed (v. 2829), attitudes that foreshadow their eventual spiritual evolution. The technique is often used in typology. On the tympanum of the church of Saint-Gabriel (Bouches-du-Rhône), Adam and Eve in the Garden of Eden are paired with Daniel in the lions' den (*Fig. 26*):

> on signifie par là que les deux scènes sont antithétiques et se répondent aux deux entrémités de l'histoire du salut. Adam a introduit la mort dans l'humanité; Jésus, nouvel Adam, rend la vie éternelle à la nouvelle humanité: ces deux personnages du tympan ont le même visage. Les attitudes sont, elles aussi, antithétiques: Adam et Eve couvrent leur nudité que le péché leur a rendue honteuse; Daniel habillé—mais tout juste!—pour être une figure décente du Christ, ouvre les bras en un geste enfantin d'une totale innocence. Si l'on ajoute que les lions sont un symbole fréquent de la *luxure* (le vice qui dévore furieusement), on est amené à penser que l'artiste a interprété le péché originel non pas, bien sûr, comme un vulgaire péché de luxure, mais dans sa conséquence qui fut d'introduire le trouble et même la honte dans un domaine qui était sorti tout pur des mains du Créateur: "et ils virent qu'ils étaient nus." Le recouvrement de la grâce d'innocence sera souvent symbolisé par une nudité rayonnante de pureté, affranchie de toute gêne.[444]

A related type of figuration lacks the inverted aspect alluded to here and depends heavily for its ironic impact on the known moral reprehensibleness of the individual involved. Northrop Frye aptly refers to "the deliberate reversal of the customary moral associations of archetypes" as demonic modulation,[445] but it is more fitting, in a medieval context, to term this process aping.

Patristic writers, mindful of the ape's mimetic proclivities and of the fact that the devil had the ambition to imitate the Lord, viewed this beast as a *figura diaboli* and applied the term *simia* to all enemies of Christ and his Church.[446] They also considered the ape to be the image of man as sinner (naturae degenerantis homo),[447] both laughable and contemptible, and associated it with the notion of vice masquerading as virtue.[448] The ape often represents Avarice[449] and, beginning about 1200, is frequently depicted eating an apple, thus symbolizing the Fall of Man.[450] In Gothic drôleries, finally, apes appear repeatedly in inversions and parodies satirizing the fact that every man has his foible.[451]

The complicity between the author and his audience must be fully grasped in such situations: Just as the ape is not amusing or appealing in such depictions, but an incarnation of evil, a personage's wicked nature in the *Song of Roland* necessarily taints his character and the things with which he is associated.

Thus Saracen attributes and qualities—the epithets *bel*, *fier*, *prod*, *sage*, *vaillant*, *vassal*, *vertuos*, Marsile's *faldestoel*, his Twelve Peers, the uncle-nephew relationship, Baligant's sword[452] and war cry *Precieuse* —while resembling superficially those of the Franks, are never without their peculiar blemish, and the pagan gods are but weak imitations of the Trinity. Saracen stances are derisive when compared with the attitudes and postures on which they are clearly modeled, as when Baligant spurs his horse forward to be, like the dying Roland, ahead of his men (vv. 2842, 3324), and when his horse, like Charlemagne's, takes a mighty leap (vv. 2997, 3166). Even gardens and trees, when associated with Saracens, reflect pagan perversity.

Pinabel's expressed desire to sustain the honor of his relatives (v. 3907) is an instance of aping by a Christian villain, Roland's concern for his family's honor (vv. 1063, 1076) offering the model. Aping assumes a far more alarming complexion when it refers to Christ, as in the Saracens' blasphemous imitation of the Entry into Jerusalem (COMMENTARY, 2), or Ganelon's shocking assumption of the Savior's attitude in the Scourging and in the Arraignment before Pilate (COMMENTARY, 45). A disturbing effect is also produced when Ganelon implies, in the apple anecdote, that Roland is a diabolic seducer leading Charles and the Franks to their perdition, when in fact it is the traitor himself who, in this poem, is—but not just for the sake of argument! —the devil's advocate (COMMENTARY, 6).

H. Space and Time Conventions

In an effort to move his story along at an accelerated pace, Turoldus at times has individuals or entire armies cover considerable distances in a short time as, for example, Ganelon's voyage to and from Saragossa, and the various advances and withdrawals of Charlemagne's forces.[453] The audience is so absorbed by the events in question and so drawn along by the narrative momentum that, in general, it is barely aware of what to some scholars constitutes stretching plausibility too far.[454]

In general Turoldus tells his story chronologically, but on occasion he makes use of flashback and flashforward techniques.[455] In one instance he provides a synchronic overview.[456] Simultaneous actions take place from time to time: Marsile's movements in Laisses 55 and 68, for instance, coincide with Charlemagne's,[457] and the last French survivors at Roncevaux fall as the Emperor vainly tries to reach them.[458] The interlacing of these events is effected with consummate skill and produces considerable dramatic impact.

There are few, if any, gaps in time, although the duration of many actions is quite vague, for instance, the return to Aix and the summoning of the judges.[459] This does not mean that all time periods are realistic. The stopping of the sun casts an aura of awe over the rout of Marsile's army, but it also serves as an escape valve for the bursting calendar of events on the day Roncevaux takes place. Turoldus's penchant for plethora is no less apparent in the schedule of the day on which Charles meets and destroys Baligant.

Artists of all times have condensed or selected elements in a scene rather than depict them explicitly and in all their details. This is particularly frequent when some of the components are repetitive. Thus, in Romanesque iconography, the Three Temptations of Christ, the Three Denials of Peter, and the Three Kings before Herod (Herod's consultation of the chief priests followed by his meeting with the Magi) are often reduced to single actions or figures, or a city by one or more towers or a crenelated wall.[460] Romanesque artists did not adhere to the laws of proportion and perspective developed later in the Middle Ages and especially during the Renaissance.

Condensation or selectivity is to be found in Turoldus's suggestion of a forest by means of a solitary tree (v. 366), of a large council by dialogues between three or four individuals,[461] or of a battle by a series of isolated duels, formulas also found in contemporary art. An iconographic parallel for the narrative economy involved in disposing of a lengthy voyage in a few words can be found in a miniature of a fourteenth-century manuscript of *Girart de Vienne* (*Fig. 27*). Oliver sets out from Vienne to parley with Charlemagne, who is camped nearby: The hind legs of his horse are still inside the gate of the city, while its forelegs touch the Emperor's tent![462] A locution such as *Tant chevalcherent . . . que*, particularly when repeated in close proximity, as in vv. 402–403 and 405–406, does, however, convey the impression of great distance and elapsed time with considerable force.[463] The concision occasioned by the exigencies of literature intended for oral delivery is not unlike the tyranny of spatial limitation (la loi du cadre) forcing the artist to adapt his work to small or awkwardly shaped surfaces.[464]

The linking of remote armies by means of the oliphant's sound has been shown to be a remarkably effective narrative device for bridging space and time.[465] Flashbacks and flashforwards, and the freezing phenomenon (COMMENTARY, 20) are worth mentioning in this regard.

Of comparable interest is Turoldus's sense of historical time.[466] Since the Middle Ages men have become increasingly sensitive to the changes that separate them from preceding generations, and three centuries strike moderns as a yawning chasm on whose far side lived a race of total strangers. Turoldus felt no such disjunction with respect to the men of Charlemagne's day. Like contemporary artists, he dressed his personages in eleventh-century garb and ascribed familiar manners and mores to his heroes, largely perhaps out of ignorance of Carolingian apparel and modes of behavior and thought, but also as a reflection of the prevailing notion that nothing fundamental had really changed since then.

The so-called archaisms in the *Song of Roland* are of a superficial nature and in no way constitute an expression of true historical discontinuity.[467] The celebrated opening strophe of the tenth-century *Vie de Saint Alexis* bemoans the decline of morality since the age in which the hero lived,[468] but the very term *ancessor* (< *antecessorem*, accusative of CL *antecessor* < *ante* + *cedere* 'to go before') has a decidedly filial quality in this passage, and it strongly implies that the anonymous poet feels as one with those who preceded him:

> Bons fut li siecles al tems anciënour,
> Quer feit i eret e justisie ed amour,
> S'i ert credance, dont or n'i at nul prout;
> Toz est mudez, perdude at sa colour:
> Ja mais n'iert tels com fut as anceisours.[469]

The reason for this emerges a few verses later: *Nostre anceisour ourent crestiantet* (v. 12).

Several different schemes were devised during the Middle Ages for dividing history into three, four, five, or seven ages, but the most recent phase invariably began with the birth of Christ.[470] Thus Turoldus's historical perspective resulted in a feeling of solidarity with the early martyrs and with the legendary heroes of Charlemagne's day, whose exploits in Christ's name he viewed with the same awe and wonder.[471]

19. Character Portrayal

Nowhere is the distance between modern practice and the art of the *Song of Roland* greater than in the depiction of characters. It has been said that Turoldus's personages lack depth and that they tend to conform to stock types: the Hero, the King, the Traitor.[472] Much of the discussion concerning Roland gravitates about the notion of *hybris*,[473] but the use of Aristotelian views (cf. the recurrence of such concepts as tragic flaw [Gr. *hamartia*][474] and recognition [Gr. *anagnorisis*])[475] to explain medieval epics can be just as misleading as the application of critical notions developed during any other period.

A. Individualization and Role-Playing

Distinct characterization such as we find in modern literature—often aided by details concerning physical appearance, clothing, gestures, speech mannerisms, and quirks of various sorts—is absent, for the most part, in the *Song of Roland,* just as it was in the art of the period. A few scattered indications, notably concerning Charlemagne (deliberateness, fierceness, regal bearing, sensitivity), Ganelon (arrogance, deceitfulness), and the Saracens (diabolism), provide revealing glimpses of personality, but Turoldus does not always rely on such particulars to convey character traits. In fact, individuals tend to look and think a good deal alike and to use the same kind of language. Indeed, personal information rarely imparts meaning in absolute fashion, identical attitudes or features often being subject to widely divergent interpretations.

Characters each have a nature, good or bad, identified from the outset of the poem by an epithet or a phrase (e.g., v. 172: E de Gascuigne li proz quens Acelin; v. 178: Guenes i vint, ki la traïsun fist), by being Christian or Saracen, or simply by being one of us (v. 1: Carles li reis, nostre emperere magnes).

The more important the character, the more his goodness shines forth or his villainy looms large. This is the literal meaning we must attach to the word *cler*, for example, in descriptions of physiognomy or laughter (vv. 619, 628, 895, 1159, 3116, and 3160), the connotation being good or bad depending on the referent.[476] The character traits one can read in another's face, combined with the advice evildoers receive from Satan, explain how the Saracen messengers are able immediately to identify Charlemagne even though they have never seen him before (v. 119), and they suggest the reason why Blancandrin, on the road to Saragossa, seems to know that Ganelon will prove to be treacherous.

This categorization (v. 1015: Paien unt tort e chrestïens unt dreit) governs behavior and outlook to a remarkable degree, for, as a rule, individuals do not change their essences. Good characters learn, acquiring knowledge or experience that edifies or scandalizes them in the etymological sense, that is, builds up or acts as a stumbling block to their faith. Evil characters become more villainous as their despair grows darker. The only exception is the convert, epitomized by Bramimonde, whose complete transformation from evil to good is wrought through the miracle of grace. Other personages simply do not change or develop in the modern acceptation of these terms.

Characterization in the *Song of Roland* is often strongly affected by role-playing. Thus while relatively few exterior traits distinguish Charlemagne, Roland, or Ganelon, the modeling of a character after a well-known archetype (e.g., Abraham, Christ, Judas) tends to add the prefiguration's virtues or vices to the individual's portrait.[477] This rubbing-off of personality is an important part of the poetic process. Scenic formulas and transpositions produce the same sort of effect upon the protagonists as does role-playing in these figural representations.

A distinction needs to be drawn between conscious and unconscious role-playing. Evil characters, notably when aping, are totally unaware of the image on which they are patterning themselves, and with such derogatory effect upon the audience.[478] On the other hand, as Charles and Roland probe ever deeper into the mysteries of faith and martyrdom, they grow increasingly aware of the archetypal figures whose sublime deeds they reenact.

B. *Virtues and Vices*

Turoldus conceived of his characters in medieval fashion, that is, as being motivated by a central virtue or vice, each of these traits being associated or in conflict with corresponding qualities or faults.[479] Although this system of virtues and vices is firmly rooted in biblical and patristic sources, the mundane aspect of moral strengths and weaknesses is also depicted. Thus while Largesse, the chief virtue of the king, is at times viewed as a reflection of divine Largitas, it can also refer to more familiar forms of liberality.

Chivalric virtues, which figure prominently in the *Song of Roland*, had not yet been reduced to the rigid code one begins to notice increasingly in the second half of the twelfth century, when the Church's influence also becomes apparent.[480] However, it is a mistake to assume that the only virtue expected of a knight in Turoldus's day was manly courage and that loyalty was merely a contractual obligation between lord and vassal.[481] There can be no denying the fact that the twelfth century witnessed important cultural changes,[482] but the evolution in institutions and in manners and mores was gradual, and sporadic early manifestations of what were later to become highly developed traditions are sometimes noticed. When, in the *Pèlerinage de Charlemagne*, Oliver courts King Hugo's daughter, and when, in the *Pseudo-Turpin Chronicle*, Roland places a pillow under the head of his resting adversary during a truce, these gestures foreshadow the courtesy epitomized by Chrétien de Troyes's knights.[483] One must be careful to distinguish between idealized views and reality, for literature is the province of enhanced images. The fact that the eleventh century may actually have seen little of the heroic stances or of the magnanimity found in the *Song of Roland* did not prevent Turoldus from visualizing such behavior. Moreover, in all likehood, the poet's portrayals helped shape later conceptualizations of ideal conduct.

C. *Point of View*

A character's virtues or vices are chiefly manifested through his actions and words. Physical appearance provides important clues to an individual's nature, but looks can also be deceiving (INTRODUCTION, 10, B, 2). Impressions of a different sort are gained when the poet himself intervenes, praising or condemning deeds as they occur, or in retrospect. An individual's observations about another—whether in the form of an assertion, an anecdote, or an insult—furnish us with information of yet another kind, for they must always be carefully weighed in light of the fact that the speaker represents a point of view that is not necessarily shared by the author. The stories Ganelon tells about Roland to Blancandrin and later to Charlemagne are intended to vilify his stepson.[484] Oliver's description of his companion's anticipated behavior, when the hero volunteers to go to Saragossa (vv.

256–257), is self-serving—he himself wishes to go on this mission—and therefore suspect.[485] His characterization of Roland's decisions in the oliphant debate represents a very understandable reaction, but it also constitutes a refusal to come to terms with the deeper meaning of his friend's stand.

Finally, an individual may provide important insights into his own psychological make-up while boasting or talking about others, especially in tense moments.

Self-praise strikes the modern reader as being unseemly in the hero. However, the medieval audience drew a distinction between truthful claims and hollow assertions.[486] Thus Roland's detailing of his past and future accomplishments[487] not only constitutes behavior that is quite acceptable but also provides information which is essential to the narrative. However, the Saracens' *gabs* are repeatedly shown to be vain. Formal laments, which laud a fallen companion's qualities, and insults, which bring out an adversary's villainy, are similarly viewed with suspicion today because each occurs under circumstances notorious for fostering extravagant speech. When reading the *Song of Roland*, it must always be assumed that praise for a Christian and scorn for a pagan are well merited, and never the reverse. On the other hand, Ganelon's attempts, in the apple anecdote, to portray Roland as a diabolic seducer and, during the trial, as a felon motivated by greed, unwittingly show his own true colors.

If the battlefield discussion concerning the sounding of the oliphant is viewed as an externalization of an internal debate—the form is identical in each case—Oliver's words can be interpreted as an effort to convince himself that he should assume Roland's stance, or as a reflection of Roland's agony of decision. This explains in part Turoldus's emphasis, in the lines following v. 1093 (Rollant est proz e Oliver est sage), on the equality of worthiness found in the two companions-in-arms.

D. *Reflections*

One aspect of character depiction, indirect delineation of personality traits, is worthy of special note: Turoldus projects facets of an individual's psychology and spirit on certain objects in his possession.

The praise that Roland lavishes upon Durendal represents a detailing of the hero's own valor and stunning achievements. The sword's brilliance is literally a reflection of the hero's virtues.[488] This radiance corresponds exactly to the shining quality of the gold ground in Emperor portraits of the day.[489] The jewel-encrusted ivory oliphant, like Durendal's priceless ornamentation, symbolizes its owner's matchless qualities, and the horn's ascending voice evokes Roland's undying spirit. Joyeuse plays a similar role in portraying aspects of Charlemagne's character. These emanations link Emperor and nephew in mystical fashion. Conversely, the very name Precieuse is a mocking reflection of Baligant's hollowness, and Murgleis and other sinister names cast an evil glow—like that of the lantern-lit Saracen ships (COMMENTARY, 29)—on the persons with whom they are associated.[490]

Roland and Oliver are brothers-in-arms, but the resemblance between Charlemagne and his nephew goes far beyond community of interest and solidarity of purpose. The hero is the Emperor's right arm (vv. 597, 727, 1195), a physical union symbolizing moral and spiritual oneness as well.[491] The lance is an apt symbol for Roland (INTRODUCTION, 10, A, 1) and it is specifically identified with the hero in the first of Charlemagne's dreams (COMMENTARY, 10). The poet doubtless wishes to suggest that Roland, like his weapon, is straight and strong. But Roland's lance is also an extension of his arm and is thus associated with the right-arm image. Uncle and nephew maintain their separate individualities, but such integration implies remarkable psychological compatibility. Each character's personality reflects various facets of his counterpart's being. Nowhere in the *Song of Roland* is the fact that weapons often mirror their owner's moral excellence or depravity more in evidence than in the case of Durendal and Joyeuse, whose brilliance, holiness, and invincibility are virtually indistinguishable, pointing to the poet's similar concept of Charles and Roland (COMMENTARY, 25). Thus the debate over whether Charles or Roland is the chief hero of Turoldus's poem is pointless: One character is the extension of the other, and the author clearly had no intention of according one precedence over the other.[492] Roland and Alda are also closely linked and reflect each other by virtue of their betrothal, their shared death—including a similarity of phrasing in this respect (vv. 2392 and 3723)—and their virginity (INTRODUCTION, 19, F).[493]

E. Charlemagne

The Emperor is the most complex figure in the *Song of Roland*, for aspects of his personality enjoyed an independent existence exceeding by far the limits of the poem. Other personages in Turoldus's epic are historical figures, and legends about a number of these individuals, notably Roland, had doubtless been elaborated before the present work was composed. However, these stories pale beside the Charlemagne myth, which experienced an extraordinary growth throughout Europe, particularly in France and Germany in the centuries following the Emperor's reign.[494]

A firm grasp of what anthropologists refer to as the culture-hero is vital to our understanding of this development:

> Many races believe in culture-heroes, whom they suppose to have brought fire, water, or other indispensable blessings to man. Frequently these culture-heroes are treated as gods—that is, worshipped through ritual. But in other cases no divine attributes are ascribed to them, and they are regarded as great men of the past, and sometimes as ancestors of a particular tribe. Yet, whether as gods or not, these culture-heroes usually play the principal part in a whole cycle of myths or legends.... The distinction between religious and profane legends is not always clear. When heroes and legendary figures are not actually worshipped, but merely represented from time to time in an historical celebration, the religious significance may be lost altogether. Very often there are a whole host of subsidiary figures—good and evil spirits which play a part as masks in the ceremony, either alone or in conjunction with divinities and heroes.[495]

The historical Charlemagne did in fact promote the well-being of his subjects and their descendants, notably in the area of administration and in the realm of arts and letters, but his accomplishments and benefactions were greatly exaggerated in later times. A religious cult, attested soon after the Emperor's death, was considerably offset by the legend of an unconscionable sin later identified as incest.[496] Charlemagne was canonized on 29 December 1165, at the instigation of Frederick Barbarossa.

The religious aspect of the legend was intensified by the frequent comparisons made during Charlemagne's own lifetime between the Emperor and David, and, soon afterward, between Charlemagne and Constantine.[497] By the eleventh century the idea of kingship had become firmly Christ-centered, and the *basileus* notion had spread from the Byzantine court to that of the Holy Roman Emperors.[498] Focusing now on the image of Charlemagne in the *Song of Roland*, it is important to bear in mind that the priest-king concept applied to Jesus in Hebrews 4:14, stems from Psalms 110:4: "You are a priest of the order of Melchizedek, and for ever."

Melchizedek, King of Salem, makes a mysterious appearance in Genesis 14:17–20, bringing bread and wine to Abraham. Medieval exegetes saw in this royal personage a prototype of the Messiah and, in this episode, a prefiguration of the Eucharist.[499] The iconographic formula showing Melchizedek in priestly vestments, is best known in the thirteenth-century Reims version, a bas-relief popularly known as "La Communion du chevalier"[500] (*Fig. 28*). Here Abraham is depicted in chain mail, receiving holy communion from Melchizedek's hand. The Reims sculptor visualized an armed figure in accordance with the account in Genesis, which situates the encounter after Abraham's defeat of Chedor-laomer, King of Elam. Melchizedek alludes to this victory in his blessing: "Blessed be Abram by God Most High, creator of heaven and earth, and blessed be God Most High for handing over your enemies to you."

Lejeune and Stiennon regard the Reims figures as the representation of Turpin serving communion to Roland on the battlefield of Roncevaux.[501] While the Melchizedekian interpretation of the bas-relief is certain, the communion scene in the illustrated manuscript of Conrad's German translation (*see Fig. 6*) does bear a striking resemblance to this depiction.[502] It is quite possible, then, that contemporaries, at least those who were more familiar with epic material than with liturgical symbolism, read the same meaning into the Reims sculpture. The Abraham archetype and the nexus of sacrificial symbols in the *Song of Roland* favor such an interpretation.

Biblical associations abound in Turoldus's depiction of the protean figure of Charlemagne, for he is successively—at times simultaneously—Abraham, Christ the Judge, Joshua, the Ancient of Days,[503] Christ the Reaper, Constantine, and Job.[504] First and foremost, however, Charles is a Messianic figure who incarnates Sapientia and plays the role of Abraham (INTRODUCTION, 11, C, and 13, C).

The narrative of the Sacrifice of Isaac in Genesis mentions no emotion on Abraham's part. Charles evinces the same blind and spontaneous obedience to the strange promptings of the Almighty. However, Turoldus portrays him in a more human light, repeatedly stressing the Emperor's great anguish as the dimensions of his role are gradually revealed to him by the omen of the dropped gauntlet,

Ganelon's nomination of Roland to the rearguard, the premonitory dreams, and, finally, the traitor's attempt at deception when the sound of the oliphant is heard.

It has been stated that the vagueness of the warnings received by Charles—he knows who will betray him but not how the deed will be perpetrated—explains the Emperor's inability to stay the onrushing catastrophe.[505] Charlemagne is guided by an inner light that, the poet makes clear, comes directly from God (v. 535: De tel barnage l'ad Deus enluminet). He may not know all, but this is not the point. In the gospel narrative of the Last Supper, the details of Christ's knowledge of Judas's treachery do not concern us. What matters in the New Testament and in the *Song of Roland* is the determination to play the role assigned by God to the bitter end.[506]

Charles survives his nephew,[507] and it is obvious that Turoldus attached a good deal of importance to his serving as a posthumous witness to Roland's edifying death. The author of the *Pseudo-Turpin* felt a similar need to emphasize this aspect of Charlemagne's role, for he has Baudouin and Thierry transmit in person the manner of Roland's passing. Also, Archbishop Turpin, having been favored with a vision of a choir of angels bearing the souls of Roland and his companions to Paradise, reassures Charles in this regard.[508]

F. Roland

Jenkins and Faral provided analyses of Roland's character, which influenced many subsequent writers on this subject.[509] For the American scholar Roland's essential virtue is his loyalty, that is, the unswerving allegiance he gives to his friends, his family, his king, his country, and his faith. To sustain him in his fidelity, the poet grants him exceptional courage but also the fault of his virtue, rashness. According to Jenkins, this tragic flaw, coupled with excessive sensitivity as to his military reputation, brings about the disaster. Roland recognizes his error, has a change of heart, and atones for his misdeed by his suffering and his death. Conversely, Faral considers valor to be the hero's chief quality, and, while he concedes that Roland's bravery borders on recklessness, he insists that Turoldus merely wished thereby to enhance the beauty and grandeur of his heroism. Roland remained true to himself and in no way felt the need to expiate any sin or wrongdoing.

Jenkins points out that it is only Roland's enemies who accuse him of pride and that Oliver's charge of recklessness comes "in the heat of battle and the exasperation of defeat."[510] This distinction, which is not drawn by Faral or by most of the critics in either scholar's wake,[511] is crucial to our understanding of the poet's intention.[512]

Jones has shown that fierceness and justifiable pride (fiertet) are always praiseworthy in the *Song of Roland*, as opposed to arrogance and haughtiness (orgoill), which are treated with contempt.[513] "Nevertheless, this professed disapproval of arrogance must have been largely theoretical; for most of the characters of the epic behave arrogantly, especially the most admirable ones. Certainly Roland's braggadocio is the epitome of haughtiness (2316–2334)."[514] Jones could not have selected a less suitable passage to support his assertion, for it refers to Roland's apostrophe to his sword.[515] Few words in Turoldus's poem have any absolute value. Applied indifferently to both good and evil characters and situations, terms such as these derive much of their force from a rigid categorization assumed from the start. Superbia in the *Song of Roland* is incarnated first and foremost by the Saracens, notably Baligant, and it is symbolized by the mountain citadel of Saragossa. It is also a trait associated with Ganelon. There is no textual support for any *psychomachia* within Roland; there is no evidence that he undergoes any change whatsoever.[516] The view that the hero experiences a conversion or transformation is a lame assertion.[517]

Roland is the ideal knight, his *proece* combining all chivalric virtues, the ability to impart sound advice (consilium) as well as the courage and strength to be of formidable assistance in combat (auxilium). In view of the traditional interpretations of Roland's character, it may seem paradoxical to maintain that, on a spiritual plane, beyond worldly chivalry, the hero personifies Humilitas. In medieval thought true humility consisted in recognizing one's lowly condition compared with God's greatness, one's need to surrender oneself completely to the dictates of the divine Will, and one's total dependence upon grace.[518] Having demonstrated his humility in his speech in Laisse 14, urging Charles to carry on the struggle against Marsile,[519] and in his debate with Oliver, maintaining that Folly is Wisdom, Roland begins his spiritual ascent. Saint Anselm, in a letter to Turoldus, monk of Le Bec, dated before 1109, states: "to spiritual eyes they who humble themselves never appear to descend, but to mount up the heavenly hill whence one ascends to the celestial kingdom."[520]

The characterization of Roland as the incarnation of Humilitas is in complete harmony with the Ascent metaphor (INTRODUCTION,

15, c). Also, the virtual synonymity of this concept with that of Sapientia explains the litany of virtues in the metrical planctus following the hero's death in the *Pseudo-Turpin Chronicle:*

Non decet hunc igitur vacuis deflere querelis
  Quem laetum summi nunc tenet aula poli.
Nobilis antiqua decurrens prole parentum,
  Nobilior gestis nunc super astra manet.
Egregius, nulli de nobilitate secundus,
  Moribus excellens, culmine primus erat.
Templorum cultor, recreans modulamine cives,
  Vulneribus patriae fida medela fuit.
Spes cleri, tutor viduarum, panis egentium,
  Largus pauperibus, prodigus hospitibus,
Sic venerabilibus templis, sic fudit egenis,
  Mitteret ut celis, quas sequerentur opes.
Dogmata corde tenens, plenus, velut arca libellis:
  Quisquis quod voluit, fonte fluente, bibit.
Consilio sapiens, animo pius, ore serenus,
  Omnibus ut populis esset amore parens.
Culmen honoratum, decus almum, lumen opimum,
  Laudibus in cuius militet omne decus.
Pro tantis meritis hunc ad celestia vectum,
  Non premit urna rogi, sed tenet aula Dei.[521]

Finally, in an appendix to the Latin chronicle, the following etymology of the hero's name is provided: "Rotolandus interpretatur rotulus scienciae, quia omnes reges et principes omnibus scienciis inbutus excellit."[522]

Far too much emphasis has been placed on the negative views of Roland derived from statements made by Ganelon and Oliver. Turoldus's own characterization of the hero is reflected in Charlemagne's perception of his nephew, notably in his lament (Laisses 207–210) and in his anecdote recognizing the prophetic significance of the hero's words at Aix (vv. 2860–2867).

Another important aspect of Roland's character should be discussed here. Anna Granville Hatcher, in an article seeking to explain why the heroine of the Old French *Sequence of Saint Eulalia* (ninth century) elects to suffer martyrdom rather than lose her virginity, has equated physical virginity with Christianity.[523] But, as F. J. Barnett has pointed out, the Church never stipulated physical virginity as a condition for salvation.[524] Barnett argues persuasively that what is involved in *Eulalia* is virginity of the heart, mind, or soul, which the Church Fathers, notably Saint Augustine, stressed repeatedly. This is the same as the notion of the "pure in heart" (mundi corde), who shall see God (Matthew 5:8), the opposite of the hardness of heart that characterizes Marsile (INTRODUCTION, 19, L).

In Christian tradition only three personages looked on God and remained alive: Moses, Elijah, and Paul.[525] The Church considered these individuals to be preeminent mystics and explained that they were accorded this extraordinary grace because their hearts were pure, that is, because they were virginal in spirit. As he lies dying, Roland, in the *Pseudo-Turpin*, makes this astonishing statement: "Omnia terrena michi vilescunt; nunc enim, Christo donante, intueor quod occulus non vidit, nec auris audivit, et in cor hominis non ascendit, quod praeparavit Deus diligentibus se."[526] The hero's claim was doubtless influenced by Saint Paul's affirmation that he was caught up into the third heaven and "heard things which must not and cannot be put into human language" (2 Corinthians 12:4).[527]

In the *Song of Roland* Virginitas[528] and the related concepts of intactness (entireness, quality of being uninjured), integrity (quality, state of completeness, of being unimpaired), and inviolability (unassailability)[529] lead inexorably to the hero:

—Roland dies but suffers not a single wound,[530] except that his temples burst from sounding the oliphant. The major threats he overcomes in this respect are Oliver's blow (v. 1997) and the Saracen army's assault (v. 2159), but in each case the hero remains unscathed.

—Durendal reflects Roland's many shining virtues, but the fact that it cannot be destroyed, even after repeated attempts by its owner, implies that nothing can break the hero's spirit. Compare the image of the shattered lance in Charlemagne's first dream (COMMENTARY, 10; see also COMMENTARY, 16).

—Roland prays to the Virgin (v. 2303) and his sword holds a relic of her clothing (v. 2348).[531]

—Roland carries a white ensign lashed to the tip of his spear (v. 1157); at Roncevaux his heart is placed in a white casket (v. 2966) and, later, his body in a white coffin (v. 3692). Whiteness is associated with martyrdom (COMMENTARY, 34, note 9) but also with chastity, purity of heart, and virginity (Blaise, par. 492).

Conrad, sensing the primary importance which Turoldus attached to the concept of Roland as virgin, gave the hero a helmet called Venerant[532] (venerable, sacred) bearing the inscription:

> Elliu werlt wafen
> Di muzen mich maget lazen.[533]
>
> (All the weapons of the world
> Will leave me unscathed.)

The literal meaning of *maget* (= OHG *magad*) is 'maiden, virgin'.[534]

One may also add that the hero of the *Song of Roland* is referred to by Charles in his lament as a *juvente bele* (v. 2916) and that he is engaged, not married, to Oliver's sister.[535] When Alda learns of his death at Roncevaux, she immediately falls dead at Charles's feet and is buried in a nunnery (v. 3730). Her maidenhood is never in doubt and, because she is linked to Roland, her virginity may be said to reflect his (INTRODUCTION, 19, D).[536] Throughout the Middle Ages Roland, in legend and song, never weds, nor does he dally with women.[537] The opposite is true in the case of Oliver, who early on acquires the reputation of a ladies' man.[538]

G. *Ganelon*

It is difficult for present-day readers to accept that a character can be all bad, and there is a tendency—especially since the Romantic period—to view villains as alienated, misunderstood, or, for one reason or another, not entirely to blame for the crimes they perpetrate. Many critics feel a decided sympathy for Ganelon and suggest that he is goaded into his fury and treason by a tactless Roland, shows courage in his dealings with Marsile, and has a strong case when he pleads justifiable homicide during the trial at Aix.[539] The plain fact is that Turoldus and his contemporaries considered Ganelon to be completely evil. Like the Saracens or Satan himself in the *Song of Roland*, Ganelon has no redeeming trait whatsoever.

Scholars have long puzzled over the question: Why does Ganelon hate Roland?[540] Turoldus makes it thoroughly clear that the villain *sold* the rearguard (v. 845: Del rei paien en ad oüd granz duns; v. 1407: Qu'en Sarraguce sa maisnee alat vendre), and the greed motive is confirmed by Roland (v. 1148: "Pris en ad or e aveir e deners") and by Charlemagne (v. 3756: "Les .XII. pers ad traït por aveir").

Ganelon's claim that he was cheated out of gold and riches by Roland (v. 3758) (INTRODUCTION, 19, C) reveals more about himself than about his stepson, and his claim in v. 3771 that it was the hero who hated him, not vice-versa, should be interpreted in similar fashion. Finally, there is no quarrel between father and stepson in the *Pseudo-Turpin Chronicle*, but the idea of betraying for money is clearly spelled out:

> Ganalono vero viginti equos argento et auro et palleis honeratos fraudulenter obtulerunt, ut pugnatores in manibus illorum traderet ad interficiendum. Qui concessit et pecuniam illam accepit.[541]

Most critics, however, are inclined to believe that the real reason for Ganelon's betrayal is the slight he suffers in the scene where Roland nominates his stepfather for the perilous mission to Saragossa.[542] Others suggest that a feud between Ganelon and Roland has been smouldering for some time before the poem begins.[543] At any rate, the allegation of greed is generally viewed as a secondary motive at best, when it is not dismissed out of hand as totally irrelevant.[544]

Such an interpretation reflects modern values, which regard avarice as a lesser vice and a certain amount of acquisitiveness as justifiable and even normal.[545] In Turoldus's day Pride and Avarice were considered to be the root of all evil, a view based on Scripture.[546] In fact, Lester K. Little has shown that Avarice begins supplanting Pride as the mother of vices precisely in the eleventh century.[547] Covetousness was Judas's sin and the mortal enemy of Caritas, the chief virtue counseled by the New Law.[548] Charity involved much more than mere generosity in almsgiving and the like, and it referred in this context to a magnanimous imitation of the Lord's love for and liberality to mankind.[549] Avaritia, its antonym, alluded to the arrogance of those who rely on their own wealth and think they can do without God.

Once Avarice has been placed in its Romanesque setting, one is in a better position to appreciate what Turoldus repeatedly states about Ganelon's essential motivation for betraying Roland. Greed nurtured his hatred for his stepson and, when the poem opens, had already pushed him to the edge of the precipice, over which he falls in the quarrel scene. Each successive episode reveals a new facet of his growing depravity. The affront merely serves as a catalyst for vicious proclivities in Ganelon antedating the poem but successfully masked until that moment.

The mainspring of Ganelon's actions is Avarice, then, but it is equally important to understand that this moral fault was believed to engender such ancillary vices as Proditio, Fraus, Fallacia, Perjuria, Inquietudo,

Violentiae, and Obdurationes cordis contra misericordiam. The twelfth-century *Hortus Deliciarum* (*Fig. 29*) cites this list, which seems to originate with Gregory the Great (d. 604),[550] and depicts Avaritia in a chariot drawn by a fox and a lion holding in their jaws a scroll that reads: "Avaritia dicit: Lingo fraude dolo quasi vulpes vel vi sectans[551] lucra rodo ut leo crudelis."[552] The reference to the fox's deceitful licking evidently alludes to Avaritia's practice of masking as a virtue, one of the activities in which she engages in the *Psychomachia* (vv. 549–553).[553] In Prudentius's poem Greed also instigates family discord, a soldier slaying his own brother for his jewel-studded helmet and a son stripping off his dead father's belt and armor (vv. 470–479).[554]

One can better understand now Ganelon's deceitful pose (Fraus) in the first French council and his willingness to risk all in a wild scheme involving an annual gift and, presumably, protection from the Saracens upon his return to France (COMMENTARY, 4 and 7). Ganelon lies (Fallacia, Perjuria) to achieve his ends to such an extent that one cannot believe a single word he utters throughout the entire poem.[555] His greatest crime stems from the related vice of treachery (Proditio), which causes the death of the French rearguard.

The violent side of Greed is well illustrated by the lion pulling Avaritia's chariot in the sketch in Herrad of Landsberg. Gérard Cames has shown that the lion incarnates ambition and cruelty but notes that the fox, too, was known for its destructive habits (Song of Songs 2:15).[556] Six other animals surround Greed's chariot in the *Hortus Deliciarum*: a bear, a wolf, an ox, a dog, a pig, and a vulture, each with an identifying scroll ("Violentia est ursus," "Rapacitas est lupus," "Fames acquirendi est bos," "Tenacitas latrans ut canis," "Sorditas est sus," "Philargyria, id est incontinens appetitus acquirendi, est vultur") and further comments.[557] The wolf recalls once again Ganelon's fraudulent behavior in the French council, for it is an obvious allusion to Matthew 7:15 (Beware of false prophets who come to you disguised as sheep but underneath are ravenous wolves).[558]

The convergence of imagery in Turoldus and Herrad of Landsberg is most striking in the bear. When the traitor is arrested, he is chained *altresi cum un urs* (v. 1827) and, in one of Charlemagne's dreams, he will be portrayed in identical fashion (*brohun*, v. 2557).[559] The bear in Herrad has a scroll proclaiming "Violentia est ursus" and "Terret clamore minisque avaritia."[560] It seems likely, therefore, that for Turoldus the violent side of Ganelon's nature, symbolized by the bear, was one of the nefarious effects of his avarice.[561]

To sum up, Ganelon is essentially a Judas figure,[562] and it is Avarice that leads him to betray Roland and, by implication, Charlemagne and God. Unable to elude the snares of the devil, a weakness recognized by the Emperor (v. 746), he resorts to lying in a vain attempt to cover up his misdeeds. His handsomeness is part of the fraudulence traditionally associated with Covetousness (and Satan!), and his alleged courage before Marsile needs to be interpreted in this light (COMMENTARY, 7). It is Avarice, too, that makes Ganelon jealous of Roland's sway over his companions and over Charles. It is possible of course to maintain that Ganelon is primarily motivated by Envy or Malice.[563] However, the concordance of the evidence points to the specific hierarchy of vices detailed here.

H. Oliver

In discussions of the various characters in the *Song of Roland*, Oliver usually receives the most favorable comment. Most scholars agree that Roland is the central hero, yet they find one aspect or another of his behavior repellent. They either conclude that Turoldus himself disapproved of Roland or assert that he represents a value system that is completely discredited today. Oliver, however, is generally well liked. He is, according to a typical assessment, "the most lovable of all the characters."[564]

Jenkins underscores Oliver's role as Roland's companion-in-arms.[565] Equal in courage, he is more prudent or perhaps more anxious than his friend, to whom he is bound by great affection. There is goodnaturedness and humor in their relationship, but above all there is pathos, for, Jenkins points out, in the end they must part. However, Faral's opinion of Oliver is more representative of the view that has prevailed since Bédier.[566] For him, "Olivier est le sage Olivier." Brave like Roland, he is better adjusted and shows more equilibrium. Faral does recognize that he is a secondary character and exists primarily to set off his companion's qualities. The archetypal comrade-in-arms, Oliver simply has a different concept of duty from that exemplified by the hero.

Oliver is without a doubt the most difficult character to interpret in Turoldus's poem. One misconception has confused the issue. *Sage*, in modern French, can mean 'modéré, retenu, maître de ses passions, réglé dans sa conduite', but this sense was not attested to at this time, or indeed until the seventeenth century.[567] In Old French, *saige* or *saive* refers primarily to unusual understanding of people or situations, judiciousness, or skill. This is not at all the same as the caution as to danger or risk, or the careful weighing of all possible consequences before taking action, which are inherent meanings in the present-day concept.

Modern critics have been unduly influenced by the classical notion that *fortitudo* and *sapientia* are the essential virtues of the warrior, and that one quality balances the other in the ideal hero (INTRODUCTION, 3). Valuable as this ideal may have been in antiquity, or may even be for us today, it would be a mistake to assume that Turoldus held it in similar esteem.

Oliver is really very much the same as Roland, and Turoldus makes it clear that both individuals have all the chivalric virtues. Proper balance in no way distinguishes one from the other, Oliver's claim notwithstanding. The crucial battlefield debate is not designed to contrapose Oliver's wisdom with Roland's folly; rather it serves to highlight the nature of the hero's agonizing choice (COMMENTARY, 14). Oliver is a hero, possessing every human quality; Roland is a super-hero having Sapiential vision as an added attribute, and therein lies a world of difference. In other words, if one considers each character without proper regard for the martyr-ideal Roland incarnates, one misses the author's point completely. The modern reader is free of course to conclude that Oliver's advice should have been followed, but it would be a serious error to believe that Turoldus felt that way. Such a view is out of keeping with clerical values and with what is manifestly the *Song of Roland*'s central meaning.

I. Prophetic Figures: Turpin, Ogier, Alda

The role of Archbishop Turpin as a vigorous, warlike prelate poses no particular problem, for examples of such militancy on the part of contemporary clergymen come readily to mind.[568] Everyone recognizes, too, that Turpin's presence on the battlefield helps to give the struggle a religious character.[569] This is apparent in the Archbishop's intervention in the debate between Roland and Oliver, and in his statements and activities relative to death and its meaning in the poem.

One aspect of Turpin's role, however, deserves further clarification, for the Archbishop is linked in an unsuspected way to Ogier and Alda. In vv. 2255–2256 Roland praises the slain prelate by affirming that

"*Des les apostles ne fut hom tel prophete / Pur lei tenir e pur humes atraire.*" In his commentary on this passage, Bédier writes:

> Cet éloge, décerné à Turpin, surprend un peu. Mais il faut remarquer que la qualification de "prophète" dans les Ecritures, ne s'applique pas exclusivement à des personnages qui ont des vues sur l'avenir. Alain de Lille, en ses *Distinctiones* (*Patrologie* de Migne, t. CCX, col. 912), le marque en ces terms: "Propheta *dicitur sapiens a Deo instructus, unde Dominus ad Abimelech de Abraham dixit:* Nunc igitur redde vero suo uxorem, quia propheta est." Appliqué à Turpin, *prophete* signifie donc simplement "homme de Dieu." Le vers semble d'ailleurs traduire cette phrase du *Deutéronome* (34:10): *Et non surrexit ultra propheta in Israel sicut Moyses.*[570]

The reference by Alain de Lille is to the story of Abimelech, King of Gerar, who took Sarah to wife, having misinterpreted Abraham's expression "She is my sister." God appeared to the king in a dream and ordered him to return Abraham's wife, explaining: "He is a prophet and can intercede on your behalf for your life" (Genesis 20:7). Modern biblical scholars gloss the word prophet in this passage as "one of privileged standing before God and therefore inviolable, Ps 105:15, and a powerful intercessor, cf. Dt 34:10; Nb 11:2; 21:7."[571]

Bédier's interpretation, while generally adequate—the Turpin-Moses parallel has possibilities—does not sufficiently explain the notion that Turpin is a prophet *Pur lei tenir*. Turoldus was probably thinking of the Old Testament prophets who, as the etymon implies, spoke *for* God when they sternly admonished kings not to fail in their duty (COMMENTARY, 23).[572] Ogier plays this role when he threatens to call down the wrath of God if the Emperor fails to act decisively in the battle against Baligant (vv. 3538–3539). In similar fashion Alda reminds Charles of Roland and of his obligation to see to it that justice is done (Laisse 268).[573]

J. Bramimonde

The Saracen queen is a prophetess of a different sort, for her initial intuition that Baligant's arrival will change nothing insofar as pagan fortunes are concerned (vv. 2602–2607) later becomes a bitter prediction of things to come (v. 2721). Witness to Ganelon's treachery at Saragossa, to Marsile's humiliating return from Roncevaux, and to the rout of Baligant's forces, Bramimonde is the only Saracen dignitary who survives the stunning double defeat. Her repeated references to Charlemagne (vv. 640, 2605–2608, 2721, 2736–2740) are a clear indication that her role is inextricably linked to that of the Emperor. In fact, the notion of winning the hearts of the Saracens in the *Song of Roland* usually involves Charlemagne, and it is he whose magnanimous gesture, after the fall of Saragossa, makes the edifying conclusion of the poem possible. But it is Bramimonde's repudiation of her pagan gods and her adoption of Christianity *par amur* that offer the most significant manifestation of the Theme of Conversion in Turoldus's epic. The conquest of foreign lands and Bramimonde's submission at Saragossa play an obvious part in the narrative of defeat turned into victory, but such images also figure in the poem's religious dimension.[574]

K. The Franks

Paien unt tort e chrestïens unt dreit, asserts Turoldus in a formula celebrated for its glaring simplicity (v. 1015). Turoldus's world view has decidedly black and white characteristics; bad on one side, good on the other. In general the men who make up Charlemagne's army display traditional chivalric virtues, notably bravery and loyalty, and their Christian convictions are unshakable. Their contentiousness, propensity for warfare, and thirst for revenge are doubtless accurate reflections of eleventh-century aristocratic behavior, but they should also be viewed in light of the poem's agonistic theme—the struggle of the virtues and vices for man's soul.

Turoldus nonetheless does ascribe one major weakness to the faceless Franks and even, on occasion, to individuals designated by name or nationality. The Franks vacillate, tend to agree with whoever has spoken last and, above all, cannot be relied upon to give sound advice.[575] This disturbing characteristic is evident in the first French council, when Roland's plea to reject Marsile's proposals, which the audience knows are deceitful, are ignored; whereas Naimes's fateful speech, in effect seconding Ganelon's base counsel, wins immediate general approval (vv. 217, 243). In his initial speech Roland does not hesitate to pillory the advice the Emperor is likely to receive from the Franks, reminding Charles of an earlier parallel occasion involving messengers bearing olive branches, similar proposals, and the ill-fated

Basan and Basile (vv. 205–206: "A voz Franceis un cunseill en presistes, / Loërent vos alques de legerie").

The Franks are quick to agree with Roland's momentous nomination of Ganelon to carry the Emperor's counterproposal to Saragossa (vv. 278–279) and doubtless misinterpret the significance of the gauntlet dropped by Ganelon (vv. 334–335). Their untrustworthiness in council is nowhere more apparent than in the trial of Ganelon, where, intimidated by Pinabel, they ask Charles to drop the case against the traitor. Characteristically the Franks agree to another solution—the judicial combat (v. 3837). After Pinabel's menacing presence has been removed, they finally come up with an equitable verdict.

Duke Naimes, Charlemagne's private counselor, is one of the most complicated of the minor French characters in the poem. In the early scenes he recommends mercy when perseverance is called for (COMMENTARY, 4), and his suggestion that Charles offer half his army to his nephew is brushed aside by Roland (COMMENTARY, 11). Privileged to share in the knowledge imparted to Charles by a celestial messenger —to be sure, he may only have an imperfect grasp of the meaning of the dream—he plays the mute (COMMENTARY, 11), until it is too late (COMMENTARY, 19). In the Emperor's hour of greatest need, he stands by while Thierry champions Charlemagne's cause (COMMENTARY, 45). Clearly Thierry surpasses Naimes in *auxilium*, Ogier outdoes him in *consilium* (INTRODUCTION, 19, I).

In the trial of Ganelon fear obviously inhibits the Franks' capacity to offer proper counsel, and, in retrospect, one wonders whether, in the first council, the traitor's commanding and perhaps threatening presence may not have been a factor motivating their prompt concurrence in Naimes's proposal. Militating against this view is the fact that the Franks just as quickly endorse Roland's nomination of his stepfather for the mission to Saragossa. It seems very likely, too, that war-weariness rather than anxiety or lack of courage prompts them to support any proposal that will bring their seven-year involvement in the Spanish campaign to an honorable end in the most expeditious way.

If fear cannot be said to be at the root of the Franks' *legerie*, their constant weeping offers another possible explanation. Emotionalism corresponds to irresolution and often leads to hasty and injudicious decisions. But crying is a conventional expression of concern or grief in medieval epics, and Turoldus's heroes—Charlemagne in particular, who is associated with Sapientia—not infrequently shed tears.[576]

In the final analysis the unreliability of the Franks in council, like the circularity of Oliver's argumentation in his debate with Roland, appears to be a device used by the poet to bring out the vanity of worldly wisdom and the transcendence of Sapientia. Viewed from this perspective, the Franks in the *Song of Roland* are the inverted image of Charlemagne. On occasion Christ upbraided his disciples for being men of little faith and for requiring signs and wonders (e.g., Matthew 8:26, 14:31). Similarly, the faith of Charlemagne's men needs constant bolstering with miraculous occurrences, such as Roland's death and Thierry's victory over Pinabel. However, it must be said to their credit that, having seen a sign from Heaven, the Franks take prompt and appropriate action. Also, whatever human failings they may have pale into insignificance when the Franks meet their end in edifying fashion as martyrs.

L. The Saracens

What few contacts French merchants, soldiers, and travelers had with the Muslim world in the eleventh century contributed little if anything to Turoldus's knowledge of the Saracens. The enemies ranged before the Christians are a strange amalgam of folk beliefs, feudal institutions and practices, scraps of information ultimately derived from classical sources, and stereotypes stemming from the Bible.[577] The conventional portrait of the Saracen, which emerges from a reading of the *Song of Roland* as well as other chansons de geste, has been studied in detail by a number of scholars.[578]

What is perhaps most singular is the lumping together of disparate groups from Islam and from other parts of the world, notably from Eastern Europe.[579] The cartographers of Turoldus's day recognized three major geographical areas—Africa, Asia, and Europe—but clerks tended to classify nations according to whether they lived under the Old Law (Jews), the New Law (Christians), or the False Law (Saracens, see v. 3638): *De ces trois manieres de genz est establiz li mondes*, writes the author of the *Perlesvaus*.[580]

The greatest misconception concerns religion.[581] The Saracens are characterized by Turoldus as idolaters and worshippers of the trinity of gods Apollo, Mohammed, and Tervagant. Their land, like Egypt to the Fathers of the Church, is held to be a place of darkness inhabited by hardhearted men given to sorcery and other vile practices.[582] Two centuries earlier Einhard had characterized Charlemagne's Saxon enemies in the same way:

> Saxones, sicut omnes fere Germaniam incolentes nationes, et natura feroces et cultui daemonum dediti nostraeque religioni contrarii, neque divina neque humana jura vel polluere vel transgredi inhonestum arbitrabantur.[583]

Although Saracens in the *Song of Roland* are at times outwardly indistinguishable in their appearance and behavior from the Christians—certain descriptive adjectives are used interchangeably for either group—the very thought of Saracens triggered a negative reaction in contemporary audiences. The latter considered all pagans to have perverted natures and expected them to be forever engaged in evil activities. The Saracens were universally regarded as being possessed by the devil, a belief that accounts for their impurity, swarthiness, and ugliness in medieval literature.[584] Their pride, that is, their false reliance on their own strength, is underscored in v. 1941 (Entr'els en unt e orgoil e cunfort; cf. also v. 2279), and it is only fitting that such treacherous individuals should consort with the traitor Ganelon.[585] There is some evidence of admiration for the Saracens in later chronicles,[586] but none is to be found in the *Song of Roland*. Epithets seemingly implying a favorable opinion of the Saracens belong to the category of terms denoting lying exteriors.

The pagan leaders Baligant and Marsile deserve special note. As to be expected in such a biased account, the Saracens in question are incarnations of every imaginable vice. Baligant appears far more haughty, and his role, which is to oppose Charlemagne in an apocalyptic confrontation, is clearly affected by the image of Antichrist. His behavior, moreover, involves contemptible aping of the Emperor and Roland. Marsile, on the other hand, suffers one indignity after another, and the chronicling of his despair, growing deeper with each succeeding episode[587]—the first syllable of his name (*Mar* < Lat. *mala hora*) is an expression of woe in Old French—constitutes a scathing denunciation of pagan life and worship.

The word *tirant* does not appear in the *Song of Roland*, yet Saracens, especially their leaders, were frequently associated with cruel tyrants throughout the Middle Ages. It is safe to assume that such a notion influenced Turoldus's conception of Baligant and Marsile.[588] The medieval iconographic formula for the tyrant—a crowned and enthroned figure often shown in profile rather than frontally—comes particularly to mind when the Saracen chieftains are described by Turoldus as seated[589] (*Fig. 30*). In the Middle Ages tyrant conjured up less the notion of absolutism than that of a monstrous and relentless persecutor of Christians.[590] Religious overtones are clear, for instance, when the individuals who crucified Jesus are referred to as *tiranz* in *Les Chétifs*.[591] It seems reasonable to conclude, therefore, that the poet's idea of Baligant and Marsile is not entirely foreign to that of Herod, murderer of the Holy Innocents (cf. v. 1480: "As Innocenz vos en serez seant"), and the succession of diabolic magistrates and rulers who cause the martyrs to suffer unspeakable tortures in the saints' lives.[592] In the end, all are frustrated by the hero's victorious death.

One of Turoldus's most disconcerting habits, insofar as the modern reader is concerned, is to portray Saracens thinking like Christians. The poet goes far beyond showing Muslims wearing Western armor or living under the feudal system, for he also implies they are thoroughly familiar with the Bible. Thus, for example, Marsile has his ambassadors imitate Christ's Entry into Jerusalem; the same messengers presumably grasp the significance of the Last Judgment scene that greets them on their arrival in Charles's camp; and Ganelon, on the ride to Saragossa, expects Blancandrin to understand the allusion to Roland as a diabolic seducer (COMMENTARY, 2, 3, and 6). Such depictions should not be scorned for their lack of realism but viewed in terms of their own esthetic: A biblical reference is a natural and effective way of imparting an aura of blasphemy to foul deeds.

20. Rhythm

Although accent, meter, assonance, and other standard elements of versification in the *Song of Roland* have been studied in considerable detail, much remains to be said about the way in which the poem flows. A frequently cited chapter in Erich Auerbach's *Mimesis* makes much of the fact that Turoldus's epic is paratactic,[593] but it is perhaps just as important to stress that, more often than not, the poem moves forward in breath and sense groups of two and three verses. In the three-verse patterns one notes two variations:

(pause)

and:

(pause)

The possibilities afforded by modern punctuation (comma, colon, semicolon, dash) are virtually limitless, and editors suggest variant configurations of verses within the laisse by means of these conventional and, at times, arbitrary signs. Nevertheless there is meaning to be found in these conscious or even chance arrangements. The length of individual laisses also lends itself to various interpretations, as does the alternation of tenses within a single verse or group of verses. Observations along these lines are scattered throughout many scholarly works, but no systematic study has yet been published.

21. Oral Interpretation: The Gestural Script

When analyzing medieval French epics it is essential to bear in mind that the poem involves not only an author and his work but also an interpreter and his audience.

Scholars have long recognized that the early chansons de geste were not intended for silent reading but for oral delivery. Maurice Delbouille has suggested that many, perhaps most, jongleurs chanted their epics with a manuscript before them, possibly on a lectern, serving as a kind of promptbook.[594] The oral version sung by the jongleur may have been closely related to the written texts that have survived, but it represents a distinct form of the poem. Jongleurs, like storytellers and folksingers in other times and other places, probably learned the plot or story line, and no doubt certain key phrases from others but improvised the rest while singing. This appears to be what is meant when the narrator in certain chansons de geste says he knows very well the epic he is about to tell. It is true, however, that singers of tales have been known to memorize long poems. The poem entitled "Deux Bordeors ribauz" concerns two jongleurs who each claim to know by heart a large number of epics, fabliaux, and songs.[595]

Was the *Song of Roland* chanted on a single note? Was it intoned on a few musical phrases endlessly repeated in a singsong manner? Or was there, as Jacques Chailley has argued, a straight-line development from the melodic technique used in singing saints' lives to the chansons de geste?[596] There is unfortunately no conclusive evidence supporting any one of these views.

On the other hand, it is certain that at times, at any rate, the jongleur's recitation was accompanied by music, which he played on a three-stringed violinlike instrument known as a *vielle*.[597] In fact, the viol is the one unmistakable attribute of the jongleurs in medieval illustrations, although one can never be certain, of course, that the individual playing the instrument is singing an epic.[598]

Singing a poem while playing a viol required skill. A passage in the *Roman de la Violette* makes it clear that the hero, Gerard, who has disguised himself as a jongleur, has difficulty doing what he has never learned to do, that is, *chanter et vieler ensamble*.[599] Jongleurs were individualistic and guarded their repertory jealously, but they also traveled from town to town and from castle to castle in groups. At times one jongleur may have recited while another accompanied on the viol. Perhaps individual jongleurs varied their presentation by dramatizing stretches of narrative with different intonations and gestures, accompanying the remaining passages by music only. In the *Song of Roland* certain dialogues lend themselves to dramatic rendition, while others—laments, for example—call for music.

The quasi-universality of the techniques of oral interpretation throughout history constitutes a strong argument in favor of viewing the performance of the chansons de geste as one involving expressive and mimetic voice modulation and body movement. What follows is a series of conjectures concerning the oral interpretation of the *Song of Roland*. However, it should be borne in mind that the poem may never have been recited or chanted in the form preserved in the Oxford manuscript (INTRODUCTION, 2).

The prevalence of direct discourse in Turoldus's epic afforded excellent opportunities for impersonation as, for example, when the poet says that a character cried out or said something while laughing or weeping. Jeanne Wathelet-Willem has detailed the formulaic locutions signifying the acts of buckling on a sword, drawing it from its sheath, brandishing it, and striking someone—all seemingly static expressions when considered in that fashion—yet the formulas leap to life if one imagines the jongleur acting out these motions.[600] In a crucial scene Ganelon defiantly throws off his furs; in another he braces himself against a tree. Roland's placing of the oliphant against his lips is carefully described, and it is difficult to forget the portrait of the hero riding off to battle, holding his sword in one hand, and turning the white pennant lashed to the tip of his spear against the sky in the other. Turoldus's frequent use of the locution *As/Ais vos/vus* and *As les vus* (vv. 263, 413, 889, 1187, 1889, 1989, 2009, 3403) imparts a sense of immediacy to the narration, but it also implies pointing by the jongleur to draw the audience's attention to the approach of an imaginary walking or riding figure.[601]

With or without his viol, the jongleur surely mimicked certain scenes in Turoldus's poem, grimacing and raising his voice in imitation of Ganelon's anger at Roland's sarcastic rejoinder, facing or even stepping from side to side to impersonate speakers in a dialogue,[602] intoning solemnly and raising his hand in benediction as Charlemagne says farewell to his messenger leaving for Saragossa, muttering between clenched teeth to his sword where the text states that Ganelon prepares to defend himself against Marsile's ire.

When Ganelon draws his sword the width of two fingers from its scabbard (v. 444: Cuntre dous deie l'ad del furrer getee), the reader's first impulse is to consider this gesture unique. However, Wathelet-Willem has shown that an identical action occurs in the *Chanson de Guillaume*, when the hero shows his anger against his sister, and in the *Couronnement de Louis*, when William threatens Arneïs before deciding to beat the traitor to death with a blow from his fist.[603] Examination of the early French epics reveals, in fact, that while the phrasing may not always be formulaic, the gestures described or alluded to are identical in numerous circumstances. Some fifty-odd gestures in the *Song of Roland* recur in at least one and at times several of the same nine epics studied by Rychner.[604] Gestures, which, like spoken utterances and the written word, are a form of communication between humans, are conventional and may be compared with formulas.[605] The jongleur doubtless used the same stylized gestures in the same places during his presentation, with the result that one may speak of a gestural script. The latter can be reconstructed to a surprising degree.

Rhetorical tradition dating back to the Greeks and Romans stipulates that the gestures that an orator uses are to be executed a certain way.[606] Actors and mimes adhered to similar conventions. But the best sources of knowledge about the jongleurs' gestures are the epics themselves.

There are numerous deictic elements—demonstratives calling for gesture—in Turoldus's poem.[607] Oaths are perhaps the most obvious instance of this practice (vv. 47–48: "Pa *ceste* meie destre / E par la barbe ki al piz me ventelet"; v. 249: "Par *ceste* barbe e par *cest* men gernun"; v. 261: "Par *ceste* barbe que veez blancher"; v. 1719: "Par *ceste* meie barbe"; v. 3954: "Par *ceste* barbe dunt li peil sunt canuz"). As Roland lies dying, a Saracen warrior makes bold to steal Durendal. He crawls toward the hero, using an expression that implies a gesture on the part of the jongleur (v. 2282: "*Iceste* espee porterai en Arabe"). Pledging usually involved holding an article of clothing, representing the whole person (a glove or the edge of a cloak), or an object symbolizing the fief (a sheaf of wheat, a clod of dirt),[608] and oaths at times resemble this custom. However, an oath taken on relics was an entirely different matter. In a scene from the Bayeux Tapestry (*Fig. 31*), Harold swears by placing his left hand upon an altar and, more characteristically, by touching a chest containing relics with the outstretched index and middle finger of his right hand.[609] In the illustration in the *Rolandslied* of Ganelon's perfidious vow made at Saragossa to destroy Roland and the French rearguard (*Fig. 32*), the artist portrayed Ganelon and Marsile each raising an index finger toward a pagan idol.[610]

Philippe Ménard has shown that in some forty French epics the gestures indicated, on the one hand, by the locutions *tenir le chief enbronc* or *enclin*, and *croler le chief* 'to lower one's head', and, on the other, by the expression *la main a la maissele* 'hand on the cheek', always symbolize sorrow and distress.[611] To be sure, one detects various nuances of meaning, since the circumstances are often quite distinct. Yvonne Labande-Mailfert had earlier studied the iconography of sorrow and death in Romanesque and Gothic art and found the same gesture with several variations, such as the face held in both hands or both hands held up, palms outward[612] (*Fig. 33*).

While not specifically alluded to in the *Song of Roland*, a number of gestures the jongleur executed may be inferred from medieval art. Mary Laura Heuser's doctoral dissertation[613] and, above all, Karl von Amira's monumental study of early-fourteenth-century illuminations of the *Sachsenspiegel*, a compilation relating to common law and other customs in Germany, [614] offer valuable data in this regard. Here one finds, for example, stylized gestures indicating accusation, acquiescence, command, compassion, conversation, deference, incapacity, joy, pleading, refusal, regard, threat, and so on. These attitudes and postures were probably not all employed by the jongleur in systematic fashion. However, considering the fact that certain positions of the hands and other parts of the body specifically mentioned in Turoldus's poem, as well as in other medieval French epics, were widely attested in contemporary art,[615] there is an excellent chance that many of the other attitudes found in iconographic sources were also part of the jongleur's gestural repertory.

II

Commentary

1. A Historiated Initial

Laisse 1 (verses 1–9)

Many chansons de geste, like Old French saints' lives,[1] begin with a preamble or prologue that, characteristically, contains an injunction to silence, an invocation to God, the subject to be narrated, and a reference to the source.[2] The oldest French epics generally forgo such preliminary matter,[3] although Venice IV opens conventionally enough:

Chi voil oïr vere significance?
A San Donis ert une geste, in France;
Cil ne sa ben qui par l'escrit inçante,
N'en deit aler a pri ç'ubler que çante,
Mais çivalçer mul e destreire d'Erabie.
Desor comença li traïment de Gayne
E de Rollan, li nef de Çarle el Mayne.
Çarle li reis, nostre inperer de France,
Set ans tut plens a estez in Spagne . . .[4]

It is often said that the *Song of Roland* begins *in medias res* or *ex abrupto*.[5] Actually the initial impression is of a long story about to end. A final challenge remains to Charlemagne's total victory in Spain. His archenemy Marsile continues to hold Saragossa, the pagan leader's last remaining fortress. However, powerful and seemingly relentless forces are at work: Charles cannot help but win, Marsile cannot possibly avoid disaster. The concluding aspect of the opening laisse is reinforced by the poet's choice, in his first indication of time, of the biblical number seven (v. 2: Set anz tuz pleins ad estet en Espaigne),[6] which, since Genesis 2:2, suggests a great task being brought to a satisfying close.[7] This poem, which begins, as it were, with an ending, will also end with a beginning (Commentary, 49).

Charles's ultimate triumph seems to be at hand, then, but disaster lurks. The *mals* in v. 9 refers to Marsile's impending doom, but another death is also foreshadowed, that of Roland. It will be no mere coincidence when Turoldus uses the same locution *Nes poet guarder que* in v. 95 to mark the point in the narrative when the tragic outcome is set in motion. Death and the Theme of Victory, with its majestic ambiguities, permeate the poem from beginning to end.

Jenkins points out that the opening laisse is a "preamble," Le Gentil refers to an "exorde," Rychner to a "laisse d'exposition."[8] If we agree with these scholars, the first nine verses of the *Song of Roland* are designed to impart certain particulars that situate the action and the characters in a given locale. While such a view is correct in a general way, the terms imply that we are dealing here with something external to the story proper, whereas the opposite is true.

The nature of the first laisse may more readily be grasped by comparing it with historiated initials, which highlight the essential or most dramatic elements of a following story in certain medieval manuscripts. A striking parallel between this artistic procedure and that used in the opening verses of Turoldus's poem is found in a thirteenth-century manuscript of the *Pseudo-Turpin Chronicle*, preserved in the Bibliothèque de l'Arsenal[9] (*Fig. 35*). Three scenes, corresponding to the principal divisions of the story, illustrate this tale in the earliest manuscript tradition: (1) Saint James appears to Charlemagne; (2) Charlemagne and his army leave for Spain; (3) Charlemagne and his veterans return to Aix.[10] However, the Arsenal copy illuminator broke with this tradition and elected instead to show Charles before the walls of a Spanish fortified city, a scene that represents no particular event but symbolizes rather, in Lejeune and Stiennon's words, "la conquête de villes sarrasines par l'empereur et ses chevaliers."[11] As in most early medieval depictions of sieges, the city is reduced to a single tower and gate, the defenders to one or two figures emerging from the battlements, and the attacking army to a few horsemen.

In the *Song of Roland*, as in the historiated initial, the artist chose to depict not the beginning of the story[12] but the essence of the narrative. The siege of Saragossa will actually take place only toward the end of the poem—in Laisse 265—and the various investments of the *Pseudo-Turpin Chronicle* occur after the Vision of Saint James and the departure of Charles's army. In both instances what the initial image emphasizes is the fateful clash of two worlds. On the level of plot the conflict epitomized in the opening laisse of the French poem is between the

Emperor and Marsile, but it soon becomes apparent that, on a metaphorical plane, the eternal struggle for man's soul is also symbolized. Synchronic overview is perhaps a more apt designation of the narrative technique involved here than flashforward, for this suggests that the poet—in a manner suggesting God's perception of the full scope of world history—is able to transcend the dimension of time.[13]

Everything underscores the magnitude of the confrontation between Charles and his Saracen rival: the Emperor's greatness (nostre emperere magnes),[14] the lengthy duration of the campaign (Set anz tuz pleins), and the vast expanse and diversity of the already conquered territory (Tresqu'en la mer, castel, mur, citet). But this is no ordinary struggle, and the reader can begin to perceive its profound significance when it is noted that Christian warriors, aided by their Supreme Being, are about to give battle to pagans, whose appeals to their false gods will be in vain. In this concise thematic overture the poet presents an elemental conflict between Good and Evil, symbolized by the opposition between Charles and Marsile, Christian and Saracen, true God and pagan divinities, heaven and earth,[15] land and sea, mountain stronghold and besieging army.

Why does the author situate Saragossa on a mountaintop when the city in reality lies on a plain? Was it simply an error on his part?[16] There will be other passages suggesting rather vague notions of Spanish topography on the part of the French poet. Jenkins notes rather lamely that Saragossa "is situated in a hilly country. Monte Terrero, to the south, commands the city (height 235 meters)."[17] Aurelio Roncaglia suggests that *muntaigne* is a hispanicism meaning 'woods'.[18] Unfortunately this ingenious interpretation is undermined by Turoldus's use of the same term in its normal acceptation in vv. 1084 and 2040. On the other hand, Mandach argues that Turoldus "avait le droit, comme poète, de préférer à la réalité l'image bien connue de la place forte imprenable par sa position géographique—surtout s'il avait besoin d'une rime en *-aigne*. Quel autre mot terminé par *aigne* associé à Saragosse pourrait-on proposer (le tout dans un hémistiche de six syllabes)?"[19] Such an explanation harmonizes with the view presented here that Laisse 1, taken as a whole, can be interpreted as an abstraction. Moreover, the vertical arrangement of the opening scene with Charlemagne below and Marsile in his lofty citadel conforms to a pattern of rising imagery. The Emperor must storm a mountain stronghold, a task foreshadowing Roland's dying ascent.

However, Turoldus, who characterizes Saracen Spain in v. 3 as *la tere altaigne*, doubtless situated Saragossa on an elevation not only to underscore its apparent impregnability but also to suggest a connection with Babylon, whose arrogant king thinks to himself:

> I will climb up to the heavens; and higher than the stars of God I will set my throne. I will sit on the Mount of Assembly in the recesses of the north. I will climb to the top of the thunderlands, I will rival the Most High.[20]

Thus Saragossa, like the Tower of Babel in Genesis 11:4 and the walls of Tyre in Ezechiel 26:4,[21] is a symbol of overweening pride (INTRODUCTION, 15, D). But Saragossa is doomed to fall before the forces of Righteousness, for as Yahweh says: "Were Babylon to scale the heavens, or reinforce her towering citadel, destroyers would still fall on her at my command."[22] This promise, Charlemagne knows full well—as does the audience—will be kept.

2. *The Saracen Council*

Laisses 2–7 (verses 10–95)

After an opening scene showing Charles and Marsile frozen in a stylized confrontation, the action proper begins as the Saracen king proceeds to a garden and lies down on a marble slab. His lieutenants cluster about him, mutely apprehensive. The lack of movement of the 20,000 massed troops and their ominous silence (v. 22: N'i ad paien ki un sul mot respundet) in this vast outdoor scene underscore the evident fright of the pagans as they ponder desperate measures. Their despondency is further emphasized by the shadows (l'umbre)[1] and by the cold blue marble (marbre bloi), a reflection of the livid faces of the Saracens.[2]

Marsile's council is one of several such gatherings, the conventional aspect of which has often been commented upon.[3] However, conventional situations and formulas do not hamper Turoldus's creative power. Not infrequently, circumstances or phrasing, which at first appear to be identical, in reality offer ironic or pathetic contrasts. Bédier noted the opposition between the despair of the Saracens here and the joy in the French camp after their stunning series of heady triumphs.[4] However, the poet checks the optimism expressed in the latter passage with a solemn warning, which parallels a phrase he has just used in the opening laisse with reference to Marsile:

9 Nes poet guarder que mals ne l'i ateignet.
95 Nes poet guarder que alques ne l'engignent.

Horrent has observed, too, that there is evidently an intended contrast between Marsile's prone posture (v. 12: Sur un perrun de marbre bloi se culched) and Charles's majestic appearance (v. 115: Un faldestoed i unt, fait tut d'or mer).[5] However, Faral's comment that the Saracen king is "étendu, à la molle manière des Orientaux" cannot be accepted without serious reservation.[6]

Turoldus does not associate lethargy with the pagans. Such stereotyping of the Oriental character dates from a later period.[7] In fact, in the *Song of Roland*, Saracens frequently resemble their French counterparts in speech and manner, and only what we know about their true nature enables us to judge their words and actions correctly.[8] Local color relative to the Orient—if indeed we may call it that—is rare.[9] It should be noted, too, that Western artists regularly transposed the Eastern reclining position at table in Byzantine art into a sitting attitude—for example in Last Supper scenes and depictions of the Wedding at Cana—even when retaining the sigma table, which was designed for recumbent dining[10] (*see Fig. 4*).

The figure of Marsile, lying on a marble slab, has undeniably sepulchral overtones. Arthurian literature, which is replete with thanatophilic associations, makes frequent use of flat tombstones in cemetery scenes. In the Raising of the Tomb episode in Chrétien de Troyes's *Charrette*, Lancelot dauntlessly lifts the heavy stone lid of his future grave. The incident was widely imitated by later writers.[11] Gawain is sitting *Sor un tonbel de mabre bis* in *L'Atre périlleux* (The Perilous Cemetery) when a devil appears.[12] The hero beheads the fiend and frees a damsel who has been imprisoned in a tomb. A similar episode is recounted in *Amadas et Ydoine*.[13] In short, Marsile's *marbre bloi* is like the cold, hard slab on which Fénice lies in her *sepolture* (sarcophagus) in Chrétien's *Cligés*.[14]

To this day, in popular belief, to peer into a grave or to sit on a tombstone is to tempt fate, and this taboo is evidently behind these literary motifs.[15] When Ovid sets the scene for the ill-fated lovers' tryst at Ninus's tomb in the shade of a mulberry tree (Conveniant ad busta Nini lateantque sub umbra/ Arboris),[16] the site casts an ominous pall over the doomed encounter.[17] The Roman poet doubtless had a mausoleum-type tomb in mind, but in the Middle Ages this was interpreted as a marble slab. Thus one reads in the twelfth-century French version of Ovid's poem:

> Ja ert assise sus le marbre
> A la fontaine dessous l'arbre,
> Ou il devoient assambler.[18]

A flat gravestone bearing the inscription HIC SITUS EST NINUS REX appears in an illuminated manuscript of Ovid's *De remediis amoris*, dated 1289.[19]

Rather than implying any notion of Oriental indolence, then, lying on a marble couch suggests that Marsile has one foot in the grave. A similar expression of utter helplessness occurs in Psalms 88:3–5:

> my life is on the brink of Sheol;
> I am numbered among those who go down to the Pit,
> a man bereft of strength:
> a man alone, down among the dead,
> among the slaughtered in their graves.[20]

The biblical image elicits pathos, whereas the depiction of Marsile evokes no pity or compassion whatsoever. On the contrary, the grave represents death in all its horror and inexorability,[21] and one thinks of Saint Eleutherius's scornful cry before the magistrate: "Tyrant, open sepulchre, if you need flesh and blood, seek out your father Satan."[22] Christ termed the hypocritical Pharisees "unmarked tombs that men walk on without knowing it" and whited sepulchres "that look handsome on the outside, but inside are full of dead men's bones and every kind of corruption."[23] A false exterior, to Turoldus's way of thinking, characterizes the treacherous Saracens.[24]

On the other hand, medieval exegetes would doubtless have associated Marsile's marble slab with hardness of heart, that is, stubbornness in sin, like that of the Pharaoh (Exodus 7:13; 13:15) or the sons of Israel at Massah and Meribah (Exodus 17:1–7; Psalms 95:8).[25] This was the significance generally ascribed to the sepulchre that figures in the Raising of Lazarus, an interpretation found, for example, in Yves of Chartres (1035–1116).[26] In the *Queste del saint graal* a marble gravestone is similarly said to signify la *durté dou monde*, and reference is made elsewhere in this romance to a tomb representing *la grant durté des Gyeus.*[27] In Conrad Charles's Saxon enemies are referred to as being hard as stone (v. 7539: di stainherten Sachsen). Such, then, may well have been the deeper significance of Marsile's marble slab for the medieval audience.

In the *Song of Roland* men in council arrive at decisions while under stress but also, and more significantly, while under the influence of otherwordly forces. Each assembly in Turoldus's poem results in either a resolve to do evil—the pagan meetings have this in common—or in a decision having tragic or at least potentially tragic consequences. This even occurs after Charles has enhanced his prospects of wisdom by hearing mass and matins (vv. 164, 670) or by holding the council on a solemn feast-day (Saint Silvester's Day, v. 3746). There is more than a suggestion here, then, of the unreliability of human and, especially, collective reason. For people living in the Middle Ages, God ruled the heavens, but the Prince of the World was Satan, whose nefarious influence was discernible everywhere. The only infallible source of Sapientia in the *Song of Roland* is the vision or dream, a form of divine grace inspiring the priest-king Charlemagne, whose final decision in the Trial of Ganelon is prompted by a sudden, apparently arbitrary, but superior intuition.

The poet often depicts the villainous Saracens with a mixture of bad and seemingly good traits. The *fortitudo et sapientia* theme is introduced, for example, with the observation that:

> 24 Blancandrins fut des plus saives paiens,
> De vasselage fut asez chevaler:
> Prozdom i out pur sun seignur aider.

These qualities are precisely what one might expect to find in a Christian worthy, but because of the equation Saracen = devil, pagans are incapable of doing what is right or good. In this instance *saive* means 'diabolically cunning', not 'wise' (cf. v. 69). Saracenic qualities were perverse, but this does not mean that pagans were felt to be any the less formidable for possessing them. Redoubtable on the field of battle, Saracens were believed to be shrewd in council.

Turoldus shows Blancandrin craftily assessing Charlemagne's fatal weakness. According to the Saracen adviser, the Emperor is cruel and ferocious—normally cause for fear or alarm—but he believes in the inviolability of pledges, especially when sealed with gifts.[28] Also, the pagans' plight may not be so desperate after all. Charles, too, has his share of problems. Many of his soldiers are hired and, consequently, unreliable mercenaries (soldeiers). He has been in Spain for seven long years and his men are without a doubt anxious to return home.[29] Finally—and this is Blancandrin's most perceptive intuition—Charles has blind faith in the mysterious workings of grace, which can bring about miraculous conversions. The keenness of Blancandrin's insight will become evident when Charles, informed of Marsile's proposal, replies as predicted here: "*Uncore purrat guarir*" (v. 156). A pledge on the Saracen king's part, sealed with gifts and hostages, and above all an indication of willingness to become a convert, will suffice, then, to bring about Charlemagne's withdrawal.[30]

The offer to seal the pact with "ten or twenty" close relatives as hostages is unconscionably callous and vile.[31] Blancandrin justifies his recommendation by affirming that the lives of a few are expendable when *onur* and *deintet* are at stake. These are lofty-sounding words, but, as Jones points out: "The honor and dignity to which he refers are goods of fortune rather than goods of the spirit, since it was shameful to betray the hostages one has given. . . . By *deintet* Blancandrin is clearly referring to the Saracens' ruling status or sovereignty in Spain; and therefore the same idea can be expressed as 'beautiful Spain' in the following *laisse similaire*."[32] The Saracen's chilling use of locutions involving the word heads (vv. 44, 58: perdent les chefs / les testes; v. 57: trecher les testes) underscores his barbarity. His selfish abandonment of his own son is an inverted image of Charles's noble sacrifice of his nephew.[33] Blancandrin's basest attribute, however, according to the feudal system of values, is his deceitfulness for even suggesting such a solution to the pagan's dilemma.

Much has been made of the animal symbolism in Charlemagne's dreams, but the feral imagery of the opening passage has thus far received little attention from scholars. Blancandrin mentions bears, lions, hunting dogs, camels, hawks, and mules. "Hawks and dogs for hunting," explains Jenkins, "but bears, lions, and camels as exotic curiosities."[34] The animals are enumerated several times, however (vv. 30–32, 89, 128–130, 158, and 183–185), attesting to their symbolic importance. Most of these animals are in fact associated with death, evil, or Satan in the *Song of Roland*.[35]

Dogs appear in Charles's second and fourth dreams, which announce Roland's death, and also in metaphors anticipating the imminent destruction of the pagans:[36]

1874 Si cum li cerfs s'en vait devant les chiens.

3527 Arguille si cume chen i glatissent.

Lions are mentioned in prayers:

2386 E Danïel des leons guaresis.

3105 Enz en la fosse des leons o fut enz.

and, notably, in a passage with clear diabolical overtones:[37]

> 2436 Que n'i adeist ne beste ne lion.

Bears play a significant role in the Emperor's third and fourth dreams and, with the packhorse, in the preliminary punishment accorded to Ganelon:

> 1827 Si l'encaeinent altresi cum un urs.
> Sur un sumer l'unt mis a deshonor.

Ganelon threatens to throw Marsile *sur un malvais sumer* (v. 481) unless he becomes Charles's vassal. Before the French heroes succumb, Turpin assures them that, once dead, their bodies will be borne in state *sur sumers* (v. 1748) and that Charles and his men will be there to prevent their bodies from being devoured by *lu ne porc ne chen* (v. 1751). Mohammed's idol is given over to dogs (v. 2591) and, at the end, Thierry will be carried in triumph *en une mule d'Arabe* (v. 3943).

In the first laisse the poet introduces Good versus Evil, Victory, and Death. In the present commentary mention has been made of Desolation and Joy, Fortitudo and Sapientia. A mere listing of some of the other story elements worked into this passage will underscore the extraordinary skill with which Turoldus interweaves several important thematic strains into his narrative at a very early stage: Betrayal, Conversion, Light and Dark, War-Weariness. In the early twelfth century Abbot Suger had these words inscribed on the façade of the church of Saint-Denis: "This golden portal announces what shines brightly within."[38]

There is no mention yet of Roncevaux. The Saracens are merely hatching a treacherous plot to avert disaster. Roncevaux will be Ganelon's doing.

Turoldus has Marsile instruct his emissaries to carry olive branches in their hands, informing them that this symbolizes *pais e humilitet* (vv. 72–73). Jenkins notes that the olive branch is a symbol of peace in classical sources and cites four instances of ambassadors bearing these tokens in the *Aeneid*.[39] After the *Roland*, he adds, olive branches appear frequently in the hands of messengers.[40] Jenkins may be correct in identifying the symbol as a classical reminiscence, but it should be pointed out that the olive branch brought back to the ark in the dove's beak (Genesis 8:11) is also generally taken to signify peace and friendship, for it indicated that God's wrath had abated.[41]

But what of *humilitet* in v. 73? Jones informs us that the term is used only once in the *Song of Roland* and asserts that it refers to "the surrender or homage promised by the Saracens. This would have caused them great humiliation, just as it would have been *viltet* if Charlemagne had done homage to Baligant (3595)."[42] The notion that *humilitet* in this passage refers to humiliation rather than to humility is suggestive. Humiliation and humility are cognates and have always had a close semantic affinity.[43] It may well be, for example, that Lancelot's humiliations have spiritual significance related to the Christian virtue of Humilitas.[44] In Conrad's version the Saracen envoys' abject prostrations—throwing themselves repeatedly at Charlemagne's feet (vv. 676, 679–680)—reinforce Jones's interpretation. However, it is possible to relate peace, humility, olive branches, and the white mules mentioned by Turoldus in v. 89 in a far more significant manner.

Having decided to deceive Charles verbally, the Saracens now set out to trick him visually as well, by aping Christ's Entry into Jerusalem[45] (*Fig. 36*). The Savior's humble mount symbolized the peaceful nature of his rule and alluded to the characterization of the Messiah as the Prince of Peace (Isaiah 9:6).[46] The gospels do not specify the color of Christ's donkey, but medieval art made it white, a sign of victory.[47] The people who acclaimed Jesus carried palms in their hands,[48] and this is the reason the Church commemorates the occasion as Palm Sunday. The kind of branches strewn in Christ's triumphal path were not identified by the evangelists, but tradition held that they were olive branches.[49]

Turoldus's thought process may be reconstructed as follows. He first imagined Blancandrin with an olive branch in his hand, as a treacherous sign of his peaceful intentions. But olive branch suggested palm branch,[50] and the idea came to him to have the pagan parody Jesus's Entry into Jerusalem, so he changed Blancandrin's mount to a white mule. *Mules* in v. 89 refers to the female of the species (the adjective *blanches* is feminine). This animal, the offspring of a male ass and a mare, is not always sterile, but it is popularly assumed to be so. This characteristic, combined with its legendary stubbornness, makes the mule a contemptible beast, compared, for example, with the more noble horse. It may be that this added irony was intentional on the poet's part.

Conrad grasped the allusion to Christ's Entry into Jerusalem in this passage and, being less given to subtleties, proceeded to remove any doubts from his readers' minds. To begin with, the Saracen messengers carry palms in their hands, not olive branches (vv. 595, 678). After

Blancandrin has spoken, Charles tells him that, since Marsile angered and humiliated him (v. 818: "Da er mich mite scande") by decapitating his two envoys, he ought to do the same:

> "Selbe der ware gotes sun,
> Fürste aller guote,
> Durch sine demüte
> Ein esel er zü Iherusalem reit,
> Du er di martir durch uns leit.
> Einem palmen uürte er in der hant.
> Nu birt ir her zu mir gesant
> Un uüret daz selbe zeichin.
> Minem zorne muz ich intwichin."

> ("But the true Son of God Himself,
> The prince of all the gods,
> Through his humility
> Rode into Jerusalem on a donkey
> Where, for our sake, He suffered martyrdom.
> He held a palm in his hand.
> Now you have been sent to me
> And you carry the same sign.
> I must therefore put aside my anger.")

As clearly perceived by the German translator, Blancandrin's aping of the Messiah is intended to mislead Charles—Conrad has Marsile state categorically that they are to *feign* humility (v. 594: "Machet uch demüte")—into believing that the Saracens have peaceful intentions and sincerely wish to become converts. The olive branches, the white mules, and the peaceful and humble demeanor set the tone visually for what the Saracens then say to Charles. In attitude as well as in words, of course, the pagans plan to deceive the Emperor.

The next series of laisses will contain an eschatological image. The peaceful Palm Sunday formula prepares a scene reminiscent of the Day of Wrath.[51] Mule-riding Saracens also point to the humiliating punishment in store for Marsile, according to Ganelon, but actually destined for the traitor himself, and to the triumphal processions returning the bodies of the slain French heroes to France after Roncevaux, and honoring Thierry after the judicial combat at Aix.

3. *Marsile's Offer Delivered to Charlemagne*

Laisses 8–10 (verses 96–156)

Les premières scènes distribuées entre deux décors aux couleurs contrastées: ici Saragosse, la seule ville d'Espagne que les Français n'aient pas encore conquise, et le verger où le roi Marsile, couché sur un perron de marbre, dit à ses ducs et à ses comtes son découragement, et combine, pour éloigner Charlemagne, ses offres de feinte soumission; —là, devant les murailles démantelées de Cordoue, le camp français, joyeux et fort; sous de grands arbres, les tentes dressées où le butin s'amoncelle, argent, joyaux, riches armures; les catapultes au repos depuis la veille; les jeux des chevaliers, des bacheliers; les vieux, sur des tapis blancs, assis aux échecs; les jeunes, qui s'escriment de l'épée; passant au milieu d'eux, sur leurs mules blanches, aux freins d'or, aux selles d'argent, les rusés messagers de Marsile, des branches d'olivier à la main; près d'un églantier, environné des Francs de France, sur son siège d'or, celui qu'on reconnaît sans l'avoir jamais vu, le grand vieillard majestueux et familier . . . ces images jouent à nos yeux et chatoient, et le poète semble s'oublier à tout ce pittoresque, et voilà pourtant qu'il a réussi à insinuer en ces premières scènes les multiples données de fait dont il avait besoin.[1]

In an effort to underscore the contrast Turoldus seeks to establish between the Saracen and French camps, Bédier chose to emphasize the "picturesqueness" of these laisses and the familiar majesty of Charlemagne.[2]

The Emperor is certainly regal, but the physical and psychological impression that emerges from a close reading of this scene is not one of serenity. Charles is handsome and initially in high spirits, and his hair and flowing beard are pure white.[3] But the most striking feature about him is the one which Blancandrin has already mentioned twice (vv. 28, 56) and which the poet specifies twice again here (vv. 118, 142), namely, his fierce and warlike demeanor.[4] The pine tree[5] and thorny sweetbrier bush near his throne (v. 114: Desuz un pin, delez un eglenter) also serve to bring out the Emperor's strength and prickly disposition. What greets the Saracens as they arrive at Cordres is a ghastly scene with disturbingly prophetic overtones.

The high walls and towers of the once proud city have been reduced to rubble by Charles's mighty catapults. The Emperor and his men have brutally slaughtered every man, woman, and child, except the ones who have accepted baptism. Seemingly oblivious to the devastation about them, the Franks engage in games or fence with wild abandon.[6] However, Charles and six of the Twelve Peers plus Geoffrey of Anjou[7] are probably positioned with an eye to achieving maximum psychological impact upon the pagan emissaries.

Viewed in panoramic fashion, the scene bears a striking resemblance to a Romanesque Last Judgment, and the terrifying implications are doubtless not lost upon the Saracen messengers. Charles, like Christ the Supreme Judge, sits upon a throne surrounded by the Peers arranged like Apostles in the role of assessors[8] (*Fig. 37*). The grisly aftermath of the destruction of Cordres and the massacre of its inhabitants suggest Hell, while the Frankish knights revel in a Paradise of booty and games, paralleling the motif of the Separation of the Righteous from the Wicked. The latter is also reflected in the terrible choice mentioned in vv. 101–102 (En la citet nen ad remés paien/ Ne seit ocis u devient chrestïen). A similar holocaust will be described in Laisses 265–266, and the Themes of Conversion, and Joy in the Midst of Desolation in this scene will appear again later (cf. v. 96: Li empereres se fait e balz e liez; v. 3682; Repairez sunt a joie e a baldur). The destruction of Cordres may thus be said to foreshadow the ultimate ruin of Saragossa, one of the climactic points in the *Song of Roland.*[9]

The spectacle before the Saracen envoys is awesome and fearful, then, but Blancandrin does not lose his nerve. As he coolly proceeds to deliver his fateful message, the Emperor's mien, initially joyous (v. 96), but which had become stern at the Saracens' approach (v. 118), now becomes pensive (v. 138). Charles will reply, but first he lifts his arms in a dramatic gesture of thanksgiving.[10]

What will the Emperor's answer be? His gravity and deliberateness create suspense. Marsile had, on a similar occasion, put two of Charles's messengers to death. Even the name of the king who formerly owned the ten mules sent as a gift by Marsile (v. 90: Suatilie) is reminiscent of *Haltilie*, the hill near which they were treacherously executed (see vv. 209, 491). Charles's expression, seemingly indicating that he is in complete control of his emotions, is but a mask hiding great inner turmoil. There will be other occasions when his public face will differ markedly from private feelings.

But Blancandrin's shrewd evaluation of Charles's character has been a valid one. The Saracens' proposal includes gifts and hostages, but, significantly, it is predicated upon a change of heart (the pagans' desire for baptism), which the Emperor is tragically inclined to believe. Such a remarkable conversion seems highly improbable to us and, as we shall presently see, to Roland, too. However, Charlemagne evidently finds it hard to accept the notion that the pagans would dare mount such a colossal hoax. A nobleman's word—and Blancandrin appears to be a nobleman—is inviolable. Partly from wishful thinking, then, but mostly—as his laconic but awed reply indicates (v. 156: "Uncore purrat guarir")—from long experience with the mysterious ways of Providence,[11] Charlemagne seems disposed to accept the pagans' offer. The Emperor may at times be motivated by secular values and a proclivity for war, but he is also a firm believer in the strange workings of the Almighty.

4. The French Council, Part 1
Laisses 11–16 (verses 157–243)

Comparison of the Saracen and French councils reveals not only a contrasting mood of despair in the former camp and of jubilation[1] shot through with ominous portents in the other, but also a number of other oppositions and parallels.

The Saracen conclave *ends* with a list of ten pagan chiefs preceded by the phrase *Li reis Marsilie out sun cunseill finet* (v. 62), reiterated verbatim, but with a slightly different word order, in v. 78; the French council *begins* with a list of French barons preceded by the phrase *Ses baruns mandet pur sun cunseill fenir* (v. 169), a word-for-word repetition, with one slight variant, of v. 166.

Roland uses a phrase that was heard at the very beginning of the poem; it will also be uttered by Turpin later in the same assembly:

2 Set anz tuz pleins ad estet en Espaigne.

197 Set anz ad pleins que en Espaigne venimes.

266 En cest païs avez estet set anz.

The smashing of fortresses by the Franks, described in vv. 4–5 and 97–98, is alluded to by Naimes in vv. 236–238.

The details of Marsile's offer, already specified in Blancandrin's proposal in Laisses 3–4, repeated by the Saracen king in Laisses 6–7, and transmitted by the king's emissary to Charlemagne in Laisses 9–10, are reiterated once more by the Emperor in Laisse 13 and alluded to by Roland and Ganelon in Laisses 14 and 15, respectively. According to Rychner, this is a prime example of *mise en train*, a stock technique of the jongleurs: The poet deliberately repeats Marsile's terms in order to make sure that the audience will not miss the all-important point of departure of the drama.[2]

Further parallels may be seen within the French council itself:

> 165 Desuz un pin en est li reis alez,
> Ses baruns mandet pur sun cunseill finer.
>
> 168 Li empereres s'en vait desuz un pin,
> Ses baruns mandet pur sun cunseill fenir.
>
> 195 En piez se drecet, si li vint cuntredire.
> Il dist al rei: "Ja mar crerez Marsilie!"[3]
>
> 218 En piez se drecet, si vint devant Carlun . . .
> 220 E dist al rei: "Ja mar crerez bricun!"

However, there are also important differences in the two councils. To begin with, both scenes occur outdoors, but the second council involves a smaller number of people. Only a thousand or so soldiers gather round Charlemagne (v. 177: Des Francs de France en i ad plus de mil),[4] as opposed to twenty times that number at Saragossa (v. 13: Envirun lui plus de vint milie humes). Only one person, Blancandrin, addresses the Saracen king, the other warriors being initially either too afraid or too confounded to utter a single word (v. 22: N'i ad paien ki un sul mot respundet). On the other hand, three Frenchmen (Roland, Ganelon, Naimes) address Charles. In the ensuing discussion Naimes, Roland, Oliver, Turpin, and Ganelon voice an opinion concerning who will deliver Charles's reply to Marsile. The French council, therefore, is much more animated. Also, whereas Marsile relies exclusively upon the advice of one clever counselor, Charles listens to a heated debate in which sharply divergent views are being expressed by several strong-willed personages.

How should we interpret the dispute between Roland and Ganelon?

A contemporary iconographic formula offers valuable insight into Turoldus's conception of the dramatic scene. In this conventional representation a seated royal personage depicted frontally is approached from the left by a figure whose hands are extended chest high in a gesture of respect. Behind and to the right of the king's throne stands another individual, often holding a sword or a spear. This disposition of figures appears, for example, in an illustration of Joseph before Pharaoh in a copy of the *Paraphrases of Aelfric*, from the first half of the eleventh century (*Fig. 38*), and in a Monte Cassino Rabanus Maurus manuscript, dated 1023.[5]

It is the use of this formula in a late-eleventh-century manuscript produced at Moissac (*Fig. 39*) that sheds light on the dispute between Ganelon and his stepson.[6] In an illustration of the *Conflictus Virtutum et Vitiorum*, Humilitas counsels Exultatio, who is being falsely advised on his left by his vassal Detractio. In Conrad's version of the *Song of Roland*, Charles becomes angered by the debate[7] and sends his advisers to parley on a hill and return with an agreement. The council within a council is depicted in a manner reminiscent of the Humilitas-Detractio opposition, although the session is presided over by a mitred figure holding a crozier, presumably Archbishop Turpin[8] (*Fig. 40*). In this pen-and-ink drawing, as well as in the next in this manuscript, which shows Charles designating Ganelon to carry his message to Marsile[9] (*Fig. 41*), the formula is the same, but the traditional attitudes and positions of hero and villain are reversed.[10]

The iconographic convention discussed above offers a valuable clue concerning contemporary perceptions of reality. Turoldus has obviously cast Roland in the role of Humilitas, Ganelon in that of Detractio.[11] What is meant by Humility here is not self-deprecation but the realization of one's total dependence on God, the exact opposite of Pride (INTRODUCTION, 19, F).[12]

The French council in Turoldus's epic has two main parts, each involving a heatedly debated decision: (1) Shall the Franks accept Marsile's offer? (Laisses 11–16); and (2) who shall carry Charles's message to Marsile? (Laisses 17–26).

The first passage centers on two parallel laisses that contain sharply contrasting points of view by Roland and Ganelon:[13]

195 En piez se drecet . . .
Il dist al rei: "Ja mar crerez . . ."

218 En piez se drecet . . .
220 E dist al rei: "Ja mar crerez . . ."

In a third speech, similarly introduced by the locution *E dist al rei* (v. 232),

Naimes appears to side with Ganelon, a move that proves to be decisive. Naimes's position seems reasonable enough but, in a way, leads to disaster as much as the quarrel that ensues.

The three speeches each hang upon a key word: *vengez* (Roland, in v. 213), *prod* (Ganelon, in v. 221), and *mercit* (Naimes, in v. 239).

Roland instinctively knows that Marsile is attempting to delude the Franks. Long experience fighting Marsile's forces has taught him that the pagan king cannot be trusted. The notorious example of Basan and Basile is reason enough for the Franks to assume perfidy on the part of the victims' assassins. His proposed course of action is clear: Seek revenge upon Marsile by smashing Saragossa.[14]

Modern critics often characterize Roland in this scene as impetuous.[15] It is more accurate to say that the hero speaks his mind immediately, from a sense of duty.[16] He begins by enumerating his personal triumphs. This exordium is a rhetorical procedure for commanding respect before an audience.[17] In 2 Corinthians 11, Saint Paul was similarly driven to sound his own praises. Roland is no hothead, as his cool decision not to sound the oliphant will later demonstrate. His stinging reminder of the bad advice given by the French on an earlier occasion (vv. 205–206: "A voz Franceis un cunseill en presistes,/Loërent vos alques de legerie") is devoid of tact, but epic heroes never mince their words. Also, Roland cannot brook the Franks' war-weariness. Ganelon evidently takes the *legerie* alluded to by Roland to be an accusation leveled against him personally and, a few moments later, will use the same expression sarcastically (v. 300: "Einz i frai un poi de legerie").[18] The promptness and anger that characterizes his retort does suggest that he identifies with the false French counselors.

Roland incarnates fortitude and perseverance, and his speech is an impassioned plea for the Strict Alternative.[19] In retrospect his advice will prove to have been sound,[20] but his words are greeted by embarrassed silence. Triumphs such as those proudly alluded to by Roland are well and good, but they are costly, too, and Charles's men long to return home.

Although Ganelon's speech strikes the French as being eminently reasonable, the audience knows from having witnessed the Saracens' perfidy that it is the height of folly. Later, when Ganelon's consuming avarice is revealed, it will become evident that the traitor's seeming moderation here masks an insatiable lust for gold and that he simply aspires to share in the Saracens' proffered bribe.[21] But Turoldus already provides two important clues to Ganelon's true nature. In a striking biblical allusion (v. 178: Guenes i vint ki la traïsun fist), the audience has been informed that Ganelon will play the part of Judas in the unfolding drama.[22] Now, in his immediate rebuttal of Roland's words, the traitor stresses the profit (prod) to be derived by accepting Marsile's terms.[23] Mentioning financial gain serves to clarify the Judas parallel[24] and to pinpoint the vice that will lead to his betrayal of the French rearguard.

There is, in Ganelon's closing words, an insulting suggestion that the hero cares not a whit about the lives of his men.[25] This notion squares well with the view expressed by Oliver in the second oliphant scene, but it is grossly untrue, as details concerning Roland's solicitous attitude toward his companions will later show beyond a shadow of a doubt.[26] Meanwhile, however, the Franks once again refrain from showing approval or disapproval and mull over these words in silence.

Naimes agrees with Ganelon's conclusion that the Franks should accept Marsile's offer, but he suggests a better one and, as it turns out, it becomes the decisive reason for adopting the course of action proposed by the traitor.[27] Marsile's might is broken: He is helpless and pleading for mercy. To refuse would be deliberate wrongdoing. To translate *pecchet* in v. 240 as anything but 'sin'[28] is to miss an essential point made by Turoldus; the necessity of showing Christian mercy even at the risk of sparing a still dangerous enemy who may abuse of it. Naimes has not taken a commonsense view of the matter, as is usually claimed. Rather, his words anticipate the Folly of the Cross aspect of the oliphant scenes and are an integral part of the Christian dimension of the *Song of Roland*. However, it is true that Naimes adds the very down-to-earth consideration that hostages will seal the pact. The nobleman simply cannot imagine anyone cold-bloodedly sacrificing a member of his own family.

The important parallel between vv. 228 and 242 ("a plus munt" / "munter a plus") has heretofore not been noted, translators having followed Bédier's lead in rendering the first of these two verses ("un conseil d'orgueil[29] ne doit pas prévaloir"). Ganelon actually says: "Wrongheaded counsel must not prevail *any longer*," and the implication is clearly that the traitor is jealous because Charles *always* listens to Roland's advice.[30] This closer translation of Ganelon's harsh and spiteful phrase helps to elucidate his bitter resentment toward Roland's hold on Charlemagne. Naimes then uses the same expression, but he diplomatically shifts the Franks' attention away from the side issue of concern over Roland's relationship with the Emperor to the central question before the council, namely, how to respond to Marsile's plea for mercy.

5. *The French Council, Part 2*

Laisses 17–27 (verses 244–365)

The stage has now been set for one of the most dramatic and controversial scenes in the *Song of Roland.* In the first part of the council, an important decision was reached concerning the Saracens' offer. Now a messenger must be chosen to take Charles's reply back to Marsile.[1] Thus far we have been involved with Plot A, a tale of Saracen treachery. The seeds of Plot B—Ganelon's betrayal—are now to be sown.

In analyzing this crucial scene, one must not lose sight of the fact that the mainspring of Ganelon's actions is avarice. The traitor is already deeply disturbed, his frustration having evidently been exacerbated by the rewards his stepson earned through feats of prowess. The affront he suffers at the hands of Roland[2] causes him to make an irrevocable decision, but Ganelon is plainly already on the downward path when the council begins. Conceivably, then, the traitor's vice could have precipitated a quarrel over money with just about anyone, but Ganelon's envy has been chiefly excited by his stepson.[3] Roland's opposition to the easy and immediate gains proffered by Marsile prompts Ganelon to term him a fool. The hero's nomination of his stepfather to deliver the message to Saragossa has been discussed by many scholars, but it will be shown to be a logical outgrowth of this first exchange between Roland and Ganelon.

What ultimately motivates the confrontation here may be clear, but the quarrel scene itself is innately ambiguous. Neither Charles nor the other witnesses become unduly alarmed at what transpires until the gauntlet is dropped, an omen that will not, for that matter, be linked to the altercation by anyone but Ganelon and his relatives. Those who witness the argument apparently dismiss it initially as being of little consequence, the sort of bickering that often happens when warriors are under great emotional stress. The Franks will have great difficulty reconstructing the incident when called upon, at Aix, to judge the traitor's deeds. Ganelon will offer a self-serving interpretation of the event in question, claiming that it was Roland who hated him and coveted his fief.

The first part of the council is structured on the basis of parallel laisses. The strophes under consideration here are constructed by means of a thrice-repeated question (vv. 244–245, 252–253, 274–276). Four candidates in rapid succession volunteer for the mission to Saragossa, only to be rejected by Charlemagne. This is followed by Roland's nomination of Ganelon.[4]

The thrice-repeated question is of course a favorite folktale device, but its ritualistic overtones should not be overlooked. This mystic aspect is also evident in the taboo that surrounds the nomination of an individual other than oneself: The nominee may not refuse. To be sure, honor may be adduced to explain the warrior's proud acceptance when publicly challenged in this way,[5] but magic and a belief in ineluctable destiny are also very much involved here. This appears most strikingly in vv. 310–311: "*En Sarraguce sai ben qu'aler m'estoet, AOI./ Hom ki la vait repairer ne s'en poet.*" It is significant, too, that the verb form *estoet* 'it is necessary' is repeated three times in the laisse in question, each time at the end of a verse, for emphasis.

The scene is presented in four parts. After some initial volunteering (Laisses 17–19), Roland proposes his stepfather (Laisse 20). Ganelon's angry reaction (Laisses 21–22) is followed by a series of decisive acts by Charlemagne (Laisses 23–26).

The Franks jump up one by one to offer their services, vying for the honor of this dangerous mission, only to be told to sit down and be silent by a worried Charlemagne. Turpin's offer to go have a look at Marsile (vv. 269–270) is felt by some to constitute grim humor, but it probably has more to do with gathering intelligence relative to pagan intentions by sizing up Marsile (cf. v. 191: "Mais jo ne sai quels en est sis curages") than with bravado.[6]

Oliver opposes the designation of Roland for the mission because his companion-in-arms would probably come to blows with Marsile (v. 257: "Jo me creindreie que vos vos meslisez"). This impulsiveness, says Le Gentil, will eventually bring about the hero's downfall.[7] However, Oliver is Roland's rival for the honor of going to Saragossa and his observation is designed to achieve a competitive edge for himself over his comrade. Jones has shown, moreover, that in the preceding verse Oliver's characterization of Roland's heart as *pesmes* and *fiers* 'fierce' is complimentary.[8] In other words, Oliver's effort to advance his own nomination is not without grudging admiration for his friend's aggressiveness. Critics do not as a rule accuse Ganelon of brashness. Nevertheless, he deliberately provokes Marsile at Saragossa, which is precisely what Oliver fears Roland will do![9]

After this initial agitation, each of the three remaining parts of the scene is dominated by a dramatic gesture.

1. Roland nominates his stepfather, who angrily rebukes him.[10] Ganelon throws off his fur mantle (v. 281: De sun col getet ses grandes pels de martre). According to Le Gentil, this is a proud gesture.[11] There is certainly more than a suggestion here that fierce pride is indeed involved, tinged no doubt, too, with anger and, perhaps, ostentation.[12] These psychological effects are secondary, however, for throwing one's cloak to the ground is essentially a sign of defiance. Ganelon feels he has been affronted and responds by challenging his adversary with a gesture as unmistakable as throwing down his gauntlet.[13] Ganelon's formal challenge to Roland, Oliver, and the Twelve Peers is made in vv. 322–326, but throwing down his cloak comes close to signifying the same thing.[14]

Why does Roland volunteer Ganelon? Is it a sudden whim?

The hero does not bear his stepfather any malice, and emulating David, who caused his rival Uriah the Hittite to be stationed in the thick of the fight and thus meet his death (2 Samuel 11), is simply not Roland's style. Nominating Ganelon to accord him honor is similarly implausible.[15] Roland proposes Ganelon in order to unmask his cowardice.

Roland had urged Charles to reject Marsile's offer and fight his enemy to the end. Unspoken but very much involved here was Roland's concept of Charlemagne's sacred mission to vanquish the Infidel. However, according to Ganelon, when his stepson gave such advice, he was showing lack of concern about his companions' lives:

> 226 "Ki ço vos lodet que cest plait degetuns,
> Ne li chalt, sire, de quel mort nus murjuns.
> Cunseill d'orguill n'est dreiz que a plus munt,
> Laissun les fols, as sages nus tenuns." AOI.

The word *sages* in this passage means 'wise men', and Ganelon is advising Charles not to run any unnecessary risks.[16] But, knowing Ganelon's vice, it is safe to assume that avarice has eroded his courage and that the wisdom he counsels actually borders on cowardice.[17]

To carry his reply to Marsile, Charles needs a messenger endowed with intelligence, tact, and, above all, courage, for the Emperor and his men are acutely aware of the fate of Basan and Basile, who were murdered at Haltille under identical circumstances. When Naimes volunteers, Charles characterizes him as *saives* (v. 248), which surely implies he has the requisite courage as well as intelligence for this dangerous assignment. After brushing aside Roland, Oliver, and Turpin, Charlemagne insists on the notion of courage (barun)[18] as he renews his appeal:

274 "Francs chevalers," dist li emperere Carles,
"Car m'eslisez un barun de ma marche,
Qu'a Marsiliun me portast mun message."

Roland thereupon volunteers Ganelon. In light of the importance attached to intelligence and, above all, to bravery as double requirements for this mission, Roland's nomination clearly constitutes a direct challenge to Ganelon's manhood. The favorable reaction of the Franks confirms the interpretation I have given of the word *saive*, for they use it to describe Roland's stepfather:

278 Dient Franceis: "Car il le poet ben faire!
Se lui lessez, n'i trametrez plus saive."

It is this very same fusion of intelligence and courage that illuminates the meaning of *saives* in the crucial passage when Roland, scoffing at Ganelon's threat, offers to go to Saragossa in his place:[19]

292 Respunt Rollant: "Orgoill oi e folage,
Ço set hom ben, n'ai cure de manace.
Mai saives hom, il deit faire message:
Si li reis voelt, prez sui por vus le face."

In point of fact, one cannot understand why Ganelon immediately explodes with anger if one does not see in Roland's reply, and particularly in his ironic use here of the epithet *saives*, an allusion to his stepfather's lack of bravery.

In summary, the semantic range of the term *sage/saive* in the *Song of Roland* encompasses the notion of courage and helps explain why Ganelon becomes infuriated by Roland's words. In their initial exchange (Laisses 14 and 15), Ganelon impugned the hero's motives for wishing to carry on the war. Roland now openly calls into question his stepfather's courage. When, having betrayed his stepson into the hands of the Saracens, Ganelon nominates Roland to the rearguard, he will not fail to allude to the hero's allegation as he seals the latter's doom:

743 Guenes respunt: "Rollant, cist miens fillastre,
N'avez *baron* de si grant *vasselage*."

Scholars have expended much time and energy debating the pros and cons of one sequence of laisses over another in this passage, underscoring the logic or lack of logic of such arrangements.[20] It is evident, however, from Turoldus's use of the laisses-similaires technique here as elsewhere in the poem that he strives less for logical exposition than for accumulation of details, which, in the aggregate, will convey the desired effect. In other words, stereoptics rather than Cartesian logic are the key to this passage. Ganelon's reactions to Roland's nomination, taunting remarks, and laughter (v. 302) show a certain progression, but probably not of the rigorous sort suggested by many critics.[21]

Turoldus's account of Ganelon's reaction includes the following elements:

(a) a gesture of defiance and challenge (throwing off his cloak).

(b) mention of Ganelon's appearance.[22]

(c) cutting remarks to Roland, the traitor all the while asserting his acceptance of the mission to Saragossa (vv. 286–288, 306–309).

(d) threats against Roland, expressed in understatement (vv. 289–291, 300–301).

(e) an expression of regret (vv. 311–316).

(f) a challenge to Roland, Oliver, and the Twelve Peers (vv. 322–326).

Ganelon sees no point in sacrificing his life for naught, yet he now finds himself in a position that will probably mean just that.

The Franks, by first enthusiastically approving Ganelon's view as espoused by Naimes (v. 243), then by just as promptly endorsing Roland's nomination (vv. 278–279), may be showing that they are aware of the ill-feeling that has long existed between Ganelon and his stepson and are therefore trying to play a conciliatory role by favoring first one, then the other. Also, the Franks in council, here as in the trial scene at the end of the poem, offer worldly wisdom, which, when compared with Sapientia, is vanity and, in the present instance, leads to disaster.

The die has now been cast: Ganelon will go to Saragossa. In his spiteful challenge the traitor specifies that he is calling out Roland because "*ço ad tut fait*" (v. 322), Oliver "*por ço qu'il est si cumpainz*" (v. 324), and the Twelve Peers "*por qu'il l'aiment tant*" (v. 325). These expressions and the locution "*Desfi les ci, sire, vostre veiant*" have a juridical ring.[23] The reasons for challenging Oliver and the Twelve Peers seem odd today, but they are based on the notion of companionage. One senses in these distinctions, too, Ganelon's alienation from the inner circle of nobles around Charles, despite his close family ties to the Emperor. At the root of this isolation, to Turoldus's way of thinking, is Avaritia, that is, the rejection of God.

2. As Charles hands over his gauntlet, an act symbolizing investiture for the mission to Saragossa, Ganelon distractedly allows the glove to fall to the ground.

This accident is immediately interpreted by everyone present as a bad omen.[24] It is an excellent example of how the poet utilizes point of view. The Franks are primarily thinking of Ganelon, who is about to embark upon a perilous voyage.[25] Ganelon, whose mind is already racing ahead with thoughts of revenge, utters a reply laden with ambiguity.[26] To the Franks he may appear to be coolly facing the dangers of the ride to the Saracen capital and engaging in a bit of bravado. Charles instinctively suspects—and the audience listening to the performance of the *Roland* knows for certain—that the traitor is hinting darkly of carrying out his threats uttered only a few moments earlier.

3. As Ganelon prepares to depart, he asks for Charles's permission to leave. The Emperor grants this request; then, in an act that strikes modern readers as unusual, he absolves and blesses him with his raised right hand. One generally considers absolution to be a priestly function and finds it quite natural when, for example, Turpin performs a similar duty on the battlefield (vv. 1133, 1141, 2205).[27] However, Charles is a priest-king and absolution is merely an extension of his role as a representative of God on earth.

The absolution Charlemagne spontaneously grants Ganelon is one of the noblest acts of charity in the *Song of Roland*. As a manifestation of magnanimity, it is to be compared to the Emperor's decision, after the fall of Saragossa, to spare Bramimonde the choice between instant conversion and death. Instead Charles will enable her to find the Way *par amur* (v. 3674). In both instances Charles turns the other cheek, refusing to return evil for evil.[28] His dreams and Ganelon's shameless manipulations—the designation of Roland to the rearguard, the effort to deter Charles from saving his nephew when the latter sounds the oliphant—will later convince him that drastic measures, rather than forgiveness, are called for, in order to eradicate this diabolical influence from the world.

The ritualistic absolution gesture is ironic and grimly prophetic, too, for its puts Ganelon's departure in a sacramental context. The traitor is already intent on killing Roland and his companions.[29] The deed is therefore initiated in an atmosphere of sacrilege and blasphemy.

6. *The Ride to Saragossa*

Laisses 28–30 (verses 366–401)

Early critics complained that Turoldus was inept in making Ganelon betray his stepson in the short space of a few lines.[1] However, concision in no way mars this passage, and the traitor's growing complicity is revealed with telling effect.

Blancandrin may have been a discreet witness to the proceedings at Charlemagne's council. At Saragossa the Saracens will withdraw for a private discussion (Laisse 38) while Ganelon, sword drawn and leaning against a pine (vv. 499–500), will observe their deliberations at a distance. As an unobtrusive onlooker, Blancandrin could easily have noted Ganelon's animosity toward his stepson, his covetousness, and his mention of a wife. Or perhaps Blancandrin simply has Satan's help. At any rate it has been said that Ganelon cunningly steers the conversation around to Roland during this voyage,[2] but the Saracen is surely in control here. Significantly, it is Blancandrin who slows down, not the traitor who hurries to catch up (vv. 367–368): Ganelon, he knows full well, is ripe for betrayal.

Recalling perhaps that Roland began his first speech with a list of conquests (vv. 198–200), Blancandrin alludes now to Charlemagne's triumphs (vv. 371–373),[3] a reference sure to trigger thoughts of Roland, the architect of the Emperor's victories. When Ganelon does not bite, Blancandrin shrewdly dangles the bait again, a bit more obviously this time, berating the dukes and counts "*ki tel cunseill li dunent*" (v. 379). Bad advice of course alludes to Roland's speech that attacked the folly of the earlier French decision to send Basan and Basile to Marsile on a similar mission:

> "A voz Franceis un cunseill en presistes,
> Loërent vos alques de legerie."

The pagan envoy has struck a raw nerve, and it is the reference to a false counselor that suggests the diabolical image which now comes to Ganelon's mind. The French emissary relates how one day Charlemagne's nephew appeared, fresh from his latest battle victory, and presented the Emperor with . . . a red apple! "Here, dear lord," said Roland to his uncle, "I present you with the crowns of all the kings." According to Jenkins:

> The bright red apple represented the gilded ball or globe, the "mound

> of dominion," or "orb," a part of the regalia of emperors. Around the golden orb were sometimes placed circlets representing the crowns of conquered kings. Here we have Count Roland's idea of a jest; Ganelon does not tell us how the flattery was received by Charles.[4]

Jenkins's explanation is unsatisfactory. Why would Ganelon choose an amusing anecdote to characterize Roland, whom he hates? Does Ganelon simply lack a sense of humor?

Other scholars have claimed that the point of this story is to underscore the hero's alleged pride. Martín de Riquer, for example, asserts:

> Ganelon rappellera . . . un curieux trait de jactance du héros, lorsqu'il offrit à son oncle Charlemagne une pomme rouge, par laquelle il voulait symboliser qu'il lui offrait les couronnes de tous les rois du monde (vers 384–386),—action que le traître veut interpréter comme étant une manifestation propre de l'orgueil de Roland.[5]

Ganelon links *orgoilz*—which, in the present context, surely means 'folly', not 'overweening self-esteem'[6]—to the hero's habit of constantly putting his life on the line and, by implication, drawing others into taking unnecessary risks. However, Ganelon does not suggest that the apple incident illustrates Roland's love of danger. Instead, the story exemplifies the notion of bad advice alluded to by Blancandrin in the preceding assertion (vv. 378–380). By turning Roland's accusation back upon the hero, Ganelon is reacting in characteristic fashion (INTRODUCTION, 19, C).[7] The apple anecdote is part of an attempt to depict Roland as a false counselor.[8]

The apple is, to be sure, a Temptation symbol.[9] However, its use here is out of the ordinary and it is best understood in the light of medieval iconography. In the south portal of the Cathedral of Strasbourg, below a Last Judgment scene, there is an illustration of the parable of the Wise and Foolish Virgins. This parable is an allegorical Last Judgment and it is frequently juxtaposed with the latter scene.[10] However, the Strasbourg sculptor invented a new figure to counterbalance Christ the Bridegroom (*Fig. 42*). This personage, referred to as the Tempter, does not have the customary diabolical features, but is depicted instead as a handsome young man, wearing a garland of roses on his head and holding an apple in his outstretched hand. The Tempter is smiling, but his true nature is there for all to see, for vile snakes, toads, and worms crawl up his back.[11] The Strasbourg statue was sculpted at the end of the thirteenth century, but the concept of the handsome devil dates back to Saint Paul who spoke of Satan disguised as an angel of light.[12]

To interpret Roland's gesture correctly, one must also bear in mind the statement that is purported to have been his in Ganelon's anecdote:

> 387 'Tenez, bel sire,' dist Rollant a sun uncle,
> 'De trestuz reis vos present les curunes.'

The allusion is clearly to the Three Temptations of Christ:

> Then Jesus was led by the Spirit out into the wilderness to be tempted by the devil. He fasted for forty days and forty nights, after which he was very hungry, and the tempter came and said to him, "If you are the Son of God, tell these stones to turn into loaves." But he replied, "Scripture says:
> 'Man does not live on bread alone
> but on every word that comes from the mouth of God'."
> The devil then took him to the holy city and made him stand on the parapet of the Temple. "If you are the Son of God" he said "throw yourself down; for scripture says:
> 'He will put you in his angels' charge,
> and they will support you on their hands
> in case you hurt your foot against a stone'."
> Jesus said to him, "Scripture also says:
> 'You must not put the Lord your God to the test'."
> Next, taking him to a very high mountain, the devil *showed him all the kingdoms of the world and their splendour*. "I will give you all these" he said "if you fall at my feet and worship me." Then Jesus replied, "Be off, Satan! For scripture says:
> 'You must worship the Lord your God,
> and serve him alone'."
> Then the devil left him, and angels appeared and looked after him.[13]

It is this double parallel with the devil as Tempter, then, that flashed into Ganelon's twisted mind. In his view Roland, the dashing young man who seemingly can do no wrong, is in reality leading Charles and all his men to disaster as surely as the Tempter with his apple or with his proffer of all the kingdoms of the world. But Charlemagne will later affirm, in a moment of extraordinary lucidity, that it is Ganelon who is the devil, not Roland:

746 Si li ad dit: "Vos estes vifs diables,
El cors vos est entree mortel rage!"

Ganelon's only moment of triumph, when he returns from his successful mission to King Marsile and offers Charles the keys to Saragossa (v. 677), will call to mind Roland's gesture in v. 386. The traitor imagines a satanic reflection in his stepson's proffered apple. The Emperor will see the devil in Ganelon.

Having succeeded in triggering the proper response in Ganelon, who now openly declares his desire to kill his stepson (v. 391: "Seit ki l'ociet, tute pais puis avriumes"), Blancandrin encourages his new ally. The Saracen has found the chink in Ganelon's armor—his envy of Roland's conquests—so he hammers away at this point by presenting the hero as a would-be Alexander, seeking to master *tute gent ... / E tutes teres* (vv. 393–394).

Blancandrin shrewdly discounts Roland's capabilities by inviting Ganelon to offer an explanation for the hero's ambition: "*Par quele gent quïet il espleiter tant?*" Ganelon immediately rises to the bait by suggesting that his stepson can dare entertain that hope because of his sway over the French and the Emperor. He commands the French soldiers' loyalty because of the booty he has given them; he holds the Emperor in his hand because he, Roland, will conquer everything from here to the Orient. These statements may be viewed as variations on the concept of Roland as Charles's Right Arm, an important theme introduced indirectly here for the first time.[14]

7. Ganelon at Marsile's Court

Laisses 31–45 (verses 402–602)

The transition between the ride to Saragossa and the messengers' arrival in the Saracen capital is marked by the parallel use of a locution frequently found in epic literature to indicate the passage of time: *tant chevalcherent ... que.*[1] Blancandrin and Ganelon give mutual pledges that they will seek to have Roland killed. No further mention of Blancandrin will be made after Saragossa.[2] However, his role there will be crucial and he will live up to his promise to the traitor.

The scene in the pagan stronghold bears many resemblances to that which opened the poem. One finds the same sinister shade (v. 11: en un verger suz l'umbre; v. 407: suz l'umbre d'un pin), the same 20,000 Saracens crowding round Marsile (v. 13: Envirun lui plus de vint milie humes; v. 410: Tut entur lui vint milie Sarrazins), the same silence (v. 22: N'i ad paien ki un sul mot respundet; v. 411: N'i ad celoi ki mot sunt ne mot tint).

But there are also important differences. A pall of doom was cast over the opening scene, whereas now excitement and anticipation fill the air. The Saracens no longer fear death and shame, and they keep silent in order to hear the news they ardently hope will be good (v. 412: Pur les nuveles qu'il vuldreient oïr). Significantly, too, the ominous marble slab, now nowhere in sight, has been replaced by an impressive throne (v. 407: Un faldestoet). A precious silk cloth, of Oriental provenance, has been placed over the throne as a sign of wealth and power but perhaps, too, as a reflection of joy and hope. Charles had appeared to the Saracen messengers seated in all his fearsome majesty, whereas Marsile may be visualized standing before the throne or even coming forward in his eagerness to greet the envoys.[3]

This passage is usually interpreted as a battle of wits, a test of nerve between two archfoes. Actually Ganelon and Marsile, the two chief conspirators in the *Song of Roland*, are both committed to a similiar objective, and the scene depicts the growing collusion of allies in a foul plot. Each instinctively grasps this community of interest the instant contact is made, and each skillfully bends all his efforts not so much to bring the other around as to make it possible for him to utter a public avowal. What is involved here is face-saving and the most villainous type of behavior in feudal society, betrayal of trust. It is Ganelon's self-image that the Saracens must bolster, but much, too, hinges on securing Marsile's enthusiastic collaboration. The Saracen king's ploy is founded on flattery, Ganelon's on exploiting the enemy's desperation.

The present episode is one of the most misunderstood passages in the *Song of Roland* and has given rise to a complete distortion of Ganelon's character. In a typical analysis, Robert A. Eisner writes:

> As for Ganelon, though he is assigned the role of villain, he is by no means unattractive. The poet stresses his splendid appearance and the impression he makes. He betrays, but he is in no sense a vile traitor. The treason he commits is unwitting. In his mind, he is doing nothing more than following the dictates of feudal life,

marked by war among barons and sworn vengeance against anyone who offends or insults.[4]

Such a view fails to take into account the all-important concept that appearances can be deceiving (INTRODUCTION, 10, B, 2). It also assumes a complexity of character that is totally anachronistic. Moral attractiveness in an evil personage is understandable in Milton's Satan or in Romantic portrayals, but it was unthinkable in Turoldus's day.

Ganelon is an aristocrat, and haughty, scornful, even brash conduct is the proper stance in such circumstances. His role as an envoy doubtless affects his behavior, too, for bravado and insolence were expected of messengers, as Clarien and Clarifan will demonstrate in a later episode of this poem, and as borne out by numerous other instances in the chansons de geste.[5] However, what is mostly involved here is playacting of a rather different sort.

Blancandrin does two things to set the stage properly for Ganelon and, in the process, also signals Marsile that an ally has been made: He holds Ganelon by the hand and praises him lavishly:

> 421 "Ci vos enveiet un sun noble barun,
> Ki est de France, si est mult riches hom."

At the end of this relatively long passage, there will be a parallel gesture of friendship on the part of Marsile (v. 647), but ushering in by the hand is much more than a device for framing this episode. Handholding is a clear indication that things have gone well, an unmistakable sign that an understanding has been reached.[6]

After an opening salutation reminiscent of his greeting to Charlemagne in vv. 123–124 (and which will be repeated almost verbatim by Ganelon in vv. 428–429), Blancandrin makes his report. He states that Marsile's message has been delivered to the Emperor, who raised both his arms and praised God but made no reply, preferring to send a messenger instead.

The report is interesting for what it withholds as well as for what it reveals. Blancandrin is a shrewd judge of men. He knows Ganelon has decided to betray Roland, but he gives the traitor an opportunity to keep up appearances. Had he quickly revealed the outcome of his conversation with Ganelon, Marsile might have treated the latter in too friendly a manner, causing him to feel shame or guilt, and to reconsider. Blancandrin realizes that Ganelon's plan is far more promising than the Saracens' original scheme, but in order for it to be carried out he must avoid alienating the individual who will play a key role in it. Blancandrin's judicious reporting enables the Frenchman to maintain his self-respect, for he is not introduced as a traitor. It also affords Ganelon an opportunity to perform center stage and to display his contempt for the enemy.

Ganelon begins innocently enough with the standard greeting and a statement reiterating the essence of the Saracen emissaries' offer to Charles:

"Iço vus mandet Carlemagnes li ber
Que recevez seinte chrestïentet."

The implication, however, is that Marsile will have to be baptized *before* the Emperor's departure.[7] This is immediately followed by the unexpected news that Marsile will no longer be sole ruler in Spain but will be forced to cede half of it to the hated invader. Ganelon, who is already cleverly bringing attention to bear on Roland—who will be identified, in Laisse 36, as the man to whom Marsile must abandon half his kingdom—now confirms Marsile's worst fears: The shame and death he was striving to avert at all costs (v. 21) are still very much present in the threats now being made in Charles's name. If Marsile does not immediately accede to the Emperor's terms, he will be captured and brought forcibly and in disgrace to Charles's capital, where he will be tried and executed like a common criminal.

Marsile's reaction is predictable. He flushes and begins to shake with anger and frustration. Brandishing his spear, he assumes an attitude aping Saul threatening to strike down David.[8] The Saracen's menacing posture is mirrored by Ganelon. The emotional tension in this scene is boldly limned by the image of Marsile being forcibly held back by his men, on one side, and by Ganelon restraining himself, on the other.[9]

Ganelon's apostrophe to his sword is a way of threatening the enemy. I will die, says the traitor, but not before causing the deaths of the bravest (v. 449: li meillor) of the Saracens. But the apostrophe also anticipates Roland's dying words to Durendal in Laisses 171–173. In fact, the fate alluded to here—dying abandoned and alone in a far-off land, but having given a good account of oneself in enemy lives[10]—is reserved for Roland.

Why has Ganelon deliberately provoked the Saracens when he has already decided to betray his own? Bédier theorized that the villain risks his life in this way in order to be in a position to oblige Roland to undertake a similarly dangerous mission (that is, assume command of the rearguard) when he returns to the French camp.[11] However, this explanation is invalidated by the fact that no allusion to having exhibited such *estultie*, or even to having encountered any danger at all, will be made by Ganelon.

The traitor's defiant posturings and brazen provocation of Marsile may be Turoldus's way of delineating a worthy adversary for Roland or perhaps of suggesting that Ganelon had the courage and strength of the devil. But viewing the scene in the context of the mutual pledge made during the ride to Saragossa (v. 403: Que l'un a l'altre la sue feit plevit) does suggest a better explanation.

More than likely Ganelon is simply being allowed by the Saracens, prompted by Blancandrin who gave Marsile the sign, to have his moment of glory. At any rate, the upshot is precisely what Oliver said would occur if Roland were sent on this mission, an ironic parallel underscored by Turoldus when he places a kindred expression (meslee = sei mesler) in the mouths of the Saracens:

> 257 "Jo me crendreie que vos vos meslisez."
> 450 Dient paien: "Desfaimes la mellee!"

At the insistence of the Saracens, especially the Caliph, Marsile now mounts his throne, a solemn act and also a sign that he has regained his self-composure and is prepared to hear Ganelon out.

The French envoy momentarily assumes the role of the offended dignitary (v. 456: "Sire," dist Guenes, "mei l'avent a suffrir"), a pose calculated to win concessions from the Saracens. Although he mouths words about his determination to deliver the message required of him by Charles, he also lets fall a broad hint concerning *tut l'or que Deus fist* and *tut l'aveir ki seit en cest païs*. The parallel with Judas, who sold his master for thirty pieces of silver, is alluded to several times in the *Song of Roland*. Ganelon's hint becomes clearer when, in a gesture of defiance, he throws off his cloak. The article of clothing is a sumptuous one, made of precious silk lined with sable, and the suggestion is evident.[12] The traitor now openly invites a violent reaction by grasping the hilt of his sword. Actually he is secure in the knowledge that the Saracens need him desperately and he has, moreover, already received Blancandrin's conspiratorial pledge. Ganelon gloats over the retreating Marsile, over Blancandrin, who receives the discarded mantle (v. 464), and over the humbled Saracens, who may be visualized making an obeisance (cf. v. 974) as they obligingly and no doubt hypocritically concede: "*Noble barun ad ci!*" (v. 467).

It is worthy of note that the Caliph, who plays a secondary but not negligible role in the *Song of Roland*, is first mentioned in this passage. Adviser to Marsile, his fame has evidently reached Charlemagne's ears, for the Emperor specifies that he is to be one of the twenty hostages to seal the understanding reached between the Franks and the Saracens. The pagans are evidently willing to sacrifice virtually anyone to rid themselves of the threat posed by Charles—even close relatives—but Marsile draws the line at his uncle the Caliph. When he returns to the French camp, Ganelon will lie to Charles to explain away the absence of the Caliph among the hostages and, in the excitement, this condition will be forgotten. The Caliph will also figure in the Baligant episode, where he will be called Marganice or Le Marganice.

Contrasting with the gestures, attitudes, and words, which are primarily for the benefit of those witnessing the scene, is the private conversation between Ganelon and Marsile (v. 468: Envers le rei s'est Guenes aproismet).[13] The traitor reassures the Saracen king (v. 469: Si li ad dit: "A tort vos curuciez"), but he immediately reiterates what appears to be the same message. However, important new details are provided by Ganelon. The kind of humiliation (the packhorse ride) and the manner of execution (head-chopping) in store for Marsile if he does not agree to the Emperor's peace terms are detailed, but, far more significantly, Roland is identified as the one who will rule over half his kingdom. The Emperor's nephew is also characterized as a madman. There is subtle irony in the fact that the alternative described earlier—being brought back in shame to Aix and being put to death after a trial—now includes the telling detail of a packhorse ride, and that all this treatment is reserved not for Marsile but for Ganelon himself after Charles has him arrested. The packhorse motif also foreshadows the solemn and triumphant rides destined for the bodies of the fallen French heroes after Roncevaux, and for Thierry at Aix.

While Ganelon continues to infuriate Marsile, he is also slyly working to focus the Saracen king's anger on Roland by the lying suggestion that his stepson will be granted dominion over half of the Saracen realm. Ganelon is proceeding rapidly from a threat to kill Roland (in the exchange at Cordres), to a pledge to kill him (on the ride to Saragossa), to a specific plot to kill him.

There is anger in Marsile's face, which, the poet relates, is drained of color (v. 485: Marsilies fut esculurez de l'ire)[14] and there is barely contained violence as he breaks the seal of the letter Ganelon has handed him and throws the wax to the ground. Marsile now proceeds to paraphrase[15] a message that comes as a surprise to him—and to the audience.

Marsile may simply be omitting that part of the message which Ganelon has already transmitted to him—that is, the matter of sharing his throne with Roland—but, from what Marsile's son will say, it seems more likely that Ganelon has lied, his purpose being to provoke the Saracen king and to channel his anger against Roland. The contents of the message, then, are surprising to Marsile because, with the exception of the specific request that the Caliph be included among the hostages, there *are* no surprises.[16] The tone of the letter is remarkably mild and the concluding phrase is, to say the least, astonishing in its understatement:[17]

494 "Altrement ne m'amerat il mie."

But Turoldus has also played a trick on the audience. Here the element of surprise is not so much the contrast between what Ganelon says the message contains and what the letter itself actually states, or between Ganelon's aggressiveness and Charles's evident conciliatory mood. It is rather the unexpected mention of Basan and Basile.

The shadow cast by the two murdered brothers is very long in the *Song of Roland.*[18] The brutal outcome of their mission had been raised by Roland during the first French council as a telling argument against any further attempt at negotiation. It had been brushed aside by Ganelon and, eventually, by the rest of the Franks in their eagerness to end the seven-year campaign in Spain. Charlemagne had seemingly been won over to Ganelon's point of view, but the audience is now unexpectedly informed that Roland's argument was given considerable weight by the Emperor.

Jurfaret, Marsile's son, breaks the ominous silence with an insulting characterization of Ganelon's statements and with a request to be allowed to execute the despised enemy messenger. Here is one person who either fails to grasp the necessity for further playacting or who refuses to participate. The game is clearly about to get out of control. Ganelon brandishes his sword, all trace of defiance and posturing now gone. He backs up to a tree to avoid being struck from behind.[19] His desperate act seems frozen in an endless moment as the mortal enemies confront each other.

But, as was suggested above, Marsile caught Blancandrin's signal. He now breaks the spell by suddenly withdrawing into a garden, taking his most trusted advisers—Blancandrin, Jurfaret, and the Caliph—with him. The council within a council plainly mirrors the French gathering the morning after the Saracen emissaries' arrival at Cordres. However, no lengthy discussion is involved here. Having earlier grasped the situation at a glance, Marsile needs only a few words now to confirm his impression that an understanding has indeed been reached:[20]

> 506 Dist Blancandrins: "Apelez le Franceis,
> De nostre prod m'ad plevie sa feid."
> Ço dist li reis: "E vos l'i ameneiz."

Blancandrin and Ganelon promptly return, hand in hand, the reiterated gesture no longer a signal but a triumphant affirmation of complicity. Ganelon's eagerness to betray his stepson is indicated by the fact that it is he who grasps the pagan's hand.[21] The shade of the trees underscores the dastardly betrayal to which they are now irrevocably committed.

In the long conversation that ensues between Marsile and Ganelon (eight laisses), one notes a conscious parallel with the discussion on the ride to Saragossa. There are also echoes of Blancandrin's statements in the first Saracen council and of a phrase used by Ganelon at Cordres.

Marsile begins with an apology and a pledge. Although Blancandrin has affirmed that Ganelon swore to aid the Saracens, the pagan king is keenly aware that the success of the plan depends upon the Frenchman's cooperation. His promise of a substantial gift by way of reparation for having threatened to strike Ganelon—which involves a repetition of the cloak-bribe motif[22]—is intended to mollify him. Ganelon's reply is curious: He asks God to reward Marsile for promising a bribe. Although irony may have been intended here, it seems more likely that Ganelon is simply using a conventional expression.

Marsile has not forgotten Blancandrin's speech in Laisse 3, for an echo of his counselor's phrasing is to be discerned:

Blancandrin:	Marsile:
35 "En ceste tere ad asez osteiet."	528 "Quant ert il mais recreanz d'osteier?"
46 "Ne nus seiuns cunduiz a mendeier."	527 "Tanz riches reis conduit a mendisted."

But the parallelism with Blancandrin's conversation with Ganelon during the ride to Saragossa is much more illuminating. Marsile begins by probing. In his mind it is clear that Ganelon is betraying Charles for gold, a matter that has been quickly disposed of by promising a suitable reward (v. 517). The Saracen king also senses that Ganelon's greed has set him against his own countrymen. Earlier, Blancandrin had had the same instinctive reaction. Both Saracens initially suppose that Ganelon has a grievance against Charles. Blancandrin's approach was to praise the Emperor. It was his expectation that Ganelon would express annoyance with or even hostility toward his sovereign if, in addition to gold, this were his other reason for betraying his own. When the Frenchman concurred in Blancandrin's flattering view of Charles, the Saracen messenger shrewdly shifted his probing to the Franks. Ganelon thereupon volunteered that Roland was the source of his irritation.

One sees now that Marsile's mind works the same way. Exploring first the possibility of a complaint against Charles, the Saracen king tries to disparage the Emperor. If he has surmised correctly, Ganelon will find the deprecation of Charles's old age and lust for warfare to his liking. When the French envoy replies by praising the Emperor lavishly, Marsile is momentarily at a loss. To gain time, he reiterates his statement about Charles, prefacing it this time with a phrase reminiscent of Blancandrin's opening words to Ganelon:

> 370 Dist Blancandrins: "Merveilus hom est Charles."
>
> 537 Dist li paiens: "Mult me puis merveiller
> De Carlẹmagne, ki est canuz e vielz."

Marsile is now expressing admiration for Charlemagne, and the allusion to his great age, here as well as in vv. 539 and 552, is made in a very different tone of voice from that which marked the Saracen king's initial observation.[23]

Ganelon does not wait for Marsile to provide him with an opening. No longer able to contain his hatred for his stepson, he blurts out: Roland must die. There has been a transition, in the traitor's statements, away from Charles in Laisse 40, to Charles's unidentified nephew in Laisse 41 (v. 544: "Ço n'iert," dist Guenes, "tant cum vivet sis niés"), and, finally, to Roland, called by name, in Laisse 42 (v. 557: "Ço n'iert," dist Guenes, "tant cum vivet Rollant"). [24] At this point Ganelon avoids mention of killing, as if it were something taboo, although the phrase *tant cum vivet*, which is repeated twice, is clear.[25]

Much has been made of Ganelon's careful differentiation between loyalty to his Emperor and betrayal of Roland.[26] In fact, Ganelon's defense will hinge upon this legalistic distinction. Charlemagne will reject this technicality, and God, through the instrumentality of the trial by combat, will show to everyone's satisfaction that the Emperor did what was right.

The traitor considers that the most effective way to shift attention away from the Emperor to Roland is to laud Charles, so as to dissuade Marsile from contemplating an attack upon the main body of the Christian forces.[27] Such an attack would only result in another smashing victory for the Franks and no doubt provide Roland with another opportunity to demonstrate his superior valor.

Ganelon affirms that it is the constellation of noble qualities expressed by the term *ber* (the nominative form of *baron*) which best describes the Emperor (v. 531).[28] Playing on the same word, he adds that Charles would rather die than abandon his *barnet* ('assemblage of barons') because of his own *barnage*, or baronlike traits given to him by God. Bédier's translation of v. 535 ("De tel barnage l'ad Deus enluminet": "Dieu fait rayonner de lui tant de noblesse")[29] implies that Charles may be visualized in a glory; in other words, that he is surrounded by rays of light. An aureole surrounding the head or body was often used in medieval art as a sign of divinity or holiness, and a halo sometimes distinguished an emperor or hero such as Roland.[30] Here, however, the expression refers to a single ray of light, such as that depicting the descent of the Holy Spirit in scenes of the Baptism of Christ (but also of the Annunciation, the Nativity, and the Pentecost) and certain emperor portraits.[31]

Persisting in his plan to allow Ganelon to take the initiative, or perhaps trying to convince himself that his army is equal to the task of defeating Charles on its own, Marsile seems to ignore the full import of the traitor's words. Can his army of 400,000 knights defeat Charles, he asks. Ganelon cuts him short, echoing a phrase he used in his speech before Charles: "*Lessez la folie, tenez vos al saveir*" (v. 569; cf. v. 229: "Laissun les fols, as sages nus tenuns").

Ganelon is aware now that Roland was right in suspecting that Marsile's proposal was mere Saracen trickery—Blancandrin doubtless apprized him of this during the ride to Saragossa—but he has brushed aside any second thoughts about his desire to seek vengeance upon Roland. What he now proposes to Marsile shrewdly combines two features of Blancandrin's original plan with a new element; the tribute and the twenty hostages:

> 570 "L'empereür tant li dunez aveir,
> N'i ait Franceis ki tot ne s'en merveilt.
> Par .XX. hostages que li enveiereiz"

is coupled with an attack upon the rearguard of the French army returning homeward:[32]

> 573 "En dulce France s'en repairerat li reis.
> Sa rereguarde lerrat derere sei."

In his excitement at the prospect of doing away with his hated stepson, Ganelon uses the present tense, as if the act were already committed, and pleads for cooperation:

> 575 "Iert i sis niés, li quens Rollant, ço crei,
> E Oliver, li proz e li curteis.
> Mort sunt li cunte, se est ki mei en creit!"

Ganelon's fascinated contemplation of the Battle of Roncevaux is prophetic to a certain degree.[33] In addition to the details concerning the rearguard and the deaths of Roland and Oliver, he also correctly anticipates the following events: (1) Charles will already be descending the far side of the mountains; (2) there will be two phases to the battle (v. 589: primes; v. 592: Altre bataille); (3) there will be many Saracen casualties. But the traitor also predicts a stunning victory for the pagans (v. 594), followed by peace (v. 595), for, with Roland dead, Charles's mighty armies will vanish and never again present a threat to Marsile's security (vv. 599–600).

Does Ganelon really believe that Marsile's armies will triumph, that Roland's death will signal the end of Charles's capacity or will to fight and the abandonment of his sacred mission? Perhaps Ganelon fully expects Marsile and all his men to be slain in the process of destroying Roland, in which case the vision of victory and peace, which he conjures up, is a shameless lie in keeping with the villain's known behavior.

However, it seems more likely that Ganelon is simply under a hallucination. Satan dangles before his eyes the prospect of a pagan victory, of sweet revenge over Roland, and of great wealth in a France where, with Saracen protection, he, Ganelon, will have great sway. In v. 653 Marsile will pledge him a huge annual gift. The villain is prepared to take an enormous risk in order to get rid of Roland and to satisfy his greed (when he returns from Saragossa, laden with Saracen gifts, and later, when the treacherous ambush becomes apparent, grave suspicions will immediately fall on him), and it can only be justified if one assumes that Ganelon is counting heavily on the devil's help to accomplish this. In other words, the traitor has sold his soul to the devil.[34] If this interpretation is correct, Ganelon is conveying to Marsile what in his desperate delusion he actually believes will occur. What he fails to appreciate is that Roland's death will not result in the simple snuffing out of the life of an importunate adversary, but in an awesome victory that will inspire the Emperor and his men to surpass themselves for God in similar fashion.

In the dialogue between Ganelon and Marsile, which begins in Laisse 39, the Saracen king repeatedly uses a wheedling expression when addressing the villain: "*Bel sire Guenes*" (vv. 512, 563, 580).[35] His flattery is interspersed with bribery. Astutely, Marsile begins with a substantial gift—his cloak worth five hundred pounds in gold (vv. 515–516)—but this is merely a token of things to come, for the pagan king eventually bestows ten mule-loads of gold on his ally and promises him an annuity of the same order (v. 653). However, before this ultimate bribe and pledge, six short laisses averaging less than eight verses long (Laisses 46–51), ushered in by Marsile's kiss in v. 601, will provide fittingly blasphemous counterpoint to these foul proceedings.[36]

8. Ganelon's Sacrilege

Laisses 46–52 (verses 603–660)

The image of Judas kissing Jesus to betray him seared the consciousness of the Middle Ages.[1] What more revolting and sacrilegious gesture could one possibly imagine? Romanesque iconography often showed a raven perched on Judas's lips[2] and, in the fifteenth-century *Passion* of Arnoul Greban, the traitor's soul must leave through his ruptured stomach because it cannot pass his defiled lips. The Judas-Ganelon association is heightened by the mention of money in v. 602, suggestive of the image of Christ's betrayer clutching his sack of money at the Last Supper or accepting the thirty pieces of silver as his master's price.[3]

The identification of the erotic with the religious still offends many sensibilities, but to maintain that there is at times a relationship between the two needs no special justification today. Indeed, the subtle link between the sacred and the sexual provides thematic unity to more than one passage of the *Song of Roland*, including the one under consideration.[4]

The implications of Ganelon's acceptance of Marsile's kiss (v. 601), which opens this scene—a comparable gesture will close this passage (v. 647)[5]—and of the exchange of kisses with the Saracen warriors Valdabron and Climborin (vv. 626, 633) are rather profound when one remembers the taboo surrounding the act of kissing an Infidel. To the medieval mind, a Saracen's body harbored Satan himself and physical contact, especially kissing, resulted in diabolic contamination. If one must find a specific moment when the devil entered Ganelon's body—one recalls how the traitor imagined Roland as Tempter! (COMMENTARY, 6)—it is surely the instant Marsile's lips touch his.[6]

In one of the *Rolandslied* sketches Ganelon touches his index finger to a pagan idol as he takes his blasphemous oath,[7] but here Marsile has Ganelon swear his stepson's death on the relics of his sword Murgleis. The name evokes ominous associations with *murdrie* 'murder, assassination'. This chilling profanation of holy remains is prophetic of the traitor's desecration of the bodies of the slain Franks, regarded as Holy Innocents, as he scoffs at the notion that the sound of Roland's oliphant could signify any real danger for the hero and his men, and later, as he blatantly disavows any responsibility for their deaths. The hilt and guard of Ganelon's sword form a cross, adding further blasphemy to the traitor's oath.[8]

Marsile now calls for the Koran[9] and, providing a fitting contrast to Ganelon's blasphemy, swears, upon the text medieval Christians reviled most, to attack Roland if he finds him in the rearguard and to kill him if he can.

The ceremonial bestowing of gifts by the Saracens upon Ganelon,[10] which follows, anticipates the religious ceremonies and rousing oath-taking of the Saracens in Laisses 69–78. Ganelon replies to each pagan gesture with a litanylike response and embrace:

616 Guenes respunt: "Ben seit vostre comant!"

625 "Ben serat fait," li quens Guenes respunt.
Puis se baiserent es vis e es mentuns.

632 "Ben serat fait," Guenes respundit.
Puis se baiserent es buches e es vis.

On the other hand, one must not mistake *amistiez* in v. 622 for anything but a convenient and temporary alliance.[11]

The mention of the value of Valdabron's sword echoes the betrayal-for-silver theme, and it is as if the poet were suggesting that Ganelon should rid himself now of the relic-encrusted sword Murgleis, which he has profaned for a more fitting Saracen weapon. This sword, as seen later in v. 1527, is the very one with which Valdabron slew the Patriarch before the baptismal font of the Temple of Jerusalem.

Climborin gives Ganelon his helmet and, it later develops, his carbuncle (v. 1488). It is not stated whether or not the magic stone, believed to glow mysteriously in the dark, is centered upon a shield as it frequently is in medieval sources, but it would seem appropriate, as helmet and buckler normally go together as defensive counterparts to the sword. Nothing will protect Ganelon from the fate he deserves at the end of the poem and one is inclined to believe that the notion of useless weapons and armor, and not merely of valuable gifts, is what the poet intended to suggest here. What is most striking, however, is Climborin's desire to dishonor Roland (v. 631). He is not satisfied with simply slaying him but would also deprive him of his dignity.

The erotic association mentioned earlier emerges most clearly with the appearance of Bramimonde. There is nothing in the text of the *Song of Roland* which states that Bramimonde is directly involved in the Saracen plot to deceive Charles. Yet it may be assumed that she was immediately informed about the outcome of the first council at Saragossa: She is quite close to Marsile, she takes part in later military and political decisions, and, above all, she plays an active role in the ceremonial sealing of the pact with Ganelon. It was no doubt Blancandrin who gave Bramimonde the idea of a gift to Ganelon's spouse. The Saracen messenger was present at Cordres when Roland's stepfather mentioned her (v. 361: "De meie part ma muiller saluëz") and betrayed the fact that he was envious of Roland's possessions.

To be sure, "*Je vos aim mult, sire*" must be translated as "I care very much for you, sir," particularly in view of the sentence that follows immediately ("Car mult vos priset mi sire e tuit si hume"). Yet Bramimonde's words become bold and suggestive when situated in their true context, for the voluptuous and amoral Saracen lady is a stock character in epic literature.[12] Indeed later versions of the *Roland* depict Bramimonde as throwing herself into Ganelon's arms and offering her body as a lure.[13] Here as elsewhere in epic tradition concerning Saracen ladies, diabolism and eroticism are closely intertwined.[14]

Turoldus has two reasons for muting these aspects of Bramimonde's appeal. First, if Ganelon were to fall a victim to a seductress' charms, it would tend to further complicate an already tangled skein of motives for betraying Roland. The poet prefers to underscore the traitor's Judas-like greed, which is the obvious reason the brooches are introduced at this particular juncture. The very name of Marsile's keeper of the treasure, Malduit (*Male* + past participle of OFr. *duire* < CL *ducere* 'to lead') suggests to what evil the passion for riches leads. Secondly, Bramimonde incarnates the Theme of Conversion in the poem, and anything but veiled eroticism here would, in retrospect, needlessly tarnish a woman already grievously sullied, according to medieval ways of thinking, by her Saracen religion.

Unlike the Saracen emissaries who spend the night in Charles's camp (vv. 157–162), Ganelon departs hastily the day he arrives (vv. 659–660), so eager is he to leave the dangerous enemy camp and perpetrate the foul deed. His abrupt leave-takings here and at Cordres (cf. v. 338) suggest that, in the *Song of Roland*, it is he who is impulsive and not, as is generally maintained, the hero.

9. *Ganelon's Lie*

Laisses 53–55 (verses 661–716)

The poet is being ironic in v. 661. It may be true that, geographically, Galne is closer to France than Cordres had been, but unbeknown to Charlemagne, the Spanish campaign is about to take a sudden and unexpected turn, altering the manner of his return. In the next few laisses a summit of joyful optimism will be reached by Charles and his men—including Roland, whose gesture (v. 707) symbolizes the elation of the moment—but in the not-too-distant wood the Saracen army is lurking. The Franks rejoice and turn homeward, duped by the treacherous Ganelon, while their enemies lie in ambush, meaning to deal them a catastrophic blow.

Like the Saracen messengers arriving at Cordres at the beginning of the poem—their deceitful mission has now been entrusted to the traitor—Ganelon comes upon a scene of utter desolation.[1] Galne, the last Saracen city to be vanquished by Roland before his death, has been visited with such destruction by the hero that nothing will stir there for a hundred years. Had Ganelon been wavering, this further demonstration of Roland's power and might would surely have been enough to confirm him in his treacherous intentions.

As in all fateful moments, Charlemagne has turned to God, rising early and hearing mass and matins.[2] He stands impatiently before his tent now, surrounded by his trusted lieutenants.

The news is sensational: The enemy has agreed to Charles's demands! The tribute alluded to in v. 666 is more than adequately met (v. 678: "Mult grant aveir vos en faz amener"), twenty hostages have been sent, and Marsile has sworn to follow Charles to France, render him homage, and become a convert to Christianity.

Only one condition has not been acceded to. Charles had insisted that the Caliph, Marsile's uncle, be one of the hostages. Charlemagne knows his enemy only too well. He realizes the Saracens are quite capable of sacrificing a number of hostages in order to deceive him, but he knows instinctively that Marsile would never dream of sending his own uncle to a certain death. Several reasons can be adduced to explain why Charlemagne uncharacteristically throws caution to the winds and believes Ganelon's story that the Caliph and his men have drowned.

First of all, Charles is caught up in the excitement generated by the news of Ganelon's safe return from a perilous mission and believes his long-awaited triumph is finally at hand. He is also completely taken in by Ganelon's great cunning (v. 675: grant veisdie). But the most decisive factor at work here is Charlemagne's sincere conviction that the world will someday be completely converted to Christianity and united once and for all under his dominion. He believes that the drowning of the Caliph is a sign from God that that day is about to dawn.

Ironically, for pecuniary reward is what originally motivated Ganelon to evolve this elaborate scheme to destroy Roland, Charles now promises to reward his brother-in-law handsomely.

Trumpets are sounded, hinting ominously—for those in the audience familiar with the legend—at the celebrated climax of the *Song of Roland*, and the army sets out for France. For Ganelon, sweet revenge appears to be certain. Before proceeding, the fabricated story concerning the Caliph needs to be examined.

When alluding to Marsile, Ganelon uses the words *li ber* (v. 680). This is a highly complimentary term for a hated enemy, for it evokes some of the most prized values of eleventh-century culture and alludes to qualities believed to come from God.[3] In fact, *ber* will be used as a synonym for *seint* in v. 2096. Generally reserved for the Franks, *ber* at times designates a worthy opponent. Thus it was the term used by Blancandrin to refer to Marsile in his first words to Charlemagne (v. 125), and it is found again, paired with *sage* (v. 648), in a flattering compliment addressed by the Saracen king to the traitor about to depart from Saragossa. In the present passage (v. 680), Ganelon's intention is doubtless to show Marsile in a favorable light, one most likely to elicit respect from the Franks.

Ganelon claims to have been an eyewitness (v. 682) to the flight of the Caliph's army. The Franks evidently have a good idea of the number of enemy troops confronting them, and when Ganelon provides the intelligence that 400,000 men have abandoned Marsile and drowned, the magnitude of this loss makes a profound impression upon them, for it means that virtually all their adversaries have been slain.[4] Unfortunately the 400,000 are anything but dead, as confirmed by v. 715.

However, it is the manner in which they have died—according to Ganelon—that strikes Charlemagne most. Ganelon knows perfectly well that one of the Emperor's most cherished beliefs is that through conquest and conversion the whole world will someday come under his sway and everyone will worship the true God. Charlemagne's conception of history impels him to the view that any and all resistance to this future order of things will necessarily be overcome. Ganelon has not simply disposed of the most serious objection the Emperor might have raised to his credibility by justifying the Caliph's absence, he has also done so in a manner implying a clear sign from God.

But, in a now familiar variation on the Theme of Sapientia, things are not what they appear to be, for even Ganelon's lie is prophetic. The traitor believes he is cleverly deceiving the Emperor. However, he is at the same time prophesying the pharaonic end of Marsile's army (Laisse 180).[5]

Verses 703–706 echo the opening lines of the *Song of Roland* and again one feels that the story is ending rather than just beginning. What is on Roland's mind as he hears the thousand trumpets sound and watches the long train point homeward at long last?

The hero is unquestionably suspicious about this anticlimax or rather nonclimax. He has passionately argued against accepting Marsile's offer and now cannot quite bring himself to believe what has transpired. Yet, on reflection, he certainly has ample reason to be satisfied with the campaign as a whole, having just recently, in the siege of Galne, achieved yet another brilliant personal victory. Suspicious, then, and ever watchful, he is nevertheless dutifully compliant to the Emperor's decision. And when the time comes to halt for the night—it is actually three days later now (see Day 5 below; for a similar condensation [approach of Baligant's ships] see COMMENTARY, 29)—it is Roland who attaches Charles's ensign to his lance and gives the signal from the top of a nearby hill.[6]

It is easy to visualize the joyous and carefree Franks in their bivouac as they set about preparing the evening meal, thousands of campfires lighting the countryside as night begins to fall. Meanwhile, the poet tells us in the same laisse, 400,000 Saracens, armed to the teeth, are riding to a desperate rendezvous. They reach a dark forest, symbolic of their perfidy.[7] The word the poet chooses here for wood is identical with another meaning 'trap' (OFr. bril, brueil) and has the harsh sound of terms like *briche*, *bricon*, *brie*, and *brin*, all implying trouble. The laisse ends with a cry from the heart bemoaning the Franks' ignorance.

In Laisse 55, the impression is initially given that the Saracens are already lying in wait for the Franks, who are making their first encampment. However, several days, required for the Saracens' preparations (Laisse 68), have actually elapsed at this point. At this juncture, the poet is evidently more interested in the dramatic impact such a confrontation will have on the audience than he is in setting forth a simple chronology of events. The technique is reminiscent of that used in the opening laisse of the *Song of Roland*.[8]

The chronology here is somewhat confusing, then, but a close reading reveals that Turoldus takes care to indicate the proper sequence of events.[9]

Day 1:

Ganelon leaves Saragossa (Laisse 52).

Day 2:

(a) Dawn at Galne: Ganelon arrives (Laisses 53, 54).

> 667 Par main en l'albe, si cum li jurz esclairet,
> Guenes li quens est venuz as herberges.
> 669 Li empereres est par matin levet.

No indication of time is provided by Turoldus for the ride from Saragossa to Galne[10] or, for that matter, from Cordres to Saragossa. In the latter instance the twice-repeated locution *tant chevalcherent ... que* (vv. 402–403, 405–406) offers little help. However, it does seem more plausible and effective, from a narrative point of view, to have

Ganelon arrive at Galne the morning after his departure from the Saracen camp.

(b) Shortly afterward, the same day: The Franks break camp (vv. 701–702). The joy with which Charles greets Ganelon's report and the immediate sounding of the trumpets (698–700), together with earlier indications of French war-weariness, imply that the order to head home is promptly obeyed.

Days 3 and 4:

The Franks retire northward.

Day 5:

(a) Late afternoon, or early evening: Roland gives the signal for the Franks to halt (vv. 707–709). The Saracens spend the entire day and possibly part of the preceding night in a forced march, coming within striking distance of the Franks. They conceal themselves in a wood in the mountains and await dawn (vv. 710–715). Laisse 68 begins a flashback[11] relating how Marsile took three days to mobilize his vast army (v. 851): This corresponds to Days 2, 3, and 4. The next day (Day 5), the French battle flags are sighted (v. 857): It is presumably late afternoon or early evening.

(b) Night: Charlemagne dreams (Laisses 56 and 57) while the Saracens take a blood oath to destroy Roland and the French rearguard (Laisses 69–78). The pagans have been fully armed during their forced march (vv. 711–713). They now put aside their armor and weapons to rest and for the oath-taking ceremony, following which they arm themselves once again (Laisses 78 and 79). As the flashback ends, they are waiting for sunrise (Laisse 55).

Day 6:

During World War II Field Marshal Erwin Rommel was quoted as saying that the first twenty-four hours of the impending invasion of Normandy would be "the longest day." No more apt phrase could be found to describe Turoldus's conception of the day on which the Battle of Roncevaux was fought.

(a) Morning: Charles sights the Pyrenees and the rearguard is constituted (Laisses 58–65).[12]

(b) The Franks' vanguard crosses the Pyrenees and views France (Laisse 66).

(c) Charles informs Naimes of his dream of the night before (v. 836).

(d) The French rearguard prepares for battle (Laisses 79–91).

(e) The Battle of Roncevaux. It is still morning when the first phase begins (Laisses 92–142), at least this is the way Marsile will later recall it (v. 2601). It is late afternoon (v. 1807) when Charles hears Roland's oliphant and gives the order for the Franks to ride to the rescue. The battle now enters the second phase (Laisses 143–161). The following laisses tell of the last rites for the French Peers and the death of Roland (Laisses 161–176), Charles's arrival (Laisse 177), and his decision to pursue the fleeing remnants of the Saracen army (Laisse 178). A miracle halts the sun and prolongs the daylight (Laisses 179–180), the Saracens are either massacred by Charles's forces or drowned (Laisse 180), and the Emperor bivouacs near the Ebro, bringing this eventful day to a close (Laisse 181).

The transition to Day 7 (the chronology of which will be discussed in COMMENTARY, 29) includes Marsile's return to Saragossa, which may be envisioned as occurring in the late afternoon or early evening of Day 6 (Laisses 187–188), and a flashback to an event having taken place seven years earlier (v. 2613: Al premer an), that is, Marsile's appeal to Baligant (Laisse 189). (For the chronology of Day 7, see COMMENTARY, 30.)

10. Charlemagne's First Dreams
Laisses 56–57 (verses 717–736)

Much has been written about Charlemagne's symbolic dreams and their significance.[1] Since Freud, dreams are usually interpreted as fanciful recreations of past experiences or emotions, but, for the poet, these two nocturnal visions are a way of informing Charles of Ganelon's betrayal *before* it is too late to alter the fateful course of events.[2] The Middle Ages distinguished between the *somnium naturale*, which it traced to bodily complexions and humors, and the *somnium coeleste* of divine origin.[3] Since the dreams in question are later referred to as *avisiun d'angele* (v. 836), there can be no doubt that Turoldus conceives of them as messages from on high.

In the first dream Ganelon seizes the ash lance, which the Emperor holds in his hand, and shakes it with such violence that it disintegrates. The lance is an extension of the arm.[4] Ganelon will destroy the weapon, that is, Roland, Charles's right arm (INTRODUCTION, 19, D), but the hero's soul, like the fragments of the lance, will soar heavenward. The shattering lance may intimate something far more distressing to Charles than the death of his nephew. It may suggest the breaking of Roland's spirit. (Cf. the concept of Virginitas in INTRODUCTION, 19, F). When the Emperor finds the hero's sword intact—this is not actually stated but it is implied in vv. 2359 and 3017 (see also v. 2875)—he will realize that such fears were groundless.

The second dream is more obscure. If the bear (or boar) symbolizes Marsile, the leopard the Caliph, and the hunting dog Roland, the allusion is to the Battle of Roncevaux; if the bear (or boar) represents Ganelon, the leopard Pinabel, and the hunting dog Thierry, then the action takes place at Aix.

Clues abound, but they lead in opposite directions. One is even tempted to conclude that Turoldus sought to bewilder his audience.[5] Also a deliberate confusion of Ganelon and Marsile is not to be ruled out.

However, in the final analysis, the locale (v. 726: en France, a sa capele, ad Ais) and the place whence help will come in Charles's moment of greatest danger (v. 728: Ardene) turn the scales.[6] They indicate that the dream anticipates Ganelon's trial and the judicial combat between Thierry d'Ardenne[7] and Pinabel. The bear Ganelon continues to bite Charles, but Charles's right arm is now revealed to be the Emperor's political and spiritual authority itself, not Roland. Pinabel, the leopard, attacks Charles's very body, but Thierry, the hunting dog, comes to the rescue.

As important as the correct identification of the various elements of this dream may be, it is even more essential to grasp the poet's intent here. The *avisiun* serves to inform Charles that Roland must die and that his own authority will be gravely shaken, not only by the catastrophic loss of his nephew but also by the combined threat of Ganelon and Pinabel.

The revelation concerning Roland's death is explicit, for the fragments of the lance flying heavenward can mean only one thing. Modern cinematographers were not the first to discover that a flashforward can be as suspenseful as the gradual unfolding of a narrative.

More than a device to create tension, the revelation of Roland's impending death serves to inform Charles of the cruel decision that he must now make and casts him in the role of Abraham. The second dream, however, is more tantalizing in that the outcome is not known. It is significant that the Franks appear in this vision. Their uncertainty as to what will transpire in the end underscores the vanity of their knowledge and their lack of conviction. The Emperor, on the other hand, has penetrating wisdom and unshakable faith.

The dreams function as a corrective, then, giving Charles and the audience privileged information about Ganelon's perfidy. The audience has known from the outset, of course, who the traitor is (v. 178: Guenes i vint, ki la traïsun fist) and has witnessed the events at Saragossa. Ganelon's ghostly appearance now confirms the Emperor's suspicion, first aroused by the dropped gauntlet and soon to be reinforced by the villain's vengeful nomination of his nephew to the rearguard.[8]

11. Roland Named to Command the Rearguard
Laisses 58–68 (verses 737–859)

Coming, as it does, hard upon the dreams prophesying the betrayal and death of Roland, Ganelon's blunt and ironic reply to Charles's query concerning the rearguard constitutes a stunning blow. Ganelon's term *fillastre* (v. 743) could conceivably have the harmless meaning 'stepson' but is naturally to be taken in the pejorative sense 'poor imitation of a son'. It echoes *parastre* in v. 277 and is uttered tauntingly.[1]

As seen in Laisses 17–19, Charles is able to turn down volunteers for a dangerous mission. Now he appears to be either bound by tradition or unwilling to see an individual whose name has been proposed by someone else denied the opportunity to accept this challenge. However, the Emperor's decision to accept Ganelon's nomination is also motivated by a sense of history. Charles must prolong and relive the past by playing Abraham, who unhesitatingly accepted to do God's will.[2] He mutely accepts Ganelon's proposal, but he also brands the perpetrator of this foul deed for what he is: "You're a living devil," he cries. "A deadly frenzy has entered your body!" The Emperor's reaction underlines Ganelon's consuming vice, for, as the *Hortus Deliciarum* makes clear: *Avaritia, id est Diabolus.*[3] This chilling reply is accompanied by a ferocious look, a combination about to be seen in Roland.

Were he not utterly convinced of Roland's imminent death and were his decision to accept it not so final, Charles would never level such a charge. His ire is not to be mistaken for mere frustration: It is the anger of the righteous. The scene, which in the preceding laisses focused on Charlemagne, now shifts dramatically to Roland.

It is important to read the following laisses cumulatively and not as a passage intended to provide logical progression or simple contrast.[4] Roland's reaction to being volunteered for the rearguard and to Ganelon's spiteful words and deeds is understandably one of anger (v. 762: Ireement; v. 777: irascut).[5] The hero nevertheless remains cool. He maintains a proud mien and is able to confront the villain, whose apparent triumph will turn out to be hollow.

Roland phrases his reply carefully, thanking his stepfather for the honor of leading the rearguard, the most dangerous position and, consequently, the one requiring the bravest men when an army is withdrawing from enemy territory.[6] He quickly makes it clear that Charles can now be absolutely sure of the most vigorous kind of protective action.[7]

Chivalry implied a certain civility in most circumstances, but it never excluded the well-turned insult when merited.[8] Mincing no words, Roland reminds Ganelon that he nervously allowed the staff, which Charles was handing him, to fall to the ground. You can be sure, he asserts with finality, that I won't be guilty of such timidity.

Ganelon's response (v. 760) is open to various interpretations. It is tempting to see in the expression "You speak the truth, I'm sure," an admission of defeat and even a grudging admiration for his stepson's remarkable courage in the face of great danger. However, it seems more in keeping with Ganelon's evil character to assume that this reply is made in a sarcastic tone of voice.[9]

Throughout this episode, and not infrequently afterward, Charles weeps profusely. The Emperor's overwhelming grief is not a sign of weakness or merely a classical reminiscence. The public shedding of tears by men would later be regarded as unseemly, but this is not true for the Middle Ages, when mention of weeping could be expected to evoke corresponding emotions from the audience.[10]

Naimes now intervenes in an interesting fashion.[11] Common sense calls for compromise here in order to enable the antagonists to save face. Charles has still not made the decisive move of handing over the bow, symbolic of command,[12] to his nephew. The Emperor turns to his trusted and resourceful adviser. What's done is done, Naimes says. Give Roland the bow . . . but also plenty of companions! Naimes's proposal is excellent, for what purpose would be served by needlessly risking the life of the Emperor's stalwart leader? There is, moreover, the very real possibility of treachery. As anyone can plainly see, this may be Ganelon's last chance to settle old scores and recent provocations.

Naimes should have known better. In Roland's eyes Charles's offer of half his army, well-meaning though it may be, lessens the honor attached to this undertaking, and the hero will hear nothing of it.[13] Charles makes the offer anyway, but understanding his nephew only too well and being fully conscious of the fact that events must run their tragic course, he does not insist too strongly. His use of the word *salvement* is a final, desperate signal to Roland, but the hero does not or will not heed it. At least Charles has the satisfaction of knowing that he has enhanced his nephew's reputation. Finally, on a symbolic level, Roland's gesture in turning down the Emperor is reminiscent of David refusing Saul's armor before his encounter with Goliath (1 Samuel 17:38–40).[14]

What follows is a scene that bears a certain similarity to Ganelon's departure for Saragossa in Laisse 27 and may have been designed to contrast sharply with that tearful leave-taking. Once again, one finds a central figure, mounted on his war-horse (vv. 347, 792), surrounded by well-wishers. However, there are no tears now, no sad farewells, although the situation is plainly as dangerous as Ganelon's mission to Saragossa.[15] What impresses the audience is the quiet determination and the unquestioning loyalty and devotion of Roland's companions to their leader, as one by one the French Peers, headed by Oliver, come to the hero's side.

As Roland gives his orders to Gautier de l'Hum, who acknowledges them,[16] mention is made of some of the same reasons the hero will give to Oliver for not sounding the oliphant:

804 France, nostre tere (cf. 1090: France).

806 l'emperere (cf. 1092: l'emperere).

807 Pur vos (cf. 1054, mun los).

Throughout history, love of king, country, and family, and notions of honor and loyalty to one's comrades, have figured prominently in appeals to courage in the face of danger. God is not specifically mentioned here, but in the present context *France* and *emperere* are highly affective terms signifying all that Roland and his men hold dear, values that include, notably, Christian beliefs and ideals.[17]

Gautier and a thousand Frenchmen are ordered to hold the heights and mountain passes. The poet names the Saracen king (Almaris del regne de Belferne), who will attack them that very day, but the king is not mentioned again in the poem. However, Gautier will make an unexpected appearance shortly before Roland expires.

Halt sunt li pui e li val tenebrus, / Les roches bises, les destreiz merveillus (vv. 814–815) is the first use of a refrain that recurs several times in various forms until Roland's death (INTRODUCTION, 16, A).[18] It is an extremely effective rhetorical device suggesting, rather than describing, the wild mountain locale and shrouding the events about to transpire in an aura of anguish, fear, and mystery. The repeated use here and elsewhere of words in *-us* and *-ur* is a major factor contributing to the ominous tone of this part of the *Song of Roland*,[19] and the poet skillfully implies that the natural surroundings are unwitting conspirators against the Franks. The most frequent pattern is the initial hemistich *Halt sunt li pui*, underscoring the theme of noble aspiration and painful ascent.[20]

While the rearguard is still slowly wending its way through the dangerous defiles, the vanguard of the Franks is descending the other side of the Pyrenees, where they see France stretching below. After years of hard campaigning, during which they have had to put such thoughts behind them, Charles's men, suddenly reminded of their homes and families, weep for joy.[21] The Franks' eagerness to rejoin their women seems genuine. However, medieval attitudes toward women must be borne in mind, lest this relationship be oversentimentalized.[22]

Charlemagne is moved to tears for a different reason: He knows he must suffer a tremendous loss before the day is over.[23] After vainly trying to hide his anguish under his cape (v. 830), he reveals his secret to Naimes. Men have always been prone to have reservations about other men's dreams. Whether this is the case now, or whether Naimes is struck dumb by the enormity of his miscalculation of Marsile's intentions, one cannot say for sure. At any rate, Naimes will remember this revelation when he urges Charles not to listen to Ganelon's promptings and rush to Roland's side (Laisse 135). Only then will he begin to grasp the full import of Charles's words concerning the betrayal (COMMENTARY, 19, v. 1792) and perhaps also the profound significance of the equation France = Roland = lance (cf. COMMENTARY, 14).

Determined to relive Abraham's agony, Charles has resolutely borne his sorrow, but now he approaches a crisis. His profuse weeping and his confession to Naimes indicate that he has reached a breaking point, but it is his last sentence that expresses most clearly the depths of his despair: "*Deus! se jol pert, ja n'en avrai escange!*" (v. 840).

If he loses him? Is Charles on the verge of refusing to play the role that has been thrust upon him by a relentless God? Is the Emperor about to take whatever steps may be necessary to save his nephew? No. When the poet ascribes these words to Charles, he has an altogether different purpose in mind. He is not suggesting that Charles may fail to live up to what God expects of him. Instead, Turoldus is drawing a parallel with Christ's agony in the Garden: "My Father, if it is possible, let this cup pass me by."[24] Charles, like Christ at Gethsemane, says "if." The point, of course—and Turoldus is too great an artist to make the parallel any more explicit than he already has—is that Christ immediately went on to say: "Nevertheless, let it be as you, not I, would have it."

"Laisse 68 de transition," writes Rychner laconically in his outline of the *Song of Roland*.[25] The recitation has thus far lasted an hour or less and, consequently, no excessive physical demands have been made on the jongleur or his audience.[26] Why, then, does the poet recapitulate at this particular juncture? Perhaps he wishes to build up tension by delaying the progress of the narrative or by emphasizing key points. A brief summary may also be a way for the jongleur to provide essential facts for late arrivals in the audience.[27] More than likely, however, Turoldus simply wishes to shift the scene to Marsile now, and he resorts to a technique consisting of thought-association. This procedure is worth examining in detail:

841 *Charles* is weeping.

842 *The Franks* are moved to tears at the sight of Charles.

843 *Roland* is a cause for great concern.

844 *Ganelon* betrayed him.

845 *Marsile* bribed Ganelon.

If one looks only at the italicized names, one gets the impression that the poet is jumping wildly from one individual to the next. However, each line is adroitly linked to the preceding as well as to the following verse by a common thought:

841–842 tears (and Charles).

842–843 Charles and Roland (and tears).

843–844 Roland and Ganelon (and Charles).

844–845 Ganelon and Marsile (and Roland).

The point of view switches from Charles, suffering from privileged knowledge of Roland's destiny, to the Franks, who can only assume that the Emperor's anguish concerns Roland, then becomes that of the poet reminding the audience of what they are privy to but the Franks do not know.

The Franks could reasonably be expected to piece together the quarrel between Ganelon and Roland, the lavish gifts Ganelon brought back from Saragossa, and the traitor's spiteful nomination of his stepson to the rearguard, and conclude that Charles's tears concern the danger Roland now faces as a result of a possible betrayal. However, ordinary Franks in the *Song of Roland* are not particularly perceptive.[28] They can be roused to fight superbly in pitched battles, but they usually do not show much eagerness for combat. They are, in fact, easily misled by appearances and avoid making hard decisions whenever possible. At most, then, the Franks sense dully that something is amiss and they tremble for Roland. But nothing will be done.

The scene now shifts again from Charles to Marsile. After assembling his army, the pagan king has, by forced marches, positioned his army, one would assume, between the rearguard and the main body of the enemy. However, in v. 1021 Oliver announces that the Saracens are coming from behind or perhaps from the flank (Devers Espaigne).

Turoldus's notions about Mohammedanism are notoriously false and doubtless derive in large measure from stories about pagan cults recounted in the Bible. Medieval artists represented idols as little statues of humans or devils mounted on a pedestal, and this is the formula one finds, for instance, in the sculptures at Angoulême and Chartres, and in a miniature illustrating the Wolfenbüttel manuscript of *Karl der Grosse*.[29] A bovine creature, perhaps stemming from the story of the golden calf in Exodus 32, or intended to depict Astaroth (Astarte), the Phoenician goddess of love associated with Baal, also figures in medieval conceptions of idolatry.[30] In the Heidelberg manuscript of the *Rolandslied* (*Fig. 32*), this is the form of the idol that Ganelon touches with his index finger as he swears to kill Roland.[31] It is also that found in the scene where Bramimonde has the Saracen idols smashed following Marsile's defeat.[32] The pagan Trinity, according to Turoldus—here doubtless intending a parody of the triune God of the Christians—was comprised of Apollo, Mohammed, and Tervagant. In Laisse 68 it is the image of the deified Mohammed, which is raised at Saragossa, and the word for the mosques at Saragossa (v. 3662: *mahumeries*) is derived from his name. Medieval authors, in keeping with biblical custom, at times use the collective name Baal to designate false gods, and the name Baligant may be related to the latter term.[33] Aelroth, whom the reader encounters for the first time in the next laisse but whose name appears only in v. 1188, is perhaps a distortion of Astaroth.[34]

Structurally, the raising of the idol of Mohammed on Saragossa's highest tower, symbolizing the zenith of Saracen hopes in the *Song of Roland*, is part of a frame and marks the beginning of the Battle of Roncevaux. The frame will be completed when the final rout of Baligant's forces is observed from a tower by Bramimonde in the company of her high priests (Laisse 264).[35] Viewing from afar is a device that a great many poets have put to effective use in Old French literature, and its recurrence is an excellent example of *rhétorique coutumière*.[36] The spectacle before Bramimonde's eyes is perhaps the most striking instance of this technique in the poem, but vision and, above all, other perceptions of reality are repeatedly underscored in Turoldus's epic. The passage under consideration affords us a good example. To emphasize the proximity of the two armies but also the fact that the Saracens, for the moment, are keeping a safe distance, Turoldus describes the pagan forces as riding hard through valleys and over mountains until they spy from afar the banners of the French.

12. The Saracen Oaths

Laisses 69–78 (verses 860–993)

Fifteen thousand years ago in the Dordogne region of southwestern France, a tribe of primitive men gathered in a deep cave in what is now known as Lascaux to perform a ritual not unlike that which one witnesses in the next few laisses of the *Song of Roland*.[1] The walls at Lascaux are covered with paintings of bisons, bulls, stags, and other animals, and a strange assortment of spearlike lines, patterns of dots, and mysterious objects resembling rakes and checkerboards, all in vivid reds and blacks. In a pit several yards deep is to be found the most singular scene of all: A huge, crudely drawn bison appears to be charging a man, who is lying on his back. A staff surmounted by a stylized bird appears at his side.

The prehistoric men who painted these scenes by torchlight were hunters, and the drawings were a ritualistic enactment of kills they hoped to make. The mysterious objects were probably intended to represent traps and some of the spears are shown piercing the animals' bodies. The significance of the bison attacking the prostrate man is obscure, but the bird-staff is plainly connected with a ceremony designed to cast a spell on the animals or to ward off evil.

The Saracen boasts and oaths unconsciously imitate rituals that have taken place since the beginning of time and which are performed even today among primitive peoples.

Prehunt or prebattle rituals of this sort stimulate individuals and the group to a fever of excitement—in v. 992, 100,000 Saracens are said to be burning to fight, thereby enhancing the prospects of peak performance culminating in a successful endeavor. Less obvious but of equal importance is the fact that incantations and symbolic enactments are felt to actually *cause* the event to happen.

This incantatory and diabolical rite stands out in sharp contrast to the manner in which the Franks will muster their courage for battle, notably as they kneel to receive Turpin's absolution and solemn benediction.[2] An effort should be made to reconstruct the sights and sounds of the tumultuous pagan scene the way the poet visualized it.

Turoldus does not specifically state that the Saracen oath-taking occurs at night, but it fits here chronologically (see COMMENTARY, 9, outline of Day 5), suits the needs of ritual (like the somber cave at Lascaux), and serves as a grisly counterpoint to Charles's fitful dreaming.[3]

The scene involves a good deal of movement. It is not clear whether Marsile is on horseback, standing, or seated on a throne; however, he is a figure exerting a kind of centripetal force as the Saracen leaders, all mounted,[4] gallop toward him from all directions and remain crowded around him. The movement of the mounted Saracens and the bunching together in front of Marsile are indicated in the following verses:

860 Li niés Marsilie, il est *venuz avant*,
Sur un mulet, od un bastun tuchant.

885 Reis Corsalis, il est de *l'altre part.*

889 As vos *poignant* Malprimis de Brigant.

900 *Devant Marsilie* cil en est escriet.

911 *Devant Marsilie* ad faite sa vantance.

916 *D'altre part* est Turgis de Turteluse.

919 *Devant Marsilie as altres si s'ajustet.*

931 *De l'atre part* est Escremiz de Valterne.

933 *Devant Marsilie* s'escriet *en la presse.*

940 *D'altre part* est uns paiens, Esturganz.

943 Ço dist Marsilie: "Seignurs, *venez avant*!"

955 *Curant* i vint Margariz de Sibilie.

961 *Vint en la presse*, sur les altres s'escriet.

975 *De l'altre part* est Chernubles de Munigre.

The forward movement is symbolical, for it demonstrates the Saracens' enthusiastic response to Marsile's call to action and appeal for volunteers to lead his army:

943 Ço dist Marsilie: "Seignurs, venez avant!
En Rencesvals irez as porz passant,
Si aiderez a cunduire ma gent."

Throughout this wild ceremony, which involves boisterous shouting and laughing (v. 862: Dist a sun uncle belement en riant; v. 891: cil s'escriet mult halt; v. 900: cil en est escriet; v. 933: s'escriet en la presse; v. 961: sur les altres s'escriet), a dialogue is taking place between Marsile and his chieftains. Marsile's men do most of the talking, but two-way communication is indicated at several points: in Laisses 69–70 a gauntlet is given and received; in Laisses 72 and 76 there is a verbal exchange; in Laisse 77 Marsile acknowledges an oath with a deep bow. The scene is one of mutual exhortation, and the Saracens' words stress solidarity (v. 881: e jo e vos irum; v. 920: Ne vos esmaiez unches! v. 922: l'onur del camp ert nostre; v. 949: Noz espees; v. 950: Nus les feruns; v. 962: Ne vos esmaiez mie!), a conviction that the outcome will be a favorable one for their side, and comradely rivalry to seek out and find Roland and the Twelve Peers—and to strike the mightiest blows.

At one point (v. 911), Turoldus characterizes a Saracen's words as a *vantance*, and what the pagans say here is customarily referred to as a *gab* 'boast'. Boasting is generally disapproved of today,[5] and we expect our heroes to affect modesty; but in the Middle Ages it was a way of committing oneself totally, for, if the deed was not accomplished, one's reputation suffered. Also, as in the case of Roland at Cordres (COMMENTARY, 4), Aelroth's boasting in vv. 863–865 is a way of commanding attention and respect before requesting a boon.

The boasting in this scene, however, is of secondary importance; the blood-oaths are far more significant. Foulet's translation of *male vode* in v. 918 (*Glossaire*, p. 499: "L'expression *male vode* [< *mala vota*] signifie originairement 'souhaits de malheur' [Bédier translates *De chrestïens voelt faire male vode* as "Aux Chrétiens il souhaite male mort"], mais a fini par prendre le sens de 'calamité', 'ruine', 'carnage': 'carnage' serait le mot juste au v. 918") loses sight of the fact that, one after another, the Saracens make a formal pledge before witnesses ("Jo vos plevis," says Margariz in v. 968).[6]

The vows are diverse, but a number of elements recur, chief among which is the notion of killing[7] (Roland seven times [vv. 866, 893, 902, 914, 923, 935, 963], the French six times, the Twelve Peers four times, Oliver three times, and the rearguard once); going to Roncevaux (eight times);[8] and finding Roland (five times).[9] Repetitions of the name Roland here function as a kind of incantation. The Saracens seem to invoke infernal aid to destroy him.

In vv. 877–878 Aelroth asks his uncle Marsile to select twelve Saracen barons to fight the French Peers.[10] It is significant that the Saracens vow to kill Roland *if* they find him (vv. 893, 902: Se truis Rollant; vv. 914, 935, 986: Se trois Rollant). Identifying the French leader may indeed be a problem (see COMMENTARY, 15), but such hedging may also be a sign of cowardice.

Mentioning the sword, as the Saracens do repeatedly here, gave the jongleur an opportunity to execute a fierce brandishing or a slashing gesture. However, it was customary to swear an oath on a sword, which is shaped like a cross, and the passage suggests the aping of a Christian practice.[11] Such an interpretation adds a new dimension to what is doubtless the main reason for introducing the sword toward the end of the oath-taking ritual; namely, adding horror to the scene. The sword is repeatedly associated with blood (v. 950: Nus les feruns vermeilles de chald sanc; v. 968: en vermeill sanc ert mise; v. 985: jo la teindrai vermeille).[12] Aelroth's laughter,[13] the prayer to Mahomet, the mention of black arts and of Munigre (an accursed land where the sun does not shine, wheat does not grow, rain does not fall, dew does not form, where all stones are black, and where some say devils reside), the idea of laying waste to France and of the Saracens sleeping in Saint-Denis, the place the French hold most sacred,[14] and repairing to a secluded pine grove immediately after the oaths, add to the sinister aspect of this passage.[15]

Each laisse focuses on one or two of the Twelve Saracen Peers, who are matched against the French Peers. Aelroth, Marsile's nephew, who will only be identified in v. 1188 (not naming an individual in this sort of enumeration is a way of centering attention on him[16]) is Roland's counterpart, just as the Saracen king corresponds to Charlemagne. Turoldus individualizes, to a certain extent, the Saracen Peers by giving them evil-sounding names and by providing biographical information or details about physical appearance. Further particulars are added beginning with Laisse 93. Aelroth is probably derived from the name of the Egyptian goddess Astaroth.[17] Escremiz, Estramariz, and Esturganz are names formed with the same initial syllable, recalling *Espaigne*. Falsaron and Malprimes contain epithets meaning 'false' (i.e., false religion) and 'evil'.[18] Turoldus is particularly fond of associating Saracens with wrongdoing, other pagans being named Malbien (v. 67), Malcud (v. 1551), Malduit (v. 642), Malpalin (v. 2995), Malquiant (v. 1551), Maltraien (v. 2671), and Malun (v. 1353). Baligant's spear is called Maltet (v. 3152), and giants from Malpreis (v. 3285) and Malprose (v. 3253) appear in the third and tenth squadrons of Baligant's army. Finally, Margariz may be the same as OFr. *margari*, attested in the meaning 'apostate' in the epic *Gormont et Isembart*.[19]

One of Turoldus's favorite clichés is to associate each Saracen, as he is being introduced, with a homeland, a fief, or a relative. An analogous technique is mentioned in the Introduction.[20]

Two seemingly contradictory elements appear in the descriptions of the Saracens here and elsewhere in the poem: They are either *felun* (vv. 910, 942, 1216), *glutun* (v. 1251), *traïtur suduiant* (v. 942)—terms roughly synonymous in the present context—skilled in the black arts (v. 886), have a broad forehead (v. 1217–1218), that is, all bad qualities,[21] or they are brave (vv. 887–888, 898), fair of face and body (vv. 895, 957, 1312),[22] fierce (vv. 875, 895, 897), fleet of foot (vv. 890, 1312), laughing (v. 862), and strong (v. 1313), seemingly favorable attributes. Considering the widespread misogyny of the Middle Ages, designating someone as a ladies' man is not necessarily flattering,[23] yet in his sketch of Margariz, the individual in question, Turoldus uses the term *chevalerie* (v. 960), which refers to all the virtues desirable in a knight.

The adversary must be made to appear formidable or worthy in order to enhance the hero's ultimate triumph. However, such an approach does not adequately explain Turoldus's apparent partiality to certain Saracens. What is also involved here is the concept of the lying exterior.[24] Turoldus is not simply resorting to stereotypes, and even less is he drawing a distinction between good Saracens and bad. All pagans are intrinsically evil and, when the poet affirms in v. 899: *Fust chrestïens, asez oüst barnet* ('If he were a Christian, he would be a very worthy knight'),[25] the disclaimer contains no tinge of wistfulness. It expresses nothing less than complete and utter condemnation.

13. The French Prepare for Battle

Laisses 79–82 (verses 994–1048)

The arming of the Saracens in Laisse 79 is an epic cliché and serves to heighten tension immediately before the battle begins.[1] The pagan army, after having lain in ambush all night, now shows itself in a fashion calculated to strike fear in the hearts of the French. The oath-taking scene was loud, but, as the army advances in the bright sunlight, the din of the thousand Saracen trumpets becomes deafening.[2]

The reverberation of a horn will play a key role in a later passage of the *Song of Roland*. The blasts of the pagan bugles and of the oliphant function as a frame within a frame, towers marking the outer limits of the battle scenes (COMMENTARY, 11). A trumpet sound also serves here and elsewhere in the poem to shift the scene from one opposing army to the other. The Saracen clarion call is characterized as *bel* 'beautiful', and so it must appear to the pagans who are emboldened by it and to the poet, too, for one senses Turoldus's undisguised excitement as he visualizes the Muslims moving forward in close array to meet the enemy. To the startled French, however, the trumpets' pealing is no doubt shrill and terrifying. In retrospect the echoing of the Saracen trumpets will seem jarring and discordant as compared to the haunting and portentous sound of Roland's oliphant.

It is possible to interpret what ensues literally, that is, to follow Oliver up and down the mountainside twice and note a certain evolution in his reaction. However, as in other laisses similaires, it is better to consider Laisses 80–82 as an entity, for an overall impression supersedes logical development here. There is progression, to be sure, in that the poet indicates that the French hear (Laisse 79), then, through Oliver's eyes, view (Laisses 80–82) the advancing army. However, reading the entire passage as a unit reveals a crucial preliminary and general reaction on the part of the French, including Oliver.

It is a surprisingly calm and courageous stance, as expressed, notably, in the remarkable understatement:[3]

> 1006 Dist Oliver: "Sire cumpainz, ce crei,
> De Sarrazins purum bataille aveir."

In no way do Oliver and the French panic or seem unduly distressed.[4] Oliver experiences bewilderment and consternation (v. 1036: E[5] lui meïsme en est mult esguaret), but *esguaret* here is close to its etymological sense of having lost one's bearings, usually momentarily. It is a world apart from the meaning *égaré* can have in Modern French: distraught, even deranged, frenzied, or wild. Bédier's translation ('grandement troublé') was no doubt carefully considered, but it conveys more fear than the poet intended. On the other hand, the French scholar is in error when he renders *irur* in v. 1023 as 'grande angoisse' ("Icist ferunt nos Franceis grant irur"), for, as Jones has shown, *irur* means anger.[6] Oliver's mental attitude can best be characterized as sudden realization that a battle is about to take place. His first reaction is to utter a stirring and prayerful exhortation to the French to stand firm:

> 1044 "Bataille avrez, unches mais tel ne fut.
> Seignurs Franceis, de Deu aiez vertut!
> El camp estez, que ne seium vencuz!"

The French do not disappoint him as they echo his courageous words:

> 1047 Dient Franceis: "Dehet ait ki s'en fuit!
> Ja pur murir ne vus en faldrat uns." AOI.

In fact, the strongest emotion expressed in this passage is one of hatred for Ganelon as the scales fall from Oliver's eyes:

> 1024 "Guenes le sout, li fel, li traïtur,
> Ki nus jugat devant l'empereür."

Roland's response to this accusation is not, as is sometimes stated, one of disbelief or stubborn loyalty to his stepfather.[7] His true feelings will be revealed in Laisse 90, and there is no reason to suppose that he has learned anything new or has changed in the interim. The hero's words are in keeping with the contempt he expressed earlier for Ganelon's proposed abandonment of the siege of Saragossa and, later, for his craven behavior when selected to carry Charles's message to Marsile. Roland simply says he cannot bear to hear his stepfather's name mentioned again. It is interesting to compare the intuition that the two companions-in-arms have of Ganelon's betrayal, which can be nothing more than an educated guess, with Charles's apprehension of the same event through divine revelation.

Oliver instinctively implores God's strength (v. 1045: vertut) for the French so they will not suffer ignominious defeat at the hands of the Saracens. It is Roland, however, whose clear-ringing initial reaction to the prospect of battle with the Infidel is most significant in this passage: "E Deus la nus otreit!" (v. 1008). Oliver steadfastly faces up to the Saracen threat and appeals for divine assistance, whereas Roland prays God for an opportunity to serve Him.

Many critics have failed to grasp the profound meaning of this crucial invocation. Roland, they say, is quite prepared to die for Charlemagne (v. 1009: "pur nostre rei") and seems to be primarily driven by a desire to protect his good name (v. 1014: "Que malvaise cançun de nus chantet ne seit!"; v. 1016: "Malvaise essample n'en serat ja de mei"). These sentiments are not Christian, they insist. They stem, rather, from a sense of feudal obligation to a sovereign lord[8] and betray the outlook of a pagan shame culture.[9]

It is difficult for someone living in the twentieth century to equate these things, but, for Turoldus and the men of his time, Emperor and God are one and the same notion.[10] When Roland says the French must be prepared to suffer everything in the King's name, he means literally that Christians must be willing to face death in God's name.[11] Charles's cause is God's cause and the Spanish campaign is a holy war. In Turoldus's poem Election is embodied in the figure of Charlemagne.[12] If added proof is needed of the symbolic significance of Roland's exhortation,[13] one need only consider the fact that the hero's speech echoes almost word for word a passage in the *Gesta Francorum*, where hardships are endured by the Crusaders for Christ's sake:

> Fratres, nos oportet multa pati pro nomine Christi, videlicet miserias, paupertates, nuditates, persecutiones, egestates, infirmitates, fames, sites et alia huiusmodi.[14]

In the *Pseudo-Turpin Chronicle* hunger, thirst, and other physical suffering borne in Christ's name appear, significantly, in Roland's dying prayer:

> Domine Ihesu Christe, pro cuius fide patriam meam dimisi in hisque barbaris horis ad exaltandam christianitatem tuam veni, multa

> perfidorum bella, tuo munitus auxilio devici innumeras alapas, ruinas, vulnera multa, opprobria, irrisiones, fatigaciones, calores, frigora, famem, sitim, anxietates pertuli, tibi in hac hora commendo animam meam.[15]

The source of this idea is a passage in which Saint Paul relates his sufferings *in labore et aerumna, in vigiliis multis, in fame et siti.*[16] The theme appears frequently in medieval devotional literature.[17] In the *Song of Roland* it is an excellent example of the transposition of a formula with virtually all the content of the original being carried over (INTRODUCTION, 12).

The phrase "*Paien unt tort e chrestïens unt dreit*" (v. 1015) has been deliberately inserted by Turoldus at this juncture in order to drive home this point.[18] The Christian religion has been mentioned several times thus far in the *Song of Roland*, and it has nearly always been related to the Theme of Conversion (vv. 38, 85, 102, 155, 190, 431, 471, 686).[19] But v. 1015 marks an important turning point in the narrative. It is the first time the hero refers to the French not by their nationality but by their nobler designation, Christian.

14. The Prebattle Debate

Laisses 83–92 (verses 1049–1187)

The dialogue between Roland and Oliver, which began in Laisse 79 but now becomes a heated debate, has caused more ink to be spilled than any other single episode in Turoldus's epic.[1] Bédier considered that the poem was born when Turoldus hit upon the idea of opposing two characters in a crucial scene, the one representing audacity, courage, valor, the other discretion, prudence, reserve.[2] It is without a doubt the debate's "Cornelian" aspect that has cast it in the limelight.[3] This focusing of critical attention has been unfortunate. The passage is certainly charged with emotion—the debate device accomplishes this—but whether or not Oliver will succeed in winning Roland over to his point of view is simply not the pivot on which the whole poem turns. As stated in the Introduction, the central meaning and related themes and metaphors of the *Song of Roland* have to do with other concerns. Roland's decision is a crucial one, but it is never in doubt.

Was Roland right to insist on fighting the enemy without calling Charlemagne, or should he have heeded Oliver's commonsense advice?[4] Bédier felt that Turoldus was unable to choose between the two, yet the French scholar described Roland's silence at the conclusion of the argument (Laisse 131) as ambiguous and sublime.[5] Many critics have not agreed with Bédier's view and have argued that the context makes it clear which protagonist he favors. A case for either side can certainly be made, but to justify only Roland is to neglect the poignant human tragedy; to vindicate only Oliver is to deny the poem's sublime spirituality. It is inconceivable that Turoldus viewed the hero's fateful decision as a mere tactical error or, worse, as a sin. The injection of *fortitudo et sapientia* into this discussion has only clouded the issue.[6] Roland's grace under pressure—not the style referred to in Hemingway's definition of courage, but the charisma mentioned by Saint Paul[7]—gives him the power to act decisively and unhesitatingly in his greatest crisis. Whatever emotion he may feel, whatever common sense he may have, is hidden behind a mask of imperturbability that Oliver finds infuriating. Be that as it may, Roland makes his choice and it is manifestly and wholeheartedly approved by Turoldus.

Before proceeding any further, some simple facts need to be clearly understood. First of all, the debate is in two scenes: The first immediately precedes the battle, the second takes place just prior to the final Saracen assault.[8] The two-part debate is a private one, but in each instance a third person, Archbishop Turpin, intervenes. The scenes are part of the parallel structure of the poem. Roland's argument for not sounding the oliphant[9] in the initial encounter is turned back upon the hero by Oliver in the ensuing discussion.[10] Finally, while the debate involves a psychological confrontation and presents opposing analyses of the military situation, one must above all not lose sight of its spiritual significance. In other words, discussion cannot simply be limited to the consequences of Roland's decision insofar as winning or losing the battle against the pagans is concerned, but the religious meaning Turoldus intended it to have must also be considered.

Debating was one of the methods devised by the ancients for training orators and lawyers, and in the Middle Ages the *altercatio* or *disputatio* assumed a very great importance in the schools as a means of testing knowledge and developing rhetorical skills.[11] Public disputation between Christians and pagans and between Christians and Jews is widely attested in historical sources.[12] Its literary manifestation appears frequently in the saints' lives. The future martyr engages his persecutor in a debate over the relative merits of the Christian versus the pagan religions and invariably wins the argument hands down.[13] There are two such *disputationes* in a source very close to the *Song of Roland.* In the *Pseudo-Turpin Chronicle* Charlemagne engages the African king Aigolandus, who had invaded Spain, in a theological debate, and Roland vanquishes the Saracen giant Ferracutus in a similar discussion.[14] The fact that these debates both take place on the battlefield is an important point of contact with the Roland-Oliver exchange.

The debate was a popular literary genre in its own right. There were first of all, debates in which right triumphs over wrong. Ambrose of Autpert's *De Conflictu Vitiorum et Virtutum* (c. 778), a *psychomachia* in which twenty-four vices dispute an equal number of virtues, is a model of the type.[15] In sharp contrast with this sort of text where the author clearly takes sides, one finds works such as the twelfth-century *Altercatio Phyllidis et Florae*, which involves a dilemma, the poet giving equally defensible arguments to each debater.[16] The most celebrated of these exercises in the casuistry of love was the *Débat du Clerc et du Chevalier.*[17] Abelard utilized a similar principle in his *Sic et Non* (c. 1122), a treatise presenting in systematic fashion seemingly contradictory passages from Scripture and the Church Fathers relative to 157 theological questions.[18] In regard to circumstances, then, the debate between Roland and Oliver is an interlude between battles, resembling the *disputatio* in the *Pseudo-Turpin.* However, the arguments themselves participate in the tradition of the *Débat du Clerc et du Chevalier* and the *Sic et Non.*

Considered as a whole, Laisse 87 clearly refers to the second type of debate. Turoldus repeatedly stresses the fact that the two companions-in-arms are equally worthy:[19]

> 1093 Rollant est proz e Oliver est sage:
> Ambedui unt meveillus vasselage,
> Puis que il sunt as chevals e as armes,
> Ja pur murir n'eschiverunt bataille;
> Bon sunt li cunte e lur paroles haltes.

At first glance v. 1093 would appear to militate against such an interpretation, for the line has been assumed to mean 'Roland is brave but Oliver is wise'. If this translation were correct, the natural inclination would be to favor Oliver. However, the two parts of this sentence are not linked by the conjunction *mais* 'but', which is what one might expect if the poet had a sharp contrast in mind.[20] The conjunction *e* 'and' implies quite the opposite. It indicates that what is being compared in the two hemistichs is identical.

The crux of the matter resides in the word *proz*.[21] If one leaves aside the many meanings of *prod* when used as a substantive or as an adverb,[22] what connotation does this term have when it functions as an adjective referring to a person? As its etymology, which is linked to the notion of utility, suggests, the basic meaning of OFr. *prod* is 'worthy'.[23]

There is no evidence to support the contention that, primitively, *prod* referred exclusively to physical courage, and only later, about 1150, under the influence of courtly ideals, did it begin to denote intellectual traits too.[24] Turoldus uses the term in both senses. When a knight in the *Song of Roland* is *prod*, he is worthy, that is, he is brave, loyal, pious, trustworthy, or wise, depending on the circumstances, but usually he possesses *all* these qualities.[25] However, it is also true that *prod* often points to one quality or another according to the needs of a particular moment. Thus in vv. 576, 2905, 3180, and 3186,[26] where the epithet appears in a neutral context, *prod* conveys the notion of general worthiness, but in vv. 1441, 3546, and 3915, which occur in battle scenes, the word underscores the character's strength and valor.[27]

On the other hand—and this is the key to v. 1093—a man could hardly be considered excellent without being intelligent, so *prod*, in the *Song of Roland*, comes naturally to refer to a person's wisdom:[28]

172 E de Gascuigne li proz quens Acelin.
176 E Oliver, li proz e li gentilz.

These verses appear in Laisse 12, where the Emperor has just summoned Acelin and Oliver to a council (vv. 166, 169). In this circumstance Charles will need good advice rather than valor, although one need not exclude the other. Ideally, the two go hand in hand.[29]

In short, far from contrasting Oliver's wisdom with Roland's valor, Turoldus, in v. 1093, lauds both knights as being equally worthy, that is, *prod* and *sage*. Here as in v. 3691 (E l'arcevesque, ki fu sages e proz), the epithets are plainly synonymous.[30] Oliver maintains that in the face of a vastly more numerous enemy the oliphant must immediately be sounded to bring Charles and the main body of the army to the rescue. Roland counters that the French must make a stand here and now, and at all costs, in order to uphold Christianity.

Like Abelard, Turoldus presents a dilemma, and either solution, viewed in purely human terms, is equally unsatisfactory.[31] But, as in the *Sic et Non*, the dilemma is only an apparent one, for, considered from the perspective of Eternity, upholding Christianity is far superior an alternative to merely surviving.

Earlier, in Laisse 82, Oliver urged the French to stand firm. Roland's speeches in the ensuing passage are an extension of his companion's initial posture. Turoldus utilizes the debate device to underscore the agony of Roland's decision. Seething with excitement, he is nonetheless inwardly torn by strife. The artifice of the *disputatio*, whether, as here, it involves two individuals, or, as in Chrétien's *Charrette*, an internal dialogue between Love and Reason,[32] tends to put off modern readers. In Turoldus's day the coventional debate was evidently capable of conveying far greater emotion than it does today.

Oliver is not afraid of dying. He simply believes that a lonely stand by the rearguard against overwhelming odds would be pointless. His statements in this phase of the debate are brief, but it is fair to assume that he feels the destruction of the rearguard will weaken the Franks to such an extent that, at the very least, the fruits of the entire campaign will be lost. What is more, the Empire itself may fall prey to the Saracens. His argument unwittingly parallels that of Ganelon, who was able to persuade Marsile that if Roland were to be destroyed, Charles would become powerless.[33]

Roland considers that calling for help would have even more disastrous effects. His thinking is not expressly detailed either, but the consequences he is determined to avert appear to be twofold. Sounding the oliphant would be an open concession by the French that they cannot cope with the situation, an avowal certain to buoy up the Saracens' hopes and give them a psychological advantage.[34] It would also be a catastrophic blow to the French army's morale, which, presumably, has never been subjected to such behavior on the part of their hero.[35]

Once again, laisses similaires are involved. Consequently it would be a mistake to try to discern much logical development here.[36] The thrice-repeated plea "*Cumpaign Rollant, kar sunez vostre corn*" (v. 1051 with slight variants in vv. 1059 and 1070) has cast a spell on critics. Trinary patterns abound in the *Song of Roland*, but their importance and possible symbolic significance should not be exaggerated here.

The passage consists of a reiterated plea by Oliver, on the one hand, and a stubborn ticking off of reasons why not by Roland, on the other. Oliver's appeal is a simple variation on the theme: They are many, we are few.[37] Roland's answers contain an argument and an oath. The oath (vv. 1058, 1069; cf. v. 1072), with its fixation on the sword Durendal dripping with Saracen blood, echoes the blood-oaths of the pagans (COMMENTARY, 12).

As for Roland's argument, the importance *mun los* (v. 1054) assumes by virtue of being cited first troubles many who are influenced by modern values, which tend to interpret great concern for personal reputation as selfish and prideful. This view, however, assumes that *los* has only one meaning in this passage.[38] Actually, Roland rings the changes on this concept. For him family (vv. 1063, 1076), France (vv. 1064, 1090), and Emperor (v. 1092) are inextricably intertwined with the idea of personal pride. In identical fashion Charles, too, made no distinction between Roland and France (COMMENTARY, 11, v. 835). Defining what it is he is willing to die for, the hero offers a litany of things he holds dear. The word *los* sums up all these values. If one remembers that in Turoldus's poem Emperor means God,[39] and if one bears in mind, too, that Roland repeatedly invokes the Deity in this passage (vv. 1062, 1073, 1089), it becomes apparent that the hero refuses to sound the oliphant out of a sense of duty to uphold Christianity.

There is a strikingly similar fusion of concepts in the *Psychomachia*, when Sobrietas, "mingling appeals with her reproaches to awake their courage" (v. 350: Exstimulans animos nunc probis, nunc preca mixta), addresses her troops:

> State, precor, vestri memores, memores quoque Christi.
> Quae sit vestra tribus, quae gloria, quis Deus et rex,
> Quis Dominus meminisse decet . . .[40]

(Stand, I pray you. Remember who ye are, remember Christ too. Ye should bethink yourselves of your nation and your fame, your God and King, your Lord.)

To fail to grasp that, to Roland's way of thinking, *mun los*, family,[41] France, and Emperor are the equivalent of Christianity, is to miss the entire point of the *Song of Roland*. Oliver's argument is realistic, but Turoldus's epic is a poem designed to edify; it is not a manual of military tactics. Roland's statements may be less practical, but their teleological thrust is unmistakable. To spell it out any more clearly would have done violence to the work's poetic essence.

In the debate Oliver's argument was based on an antithesis concerning the disproportionate size of the two armies: They are many, we are few. In Laisse 87 Roland's companion, having concluded that further discussion would be fruitless, now contrasts distances: The Saracens are near, Charlemagne is far.

The first part of the *Song of Roland* is an arduous ascent, culminating in glory. In vv. 1103–1105 Oliver observes the rearguard wending its way up the mountain side and laments its imminent destruction.[42] One sees, then, that Roland and Oliver are at the tail of the French column protecting Charlemagne, the position offering the greatest danger and therefore involving the greatest honor. When Bramimonde watches from her tower as Baligant's fleeing army approaches Saragossa, she will gaze downward, and her perspective will be the traditional one.[43] The present scene is an effective variation on this tragic viewing and at the same time a poignant use of the poem's symbolic Theme of Ascent. Roland's reply in Laisse 87 echoes Oliver's brave words in Laisse 82; in Laisse 88 the hero repeats the words he spoke in Laisse 79, thus providing a frame for the first debate. The "lord" for whom Roland says one must be prepared to endure all suffering (v. 1117) is Charlemagne, the sovereign of the Franks, but also, as indicated above, the Lord God.[44]

Scholars have usually discussed the companions-in-arms debate in purely worldly terms: Roland insists on the need to safeguard reputations; Oliver counsels prudence. Archbishop Turpin's speech in Laisse 89 is said to provide, for the first time, spiritual significance to the struggle, which is about to commence.[45] However, Roland, too, has been talking about spiritual matters. The most important indication of this thus far is the value that the people of his day attached to the notion of king. Turpin now mounts a pulpitlike hillock and preaches to the Franks, who have gathered before him. His sermon supports the Christian interpretation given here to Roland's words.

We must be prepared to die for our King, says the Archbishop, echoing precisely the religious symbol used by Roland.[46] If a shadow of a doubt remains that the idea of king involves more than a political or feudal connotation, it will immediately be dispelled in the very next sentence, when Turpin implores the French to help sustain Christianity. The Archbishop then states that the Christian soldier girds himself for battle through confession.[47] Thus you will be in the state of grace, he says, and should you be killed, you will die as martyrs and enter directly into Heaven.[48]

It may be useful to discuss briefly the concept of martyrdom expressed in v. 1134. Jenkins records Tavernier's view that this idea is "hardly thinkable before the Council of Clermont." Confession and true contrition were then and continue to be today essential prerequisites for absolution.[49] From the earliest days the Church imposed public penitance, notably for sins of a scandalous nature, but it eventually introduced a system of indulgences in lieu of some of these acts of self-abasement and mortification. In the tenth century the temporal punishment due for sin could be worked off by church construction and pilgrimages to holy places. At the end of the eleventh century participating in a crusade became a new way of remitting punishment.[50] However, Urban II apparently went even further. In his famous speech on 27 November 1095, the Pope exhorted the assembled lords and knights to cease internecine warfare and brigandage and become *milites Christi*.[51] The locution 'soldiers of Christ'[52] had regularly been applied to the early martyrs of the Church, but Urban is believed to have expressly stated that anyone dying in the siege of Jerusalem or even on the way to the Holy Land would in fact be suffering martyrdom and his soul would go to heaven.[53] This was said to be a new way of salvation.[54] Turpin's speech is equally specific and his statement in v. 1138 (Par penitence les cumandet a ferir) should be viewed in the light of these historical circumstances.

In Laisse 91 the hero, astride his war-horse Veillantif, brandishes his lance and twirls the white pennant that decorates its tip against the sky.[55] One readily visualizes the jongleur miming Roland's dramatic pose as he recited this passage. Our eyes, drawn upward by the movement of Roland's lance, perceive the hero in all his glory, his strong body, his smiling face, the pure white banner (INTRODUCTION, 19, F) silhouetted against the heavens as he calmly rides forward to meet his destiny.

Roland's threatening looks toward the Saracens, contrasting sharply with his gazes toward the French, have been identified as a literary commonplace dating back to Greek antiquity.[56] Jones is quite correct when he affirms that the expression *humeles e dulcement* (v. 1163) conveys none of the meekness and modesty generally associated with Christian humility. Mildness of temper would certainly be out of place as the French prepare for battle. The key to this passage is provided by the term *dulcement*, which expresses the affection and quiet confidence Roland feels toward his men at this moment in light of what they have already achieved and can now be expected to accomplish together. A sense of optimism and well-being is reflected in Roland's bright and cheerful expression (v. 1159). The pairing of the adjective *humeles*—

used adverbially here[57]—with *dulcement* indicates that the former term connotes friendly rapport, a meaning also associated with *umeliance* in Benoît de Sainte-Maure's chronicle, dated 1160.[58]

Much has been written about the early evolution of the term *corteis*.[59] Jones asserts that in the *Song of Roland corteis* and its synonym *prod* are devoid of overtones of kindness and imply only strength and courage, the qualities he insists were valued almost exclusively at court at this time.[60] However, it has been seen that *prod* could actually refer to a broad range of knightly virtues including, most significantly, the treasured ability to give sound advice. The use of *curteisement* in v. 1164, to describe the manner in which the hero addresses his men, is a particularly fortunate attestation, then, for, like *humeles e dulcement*, it doubtless suggests brotherly affection.[61] The French equivalent of companionage does not appear in the *Song of Roland*, although the kindred terms *cumpaign*, *cumpaigne*, and *cumpaignie* are frequently found. Yet one can think of no more fitting concept to describe the bond that unites Roland and his men and what is implied by *humeles*, *dulcement*, and *curteisement* in this passage.

Two crucial statements are made just as the French and Saracens collide. Roland, addressing his companions with confidence and devotion born of long association, quietly urges them on, absolutely certain that Right will prevail. *Martyrie*, originally part of the religious vocabulary, means 'massacre' in the present passage. The term may have a sarcastic edge to it here, however, for in Roland's view only Christians can aspire to the privilege of martyrdom.

Léon Gautier and the many translators who followed him, including Bédier, have ascribed an unworthy thought to Roland as he addresses his men. The Oxford version reads: "*Encoi avrum un eschec bel e gent*" (v. 1167), which Gautier translates as: "Le beau butin que nous aurons aujourd'hui!" (Bédier: "Avant ce soir nous aurons gagné un beau et riche butin").[62] The word *eschec* is found only in the Oxford manuscript, but the traditional interpretation is supported by Châteauroux, Venice VII, Paris, and Lyon, which substitute the term *gaaing*. The taking of spoils was a widespread practice during the Middle Ages and great concern was shown about dividing up the booty fairly at the end of a campaign.[63] Soldiers easily lost interest in military operations and often turned to plundering.[64] However, clerks continually castigated these abuses.[65] Filled with thoughts of striking a mighty blow for Christianity and twirling the pure white banner symbolizing the rightness of his cause, Roland appears to sound a jarring note here.

In fact, he does no such thing. OFr. *eschec* does at times reflect its Germanic root (*Schach* 'booty') and that is the meaning in v. 99 of the *Song of Roland*. However, the term had also acquired the sense 'battle' and that is plainly what Roland is thinking about here.[66] The Venice IV redactor evidently anticipated the possibility of this gross misinterpretation, for he substitutes the unambiguous word *çambel* (OFr. *cembel*), indicating that he understood *eschec* here to mean 'battle'.[67] The expression *gent* is used regularly in this poem to refer to violent deeds.[68] "*Gente est nostre bataille*," Oliver will say in v. 1274; "*Colps i ai fait mult genz*," Roland will echo in v. 1712. Turoldus himself will affirm in v. 2099: *Li quens Rollant gentemet se cumbat*. There is definitely a note of eagerness here of course, a relish for battle already found in the hero's initial reaction in Laisse 79. Conrad describes the French advancing as if they had been invited to a banquet.[69]

In the *Song of Roland* the adjective *vaillant* most frequently describes men and often suggests strength and physical courage.[70] However, its etymology parallels that of *prod* and at this time can refer to other notions concerning worth. It is safe to conclude, then, that while the imminent battle to which Roland alludes in v. 1167 will be grand and mighty, the hero has the vision to realize that it will also have tremendous historical consequences: "No king of France ever had such a worthy challenge," he says.[71]

A few fleeting seconds separate Roland's statement from Oliver's (v. 1169: A cez paroles vunt les oz ajustant; v. 1187: Francs e paiens, as les vus ajustez), which comes just before the two armies collide.[72]

The command decision to stand and fight has been made by Roland, but Oliver, who tried in vain to dissuade his companion and leader from such a glorious but suicidal course of action, cannot bring himself to comply without further argument.[73] His statements at this point are usually viewed as bitter (v. 1101: "Vostre olifan, suner vos nel deignastes"), his utterances in the second horn scene as sarcastic. However, this casts Roland's companion in a dubious role. It is more accurate to interpret his statements as those of an old campaigner who likes to complain but who can always be relied upon to do his duty when it is time to fight a battle. This character type is very much in evidence in the literature of both World Wars and was immortalized under Napoleon as the *grognard*. As can be seen here, the tradition goes back much further than the era of the Vieille Garde.

Oliver uses the expression *deignastes* three times when addressing his friend (vv. 1101, 1171, 1716). OFr. *deignier*, like Modern English 'to deign', assumes a lowering of dignity, for example, when it is used in prayers.[74] Here it obviously involves irony or mild derision on the speaker's part. However, Oliver is not implying that Roland is arrogant or full of pride. He is merely suggesting that he considers his companion's moral plane to be too high. For dignity is the essence of the hero's stance. Dignity, like honor, integrity, and nobility, is not to be taken here only in a worldly sense, but as an expression of man's noblest aspiration. It is that spark in man that brings him closest to God.

At any rate, once Oliver has indulged in a final bit of carping about Roland's refusal to sound the oliphant, he promptly shouts his encouragement to the French, reiterating Roland's cry in Laisse 79 and his own in Laisse 82.

The triple allusion to the stirring battle cry *Monjoie* (v. 1179: L'enseigne Carle; v. 1180: sunt Franceis escriet; v. 1181: Munjoie),[75] the poet's exclamation (v. 1183: Deus!), and the vision of the French furiously spurring their steeds (v. 1184),[76] contribute to the mounting excitement. A skillful jongleur doubtless elicited vocal responses from the audience, who, caught up in the spirit of the poem, perhaps joined in, shouting *Monjoie!* individually or as a chorus. The rhetorical question *que fereient il el?* in v. 1185 functions quite effectively as a way of heightening tension.[77]

The question also expresses helplessness on the poet's part before a double fatality. The tragic collision of the two armies is about to occur. Nothing can stop the action now. This is a fatalistic situation, since the French are vastly outnumbered. But it also seems as if the Christian characters become autonomous here, escaping from the poet, who no longer has control over the modalities of their existence.[78] Their wild ride resembles King Theodoric's mad pursuit as depicted in the portal of Saint Zeno at Verona.[79] Suddenly, however, this momentary impression of literary disintegration is arrested by the chilling spectacle of the Saracens, who take the shock of the French charge without fear (v. 1186).

Fragmentation does occur in a sense, however, as the poet shifts now from a panoramic view of converging armies to a series of duels pitting one French knight against a Saracen adversary.[80]

15. *Roncevaux, Part 1*

Laisses 93–104 (verses 1188–1337)

As recreated in Turoldus's imagination, the Battle of Roncevaux consists of four phases:[1] (1) the destruction of the first wave of 100,000 Saracens by the French rearguard, highlighted by the encounter of the Twelve French Peers with the Twelve Saracen Peers,[2] which results in the death of all but one of the latter (only Margariz will escape with his life); (2) the gradual elimination of all but sixty men in the French rearguard by Marsile's second wave, which suffers enormous losses in the process; (3) the death of the remaining French heroes, including Oliver, Turpin, and Roland; (4) the arrival of Charles and the rout of the shattered remnants of Marsile's army.

At first glance the dueling personages in the initial encounter resemble figures in a tediously repetitious Romanesque frieze. Rychner has noted the similarities in these two-man fights.[3] The complete motif consists of the following seven elements, but various combinations appear frequently: (1) spurring one's horse; (2) brandishing the lance;[4] (3) striking; (4) smashing the adversary's shield; (5) piercing his hauberk, or coat of mail; (6) piercing his body with a lance, or, missing him, only scratching him; (7) knocking him off his horse, usually killing him. An important cue as to the outcome of each duel is provided by the fact that the attacker is always the winner. The only exception is Margariz, whose attack on Oliver is thwarted by divine intervention (cf. COMMENTARY, 17).

But to view the first phase of the Battle of Roncevaux in this light is to consider externals only. Such a classification may answer present-day requirements for ordering things and appeal to sensibilities sharpened by the comparative method, but it would not have made sense to a person living in the Middle Ages.

The medieval audience would very likely have associated such duels, especially in the early phase of the battle when Christians systematically vanquish Saracens, with the triumph of the virtues over the vices.[5] In medieval art the portrayal of warriors arrayed against each other can have different meanings, but it usually symbolizes the struggle for man's soul.[6] Turoldus did not model his characters after personages in the *Psychomachia*. However, his recital of the felling of one villain after another by a heroic Christian could not fail to remind medieval audiences of the humbling of Superbia in Prudentius's poem.[7] Among the recurring expressions characterizing the defeat of the Saracens in this passage is *trestorner mort* (vv. 1287, 1357, 1385), which indicates that the slain adversary falls backward as he is unhorsed. The head-downward tumble of the Saracen results from the force of the lance thrust, but the context of a battle between Good and Evil also suggests Pride's fall[8] (*Fig. 44*).

Jenkins itemizes several precedents in classical sources for Aelroth's taunt (notes to vv. 1195 and 1207),[9] the manner of presenting Abisme (note to v. 1470), and Grandoine's fear at the mere sight of Roland (note to v. 1639). Classical influence is quite possible, but the theory of *rhétorique coutumière* is also adequate to explain such stylistic commonplaces.[10] A comparison with the manner in which medieval artists absorbed classical formulas is particularly revealing here. When manuscript illuminators came to depict various scenes in Prudentius's *Psychomachia*, they borrowed from Roman art traditional gestures of address and command and the motifs of trampling on an adversary and of falling off a horse.[11] In the iconography of Prudentius's allegory, as in the narrative art of Turoldus's epic, new content was given to ancient forms.

The Saracen Peers appear here in exactly the same order as in the oath-taking ceremony. Does this series of duels take place before the confronted armies? How is it that the Saracens manage to find their French counterparts?[12] Do the French Peers have some sort of distinguishing armor, shield, pennant, or other device that enables the Saracens to identify them? In contemporary art Saracens are often dressed exactly like Frenchmen, although some artists provide pagans with round shields, Christians with kite-shaped bucklers. In the *Pseudo-Turpin* Roland ties up a Saracen prisoner until he tells him who Marsile is. The latter is identified by round shield and red horse, indicating that medieval authors recognized the problem of ascertaining opponents in combat.[13] Turpin can be visualized with crozier and mitre even in battle, a notion that did not strike the Brindisi artist or the Conrad illustrator as curious.[14] Accepting to lead the rearguard, Roland, in v. 767, requests and presumably receives a bow, the symbol of command.[15] In v. 1157 Roland waves a pure white banner at the tip of his lance. The hero of the *Song of Roland* is never mentioned as bearing the *oriflamme*, Charles's red banner, an honor reserved for Geoffrey of Anjou (vv. 106, 3093).[16] Can the Saracens pick him or any of the French Peers out of the melée?

Actually, in this episode it is the French heroes who, in every case but one, attack the Twelve Saracen Peers. Margariz initiates one clash but has no way of knowing his adversary is Oliver. In at least two instances (Aelroth, v. 1189; Falsaron, v. 1220), a Saracen rides out ahead of his men, making it possible for the French to single out a leader.[17] One of the Saracen chieftains is a king, implying a crown (v. 1235, Corsablix).[18] Others have impressive titles suggesting some distinctive device (v. 1213: duc . . . Falsaron; vv. 894, 1269: amurafles . . . de Balaguez; vv. 909, 1275: almaçurs . . . de Moriane). Still others are distinguishable by their physical appearance: Margariz by his handsome features (mentioned twice, vv. 957, 1312); Chernuble by his long hair reaching to the ground (v. 976). The remainder are probably very ugly or terrifying.

The exchange of insults between Aelroth and Roland is an extension of the battlefield debate between Oliver and his companion-in-arms.[19] Three of the reasons given by the hero for not sounding the oliphant are echoed here: sweet France's good name (vv. 1064, 1090 = v. 1194), that of the Emperor (v. 1009 = v. 1193), and that of Roland himself, here symbolized as Charlemagne's right arm (v. 1054 = v. 1195).[20] The highly emotional vocabulary of insult is also reiterated: *felun* (v. 1057 = v. 1191), *fol* (v. 1053 = v. 1193). There is also the matter of betrayal (v. 1024 = v. 1192).

After Roland's savage attack on his adversary, his nearly word-for-word repetition of Aelroth's taunt is anything but formulaic in the routine sense. It is rather a systematic denial of the Saracen's baseless assertion. Eugene Dorfman has made an interesting suggestion:

> Aelroth cannot be accusing Charlemagne of betraying Roland by placing him in command of the rearguard and leaving him to the mercy of the Saracens, since the emperor was simply following the mandates of protocol in council and, indeed, Roland's own expressed wishes. The only plausible interpretation is that Aelroth is referring to the treachery of the renegade. As an envoy on a mission of public trust, Ganelon was under obligation to "guard" the interests of the Franks. This he had signally failed to do. There is no longer any reason for Aelroth to conceal the fact, since the victims cannot escape from the trap. Forced to accept as true the accusation that treachery has been committed, Roland must now face squarely the treason charge involving his mother's husband.[21]

Dorfman's view finds important support in the rhymed version, which, in a recasting of this passage, identifies the traitor as Ganelon: "*Mot est fel Guenes et plens de tricherie*" (Châteauroux, v. 2109).[22] Nevertheless, a close reading of the passage in question in the Oxford version makes this interpretation highly unlikely. Roland's words correspond very closely to Aelroth's and would lose much of their irony if the parallelism were not complete:[23]

1192 *Traït* vos ad ki a guarder vos out (Aelroth).
1208 Ne *traïsun* unkes amer ne volt (Roland).

1193 *Fols est li reis* ki vos laissat as porz (Aelroth).
1209 Il fist que *proz* qu'il nus laisad as porz (Roland).

1194 Enquoi perdrat France dulce sun *los* (Aelroth).
1210 Oi n'en perdrat France dulce sun *los* (Roland).

The use of *prod* (v. 1209) as the antonym of *fol* (v. 1193; see also v. 1207: "Ultre, culvert! Carles n'est mie fol")[24] offers valuable proof that it is a glaring error to translate the former term as 'brave' or 'courageous' (e.g., Bédier: "nous laisser aux ports, ce fut agir en preux") when Turoldus is plainly concerned with wisdom.

Aelroth, whose name appears to have a biblical origin (COMMENTARY, 11), is presented as an evil person uttering ugly falsehoods in a curse.[25] Biblical associations and malediction are similarly joined in Laisse 94. Marsile's brother Falsaron, whose one-line curse echoes precisely one of his nephew's phrases (v. 1194 = v. 1223) and who is said to be one of the vilest scoundrels on earth (v. 1216), holds the land of Dathan and Abiram as his fief. Abiram, together with Core, son of Isaar, led a revolt against Moses in Palestine and were punished when the earth split open and swallowed them alive (Numbers 16:1–35). The fate of Dathan and Abiram was familiar to medieval audiences, since it appeared in formulas used in wishing evil on someone.[26] The very name Falsaron suggests a connection with *falserie*, which, among other things, conjured up witchcraft and black arts, believed to be practiced in Saracen places of worship (vv. 3661–3665). This is yet another instance where Turoldus assimilates Old Testament figures and situations with the despised Saracen Infidel.

The physical description the poet gives of Falsaron, the space between whose eyes is a full half-foot wide, suggests his giant size—a formidable adversary, then, for Oliver—and his evil nature. A large forehead and a wide space between the eyebrows are stock features in contemporary descriptions of ideal beauty,[27] but the fact that Falsaron's eyes were so far apart would naturally have been considered to be grotesque. Similar exaggeration of the space between the eyes appears in portraits of ideal ugliness found in other early French epics.[28] To the medieval mind such a repulsive exterior corresponded to inner malevolence.[29]

The detailing of Oliver's blow, and of other mighty strokes in the *Song of Roland*, is an epic cliché that will give rise to Rabelais's amusing parody describing with anatomical precision the downward slash of Jean des Entommeures's sword through an adversary's body.[30] But Turoldus's descriptions are hardly devoid of emotion. The evident relish with which he narrates the slaying of the Saracens is often explained as the reflection of a crueler era. There is no denying a certain evolution in popular sensibilities over the centuries, but the reaction of medieval as opposed to present-day audiences in this respect has been overstated. Persons listening to the *Song of Roland* doubtless experienced mixed feelings, just as we do when watching violence on popular television programs or at the cinema. The modern spectator's grunt when the hero throws a well-placed punch and blood spurts from the villain's nose and mouth is partially in admiration, partially in disgust. While it is easy to imagine the medieval audience cheering as the jongleur reenacted—no doubt quite energetically—the multiple slayings in this episode, it probably experienced revulsion too. The difference is that we usually find ourselves directing our anger at the author for subjecting us to such a savage spectacle, whereas the medieval audience channeled its hostility toward the despised pagans for having invited such brutality in the first place.

Much of this of course is conditioned not so much by a particular zeitgeist as by circumstances. A threatened people feels that the source of the menace has only itself to blame for any evil that befalls it. The justification of wartime atrocities from the beginning of time is based on this premise. It is simplistic, then, to view bloody battle descriptions in the *Roland* as sadistic, when in fact they served to stimulate hatred of the Saracens in the same way as did the narrative of their foul deeds or the notion of their ugliness. (See COMMENTARY, 24, for a discussion of a different stylistic use of battlefield gore.)

Although a general melée is in progress,[31] Turoldus focuses on isolated duels. It is often evident that the struggle between two antagonists is observed by other participants in the battle. The French (and the audience too) witness a kind of deadly tournament. Individuals enter the list in succession and fight their opponents to the death while everyone else seems to be watching.[32] Following the first three clashes in Laisses 93, 94, and 95, Roland, Oliver, and Turpin urge their French companions to strike (Roland, v. 1211: "Ferez i, Francs"; Oliver, v. 1233: "Ferez i, Francs"; Turpin, v. 1258: "Ferez, Franceis"). Oliver may be commenting on the general situation in v. 1274 (Dist Oliver: "Gente est nostre bataille!"), but Archbishop Turpin praises Samson's blow in Laisse 98 (v. 1280: Dist l'arcevesque: "Cist colp est de baron!"). A similar remark is made by Roland apropos of Anseïs's deadly action in Laisse 99 (v. 1288: Ço dist Rollant: "Cist colp est de produme!").

Incidentally, Roland's justifiable pride in having struck a successful first blow (v. 1211: "nostre est li premers colps!") mocks Aelroth, who rashly, as it turned out, sought and obtained the right to initiate the battle (vv. 866, 873, 874, 876). Turpin makes a similar claim (v. 1259: "Cist premer colp est nostre"), indicating that in the second instance *premer* must be taken to mean that the Archbishop shares vicariously, as it were, in this honor. All this suggests a shifting back and forth from one part of the battlefield, where presumably the Peers are fighting within view of one another and of a number of their companions, to the rest of the conflict.

Early artistic portrayals of small actions within a broader tableau readily come to mind. One thinks of the Utrecht Psalter (*Fig. 45*), executed at Reims about 832, and of the late-tenth-century Canterbury Psalter (*Fig. 46*), which is derived from it.[33] Here the clustering of groups of figures, the direction in which individuals face, their gestures, and the use of buildings, natural contours, and curving horizontal lines serve to isolate various parts of the action while maintaining overall harmony. On the other hand, the masters who designed the Bayeux Tapestry (late eleventh century) and the ceiling at Saint-Savin (*Fig. 47*) had unusually long surfaces to work with and repeated scenes over and over again, assuming the eye would move along, grasping each new context after a momentary adjustment.[34]

Turoldus's technique differs considerably from these two distinct narrative styles. Like the Conrad illustrator (*Fig. 48*), the *Roland* poet concentrated on the French Peers.[35] The larger battle of 100,000 Saracens against 20,000 men in the French rearguard is merely suggested by a few references to the "French" and the "Saracens." Turoldus's manner here, then, is one of simplification and condensation.[36] The similarity of the characters in the *Song of Roland* and the repetitiousness of their duels can also be compared with the isocephalism and figural redundancy in the Conrad sketches. The very monotony of a particular feature is an effective device suggesting infinite repetition and, consequently, multitudes.

Corsablix eschews hurling an insult directly at the enemy, preferring instead to address his own men. His words of encouragement are shouted, ostensibly so that the Saracens may hear them over the din of battle, but plainly, too, because they are intended for Turpin's ears. The idea that the Saracen's words are lies, implicit in Roland's point-by-point rebuttal of Aelroth's vaunt in vv. 1207–1210, is reiterated by Turpin in v. 1253 in a similarly systematic manner (v. 1241 = v. 1254; v. 1242 = v. 1257). The French may be stung by the pagan insults, but they derive great strength (v. 1246: grant vertut) from their conviction that they are in the right, the pagans in the wrong (v. 1212).

The pattern of savage French onslaughts, which result in stunning Saracen defeats, of shouted insults followed by redressing of falsehoods, and of mutual encouragement on the part of the Christians is broken in Laisse 103, when Margariz—first among the pagan leaders to do so—spurs his steed forward to attack Oliver. A significant change is also indicated by the fact that Roland's companion is the first knight to engage in a second tilt. Thus far attack portends victory, and for a wild instant it appears as if Margariz will succeed.

Margariz survives in order to carry the shattering news of the death of the other eleven Saracen Peers to Marsile.[37] Critics are unanimous in their judgment that one or more laisses recounting Margariz's arrival at the pagan king's camp is missing in the Oxford copy.[38] Bédier also points out that this bearing of bad tidings parallels the Gautier de l'Hum episode just before Roland's death.[39]

Scholarly concern has focused, then, on Margariz. No one thus far has commented on the fact that Oliver has also been spared. For the second time in this poem—Charles's dream was the first such manifestation—God intervenes directly (v. 1316: Deus le guarit, qu'ell cors ne l'ad tuchet).[40] Oliver's death is averted and, as in the case of the nocturnal angelic visitation, one must try to discern the reason for such a sign from above.

The most obvious explanation is that Oliver has been spared for the time being because he is destined to have a second confrontation with Roland, an episode that, however one interprets it, plays an important role in the story. Oliver's brush with death is also a chilling portent of things to come, for the fortunes of the French will soon take a turn for the worse. The incident's most significant aspect, however, is that it proves that God is on the side of the French.

There is a curious ambiguity in this. Should they perish, the French fervently believe that this would be a sign of divine favor. Not only will they all go to Heaven, but they will also be imitating the early martyrs who died for Christ.[41] On the other hand, the Christians trust that God will protect them and make them victorious in order to show that they are His Chosen People. In other words, whatever happens is interpreted by the French as a Providential sign. The audience, listening to the *Song of Roland*, must have viewed Oliver's escape without a scratch in that light. It had to suspend momentarily, then, its foreknowledge of the fate that would inevitably overtake everyone in the French rearguard, including Oliver, in order to experience, at this juncture, joy in God's great deed.

16. Further French Triumphs

Laisses 105–110 (verses 1338–1437)

The first part of this scene concluded with Roland's mighty blow cleaving Chernuble and his horse in two, not one of the French heroes suffering so much as a scratch. This marks the first appearance of Durendal, in fact the first use of a sword in battle.[1] Shifting away from a technique described in the preceding commentary as one of simplification or condensation, Turoldus now conveys the grandiose aspect of the battle. Staying close to Roland, Oliver, and Turpin, he follows them as they range over a broad expanse of terrain, encountering various adversaries but always triumphing over them. His refrainlike references to the battle and to the thousands of victims draw away attention from the individuals in the foreground. Our vantage point for this growing panoramic view of the battle eventually rises over the Pyrenees, to Charles, and, finally, into the clouds, as we witness, in Laisse 110, the great storm raging over France. At first the tempest in the heavens merely seems to reflect the convulsion on earth—there was similar earth-sky opposition in Laisse 1—but the wild hailstorm rapidly assumes both a symbolic and a prophetic aspect.

The near-disastrous encounter between Oliver and Margariz was a portentous sign. Now the French lances begin to shatter ominously, first Oliver's in Laisse 106, then those carried by Gerin and Gerier in Laisse 108, reminiscent of the flying shards in Charlemagne's dream (v. 723).[2]

But it is the blood spattered over Roland in Laisse 105 that is the surest indication of things to come. Once again, our reaction to such gore, like that of the poet in vv. 1341–1342, is one of horror mixed with fascination. Oliver, too, will share in this sensation, in v. 1711. Roland already wears the badge of his martyrdom, a fate he literally embraces with both arms (v. 1343). Thus far, however, the blood is pagan blood. Turpin's cry in v. 1349 is partly an exultant thanksgiving for such God-given strength (cf. v. 535), partly an encouragement to the French.

After his brush with death Oliver attacks all the more vigorously. The shaft of his spear becomes shorter and shorter, breaking off with each thrust, until he holds a mere stump in his hand.[3] Jenkins terms Roland's remark in vv. 1360–1361 a warrior's jest and imagines that it produced "frenzied applause." A club was considered to be a lowly and humorous weapon (cf. Rainouart's *tinel* in the *Chanson de Guillaume*),[4] but Turoldus, in connivance with the audience, which knows of Charlemagne's dream, may well be suggesting that Roland, suddenly overcome with inexplicable dread, simply cannot bear to look upon the broken lance.[5] There is, however, a more obvious explanation. A broken lance symbolizes defeat (one is reminded, for example, of the statue of Synagoga at Strasbourg),[6] and Roland may be chiding his companion for suggesting—unwittingly of course—such a possibility. Nevertheless Oliver's reaction is a vigorous one. Drawing his trusty sword, he swings it in a deadly arc, imitating precisely Roland's Saracen-and-horse cleaving stroke in Laisse 93.

Whether or not there is something playful in Roland's mild reproach to Oliver, this much is certain: The devil's presence is always acutely felt when there are Saracens around. Archbishop Turpin, on whom the power of exorcism has been conferred, has already dispatched Corsablix, who is *mult de males arz* (v. 886). He now slays Siglorel, a sorcerer known to have frequented Hell.[7] In just a few laisses Turpin will be locked in combat with another diabolical warrior.

The audience must be assuming that, while the Twelve Peers have thus far escaped unscathed, many of the other French warriors have fallen. The first direct confirmation of this, however, is in v. 1401: *Tant bon Franceis i perdent lor juvente*! Turoldus chooses to suggest the youthfulness (juvente) of the French warriors in this passage, one of the few in the *Song of Roland* that gives equal space to mothers, wives, and comrades-in-arms.[8] The bond of affection between the doomed French and their families serves as a narrative link between the rearguard, as it fights its desperate battle in the Pyrenean defile, and Charles, who anxiously awaits them on the other side of the mountain.

The Emperor, in v. 1404, sheds tears of apprehension, but also tears of foreknowledge.[9] Sensing clearly what is transpiring, Charles nevertheless acknowledges his profound obligation to play out his role as an Abraham figure. The unbearable tragedy of the instant is momentarily relieved by the flashforward of Ganelon's trial at Aix, where the evil deed will be punished.[10]

A Rychnerian analysis of vv. 1406–1411 might suggest that the jongleur here was chiefly concerned with providing any late arrival in the audience with information he will need to understand what follows.[11] The verses in question do indeed function as an aid to narration, but, rhetorically speaking, they also serve to delay the unfolding of the story and thus to heighten tension. These two considerations have something mechanical about them, however, and the poet's achievement in this passage is anything but automatic. To appreciate Turoldus's skillful use of thought-association, one need only notice that initially, in Laisse 110, one is not certain whether the vision of what awaits the traitor is part of Charles's meditation—the Emperor's dream did include the judicial combat that ends Ganelon's trial—or an intervention by the poet for the benefit of the audience.

After a last faint echo of the Roland-Oliver debate (v. 1421: Ne reverrunt lor peres ne lor parenz), the scene shifts to the other side of the mountain—glimpsing Charles along the way (v. 1422: Ne Carlemagne, ki as porz les atent)—to France, where a storm gathers and suddenly rages.

Critics of the *Song of Roland*, showing very little interest in the literary aspects of this scene, have focused their attention on its geography, which some feel yields information about the date of the poem or of its prototype.[12] Turoldus's artistry deserves equal consideration. The howling winds and crashing thunder of a tempest are perhaps the most familiar instance in literature of the pathetic fallacy, the notion that nature reflects the emotions of men in particularly dramatic circumstances. As suggested above, the storm in the heavens parallels the violence on earth. In addition, however, the wind and lightning actually suffer at the prospect of Roland's imminent death (v. 1437: Ço est li granz dulors por la mort de Rollant).[13]

The hailstorm is prophetic of the hero's passing, an announcement witnesses fail to understand, for all are filled with fear and many interpret the storm apocalyptically as the end of the world (vv. 1433–

1435).[14] This error in human judgment at one of the most crucial points in the poem echoes once again the theme of the vanity of worldly wisdom.

The essence of tragedy is knowing something terrible is going to happen but being unable to prevent it. The audience is repeatedly told through dreams and other portents that Roland will die, and it listens with horrified fascination as the story moves to its inexorable climax. What is interesting here is that the poet reveals not only what is going to transpire but also its profound significance. The midday darkness, the earthquake, and the general dismay in this passage were long ago identified as clear allusions to the narrative of Christ's Passion.[15]

If, as it appears quite possible in view of other textual evidence,[16] Venice IV preserves a laisse inadvertently omitted by the Oxford copyist, mention of the sun and the moon in this context (v. 1354: Sol ne luna no poit rendre luçerne) suggests a further connection with the Crucifixion. In medieval art Christ on the Cross is often depicted with the sun on his right, the moon on his left.[17]

These are not parallels drawn for mere esthetic ends, but a deliberate effort on the part of Turoldus to inform the audience that Roland's martyrdom is a conscious *imitatio Christi*. Like certain formulas used by medieval illuminators and sculptors, the pattern of imitation in this passage is a meaningful one.

17. Roncevaux, Part 2

Laisses 111–126 (verses 1438–1670)

There is a brief lull in the battle. The poet surveys the battlefield, strewn with thousands of French and Saracen dead. Turpin's reaction is one of pride in his men for their courageous and successful struggle. The allusion in v. 1443 to the storied Annals of the Franks is a stock phrase in the chansons de geste, but it usually figures in passages where the poet is speaking.[1] In such circumstances it imparts an aura of authenticity to what is being reported. The verse that follows has been referred to as a *locus desperatus*.[2] It is therefore hazardous to venture an interpretation of what the chronicles say according to the Archbishop. Most of the related texts have Turpin reiterating the thought found in v. 1441—that his men are courageous. Bédier was upset to find the epithet *vassals* affixed to *nostre empereür* ("l'idée est d'une rare insignifiance").[3] However, as Foulet points out, the adjective is never used to indicate feudal subservience in the *Song of Roland* and suggests rather a laudable combination of chivalric virtues, courage in particular.[4] Foulet notes that in v. 3343 the French use an identical expression when referring to Charles (Dient Franceis: "Icist reis est vassals!"), a line which Bédier had no trouble rendering ("Les Français disent: 'Le roi est un vaillant!' ")[5]

There is nothing inconsistent in having Turpin mention the Emperor's valor at this particular juncture. On the contrary, the Archbishop earlier (v. 1128) alluded to Charles as the exemplar for whom the French should be prepared to die, identifying him, in the very next breath, with the cause of Christianity.

The connection with the *Geste Francor* is far more puzzling. Perhaps Turoldus is suggesting that Turpin is acutely aware of the historic role the rearguard is playing; that it is one worthy of being recorded in the annals of France, alongside the deeds of the Emperor; that Charles is a legend in his own time, a living Christ surrogate. If this interpretation is correct, what emerges is a fascinating glimpse of how Turpin views time.[6] For him history is a process linking God, Charles, and the Franks, on the one hand, and the events related in the Bible, the Annals of the Franks, and those occurring in the present, on the other, in a vast continuum, all else being vanity. Turpin's meditation on the meaning of life is triggered by a heartrending panoramic view of dead and dying warriors lying on the battlefield. The survivors wander, like lost souls, in the midst of the carnage, lamenting their dear, departed relatives (vv. 1445–1447). It is interesting to compare this passage with that describing Charles's arrival upon the same desolate scene (COMMENTARY, 27, *ubi sunt* motif).[7]

Turoldus often employs the final line of a laisse to great effect. Interrupting his narration of Turpin's profound meditation, as spectral figures mournfully thread their way among their fallen comrades and relatives, he announces, suddenly, the unexpected arrival of the main body of Marsile's army.

The Oxford manuscript is considerably at variance with other versions of the poem with respect to the order of laisses in this passage:[8] (1) several laisses recounting how Margariz informs Marsile of the initial disaster appear to be missing; (2) in the Oxford manuscript a rearrangement of laisses creates the impression that a single decisive battle is involved. In the other versions Marsile divides his army in two: After the first corps has been vanquished by the French, the Saracen king launches a final attack with the remainder of his forces. In the Oxford copy the Turpin-Abisme duel inaugurates the Battle of Roncevaux, Part 2; elsewhere, Turpin's encounter with Abisme occurs in the second (and last) phase of this part. It is difficult to say whether the disposition of laisses in the Oxford version results more from design than from accident.[9] On the other hand, what seems clear is that the other versions, as opposed to that found in the Oxford copy, reflect more faithfully the order originally conceived by Turoldus. Consequently, in the present edition the order of laisses has been altered to conform more closely to the other versions in this passage.

Marsile's startling irruption upon the field is emphasized by his stealthy approach along a valley (v. 1449), the sudden flash of armor (vv. 1452–1453), and the ear-splitting blast of 7,000 trumpets sounding the charge (v. 1454).[10] Such bursting forth implies treachery and deceit, and that is doubtless what prompts Roland's remark about Ganelon's betrayal in vv. 1456–1459. The statement echoes Oliver's observation in v. 1024. For Oliver the only solution is still, no doubt, to sound the oliphant. However, Roland is content to know that the Emperor will avenge their deaths (v. 1149 = v. 1459). Thoughts about Charles's revenge are not, as has been suggested, the hallmark of a pagan ethos,[11] but are yet another reflection of the identity of Emperor and God in the hero's mind. According to this view of things, retribution will be meted out in this world or the next, and it really matters little which.[12]

At the sight of the Saracens, the French instinctively turn to the source of their strength: Roland, Oliver, and the Twelve Peers. The pattern here is one that has already been observed earlier: (1) an overwhelming enemy is sighted; (2) the French turn to their leaders; (3) the leaders harangue their men, impressing upon them the sacredness of their mission; (4) the French face the enemy in a state of exaltation.

The play on the word *guarant* in this passage is worth noting. In v. 1470 the French appeal to their leaders to aid and protect them (qu'il lor seient guarant); in v. 1478 Turpin guarantees that Heaven awaits them ("Mais d'une chose vos soi jo ben guarant"). The Archbishop gently but firmly diverts the attention of his men away from thoughts of mere physical safety and urges them to think rather of the eternal reward that is theirs if they fight courageously. The French,

Turpin suggests, should not rely on others but upon the strength that comes to them from God. Death is surely in store for them (v. 1476: "Pramis nus est," is another variation on the notion implicit in *guarant*), but they have the promise of eternal life.[13] The key phrase, then, is in v. 1472: "*Seignors barons, n'en alez mespensant*". OFr. *mespenser* means to have a false notion, to be wrong about something.[14] It is the prospect of becoming Holy Innocents that overjoys the French and firms their resolution to fight well.[15] Here one finds the curious paradox implicit in viewing oneself as a harmless child, murdered for the sake of Jesus, in order to steel oneself for combat.[16] For twentieth-century man this is a rather odd notion, yet only by reconciling these two seemingly contradictory concepts can one expect to penetrate the mind of the Middle Ages.

The duels that ensue are structured according to a very well-defined plan. Most of the French Peers die, but the Saracens pay a heavy price. No pagan must be allowed to savor his triumph over a French hero. There is ominous symmetry in the fact that at the beginning of this phase of the battle Climborin's defeat of Engelier is avenged by the latter's death and by that of Alphaïen, Escababi, and seven other Saracens, all by Oliver's hand, whereas, at the end, Grandoine's victory over five French heroes[17] will result in his death alone. One is able to anticipate who the victor will be, for it will invariably be the individual who takes the initiative, spurs his horse, and rides forward to strike his opponent (see COMMENTARY, 15). In view of such cues, alert audiences must have grown accustomed to cheering or groaning as alternating laisses in this passage began with either a revered or a despised name.

Four main events are narrated here. As indicated above, two—one at the beginning and one at the end—involve several combatants, but all four events are essentially triangular in that a Saracen warrior (Climborin, Valdabron, Malquiant, and Grandoine), momentarily victorious, will be brutally eliminated by a French avenger (Oliver, Roland, Turpin, and, once again, Roland). The entire passage hinges on the notion that each French death must be *appropriately* avenged.[18] Oliver's multiple triumphs after Engelier's demise is the most striking example of this. When Grandoine's fivefold victory over the French is matched by a single Saracen death, the inadequacy of this revenge, although not explicitly stated by the poet, cannot fail but reverberate frighteningly among the French.[19]

The duels in this passage are highly conventional, yet Turoldus manages to impart an extraordinary amount of other information in the process. One notes, first of all, a return to the technique of condensation. The listeners' attention is focused on the exploits of a handful of men, but the impression of a general battle raging all around them is also suggested. This is accomplished in each laisse by means of: (1) a hortative dialogue between the main protagonist and his comrades-in-arms (Climborin addresses the pagans, vv. 1499–1500; Valdabron also, v. 1535); (2) railing at the enemy (Roland addresses the pagans, vv. 1548–1549; Turpin addresses Malquiant, vv. 1565–1566; Roland addresses Grandoine, vv. 1589–1590);[20] or (3) a group reaction to an individual exploit (the French lament Engelier's death, v. 1501; the French cheer Roland's blow, v. 1609; they lament Samson's death, v. 1536, Anseïs's death, v. 1561, and the death of five French heroes, v. 1585; Roland and Oliver discuss Engelier's death, vv. 1502–1505; Roland praises Oliver's blow and urges the French on, vv. 1515–1517; the Saracens lament Valdabron's death, v. 1547; the Saracens rejoice at Grandoine's multiple slayings, v. 1584; the French cry of distress at the multiple slayings of their own is heard by Roland, v. 1587). Finally, more than any other expression, the term *presse* in v. 1500 suggests the tumultuous confusion of the wider battle raging opposite the individual duels.[21] This alternation between background and foreground occurs elsewhere in the laisse, but Turoldus makes particularly effective use of the last line for this purpose.

One way of explicating the author's reference, in Laisses 114 and 116, to Saracen connections with Ganelon is to allude to the jongleur's need to recapitulate from time to time.[22] However, such an explanation is inadequate, for Turoldus must surely be given credit here for thematic as well as for purely narrative concerns. The poet is not merely putting the audience in mind—or informing late arrivals—of key prior events necessary for understanding what is being related at this point in the story. His references to Ganelon are part of a pattern of constant reminders throughout the *Song of Roland* of the traitor's perfidy.

The references to Ganelon's blasphemous oath and above all to the Judas-like kiss and bribe, recall the nature of the villain's deed, as does the story of Valdabron's treacherous and sacrilegious deed at Jerusalem, specifically associated with Ganelon in vv. 1523–1527.[23] Mention of Saragossa in v. 1483 is yet another indirect allusion to the same theme.[24] The insistence on father-son and uncle-nephew relationships among the Saracens (Blancandrin sacrifices his own son as a hostage, v. 149; Marsile is the Caliph's nephew; Jurfaleu is Marsile's son, Aelroth is his nephew; Malquiant[25] is the son of King Malcud; Grandoine is the son of Capuel, King of Cappadocia)[26] is characteristic of the Old French epics,[27] but in the *Song of Roland* it repeatedly echoes the crucial Charles-Roland and Ganelon-Roland family connection.[28] Ganelon's ghostly presence at Roncevaux is designed to prepare the audience for the final act, when the traitor will be tried for his felony. It serves as an important corrective to any inclination the audience might have to pity Ganelon or to agree with his defense of his actions. The ghostly appearances of Ganelon function in the same way as Charles's dream, insofar as both provide essential but privileged information to the audience, on the one hand, and to the Emperor, on the other.

On a purely stylistic level, there is use of irony in what at first appears to be a formulaic expression (v. 1485: Ço est Climborins, ki pas ne fut produme).[29] The locution recurs a few verses later in the touching lament for Climborin's victim Engelier (v. 1501: Dient Franceis: "Deus, quel doel de prodome!"). One of Turoldus's favorite devices is understatement, two examples of which are found here (v. 1515: Ço dist Rollant: "Mis cumpainz est irez!"; v. 1548: Respont Rollant: "Ne pois amer les voz").

Grandoine, Roland's final adversary in this episode, is depicted as possessing the kind of warlike qualities that would make him redoubtable to any man (vv. 1593–1594), and his methodical dispatching of the five doomed French heroes is an awe-inspiring performance. The other versions single out Grandoine even more.[30] He bears Marsile's golden banner and commands the first corps to attack the French in this phase of the battle, although it is Climborin who actually leads the assault. However, he shows his true colors when he spies Roland.[31]

Whereas the Saracens have all sworn to slay Roland *if they can find him in the melée*,[32] nothing would appear to distinguish the French hero from the other Peers. Yet Grandoine recognizes him instantly:

> 1596 Enceis nel vit, s'il recunut veirement
> Al fier visage e al cors qu'il out gent
> E al reguart e al contenement.

Poetic license? Jenkins, in note to v. 1639, compares this passage with the *Iliad* (XXII: 136), which relates how Hector trembled and fled at the mere sight of Achilles. The passage certainly calls to mind this classical topos relative to fear, for Turoldus specifically informs us that the frightened Grandoine attempted flight:

1599 Ne poet muër qu'il ne s'en espoënt.
Fuïr s'en voel, mais ne li valt nïent.

It is worth noting, too, that in v. 119 (S'est kil demandet, ne l'estoet enseigner), the Saracens require no one to point out Charles, for they recognize him instantly.[33] In both circumstances Turoldus stresses handsome features and, above all, a ferocious look (v. 118: Gent ad le cors e la cuntenant fier). The poet, it will be remembered, combines these two characteristics in his portrait of Roland in Laisse 91.

Roland's fear-inspiring gaze and demeanor, then, are emphasized here. Yet, as in the portrait of Charlemagne, the poet wishes to suggest something more than ferociousness in Roland's mien. Turoldus no doubt imagines a special radiance emanating from his heroes. Elsewhere we find the epithet *cler* referring to the brightness of Roland's face (v. 1159), but a different kind of luminosity is involved here, one which has no particular reference to the face or to any other part of the body but is rather a reflection of inner beauty.[34] In the poet's mind this radiant quality is doubtless related to that of the saints, whose gaze, as captured in Romanesque sculpture, was imagined to be fixed not upon worldly objects but upon eternity.[35]

For the second time the poet's attention momentarily shifts away from individual combats—always the matter that concerns him most—to the larger battle. Turoldus is able to suggest in this way that the outcome of the battle hinges on the deeds of a few. The French have suffered the loss of the majority of their heroes and there have been ominous signs of impending disaster, yet for the time being they are still masters of the field and total victory is apparently theirs.

Laisses 123 and 124 deal with the same situation and form a unit, an impression fostered by similar initial verses and roughly the same number of lines (ten versus eight). Also in both groups of verses the scene shifts back and forth from the French to the Saracen side, suggesting a wild melée. One assumes a large number of casualties in both armies, but in his vivid description Turoldus emphasizes the violence of the French blows (v. 1611: Franceis i ferent par vigur e par ire; v. 1621: Franceis i fierent des espiez brunisant), the distress, and, finally, the panic of the Saracens.

Putting expressions like *Tere Major* (vv. 1489, 1616) in Saracen mouths strikes some as naïve, for they seem more suited for French speakers.[36] Yet in this instance, as in the oath scene (v. 952), Turoldus is being ironic. The pagans reiterate an expression they have heard Ganelon use when referring to his homeland (v. 600). The locution is utilized elsewhere by the poet to convey the emotion of the French as they first view France (v. 818), but it is often associated with Ganelon. In v. 1489 it appears as an indirect rendering of a speech ascribed to Climborin when he kisses the traitor and gives him his helmet at Saragossa.[37] Ganelon will also employ the same phrase when he treacherously attempts to convince Charles that the sound of Roland's horn is to be ignored (v. 1784). It should be noted that the possessive pronoun *la tue* in v. 1617 does not refer to *Tere Major* but to Mohammed: The Saracens ask their Deity to curse the land of the French, then pray to him to make his warriors courageous. For identical uses of the singular in addressing the Deity, see v. 2369 ("Deus, meie culpe vers les tues vertuz") and v. 3107 ("La tue amurs me seit hoi en present").[38] In an inverted image of Turpin's gentle exhortation to the French to turn their thoughts away from the Twelve Peers toward God, the Saracens pray to Mohammed, then call on Marsile![39]

The pell-mell disposition of bodies strewn over the battlefield (v. 1624: L'un gist sur l'altre e envers e adenz) is an aspect of warfare that evidently impressed contemporary artists who were trying to visualize the violence as well as the confusion of combat.[40] The lower border of the Bayeux Tapestry, in the section depicting the Battle of Hastings (*Fig. 49*), is the best-known example of this technique. However, there is perhaps another facet of the medieval imagination involved here. Bearing in mind that in these two laisses Turoldus emphasizes the fury of the French attack, which culminates in the rout of the pagans, it seems reasonable to assume that the tangled bodies littering the field are mostly Saracens. The disorder of the fallen pagans strongly evokes contemporary depictions of the damned in Hell in grotesque and topsy-turvy attitudes[41] (*Fig. 50*). This image is consistent with the poet's observation that devils take away the soul of the dying Climborin (v. 1510). The Conrad illustrator made a handsome sketch of Roland astride his horse, brandishing his sword, and galloping through a tangle of Saracen bodies[42] (*Fig. 51*). What tends to confirm this interpretation of the Saracens' postures is that Roland will take pains to align the broken bodies of his comrades before Archbishop Turpin, and that this will be an act of great significance.[43]

Ruing now Ganelon's prediction of the great initial defeat he would suffer at the hands of the French rearguard (vv. 584–591)—*martirie* in v. 1628 reiterates Ganelon's exact word in v. 591—Marsile unhesitatingly commits the remainder of his effectives to the *altre bataille* (v. 592) foreseen by his perfidious ally.

As in the first encounter one individual rides ahead of his men to open battle. Abisme, whose name means 'Pit of Hell',[44] is the most diabolical character in the *Song of Roland*.[45] The blackness of his skin is likened to molten pitch, a favorite image associated with the torments inflicted upon the damned.[46] A dragon banner does not always have an evil connotation in the Middle Ages,[47] but in this context it is plainly a symbol of the devil. According to Turoldus, Abisme is a repository for every vice imaginable and he is guilty of countless crimes. Because of his violent nature, he is highly regarded by Marsile. His shield was sent to him, via an intermediary, by a devil.[48]

The words *fel* and *felonie* further link Abisme to his sovereign, for the latter is referred to in v. 1640 as a *felun rei*. Etymologically the word felon may ultimately derive from the notion of whipping slaves,[49] but during the Middle Ages the term was most commonly used to brand cowards and traitors. However, in the present context it appears to be rather a loose term conjuring up evil and perversity. In Turoldus's mind there does not seem to be anything contradictory in a person possessing *vasselage*, on the one hand (v. 1639), and being stigmatized with *cuardie*, on the other (v. 1647), even though the concepts are opposed, for example, in vv. 887–888. Abisme's *vasselage* is courage that is useful in combat situations—an identical phrase (v. 2606: Vasselage ad e mult grant estultie) later refers to Charlemagne[50]—but it is no match for *barnage*, illuminated by God (v. 535).

According to Jenkins, in note to v. 1486, "Turpin is not ascribing cowardice to Abisme; the archbishop is communing with himself, and is perhaps not unaffected by the look of the fell Saracen." A better explanation takes into consideration the fact that *cuard* and *cuardie*, like *fel* and *felonie*, at times simply mean depravity, with no particular reference to physical courage.[51] Pagan baseness derives from the Saracens' vile religion, which instead of ennobling them corrupts their very natures. Thus Charles will later speak scornfully of the pagan faith, associating it with *felonie* and *coardise*:

> 3337 "Veez paien, felun sunt e cuart,
> Tute lor leis un dener ne lur valt."

This is why the fact that Abisme does not believe in God (v. 1634) is mentioned in the same breath as criminal behavior (v. 1633) and diabolic appearance (v. 1635).

The absence of Christianity's saving grace, then, provides adequate justification for the use of the term *herite* 'heretic' in v. 1645, for which the Archbishop provides the synonym *cuard*. There is, however, something else hinted at here. Lat. *haereticus* yielded OFr. *erege*, *irese*, but the form that Turoldus uses is *herite*, best explained as a blend with *sodomite*.[52] It may be that Turpin's ire is directed at least in part toward the unnatural sexual habits that Saracens were reputed to have and which, to his way of thinking, warrant death (v. 1646). A similar instance of veiled eroticism has been encountered in Bramimonde's conversation with Ganelon.[53]

In v. 1670 Turpin's crozier is metaphorical of course.[54] Earlier, Turpin slew another adversary with a spear (v. 1248), and Roland's mention of a spear in v. 1675 doubtless refers to the slaying of Abisme.[55] In v. 1682 the Archbishop is still holding a spear, and in v. 2089 he will wield his sword Almace. Yet medieval illustrators of the Battle of Roncevaux regularly show Turpin wearing a mitre and at times ingenuously depict him with crozier in hand.[56] If one is to visualize this scene the way Turoldus imagined it, then, one must picture the Archbishop complete with mitre and, in a manner of speaking, with crozier! Viewed in this fashion—that is, symbolically—Turpin's duel with Abisme recalls the Harrowing of Hell formula, in which Christ is represented thrusting the tip of his spearlike cross into Leviathan's gaping mouth.[57]

18. The Battlefield Debate Resumed

Laisses 127–132 (verses 1671–1752)

Turpin's duel with Abisme has opened the final and decisive phase of the Battle of Roncevaux. The outcome of this clash has been anxiously awaited by both sides before the opposing armies meet in battle. This is evident from the exchange between Roland and Oliver, both of whom have obviously witnessed the fight, and above all from the indication that, at a signal from Oliver, the struggle begins anew (v. 1677: A icest mot l'unt Francs recumencet).

Laisse 127 marks a turning point in the narrative, for although the deaths of the majority of the French Peers have been duly recorded and a good number of other Frenchmen may be presumed slain, the drastic reduction of the rearguard to a mere sixty men is now reported. There is pride in the fact that the remaining men will give a good account of themselves (v. 1690). Nevertheless Roland and his men are doomed.

18. THE BATTLEFIELD DEBATE RESUMED

The second horn scene is a reprise of the battlefield debate commented on earlier.[1] Critics have been so mesmerized by Bédier's theory that the entire poem hinges on a Roland-Oliver opposition that they have completely misinterpreted Turoldus's intention here.[2] The parallel structure of the poem and, above all, the formal aspect of the debate need to be constantly kept in mind.[3] In the first horn scene Turoldus presents a dilemma, and, far from agreeing with one set of arguments and rejecting the other, he accords each side equal weight.[4] In the second discussion Oliver resorts to turning the tables, a debating tactic known as antistrephon.[5]

In the present scene Oliver does not have the last word. Roland's so-called thoughtful pause ("Il se tait, et ce silence est la chose la plus sublime de la *Chanson de Roland*")[6] is no admission of error in judgment, no concession that he ought to have heeded his companion's advice. No change of heart transforms the poem into an epic of remorse and atonement.[7] In fact there is no pause at all: The Roland-Oliver altercation is interrupted by Turpin.

Having magnanimously and magnificently sustained Christianity, but now facing certain death, Roland proposes sounding the oliphant. For esthetic reasons the suggestion is made in the form of a thrice-posed question, but Roland's reasons are given only once. The reiteration of the query will add nothing new to what is found in the initial utterance in Laisse 128. Situations presented in the laisses similaires format are designed to be viewed as a whole and do not necessarily show logical progression.[8]

Roland says that the sight of his fallen comrades makes him realize that the end is near and that Charles must now be informed. It is what the hero does *not* say that has fascinated scholars. Roland tells us what he proposes to do, not what has prompted him to come to this decision.[9] A one-track mind is upsetting to academics who are in the habit of challenging every assertion, questioning every principle.[10] That is why critics often have little empathy with a martyr's stubborn righteousness. Yet the best explanation of Roland's behavior is that he remained true to himself to the very end. To his way of thinking, he did what had to be done. Roland's greatest concern is how to break the news to Charles (vv. 1698–1699).

Charles needs to know, then. But why? Certainly not so that he can come to the rescue. It is already too late for that. Roland needs Charles for his vindication and for his justification.[11] The betrayal of the rearguard by Ganelon and its destruction by the Saracens must be avenged. But equally important, the martyrdom of the French must be made to bear fruit. It must increase the faith of Charles and his men in the inevitability of Christian victory and it must serve as a glorious example for all mankind.[12] These thoughts, only implicit in Roland's words, will be eloquently articulated by Turpin.

Much of the scholarly discussion concerning this scene revolves around the concept of responsibility for the lives of others. In v. 1726 Oliver implies that Roland must answer for the deaths of the French at Roncevaux: "*Franceis sunt morz par vostre legerie.*"[13] The hero will lament his fallen comrades, but nowhere will he show any sign that their loss affects his conscience. Roland evidently draws a distinction between his duty to aid and protect his men—he is their *guarant* (vv. 1161, 1609), but so are Oliver and the Twelve Peers (v. 1470)—and the notion of being accountable for them. In his view each person remains an independent moral agent. Roland has a profound sense of loyalty to his comrades and he expects and receives a corresponding allegiance from them. The absence of any guilt feeling on his part clearly points to the fact that he is responding to a higher moral imperative than that which prompted Oliver's remark.

Here, as in the first horn scene, Oliver and Roland converse but do not really listen to each other. The hero's companion is bitter and angry,[14] for he does not feel that his death or that of anyone else in the rearguard was necessary. His reiteration of the arguments put forward by Roland in the first phase of the debate has a sarcastic edge,[15] but it completes a circle and thus implies that the reasons given earlier by Roland were valid (see also INTRODUCTION, 3).

Oliver echoes Roland's words but empties them of all their spiritual significance. He accuses Roland of folly, forgetting that, by definition, the Christian is a fool.[16] His lack of understanding is doubtless the greatest hardship Roland must suffer.

In his anger Oliver cries out that he will prevent the planned union of his sister Alda with Roland. The threat is interesting from several points of view. The manner in which it is expressed is another example of the discreet eroticism noted in the Bramimonde-Ganelon scene.[17] Once again Turoldus is thinking ahead to the symbolic role the female character will play at the end of the poem. Consequently, he attenuates any overt sexuality that would place their relationship in a rather different light. The statement also discloses that Oliver does not yet accept, as do Roland and Turpin, the irreversibility of the situation, for he still speaks of the possibility of returning safely to Aix (v. 1720:

"Se puis veeir ma gente sorur Alde"). However, the most revealing aspect of Oliver's remark is what it tells us about Oliver's thought processes. It is customary to regard Roland's companion as the embodiment of common sense and prudence. Yet what emerges from a close reading of the two horn scenes belies this view of Oliver. In the first part of the debate Roland offers several reasons for not sounding the oliphant, but he is in reality intent upon conveying a single, pervasive idea: The French must make a stand for Christianity. Whether or not one agrees with his position, one must at least concede that the hero is lucid and consistent in expressing his exalted view.

Oliver, on the other hand, becomes increasingly distraught and, in the present series of laisses, gives every sign of approaching mental aberration. He deliberately distorts the reasons given earlier by his companion by interpreting them literally; he blames Roland for the deaths of his men, disregarding the fact that it was Ganelon who caused the disaster and the Saracens who brought it about; he accuses his comrade of folly, a ploy that masks his own incipient madness. Feverish jumping from one subject to another betrays Oliver's mental state. After berating his companion for wishing to sound the oliphant, he stares, half distracted, at Roland's bloody arms (v. 1711: "Ja avez vos ambsdous les braz sanglanz!").[18] This situation is reminiscent of Lady Macbeth's demented vision of bloody hands (Act V, sc. 1).[19] After more accusations Oliver again, in a complete non sequitur, abruptly mentions Alda. It is as if, transfixed with horror, he could see Alda lying in Roland's bloody embrace.

In a final statement Oliver momentarily faces reality. He accepts the fact that Roland (but, pathetically, not himself) will die before the day is out (vv. 1735–1736). As his mind wanders he already imagines himself bidding a heartrending adieu to his dead companion.[20] Except for one brief, robotlike utterance (v. 1938: Dist Oliver: "Dehet ait li plus lenz!")—when Roland addresses his companion in vv. 1865–1868, the latter does not reply—and an almost word-for-word reiteration, in vv. 1976–1977, of his farewell statement in vv. 1735–1736, Oliver will speak no more until, in a final delirium, he will strike his own dear friend.

In the second horn scene the altercation between Roland and Oliver is mercifully interrupted by Archbishop Turpin, who rides up and pleads with them to desist (Laisse 132).[21] In the economy of Turoldus's poem Roland's laconism, insofar as his motivation for sounding the oliphant is concerned, is made up for by the Archbishop's statement, for there can be no doubt that Turpin merely echoes the hero's sentiment. The sound of the oliphant, he says, will bring Charles, and our deeds will be vindicated and justified: Vindicated when the remaining Saracens are crushed, justified when our achievement is recognized for what it truly is.[22]

In Turpin's prophetic vision of the justification of the French two distinct phases are to be noted: (1) ceremonial dismounting; and (2) ritualistic raising-up and lamenting.

Naturally Charlemagne and his men will be better able to search for their fallen companions on foot than on horseback, but the act of dismounting to which the prelate alludes signals the cessation of hostilities—repose following strife—and symbolizes respect. This gesture signifies that the French hold their comrades-in-arms in reverence and regard their accomplishments with admiration. Charlemagne's men do not fear death, for it brings eternal bliss, but they stand in awe of it.

Turpin reassures his men that the French, having identified their comrades, will not fail to accord their bodies proper honor. Being devoured by wild or lowly animals (v. 1751) would be an unspeakable indignity and also suggests the triumph of evil.[23]

Turpin also specifies that they will be buried *en aitres de musters*. OFr. *cimetire*, the word for cemetery (primitively, a place for "sleeping"; COMMENTARY, 26 and 44), evokes quiet repose after a life of strife against the forces of evil, and it was available to Turoldus. Nevertheless he preferred *aitre* (< Lat. *atrium*), which seems to mean the parvis or enclosed space in front of a church or nearby consecrated ground.[24] Jenkins suggests that OFr. *aistre*, a term with which it was often confused, may be involved here.[25] The latter, a derivative of Gr. *ostrakon*, meant paving stone or tile and referred to a space between the principal entrance and the altar.

The discussion of the precise place the poet has in mind for his heroes is far from idle, for the manner in which the mortal remains are disposed of often indicates how people regard the next world.[26] Entombment inside churches was common enough in the Middle Ages and the number of French victims involved here, while it may give one pause, does not offer an insurmountable obstacle. The passage may be an allusion to Psalms 92:13: "Planted in the house of Yahweh (in atriis domus Domini), they will flourish in the courts of our God." The phrase originally alluded to the just, who were so often present in the temple of the Lord that, figuratively speaking, they were "planted" there.[27]

Not only is Turoldus's word the same as that found in the Vulgate; it is also consistent with the image most frequently used by the poet to symbolize the joys of paradise, that of flowers (vv. 1856, 2197, 2898).[28] On two occasions in the *Pseudo-Turpin* (at Sahagún in Spain, and between Saintes and Taillebourg in France), the lances of the French who are to die a martyr's death in battle the following day flower miraculously.[29] The scene is illustrated in the Aachen coffer, in a stained-glass window at Chartres, in a manuscript of a late-thirteenth-century Dutch translation of the *Speculum historiale*, and in a sixteenth-century chronicle.[30] In the Brindisi mosaic (*Fig. 54*) the artist shows a long five-petal flower emerging from the heads of the five slain French warriors.[31]

Perhaps the most pervasive theme in the funereal rites of all peoples is concern for the next life.[32] From prehistoric times to the present day, man has found countless ways to manifest his belief in the unending cycle of death and rebirth. For medieval exegetes the notion of flowering symbolized resurrection (Alain de Lille provides the following gloss: "Florere significat resurgere").[33] Thus when Turpin speaks of the triumphant raising of the bodies of the French on packhorses (v. 1748), he is not only anticipating a posthumous bestowing of honor upon the victims of Roncevaux. In keeping with the floral symbolism to which he alludes in this passage, he is also suggesting a sharing in Christ's Resurrection.[34]

19. Roland Sounds the Oliphant

Laisses 133–135 (verses 1753–1795)

Roland sounds the oliphant, and it is one of the grandest and most celebrated moments in literary history.[1]

The oliphant's blast, an essential element in the narrative, awakens all sorts of emotions, notably, since Alfred de Vigny's excellent poem, a haunting melancholy.[2] For many scholars the sound of Roland's horn is the symbol of his tardy reasonableness[3] and, while its plaintive notes are admired, the hero's procrastination is either roundly condemned or profoundly lamented.[4]

These reactions were perhaps not completely foreign to the medieval audience, but other associations were doubtless more common. Ganelon's mention of a rabbit hunt, intended to mislead the Emperor and to pillory the hero as vain and frivolous, brings the reality of the Middle Ages closer to us, for the stirring sound of horn blowing accompanying the pursuit of game was forever reverberating in the countryside.[5] Horn blowers and archers are found on Romanesque tympana and friezes. Artists such as the Andlau sculptor were influenced by familiar hunting metaphors when they sought to express evil pursuing its prey, the human soul.[6] The medieval audience may have inferred, then, that Ganelon unwittingly betrayed his own perfidy with his story about a hunt (v. 1780).

Another typical association was magic. The legends and poems of the Middle Ages are replete with references to magic horns, capable of causing wondrous enchantments and of bringing about fabulous windfalls or catastrophic misfortunes. Such a magic instrument figures prominently in a 1,592–line episode known as the "Joy of the Court" in Chrétien de Troyes's *Erec.*[7] About the same time Robert Biket wrote the *Lai du Cor*, a poem about a drinking horn capable of testing a wife's fidelity.[8] Like Roland's oliphant, which was shown at Saint-Seurin in Bordeaux (vv. 3684–3687),[9] this horn, according to Biket, was to be seen at Cirencester.[10] A magic horn, to cite but one more example, is also mentioned in *Huon de Bordeaux*. It combines elements reminiscent of the *Song of Roland* and the *Lai du Cor*. No one may drink from Auberon's horn unless he is in the state of grace. Its sound, which can be heard over an extraordinary distance, lightens the heart of all who hear it, and there is, at one point, a debate over whether or not to blow it.[11]

Magic associations would naturally have come to mind when Roland gave the oliphant a mighty blast. The mention of a call heard thirty leagues away (v. 1756) is not particularly surprising in an epic full of such feats. However, in light of the tradition mentioned above, the oliphant's call suggests that the supernatural is involved.[12] The anonymous author of the *Pseudo-Turpin Chronicle* sensed this, for he caused an angel to carry the sound of Roland's oliphant to Charlemagne's ear (Cuius vox tunc usque ad Karoli aures, . . . angelico ductu pervenit).[13]

It must be conceded, too, that the carved elephant-tusk horns, which were beginning to reach France about this time,[14] were grand objects to behold and no doubt inspired reverential awe among the French.[15]

Roland's trumpet call is a signal that he is fighting a battle.[16] It is interpreted as an alarm by Charles and Naimes (the words *bataille* and *cumbatre* are used in vv. 1758, 1770, 1777, 1791), but Naimes also discerns the shrill sound of distress (v. 1795: "Rollant se dementet!").

One thinks readily of Psalm 130, traditionally connected with the liturgy for the faithful departed (De profundis clamavi ad te, Domine). By the same process of association, the medieval audience no doubt also thought of the Last Judgment trumpet, at whose fearful sound the dead would rise from the grave to meet their Maker.[17] Such a connection was natural for people who imagined the end of the world was at hand when a great hailstorm broke and the earth trembled (Laisse 110), and it is reinforced by other Roland-Christ associations in this poem.[18]

Each of the three laisses similaires (133–135)[19] is constructed on the following pattern: (1) Roland sounds the oliphant; (2) Charlemagne hears it; (3) Charlemagne says it is someone calling for help; (4) one of his men replies.

Ganelon answers the Emperor in the first two laisses of this sequence, and his false assertions offer an ironic parallel with Saint Peter denying Christ. The traitor flatly contradicts Charlemagne in a reply bordering on insolence (v. 1760: "S'altre le desist, ja semblast grant mençunge!"),[20] then, trying another tack, he makes light of his stepson's oliphant blasts.[21] In the third laisse Naimes confirms Charles's worst fears (v. 1795: "Asez oëz que Rollant se dementet!"). The awful truth of Charles's prophetic dream is dawning on him (COMMENTARY, 11, v. 1792; cf., however, COMMENTARY, 45). Ganelon's reply in the second of the three laisses, like his conversation on the road to Saragossa, contains an anecdote seeking to discredit Roland.

The story told by Ganelon is a kernel anecdote, that is, a brief narrative that was expanded into a major episode in later versions. There has been much scholarly discussion of the so-called Prise de Nobles or Noples, and the incident may antedate the Oxford *Roland*.[22] Subsequent elaborations of the story emphasize the Emperor's anger upon learning of Roland's disobedience and relate that Charles struck his nephew in the face with his gauntlet, causing drops of blood to appear. However, no trace of the field-washing motif is found in any of the later versions.[23] What is even more curious is the fact that none of the other texts of the *Roland* proper mention this deed either:

Venice IV:

1882 Ça presel Noble sença vost comant;
Fora insi Saraçin ch'era davant,
Si combate al bon cont Rollant;
Rollant in ancis cum Duridarda el brant.

Châteauroux (see also Venice VII, Laisse 182):

3089 Ja prist il Nobles tot sanz le vostr comanz.
Fors s'en issirent li Sarazin as chans;
Tuit s'entrocissent a lor espiez trenchant.
.R. li fers, li hardi conbatanz,
Se fist lever enz es pré verdoianz,
Saisi les cors a toz les combatanz
Q'il volst li sans en fust aparisanz.

Paris:

1736 Ja prinst il Nobles sans le vostre commant:
Li Sarrasin s'enfuirent as champs,
Il les ocist a s'espee tranchant;
La nos mena par les prés verdoians.

Cambridge:

1292 Hors s'en yessirent Sarrasins es champs;
Ilz les occistrent o les espees trenchans.

The laisse in question is faded in the Oxford manuscript. Also a number of alterations were made by the revisor. In v. 1775, for example, *seinz* was corrected to read *sanz*. The word *cumbatirent* two lines later was recopied very clumsily. Assuming that the subject of *lavat* in v. 1778 "must appear in the preceding line," Jenkins emends the latter to *Sis combatiet li bons vassals Rodlanz*.[24] There is an erasure after the word *ewes* in v. 1778.[25] Editors agree that *arissant* in the following line is a scribal error for *aparissant*.[26] In short, this passage is so corrupt that we should be doubly suspicious of any aberrant word or line. Curiously enough, no one seems to have been put off by the notion of Roland flooding the battlefield to rid it of blood.

In each of the other *Roland* texts washing is either omitted entirely (Venice IV, Paris, Cambridge) or one finds the locution *sei faire laver* (Venice VII, Châteauroux), presumably 'to cause (one's wounds) to be washed'.[27] On the other hand, all texts but that provided by the Bodleian copy mention a sword in this passage, and Venice IV even specifies the hero's weapon by name (Duridarda). This suggests that v. 1778 in the Oxford version, which is doubtless incorrect, represents an original *Puis od les ewes lavat s'espee del sanc*, which may be translated as follows: "Then he washed the blood on his sword in a stream."[28]

Washing one's sword in a river to remove the traces of blood can certainly be grasped more readily than the absurdity of flooding a battlefield for this purpose.[29] This reading has the advantage, too, of suggesting a connection with the folk-motif of the telltale bloodstains found, for example, in the legend of Tristan and in Chrétien de Troyes's *Charrette* (blood on the bedsheets), in Shakespeare's *Macbeth* (blood on the hands) and in Perrault's "Barbe-bleue" (blood on the key).[30]

Finally, one can see a parallel between the reconstructed verse and the following passage in Prudentius:

> Dixerat haec et laeta Libidinis interfectae
> Morte Pudicitia gladium Iordanis in undis
> Abluit infectum, sanies cui rore rubenti
> Haeserat et nitidum macularat vulnere ferrum.
> Expiat ergo aciem fluviali docta lavacro
> Victricem victrix, abolens baptismate labem
> Hostilis iuguli . . .[31]

Here is a translation of the passage:

> So spake Chastity, and rejoicing in the death of Lust, whom she had slain, washed her stained sword in the waters of Jordan; for a red dew of gore had clung to it and befouled the bright steel from the wound. So the conqueress deftly cleanses the conquering blade by bathing it in the stream, dipping it in to wash away the stain of blood that came from her foe's throat.[32]

Ganelon, then, seems to be implying that Roland cannot really wash the blood away and that now he is meeting with his just deserts.[33] The story is presumably being told to Charles for the first time and, since it reveals an act of grave disobedience, Ganelon could not have chosen a better moment to gloat over the fatal consequences of the lust for battle he had cautioned against in the first council of the Franks.[34] But it is of course the traitor who cannot wash away his sin.[35]

Beginning in Laisse 134 Turoldus notes several times the head injury received by Roland when he sounded the oliphant. According to the poet, he suffers no other wound. In fact Oliver would appear to be the only individual who actually strikes the hero. The shielding of Roland from enemy blows serves to single him out from among his companions. There is more than a suggestion of magic in the fact that the hero sustains no wound until he sounds the oliphant. One thinks of Yvain, who is given a ring that, so long as he is a true lover, preserves him from loss of blood, and of the catastrophic effects the horn sounding is supposed to have in Chrétien de Troyes's *Erec.*[36] However, in the present poem invulnerability is chiefly associated with Roland's undying spirit.[37]

The bursting of Roland's temples magnifies the mighty blast that the hero gives on his oliphant. The long agony that he must endure, his life slowly ebbing away as the blood oozes from his temples—believed throughout the Middle Ages to be the abode of the Holy Spirit[38]—accentuates the parallel with the Passion of Our Lord, who, the Evangelist John (19:33) carefully points out, was already dead when the soldiers came to break his legs and pierce his side.

Roland begins to die now. But the peal of his oliphant has reached Charlemagne and, like other sounds throughout the poem, serves as a link between the sixty French heroes at bay and the anxious Emperor, finally impelled to action.

20. Charlemagne to the Rescue

Laisses 136–139 (verses 1796–1850)

Time now slows down to a virtual standstill. To express the seeming eternity of Charlemagne's army struggling to rejoin the doomed rearguard, Turoldus resorts to two contrasting tableaux. The first (Laisses 136–139), in which the Emperor strives valiantly but ineffectually to traverse the thirty leagues that separate him from Roland, would seem to be all movement but, in reality, is frozen stillness; the second—exactly the same duration but stretching over no fewer than thirty-six laisses (to Laisse 177)—appears to relate very little but, paradoxically, is full of action.

The series of four laisses depicting the Emperor's efforts can most usefully be compared with the sequence in which Turoldus narrates the convergence of the French and Saracen armies in Laisses 90–92.[1]

Both tell of arming,[2] of mounting steeds, of banners waving, of spurring forward. The most significant detail is that both contain an expression of helplessness before fatality (v. 1185: que fereient il el? Cf. vv. 1806, 1840: De ço qui calt?). Thus far one notes a point-by-point similarity. However, in the first sequence Roland and his men seem to escape momentarily the poet's power and rush headlong to meet their destiny as autonomous characters. Exactly the opposite occurs in the present series of laisses, for, not only does the poet control the movement of the Emperor's army, he also deliberately impedes its progress forward.[3] Charlemagne and his men appear to be on a giant treadmill, straining strenuously—panting, pawing, plying—all to no avail. In a similar fashion the Egyptian army could scarcely make headway as it tried to cross the Red Sea on dry ground behind the sons of Israel (Exodus 14:25).

As in other laisses similaires, one should not try to discern emotive gradation but an overall complexity of sentiment. Thus the impatience and trepidation of the French relate at the same time to their desire to share once again the exhilaration of fighting at Roland's side (vv. 1804–1805, 1845–1847) and their panic-stricken but prayerful concern for his safety (vv. 1815, 1837).

At first glance the leitmotif in this passage is the sorrow and, especially, the anger of the French (vv. 1812–1814: Li empereres cevalcet par irur / E li Franceis dolenz e curuçus. / N'i ad celoi ki durement ne plurt; vv. 1834–1836: Li empereres chevalchet ireement / E li Franceis curuçus e dolent. / N'i ad celoi n'i plur e se dement; v. 1842: Par grant irur chevalchet li reis Charles; v. 1845: N'i ad icel ne demeint irance), but the operative concept is clearly one of frustration at the impeded progress.

Those who believe that an individual is presumed innocent until proven guilty naturally find the treatment accorded to Ganelon in this scene both cruel and unfair, or at least a bit premature.[4] However, medieval justice—that found in literature, at any rate—is characteristically prompt. Also, the audience is privileged to have all the facts. By this foretaste of what lies ahead for Ganelon, Turoldus relieves the tension built up by the traitor's gloating and bald-faced lying at the very instant of Roland's supreme agony. Naturally the audience fully appreciates the fact that Charles's inner vision enables him to grasp the truth of the matter. To the medieval mind the Emperor is actually showing a good deal of forebearance in allowing the drama to run its full course.

Frederick W. Locke has suggested that the punishment meted out to the villain is symbolic, in that the cooks portend the treatment he will be accorded in the fire and brimstone of "Hell's kitchen."[5] However, it is apparent that there is more than culinary symbolism here. Chaining the culprit "like a bear" (v. 1827: Si l'encaeinent altresi cum un urs)[6] recalls Charlemagne's dream (Ganelon the bear).[7] The humiliation of being forced to ride on a packhorse[8] has also been foreshadowed by

Marsile's gifts to Charles and his bribes to Ganelon, hinted at again in the latter's taunting of the Saracen king (v. 481) and echoed in Turpin's vision of posthumous honors (v. 1748). Above all, however, the detailing of Ganelon's preliminary punishment serves to alleviate the audience's frustration, which, at this point, is becoming unbearable.

Why do the French, in their desperate urgency to reach the rearguard, seem preoccupied with Roland at this particular juncture? Charlemagne's nephew is, to be sure, the guarantor of the French as well as a central character in this poem. However, this fixation on Roland is also a way of expressing French concern for the Christian cause the hero symbolizes.

The mixture of admiration, affection, and pity that the French have for their threatened leader may very well be translated by the poet's use of a title that appears here for the first time in the *Song of Roland* (vv. 1846, 1850) and which is usually reserved for the hero.[9] OFr. *chataigne* (Anglo-Norman *cataigne*), ultimately derived from Vulgar Latin **capitaneum* (< CL *caput* 'head'), attested in Carolingian times,[10] relates to military rank. However, the term did not have the technical meaning usually ascribed to modern *captain.* The word *chataigne* resembles and may be associated here with OFr. *chaitif* (< VL *cactivum* < CL *captivum* 'captive').[11] The latter generally designates the captive state and, by analogy, the wretchedness that accompanies this predicament (cf. MFr. *chétif* 'weak, puny, sickly [person]').[12] OFr. *chaitif* was part of the terminology of repentance.[13] It also expressed endearment mixed with sympathy, a meaning *cataigne* seems to have in the present context.[14]

In this congealed time frame one notion more than any other emphasizes the tragic powerlessness of everyone concerned. While the French struggle to overcome space, which never seems to diminish, time, expressed here by waning daylight (v. 1807),[15] moves inexorably on. The lengthening shadows, sealing Roland's doom, will be suddenly and miraculously halted, too late to save the hero but in time for Charles to avenge him. However, the audience knows nothing of this future development.

Earlier, the oliphant conveyed the desperateness of the hero's situation (v. 1795: "Asez oëz que Rollant se dementet!"). Now, the French sound their bugles in a frantic effort to tell Roland and his cornered men that help is on the way (v. 1833). However, in the next thirty-six laisses, not a single echo of the Emperor's trumpets will bolster their failing hopes.[16]

21. *The Rearguard's Stand at an End*

Laisses 140–155 (verses 1851–2098)

Roland, who will keep the stage now until he dies, does not listen for Charlemagne's trumpets. The hero looks toward the mountains (v. 1851), an attitude taken from Psalms 121:1 ("I lift my eyes to the mountains; where is help to come from?"),[1] one of the most celebrated of the "pilgrim songs" and a lyrical expression of confidence in God. The phrasing will recur in v. 2235.[2]

Roland's prayerful gaze is immediately followed by a lament. Paul Zumthor has shown how the lament in the *Song of Roland* assumes a highly stylized form.[3] However, stereotyping in no way negates sincerity. After all, most prayers and expressions of sorrow are formulaic. There has been much discussion as to the meaning of certain verses in this passage. The debate centers on the question of whether or not Roland assumes responsibility for the death of the companions he mourns. Nothing indicates that Roland finally recognizes his guilt here.[4] The hero regrets the loss of his companions but unswervingly holds to his conviction that his decision was the right one. Divergent interpretations of this passage have had the unfortunate effect of distracting critics from a much more significant development.

The lament in Laisse 140 ushers in the ritual death of the hero.[5] Virtually everything that follows, except for the remaining combats, is characterized by formal acts and ceremonies. Some—for instance raising eyes toward the mountains—are easily recognizable as religious; others, such as the proffered gauntlet, are more obscure in their symbolism. However, all reflect great concern on the part of the poet that the passage from life to death be marked with repeated affirmations of the nature of these two states.

The lament expresses the same confidence in the Lord as is symbolized by looking toward the mountains. "God have mercy on you," says Roland to the departed. The Franks have served Roland (v. 1858). However, it should not be forgotten that OFr. *servir* (v. 1858) had long been associated with doing God's will.[6] The expression *ki unkes ne mentit* in v. 1865,[7] which implies a pledge of salvation in return for loyal service, is a reaffirmation of the unswerving faith the hero indicates by gazing toward the mountains.

In this passage the terms *emperere* and *France* (vv. 1860, 1861) connote God's instruments. Bédier's translation of v. 1860 ("L'empereur nous a nourris pour son malheur") needs to be emended to reflect an important semantic distinction.[8] OFr. *mar*, probably derived from Lat. *mala hora* (not to be confused with CL *augurium* 'omen' > VL **agurium* > OFr. *aür*, *eür*, the ultimate source of MFr. *bonheur*, *malheur*) means 'in an evil hour, to one's misfortune' in such verses of the *Song of Roland* as vv. 196 and 220 (the exchange between Roland and Ganelon: "Ja mar crerez . . ."). However, in the present context, as well as in those that immediately follow, it is a manifestation of grief and admiration and does not reflect guilt feelings. Similarly, the *pur mei* in v. 1863 ("Barons franceis, pur mei vos vei murir"), far from being a confession of guilt, is merely an expression of gratitude mixed with sorrow.[9]

Roland's statement concerning the unbearable pain he is suffering (v. 1867: "De doel murra, se altre ne m'i ocit") is classical in phrasing but also prophetic. Ominous, too, is the fact that the hero's lament shifts almost imperceptibly into a conversation with Oliver, whose death, unbeknown to the two friends, is even more imminent. Turoldus does not specify what thoughts are in Oliver's mind, but, since Oliver is standing nearby, he is presumably reflecting along the same lines as his companion-in-arms.

After this interlude Roland returns to the battle and, according to Turoldus, slays no fewer than twenty-five adversaries (vv. 1871–1872). The image of the Saracens fleeing before the hero like a stag chased by hunting dogs is well known.[10] Hunting similes to describe pursuit in combat are very frequent in Old French literature: *Gormont et Isembart*, vv. 609–610 (stag fleeing); *Chanson de Guillaume*, v. 863 (dogs attacking a bear); *Couronnement de Louis*, vv. 1073–1074 (dogs chasing animal in woods); *Charroi de Nîmes*, v. 361 (fleeing like a cowardly greyhound); *Aye d'Avignon*, v. 1498 (dog attacking a dying boar); *Tristan de Thomas*, 1:342 (dogs chasing a rabbit); *Perlesvaus*, lines 4413–4414 (hunting dog fleeing before a lion), lines 6918–6919 (rabbit hiding from dogs), lines 7666–7667 (boar attacking dogs); *Prose Lancelot*, 5:135 (lion chasing does), 175 (famished wolf in an enclosure of sheep), 427 (famished lion chasing wild animals).[11] One is therefore tempted to dismiss the expression as merely another instance of formulaic diction. However, Lejeune and Stiennon have noted the recurrence of the stag-hunt image in sculpture associated with the *Song of Roland:* in the lintel of the Cathedral of Angoulême, the tympanum of Santa Maria della Strada, and a fragment belonging to Notre-Dame-de-la-Règle at Limoges.[12] Not only does the poet use the hunting simile, but Ganelon also associates Roland with a hunt in v. 1780.[13] It seems likely that the stag-chase metaphor was suggested to the poet by the sound of the oliphant.

The presence of stag hunts in church sculptures is explained by Lejeune and Stiennon as imagery related to the struggle between the virtues and vices, the theme "se rapportant à la prédication de l'Evangile, cette 'chasse des âmes' menée par le christianisme."[14] They add that the illustrations were purely religious at the outset but later associated with Roland.

The hunt is one of the richest motifs of Christian iconography. The funeral monuments of late antiquity and early Christianity often depicted hunting scenes in conjunction with banquets, the former representing the exercise of virtue, the latter the celestial reward.[15] The stag was also reminiscent of Psalms 42:1, where the soul's desire for God is compared with the doe's longing for running waters.[16] However, the biblical passage offering the most suggestive connection with the simile used by Turoldus is found in Jeremiah 16:16, where, according to the prophet, Yahweh cried out: "I will send many huntsmen, and these will hunt them (that is, the idolatrous enemy) out of every mountain, every hill, out of the holes in the rocks."[17]

Archbishop Turpin's enthusiastic reaction to Roland's feats of arms reflects admiration for the hero's strength and valor, but it also contains what some interpret as scarcely veiled contempt for monastic life.[18] Jenkins, citing Tavernier, strenuously denies any such scorn: "each is useful, nay indispensable, in his own field. Feudal society viewed itself as divided by function into 'defensores, oradores, labradores,' to use the terms of the Spanish *Siete Partidas*; during the Crusades, abbot and bishop were more than the equals of the chevaliers in authority."[19] The observation is valid insofar as medieval society's self-image is concerned, but it is seemingly contradicted by Turpin's bellicose acts. Lejeune points out that Saint Bernard, for one, vigorously disapproved of warring ecclesiastics and notes that the remark was either watered down or eliminated in later versions of the poem.[20]

Turoldus plainly sees no contradiction in having the prelate play an edifying role one moment and stain his hands with Saracen blood the next. Numerous historical and literary examples of combative clergymen have been cited,[21] but the fusion of such seemingly contradictory propensities in one individual deserves a more adequate explanation. For Turpin:

> There is a season for everything, a time for every occupation under heaven .... A time for killing, a time for healing .... A time for

> tears, a time for laughter; a time for mourning, a time for dancing.... A time for keeping silent, a time for speaking.... A time for loving, a time for hating; a time for war, a time for peace.[22]

Ecclesiastes's celebrated meditation was a reflection on the vanity of man's efforts to penetrate God's scheme of things and to modify the course of events. However, the biblical sage's words are often cited when one wishes to represent a vigorous response to the vagaries of existence and the accidents of one's estate in life. Turoldus's conception of Turpin reflects this idea.

Marsile no longer appears as a treacherous plotter or evil individual proffering a bribe, but *en guise de barunt* (v. 1889). His ability as a fighter is stressed in order to present him as a worthy opponent for Roland, who is described in precisely the same terms a few verses later, in the same laisse (v. 1902). The Saracen king kills Bevon and three of the remaining French Peers in quick succession. Roland reacts immediately but succeeds only in maiming his adversary.

Loss of a hand or arm by an evildoer is a common enough wound in Old French literature.[23] The following examples attest to the popularity of the motif: *Huon de Bordeaux*, v. 2094; *Gaydon*, vv. 1726–1727; *Tristan de Thomas*, 1: 22, 222–223; *Conte del graal*, v. 7028; *First Continuation*, T 4807; *Ipomedon*, v. 4935; *Prose Lancelot*, 2: 395; 5: 21, 135, 262, 443 (appendix); 7: 235; *Queste*, p. 33. [24] In the *Tournoiement Antecrit* Avarice cuts off Largesse's hand (vv. 2386–2389). Ménard notes that villains lose other limbs or parts of the body too—a leg, an ear, a shoulder, a cheek, or a nose—and that such wounds are debasing but not without humor.[25]

However, the nature of Marsile's wound is decidedly not arbitrary. The incident will be referred to several times in later episodes of the poem (vv. 2574, 2701, 2719, 2781, 2795; also indirectly in v. 2830: Marsile takes his gauntlet in his left hand) and, in v. 2809, Baligant boasts that he will take Charles's head (cf. v. 3289) to avenge Marsile's mutilation. Since Marsile is involved in the plot to kill Roland, Charlemagne's right arm, the loss of a right hand is also condign punishment.[26] From another point of view, it is only fitting that this wound be inflicted on the Saracen king, who dared take an oath (v. 612), and thus, literally, raised his hand against the hero. In a biblical parallel Judas cut off Nicanor's head "and the right hand he had stretched out in a display of insolence; these were taken and displayed within sight of Jerusalem" (1 Maccabees 7:47; see also 2 Maccabees 15:32). Nicanor, an enemy general, had blasphemously stretched out his hand and sworn to destroy the altar and dedicate the temple to Bacchus (2 Maccabees 14:33).[27]

If the cutting of the bear's ear in Charlemagne's dream (v. 732) anticipates this wound,[28] it would certainly buttress the view that Turoldus deliberately chose to have Marsile's hand cut off for a thematic purpose. Lejeune and Stiennon have argued that one of the scenes of the lintel of the Cathedral of Angoulême (1120–30) illustrates this episode.[29]

Marsile's wound appears to be essentially degrading and symbolical, but it is nonetheless a mortal blow. The Saracen king will return to Saragossa, dismount reeling from his horse, collapse at his wife's feet from loss of blood (vv. 2570–2575), and take to his bed. Later, when he hears the news of Baligant's defeat, he will turn his face to the wall and die. Roland's humiliating blow will, at long last, have claimed its victim (vv. 3644–3646).

The gravity of Marsile's wound and the death of his son Jurfaleu le Blond by Roland's hand cause panic among the Saracens. They cry out to their god for help—halfheartedly, for they are already losing confidence in him—and then decide to flee. No euphemisms are used by the pagans here but rather the dishonorable word *fuïr:* "*E car nus en fuiums!*" (v. 1910).

Once again one finds the poetic exclamation of helplessness (v. 1913: De ço qui calt?). It appears to refer to the hopelessness of the Saracen cause and to the inevitability of their defeat. Momentarily buoyed up, the audience's hopes are dashed when it discovers that Turoldus's expression of powerlessness concerns not the Saracens but the French, who face the final Saracen assault. This one is led by the Caliph himself.[30]

The foe is fearsome and hideous. There can be no doubt that Turoldus meant to suggest that the black-skinned enemy are possessed by devils.[31] In Laisses 143–145 the conversations on the French, then on the Saracen sides, are triggered by a quick exchange of glances sizing up the disparity in numbers between the two armies (v. 1932: Quan Rollant veit la contredite gent; v. 1940: Quant paien virent que Franceis i out poi).

Roland speaks first, looking death in the face, yet steadfast in his determination to fight to the end.[32] His words echo precisely his reasons for having made the desperate stand (so France will not be shamed, that is, so Christianity will be exalted) and for sounding the oliphant (so Charles will be edified).[33] Contemplating the mere handful of surviving French, the Saracens come to the erroneous conclusion that Charles's cause is wrong.

The Caliph takes the initiative in spurring his horse forward, an act that invariably forecasts a successful outcome in a duel. Epic heroes do not turn their backs to the enemy, so one may safely assume that Oliver was facing another opponent. This indicates that the Caliph's blow in his victim's back was a dastardly one.[34] The word *mar* in the insult addressed by the Saracen to the mortally wounded Oliver (v. 1949: "Carles li Magnes mar vos laissat as porz!") is often taken to mean 'to *your* great misfortune' (Bédier: "pour votre malheur"),[35] but since the next line in the comment is a verbal attack on the Emperor (v. 1950: "Tort nos ad fait, n'en est dreiz qu'il s'en lot"), it doubtless refers to Charles. A further argument may be found in the fact that the Caliph's phrase echoes one used by Aelroth in v. 1193 ("Fols est li reis ki vos laissat as porz"), where the insult clearly focuses on the Emperor. In the latter case the Saracen's adversary (here it is Oliver; in Laisse 93 it is Roland) replies to the insult with a point-by-point rebuttal. In the present instance the thrust of the Caliph's remark is merely parried (v. 1959: "Iço ne di que Karles n'i ait perdut").

As Moignet astutely points out, the last part of the Saracen's insult can actually be taken as a rather high compliment ("Kar de vos sul ai ben venget les noz").[36] Oliver's triumphant answer plays on the idea of praise mentioned by his adversary (v. 1950: "Tort nos ad fait, nen est dreiz qu'il s'en lot"), for he assures his opponent that at least he will never be able to boast to anyone (v. 1961: "N'en vanteras el regne dunt tu fus"). There is something scornful, too, in Oliver's implication that the Caliph would brag to women—who cannot challenge the veracity of his claim[37]—rather than to men.

In this passage a double slaying occurs for the first time. This unique event is a way of setting off the ritual death of one of the principal heroes of the *Song of Roland*. The ebbing of life in Oliver is progressively shown by loss of vision, loss of hearing, failure of heart, and, finally, collapse of body. But it is Oliver's blindness that is stressed in this passage.

The first hint of Oliver's loss of vision occurs at the end of Laisses 146 and 147, when the warrior cries out for help to his companion (v. 1976: "Sire cumpaign, a mei car vus justez!"). Roland approaches, peers into his friend's face (v. 1978), observes his ashen features, and the blood streaking his body and spattering on the ground. The hero begins a lament intended in part, no doubt, as an encouragement to his friend. Oliver, however, evidently does not hear it. Roland's words are a mixture of admiration and compassion. Characteristically, he thinks in terms of France and Charlemagne—code words for Christianity—about to lose a great warrior.

At this point one tends to forget that Roland himself is severely injured, his temples having burst when he sounded the oliphant. His swoon—the first of several fainting spells—is an expression of grief. It is also caused by loss of blood and traumatic shock at the sight of Oliver's injuries.

The ensuing scene has a phantasmic quality: In the midst of a great battle two knights drift silently and unknowingly toward each other, the one oblivious to the slaughter going on about them, the other blinded but capable of lashing out savagely like a cornered animal. Failing rapidly but alert against the slightest movement, Oliver suddenly senses danger and swings his sword wildly. He splits open his companion's helmet but fortunately leaves him unscathed.

Rudely shaken out of his state of shock, Roland is momentarily confused and utters three disjointed phrases; but, Turoldus is careful to point out, they are addressed in a gentle tone of voice (v. 1999: dulcement e suëf). The hero has now seen his friend (v. 1998); Oliver can still only hear Roland. The poet's play on the theme of seeing/not seeing culminates in Oliver's exclamation (v. 2004: "Jo ne vos vei, veied vus Damnedeu!"). This is immediately followed by a plea for forgiveness, which Roland promptly grants "*ici e devant Deu.*" The comrades-in-arms bow gravely to each other. This, Turoldus informs us, is a sign of their mutual love.

The poet is making use here of an age-old motif. In the *Sohrab and Rustum* variant of the story, familiar to readers of Matthew Arnold, a warrior encounters a stranger, fights a duel to the death with him, only to learn, too late, that he has slain his own son. The motif is widely attested in literature and folklore, as is the idea of an unwitting fight between other combinations of relatives or friends.[38] In Old French literature a fight between a father and son who do not recognize each other is found in *Gormont et Isembart*, the *Lai de Milon*, *Beaudous*, *Richart li Biaus*, the *Lai de Doon*, the *First Continuation*, *Yder*, and the *Vulgate Merlin*; similarly, between two brothers in *Protheselaus*; and between uncle and nephew in the *Prose Tristan*.[39] There is an incognito duel between two friends in Chrétien de Troyes's *Erec*, another in *Yvain*, and yet another in the *Prose Lancelot*.[40] According to Ménard, quid pro quos are pretexts for starting up the action again, for prolonging a quest, and for delaying the conclusion. They are also often used for comic effect. He readily concedes that these duels resulting from mistaken identities are not always amusing, but suggests that there is humor in that the audience knows something characters are ignorant of.[41]

Turoldus's use of this narrative commonplace is of unusual interest. To begin with, the combat is not a duel as such. Oliver is the only one to attack and actually administers only one blow. Also, it is he alone who fails to recognize his comrade, and the latter neither defends himself nor reciprocates. In fact, the incident is more of an echo of the motif than a true usage.[42]

Oliver's abortive attack on his unsuspecting friend might readily be dismissed as of little real consequence, as a trivial case of mistaken identity frequent in the confusion of battle, were it not for the fact that it follows hard upon a heated exchange between the two companions. It was probably not this circumstance, however, that riveted the attention of the medieval audience.

Perhaps the greatest trauma experienced by a person living at the time of the *Song of Roland* was the thought of dying without having had an opportunity to confess. The terrors of *mort subite*, or *male mort*, constitute one of the fundamental themes of Hélinand's *Vers de la Mort* (c. 1195).[43] Sudden death was generally considered to be a sign of damnation,[44] and certain saints were invoked for protection against this calamity.[45] It was Roland's unexpected brush with death, then, more than any lingering hard feelings that either the hero or his companion may yet have been harboring over their quarrel, which, in the Middle Ages, caused the incident to balance on the knife edge between pure fortuitousness and profound tragedy.

Much in the *Song of Roland* has to do with wisdom and conversion. Blindness, a common metaphor for lack of faith and hardness of heart, is the cause of man's downfall.[46] The medieval audience may very well have felt that Oliver's groping symbolized the plight of the unrepentant sinner. It is significant in this respect that the conversation between Roland and Oliver involves a plea for and a granting of forgiveness. The theme of seeing/not seeing reaches its culminating point when Oliver prays that God gaze favorably upon the friend he has offended.

Modern readers tend to feel that Oliver may have struck Roland, but it is the hero who should beg his friend for forgiveness for the greater offense of having brought about the catastrophe in the first place.[47] But that is not what Turoldus wrote. An attempt has been made here to plumb the workings of the poet's mind rather than to render judgments according to twentieth-century values.

Oliver's dying attitude has been studied by Mario Roques.[48] Turoldus tells us that two separate phases are involved. First, the warrior lies supine, his joined and raised hands representing the elevation of his heart in prayer. Before he dies, however, his body assumes a prone position (v. 2025: Gesir adenz, a la tere sun vis), which is an attitude expressing contrition.[49] It is safe to assume that God, taking Oliver's repentance and suffering into account, grants him remission of his sins.[50] The poem indicates that Oliver confesses his sins aloud (v. 2014: Durement en halt si recleimet sa culpe),[51] but, as in the case of Roland, no particular offense is specified.

Oliver's dying prayers concern first and foremost his own immortal soul (v. 2016: Si priet Deu que pareïs li dunget), but they also include a plea for Charles and for France, that is, for the continued success of their sacred mission. Interestingly enough, Oliver's last and most insistent request is for God's blessing on Roland (v. 2018: Sun cumpaignun Rollant sur tuz humes). If the expiring hero symbolizes anything, it is unflagging loyalty to his companion. The moment of death is signaled by the sudden forward inclination of Oliver's helmet (v. 2019), marking the instant his life-sustaining soul leaves his body (v. 2020).[52] The Struggle, so far as Oliver is concerned, is over.

Roland's lament parallels Turoldus's appraisal of the debating companions-in-arms in Laisse 87 (Ambedui unt meveillus vasselage . . . Bon sunt li cunte e lur paroles haltes), which stresses the identity of the two in all things.[53] The key word in the present passage is contained in v. 2028: "*Ensemble avum estet e anz e dis.*" Here the term *ensemble* means 'together', but it also retains part of its etymological sense (Lat. *simul* 'at the same time' akin to Lat. *sem* 'one' and *similis* 'alike').[54] "*Quant tu es mor, dulur est que jo vif*" (v. 2030) is not just a stylized antithesis of the type recommended by writers of rhetorical treatises. Roland is saying that Oliver shared in his existence and that, when he died, a part of his own nature expired.[55] Roland's swoon can be interpreted as a symbolic death and thus as a gestural extension of the thought expressed in his lament. Anyone who believes that Roland's bereavement is caused by nagging remorse over the command decision that led to Oliver's death must explain how the hero can baldly assert "*Nem fesis mal ne jo nel te forsfis*" (v. 2029). Even unconscious, Roland sits straight in his saddle, his firm posture (v. 2033) symbolic of the rectitude and uprightness that have guided all his acts.

Roland's swoon is also a convenient device to account for the passage of time needed to eliminate the remaining men around the leader.

Perceval's trance in the *Conte del graal* also bridges a time gap and affords the author an opportunity to pick up the narrative elsewhere.[56] The sudden appearance of Gautier de l'Hum—dispatched earlier (vv. 800–813) by Roland to occupy the high ground on the rearguard's flank—has puzzled many commentators.[57] Structurally (especially if one considers the laisse supplied by most of the other sources),[58] it corresponds to the arrival of Margariz in Marsile's camp in a passage also missing in the Oxford manuscript.[59] The strophe that follows Laisse 152 in the other versions contains a phrase reminiscent of Augustus's haunting exclamation after the death of Varus and the destruction of his three legions in Germany: "Vare, redde legiones" (Suetonius, chapter 23).[60]

However, there is adequate development in Laisse 152 to make it clear that Gautier's flight and appeal to Roland for help (v. 2044) are intended to underscore the desperateness of the French situation.[61] Lejeune suggests that Gautier's arrival makes it possible once again, following Oliver's death, for the action to center on a triad of French heroes.[62] Threefold modes of expression are frequent in this epic, and Conrad's translation states that Roland, Turpin, and Gautier return to the fight "in the name of the Trinity of Our Lord" (v. 6583). Gautier's plaintive cries, in particular the references to the broken lance, and the pierced shield and hauberk of vv. 2050–2051 (cf. vv. 2077–2079), recall phrases in the Psalms, notably the prayers in time of distress.

The effectiveness of the Saracen attack diminishes in proportion to the size of the French rearguard, to the point where 40,000 pagans are fought to a standstill by the three remaining worthies. Roland, Turpin, and Gautier charge the enemy like the invincible phantom triad that came to the aid of Christian armies in contemporary accounts.[63] The outcome of the battle now hangs in the balance as the Saracens, their will to fight broken, eye their formidable adversaries warily and from a distance.

At this point Turoldus returns once again to a theme mentioned earlier in this commentary relative to vv. 2028–2030, that is, the equality in worthiness of the French heroes.[64] Valor is stressed in the two passages in question (Laisses 87 and 154), but it is clear that the combination of personal qualities felt to be present in the ideal knight is what is principally being alluded to. It is remarkable that the terms *proz* and *bon*, which refer to chivalric perfection, are found in both contexts (v. 1093, proz = v. 2068, prozdom; v. 1097, bon = v. 2067, bon). One is also afforded an excellent opportunity to observe how *noble* in v. 2066 is plainly synonymous with these terms. Courage is high on the scale of knightly virtues, but loyalty to one's brother-in-arms has equal importance. While the special relationship technically referred to as companionage exists between Roland and Oliver, it is evident that combat gives rise to a comparable sense of fidelity binding together men fighting for the same cause. This battlefield allegiance is expressed by the notion of inseparability or not wanting to leave one's companion, a concept found in v. 2069 (Li uns ne volt l'altre nïent laisser), implicit in the term *ensemble* in v. 2028, and adding an important dimension to the terms *departie* and *desevrer* in vv. 1736, 1977, and 2009.

Realizing that they will never overcome the handful of French knights in hand-to-hand combat, the Saracens resort to throwing spears, a less manly tactic.[65] The profusion of terms suggests the murderous rain of weapons descending upon the French. The cowardly nature of their attack—the modern term overkill conveys similar horror—is emphasized by the fact that Turpin's shield, helmet, and hauberk are rent asunder, and that no fewer than four spears pierce him through and through. Still further missiles are implied in the slaughter of the Archbishop's horse.

Gautier is summarily despatched by the shower of projectiles and never mentioned again. Once he has played his brief but important role in the poem, he becomes a mere supernumerary, joining now the faceless multitudes bearing mute testimony to the grandeur of the rearguard's deed.

The dying perambulations of the French heroes increase as their numbers dwindle, suggesting the relative strength of the individuals concerned and adding to the pathos of the scene. After each has been mortally wounded, he will continue to fight, then confess his sins, assume an appropriate posture, and die. Oliver dies five laisses after receiving his mortal blow. Turpin perishes in the twelfth laisse following the rain of spears. From the oliphant scene, which marks the beginning of the end for Roland, to the moment of the hero's passing, the narration will require no fewer than forty-three laisses.[66]

Although the events related between the sounding of the oliphant to the present laisse are many and diverse, the scene continually focuses on Roland, who is always uppermost in the thoughts of the French. The French call their hero for help in their moment of greatest need: Oliver in vv. 1964 and 1975; Gautier in v. 2044. Now it is the Archbishop's turn (v. 2086).

The French look to Roland for moral encouragement and physical aid, but also to witness their acts. Roland functions as an Emperor surrogate, Charles being the individual who will ultimately testify to their glorious deeds. Roland sounds the oliphant not in the hope of being rescued, for it is already too late for that, but so that the Emperor will come and take cognizance of what has transpired. This explains why Turpin affirms to Roland that he remains undaunted (vv. 2087–2088), a claim that leads the poet to observe, in v. 2091, that Charlemagne was duly impressed. The purpose is edification in the etymological and mystical sense of building up the Church and the Kingdom of God.[67] What the French are doing at Roncevaux corresponds symbolically to the construction of monasteries and churches by Charles after his conquest of Spain, according to the *Pseudo-Turpin Chronicle*.[68] Edification is not conceived of as altogether altruistic, for such work is regarded as weighing heavily on the scales in the hereafter. Thus, according to the Archbishop's vision in the *Pseudo-Turpin*, when Charles is judged after his death, devils come to take away his soul, but Saint James appears on the scene and throws the churches built by the Emperor in the balance, far outweighing any evil he may have committed.[69]

From time to time ghostly presences, that is, characters who, although physically absent, play a role in the action, are felt in this poem. Mention is made now of another kind of apparition, this time by someone in no way implicated in the events being narrated by the author.

One of Turoldus's great concerns throughout the *Song of Roland* is credibility. The modern reader is quite capable of suspending his disbelief of highly implausible deeds in order to get into the spirit of the epic. This is the mental process by which one accepts the poem on its own terms. One learns at an early age that an epic may be based on historical fact, but that events therein are imaginatively recreated. One expects historical chronicles to be scrupulously accurate, but one allows poets a good deal of leeway in telling their version of what happened. Medieval chroniclers and jongleurs were not as naïve as they are often reputed to be—for instance, they often accuse other authors of being ignoramuses or liars—and they did take their work seriously. Authors usually endeavored to relate essential facts as they knew them, and much of what they passed on was based on an oral or written tradition of some sort.

Eyewitness accounts exist throughout history,[70] but most chroniclers have always had to rely on others for their information. In the Middle

Ages certain individuals, chronicles, and monastic archives acquired a reputation for veracity, and writers began citing these authorities, often without ever having consulted them, in order to lend plausibility to their narratives.[71] Considering the fact, then, that some of the sources alluded to in the chansons de geste are known to have existed, whereas others are purported authorities only, what is one to make of Saint Giles's narrative referred to, in v. 2095, as the guarantor of what has just been related?

No such chronicle, if there ever was one, has survived. Early on, however, the seventh-century saint became associated with the legend of Charlemagne.[72] A tenth-century Latin *Vita Aegidii* relates that Charles asked the saint to say special prayers for him because he had committed a sin so shameful he dared not confess it.[73] A few days later, an angel appeared to Giles as he was saying mass. The celestial messenger left a scroll revealing the nature of the Emperor's offense and passed on the welcome news that, thanks to the saint's intercession, the sinner was forgiven. Charles had only to repent and never commit the same sin again. By the end of the twelfth century, Charlemagne's sin had been identified as incest with his sister, from which relationship Roland was born.[74] It is not certain that Turoldus was cognizant of this legend.[75] Saint Giles's mass is depicted in a mural dated about 1200 at Le Loroux-Bottereau and in a miniature illustrating a psalter dated 1255–60 preserved at Liège.[76] The legend appears with scenes from the Battle of Roncevaux in the Aachen casket (1200–1215) and in the famous early-thirteenth-century Charlemagne window at Chartres.[77]

The passage in question in the *Song of Roland* states that Saint Giles was present at Roncevaux and recorded what he saw in a manuscript preserved in the monastery at Laon.[78] Since Turoldus later makes it clear that there were no survivors, it would appear that Saint Giles saw the battle in a vision. The *Pseudo-Turpin Chronicle* provides an incident with which it is useful to compare this passage.[79] According to the latter narrative, the Archbishop was with Charles rather than with Roland and was informed of the details of the hero's death by Thierry, who witnessed the event.[80] Just before Thierry's arrival, Turpin had a vision while saying mass.[81] In reply to a query several devils, looking as if returning from a foray, say they are carrying the souls of Marsile and his men to Hell and that Saint Michael is bearing those of Roland and his companions off to heaven. Following Charlemagne's death, Turpin has the second vision, mentioned above. The miniature illustrating the initial apparition in the *Codex Calixtinus* shows the bodies of Roland and his men in a lower register and two angels bearing their souls heavenward immediately above.[82]

In the *Pseudo-Turpin Chronicle* the physical witnessing by Thierry and the mystical "presence" of Turpin at the Battle of Roncevaux are plainly intended to lend credibility to the narrative.[83] A Pseudo-Giles version of the same events may have existed, but it seems more likely that Turoldus was merely endeavoring to make his narrative sound plausible at this particular juncture. The great importance he attaches to trust is epitomized in v. 2098 (Ki tant ne set ne l'ad prod entendut), which can be compared to Philosophy's query in Boethius's *De Consolatione Philosophiae*: "Do you hear my words or are you like an ass before a lyre?"[84] (*Fig. 52*).

22. Charlemagne's Approach

Laisses 156–164 (verses 2099–2221)

The weakness of Roland's final blast on the oliphant underscores not only the hero's failing strength but also his determination to signal his uncle. The sound of the horn is clearly magic, for although it is feeble it still carries all the way to the Emperor. The latter interprets it as a trumpet of doom (v. 2108: "Ja oi al corner que guaires ne vivrat"). In the laisses that follow a persistent leitmotif, which stresses the return of Charlemagne, is not described directly but related through the reactions of others (v. 2114: "Karlun avrum nus ja!"; v. 2115: "L'emperere repairet"; v. 2117: "Se Carles vient"; v. 2133: "Carles repairet"; 2149: "Carles repeiret"). The Emperor's answering calls seem to be enchanted too. Sixty thousand trumpets are sounded (v. 2111), the mountains and valleys shudder from the blast, the Saracens hear them and quake, but—mysteriously—the French do not react. It is as if an impenetrable wall of air—like the one that surrounds King Evrain's enchanted garden in Chrétien's *Erec*—seals them off.[1] In v. 2145 Turpin says: "*Carles repairet,*" but this is an expression of hope and confidence, not an announcement.

The thought of the Emperor's arrival strikes fear into the hearts of the Saracens, and one is reminded of the trepidation experienced by medieval people at the thought of the Second Coming.[2] For the pagans Charles's *adventus* is indeed a *dies irae*. They are torn between a desire to flee before the imminent arrival of the Emperor and the need to destroy Roland, who constitutes a deadly peril for Spain (vv. 2117–2119). The Saracens' dilemma underscores the identity in spirit of Charlemagne and his nephew. Unbeknown to them, their indecision as to whether to stay and fight Roland or to attempt to escape matters little, for in the end they will all be destroyed. In a last vain effort the Saracens hurl four hundred of their best men against Roland. In what is perhaps the greatest understatement in the poem, Turoldus says that his hero has a lot to do (v. 2123).[3]

Roland and Turpin wade in among the Saracens (v. 2129)—two against four hundred!—and, incredible as it may seem, the Saracens panic. "Let us flee, Charles is coming," they say, but it is in large part the sight of the two French heroes, prodigiously magnified in their eyes (v. 2125: Tant se fait fort e fiers e maneviz!) that makes them admit, finally, that they can never vanquish Roland (v. 2153).

The panic-stricken Saracens, who imagine their lone adversaries to be deathless and invincible, are completely deluded: Roland and Turpin have now seemingly expended the last ounce of their strength. What is it that keeps them going? What is it that infuses them with endlessly renewed vigor? Roland is grievously wounded from blowing the oliphant, Turpin stricken with at least the four lance wounds mentioned by Turoldus. Still they rise to the challenge, still they attack the enemy! The source of their strength lies in two thoughts: the idea that Charles is surely coming and the indestructible bond that joins the two warriors together. Their faith in the Emperor's return, voiced by Turpin in v. 2145, is totally blind (remember, no sound has reached French ears) and has nothing to do with the notion of rescue, which would only lead to despair since their lives are ebbing away. Their faith is founded rather upon the reaction they know the Emperor will have when he finds the evidence of their magnificent triumph.

A second thought also sustains Turpin and Roland in the last enemy assault they must withstand together. Much has been written about the companionage that binds Roland and Oliver, but it should be noted that in Laisse 159 the hero addresses the Archbishop in strikingly similar terms. One must doubtless refrain from oversentimentalizing these relationships, but the ties that join comrades-in-arms are nonetheless affectionate and strong.[4] The laments express genuine grief at the loss of a friend. Roland's gentleness with Turpin and in carrying the bodies of his dead companions to Turpin's feet also demonstrates affection. *Pur vostre amur* (v. 2139), then, conveys much of the meaning such an expression has in the modern idiom. In the next verse Roland uses the term *ensemble*, which, as noted above, implies togetherness as well as sameness and a sharing of identical fates.

In Laisse 160 Charlemagne's army is so near the Saracens that the latter hear not only their trumpets but also their mighty shouts of "Monjoie!" (v. 2151). In a final desperate and cowardly act the pagans send a second murderous hail of arrows and spears toward Roland.[5] The projectiles slay Roland's horse beneath him and pierce his shield and hauberk.[6] Miraculously, however, the hero is unscathed.[7] An invisible aureole obviously surrounds Roland's entire body, leaving him invulnerable to Saracen weapons. In medieval art saints are at times represented enclosed in a protective bubble of light[8]—the familiar elliptical mandorla surrounding Christ's person is related to this[9]—rendering them impervious to evildoers' designs, and this is evidently how Turoldus conceived of his hero.

Knights are greatly hampered of course by the loss of their mounts.[10] Turpin (Laisse 154) and now Roland (Laisse 161) are unable to pursue the routed enemy forces (v. 2166). The death of Turpin's fabulous war-horse in Laisse 154 and, here, of Roland's trusty Veillantif, is also a sign of the declining strength of the heroes. But Roland remains standing (vv. 2163, 2168). The Saracens recognize the supernatural aspect of what has transpired[11] and, instead of rushing their unhorsed adversary, they turn and flee. Roland has not been defeated. On the contrary, his defiant stance in his moment of greatest danger has vanquished the enemy.

Roland binds up Turpin's wounds as best he can, embraces him, and gently lays him on the grass. The hug he gives the Archbishop is a sign of affection, but it is also an unconscious effort to infuse some of his own vital warmth into his dying companion. One thinks of the prophet Elijah stretching himself over the widow's dead son three times, an act that miraculously restores the child to life (1 Kings 17:17–24).[12] The same life-giving hug has been repeated in countless death scenes. Primitively, the death embrace was probably an attempt to prevent the ghost-spirit from leaving the body.[13] Medieval people visualized the soul's departure graphically (*see Figs. 18 and 64*), and such considerations may have a bearing on what is transpiring here.[14]

Having made Turpin as comfortable as he can, Roland begs leave to seek out his companions and bring them back to the spot where the Archbishop lies. They were dear to us, the hero says, and we must not leave them (vv. 2178–2179).[15]

The conversation between Roland and Turpin is curiously formal: "La politesse, dans l'ancienne épopée, est rigoureuse et souvent cérémonieuse. On ne se quitte jamais sans demander expressément congé." Jenkins, who quotes this observation by Gaston Paris, wonders: "Or, has Roland in mind that, at v. 2141, he had promised formally not to leave Turpin alone? May the Saracens not return? Is there not still some danger? Cf. vv. 2274 ff. [the Rash Saracen incident]."[16] There is, however, no such concern on their part, for the idea of having achieved a definitive victory is uppermost in their minds at the moment: "*Cist camp est vostre, mercit Deu, vostre et mien,*" says Turpin (v. 2183).[17] The theme of triumph in death, which becomes so important later on, is already implicit in the Archbishop's words. Paying strict attention to Roland's words, one sees that his intention is essentially to identify his deceased comrades. The etymology of *entercier* in v. 2180 is helpful here. The term is derived from VL **intertiare* (< Lat. *tertium* 'third') and indicates the act of placing aside or of giving something to a third party. After a battle it is often a real problem of course to distinguish friend from foe and to identify individuals in one's own army.[18] The search for the bodies of the French Peers will be a gripping moment in the *Song of Roland.*

The ritual alignment of the bodies of the fallen Christians has thus far elicited no scholarly commentary.[19] To begin with, it is the French Peers, not just any Christians, who are brought before Turpin. The bodies are carefully disposed *en reng* (v. 2192), which can mean 'in a row or rows' (Bédier: "sur un rang") or, possibly, retaining its etymological sense, 'in a ring', that is, a semicircle. The latter disposition suggests the council of the Franks, where the same term was encountered (v. 264).[20] Turpin's benediction (v. 2194) of the symmetrically arranged bodies recalls the image of Abbot Raganuldus blessing the people in the Marmoutier Sacramentary[21] (*Fig. 53*).

More important, however, the painstaking search for and arrangement of the bodies shows once again the great importance the French attach to the manner in which Charlemagne will find their remains. Roland and Turpin, who know full well they will not live to see the Emperor (v. 2199: "Ja ne verrai le riche empereür"), want to send him a message beyond the grave. The orderly disposition will serve as a means of identification because the Peers will be found together, a sign of their companionage,[22] and because this symmetry, as opposed to the tangled state of the Saracen cadavers, suggests inner peace.

There may be further significance to the arrangement. One of the most striking Christian theophanies is John's vision of Christ in Majesty appearing before the Twenty-Four Old Men (Revelation 4:2–11).[23] The Elders bow down and adore the Lord and sing his praises. Various interpretations have been proposed for this portion of the Johannine narrative. One of the most widely accepted medieval views is that they represented the Twelve Prophets and the Twelve Apostles, that is, the Old and New Testaments together.[24] The Twenty-Four Elders are a familiar motif in the art of the Middle Ages and are frequently accorded a place of honor in apse murals or on the tympanum over the main portal in Romanesque churches.[25] In these representations the number of figures and their attributes vary, but, whether seated, standing, or in prostration, the Elders are invariably depicted with heads thrown back and eyes elevated in adoration and ecstasy.[26] Since the deed accomplished by Roland and his men at Roncevaux is edifying, the careful alignment of the Peers may be intended to suggest the perpetual laud of the Elders of the Apocalypse. Certainly Turpin's gesture of benediction (v. 2194) recalls the hand raised in blessing of the Majestas Domini.[27] *Deus li Glorius* in v. 2196 is the equivalent of Rex Gloriae, a possible allusion to the same Johannine vision.[28] Finally, the Archbishop's prayer that the souls of the departed French Peers be received by God and that He place them among the holy flowers of Paradise is yet another reference to Heaven in this passage.[29]

A separate trip, symbolic of the special relationship between the two companions, is needed for Roland to bring Oliver to Turpin. Roland's embrace recalls his hugging of the Archbishop in spite of the fact that Oliver is already dead.[30] The Brindisi mosaic depicts Roland carrying his friend on his shoulders in an attitude that cannot fail to suggest the Good Shepherd[31] (*Fig. 54*). For the Brindisi artist the scene evoked an image of Christ with the strayed sheep on his shoulders,[32] and it seems reasonable to suppose that, in the medieval audience, persons inclined to make such connections interpreted the act in that fashion.

For medieval exegetes Christ the Good Shepherd was prefigured in Psalms 23:1–4: "Yahweh is my shepherd, I lack nothing. In meadows of green grass he lets me lie. To the waters of repose he leads me; there he revives my soul. He guides me by paths of virtue for the sake of his name. Though I pass through a gloomy valley, I fear no harm; beside me your rod and your staff are there, to hearten me." Symbolically, the lost sheep is the repentant sinner that Christ brings back to the fold.[33] The Archbishop makes a sign of the cross over Oliver and gives him posthumous absolution (v. 2205). This association with penance should give pause to anyone who believes that the poem centers on the idea that Roland is the sinner and that it is his comrade-in-arms who vainly strives to bring him within the pale. The occurrence of a penitential image at this juncture does not necessarily mean that Turoldus wishes to associate the notion of savior or sinner with either Roland or Oliver.[34] More than likely the poet simply wishes to suggest God's forgiveness and mercy in a general way.

Roland's lament for Oliver (vv. 2207–2214) praises his *fortitudo* and his *sapientia*, a combination of virtues said to reside in the ideal knight. To complete the portrait, mention is made of Oliver's father, Duke Renier, the implication being that such qualities are inherited. Nobility is being alluded to here of course. Lat. *nobilis*, akin to Lat. *gnoscere*, *noscere* 'to come to know', meant 'famous, well-known' hence 'well-born', but it was the latter sense that yielded the word *noble*.

23. The Death of Turpin

Laisses 165–167 (verses 2222–2258)

Two interlocking narrative circles, one passive, one active, are important patterns in Laisses 165–167. Oliver's death triggers a sympathetic reaction from Roland, whose swoon stirs Turpin to a final effort culminating in his own passing, which in turn elicits another lament from Roland. This chain of grief is intertwined with a distinct series of narrative links having to do with reciprocal acts of charity. Roland, who has been tending Turpin, faints, whereupon the Archbishop endeavors to come to his assistance by obtaining water, a charitable act to which the hero responds by arranging the prelate's hands in a posthumous prayer and gesture of repose.[1]

Very few details in the *Song of Roland* are apt to intrigue scholars inclined to symbolic interpretations as much as the presence of a stream at Roncevaux.[2] The fact that Turpin takes Roland's oliphant and dies while trying to reach the water is also pregnant with possibilities. It matters little that there are in fact two streams at the traditional site, as well as a spring in the village that bears the name of the famous battle itself, any or indeed all of which may have been known to Turoldus.[3]

The metaphor of the stag longing for water, an important image of the Christian's desire for God, was mentioned earlier,[4] and it is possible to interpret Turpin's efforts to reach the spring as a similar expression of his enduring faith. The direction of his dying steps would not have been lost on Charlemagne, the eventual witness of the Christians' dying attitudes. Indirectly, too, the Archbishop's effort to obtain water points to Roland's great thirst, an aspect of the latter's imitation of Christ's Passion.[5]

However, the context rather suggests a connection with the sacrament of Penance.[6] The French heroes all confess their sins and, in their final moment, adopt attitudes expressive of their contrition or symbolic of their attitude toward their past transgressions. It must be clearly understood that the confessions are general and have nothing to do with the decision leading to their martyrdom at Roncevaux. Turpin is, to be sure, involved in an act of charity, which is edifying in its own right, but water in this instance has a powerful association with purification and rebirth, symbols of Penance, and it probably has that function here.[7]

It should be noted that Turpin's tripping steps (v. 2228), which arouse pity, provided an opportunity for the jongleur to mime this act.[8] He could easily have dramatized the Archbishop's death, too, by slight forward body and head movements suggesting Turpin's final collapse. There was doubtless a pause for effect, too, between Laisses 166 and 167, after Turpin had expired.

Roland revives just before the Archbishop dies. It had not been clear in Laisse 150 whether or not Roland witnessed Oliver's last gasp, although Roland was uppermost in Oliver's thoughts. The hero has an anxious moment as he regains consciousness, for the Archbishop is nowhere to be seen. After a brief search—Roland's glances toward the mountain (v. 2235) are partly an effort to find the missing prelate and partly a prayer on his behalf[9]—he spies him lying on the grass, where he fell trying to reach the stream. Turpin beats his breast and, with a last effort, raises his joined hands in a final supplication.[10]

The portrait of Turpin that emerges from the glowing tribute accorded to him by the poet in Laisse 166 and from Roland's lament emphasizes the long service he has rendered God. The Archbishop's nobility (vv. 2237, 2252) appears to be directly related to the fact that he answered God's call and acted in his name (v. 2238). The notion of altruistic service is reiterated in the expression *campiuns* (< Lat. *campus* 'field [of battle]') in v. 2244, for primitively, a champion was a person who fought a judicial combat on behalf of someone else.[11] Once again one notes that warring for Charles is identical with fighting for God (v. 2242).

According to Turoldus God's service in these perilous times entails, essentially, a struggle against the Infidel. What is generally stressed in discussions of Turpin's character is his warlike behavior. It is true that he fights valiantly when called upon to do so and evinces a propensity for combat and strife as indicated by his eagerness to take Charles's message to Marsile (Laisse 19), his volunteering to be part of the rear-guard (v. 799), and his remarkable energy on the battlefield. In the passage under examination, Turpin's ardor for combat is mentioned in passing (v. 2242: le guerreier Charlun), but the *granz batailles* alluded to in the following line are equated with his hortatory activities. The latter contribution to the war effort is often not accorded the attention it warrants.

Turpin's interventions were crucial in both phases of the Roland-Oliver debate.[12] The fine *sermons* alluded to in v. 2243 probably refer in part to the speeches made on these occasions, for the term was used not only for homilies delivered from a pulpit but also for any kind of edifying discourse.[13] However, it is clear from the context that formal sermons were also preached on earlier occasions by the Archbishop as part of a sustained effort to enlist support for the war against the pagans.[14]

The term "prophet" (v. 2255) was at times loosely applied to holy men in general,[15] but it refers here to the Archbishop's vigorous exhortations. Turpin's crusading appeals are likened to the ceaseless admonitions and promptings of the Old Testament prophets whom God also "sent in His name" (v. 2238).[16] His urgings were designed to uphold the Christian religion, a rather vague concept to be sure, but Turoldus joins it to a phrase that leaves no doubt that exalting Christianity was to be accomplished by becoming involved, by joining a crusading venture (v. 2256: Pur lei tenir e pur humes atraire).

The grisly details of the Archbishop's wounds may shock the modern reader, but they were doubtless intended to suggest a community of martyrdom with Christ.[17]

The last two phrases in Roland's lament for Turpin are a prayer for the latter's soul, which is conceived of as on its way to heaven.[18] Translations have usually rendered *sufraite* in v. 2257 as 'privations' (cf. Moignet: "Que votre âme ne manque pas d'être comblée"),[19] and that is the meaning this term has in other passages of the poem. OFr. *sofraite*, a derivative of the verb *sofraindre* (< VL **suffrangere* for CL *suffringere* 'to break') also meant torment, that is, suffering not only from lack or want, but pain of any sort, a sense reinforced by the proximity of OFr. *sofrir* (< VL **sufferire* for CL *sufferre* 'to support, to bear') 'to suffer'.[20] The distinction is not a frivolous one, for it offers an insight into how the French conceived of the transition from an earthly to a celestial existence at the time of the *Song of Roland.* The hero prays that the Gates of Heaven[21] be open for Turpin's soul and that it not be obliged to endure tortures, a clear allusion to Purgatory.[22]

24. The Rash Saracen

Laisses 168–170 (verses 2259–2296)

Roland now faces death alone. In the long series of laisses that follow, rescue by Charlemagne's army or at least the Emperor's arrival on the scene, which seemed imminent a few moments ago, is completely forgotten. The hero has only three thoughts on his mind: (1) prayer; (2) the oliphant and Durendal; and (3) an appropriate dying attitude. These ritualistic concerns engross him to such a point that any intrusion will strike him as insufferably blasphemous.

Laisse 168 sums up Roland's concerns. Too much importance should not be attached to the distinction he draws in his prayers at this point —he prays God to call his Peers to Him, whereas he himself prays to Gabriel—but one is entitled to wonder why he thinks of the archangel in particular. Except in one instance, when both Michael and the angel referred to as Cherubin also descend to take Roland's soul to heaven,[1] Gabriel is the only celestial messenger to appear in the poem. He has a predilection for Charlemagne: He inspires at least two of his visions (vv. 2526, 3993), protects and blesses him (vv. 2847–2848), and comes to his aid in the battle with Baligant (vv. 3610, 3612).[2] The closeness of the relationship between the Emperor and his nephew (INTRODUC-

TION, 19, D) suffices to explain why Gabriel favors Roland too. It is worth noting that in addition to his duties as a messenger, one of the functions traditionally ascribed to him,[3] Gabriel assumes a task usually associated with Saint Michael, Prince of the Heavenly Hosts, namely, help in time of war.[4] It is Saint Michael, too, who customarily leads souls to heaven and weighs them on his scales.[5]

It was not uncommon for persons in the Middle Ages to confuse these angelic functions, and Turoldus, like other writers, even individualizes Cherubin, actually a plural word. Perhaps Roland prays to Gabriel simply because a messenger will be needed to carry his gauntlet to heaven.[6] Another explanation for Roland's prayer to Gabriel rather than to anyone else resides in the fact that this archangel, like Michael, was felt to be particularly effective in warding off evil.[7] This is the reason the two archangels often figure on church portals and why they are referred to in Greek as *propylaios*.[8] Life-size statues of Roland and Oliver stand out in the portico of the Cathedral of Verona.[9] Lejeune and Stiennon believe that the reason Niccolò's sculptures, dated 1139, guarded this entrance was that the French heroes were revered as defenders of the faith.[10] Thus the association between Roland and Gabriel, both stalwart protectors of the Church, was a natural one.

The hero now begins his final ambulation. His intention, stated later,[11] is to position his body in a manner signifying to Charlemagne that he kept his word and died courageously at the head of his men, having taken a symbolic additional "step" toward Spain to demonstrate his defiance of the Saracens and his valor in the face of the enemy.[12] The Emperor, recalling his nephew's solemn vow at Aix, will be looking for precisely this message when he searches the body-strewn field of Roncevaux for Roland.[13]

Roland's dying moments are related in a series of laisses similaires, a stretching device used to great effect by Turoldus for lyrical purposes and for dissecting and scrutinizing a brief action. It is easy to lose track of the actual distance covered by the hero and the relatively short time involved. What happens is simply this: Roland moves forward, advancing perhaps as much as a few hundred yards—the distance traversed by a bolt fired from a crossbow, Turoldus tells us (cf. vv. 2265, 2868)—climbing a hill in the process, and finding a spot with two trees,[14] four marble objects, and a dark stone.[15] There he has a brief encounter with the Rash Saracen, whom he slays with a blow from the oliphant.[16] Roland then strikes the dark stone with his sword in an effort to make his weapon useless to the enemy. The demolished stone will constitute another sign for the Emperor.[17] After running forward once again toward a pine tree, he lies down prone, his face turned toward the enemy to signal Charles that he died victorious. He confesses his sins and, just before he expires, raises his gauntlet in a gesture intended, for once, not for Charlemagne but for God. What follows is an examination of each phase of the hero's final moments.

The most obvious meaning one can read into Roland's agonizing ascent and death on a mountain near a tree is that it is an imitation of the Passion. The hero's suffering, especially his thirst, echoes that of Christ, the hill represents Calvary, the tree the Cross.[18] The parallel fits the overall typology of Abraham and Isaac, the latter being universally associated throughout the Middle Ages with God's sacrifice of his own son.[19] Roland predicted the manner of his death,[20] which is brought about by Ganelon's Judas-like betrayal and is announced, as in the gospels, by an earthquake and storm.[21]

In another epic narrative the dying hero also imitates Christ. Having observed, in the recital of Vivien's suffering in the *Chanson de Guillaume*, some probable allusions to Saint Peter denying his Savior, to the "calice d'amertume, épuisé jusqu'à la dernière goutte, dont Jésus parle symboliquement," and to Christ's momentary weakness at Gethsemane,[22] Frappier affirms that "le poète avait formé le dessein très conscient de transposer dans le mode épique certains aspects du drame de la Passion."[23]

But, as is the case for other motifs in the chansons de geste, the death of the hero is often and above all merely a variant of a conventional scene.

In the *Song of Roland*, in the *Chanson de Guillaume*, and elsewhere, the topos retains a number of traditional features: the hero's suffering; his last prayers including the "epic credo"; his final gestures, notably the mea culpa and the hands joined or raised, or the arms crossed; and the angels who witness his last moments and who accompany his soul to heaven. This is followed by laments, the embalming ceremony, and, finally, burial. Some of these elements are missing at times and, in the *Song of Roland* and the *Chanson de Guillaume*, certain details have been rearranged, yet the conventional aspect of these scenes cannot be denied.[24]

Scholars have focused to such an extent on isolated elements in the epic death scene that the motif taken as a whole has been seriously neglected. The epic motif of the dying hero is clearly patterned after the topos of the dying martyr in the saints' lives. The latter bears unmistakable signs of having been influenced by the narrative of the death of Christ. For example, the Passion no doubt had an effect on the earliest (second century) Latin *passio*. Bollandist Father Hippolyte Delehaye, having noted that Saint Polycarp predicts his own death, is betrayed by a Judas-like figure, and accepts God's will, draws the following conclusion: "L'idée-mère de la *Passio Polycarpi* est un parallèle du martyr avec le Christ souffrant: les détails sont, sinon inventés, du moins choisis et mis en lumière à cet effet."[25] The hagiographs were to remember Christ's Passion on countless occasions:

> Toute l'antiquité est pénétrée de cette pensée que le martyr souffre avec le Sauveur et reproduit sa passion en lui. On la retrouve un peu plus tard dans la lettre des Eglises de Vienne et de Lyon, dans Hégésippe à propos de Jacques le Juste, dans la Passion de Perpétue et Félicité, et dans beaucoup d'autres textes.[26]

It is clear, then, that the jongleurs who composed the Old French epics were influenced not only by the conventional death scene in the saints' lives but also by the traditional association of the death of the martyr with that of Christ. This is what explains the Good Friday reminiscences that are found, for instance, in the *Chanson de Guillaume*, in the *Pseudo-Turpin Chronicle*, and in the *Guide du Pèlerin*.[27] This is what explains their presence in the *Song of Roland*.

The locale imagined by Turoldus for Roland's death is unique in that it contains four marble objects. Bédier has suggested that *quatre perruns* constitute "un emplacement carré ou rectangulaire, où la main de l'homme avait planté deux beaux arbres et disposé des marbres bien taillés."[28] He goes on to say that the slabs were boundary markers:

> Dès lors, on entrevoit ce que le poète a voulu dire. Il devait bien savoir que la plaine de Roncevaux était, depuis des siècles, terre habitée et terre chrétienne: son imagination a planté sur ce tertre, comme en un lieu solennel, des bornes pour marquer la limite entre la chrétienté et la *paiënie*,—la frontière.[29] S'il en fut ainsi, on comprend (et je n'arrive à le comprendre qu'à la faveur de cette hypothèse) que Roland ne veuille pas mourir là, mais, pour mieux prouver sa victoire, plus loin, au-delà de la frontière, en terre sarrasine. Ainsi s'explique son suprême effort.[30]

To my knowledge Bédier's interpretation has not been seriously challenged,[31] but it has probably not convinced many scholars who have taken the time to examine the passage in question critically either.

Its chief merit is that it ascribes symbolic meaning to Roland's act: The hero flees the boundary marker as part of his message to Charlemagne.

Bédier believed that the stone or stones that Roland strikes with Durendal (vv. 2300, 2312, 2338) were the same as the four marble slabs, and that the hero fled this spot (v. 2357: Desuz un pin i est alet curant). However, Turoldus distinguishes carefully between the four hand-shaped shiny marble objects near the two trees located on the hill:[32]

> 2267 Muntet sur un tertre, desuz .II. arbres bels,
> Quatre perruns i ad, de marbre faiz.

> 2271 Halt sunt li pui e mult halt les arbres,
> Quatre perruns i ad luisant de marbre.

the grayish-brown natural rock or rocks he strikes with his sword:

> 2300 Dedevant lui ad une perre byse.

> 2312 Rollant ferit el perrun de sardonie.

> 2338 Rollant ferit en une perre bise.

and the solitary pine, which is his final resting place:

> 2357 Desuz un pin i est alet curant.

> 2375 Li quens Rollant se jut desuz un pin.

On the other hand, the knoll, the two trees, the four marble objects, the grayish-brown stone or stones, and the pine tree are all within a few feet of one another. The pine is no further than the few remaining steps that Roland manages to take in his dying condition.

After the destruction of Marsile's army, Charlemagne will find this exact spot and, having climbed the knoll (v. 2869),[33] he comes upon the two trees (v. 2874) and the stone or stones (v. 2875) struck by his nephew. The Emperor faints at the sight of Roland, whereupon his men lean him up against *un pin* (v. 2884), presumably the same pine mentioned in vv. 2357 and 2375. Until now it has not been clear whether Roland strikes one or more stones, *une perre byse* or *bise* (vv. 2300, 2338) being compatible with the *perrun de sardonie* in v. 2312. However, in v. 2875 Turoldus will state that the Emperor *Les colps Rollant conut en treis perruns*, which seems categorical enough, until one notes that the corresponding verse in Venice IV reads: *Li colp de Rollant cognos in le peron.*[34] The Oxford copyist may have mistaken *en le* for *en .iii.*, or he may have rationalized that Roland's blows fell on three stones, the triple mention of sword strokes in vv. 2300, 2312, and 2338 appearing in laisses similaires and lending themselves to interpretation as one stone or three. It should be noted that the preceding line in Venice IV has Charlemagne finding the stone near a single tree (Desot d'un arbre e parvegnu amo), while in the Old Norse *Saga* and Conrad's version one reads that Roland is lying in the midst of four (marble) stones.[35]

The situation is a complex one, then, yet a number of facts seem clear: (1) the two trees are distinct from the pine in Turoldus's mind and he does not confuse the four marble objects with the stone or stones; (2) these landscape features are all very close to one another; and (3) Roland's blows fall, not on the marble but on the dark stone or stones. The relevance of these three points emerges from what follows.

Bédier's allegation that Roland fled from the marble blocks is baseless in view of the proximity of the objects in question. The major argument he presents in favor of the stones being a border marker is that one manuscript of the rhymed version (Paris, v. 2611) offers the following variant for v. 2300: *Il esgarda, une bosne a veüe.*[36] OFr. *bodne* (< Medieval Lat. **bodina*) is the ancestor of MFr. *borne* 'boundary stone'. However, this evidence consists of an isolated substitution by a scribe copying in the second half of the thirteenth century and, moreover, concerns the stone that Roland strikes, not the marble. Finally, although the French scholar understood that four marble objects constitute a man-made square or rectangle, his notion that this was done "pour la symétrie"[37] is lame and in no way clarified by the boundary-stone hypothesis.

The term *perrun*, like its Modern French counterpart *perron*, usually refers to a stone block, a step, or a platform presenting a flat horizontal surface such as one might find, for instance, in front of a church door.[38] In the *Song of Roland* it refers additionally to the stone step used to facilitate dismounting from a horse (vv. 2704, 2819, 3697) and to Marsile's couch (v. 12).[39] But the standard Old French dictionaries also provide numerous examples of *perron* referring to vertical stones, monuments of various kinds including megaliths and statues, and, most significantly, columns and pillars.[40] The column at Liège, which symbolizes the city's franchises and appears in the municipal coat of arms, is termed *le Perron*.[41] The Pillars of Hercules at the Straits of Gilbraltar are alluded to in a thirteenth-century source as *les bones et petrons que Ercules mist.*[42]

In one of his nocturnal visions Charlemagne dreams *Qu'il ert en*

France, ad Ais, a un perrun, / En dous chaeines s'i teneit un brohun (vv. 2556–2557). Bédier, who reads *s'i* as *si* (see OXFORD TEXT, ENGLISH TRANSLATION, v. 2557), translates: "qu'il était en France, à Aix sur un perron, et tenait un ours enchaîné par deux chaînes" (Owen: "He was in France at Aix on a stone step / And held a bear there fettered with two chains"). That the incident occurs in front of his palace is confirmed by v. 2563: *De sun palais uns veltres i acurt.* Everyone agrees that the apparition refers to the events which occur later at Aix and that the lines in question correspond closely to vv. 3734–3737:

Li emperere est repairet ad Ais.
Guenes li fels, en caeines de fer,
En la citet est devant le paleis.
A un estache l'unt atachet cil serf.

The apparent discrepancy between *a un perrun* (v. 2556) and *A un estache* (v. 3737) is resolved when one understands that a pillar, or post, is intended in both passages. OFr. *estache* usually referred to a wooden stake, but sometimes, as in the present instance, indicated a stone column.[43] (The symbolic aspect of the pillar to which Ganelon is chained is discussed below, in COMMENTARY, 45.)

A telling argument in support of the interpretation offered here of the four marble objects at Roncevaux is found in the illustration of the Rash Saracen scene in Conrad's translation (*Fig. 55*),[44] which shows Roland in the midst of four rectangular columns.

There is ample reason to believe, then, that the *quatre perruns* were four marble pillars. Such being the case, the stone shafts were doubtless associated in the poet's mind with the four columns on which the tabernacle veil was hung in the Temple of Jerusalem (Exodus 26: 31–33.).[45] The veil symbolized the sky separating earth from ḥeaven[46] and, as noted below,[47] can be visualized when Roland's soul is borne heavenward or is said to be in Paradise. The pillars were held by medieval exegetes to represent the four corners of the world, the Evangelists, or "the powers of the celestial hosts, adorned with the four virtues."[48] The sky-curtain appears in numerous Carolingian and Ottonian miniatures, including the Christomimetes (*see Fig. 2*); the four Living Creatures or Tetramorph (Lion, Ox, Man, and Eagle) are often substituted for the pillars.[49] The ciborium, that is, the four pillars supporting a cupola, a structure that traditionally encloses the altar in Christian churches, is also a symbolic representation of the Temple columns and veil[50] (*Fig. 56*).

The significance of the mysterious marble objects is now obvious. Roland is about to pass from this world into the next,[51] and this transfer will take place in a locale suggesting the Jewish tabernacle. His death, like that of Christ, is a sacrifice on a symbolic altar.[52]

The parallel with Christ, which became evident with the emergence of the archetype of Abraham and Isaac and Roland's imitation of the Passion of Our Lord, is underscored by the imagery of the two trees and the pine.

One of the most fertile images of the Middle Ages is the contrast between good and evil symbolized by two trees.[53] The metaphor stems from Matthew 7:11 ("A sound tree produces good fruit but a rotten tree bad fruit"), but there were other influences, too, in particular that of the Tree of Knowledge of Good and Evil[54] as opposed to Christ, the Tree of Life.[55]

In Romanesque art—for example, in the New Minster of Winchester Psalter (*Fig. 57*) and the Gospel Book of Saint Bernward[56]—the Cross is sometimes flanked by two trees representing the Garden of Eden. A miniature of the *Hortus Deliciarum* (*Fig. 58*) conveys more explicitly the idea that Christ, through his Passion, reopened the Gates of Paradise, which had been closed by Adam and Eve's sin.[57] Under an ornate cupola depicting the firmament, the Tree of Life (*Lignum Vit*[*a*]*e*)[58] is framed by two other trees and the symbols of the four rivers of Paradise mentioned in Genesis 2:10.[59] The composition is labeled *Paradisus Voluptatis* 'Garden of Delights'.

There is a striking resemblance between this drawing and the setting imagined by Turoldus for Roland's death. In both cases, the four pillars, primitively Temple columns, are associated with three trees. This combination of Edenic and Crucifixion imagery symbolizes Paradise Regained.[60]

The intrusion of the Rash Saracen on this hallowed ground just as the hero prepares to meet his Maker provokes a violent reaction.[61] The pagan's deceitfulness in feigning death, and his face and body soiled with the blood of others (vv. 2275–2276),[62] indicate his diabolic nature.[63] Symbolically, the Saracen represents the surreptitious enemy whom Christians pray will not prevail against them at the hour of their death.[64]

Similar instances of Saracen trickery in the *Chanson de Guillaume* and the *Chevalerie Vivien* have been adduced by Skidmore,[65] and the pagan's boast to have vanquished Roland (v. 2281) is also reminiscent of the evil Seneschal of the King of Ireland, who pretends to have killed the dragon, already slain by Tristan, in order to obtain Isolt's hand in marriage.[66] The Rash Saracen may be handsome and brave (v. 2278) but pride causes his downfall (v. 2279).[67]

Robbing the bodies of the dead on the field of battle is an age-old practice. In Prudentius's *Psychomachia* Avaritia impels men to loot the bodies of the fallen even when they are relatives.[68] The same lust for gold and silver prompts certain Christians in the *Pseudo-Turpin* to steal from dead bodies after Charles defeats King Aigolandus (INTRODUCTION, 10, A, 7).

Earlier (v. 1754), Roland had sounded a mighty blast, then (v. 2104) a weaker one. The split at the wide end of the oliphant (v. 2295) appears now to have rendered the horn useless. However, in a later passage (v. 3119) the sound of Roland's oliphant will again be heard. The break in the horn, then, underlines the violence of the blow to the Saracen's head and, like the diminished call, symbolizes that the hero's life is rapidly ebbing.[69]

25. *Roland Attempts to Destroy Durendal*

Laisses 171–173 (verses 2297–2354)

The foiled attempt to steal Durendal reminds Roland that he must ensure that his sword not fall into Saracen hands. The splitting of the oliphant presumably renders the object less attractive as potential booty, but its utility has not been impaired, for it will reappear in Guinemant's charge in the Baligant episode (v. 3017) and will eventually be enshrined on the altar of Saint-Seurin at Bordeaux (v. 3685).[1] The repeated attempts to destroy Durendal bear a striking resemblance to Arthur's efforts to dispose of Excalibur, a connection made even more apparent in later accounts where the hero throws it into a lake or stream.[2] Roland's sword survives and is borne by Rabel in the battle against Baligant (v. 3017).[3]

Roland's apostrophe to his sword[4] is essentially an amplification of the following themes:

1. concern that he can no longer care for it (vv. 2304–2305) or that it may fall into the hands of a coward (vv. 2309, 2351) or a pagan (vv. 2335–2336, 2349–2350).

2. praise for the many victories it has occasioned (vv. 2306–2308, 2322–2334, 2352–2354).[5]

3. praise for its goodness (v. 2304), beauty, brilliance (vv. 2316–2317, 2344),[6] and holiness (vv. 2344–2348).[7]

Although Turoldus specifically refers to Roland's words as a private lament (v. 2315: A sei meïsme la cumencet a pleindre; v. 2343: Mult dulcement la pleinst a sei meïsme), and although both the hero and he utilize the vocabulary of grief (v. 2301: par doel e par rancune; v. 2304: "si mare fustes!"; v. 2335: "Pur ceste espee ai dulor e pesance"), there is relatively little sorrow in this passage. Roland's praise of Durendal's qualities far outweighs his expressions of concern.

The hero's laud of his matchless weapon is closely related to his initial speech in Laisse 14 extolling his many conquests, which introduces the Theme of Victory in the poem.[8] By recalling his glorious deeds, Roland, in the earlier passage, sought to persuade the Franks to heed his advice. Now, in similar fashion, he beseeches God to pay attention. The hero's apostrophe to his sword is intertwined with prayers (vv. 2303, 2337) and immediately precedes his moving mea culpa. His breast-beating echoes Durendal's repeated blows upon the stone.[9] The roll call of victories is therefore part of Roland's dying supplication and, like the proffered gauntlet, closely parallels the way the Emperor tips the scales in his own favor in the particular judgment narrated in the *Pseudo-Turpin Chronicle*.[10]

The praise of Durendal begins, indirectly, in the Saracen oath scene (vv. 926, 988), where it must be assumed that Ganelon had earlier told the pagans the name of Roland's sword. In that passage the pagans' dream of "conquering" Durendal is an inverted image of the Theme of Victory. Other reflections of the same theme occur whenever the hero or the poet mentions Durendal (vv. 1055, 1065, 1079, 1120, 1324, 1339, 1462, 1540, 1870, 2143, 2264, 2780). As Roland prepares to leave this world, in a scene symbolizing the Christian concept of victory over death, it is only natural that the poet should choose to have his hero recite a long litany of Durendal's triumphs. Martyrdom has always been associated with invincibility.[11] The achievements in question were effectuated for Charles (vv. 2308, 2334, 2353) and for France (vv. 2311, 2337), synonyms for Christianity.[12] The hero affirms that Durendal must be served by Christians (v. 2350)[13] and, in the last line of this sequence (v. 2354), maintains that it is one of the important sources of the Emperor's power and might. As Foulet has observed,[14] expressions such as these are filled with religious fervor. This is in keeping with the idea that Durendal, like Roland's lance, is an extension of the hero's arm, the latter being a manifestation of the Emperor's strength. Roland, a prolongation of Charlemagne, shares in the sacredness associated with the Emperor's person (INTRODUCTION, 19, D).

Addressing an object implies that it can hear; in other words, that is has a life of its own.[15] Durendal's biography includes an impressive list of conquests and a supernatural origin. Charles's role as intermediary (vv. 2318–2321) provides another mystical bond between the two closely related characters.[16] The living nature of Roland's sword and its celestial provenance are effectively brought out when it rebounds toward heaven as the hero vainly tries to destroy it (v. 2341: Cuntre ciel amunt est resortie). The leaping motion recalls the upward flight of the lance shards in the Emperor's dream (v. 723) and Roland's spear silhouetted against the sky (vv. 708, 1156), and it anticipates the sparks that will fly from the clash of Pinabel's and Thierry's swords (v. 3912). Above all, as it vaults in the air, Durendal foreshadows the ascent of Roland's soul to heaven.

Durendal's brilliance (vv. 2316–2317)[17] and the relics in its handle (vv. 2345–2348) constitute yet another dimension of the sword's holiness.[18] The weapon's luminosity functions precisely as does the gold ground in contemporary religious art, since it symbolizes the character's holy and shining qualities.[19] However, it is the sword's unbreakable quality that, more than any other attribute, underscores its sacredness.[20] Firmness and solidity are associated with ideal Christian faith,[21] but intactness and inviolability lead down a different mystical path, for these are the attributes of the Blessed Virgin.[22] It may not be fortuitous, then, that Roland prefaces his lament for his sword with an invocation to Mary (v. 2303: "E!" dist li quens, "seinte Marie, aiue!") or that Durendal contains a relic of Mary's clothing (2348).[23]

Medieval exegetes would doubtless have read meaning into Roland's blows to the stone, for the rock that Moses smote in the desert of Sin (Exodus 17:6; Numbers 20:11) was associated with Christ (1 Corinthians 10:4: Haec petra erat Christus).[24]

26. *The Death of Roland*

Laisses 174–176 (verses 2355–2396)

The series of laisses similaires recounting Roland's final moments has been admired by many commentators, who have stressed its remarkable cumulative effect.[1] Roland makes a general confession. There is no reference here to any specific sin he has committed, no allusion whatsoever to the accusations leveled against him by Oliver in the horn scenes (INTRODUCTION, 3).

As death descends inexorably from the hero's head to his heart, a movement also followed in Oliver's last agony (vv. 2010–2020),[2] Roland's confession mounts heavenward. In v. 2369 ("Deus, meie culpe vers les tues vertuz"), the hero does not, as Jones believes, compare his own sins (culpe) with God's strength (vertuz):[3] *meie culpe* is simply a literal transposition of *mea culpa*, an expression of remorse visualized here as rising upward.[4]

One of the most striking things about this memorable scene is the meticulous detailing of the hero's dying attitude. Roland lies prone (v. 2358)[5] over his sword and oliphant (v. 2359), his face turned toward the pagan foe and Spain (vv. 2360, 2367, 2376).[6] The significance of this posture is explained by Turoldus: Roland assumes it so that Charles and all his men will say that he died victorious (vv. 2361–2363).[7] The hero cries out his sins over and over (v. 2364: Cleimet sa culpe e menut e suvent; v. 2383: Cleimet sa culpe, si priet Deu mercit)[8] and mimes this act by beating his breast with one hand (v. 2368: A l'une main si ad sun piz batud). Bédier evidently interprets *menut* in v. 2364 to mean 'small, weak' as in v. 2370, for he translates: "A faibles coups et souvent." The two adverbs are clearly synonymous, otherwise *clamer* and *menu* would be contradictory.[9] *Menu* in this context obviously suggests closeness, rapidity, and perhaps a certain feverishness, each utterance falling hard upon the other (cf. Bédier's translation of v. 1426: "La foudre tombe à coups serrés et pressés").

Roland's penultimate gesture is the proffering of his gauntlet to God for his sins (vv. 2365, 2373, 2389).[10] The hero then joins his hands (v. 2392) just as his head drops over his arm in an attitude of peaceful slumber.[11] For Christians death is but a sleep, and cemetery is a word that originally meant a place for sleeping (Late Latin *coemeterium* < Gr. *koimētērion*). To the Fathers of the Church this served as a reminder of the coming resurrection before the final judgment, but also of the eternal rest earned by the just.[12]

It is only fitting that the hero's last thoughts should be the culmination of the long series of associations noted earlier: conquest, France, family, and Charlemagne.[13] These are all variations on the Themes of the Struggle and of Victory. Roland's final prayer links him with the unbroken chain of martyrs and saints who, from the era of the Catacombs, reminded God, in their hour of greatest need, that he raised Lazarus from the dead and protected Daniel in the lions' den.[14] The hero implores his Maker to save his soul from the peril it now faces.[15] God is infinitely merciful, but he is also infinitely just, and all Christians, however firm in the Faith, fear his judgment. What makes the suspense bearable and Christians eternally hopeful is implied in the initial phrase of Roland's prayer: "*Veire Patene, ki unkes ne mentis*" (v. 2384). The guarantee of salvation in spite of one's sins (v. 2388) is contingent upon a single, solitary condition: One must present evidence that one's end of the bargain has been kept. This concept is what explains the proffering of the gauntlet by Roland.

In each of the three laisses similaires, nearly identical phrasing is used with respect to Roland's gesture. There is no Modern French equivalent for the verb *poroffrir* used in two of the laisses, but Modern English 'to proffer', that is, to tender, to offer for acceptance—often something owed or due—has the same meaning. In Old French and in Modern English, the word is most often utilized to express an offer that is legally binding, a pledge, or, to use an Old French word, a *gage*. The middle laisse, on the other hand, contains the verb *tendre* 'to tender', which implies a less formal offer.

Scholars are in accord that the gesture is a feudal one. The most commonly held view is conveniently summed up in a note found in the Nouveaux Classiques Larousse edition of the *Roland*: "Ce geste est féodal: Roland considère que Dieu est une manière de suzerain auquel il offre son gant, symbole de la personne même. *Remettre son gant* à un ambassadeur, c'est lui donner plein pouvoir; *offrir son gant*, c'est livrer sa personne entière; *jeter son gant*, c'est mettre en avant sa force et son courage pour appuyer ce qu'on avance."[16]

This interpretation dates back to Gaston Paris, who, in his selections from the *Roland*, published in 1887, stated: "Roland regarde Dieu comme son seigneur suzerain, envers lequel il se conduit comme un loyal vassal . . . offrir son gant, comme ici, c'est abandonner sa personne entière."[17] Jenkins accepted this view, adding: "In the absence of Charlemagne, his feudal lord, Roland surrenders himself *in toto* to God, proffering his glove as a symbol."[18]

In feudal society vassal relationship was established by the contract of commendation, a ceremony consisting of two formal acts: homage and the oath of fealty.[19] These acts were frequently accompanied by a ceremonial kiss, especially in France.[20] The rite of homage referred to by Gaston Paris is the self-surrender of one person to another.[21] However, this act was invariably symbolized by *immixtio manuum*, or the placing of the hands of the vassal between those of the lord.[22] All the expressions referring to homage mention *manus* 'hand': for example, *manus alicujus venire* 'to come into the hands of someone', *manus alicui dare* 'to give one's hands to someone', *aliquem per manus accipere* 'to receive someone by the hands', and *alicujus manibus junctis fore feodalem hominem* 'to become by joined hands the vassal of someone'.[23]

Gaston Paris and those who accept his interpretation of Roland's dying gesture confuse the meaning ascribed to homage and the act of investiture.[24] The latter followed commendation, generally at once, but was distinct from it. Investiture was the conferring of a fief by the lord to the vassal, and the rite consisted in the handing over by the lord of some symbolic object intended to represent the act of concession. This could be a scepter, ring, glove, and so on, but the lord always retained the object employed.[25] At times an item was actually handed over to the vassal, but this was a cornstalk, a piece of turf, a banner, or something that clearly symbolized the fief itself. The renunciation of a fief was enacted by a similar ceremony. The vassal divested himself of the fief by placing his hands between those of his lord. Then he handed back an object similar to the one that had been received.[26]

Bédier gives a somewhat different interpretation of Roland's dying gesture.[27] Referring to what he terms "le seul trait qui distingue Roland des autres chrétiens,"[28] the French scholar characterizes Roland's gesture as nonliturgical and exclusively feudal. Roland holds up his gauntlet to God: "en signe qu'il lui rend le fief reçu de lui, le fief du martyre sans doute et de la bonne mort, et qu'il s'abandonne tout entier à son seigneur."[29] Bédier accepts, then, Gaston Paris's interpretation, that is, self-surrender, but he qualifies it by separating the homage concept from that of investiture, or rather from that of the opposite ceremony symbolizing the renunciation of a fief.[30] For Bédier this fief was martyrdom or dying in the state of grace.

Dorothy L. Sayers proposes a slight variation on Bédier's view: "The glove is offered and accepted in token of Roland's surrender to God of the life which he holds as a fief from Him."[31] Eugene Vinaver alludes to the renunciation of a fief but does not tell us what the fief is: "Roland rend à Dieu le fief qu'il a reçu de lui."[32]

A third interpretation is provided by Faral.[33] Terming Roland's action a "rite obscur," he believes it is a sign that the dying hero recognizes God's jurisdiction. He notes a similar gesture on the part of Pinabel and Thierry at the end of the poem. Ganelon has been accused of treason by Charles and, after making his formal defense, is championed by his friend and peer Pinabel. Thierry comes forward to defend the Emperor's cause and the issue is to be decided by single combat. Before the ordeal begins, however, Pinabel and Thierry both offer their right gauntlets to Charles, who accepts them. This gesture, Faral says, is a sign that the two adversaries recognize Charlemagne's jurisdiction in this trial by combat. "De même fait le comte Roland: il tend son gant droit à Dieu pour qu'il le juge, geste d'un vassal aux yeux duquel le mystère religieux revêt les apparences d'une institution féodale."[34] When God accepts Roland's glove, he shows that he looks favorably upon Roland's service. Faral concludes: "Roland, devant Dieu comme devant les hommes, est le plus grand."[35]

If one accepts Faral's view, Roland's gesture has little real significance, for the hero will be judged instantly and decisively by his Creator whether or not he voluntarily submits to the latter's jurisdiction. The author states that Roland's soul is immediately transported to heaven by angels, clearly a way of saying that the particular judgment—there will also be a Last Judgment of course—has been rendered, as in the case of the pagan soldiers, whose souls are dragged off to hell by devils.[36]

Faral's interpretation has been accepted by Jones, who believes that the hero is motivated by feelings of chagrin and vindication, characteristics of a pagan shame culture, not a Judaeo-Christian guilt culture: "It is significant that the dying Roland proffers his right-hand glove to God when dying, for it was a feudal custom for a vassal to offer his glove as a pledge when submitting himself to his lord's jurisdiction."[37]

Thus far, then, it has been shown that the gesture cannot be interpreted as self-surrender, for homage was symbolized by placing the hands between those of the lord, not proffering a glove; also, it has been observed that when Roland's dying gesture is interpreted as the renunciation of a fief, vague and contradictory meanings are ascribed to the fief. These explanations all fail to take into consideration the context of Roland's final gesture and the testimony of the other early versions of the poem.

The three laisses similaires, which relate the climactic scene, focus progressively upon one central deed, Roland's dying act of contrition.

In all three laisses the hero beats his breast and begs forgiveness for his sins. In all three laisses the phrase "for my sins," in either direct or indirect discourse, is ascribed to Roland in connection with the gesture of the proffered glove. In the first laisse, in fact, the association is in the same line: *Pur ses pecchez Deu en puroffrid lo guant* (v. 2365).

The importance of situating Roland's gesture in its proper setting has recently been underscored in two contributions by British scholars.

> Dr. Hackett's recent article on this topic in *Romania* (1968) is wholly convincing. The dying Roland confesses his sins and offers his glove to God. In Dr. Hackett's view the glove here is a token of the desire to obtain forgiveness. She links the proffered glove with similar gestures in the epic where a knight offers to put right a wrong and seeks forgiveness. My own paper supports Dr. Hackett's contention and brings grist to her mill. In particular, I have found in a charter historical evidence, dated ca. 1075, that the proffering of a glove was a propitiatory gesture. Moreover in this historic account a knight ostensibly on his death-bed dispatches his own brother as a messenger to place his glove upon an altar and thus to "offer it to God." Here are resemblances of date and of situation closer to the *Roland* than any other example so far cited. In the charter the wrong to be righted is the expropriation of land, as is also the case in the late XIIth century Anglo-Norman romance of *Protheselaus.* More expansive on the theme of proffering a glove than any other writer I know, Hue de Rotelande supplies details useful to a comprehension of the gesture. Another late XIIth century romance *Partonopeus* uses the proffered glove as a means to end a misunderstanding between two sisters. In Jean de Meung's *Roman de la Rose* Pygmalion holds out a gage in order to make amends for belittling the statue he has made. In a recent book, Mr. John V. Fleming has published a XIVth century miniature of this scene with Pygmalion proffering a white glove. In conclusion, we have in chronicle, in romance and in iconography clear examples of the glove proffered in a conciliatory gesture from the XIth to the XIVth centuries.[38]

Hackett and Lyons have correctly identified Roland's gesture as a propitiatory one,[39] an outward sign of his remorse for his sins. Roland's act of contrition is accompanied by breast-beating, symbolizing the striking of the fault, and weeping and sighing (v. 2381), expressing intense sorrow for his sins.[40] His prone position (v. 2358) is a similar manifestation.[41] Other familiar penitential postures and gestures not present here include kneeling, bowing the head, hand-wringing, tearing out hair, and scratching bits of flesh from the face.[42] However, an essential element is still missing in the explanation presented thus far for Roland's proffered glove.

A corresponding passage in one of the rhymed versions of the *Roland* and a parallel dying scene in the late-twelfth-century epic *Aliscans* provide valuable clues in this regard. Where the Oxford text reads *Pur ses pecchez Deu en puroffrid lo guant* (v. 2365), the Lyon manuscript states *Per ses pechiez, vers Deu son gage rant* 'for his sins he tenders his gage toward God'. As Vivien lies dying, in *Aliscans*, he beats his breast and, the author tells us, *A Damedieu va son gage rendant* 'He renders back his gage to the Lord God'.[43] Roland's gauntlet, then, is a gage, that is, a token or sign of something pledged or owed to someone else.

In the Middle Ages repentance was viewed as the paying off of an obligation or debt.[44] Medieval penitential doctrine viewed sin as a debt incurred of God, and remorse as the only way in which man can rid himself of that debt and be reconciled to God.[45] This view of repentance as the payment of an amount due, referred to as the tariff concept, derives ultimately from the Lord's Prayer where the sinner is placed in the position of a debtor: *demitte nobis debita nostra* 'forgive us our debts'.[46]

When Roland proffers his gauntlet, then, it is an outward manifestation of his remorse, but it is important to understand that he views himself as a debtor offering to pay back—as he must, in order to be saved—the amount due.[47] It is helpful to bear in mind here the Old French locution *estre quite de pechiez* 'to be free from sins'.[48] After Turpin blesses the French soldiers before the Battle of Roncevaux and orders them to strike the enemy for penance, the French rise to their feet, and *Ben sunt asols e quites de lur pecchez* (v. 1140) 'They are completely absolved and free from their sins'. 'To proffer' and 'to acquit', in these related passages of the *Song of Roland*, are penitential terms derived from medieval juridical phraseology.[49]

Roland's proffered glove emerges, therefore, not as a feudal homage rite, or as a renunciation of some vague fief, or as a recognition of the Lord's jurisdiction over him, but rather as an extension of his act of contrition and as a moving expression of remorse. The hero's dying gesture thus constitutes a fitting transition between pitiful breast-beating and hands joined together in peaceful death.

At one point in his prayers, Roland says: "*Tresqu'a cest jur que ci sui consoüt*" (v. 2372). Bédier translates this verse as follows: "Jusqu'à ce jour où me voici abattu."[50] OFr. *consoüt* does indeed have the meaning 'struck down', but an alternative reading (*consoüt* 'overtaken') has interesting possibilities. The image conjures up the Furies of Roman mythology tracking down their prey with a mad vengeance. However, a classical allusion seems inappropriate in such intensely Christian circumstances and Turoldus's thought processes were doubtless of a rather different order. The verb *consequi* in Ecclesiastical Latin is regularly used in the meaning 'to obtain (through prayers)',[51] and it appears likely that this initial idea was transformed into a notion suggesting pursuit because of the kindred nature of the two expressions in Old French.

In the Middle Ages the departure of the soul from the body was frequently depicted as a small naked figure emerging from the dying person's mouth (*see Fig. 18*). In a related conceptualization, the soul was often shown being borne heavenward by means of a scarf held sling fashion by two angels.[52] Turoldus doubtless imagined in this manner the act related in v. 2396 (L'anme del cunte portent en pareïs), an interpretation amply supported by a full-page illumination in the *Codex Calixtinus* of the *Pseudo-Turpin*, a thirteenth-century historiated initial, and two fourteenth-century miniatures of this scene[53] (*see Fig. 12*). The scarf is the same as the one that separates the celestial regions from earth in contemporary iconography (*see Fig. 2*). It stems from the tabernacle veil that hung from four columns in the Temple of Jerusalem, imagery also associated with Roland's death.[54] Turoldus may have had the same cloth in mind when he states that Roland is in heaven (v. 2397: Morz est Rollant, Deus en ad l'anme es cels), for the scarf is found in the iconography of Abraham's Bosom (*see Fig. 13*), a metaphor for Paradise.[55]

27. Charlemagne's Revenge

Laisses 177–184 (verses 2397–2524)

The ethereal peace and beauty of the ascension in the preceding passage suddenly gives way to a scene of a very different sort.[1] The Emperor arrives at Roncevaux along an infernal path strewn with French and Saracen cadavers. Charles's return is punctuated with cries for the

Twelve Peers, a desperate call for survivors that is transformed into a lament as the enormity of the catastrophe becomes evident. Charles's plaintive cries are clearly modeled on the *ubi sunt* motif, a form traditionally expressing the vanity of things of this world but metamorphosed here into a hymn of praise for the fallen French heroes.[2] However, there is more than a trace of the original content in Turoldus's allusion to the hopelessness of the calls (v. 2411) and to Charlemagne's great anger and frustration at having arrived too late (vv. 2412–2414). The 20,000 knights who fall into a swoon correspond exactly to the number of dead in the French rearguard, a way of expressing the army's solidarity in suffering. But the significance of the French deed at Roncevaux will not be lost sight of even in the shock of this unexpected discovery.

At a distance of two leagues (v. 2425), a telltale cloud of dust can be seen pointing, like an accusing finger, at the source of the misdeed.[3] Naimes, the voice of the blood of the French,[4] cries out for revenge.[5] Having once already this day suffered the consequences of being too late, Charles appeals to God for help in making justice prevail.[6] The Saracens have taken the flower of the French army from him and Charles claims his right to make them pay for this pernicious act. Here as elsewhere in the *Song of Roland*, one notes the appropriation of God's vengeance by the Emperor, who asserts his right to convert it to his own use. In a sense Charles's supplication merely participates in the long tradition of calling down the Lord's vengeance on one's enemies, but, in this poem, it is further characterized by the identification of France's cause (v. 2431: "De France dulce m'unt tolue la flur") with that of Christianity, and by the invoking of rights in this regard (v. 2430: "Cunsentez mei e dreiture e honur").

Before setting off in pursuit of the Saracens, Charles orders Oton, Geboin, Tedbald of Reims, and Milon to guard the battlefield and surrounding hills and valleys. A thousand men are retained for this purpose. Ghoulish looters are always to be feared. Some other Rash Saracen could make off with a battlefield trophy. Bédier points out that the wild animals from which the French dead are to be protected were alluded to by Turpin in v. 1751, but he notes that lions (v. 2436) have never been known to roam the Pyrenees:

> Je ne vois qu'un moyen d'écarter la bizarrerie, et c'est de rappeler les formules liturgiques où le lion et le dragon sont les types du Démon et de l'Enfer: "Non se ei opponat leo rugiens et draco

devorans, miserorum animas rapere consuetus ..." "Libera eas animas de ore leonis." C'est Satan que Charlemagne veut désigner, ou bien les démons, car le pluriel se rencontre aussi dans les textes ecclésiastiques; ainsi, dans une prière attribuée par un récit antique à saint Joseph mourant: "Neque irruant in me leones."[7] L'usage, aujourd'hui subsistant, de veiller les morts n'a pas d'autre raison d'être que de les préserver des démons.[8]

According to Jenkins, repetition of *adeist* in vv. 2436, 2437, and 2438 is "very natural under the circumstances: Charles's agitation is so great that his orders are querulously explicit."[9] This does little to explain the Emperor's insistent interdiction, which borders on a taboo. One is reminded, in fact, of Christ's *Noli me tangere*: "Do not cling to me, because I have not yet ascended to the Father."[10] The notion of taboo—perhaps sacredness would be a more accurate term—affecting the bodies of the slain Frenchmen is reinforced by the fact that *esquier* and *garçun* (v. 2437) are specifically prohibited from going near the remains. This suggests a connection with the *cumpaignons de la quisine* (vv. 1821–1822), who treat Ganelon with indignity after his betrayal of Roland has been unmasked.[11] In such cases the low station of the individuals involved is felt to have a contaminating effect upon whomever they touch. The corpses of the martyred Roland and his men, it should not be forgotten, have become holy relics.

However, it is also apparent that Charles seeks some kind of sign that will enable him to isolate the Twelve Peers from the tangle of lifeless forms lying helter-skelter on the battlefield.[12] Although Turoldus tells us nothing of the Emperor's reaction on finding the mortal remains of Turpin and the Peers, who had been carefully arranged around him by Roland (Laisse 213), considerable attention will be accorded to the anecdote concerning Roland at Aix and to the semaphore message his body conveys.[13]

The Emperor's pursuit of Marsile's remaining forces begins, in Laisse 179, with the sounding of trumpets, as had his ill-fated attempt to rescue his nephew (vv. 1796, 1832). This time, however, the French are not guided by the sound of the oliphant to an expiring comrade, but by a portentous cloud shadowing a fleeing enemy.[14]

Shattered by the spectacle of the annihilated rearguard he was unable to rescue and realizing that time may once again frustrate his efforts, Charlemagne pleads with God for a prolongation of the day. In pre-Copernican times such retardation was conceived of as halting the sun in its course.[15] The miracle seems to be an obvious reminiscence of Joshua 10:12–14, where the victorious siege of Gibeon was assured in this manner,[16] but Turoldus may also have been thinking of a similar occurrence associated in legend with Charlemagne as early as the *Annales Anianenses* (c. 946).[17] However, the connection of Charles with Joshua is specified by Conrad (vv. 7017–7022)[18] and is confirmed by the miracle of the tumbling walls of Pamplona in the *Pseudo-Turpin*, unquestionably an allusion to the fall of Jericho.[19] It is worth mentioning that medieval exegetes read eschatological significance into both biblical events. The staying of the sun was interpreted as the postponing of the Last Judgment by Christ to enable sinners to be saved;[20] the blowing of the trumpets and the collapsing walls at Jericho were also viewed as a prefiguration of the final judging of mankind by God.[21] The sound of Roland's oliphant surely triggered similar associations in the medieval audience.[22]

The answer to Charlemagne's prayer comes swiftly and decisively. An angel, the one "who regularly speaks with him" (v. 2452)—Gabriel, no doubt—addresses him with the peremptoriness of the celestial captain of the Lord's host at Jericho:[23] "*Charle, chevalche, car tei ne falt clartet*" (v. 2454). It is as if the celestial light that flows from God to Charles (v. 535) and radiates brighter than the sun from his sword Joyeuse (vv. 2502, 2990)[24] had now been brought to a focus in order to illuminate the darkening landscape. The miracle of the sun is accompanied by the specific granting of permission to wreak God's vengeance on the Infidel (v. 2456).

The French army is now loosed and it pursues the Saracens like the avenging angels of Revelation 9:14–15.[25] Marsile's forces are overtaken in the *Val Tenebrus* (v. 2461). The designation has ominous overtones, for the devil was referred to as the *princeps tenebrarum*, and the *tenebrae exteriores* or *inferni tenebrae* were a symbol of Hell.[26] Unbelievers were also said to reside in the darkness of ignorance.[27] The contrast between the Christians pursuing in the light of day—thanks to the miraculous staying of the sun—and the Saracens finding their way in the darkness of the *Val Tenebrus* was doubtless intended by Turoldus.[28]

The Saracens now find their retreat to Saragossa barred by the formidable Ebro River. Their watery grave, foreshadowed by Ganelon's lying tale of the Caliph's destruction,[29] conjures up the drowning of the Pharaoh's host (Exodus 14:21–29). For medieval exegetes such an association would have had baptismal overtones, for the Crossing of the Red Sea symbolized Salvation through Christ's blood as well as Damnation, represented here by the drowning of the pagans.[30]

The episode presents another striking contrast. The Saracens, thrashing about wildly in the swirling waters, implore Tervagant to save them, but their prayers are in vain.[31] Divided into three groups like examples drawn from a parable (Li adubez . . . Li altre . . . Li miez guariz . . .), their sinking bodies[32] foreshadow the fall of the pagan idols.[33] Meanwhile the French, surveying from the banks of the river the mighty spectacle of God's wrath, cry out Roland's name. Their shout is steeped in misery and compassion (v. 2475: "Mare fustes, Rollant!"), but it is as if, too, the French call their lost leader to witness the consummation of his revenge.[34]

The destruction of Marsile's army is wrought by God, but Turoldus makes it clear that French steel was also involved, a point skillfully made in Bédier's rendering of v. 2477: *Alquanz ocis e li plusur neiet* 'les uns tués par le fer, et la plupart noyés'.[35]

The solemnity and the religious intensity of the circumstance—the sublime expression of grief and vindication by the French in v. 2475 is followed by Charlemagne's ritual prayer of thanksgiving (v. 2480: Culchet sei a tere, sin ad Deu graciet)—seem at first glance to be marred by the poet's observation in v. 2478: *Mult grant eschec en unt si chevaler*. It was pointed out earlier that imputing an interest in booty to Roland just as he prepares to meet the Saracens for the first time is completely inconsonant with the other emotions that fill him at that precise moment, and that the correct equivalent for *eschec* in v. 1167 is 'battle'.[36] But the struggle against Marsile is over now and, consequently, orderly taking of spoils is perfectly justified here as it was after the siege of Cordres.[37]

His ends achieved and his profound gratitude having been expressed to God, Charlemagne rises[38] and, as if it had been waiting for this signal, the sun now dips below the horizon (v. 2481).[39]

The fury of battle is followed by an idyllic interlude suffused with a mood of peace and repose.[40] The central metaphor in this passage is the horse. Often, in medieval sources, a symbol of incontinence and lust that must be curbed by reason,[41] this animal represents here as in Revelation 6:1–8, the passions unleashed in armed conflict or righteous indignation.[42] Unsaddling and removal of bridles (vv. 2485, 2490–2491) are signs of the cessation of hostilities. The exhausted steeds are allowed to rest in a verdant meadow (vv. 2486, 2492), a traditional image of peaceful rest.[43] The men lie down, utterly drained of emotion and strength. The completeness of their victory is indicated by the relaxing of the guard (v. 2495). For medieval exegetes, however, a lapse of vigilance had great spiritual significance. The true Christian, symbolized by the rooster on the church steeple, was expected to be eternally watchful.[44] Such an attitude is suggested by Charles, who sleeps fully armed, girt with Joyeuse, his great spear close at hand (vv. 2496–2501).

The moon, which bathes this nocturnal scene with its mournful light, recalls that celestial body's weeping in the iconography of the Crucifixion.[45] The Emperor's thoughts drift back to the dead lying on the plain of Roncevaux and he sobs in splendid isolation as the French sleep. The meditative champing of the stolid horses forms a muted accompaniment to his lament. Charlemagne's heart is heavy with sorrow, but, paradoxically, he experiences joy too. For, having wreaked his vengeance upon the Infidel, his thoughts focus naturally on Roland (v. 2513). With growing fascination, one peels off layer after layer of interrelated concepts in this scene until one arrives at the core, which is joy.

The spear that is planted firmly in the ground next to the Emperor's slumbering head (v. 2497)[46] is constantly linked with the hero in this poem, and it serves here as a reminder of that relationship. One of the last images of Roland was of the hero vainly trying to smash his sword against a stone, a violent act contrasted now with the portrait of the Emperor in repose, his sword at his side. It is no accident that at precisely this point in the narrative, Turoldus introduces a word-portrait of Joyeuse, whose kaleidoscopic reflections emanate from the holy relic of the Lance encased in its handle.[47] The matchless weapon's name corresponds to the Christian's emotion at the thought of the Lord's Passion, source of man's redemption.[48] One may assume, too, that Charlemagne's overriding thought is one of bliss as he considers the joyful implications of Roland's martyrdom. This line of thought leads the poet to mention the French war cry "Monjoie!" (v. 2510), which he believes is related to this concept.[49]

Henceforth, whenever the French utter that cry, it will express this entire nexus of associations centering on joy. Such all-encompassing mystical power, Turoldus says in v. 2511, makes the French invincible. And it is to this profound insight into the paradoxical nature of things, into the interpenetration of joy and sorrow at the thought of Roland's martyrdom, that the poet alludes when he says, summing up this experience: *Mult ad apris ki bien conuist ahan* (v. 2524).[50]

28. *Charlemagne's Second Dreams*

Laisses 185–186 (verses 2525–2569)

Charlemagne's men have lulled themselves into believing that the threat posed by the Saracens has been completely and definitively dispelled, but the Emperor himself remains instinctively alert.[1] His intuition that the struggle is far from over is now confirmed by another angelic visitation.

Gabriel does not simply deliver his message to Charlemagne and then depart. Obedient to the Lord's command, the celestial messenger spends the night watching at his bedside, like a benevolent guardian angel. The archangel's role in warding off evil has been mentioned before,[2] and here again one finds him keeping vigil at the door, as it were.

But the greatest service Gabriel can render the Emperor at this moment is to advise him of an impending danger. As in the earlier dreams, the visions constitute a monition, and Charles, although amply forewarned, will again elect to play out his role. There is no controversy as to the significance of these new dreams: They announce the battle with Baligant[3] and the judicial combat between Thierry and Pinabel.[4]

A number of elements in the present dreams are reminiscent of the Emperor's earlier visions, but their significance has changed now. The shattered lance, which represented Roland, reappears, but it is multiplied this time, referring to nameless French knights. The locale in two instances is Aix. Some of the same wild animals are present and Charlemagne is personally attacked on both occasions. Finally, the wood in v. 2549 recalls the forest with which *Ardene* in v. 728 is associated,[5] although the allusion is to the homeland of Ganelon's relatives. In the earlier nocturnal experience, Turoldus gave no indication of accompanying physical torment on Charlemagne's part, but in a later scene (Laisses 67–68), he was visibly troubled by the phenomenon and tried to conceal his chagrin beneath his cloak (v. 830). In the second visions the Emperor suffers "like a troubled man" (v. 2525), an outward manifestation of the increased gravity of the traumatic experience. In neither instance does Charles know what the outcome will be (v. 735: Il ne sevent liquels d'els la veintrat; v. 2553: Mais ço ne set liquels abat ne quels chiet; v. 2567: Mais ço ne set liquels veint ne quels nun), but only on the second occasion is he acutely aware of being helpless to intervene (v. 2548: Aler i volt, mais il ad desturber).

The third dream (the first here) is quite elaborate and, from a literary point of view, probably the most interesting of the Emperor's nocturnal fantasies. It has three different phases. First, Charles's eyes are attracted heavenward, where what at first appears to be a gathering hailstorm (cf. the meteorological disturbance announcing Roland's death in vv. 1424–1426)[6] takes on a vastly more sinister aspect when flames (v. 2535: E fous e flambes) are detected. Lightning flashed repeatedly in the earlier tempest, splitting the sky in great rents (vv. 1426, 1432), but the thunderbolts merely seemed to strike the ground while the earthquake cracked house walls (vv. 1427, 1430). Now, however, the storm and the infernal fire come together like a molten mass and suddenly pour down on Charlemagne's men. The connection with Sodom and Gomorrah is obvious, and the horrifying image of the French, like their calcinated lances, being burned to a cinder from a celestial discharge implies that they are being punished by the Almighty for an obscure but terrible sin.[7] Later it will become clear that the battle against Baligant is a test (Job motif), not a punishment.[8]

Such a vision of sulphur and fire would naturally be taken by medieval commentators to be a reflection of Hell, where the damned will be consumed in an eternal gehenna.[9] This interpretation is reinforced by the image of Charlemagne watching powerlessly as his men cry out to him for help (v. 2546–2548: E Franceis crient: "Carlemagne, aidez!"/ Li reis en ad e dulur e pitet,/ Aler i volt, mais il ad desturber). One is reminded of the parable of the Rich Man and Lazarus: Dives, tormented by flames, pleads for the Father to send the poor man, who once lay at his gate and is now in Abraham's bosom, to dip the tip of his finger in water and cool his tongue. But between Charles and his men, as between Lazarus and Dives, a great gulf has been fixed to stop anyone wishing to cross from one side to the other (Luke 16:19–26). This apparition is abruptly transformed into another scene with specific diabolical overtones: Bears, leopards, serpents, dragons, devils (v. 2543: averser), and 30,000 griffins are now unleashed on the hapless Franks and seek to devour them. Surely the Christians are facing their greatest peril, for not only their bodies but their souls are evidently at stake in such a struggle.

In a third and final phase of the dream, a ferocious lion symbolizing Baligant emerges from a forest and attacks Charlemagne himself. The outcome of the fierce hand-to-hand struggle that ensues literally hangs in the balance, for as they tumble over, it is uncertain which of the two forces the other down and which one falls (v. 2553: Mais ço ne set liquels abat ne quels chiet).

The second dream,[10] a much shorter narrative, finds the Emperor outside his palace at Aix. He is near Ganelon, who is chained to a *perrun* (v. 2556), a clear allusion to the traitor's later humiliation.[11] Perhaps the most arresting feature of this vision is the fact that the thirty bears speak *altresi cume hum* (v. 2559). Turoldus gives them human voices to stress how Ganelon's relatives and, above all, the villain himself will debase language as they seek to justify what has transpired.[12] Ganelon is a liar and a traitor, and the skillful but evil way he uses speech is Judas-like.[13]

29. Marsile at Saragossa

Laisses 187–191 (verses 2570–2645)

Before proceeding any further, it may be helpful to situate what transpires next with reference to the days outlined in COMMENTARY, 9 and 30. Day 6, it will be recalled, ends with the Emperor camping near the Ebro after defeating Marsile's forces. The Saracen king's return to Saragossa (Laisses 187–188) is narrated after Charlemagne's dreams (Laisses 185–186), thus constituting a slight flashback,[1] for, as Bramimonde states, the events at Roncevaux occurred *oi matin* (v. 2601). The words *en l'umbre* (v. 2571) suggest that the sun has not yet set, an event mentioned in v. 2481.[2] Nocturnal gloom would seem to be an appropriate setting for Marsile's disgraceful return, but Turoldus prefers to emphasize darkness when describing Baligant's sinister approach (vv. 2630–2644), thus contrasting evil goings-on with the Emperor's dreams in precisely the same manner he had earlier opposed the Saracen oaths to Charlemagne's first nighttime visions.[3] It should be noted, finally, that the news of Baligant's approach reaches Marsile during the same fateful night, between Day 6 and Day 7 (v. 2638).

The narrative of Marsile's return to Saragossa, which is presented in the form of a diptych—the scene outside the palace being followed by another inside the royal residence—limns the descending curve of Saracen power.

The shameful character of Marsile's mutilation and the olive tree, which, as was the case during Ganelon's ride to the same city, symbolizes despair,[4] underscore the fact that he is now a broken man, physically and spiritually.[5] He dismounts, sheds his sword, helmet, and armor, and falls half-dead at Bramimonde's feet, his right arm a bleeding stump. Below a sculpture dated about 1120 depicting Christ between Peter and Paul in the tympanum of the Cathedral of Angoulême, there is a lintel showing a group of horsemen engaged in combat and, on the right, figures arranged in front of or inside a castle or walled city.[6] The scene has puzzled scholars. Lejeune and Stiennon suggest that the two personages on the extreme left are a representation of the duel between Archbishop Turpin and the Saracen leader Abisme, while the pair of horsemen on the right illustrate Roland in the act of cutting off Marsile's hand. On the extreme right Bramimonde may be among the standing figures arranged in a group if, as the Belgian scholars conjecture, the faltering individual is Marsile.[7]

A few verses later the Saracen king is carried off to his bed chamber,[8] where he dreams of Baligant coming from far-off Babylon to avenge his catastrophic defeat. However, Bramimonde senses the inevitability of Christian victory,[9] wishes Charles dead, and vents her anger by ordering the pagan idols destroyed.[10]

If the Baligant episode is an interpolation made by Turoldus, it must be said to his credit that he developed the character Bramimonde with great skill. Her attitude stands out in sharp contrast to that of her husband. The queen's two speeches, alternating with the narrative of Marsile's arrival and the latter's idle fantasies (Marsile, vv. 2570–2575; Bramimonde, vv. 2576–2591; Marsile, vv. 2592–2594; Bramimonde, vv. 2595–2608), reveal a lucid and even a prophetic mind. The Saracen queen, as opposed to her stubborn spouse, intuitively senses the significance of Marsile's defeat and the Battle of Roncevaux.

Bramimonde causes the idols to be smashed,[11] a manifestation of her anger, but their destruction also announces her conversion.[12] The flashback to an earlier episode during which Marsile threatened to renounce his gods if Baligant did not come to his aid indicates that the Saracen king, as opposed to his wife and his men, has not completely abandoned them. For Bramimonde, however, Baligant's long-awaited arrival offers no real hope, because, down deep, she knows that Charles will certainly rout the latter's forces. She ends up rending the air with a cry that betrays her rage but also her barbarity: "*Mult est grant doel que n'en est ki l'ociet*!" (v. 2608).[13] Bramimonde would be capable of performing this act herself if afforded an opportunity to do so, for the Saracen queen has the heart of a Judith.

The cries of desolation that greet Marsile's arrival at Saragossa differ from the French lamentations in that the latter never, even in great adversity, show any ill-will toward their God.[14] The faith of the Saracens is thus revealed to be much less firmly anchored. Their despair is both prompt and violent. It is surely not without meaning that the pagans begin by cursing Charles and France, and that 20,000 Saracens, the exact number in the Emperor's rearguard,[15] inveigh against them, for these are symbols of the countervailing faith. The God of the Christians is honored in imposing churches and monasteries, the Saracens relegate their idols to a mean grotto (v. 2580).

A careful reading of the passage describing the destruction of the idols reveals that each god is individualized:[16] Apollo has a crown and scepter (v. 2585), suggesting that he is perhaps the chief deity in the pagan trinity;[17] Tervagant has a carbuncle (v. 2589), that is, a precious stone that was believed to have magical properties and glow in the dark;[18] Mohammed is thrown into a ditch and defiled by being stepped on and devoured by dogs and swine. There is a suggestion of condign punishment in the latter instance as well as in the beating of the sceptered Apollo with staffs (v. 2588).[19] It was long ago suggested that there may be an allusion here to the legend that the body of Mohammed was torn to pieces by dogs, a fate reminiscent of that of Achab and of Jezebel (1 Kings 21:23–24; 22:38; 2 Kings 9:36).[20] In the *Pseudo-Turpin* the idol of Mohammed at Cadiz is called Salam and is said to enclose a legion of devils fatal to Christians but harmless for Saracens. It holds a key that will fall from its hand the year the French king who conquers all Spain is born.[21]

The mention by Bramimonde of the defeat at Roncevaux *this morning* (v. 2601)—confirmed, the following day, by repeated references to the same event having occurred *ier* (vv. 2701, 2772, 2791; cf. v. 2745: her seir, and v. 2758: anuit)—is consistent with the darkness covering the stealthy approach of Baligant's fleet (Laisses 190–191). The Emir disembarks at Saragossa the very next morning. Such is the economy of Turoldus's narrative that not a single day is lost in the process. To be sure, this coincidence subjects the audience's credibility to a severe test, but the timing of Baligant's arrival is meant to be an indication of the unremitting character of the Saracen menace in the *Song of Roland: Gent paienor ne voelent cesser unkes* (v. 2639).

Actually the poet does remind his audience at precisely this juncture, in another flashback,[22] that the Spanish campaign has lasted seven long years and that Marsile *al premer an* (v. 2613) requested help from Baligant. Also the Emir's septennial delay,[23] the great distance he must travel, and the forty kingdoms he summons to his banner serve to magnify the tidal wave that is about to break on Charlemagne.

The need for a second battle has been challenged by some scholars who believe that, in the original poem, Charlemagne proceeded directly from Marsile's defeat and the recovery of the bodies of the French at Roncevaux to the attack at Saragossa.[24] Whether or not this is so, all the French versions of Turoldus's poem except Lyon contain the Baligant material and ample justification can be made for its existence. Turoldus obviously felt the need for enhanced revenge for the ignominy perpetrated by the Saracens and imagined a cosmic confrontation. Scholars have often noted that the Baligant-Charles battle has a decidedly apocalyptic aspect and have maintained that the poet conceived of Baligant as an Antichrist figure.[25] This interpretation is very sound. However, this conception does not differ significantly from that found in the remainder of the poem, for the latter is suffused throughout with Old Testament figures and with Christian allusion and metaphor.

Some specialists have detected stylistic differences in the two parts, a number of them more significant than others.[26] However, the notion that Turoldus simply joined two distinct poems together with a minimum of alteration is so far-fetched that it merits no more than passing mention here.[27] The possibility remains that Turoldus expanded an already cohesive and well-structured poem. If that is the case, to what extent did he transform other parts of the poem as he worked on his expanded version? This line of speculation is fraught with difficulties, most of them insurmountable. In any case the entire poem appears to be sufficiently the work of one poet to warrant the type of connected analysis provided here.

Baligant, whose very name may echo the generic designation for the pagan gods of biblical times (COMMENTARY, 11), is the Emir of Babylon. According to most authorities,[28] *Babilonie*, the place where one first encounters the new Saracen menace and which is considered his capital, is another word for Cairo in Egypt.[29] However, to the medieval audience such a toponym doubtless also conjured up Old Testament associations.[30] In the Bodleian manuscript only there is a curious allusion to the Emir's great age (vv. 2615–2616). This is an obvious parallel with Charlemagne, whom the Saracens believed to be two hundred years old (vv. 524, 552), but the expression in v. 2615 (le viel d'antiquitet) has a decidedly biblical resonance.[31] The association with Virgil and Homer is not an idle one, for while clerks recognized them as celebrated authors,[32] the names also brought to mind certain legends that had cropped up around these figures, and their works were roundly condemned in monastic circles.[33] Virgil, in particular, acquired a reputation for dealing in the occult.[34] There is nothing flattering intended here, for Turoldus explicitly condemns magic as the work of the devil.

The Emir's formidable flotilla presents an eerie sight as it glides silently over the waters, lanterns and carbuncles emitting a mysterious glow from the mastheads.[35] *Par la noit la mer en est plus bele* (v. 2635) echoes v. 1004: *Sunent mil grailles por ço que plus bel seit*. In both cases *bel(e)* has nothing to do with true beauty but refers instead to the fascination that evil exerts on the unwary, a charm comparable to the song of the sirens.[36]

Several weeks, perhaps months, are presumably involved in transporting Baligant's forces from Alexandria (v. 2626) to Saragossa (v. 2645),[37] but the lengthy action is distilled by Turoldus into a vision of lantern-lit ships slipping through the darkness. Then, in a further condensation, this gloomy scene changes imperceptibly into the night before Baligant's arrival at Saragossa.[38]

30. Baligant's Arrival

Laisses 192–193 (verses 2646–2685)

Baligant's first appearance is marked by a procession (vv. 2647–2650), traditional symbol of pagan spectacles and idolatry, and of the seductions of the devil.[1] It is clear that the Emir is the personification of Superbia, the root of all evil, whose followers customarily include the principal vices.[2]

Envious of Charles's *majestas*, Baligant seats himself on a similar *faldestoed* made of ivory (v. 2653; cf. Charlemagne's golden throne, v. 115),[3] under a tree (v. 2651 = v. 114),[4] before a white rug (v. 2652 = v. 110).[5] Whereas Marsile would have been content simply to rid himself of the Emperor, Baligant arrogantly claims that Charles's very existence depends on his whim. He emphasizes this with a slap on the knee (v. 2664) and rashly pledges that he will carry the war into France itself. Slapping the thigh is a gesture of mourning in the Bible,[6] but it is also a phallic oath, the knee or thigh being a euphemism for the private parts.[7] An erotic allusion here is consistent with other images associated with the Saracens.[8] Throwing caution to the winds, Baligant boasts extravagantly that Charles will have to crouch at his feet, beg for mercy,[9] foresake Christianity or be destroyed.[10] The Emir is at the top of the Wheel of Fortune,[11] but he is about to tumble down, for if Roncevaux was a disaster for the Saracens, Baligant's defeat will signal their utter annihilation.

Several echoes of earlier disasters hint darkly at the outcome of Baligant's unbounded insolence. The dispatching of two alliteratively named messengers, Clarifan and Clarien (v. 2670), recalls the fate of Basan and Basile beheaded on Haltille. Their father Maltraien brings to mind individuals with like-sounding names now lying dead on the plain of Roncevaux. The advice proffered by Baligant's men (v. 2668) harkens back to Marsile's council. The very mention of doomed Saragossa and the dying Marsile (vv. 2673, 2674) augurs ill, as does the gauntlet, which evokes Ganelon's calamitous mission. Most portentous, however, is the request that Marsile place Baligant's glove on his right hand, for the audience knows that it has been lost in the Saracen king's encounter with Roland.[12]

Roland is often associated with impetuous courage, but in Turoldus's mind there is a world of difference between Christian zeal leading to exalted self-sacrifice and pagan frenzy conducive to disaster.[13] It is the difference between *gloria* and *vanagloria*, between *caritas* and *odium*,[14] between *humilitas* and *superbia*.

Here, for the sake of clarity and with reference to the chronology of Days 1 through 6 detailed in COMMENTARY, 9 and 29, is an outline of the events that occur on Day 7.

(a) Morning: Baligant lands at Saragossa (Laisse 192) and dispatches messengers to Marsile (Laisse 193). Their message delivered (Laisses 194–198), Clarifan and Clarien report back to Baligant (Laisses 199–200), who promptly visits Marsile, then sets out after Charles (Laisses 201–202). Meanwhile, Charles rises at dawn (v. 2845), returns to Roncevaux, laments the French martyrs, and sees to it that they are given proper funeral rites (Laisses 204–213). The initial phases of the encounter between Charles and Baligant, including the marshaling of the French army, occur in the morning, for in v. 3098 (Charlemagne's prayer) reference is made to the rising sun.

(b) Afternoon: The events narrated from Laisse 227 (Charles rides to meet Baligant) to Laisse 265 (Capture of Saragossa) may be envisioned as occurring in the afternoon, although the return of the Saracen messengers (Laisse 227) and the marshaling of the pagan army (Laisses 228–236) may take place simultaneously to Charles's preparations, that is, in the morning.

(c) Night: Evil is extirpated from Saragossa as the Saracen cult there is destroyed; Bramimonde is spared (Laisse 266).

The next morning (v. 3675) the Emperor begins his voyage home.

31. Saragossa

Laisse 194 (verses 2686–2704)

One finds now, for the first time, a brief description of Saragossa with its ten gates, four bridges, streets inhabited by *burgeis*,[1] and palace rising from the fortified citadel (vv. 2690–2693).[2] In a later passage a main gate (v. 3650) and sixty towers will be mentioned (v. 3656: Les dis sunt grandes, les cinquante menues), as will the presence of *sinagoges* and *mahumeries* (v. 3662). If the number of persons baptized following the siege is any indication, the city had over 100,000 inhabitants (v. 3671: Baptizet sunt asez plus de .C. milie),[3] quite high by eleventh-century standards, but less than a third the size of present-day Zaragoza.[4]

Boissonade believed these details constituted a realistic description of the medieval city of Saragossa: "Il embellit le tableau, mais le fond est assez conforme à la réalité."[5] However, it is almost certain that this portrait is a figment of Turoldus's imagination, comparable to the conventional cities in contemporary art. Pierre Lavedan, who studied a representative number of the latter, concluded: "Si nous laissons de côté les pures fantaisies . . . on peut dire que jusqu'au XIVᵉ siècle, en Occident, la ville n'est guère qu'un idéogramme . . . une enceinte flanquée de tours [et] quelques monuments: une ou deux tours ou bien une ou deux basiliques."[6]

In the Middle Ages the city of Jerusalem was usually drawn as a circle with four towers, four doors, and four quarters, with Solomon's temple at the center.[7] Other cities were usually drawn as a hexagon with angle towers and included a few persons and stylized buildings.[8] Slowly the hexagon began to assume the form of a circle.[9] Only in the thirteenth century do cities begin to have distinctive characteristics, for example in the itinerary from London to Jerusalem ascribed to Matthew Paris.[10]

On the other hand, early itineraries and "crusade" chronicles do provide details concerning civic and religious architecture—for example, the Cathedral of Santiago de Compostela in the twelfth-century *Guide du Pèlerin*.[11] The contemporary *Pèlerinage de Charlemagne* mentions the *clochés*, *eglés*, and *punz relusanz* ('bell towers', 'churches', and 'cupolas, or domes') of Constantinople, rather vague features, to be sure, but not entirely devoid of local color.[12]

In the present passage Turoldus again makes use of one of his favorite devices: The linking of distant or converging groups by means of sound.[13] The wailing and lamenting of the palace inhabitants, constituting a *grant fremur* (v. 2693), reaches the ears of the approaching envoys.[14] The Saracens equate the erosion of faith in their gods, whose idols they have destroyed, with the disability suffered by Marsile and the loss of Jurfaleu, both at the hands of Roland. In their eyes the hero lives on by virtue of the fact that Spain is still at the mercy of the Franks.

32. The Saracen Messengers

Laisses 195–198 (verses 2705–2764)

In the midst of this desolation, Baligant's two messengers behave in a curious way. After dismounting and leaving their horses in the care of two Saracens, the emissaries climb the stairway to the palace. Jenkins translates v. 2707 (E li message par les mantels se tindrent) as 'The messengers held each other by their cloaks'[1] and explains: "If the reading is correct, the purpose of giving this detail can hardly be other than to ridicule the customs of the paynims. The romances, which give so much space to matters of social etiquette, prescribe that the cloak must be laid aside whenever a person of lower degree presents himself before royalty."[2]

The detail does seem curious to modern readers but I do not believe that ridicule is intended here. The messengers hold each other by the cloak as a courteous act as they climb the palace stairs, mentioned in vv. 2821 and 2840. In a comparable scene in the *Chanson de Guillaume* (vv. 2387–2391), Guillaume holds his wife's long sleeves as they mount a marble stairway. Then she fetches water and a towel for her husband:

Dunc prent s'amie par les mances de paille,
Sus munterent les degrez de marbre.
Ne trovent home que service lur face;
Dame Guiburc li curt aporter l'eve,
E aprés li baillad la tuaille.[3]

However, it is the manner in which the messengers make their greeting on reaching the palace that has puzzled scholars. According to Turoldus: *Par bel amur malvais saluz li firent* (v. 2710), which seems to be a contradiction in terms.[4] Jenkins cites Ker's suggestion that the verse in question is a rare instance of a "turn upon words."[5] "The reading, however," adds Jenkins, "is too uncertain to be valuable." *Par bel amur* does look suspicious, and so it may have seemed to the author of Venice IV, which has no trace of the hemistich (Vene al roi Marsilio, salu li dixe). However, the reading in the Oxford copy is supported by Châteauroux and Venice VII (Cil le salue soef par bon talent), Paris (Si la saluent et bel et gentement), and Cambridge (Par bonne amour si ont leur reson dite), and the characterization of the greeting as a *malvais saluz* is echoed in Conrad's translation ("They greeted the King disrespectfully, they did so with an evil design in mind").[6]

The solution to this perplexing matter may be that Turoldus is recalling earlier messages. The first was delivered by Blancandrin to Charlemagne:

E li message descendirent a pied,
Sil saluerent par amur e par bien.
Blancandrins ad tut premereins parled
E dist al rei: "Salvet seiez de Deu,
Le Glorius, que devuns aürer!"

In the latter passage it is clear that Blancandrin, who is bent on deceiving the Emperor, has nothing but feigned *amur* in his salutation and no intention whatsoever of one day adoring the Christian God. The Saracen envoy's calculation is mirrored in Ganelon's message to Marsile at Saragossa:

Mais li quens Guenes se fut ben purpenset.
Par grant saver cumencet a parler
Cume celui ki ben faire le set
E dist al rei: "Salvez seiez de Deu,
Li Glorius, qui devum aürer!"

Having conspired with the Infidel to betray his stepson and Charlemagne, Ganelon returns to the French camp:

674 Guenes i vint, li fels, li parjurez,
Par grant veisdie cumencet a parler
E dist al rei: "Salvez seiez de Deu!"

There is great cunning (veisdie) in his message, but the audience knows that Ganelon is a felon and a perjurer. There can be no mistaking either the traitor's contempt for God or his hypocritical concern for Charlemagne's welfare. Thus the poet qualifies the true meaning of *amur* in v. 121 by associating it with the lying Ganelon's *grant saver* (v. 426) and *grant veisdie* (v. 675). The connection with Ganelon also illuminates Clarien and Clarifan's malevolent salutation at Saragossa.

Upon their arrival the Saracen envoys get wind of the disaster at Roncevaux and of their allies' rejection of Tervagant, Mohammed, and Apollo (vv. 2696–2697). Now, with devastating sarcasm and mocking airs, they invoke the feckless gods' protection for the unfortunate Marsile and his spouse (vv. 2711–2713).

There has been much consternation among scholars over the fact that the Bodleian copy has the messengers address their insulting remarks to *li*. Bédier,[7] for example, says:

> A qui se rapporte *li*? Müller et Petit de Julleville ont imprimé: *Marsilie saluz firent*; Gautier et Clédat, *malvais saluz i firent*. Quant à Jenkins, il a introduit dans son texte un vers 2709 *a: Le rei troverent, devant lui la reïne.*[8] Seul, Stengel a maintenu la leçon du manuscrit. Elle peut se défendre, je crois. La *cambre voltice* a été décrite plus haut (v. 2592): nous y avons été introduits, nous y avons vu Marsile gisant, assisté par la reine. Marsile n'est pas nommé, il est vrai, au v. 2710, mais il l'a été dix vers plus haut. Qui donc les messagers salueraient-ils à leur entrée dans cette chambre, sinon lui? Etait-il nécessaire de le désigner par son nom?[9]

However, there is a simpler way out of the difficulty: One may interpret *li* to mean *lur*.[10] A comparable situation is to be found in v. 820 (Dunc le [for *lur*] remembret des fius e des honurs) and in v. 2762 (De Sarraguce les clefs li [for *lur*] ad livrees). Whether *li* in v. 2710 is a scribal error or a genuine form, the proposed interpretation offers the added advantage of meshing nicely with v. 2713: "*Salvent le rei e guardent la reïne!*"

At any rate the mocking allusion to the Saracen trinity is not lost on

Bramimonde (v. 2714: "Or oi mult grant folie!"). She reiterates the general lamentation over the disastrous consequences of Marsile's encounter with Roland at Roncevaux, emphasizes the fact that the pagan gods abandoned their people (vv. 2715, 2717, 2718: en recreantise, lesset ocire, faillirent), and wishes herself dead (v. 2723: "E! lasse, que n'en ai un hume ki m'ociet!").

The death wish betrays a profound change of attitude in Marsile's spouse. Contrasting sharply with the energetic posture, reminiscent of Judith (v. 2608: "Mult est grant doel que n'en est ki l'ociet!"), it shows that Bramimonde is in the depths of her despair. Her fixation on Charlemagne, whose victory over Baligant she prophetically announced in an earlier lament for her mutilated husband (vv. 2605–2607) and reiterates here (v. 2721), is due of course to his being the major cause of her despair.[11] However, the Emperor will also be her salvation. The fact that she cannot, despite everything, keep herself from admiring him foreshadows the edifying end of the Theme of Conversion in the *Song of Roland.* It should be noted that the use of the demonstrative in the expression *Cest mien seignur* in v. 2718 afforded the jongleur an excellent opportunity for appealing to the audience's creative fancy, for he doubtless assumed a disconsolate mien, used a plaintive inflection, and pointed downward to an imaginary couch.

Persisting in the arrogance associated with messengers in Old French epics,[12] Clarien brushes Bramimonde aside and proceeds to vaunt Baligant and his massed forces. Turoldus has no qualms about placing the insulting epithets *paien* (vv. 1500, 1535, 2844, 3136, 3326, 3397, 3524, and here in v. 2725) and *averse* (v. 3295) in the mouths of the Saracens when they are referring to themselves.[13] A fleet ordinarily implies great power, and it obviously does to Clarien, who revels in his vision:

> 2728 En Sebre avum .IIII. milie calant,
> Eschiez e barges e galees curant;
> Drodmunz i ad, ne vus sai dire quanz.

However, persons familiar with the Bible doubtless saw an allusion here to the ships of Tharsis, a symbol of human pride soon to be abased.[14]

Already the Saracen envoy fancies Baligant storming France itself, and mighty Charlemagne surrendering abjectly and even dead (vv. 2731–2733). In a slashing rejoinder Bramimonde dryly points out that the Emir will not have to travel so far, for the Emperor is at Saragossa's gates.[15] The queen's allusion to the fact that Charles has been marauding upon Marsile's domain for the past seven years is a scathing reflection upon the Emir's procrastination.

Marsile, who thus far in this scene has been cast in the role of silent consort to a wrathful spouse, now begins to assert himself. Stubbornly optimistic, despite the fact that he is near death and does not even have the comfort of an heir who will survive him (v. 2744), he pleads with the messengers to prevail upon Baligant to come to his bedside. He promises the Emir everything if he will only defend his realm against Charles. The French ruler, he says, can be vanquished in a month (v. 2751).

One wonders what possesses Marsile, as he reviews the catastrophic events of the past seven years and, especially, of the preceding day—his men annihilated at Roncevaux, his land devastated, his cities ravaged with fire and sword (vv. 2756–2757)—to take heart at the news of Baligant's arrival. Even as he informs the envoys how close Charlemagne has camped the night before, his intention being to impress upon the Emir how easy it will be to reach the enemy and cut off his retreat (see vv. 2799–2801), his words assume a plaintive form: "*Jo ai cunté, n'i ad mais que .VII. liwes*" (v. 2759), echoing the Psalmist's lament: "I can count every one of my bones."[16]

33. Baligant at Saragossa

Laisses 199–202 (verses 2765–2844)

The note of despair in Marsile's voice makes a profound impression upon Clarien and Clarifan, who are next seen galloping from the city *esfreedement*. The lengthy recapitulation of Marsile's defeat at Roland's hands and Charlemagne's victories—the fourth in the relatively short space of seven laisses (vv. 2700–2703 [the pagans in the streets of Saragossa], vv. 2716–2721 [Bramimonde's lament], vv. 2755–2759 [Marsile's account], and now in vv. 2771–2785 and 2790–2799 [Clarien's report to Baligant])—may be designed in part to remind the audience of what has occurred thus far.[1] However, it also serves to underscore the fact that the upcoming battle is not simply a confrontation between Charles and the Emir, but a direct consequence of Roland's mighty deed at Roncevaux. To Baligant's way of thinking, Marsile must be avenged (v. 2808), and the logical victim is Charlemagne. Roland's long shadow may be discerned in the extension of the right arm/right hand motif to Charlemagne's head (v. 2809: "Pur sun poing destre l'en liverai le chef"). The image in question began with the Emperor, whose right arm is Roland, and reverts now to Charlemagne. The symbol has thus come full circle.

There is a parody in this scene, too, of the Emperor's simultaneous joy and sorrow at the thought of his nephew's martyrdom.[2] As Baligant listens to the narrative of Marsile's trials and tribulations, he becomes so grief-stricken that he nearly loses his mind (v. 2789: Si grant doel ad por poi qu'il n'est desvet). This emotion does not overwhelm him completely, however, for the same recital by Clarien, recounted by Turoldus in a laisse similaire but culminating this time in the prospect of sweet revenge, now fills his heart with joy (v. 2803: En sun curage en est joüs e liet).

The Emir's stirring call to action is accentuated by the act of rising from his throne (v. 2804). His appeal is vigorous and direct. There is doubtless satiric intent on Turoldus's part here, a desire to underscore the precipitateness, noted earlier, in Baligant's first appearance as contrasted with Charlemagne's habitual reflection. The Saracen's eagerness to avenge his relative this very day (v. 2808: enqui), which can be attributed in part to the chronological economy of the poem, serves mainly to bring out this character's rashness. Baligant's men rush headlong from their ships and, symbolic of the recklessness of the whole enterprise, begin their madcap ride toward Charlemagne's army. As usual Turoldus's aside (v. 2812: que fereient il plus?) indicates helplessness on his part to impede the action, but this time it is uttered with a disbelieving wag of the head. As if in an afterthought, Baligant hastily designates one of his men to lead his troops, for he will be momentarily diverted by a visit to Marsile at Saragossa (v. 2815). The person he chooses bears a name that announces the inevitable outcome of all this haste: Gemalfin.[3]

Bramimonde intercepts Baligant on the stairway leading to her husband's chamber (vv. 2821–2822), utters a plaintive cry, and faints at his feet.[4] In this new diptych the Saracen queen's swoon may be said to be the inverted image of her eventual spiritual ascent, just as a few verses later, in the second part of this scene, Marsile's rising motion as he tries to lift himself in his bed (v. 2829), is the reversed reflection of his final downfall.[5] For the Theme of Conversion, introduced at the very outset of the poem and until now developed by Turoldus in various subtle ways, is about to emerge triumphant.[6] First, however, Bramimonde must be purged through suffering.

In the Saracen queen's single utterance to Baligant, as well as in the few sentences her husband manages to speak to the Emir, what is stressed is the loss they have both experienced, the shame, and, above all, the emptiness that is theirs (Bramimonde, v. 2824: "A itel hunte, sire, mon seignor, ai perdut!"; Marsile, v. 2834: "Mei ai perdut e tute ma gent"). The shame Marsile feels for having lost his men has nothing to do with Christian guilt. In a sense it is comparable to Roland's desolation at Roncevaux: He regrets the deaths of his men but feels no guilt over their loss. However, there is all the difference in the world between the hero's glorying in the achievement he shares with his men and the humiliation Marsile experiences in the common defeat. To Turoldus's way of thinking, the collective shame felt by the Saracen king and his followers stems not so much from their battlefield performance—contemptible as it may have been in many instances—but from deceitful roots: the decision to betray Charles into believing that they would become his vassals and that of having ambushed Roland and his men at Roncevaux. Marsile's disgraceful deed brought others down with him, and what Turoldus will say of Ganelon and his relatives applies equally to the Saracen leader: *Ki hume traïst sei ocit e altroi* (v. 3959).

Baligant's sorrow at Marsile's plight appears to be heart-felt—it is mentioned twice at any rate (vv. 2835, 2839)—but it is short-lived to say the least. His whole visit consists of the most perfunctory of courtesy calls (v. 2836: "Ne pois a vos tenir lung parlement"), for, as he himself now confesses (v. 2837), he is burning to confront Charlemagne. Having rapidly complied with the formality of accepting Marsile's fief (v. 2838), he hastens down the palace steps, leaps on his mount, and rushes to catch up with his advancing troops.

As the scene shifts away from Baligant, he is last seen forging ahead of his troops (vv. 2842–2844). There is intentional irony perhaps in the fact that Roland, too (v. 2865), wished to be in advance of his men.[7] Everyone recognizes that the hero's symbolic surpassing of his men at Roncevaux is fraught with significance. No one, though, seems to have noted that Baligant, in a grotesquely parallel act, apes the hero's glorious deed.

34. Charlemagne Returns to Roncevaux

Laisses 203–213 (verses 2845–2973)

Before the battle begins, Turoldus intercalates the narrative of the recovery of Roland's body and of Charles's lament over his slain nephew. In order to do this the poet must retrace his steps slightly, turning back in time to about the point when Baligant disembarked before Saragossa (Laisse 192). The Archangel Galbriel, last seen watching over Charlemagne's troubled sleep, serves as a narrative link now. His *signaculum* (v. 2848) is at once a mystical sign warding off evil,[1] a symbol of divine favor,[2] and a signal rousing the Emperor from his deep sleep.

With the light of day[3] has come the realization that before proceeding any further, the French must locate and attend to the bodies of their fallen comrades.[4] Charles has had a terrifying vision warning him of an impending battle and he feels the need to return to Roncevaux in order to fortify himself spiritually for the crucial test that lies ahead. He puts aside his armor, and all his men imitate this action (vv. 2849–2850). This solemn and ritualistic divestment signifies that they are entering the sanctuary that is Roncevaux.

Jenkins suggests that v. 2854 (En Rencesvals, la o fut la bataille) is: "A resounding line, imitated in later epics. No doubt it acquired, in time, some of the poetic suggestiveness of Wordsworth's 'For old, unhappy, far-off things, And battles long ago'."[5] It is unlikely that the line in question ever inspired the medieval audience with the Romantic melancholy to which Jenkins alludes. However, the verse does even now evoke some of the religious awe felt by Charlemagne and his men as they approach the soil consecrated by the blood of the French martyrs. Wonder tinged with fear is very much in evidence in Turoldus's choice of the expression *merveillus damage* in the preceding line. Charles cautions his men to advance reverently and insists on going before them. The Emperor hopes to find Roland's body disposed a certain way and fears that carelessness on the part of his men may make the sign unrecognizable. But he is also acutely aware of the fact that, as priest-king, he should be the first to tread on this hallowed ground.

What follows next also has a decidedly ritualistic aspect: first, the recollection of an inspired prediction by Roland, then three prophetic utterances by Charlemagne himself.

Roland's declaration at Aix occurred in one of those spontaneous boasting sessions (vv. 2860–2862) that were a popular pastime in the Middle Ages and to which there are numerous allusions in medieval literature.[6] Each hero strove to outdo his rivals by the extravagance of his *gab*.[7] The boasts were good fun and, in real life, individuals were not really expected to live up to them. However, the universe of literature has a rather different set of conventions and, in folklore, boasting is usually taboo.

It is easy to imagine Charlemagne's men engaged in just such a boisterous session at Aix, each *gab* punctuated with shouts of glee, spirits rising, and boasts growing more and more immoderate with each round of drinks. Then suddenly their charismatic leader speaks, the gravity of his voice and the deliberateness of his words contrasting sharply with the general tone thus far. What Roland says and the way he says it gives them pause, but it will soon be all but forgotten as the rowdy drinking and idle boasting resumes. However, one individual present has taken heed, and now Charlemagne recalls Roland's words. He realizes, perhaps for the first time, their fateful import and, as the Christlike aspect of predicting the modality of one's own death dawns upon him, he grasps yet another facet of the meaning of Roncevaux.

Roland died victoriously (v. 2363: mort cunquerant), a fact stressed now as Charles seeks his nephew's body (v. 2867: cunquerrantment).[8] There was a physical victory in that the hero stayed in possession of the field, moved out ahead of his men, and died without fear in the certainty of having served his Emperor well. But it was of course Roland's spiritual triumph that interested the poet above all else.

As Charles approaches the sacred spot where Roland lies, the mystical signals grow more and more apparent: the hill situated at a distance from the place where all the other Frenchmen rest in a meadow stained red with martyrs' blood (vv. 2868–2869, 2871–2872),[9] two trees (v. 2874),[10] three stones gouged in such a way it could only be the work of Durendal (v. 2875),[11] and, finally, the hero himself.

Emotion is conveyed in this passage in several ways. The attitude of *tremendum* as the French approach Roncevaux was mentioned earlier.[12] Charles weeps at the sight of the slain members of the rearguard (v. 2856), of the blood-stained flowers symbolic of their sacrifice (v. 2873), and of his nephew (v. 2943).[13] Sorrow characteristically alternates with joy in the *Song of Roland*, and this phenomenon explains in part how Charles comes to think of the festive occasion (v. 2860) when Roland predicted the manner of his death.

The Emperor's grief is so overwhelming that it borders on anger (vv. 2877, 2944),[14] and twice causes him to faint (vv. 2880, 2891).[15] He tears out his hair with both hands (vv. 2906, 2931), tugs on his beard (v. 2930), and wishes himself dead (vv. 2929, 2936, 2938–2942).[16] The French in the Emperor's entourage react similarly (vv. 2907–2908, 2932), and Turoldus himself is swept up in the general desolation, identifying with those who lament the dead (v. 2872: noz barons).

One of the characteristics of Charlemagne's lament[17] is the identification of his honor with Roland. Honor in the *Song of Roland* has little to do with the nebulous and controversial concept with which it is often associated today.[18] It is almost always concrete in its manifestations, referring, for example, to titles and property.[19] In the present instance Roland's death is felt as a diminution of Charlemagne's honor (v. 2890: "La meie honor est turnet en declin"), corresponding to a loss of physical strength and joy (v. 2902: "Cum decarrat ma force e ma baldur"). Roland is the irreplaceable mainstay of the Emperor's honor (v. 2903: "Nen avrai ja ki sustienget m'onur"). Even Roland's body conveys an impression of strength (v. 2895: Cors ad gaillard),[20] although it has lost its color and the hero's eyes are clouded over (vv. 2895–2896).[21] He is worth more to the Emperor than all his other relatives (v. 2905: "Se jo ai parenz, n'en i ad nul si proz"). While Roland was alive, his existence invigorated Charlemagne. Paradoxically, his death now serves the same purpose. Roland has now attained true glory (v. 2899), which in the *Song of Roland* is always associated with God.[22] In the litany *la meie honor* (v. 2890), *parenz* (v. 2905), *France* (vv. 2928, 2935), all identified with Charles, one recognizes once again the Christian cause as conceived by Turoldus.

Laisses 208 and 209 contain three prophetic statements by Charlemagne, the first two being quite similar: (1) The event will take place in Charles's capital city (Laon, Aix); (2) Strangers will come inquiring about Roland; (3) Charles will reply that his nephew is no more.

In the case of the *ubi sunt* motif, of which there is a faint echo here (v. 2912: Demanderunt: 'U est li quens cataignes?'),[23] it was noted that a reiterated phrase originally expressing the vanity of things of this world had been transformed by Turoldus into a hymn of praise in honor of the Twelve Peers lying on the field of Roncevaux.[24] A similar phenomenon is found here, for a familiar formula takes on rich new meaning.

Earlier, the visit of the unidentified men to Charlemagne's court (v. 2911: De plusurs regnes vendrunt li hume estrange) was characterized as mysterious and compared to an incident narrated in Genesis.[25] The arrival of men from afar asking about another individual whose fame has reached their ears is strongly reminiscent, too, of the first Epiphany ("After Jesus had been born at Bethlehem in Judaea during the reign of King Herod, some wise men came to Jerusalem from the east. 'Where is the infant king of the Jews?' they asked. 'We saw his star as it rose and have come to do him homage'").[26] The story of the Magi has always been interpreted as the first manifestation of Christ to the Gentiles and, according to medieval exegetes, was prefigured by the Queen of Sheba's visit to King Solomon ("The fame of Solomon having reached the queen of Sheba ... she came to test him with difficult questions").[27] The motif remains an epiphany in the *Song of Roland*, for it shows that the hero's fame has spread far and wide. However, Turoldus also transforms it from a joyful manifestation to an essentially pathetic device serving to bring out the enduring quality of the Emperor's sorrow.[28] The inquiries are presumably to last over a period of years. Each query will require a rehearsal of the crushing news and inflict a fresh wound on Charlemagne's grieving heart.

The third prophecy, which tells of many anticipated revolts (vv. 2921–2927), foreshadows the end of the poem[29] and underscores the Emperor's loneliness in the face of the endless struggles that lie in store for him. Roland has always been his mainstay, but now he must stand alone.

The final phase of Charlemagne's lament moves away from Roland for the first time to encompass the entire French rearguard. The shift occurs at v. 2937, where the word *maisniee*, whose literal meaning is 'household' (< VL **ma*(*n*)*sionata* < CL *mansio* 'house'), a concept that concerns Charlemagne's nephew directly, is broadened to include all the dead at Roncevaux. It is only natural that the entire rearguard that died on Charles's behalf (v. 2937: "ki pur mei est ocise") should now be considered to be part of the Emperor's "family."[30] The lament is a death wish, but at the same time it expresses the desire that both his body and soul remain close to those of his fallen men.[31] Charles seems to be trying to obliterate death by eliminating the cruel body-soul separation that has brought it about. By staying with them he will no longer have to grieve them. The thought smacks a little perhaps of the kind of rhetoric admired in the schools of the day, which strikes many modern readers as a bit forced, but it is lacking neither in vigor nor in effectiveness.

Geoffrey of Anjou seizes upon the notion of descending into the grave to help Charles overcome his anguish. Gently he pleads with the Emperor not to allow his grief such free reign and reminds him of the need to identify and bury the French who are still lying exposed where they fell. The common grave he proposes (v. 2949) and that is decided upon by Charles (v. 2954) is not merely a battlefield expedient; it also symbolizes the solidarity of the French rearguard in the fulfilment of its final duty.

The many religious who attend to the French army's spiritual needs are now called upon to render solemn funeral rites and to pronounce a final blessing over the victims. Incense (v. 2959) is traditionally a part of the honors (v. 2960) accorded to bodies that only recently were temples of the Holy Spirit, but it also symbolizes the prayers of the faithful rising to heaven.[32] The poet's expression of helplessness at abandoning the bodies of the slain Frenchmen (v. 2961: Sis unt laisez, qu'en fereient il el?) is thus tempered by the knowledge that the martyrs' souls have gone to their eternal reward.

Special honors are reserved for Roland, Oliver, and Turpin. The heart of each hero is removed from its body, wrapped in silk, and enclosed in a white marble casket. Charles insists on witnessing this ceremony, and it is clear that the intention here is to render homage to the courage of the three heroes. The medieval tradition of embalming the heart of exceptional individuals separately continued into the modern era: The heart of Richard Coeur de Lion was entombed at Rouen, that of Henry II and other English kings at Fontevrault, Saint Louis in the Sainte-Chapelle, Byron at Missolonghi, Gambetta in the Pantheon, and Saint Jean-Baptiste Vianney at Ars.[33] Other versions of the poem specify that the caskets were buried on the field of battle, a detail not recorded in the Bodleian manuscript.[34]

The three bodies are then carefully embalmed and encased in leather sacks.[35] The four nobles who had earlier been selected to guard the cadavers of the French at Roncevaux are given the assignment of accompanying the remains of the three heroes, which are placed on separate carts and draped with a silk pall.[36]

35. Battle Preliminaries

Laisses 214–225 (verses 2974–3095)

Charles is unaware that Baligant has arrived at Saragossa and assumes that the Saracen threat has been completely eliminated. As he prepares to leave Roncevaux,[1] the vanguard of Baligant's mighty army suddenly comes into view. Two Saracen messengers are dispatched and break the news of the Emir's hot pursuit to the startled Emperor. Their insulting words constitute a challenge Charlemagne cannot possibly ignore.[2]

Once again one is struck by the precipitateness of Baligant, who, having come ashore just a few hours earlier, rushed off to Saragossa and caught up to Charlemagne in what must have been a furious ride, and now insists on confronting his foe *encoi* 'this very day' (v. 2981). The Emir's rashness is further highlighted by Charlemagne's controlled anger.[3] For a brief moment, as the Emperor quietly strokes his beard (v. 2982)—one readily imagines the eyes of the entire French army riveted on this noble but hoary visage—there is a faint suggestion of indecision. But rather it is simply that Charles is still immersed in the memory of Roncevaux's desolation (v. 2983: Si li remembret del doel e del damage; cf. v. 2853: damage), from which thoughts he now wrenches himself free. Righteous indignation displaces sorrow: The Emperor's ferocious look galvanizes his weary men (v. 2984)[4] as he commands them to arm themselves for battle.

Charles quickly puts on his armor. The dressing ritual affords Turoldus an opportunity to provide details concerning Charles's luminous sword Joyeuse and, especially, his horse Tencendor.[5] As is often the case with fine mounts in the chansons de geste, the anecdote refers to a gift or a conquest involving a celebrated figure (cf. Grossaille, vv. 1649–1657).[6] The Emperor's victory over Baligant is foreshadowed in the image of the rider trampling his adversary, a formula exemplified in the tenth-century Barberini ivory preserved in the Louvre (*Fig. 59*), and reminiscent of Constantine.[7]

But it is the stirring portrait of Charlemagne galloping grandly before the massed corps of his hundred thousand men (v. 2997) that makes the most profound impression.[8] Here is Charlemagne in all his fullness, Charles the Magnificent, Charles the Unvanquished, and, as Turoldus makes clear when he depicts the Emperor invoking God and his representative here on earth (v. 2998: Recleimet Deu e l'apostle de Rome),[9] Charles the Instrument of God! The caparisoned caper is not to be mistaken for an ostentatious parade or for a barbaric celebration of the upcoming battle. It is rather a ceremonial display. The legendary Emperor shows his person in a promenade intended to inspire both bravery and holy fervor. Prebattle processions featuring sacred relics, or, among primitive people, war dances by persons having mana, serve essentially the same purpose.[10]

On the other hand, the description in Laisse 216 of the French arming does suggest the agreeable "feel" of combat gear and the stimulating sight of knights in battle array. Pennants hanging limply from lances (v. 3005) underscore the calm before the storm, and quiet confidence is very much in evidence as Charles addresses a number of his most trusted advisers. Roland's death is still uppermost in the Emperor's mind, however (v. 3012), and it is clear that the latter's surface equanimity masks a burning desire to avenge his nephew.

The ghostly presence of Roland and Oliver is further perceived in this scene with the designation of Guinemant and Rabel as surrogates for the slain heroes. Each bears one of the two instruments generally associated with Roland, *l'espee* and *l'olifant* (v. 3017), but the sword may be Oliver's weapon.[11] The lack of any distinctive memento of Oliver and, moreover, the symbolic posting of the two knights *el premer chef devant* (vv. 3018, 3195), a position where one would naturally expect to find Roland, tend to confirm the view that Turoldus did not intend to cast the two comrades in the contrasting mold critics since Bédier have assigned them.[12] The altercation at Roncevaux was a transitory affair and, while Roland is of course accorded a much more central role in the poem, Turoldus does stress the equal worthiness and inseparability of the companions-in-arms and consistently pairs them in the remaining allusions to the two heroes.

What follows is a lengthy enumeration of the ten *eschieles*, which comprises the order of battle decided upon by Charlemagne.[13] The poet proceeds in a formulaic manner. Each laisse lists the number of men in a division, their nationality, their leader or leaders—whose function is invariably referred to by the term *guier* (vv. 3022, 3034, 3042, 3050, 3059, 3067, 3074, 3083)—and one or more comments about their valor or fine appearance.[14] Laisse 217, which tells of two squadrons of French youths (v. 3020: bachelers; cf. v. 3197: bachelers . . . enfanz),[15] one of which will be commanded by Guinemant and Rabel, provides the added detail concerning Roland and Oliver. In every other case each division is characterized in a separate laisse.

Charlemagne's army numbers 350,000 men. The divisions are apparently numbered according to their size, the first being the smallest (15,000), the tenth and last the largest (100,000).[16] The French, who make up the first two and the last divisions, constituting more than a third of the entire army, are given the honor of being in the van. The poet identifies with the white-haired French veterans in the largest division (v. 3085: Cent milie sunt de noz meillors cataignes), where Charlemagne is to be found.[17]

Each division forms a natural grouping according to nationality, and their lord designates a battle commander of his choice, as is apparent in vv. 3056–3058. However, Charles exercises this prerogative in the case of the French and retains personal command of the tenth and largest division. The Emperor summons Jozeran of Provence, Duke Naimes, and Antelme of Mayence in vv. 3007–3008. From their activities it is clear that the first two serve as marshals.[18] They assemble the troops and place them in proper position for battle. The following verbs used with the noun *eschiele* refer to that function: *ajoster* (v. 3024), *establir* (vv. 3027, 3036, 3061, 3068), and *faire* (vv. 3045, 3052, 3076).

This catalogue has a decidedly formulaic aspect, but it also lends itself to parallelism, for, in Laisses 232–234, Turoldus will list the divisions in Baligant's force, once again grouping them by ten.[19] By the simple process of providing a figure for the weakest of them—which numbers 50,000 men (v. 3219)—he will be able to emphasize the vastly superior number of Saracens without specifying an exact total.

Detailing the various elements constituting the opposing armies, then, is also a device to highlight the magnitude of the conflict. There is in this list more than a suggestion of "realism." In addition to the technical vocabulary alluded to above, the mere citing of who was there—national groups, legendary heroes—enhances the illusion of historicity. Finally, as has been pointed out by generations of commentators of the *Song of Roland*, these mentions of nationalities and names may not be without intentional flattery.[20]

In his description of the tenth division, Turoldus, who earlier mentioned the oliphant, now refers to the French war cry Monjoie (v. 3092) and the oriflamme (v. 3093). The celebrated banner, says the poet, was a gift of Saint Peter and was called *Romaine*, but in that place (iloec), that is, on the battlefield, its name was changed to *Monjoie*.[21] The miraculous gift of the oriflamme to Charlemagne is recorded in the mosaic of the Lateran triclinium (c. 800)[22] (*Fig. 60*). Saint Peter seated in majesty, keys on his lap, hands the pallium to Pope Leo III, the oriflamme to Charlemagne, kneeling at his right and left, respectively. Turoldus introduces the oriflamme at this point in the narrative because it is a battle standard, and the Emperor is about to engage Baligant in a death struggle. It is no ordinary ensign, however, and its sacred character suggests the inevitable outcome of a conflict where only one side has celestial help.[23]

The historical origin and the etymology of the word oriflamme have been studied, but the significance of the anecdote itself has never been accorded the attention it deserves. In the epic universe warriors frequently receive the gift of a horse, a sword, or a similar object from a supernatural source.[24] The frame of reference is rather different here, for the oriflamme is associated, on the one hand, with the *Traditio legis* and, on the other, with the *Translatio imperii*.[25]

Beginning with early Christian art, one finds various iconographic formulas of Christ giving the New Law to Saint Peter while Saint Paul looks on, his hands raised in a gesture of acclamation[26] (*Fig. 61*). At times Christ hands Saint Paul a book, and keys to Saint Peter. The delivery of the keys and of the New Law (Traditio legis) was an important symbol of the legitimacy of the Church and of papal privilege. It was also intimately bound up with the notion that the power of the Roman Empire had been transferred to Charlemagne (Translatio imperii).[27] When one realizes that soon after his accession to the papacy in 795 Leo III sent the banner of Rome and Saint Peter's keys to Charlemagne, whom he crowned Emperor in 800, one begins to see that the oriflamme had religious as well as political significance for Turoldus and his contemporaries. It was only natural, then, that in the poet's mind the pennant was associated with Monjoie, which evoked similar thoughts. As the French gaze upon the oriflamme and utter Charles's famous war cry, they are reminded of the sacredness of their mission and of the fact that they are God's Chosen People.[28]

36. Charlemagne's Prayer

Laisse 226 (verses 3096–3120)

The Emperor now beseeches God to aid him in his hour of greatest need. His prayer, like Roland's, has references to familiar biblical figures rescued from mortal danger—the allusion to Daniel in the lions' den is identical in vv. 2386 and 3104–3105—and it is clear that virtually the same supplication can be used before combat as well as when facing imminent death.[1]

It is somewhat curious to hear Charles asking that God's love be present in him on this occasion (v. 3107: "La tue amurs me seit hoi en present!") when in the very next breath he implores his leave to avenge Roland (vv. 3108–3109: "Par ta mercit, se tei pleist, me cunsent / Que mun nevold pois venger, Rollant!"). This is a curious kind of mercy, assuming the usual acceptation of that term, which "implies compassion that forbears punishing even when justice demands it."[2] It would appear rather that the *amor*, which Charles is asking for, is synonymous in this instance with the *vertut*, that is, strength, power, associated with the Divinity in other parts of the poem, and with the sign of the cross mentioned in this passage (v. 3111: Seignat sun chef de la vertut poisant). Charlemagne, the instrument of God's wrath, seeks to punish injustice. *Mercit* should therefore be interpreted here in the general meaning of a grace or a special favor, a meaning not far removed from its etymon (< Lat. *mercedem* 'price paid, wages', a derivative of *merx* 'merchandise'). Charles's sign of the cross, the traditional gesture concluding a prayer and indicating that what precedes is being asked for in the name of the Trinity, may also allude to the fact that Roland died *cum signo fidei*.[3] The portrait Turoldus now provides of the Emperor sallying forth evokes Roland in an earlier scene:

1159 Cors ad mult gent, le vis cler e riant.

3115 Gent ad le cors, gaillart e ben seant,
Cler le visage e de bon cuntenant.

It is as if God has infused Charlemagne with the youthful vigor the Emperor believed had been lost forever at Roncevaux (v. 2916; cf. v. 1401). The French sense this miraculous rejuvenation and, when they hear the oliphant responding to the army's bugle call (vv. 3118–3119),[4] they cannot help but weep with mixed joy and sorrow at the memory and reflection of their beloved Roland (v. 3120).[5]

37. *Charlemagne's Approach Reported to Baligant*

Laisse 227 (verses 3121–3136)

The exact itinerary followed by the French as they seek out Baligant's army may puzzle those who read the *Song of Roland* with topographical survey in hand.[1] Charles leaves the vicinity of Roncevaux and heads south, so, strictly speaking, he should not encounter the haunting landscape alluded to in this passage, which is actually situated to the north. Homer caught nodding? Perhaps. But the apparent geographical disorder of this passage also suits the narrative needs of the poet. Nature recalls the suffering at Roncevaux as the French rush to avenge the infamous deed perpetrated there. The quick dash through the perilous mountain landscape, oliphant echoing trumpet calls (vv. 3118–3119, 3125–3126), stands out in sharp contrast to an earlier image of a craggy setting with bugles also responding to oliphant blasts, but with progress mysteriously impeded when the French were striving unsuccessfully to reach Roland at Roncevaux (vv. 1830–1833).[2]

In a gesture signifying defiance of the enemy[3] but also no doubt demonstrating that he is heedless of old age,[4] the Emperor proudly displays his beard (v. 3122). The act is mimed by the other grizzled veterans in his division as a sign of their undying affection and loyalty (v. 3123). The mountains and valleys, escarpments, narrow defiles, and the wasteland, mementos of the rearguard's agony, are quickly traversed, and the fateful plain is reached (v. 3129).

The scene shifts now to Baligant's camp, where the extravagant aping of everything associated with Charlemagne continues. The messenger is a Syrian Arab (v. 3131), that is, a renegade Christian,[5] suggesting a parallel with Ganelon, who betrayed the Emperor and his faith. Upon hearing the news the messenger bears, Baligant orders trumpets to be sounded, and his men immediately dismount and arm themselves, reminiscent of the scene in Laisse 136 after Charles hears Roland's oliphant call.

38. The Pagans Prepare for Battle

Laisses 228–231 (verses 3137–3213)

As noted in the preceding commentary, the arming of the Saracens is reminiscent of Laisse 136. But it is also a clear case of triplication, for there is an extended parallel with Laisses 214–216:

1. the phrasing employed in relaying the message to Charles and to Baligant:

> 2978 "Reis orguillos, nen est fins que t'en alges!"
> 3132 "Veüd avum li orguillus reis Carles."
>
> 2981 "Encoi verrum se tu as vasselage."
> 3135 Dist Baligant: "Or oi grant vasselage."

2. the leader's resounding call to arms:

> 2986 "Baruns franceis, as chevals e as armes!"
> 3136 "Sunez voz grailes, que mi paien le sacet!"

3. the dismounting:

> 2999 Par tut le champ cil de France descendent,
> Plus de cent milie s'en adubent ensemble.
> 3139 Paien descendent pur lur cors aduber.

4. the leader's rush to be the first one armed:

> 2987 Li empereres tuz premereins s'adubet.
> 3140 Li amiralz ne se voelt demurer.

5. the various items of armor and the order in which they are put on:[1]

(a) coat of mail (v. 2988 = v. 3141);
(b) helmet (v. 2989 = v. 3142);
(c) sword (v. 2989 = v. 3143);
(d) shield (v. 2991 = v. 3149);
(e) spear (v. 2992 = v. 3152).

Baligant is gigantic and there is in his features, notably his white hair and beard (vv. 3162, 3173), a reflection of Charlemagne.[2] However, the image is distorted and the handsomeness to which the poet alludes (v. 3159) and which even wrenches an exclamation of wonderment from him (v. 3164; cf. v. 3172) is manifestly diabolical, and the Saracen's expectations (vv. 3168–3171) are vain.[3] For there is a sinister echo of other evil-sounding names in the designation of the Emir's spear as

Maltet (v. 3152), and his religion is the despised Saracen idolatry (v. 3174).

The fifty-foot leap in the ceremonial parade, imitating Charlemagne's graceful *eslais* (v. 2997 = v. 3166), ominously sprinkles blood into a gaping ditch, symbolic of the abyss into which Baligant is about to plunge headlong.[4] But the poet's ironic intent is particularly apparent in the comment relative to Baligant's sword and war cry *Precieuse* in a passage where a verse has unfortunately been omitted by the Bodleian copyist.[5] There is, as noted earlier, profound significance in the joy alluded to in Laisse 183 concerning Charlemagne's fabulous sword and celebrated *cri de guerre*.[6] Mention of preciousness also suggests here the Emir's inability to grasp the reference to spiritual values and his engrossment in material things.

Laisses 229–231 present a discussion between Baligant and his son, who requests the honor of the first blow. The demand is reminiscent of Laisses 69–70, when Aelroth asked his uncle Marsile to grant him the same boon. This time, however, a new element is injected into the dialogue, for after Malprimes suggests that Charlemagne will not have the courage to show his face, Baligant contradicts his son, insisting that the Emperor is a worthy adversary (v. 3180: Dist Baligant: "Oïl, car mult est proz").[7]

It is not unusual in literature to find a father contradicting his son. Prudent senior urging brash junior to be less impulsive is an old topos. Those familiar with medieval French romances will think immediately of Baudemagu's admonitions to Meleagant in Chrétien de Troyes's *Charrette*, a situation reflected in cameo form in the *Pree aus jeus* scene in the same poem.[8] Baligant's cautionary remark echoes Bramimonde's praise of her nemesis and future savior, Charlemagne.[9] However, it is promptly followed by the assertion that since Roland is dead Charles will not have the strength (v. 3183: vertut) to withstand the Saracens. What Baligant fails to appreciate of course is that Roland—no more than Oliver, the other Peers, or the rearguard[10]—is not the sole source of the Emperor's power. God is the fountainhead of all true strength.[11]

The offer of a reward in the form of a fief to Malprimes if he triumphs over the Christians (vv. 3206–3208)[12] forms a contrast to the French, who fight for Charlemagne and for the greater glory of God. In actual practice the granting of fiefs and similar honors was often a major inducement for knights to accompany anyone on an expedition,[13] and Charlemagne, in the heat of battle, will make such an offer to his men.[14] Investiture consisted in the ritual handing over (symbolically or in fact) of an object, for instance a ring, a glove, or a banner. It represented, therefore, either the act of concession or the fief itself.[15] A gesture on Baligant's part is not specifically mentioned by Turoldus, but it appears likely that the jongleur mimed it here as he spoke the Emir's words or as he mentioned the corresponding gesture of accepting the fief in v. 3210: *Passet avant, le dun en requeillit.* Baligant may have handed over any one of several objects of little value customarily involved in investiture ceremonies. If the act of concession was merely symbolized, he may have retained the item in question, in which case *recuillir* in v. 3210 means simply a ceremonial touching of the object in question.[16] The use of the term *pan* in v. 3207 ("Jo vos durrai un pan de mon païs") suggests that Baligant may have held up a piece of his clothing (OFr. *pan* < Lat. *pannum*), perhaps the hem of his *broigne*[17]—a gesture attested in the *Sachsenspiegel*[18]—to represent the piece of land being offered to his son. In v. 3213 *vestut*, rather than the technical term *envestut*[19] (Ne il n'en fut ne vestut ne saisit), is consistent with this play on words.

Turoldus's observation here concerning the uselessness of Baligant's offer appears to be designed to reassure the audience concerning the outcome of the impending battle.

39. Baligant's Army

Laisses 232–234 (verses 3214–3264)

Enumerating the thirty divisions of the Emir's army must have required considerable virtuosity on the part of the jongleur and, judging from the many variants in the manuscripts of the *Song of Roland* that have survived, the list was probably slightly different each time it was recited. Scholars have had a field day identifying the various exotic nationalities and places mentioned in this passage, many of which are historically plausible while others are pure fantasy.[1]

The *Arrabiz*, referred to in vv. 3011 and 3081, are inhabitants not only of the Muslim Orient, an area designated by Turoldus as *Arabe*,[2] but also of Eastern Europe as well.[3] This is, then, an eleventh-century view of the world beyond the Holy Roman Empire, a concept akin to what the Greeks and Romans referred to as "the Barbarians." In the early twelfth century the latter expression was used by Anna Comnena, a Greek witness of the Crusades, to describe the inhabitants of the West between the farther side of the Adriatic and the Pillars of Hercules.[4]

Despite superficial differences, the teeming non-Christian universe in the *Song of Roland* is monolithic in that everyone owes allegiance to Baligant and worships the pagan trinity. Although Turoldus claims, in v. 3262, that his source is the *Geste Francor*, which supposedly included an account of the battle, the origins of such chimeras and stereotypes are many and diverse, and the practiced eye will detect the influence of classical and medieval geographers, and of the Bible.[5] One is reminded of a section of the tympanum of the inner west doorway of the abbey church of Sainte-Madeleine at Vézelay (*Fig. 62*), with its view of bizarre peoples remaining to be evangelized.[6]

In this passage one notes the absolute lack of anything remotely resembling the exciting sights and sounds Westerners associate with the East, particularly since the era of Romanticism. The poet is dealing here with *moral* geography, and the details concerning gigantism (vv. 3215, 3253), large heads (v. 3221), bristles (v. 3223),[7] ugliness (v. 3238), tough skin (v. 3249), and beards (v. 3260) are chosen with a view to illustrating the notion that pagans aspire only to evil (v. 3231), neither love nor serve God (vv. 3247, 3261), and are cruel felons (vv. 3248, 3251).

Virtually the same observation is made by Turoldus throughout the *Song of Roland*, including the present passage, when referring to Christians and to pagans:

1226/1902 Vait le ferir en guise de baron (Oliver, Roland).

1889 As vus Marsilie en guise de barunt (Marsile).

3054 Icil chevalchent en guise de baron (the Bretons in Charles's army).

3264 Paien chevalchent en guise de produme (the Saracens in Baligant's army).

Praise of the hated Infidel is merely a device serving to enhance the Christians' eventual triumph, for unless regenerated through the saving grace of baptism, no Saracen, in the poet's view, can have any intrinsic worth.

Such mental reservations, coupled with a propensity for depicting pagans as fiendish monsters,[8] betray considerable repressed fear of the Saracens. Much of this anxiety stems from the belief that the Saracens are creatures possessed by the devil and therefore capable of awesome feats of strength as well as revolting depravities. This biased view will evolve in time as manifested, for example, in certain favorable comments by medieval chroniclers regarding Saladin.[9] For Turoldus and his French contemporaries, however, the Saracens pose a grave threat to their spiritual as well as physical well-being. Like leprosy, they symbolize sin and constitute one of the greatest problems of the day.[10]

40. The Pagan Army Advances
Laisses 235–239 (verses 3265–3344)

Baligant's impetuousness is underscored once again,[1] this time by the curious ceremony consisting of prayers on horseback. In actual practice Muslim prayers—here corresponding to *salat*, or formal ritual prayer, as opposed to the private devotions known as *du'a*—could be said anywhere, even on the battlefield, but the prescribed movements known as *rak'a*, which include standing upright and prostration would have been impossible on horseback.[2]

The Emir has his dragon and other religious emblems brought forward. By the association of a serpent device with the pagan ensigns, Turoldus wishes his audience to understand that these objects are not merely fetishes but diabolical instruments.[3] The Cananaens, serving as pagan Levites,[4] surround these holy objects and begin shouting for the Saracens to bow down in adoration, a ritual the Saracens promptly execute. The cry resembles the muezzin's call to daily prayers, but the similarity is purely coincidental. The horseback inclination is probably intended to show the pagans in a ridiculous posture. The proximity of the French and their horrified reaction to what seems to them to be a hideous cult are indicated by their shouted insults and appeals to God to protect Charlemagne.

The strategy decided upon by Baligant is the only hint of prudence on his part, but *grant saveir* in v. 3279 denotes cunning and has nothing to do with the Sapientia associated with the Emperor.[5] The entire Saracen army will advance except for three divisions, which the Emir will hold in reserve.[6] Baligant's plan is to engage Charles and the tenth French corps with this elite body of troops. If, as Turoldus has indicated earlier (v. 3085), the Emperor has 100,000 men in his division, three Saracen units of "no fewer than 50,000 men" (v. 3219: En la menur

.L. milie en out) give the Emir decisive but, by epic standards, far from overwhelming numerical superiority. Although no exact figures are provided, this would seem to square with the Emir's known brashness. Baligant's haughty boast (vv. 3288–3289) that he will personally vanquish Charles similarly foreshadows his own downfall.

There is a certain amount of ambiguity about the theater of action referred to as Roncevaux—the battle ranges over a broad expanse repeatedly referred to as a *champ* (vv. 1338, 1869, 2434, 2999), yet hills are a prominent feature of this landscape[7]—but there is no question about the present confrontation. It takes place on a wide plain.[8] In fact Turoldus emphasizes that neither hill, nor valley, nor forest breaks up the uniform surface (vv. 3292–3293). He explains that no one will be able to hide (v. 3293: asconse n'i poet estre) and that the adversaries are in full view of each other (v. 3294). Perhaps the memory of the earlier Saracen ambush still hovers in the background, the implication being that no such deceitfulness will be possible on the present occasion. However, openness and high visibility also help to impart an air of cosmic finality to what is about to transpire. The mighty battle will decide once and for all who is in the right and who is in the wrong, for Baligant will in the end concede (vv. 3553–3554), and the whole world, which is looking on, as it were, will know the outcome.

The conflict is prefigured in the clashing war cries *Precieuse!* (v. 3298) and *Monjoie!* (v. 3300), and in the opposing trumpets (vv. 3301, 3309) as the armies edge toward each other relentlessly. However, the oliphant's blasts instill Roland's ardor into the French (vv. 3302, 3310). Baligant assures his brother excitedly that no one has ever seen the like of this battle (v. 3322). Before it has even begun, he knows it will eventually be decided in hand-to-hand combat with Charles.[9]

Frantically the Emir rushes out ahead of his troops and points the tip of his spear toward the object of his envy[10] and fury (v. 3328), acts aping two of Roland's most memorable gestures. The terms of the simile—*trespassees* in v. 3324 makes it clear that Turoldus has Roland's dying movements in mind (v. 2865: trespassast)[11]—mock the distance covered by Baligant (v. 3323: Plus qu'om ne lancet une verge pelee). *Verge pelee* is an expression frequently used in derogatory comparisons[12] (cf. v. 2265: Dun arcbaleste ne poet traire un quarrel; v. 2868: Plus qu'en ne poet un bastuncel jeter), and it has scabrous overtones.[13] Baligant's pointing spear also recalls Roland waving the tip of his weapon toward heaven on two earlier occasions (vv. 708, 1156).[14]

Laisse 239 moves the action back slightly to Charlemagne's first glimpse of Baligant. There has certainly been no dearth of hyperbole so far in the *Song of Roland*, but the view of the Saracen hordes covering the vast plain, except for the space occupied by Charles's army, is among the most grandiose images in the poem. It clearly implies that the ensuing battle will have cosmic consequences.[15] Like the Emir, Charlemagne has a premonition of the impending duel with his counterpart. His gaze seems mysteriously drawn along the invisible line projected by Baligant's spear over the heads of the pagan multitudes ranged before him until it falls on the Saracen leader riding among the symbols of the despised religion (vv. 3329–3330).

Charlemagne's impassioned appeal to his men contains an ellipsis. The missing phrase becomes immediately apparent when his speech is diagrammed as follows:

3335 "French barons, you are stalwart knights"[16]

is to

3337 "The pagans . . . are evil and cowardly"

as

---

is to

3338 "Their religion isn't worth a damn."

In this equation the Emperor not only suggests that Christianity has great worth, but he also makes it clear that French valor derives from it.

For the first time in the *Song of Roland*, the rhetorical question *d'iço qui calt?* (v. 3339) does not express helplessness on the poet's part (cf. vv. 1405, 1806, 1840, 1913), but rather Charlemagne's abiding confidence that the Christians will triumph.[17] The Emperor digs his spurs in and his mount leaps forward in four mighty bounds (v. 3342), closing the gap that remains between the two onrushing forces.

41. *The Battle Against Baligant*

Laisses 240–257 (verses 3345–3559)

The encounter with Baligant, as opposed to the Battle of Roncevaux, takes place in a location that has no name or historical basis. Disregarding for the moment Charlemagne's pursuit and annihilation of Marsile's army, which involved a miraculous prolongation of daylight, the Battle of Roncevaux and the present one last about the same amount of time. However, there were lulls in the earlier engagement, whereas the present combat continues without a break until nightfall (v. 3395).[1] The struggle between Charles and Baligant has three successive phases: (1) a series of clashes between individuals and larger groups; (2) a decisive duel involving the two leaders; (3) pursuit of the routed Saracens.[2]

Entirely different matters are at stake in the two battles, and naturally Roncevaux lends itself to many more psychological and ethical considerations. While the conflicts are intimately related and the struggle against the Infidel essentially the same, each battle pits completely different characters against one another, and its dramatic underpinnings and stylistic features deserve to be considered independently.

Turoldus shifts a good deal more from side to side in his description of the battle between Charles and Baligant. At Roncevaux each successive French triumph carried the plot along an upward-curving trajectory, reaching a high point with the flight of Margariz and the death of Chernuble. A reversal of French fortunes caused the action to arc relentlessly downward until Roland, the last remaining member of the rearguard, was eliminated. The action in the present contest will more resemble a seesaw movement.

As the French and Saracen vanguards collide,[3] the first blows are struck by Rabel and Guinemant, who attack their counterparts Torleu and, presumably, Dapamort. These duels are actually part of a broader attack by the French vanguard, but *dunc* in v. 3350 suggests that Rabel and Guinemant precede, perhaps only by a few seconds, the lead elements of their division. From a purely narrative point of view, the rest of this engagement is temporarily forgotten as Turoldus concentrates the audience's attention on two or three combats. This focus is further enhanced by the reactions of the French (vv. 3358–3359, 3365–3368), who are evidently observing these proceedings. Throughout the battle between Baligant and Charlemagne's forces, the notion that the Emperor's cause is just and that he is the instrument of God will be repeatedly stressed. It stands to reason, then, to Turoldus's way of thinking, that God will come to the aid of the French (vv. 3358–3359, 3367–3368).

Malprimes had asked for and been awarded the honor of the first blow, but this distinction has now been wrested from him by the élan of the Roland and Oliver surrogates.[4] Baligant's son turns the balance back in favor of the Saracens by a savage counterattack. His actions are initially commented upon by the narrator, who describes the Saracen's mighty blows as raining indiscriminately on any adversary he encounters, his movements having no particular orientation (vv. 3369–3372). However, the point of view immediately becomes that of the Emir, who is the first to discern Malprimes's design (v. 3373: Tut premereins s'escriet Baligant), which is to cut a swath through the French until he reaches Charlemagne himself. Perhaps this was his ambition from the moment Baligant addressed him, mentioning the Emperor's name no fewer than three times in the short space of eleven lines (vv. 3187, 3190, 3197). At any rate the Emir calls upon his men to come to his son's aid (v. 3378), and the Saracens rush forward (v. 3379). As if awaiting this signal, the poet's lens now widens to encompass the general conflict, which now involves both armies entirely (v. 3384: Justees sunt trestutes les escheles) and results in countless casualties on both sides.

Turoldus once again emphasizes the historic aspect of the struggle, looking forward and backward in time and finding nothing to match such bitter strife (v. 3382: Ne fut si fort enceis ne puis cel tens; v. 3394: Unc einz ne puis ne fut si fort ajustee). In other words, the battle is a prefiguration of Armageddon, the final conflict between Good and Evil.[5]

The voices of Baligant and Charlemagne, rising over the din and carnage, dominate this scene. Both leaders promise their men fiefs (vv. 3399, 3409–3410). However, different contexts make it clear that Baligant's offer is an attempt to corrupt and seduce, Charlemagne's to exalt.[6]

In addition to fiefs the Emir dangles the prospect of lovely maidens before his men's eyes (v. 3398).[7] The image evokes the houris, who figure among the pleasures of the Muslim paradise, but the concept of "damsels with large eyes" and other aspects of the Islamic hereafter were entirely foreign to the poet. As noted earlier, Turoldus viewed Saracen women as diabolical creatures.[8] Baligant's offer may seem tantalizing to the modern reader, but it surely elicited derisive laughter and disparaging remarks from an audience accustomed to associating such notions with the contemptible vice of Luxuria.[9]

Charlemagne's appeal to his men in Laisse 246 is at once an expression of the Emperor's high regard for and trust in his men (v. 3406: "Seignors barons, jo vo aim, si vos crei") and of his gratitude for past services in his name (vv. 3407–3408). He appeals to them now to keep the image of Roncevaux' victims before their eyes and reiterates his claim that his cause is just (vv. 3411–3413). His men promptly concur in the correctness of this assertion (v. 3414).

One of the most remarkable aspects of this passage is that it reveals the intense mutuality of the feudal bond that exists between Charles and his men.[10] The Emperor unhesitatingly demands a supreme effort and elicits a spontaneous and wholehearted response only because he himself is ready to give his all in return. Charlemagne's total commitment to his men is eloquently expressed by a simple word uttered in conjunction with his pledge of lands and financial reward (vv. 3409–3410: "Ben le conuis que gueredun vos en dei / E de mun cors, de teres e d'aveir"). The use of *cors*[11] gives this sentence a juridical turn. Feudal contracts are replete with pledges not to injure a lord "in his body" or "in his life and limbs."[12]

However, the granting of one's body is not the same as doing injury to someone's body or sustaining an injury to one's own body. Charlemagne's words recall rather the institution of the Holy Eucharist by Christ at the Last Supper: "'Take it and eat'; he said 'this is my body'."[13] Christ's words are repeated in the rite of consecration.[14] The liturgy associated with the Canon of the mass recalls the sacrifice on Calvary and that of Abraham, the Apostles, and the holy martyrs.[15] A commemoration of the Passion, the eucharistic sacrament also reminds one of Christ's love of mankind.[16] Charlemagne's words to his men, many of whom are about to die, express his great love for them, but they also associate their deed with that of Roland and his followers at Roncevaux and with the sacrifices of others, including Christ. Charles is affirming that, like the saints and martyrs before them, they will become glorious members of the mystical body of Christ.[17]

The poet's optic has been shifting repeatedly from one side to the other, effectively depicting the uncertain outcome of this momentous struggle. Now Turoldus suddenly projects the audience into the midst of this raging tempest, offering it an opportunity to observe, as in the eye of a hurricane, the terrifying maelstrom (vv. 3403–3404: Ais vos le caple e dulurus e pesmes!/Bataille veit cil ki entr'els volt estre!). The unexpected change in point of view is arresting as the Emperor makes his poignant appeal to his embattled men.

Malprimes, who has steadily been fighting his way toward Charles, must first overcome Naimes. On a number of occasions Turoldus has made it clear that the duke is one of the Emperor's most trusted counselors. While the poet provides no specific details in this respect, it is evident that Naimes is not far from Charlemagne in the tenth division, which is made up of Frenchmen.[18] It is this lieutenant's fighting qualities that will now be stressed. He gives Malprimes a fierce look, then strikes him down with his spear.

In seesaw fashion the advantage that is enjoyed by the French thanks to Naimes's attack reverts momentarily to the Saracens as King Canabeu appears on the scene and succeeds in wounding the duke. The imminence of the Charles-Baligant duel becomes more and more apparent as the Emir's kinsmen—Malprimes is his son, Canabeu his brother—fight the Emperor's closest adviser. Charlemagne rights the balance by dispatching the pagan king with a single thrust from his spear (vv. 3447–3450, 3457).

The image of the stunned Naimes, bent over, hanging on to his horse's neck (v. 3440),[19] as Canabeu prepares to strike him a death blow, is one of those moments frozen in time that appeals so much to Turoldus. It is significant that no angel appears to stay the Saracen's blade—as in the iconography of Abraham's Sacrifice.[20] Mercifully, God intervenes (v. 3439), but through Charlemagne. In this way Turoldus underscores the Emperor's messianic role.

Naimes's life hanging from a thread is also described in terms of a stifling sensation: *anguissables* (v. 3444) (< OFr. *angoisse* < Lat. *angustia* < *angustus* 'narrow') and *destreit* (v. 3456) (< Lat. *districtum*) both convey the same choking effect of death's embrace, an image mirrored in the duke's clasping of his mount's neck (v. 3440: De sun destrer le col en enbraçat). Death's hug is similarly alluded to in other passages of the *Roland* (destreit, vv. 2743, 3417, 3759; angoissier, vv. 2010, 2232, 2575; angoissos, v. 2198). It will be recalled, too, that the narrow defiles through which Charlemagne had to pass (v. 3126: ces destreiz anguisables) were haunted by the lingering memory of the hero's martyrdom.[21]

The Emperor gazing upon the suffering Naimes recalls Roland contemplating his mortally wounded comrade, grief and spattering blood uniting the two scenes (vv. 1978–1981 = vv. 3451–3453). Charlemagne and his nephew both express their unflagging loyalty and devotion to their comrades-in-arms by calling out to them to ride at their side (v. 1976: "Sire cumpaign, a mei car vus justez!" = v. 3455: "Bel sire Naimes, kar chevalcez od mei!" = v. 3460: Puis sunt justez par amur e par feid). The protective gesture of riding side by side is a symbol of their inseparability.[22]

On another part of the battlefield the Emir is also riding, desperately postponing, it would appear, the reckoning that must nevertheless take place. In rapid succession he manages to slay several Christian commanders: Guinemant, Roland's replacement and one of the leaders of the first division; Geboin and Lorant, who head the second group of French *bachelers*; and Richard, in charge of the fifth division (Normans). The Saracens are overjoyed by this feat of arms, taking heart at Precieuse's blows and seeing in the Emir—prematurely, it will develop—an invincible protector (v. 3472).

In Laisses 252 and 253 the relentless passage of time is noted by the repeated use of an exclamation involving the phrase *Ki dunc / puis oïst / veïst* (vv. 3473, 3483, 3484, 3486). Identical expressions were used earlier, in vv. 1181, 1341, 1680, and 1970, to record elapsing time, but never, as here, in short succession. In v. 3478 mention of the fact that the battle lasted until nightfall (Entresqu'al vespre) is another way of suggesting a great and lengthy encounter now drawing to a close. Although countless victims have already fallen, the toll will be greater still before the action has run its tragic course, says Turoldus in another time-encompassing expression (vv. 3479–3480). However, the most economical device for this purpose, and the one used by countless authors throughout history, is the sweeping statement listing the variety of sights and sounds involved: spear blows (v. 3475), broken lances (v. 3482), smashed shields (v. 3483), clanging hauberks (v. 3484), and grating helmets (v. 3485). The anonymity of the falling bodies (vv. 3477, 3486) and of the bestial cries (v. 3487) adds a final note of confused anguish to the battle as the poet, unable to bear any longer such a horrifying view, turns away from the scene of utter devastation (v. 3489: Ceste bataille est mult fort a suffrir).

Promiscuous noises are an important part of this description, yet in the tumult one distinguishes a sound often associated with pagans in Old French literature (v. 3487: E humes braire, contre tere murir). *Braire* is not restricted to a braying sound and may simply connote screaming or howling, particularly in a pathetic context such as this.[23] However, the presence of *Cels d'Occiant e d'Argoillie e de Bascle*—names having a decidedly harsh quality themselves—is specifically noted at the beginning of this passage (v. 3474) and, a few verses later, Turoldus uses unequivocal expressions to describe this people's whinnying and doglike yelping (vv. 3526–3527: Cil d'Ociant i braient e henissent, / Arguille si cume chen i glatissent).[24] These sounds, rising over the din of battle, are probably not without diabolical associations here and point to dying pagans.[25] It is significant, too, that Turoldus chooses to focus next on Baligant invoking gods. The Emir's idols were earlier depicted being devoured and defiled by pigs and dogs (v. 2591).

Baligant's prayer involves a parody of the Christian's obligation to serve the true God, a notion frequently alluded to in the poem (e.g., vv. 2254, 3666),[26] and a promise of a propitiatory offering (v. 3493: "Tutes tes ymagenes ferai d'or fin"). The "purchase of Paradise" through almsgiving and donations to churches and monasteries, at times taking the form of payments for construction or for statues, reliquaries, and other objects of cult, was a familiar medieval practice.[27] However, pagan idols were often represented as bovine statues mounted on pillars, and Turoldus seems to be suggesting the adoration of the Golden Calf, viewed, since biblical times, as a depraved act and a grave sin.[28]

The vanity of reliance on the pagan trinity is immediately underscored by the arrival of Gemalfin, who earlier commanded the Saracen army while Baligant called on Marsile. True to his name, he bears *males nuveles* (v. 3496). His tidings constitute two heavy blows—the Emir's son and brother have both been slain—whose severity forces Baligant's head down (vv. 3504–3505), symbolically anticipating his final humiliation.[29]

What is so overwhelming to Baligant is not the loss of his close relatives but the word picture of the legendary Charlemagne who is bent on ruining him (vv. 3502–3503), and also the realization that no one stands between them now.[30] Baligant calls a trusted counselor, Jangleu, whose name, akin to OFr. *jangler* 'to talk idly, to slander, to lie', unmasks the cunning beneath the surface of his alleged *grant saveir* (v. 3509).

It is illuminating to compare Jangleu's counsel with Ganelon's advice to Marsile. Both bluntly inform their listener that he is as good as dead:

437 "La murrez vus a hunte e a viltet."[31]

3513 E cil respunt: "Morz estes, Baligant!"

both imply that paganism is worthless:

430 "Iço vus mandet Carlemagnes li ber
Que recevez seinte chrestïentet."[32]

3514 "Ja vostre deu ne vos erent guarant."[33]

and both praise Charlemagne and his men:

534 "Sa grant valor, kil purreit acunter?"

545 "N'at tel vassal suz la cape del ciel.
Mult par est proz sis cumpainz Oliver.
Les .XII. pers, que Carles ad tant chers,
Funt les enguardes a .XX. milie chevalers.
Soüirs est Carles, que nuls home ne crent."[34]

3515 "Carles est fiers e si hume vaillant,
Unc ne vi gent ki si fust cumbatant."

Parallelism is evident, finally, in the desperate solution proposed in each instance: Send your army into battle anyway. Ganelon, of course, is only intent on bringing about Roland's downfall and shrewdly persuades the Saracens that after a costly preliminary encounter, Marsile will triumph over his enemies (vv. 588–595). It may be that he fully expects the pagans to meet with disaster, but, he muses privately, at least his archrival will have been eliminated, and that is all that matters.[35] Ganelon's abandonment of Marsile's army to its fate out of a single-minded determination to achieve personal revenge contrasts sharply with Jangleu's urgent appeal that the remainder of Baligant's forces be instantly committed to battle. Jangleu's words express acceptance of fate with resignation and even alacrity come what may (v. 3519: "Ço que estre en deit, ne l'alez demurant"). Any connection here with the Oriental concept expressed by the phrase "It was written" is purely coincidental, for Turoldus had no idea of Kismet.[36] The Saracen's plea is intended rather to emphasize the rashness and utter folly of his scheme.

Baligant's eagerness to be deluded is immediately apparent as he arrogantly fluffs up his beard, puffs himself up, and rends the air with a trumpet blast (vv. 3520–3524). The bugle call rallies his men whose yelping has diabolical overtones and produces the effect of a mad hunt.[37] With wild abandon (v. 3528: estultie), the Saracens charge, their supreme effort smashing the French lines [38] and, according to Turoldus, slaying 7,000 Christians (v. 3530).

This is the critical moment for Charlemagne. The impressive gains achieved by seven long years of campaigning now hang in the balance as the frenzied enemy runs amok in the midst of his *eschieles*. Ogier the Dane reacts vigorously.[39] A shadowy figure until now, one notes only that he was present at Charlemagne's first council (v. 170), was singled out by Ganelon to lead the van immediately after the traitor nominated Roland to the rearguard (v. 749), and was placed in charge of the Bavarians in the third division (v. 3033). Later he will parley with Thierry and Pinabel over the details of the judicial combat (v. 3856) and be found among those congratulating the victor (v. 3937). Ogier's name figures among Charlemagne's twelve "nephews," or peers, in the late-eleventh-century *Nota Emilianense.*[40]

Ogier calls three French nobles, Duke Thierry and Count Jozeran—each a leader of one of Charlemagne's divisions—together with Geoffrey of Anjou, bearer of the oriflamme. Grimly, the Dane apprises Charles of the situation. His tense nerves are much in evidence as he bluntly informs the Emperor he must strike now or risk incurring the wrath of God (vv. 3538–3539).

Jenkins notes: "This furious and successful assault of the 20th and 28th pagan divisions (vv. 3246, 3257) seems to be foreshadowed in Charles' vision, vv. 2546 ff. For a moment, Charlemagne seems paralyzed (cf. v. 2548), and his chief barons must wake him to a sense of his peril."[41] Charlemagne's dream implied that the reverse being suffered by the Christians was a chastisement from on high, the Emperor being helpless in the matter, whereas Ogier makes it clear that the exact opposite holds true here: God will be angry if Charles does not intervene. Ogier's role, then, is not to shake the Emperor from a perilous torpor but to remind him, prophetlike, of his duty.[42] Old Testament prophets were usually counselors of royalty, proclaiming not what pleased their clients but what God told them to do. The Greek etymon means one who speaks for another.[43]

The Almighty showers favors upon Charlemagne but expects untiring efforts from his champion in return. Nowhere in the *Song of Roland*, save at the very end of the poem, is Charles's burden greater as he surveys his men being slaughtered all about him, realizing all the while that still further sacrifices will be necessary. In an exquisite repetition of an earlier comment (v. 22: N'i ad paien ki un sul mot respundet; v. 3540: N'i ad icel ki un sul mot respundet)—the earlier passage describes the fearful immobility of Marsile's men in the Saracen council—Turoldus allows tension to build for a moment as violence swirls all about the Emperor. The pause expresses not indecision but great suffering. Then Charlemagne strikes.

In Laisse 256 attention was focused by the poet upon Ogier, Thierry, Geoffrey, and Jozeran in the company of Charlemagne. In the following verses, Thierry and Jozeran fade from view to be replaced by another close adviser, Naimes. The quartet surrounding the Emperor becomes a trio, reminiscent of Roland, Turpin, and Gautier de l'Hum.[44] Once again it is Ogier who distinguishes himself, the poet using the less frequently employed title *dam* to emphasize his worthiness (v. 3546: Mult par est proz danz Ogers li Daneis).[45] In a stunning action Ogier cuts his way through to Amborre, bearer of the Emir's dragon emblem, and strikes him down.[46] As he watches his standard fall, Baligant realizes to his horror that he is in the wrong and Charles is in the right.[47] Charles's exultant shout is ecstatically echoed by his men.

The importance many attach to symbols is no more strikingly apparent in the *Song of Roland* than in this passage. Jenkins cites the parallel exploit of Count Robert of Normandy at Ascalon in 1099, an event immortalized in glass at the Abbey of Saint-Denis;[48] and every schoolboy has dreamed of capturing the flag in sport if not in combat. The theatrical aspect of Ogier's feat of arms, as easy to appreciate today as it was in the Middle Ages, tends to overshadow its important symbolic meaning.

The dragon's downfall has clear apocalyptic overtones. A seven-headed monster threatens the Woman clothed with sun, crowned with stars, and with the moon under her feet, before it is overcome by Saint Michael.[49] The more familiar medieval interpretation of the Woman is that she represents the Blessed Virgin, although, early on, she was said by other exegetes (e.g., Saint Ambrose) to be a figure of Ecclesia.[50] The dragon was said to symbolize the devil, Antichrist, or profane knowledge.[51] In the *Queste del Saint Graal* Perceval has a dream of two ladies, one young and beautiful astride a lion, the other old and riding a serpent.[52] Later a *preudom* dressed as a priest interprets the vision as an allegory of the Two Laws. The young lady is the New Law astride Jesus Christ and also represents *Foi et Esperance et creance et baptesmes. Cele dame est la pierre dure et ferme sor quoi Jhesucrist dist qu'il fermeroit Sainte Eglyse.*[53] The lady astride the serpent is Synagoga, the Old Law:

> Et li serpenz qui la porte, ce est l'Escriture mauvesement entendue et mauvesement esponse, ce est ypocrisie et heresie et iniquitez et pechié mortel, ce est li anemis meismes; ce est li serpenz qui par son orgueil fu gitez de paradis; ce est li serpenz qui dist a Adam et a sa moillier: "Se vos mengiez de cest fruit vos seroiz ausi come Dieu," et par ceste parole entra en aus covoitise. Car il baerent maintenant a estre plus haut qu'il n'estoient, si crurent le conseil a l'anemi et pechierent, por quoi il furent gitié hors de paradis et mis en essil. Auquel meffet tuit li oir partirent et le comperent chascun jor.[54]

For the medieval exegete a serpent or dragon had a variety of meanings, most of them evil.[55] It is quite likely that the laying low of Baligant's dragon standard symbolizes triumph over all these evils.[56] In a close parallel a Roman coin struck after the victory over Attila in 451 near Châlons-sur-Marne shows the Emperor crushing the head of a dragon having a human head and a serpent's tail, which suggests the diabolic aspect of the Huns.[57]

42. Charlemagne Duels Baligant to the Death

Laisses 258–262 (verses 3560–3624)

The fading light of day (v. 3560) announces that the fateful reckoning is at hand.

The battle cries, which Christians and Saracens have been using for rallying purposes (vv. 3298, 3300), become a means of personal identification and a specific challenge for Charles and Baligant (v. 3566: L'un conuist l'altre as haltes voiz e as cleres). As if by prearrangement, they meet in the center of the battlefield (v. 3567). Until now the general conflict has raged all about them (v. 3561), but when the Emperor confronts the Emir, one imagines that all other action ceases, that all eyes turn to observe the supreme contest.[1]

The duel definitely has a formulaic quality: lances, then swords; on horseback, then on foot; exchange of insults; offers to give quarter rejected out of hand. Equality of adversaries (v. 3562) and tit-for-tat blows are other familiar devices designed to augment the hero's eventual triumph. The poet's remarks concerning death, which must inevitably ensue for one of the antagonists, the black-and-white opposition of right and wrong, and the celestial intervention will be reiterated in the judicial combat between Thierry and Pinabel (vv. 3577–3578 = 3913–3914; 3587–3588 = 3891, 3898; 3609 = 3923).[2] The identity of the various phases of the two duels makes it clear that both conflicts are ordeals, that is, tests to determine guilt or innocence, with the outcome viewed as a judgment of God. Charlemagne's vision, it must be remembered, could be interpreted to mean that celestial wrath was being unleashed against the French in their battle against Baligant.[3] Obviously this troubling matter must be cleared up. The similarity in scenes also suggests that the Thierry-Pinabel duel not only renders a verdict on Ganelon but also, by implication, on Charlemagne.

The miniature debate in Laisse 260 is revealing in that it shows Baligant concerned with worldly dominance while Charles speaks of the sovereignty of a supernatural Being.[4] There is in this scene a curious echo, too, of the discussion between Ganelon and Marsile, with its talk of a son being wrongfully slain (cf. Basan and Basile), of conversion, of who exercises rightful authority over Spain, and of following the rival monarch back to his homeland. The Emir seems to be aping Charles's offer to Marsile at Saragossa, all the while scheming treacherously, no doubt, to dispose of the Emperor once he has him in his power. Baligant's proposal reeks of Saracen foul play, but the rankness of Ganelon's deceitfulness lingers on, too, as it were.

Baligant's sudden blow to Charlemagne's head is a distressful development. Charles reels. No one in the poem has received such a grievous wound and survived.[5] Under the circumstances Gabriel's question (v. 3611: Si li demandet: "Reis magnes, que fait tu?") seems a bit strange. However, the edge in Gabriel's words, which strikes the modern reader as curiously unfeeling, recalls the note of impatience in Christ's voice when he admonishes his disciples who have awakened him in the midst of the storm on the lake: "Why are you so frightened, you men of little faith?"[6] The point is that Charles's fears are groundless: God will never let his champion down.

The Emperor immediately realizes this—rather sheepishly, no doubt—for the angel's voice allays his momentary fears. Bédier's translation of v. 3614 (Repairet loi vigur e remembrance) as "Il reprend vigueur et connaissance" fails to convey an important nuance found in the word *remembrance*, used here in conjunction with *vigur* meaning 'strength'. The power that comes to him is essentially supernatural, but it is intimately associated in Charlemagne's mind with the other sources of his strength, the things he values most. Analysis of the use of the verb *remembrer* in the *Song of Roland* reveals that, when in a state of agitation or in times of stress, the French constantly think of their families and fiefs (vv. 820, 2379), of Charles, their conquests, and France (vv. 2378–2380), or of the tragic personal losses they have suffered (v. 2983).[7] These things the French hold dear are summed up in the expression *Monjoie* (vv. 1181–1182).

In this moment of crisis, then, these associations that flash through the Emperor's mind—in the way that life is said to be instantly reviewed in the mind's eye at the moment of death—contribute immensely to his recuperation. It is no mere coincidence, therefore, that Charles strikes Baligant with *l'espee de France* (v. 3615) and immediately shouts

Monjoie! (v. 3620), for fatherland, sword, and war cry recall the vital strength he has summoned for this purpose.[8]

Naimes, whom Charles snatched from the jaws of death but a few moments earlier, now rushes to the Emperor's side and helps him back on his mount. At the sight of such a miraculous deliverance, the Saracens flee, propelled, as it were, by a contemptuous flick of God's finger (v. 3623).[9] The following verse (Or sunt Franceis a icels qu'il demandent), if it means what Bédier thinks it does ("Les Français sont parvenus au terme tant désiré"),[10] is related to the various images of longing found in the Psalms to describe the love of God,[11] and to the metaphor of reaching a port, used by classical as well as mystical writers.[12]

43. The Subjugation of Saragossa
Laisses 263–267 (verses 3625–3704)

With total victory now in sight, the French give chase to the panic-stricken Saracens. The phrase *Damnesdeus le volt* (v. 3625) is a prime example of the crusading zeal that is very much in the air when Turoldus is composing his epic. It became one of the most successful slogans of all times following its use in a rousing speech by Pope Urban II at Clermont in 1095.[1] Here again, as after the Battle of Roncevaux (cf. v. 2428: "Car chevalchez! Vengez ceste dulor!"),[2] the great evil generated by the Saracens must be avenged. To Charlemagne's way of thinking, the deaths of the Christians caused great sorrow but also contaminated those who witnessed such a foul deed. French hearts and minds must be made free from defilement in the same way that the soul must be purged from sin (v. 3628: "Si esclargiez voz talenz e voz coers").[3]

The rout of Baligant's army is first narrated as if seen by a spectator on the battlefield itself (Laisses 262–263), then, as the remnants of the Saracen horde, shrouded in a sinister cloud of dust (v. 3633),[4] approach the gates of Saragossa,[5] the point of view changes—this shift is marked by the phrase *d'ici qu'en Sarraguce* in v. 3635—to become that of Bramimonde.

Turoldus has left us an unforgettable portrait of the Saracen queen's final agony. One notes, first, a difficult and fearful climb up the steps of a tower, accompanied by clerics and canons of the religion she has come to despise (vv. 3636–3638), then the ghastly spectacle of an army in full rout (v. 3640).[6] Bramimonde has definitely renounced her gods, but she remains a creature of habit. Her piercing cry (v. 3641: A halte voiz s'escrie: "Aiez nos, Mahum!") is hardly an invocation. It is a mere reflex or, more likely, it voices the heartrending realization that life is no longer worth living. Bramimonde cries out from her tower the news of Baligant's shameful death (v. 3643), and her shout pierces Marsile's heart like a fatal arrow. Her husband now dead, nothing remains for the Saracen queen but to cast herself down, Hero-like, from the tower.[7] But the departure of the devils with Marsile's soul (v. 3647) saves the future convert.[8]

The narrative of the capture of Saragossa is made up of elements borrowed from the Apocalypse and from the gospel according to Saint Matthew.[9] Turoldus, who conceived of the conflict between Charles and Baligant in terms of Christ's struggle against Antichrist, now draws upon the same scriptural material to depict the Emperor as an instrument of divine retribution come as a reaper to cut down the wicked of the earth.[10] The grim choice between baptism and the sword doubtless reminded contemporary listeners of events that actually took place during the Crusades, either on the way to Jerusalem or, earlier in the eleventh century, in Spain.[11] On a symbolic level Charles appears in the guise of Christ the Judge, separating the Just from the Damned (Matthew 25:31–46).

But Charles is not merely bent on revenge; his deeds at Saragossa prove he also has magnanimity.[12] In their superb study of the iconography of the Roland legend, Lejeune and Stiennon give the following description of the drawing (*Fig. 63*) that illustrates this episode in MS. P of the *Rolandslied*:

> Charlemagne triomphant arrive avec son armée devant Saragosse. La foule se presse sur les remparts de la grande cité païenne où le roi Marsile est mort de ses blessures.
>
> Couronnée, la chevelure flottante, vêtue d'une robe à manches très amples, assistée d'une suivante dont la silhouette se dessine dans l'encadrement de la porte ouverte de la ville, la reine Brechmunda (la Bramimonde de la *Chanson de Roland*) s'est portée à la rencontre du vainqueur. Elle s'incline devant l'empereur en gage de soumission. Non seulement elle rend la ville, mais elle demande à se faire chrétienne.[13]

The Belgian scholars show that the artist clearly drew upon a well-known formula in Romanesque art: a monarch on horseback being approached by a submissive queen.[14] Art historians have provided several different interpretations of this theme, the most plausible being that the figure represents either Constantine and the Church, or a symbolic crusader triumphing over Islam.[15] Lejeune and Stiennon conclude:

> Le contexte explicite dans lequel s'insère le dessin du *Ruolantes Liet* permet de supposer que la reddition légendaire de Saragosse par une femme à Charlemagne, nouveau Constantin, pourrait n'être pas étrangère à certaines sculptures du genre de celles qui viennent d'être évoquées.[16]

It should be emphasized, however, that the association of ideas which led the twelfth-century illustrator of a version of the *Song of Roland* to choose this formula also sheds light on the symbolic meaning of Turoldus's poem. The poet drew upon the same fund of images in the composition of his epic as the contemporary German artist did for his drawing. Thus the surrender of Saragossa by Bramimonde, which represents, at the level of the plot, the culmination of Charlemagne's expedition into Spain, succeeds at the same time in expressing, on a metaphorical level, the idea of spiritual conquest, a simple variation of the Theme of Conversion.[17]

Turoldus's comment at the moment Bramimonde surrenders Saragossa has a proverbial ring: *Mult ben espleitet qui Damnesdeus aiuet* (v. 3657).[18] In the discussion that Blancandrin had with Ganelon on the way to that pagan city, the Saracen inquired of Roland: "*Par quele gent qüiet il espleiter tant?*" (v. 395). Ganelon replied that his stepson relied on the French. The use of the same verb in the present passage indicates that the traitor omitted a very important qualification in his answer, for it is evident that God's hand is visible in the French exploits.

The subjugation of Saragossa lasts far into the night, darkness being a fitting accompaniment for the ugly duties the French must now perform.[19] However, the light of the moon and stars symbolizes the fact that the saving grace of Christianity now shines forth where only heathen gloom once reigned (vv. 3658–3659).[20] First, paganism must be rooted out, and the French quickly break into the city's mosques and smash every idol they find with hammers and axes (v. 3663).[21] Black arts associated with pagan religion (v. 3665) are an Old Testament legacy.[22] Charles orders those who refuse baptism to be seized, burned, or put to the sword (v. 3670).[23] The axes (cuignees) and fire recall John the Baptist's words to the Pharisees and Sadducees coming to his baptism: "Even now the axe is laid to the roots of the trees, so that any tree which fails to produce good fruit will be cut down and thrown on the fire."[24] The iconography of the Baptism of Christ in the Jordan—for example, in the eleventh-century mosaic of the Baptistery of San Marco at Venice—includes an axe stuck into the trunk of a tree.[25] The motif is also associated with Saint Boniface, who is said to have felled a sacred tree venerated by pagan tribesmen in Germany.[26]

The smashing of the Saracen idols has many Old Testament antecedents and is a hagiographic commonplace.[27] One of the apocryphal gospels (Pseudo-Matthew, 23) tells how idols fell of their own accord when the Holy Family entered Egypt in fulfillment of Isaiah 19:1: "See! Yahweh, riding a swift cloud comes to Egypt. The idols of Egypt tremble before him."[28]

The joy of the French as they set off for home (v. 3682)[29] is highlighted by the brightness of day (v. 3675)[30] and the happy prospect of the triumphal return to Aix with the Saracen queen. Bramimonde is a symbol of the total subjugation of the enemy and of the conversion of the surviving Saracens. The Emperor leaves a trail of relics behind him: Roland's oliphant on the altar of the collegiate church of Saint-Seurin at Bordeaux, and the bodies of Roland, Oliver, and Turpin encased in white[31] marble caskets in the church of Saint-Romain at Blaye. The enshrinement there takes place with all due solemnity (v. 3694).[32]

It is clear from the text itself (v. 3687: Li pelerin le veient ki la vunt)[33] that the objects venerated at Bordeaux and Blaye were believed to be genuine mementos of the heroes of Roncevaux.[34] Turoldus chooses to mention them for two reasons. They lend an aura of authenticity to his account, for the legend that predates the poem is already associated with these items in the localities in question.[35] However, first and foremost, they constitute a device enabling him to move Charlemagne and his army from Spain to Aix with the image of Roland and his companions constantly before our eyes. The ceremonies in churches along the way repeatedly emphasize the religious aspect of the events at Roncevaux. Charles's ever-present sorrow, not merely narrative economy, explains why he will call his barons together for the purpose of trying Ganelon the moment he arrives at his palace at Aix (vv. 3699–3704). It also ushers in and sets in proper perspective the strangely moving scene in which Alda confronts Charlemagne.[36]

44. *The Death of Alda*

Laisses 268–269 (verses 3705–3733)

Charlemagne's arrival at Aix, with its dramatic summons, is clearly in the Adventus tradition: The monarch's approach is likened to the Second Coming.[1] Advent liturgy celebrates not only preparation for a spiritual arrival but also the Parousia, this definitive occurrence to take place in the fullness of time.[2] The Last Judgment will be a day of wrath (dies irae), but also the moment of deliverance when the Redemption will finally be complete.[3]

Verse 3704 appears to constitute a demarcation line setting off Ganelon's trial from what precedes: *Des ore cumencet le plait de Guenelun.* One notes, however, a curious interlacing of events in this passage.[4]

1. Charles travels from Saragossa to Aix; stages along the way are indicated (v. 3683: Nerbonne; v. 3684: Bordeaux; v. 3689: Blaye), but speed is emphasized (v. 3696).
2. Charles arrives at Aix (v. 3697).
3. In his palace at Aix Charles summons his judges from every corner of the Empire (vv. 3698–3703).
4. Arriving at his palace at Aix, Charles encounters Alda (vv. 3705 ff.).
5. That night, there is a wake for Alda and she is buried the following day (vv. 3731–3732).
6. Charles is at Aix; Ganelon is flogged and awaits his trial (vv. 3734–3741).
7. Charles summons his judges (v. 3743).
8. The judges assemble at Aix (v. 3744).
9. The trial of Ganelon is held on Saint Silvester's Day (vv. 3745 ff.).

The chronology is evidently 1, 2, 4, 5, viewed as consecutive actions. Items 3 and 7 are one and the same event and occur later, simultaneously to 6. Items 8 and 9 take place at approximately the same time and are the culmination of all these activities. Item 3, then, appears to be the only incident narrated out of order, and this flashforward serves to highlight the occurrence. The framing of Alda's death with two separate allusions to the summoning of the judges underscores the inseparability of the two events.[5]

Charles's return to Aix clearly parallels Baligant's visit to Saragossa.[6] Bramimonde had rushed out of the hall to meet the Emir as he mounted the palace steps:

2821 Par les degrez el paleis muntet sus
E Bramidonie vient curant cuntre lui.

Four verses later, Baligant and the Saracen queen entered the hall: *Sus en la chambre ad doel en sunt venut.* In similar fashion Alda now accosts the Emperor just after he has mounted the palace steps and entered the hall (vv. 3707–3708).[7] A further point of comparison resides in the fact that both women collapse in the arms of the monarch they have come forward to greet:

2825 Chet li as piez, li amiralz la reçut.

3720 Pert la culor, chet as piez Carlemagne.[8]

Turoldus has evidently drawn this parallel with a specific purpose in mind.

The key lies in the juridical situations that are contrasted here. Both scenes are a prelude to an effort to right a wrong. Bramimonde's shameful loss (v. 2824: "A itel hunte, sire, mon seignor ai perdut!") demands retribution, yet she has little hope that Baligant can rectify it. Her mock death expresses despair. Alda's glorious loss fulfills her and she has no further raison d'être. She brushes aside the offer of someone to take Roland's place and dies. It is reasonable to assume that she succumbs secure in the knowledge that justice will be served. She is certain that Charles will see to that because her prophetlike query and prayer (cf. vv. 3538–3539) have reminded the Emperor of his duty.[9]

There is no question of a broken heart here: Alda speaks only of a solemn pledge to marry (v. 3710: "me jurat cume sa per a prendre"). For individuals of Roland and Alda's social rank, such an agreement was usually a legally-binding contract arranged between two families.[10] The personal preferences of the future wife were given little if any consideration.

Under ordinary circumstances, then, Alda would probably have been quite content with the proposed substitute. After all, Louis is the Emperor's son and heir and in a sense a *mult esforcet eschange* (v. 3714).[11]

However, a strong bond plainly unites Alda to Roland. It is not romantic love, to be sure,[12] but it is much more than a purely legal tie. Turoldus expresses this in two ways. First he has the beautiful maiden[13] refer to her fiancé as *Rollant le catanie* (v. 3709), a term that indicates both sorrow and affection.[14] Evidently Alda already suspects the worst when she queries Charlemagne about the missing Roland. Secondly, the fiancés are mystically linked in death. The poet suggests this union by identical phrasing:[15]

2392 Juntes ses mains est alet a sa fin.

3723 Alde la bel est a sa fin alee.

In each instance the idea of accepting death willingly is implied, and the individual's sacrifice is regarded as an immolation. Alda's days were numbered the moment Roland died, and her death is an extension of her fiancé's. However, her chief role is to remind everyone that righting the wrong perpetrated at Roncevaux will require a higher form of justice than that which ordinary men are capable of rendering.[16] This is probably what Conrad means when he says apropos of Alda's death: "In this, God revealed his secret thoughts" (v. 8727).

The seemingly equitable offer of a substitute husband strikes Alda as strange (v. 3717: Alde respunt: "Cest mot mei est estrange"), an expression fraught with significance (INTRODUCTION, 17). As her next utterance clearly indicates (v. 3718: "Ne place Deu ne ses seinz ne ses angles"), she is absorbed by thoughts of the next world. In the final analysis Alda's rejection of the new proposal of marriage is a way of foreshadowing Charlemagne's refusal, in Laisse 276, to concur in the "reasonable" recommendation of the court, and of his decision to achieve true justice by means of a *judicium Dei*.

The endowment made in Alda's honor reflects her high station in life, but it also reinforces the notion that her death was a kind of martyrdom. Interment in a convent (muster de nuneins)[17] further associates her with the victims at Roncevaux (v. 1750: "Enfuërunt en aitres de musters").

Turoldus probably visualized Alda's demise in terms of the iconographic formula of the Death of the Virgin[18] (*Fig 64*). Contemporary artists depicted Mary as a horizontal figure surrounded by the grief-stricken Apostles and attendant angels. The Passing of the Virgin in Romanesque art is represented as a *Koimēsis*, that is, a falling asleep, an apocryphal tradition based on the cult of the Assumption of the Virgin into Heaven.[19] Like Mary, Alda is a virgin,[20] and her passing, which is so peaceful it completely deceives Charles into believing she has merely fainted (v. 3724), is an awe-inspiring dormition.[21]

45. *The Trial of Ganelon*

Laisses 270–280 (verses 3734–3872)

In the narrative of Ganelon's trial, Turoldus uses a number of technical terms quite correctly and shows that he is familiar with the juridical practices of his own time and, possibly, those of a bygone day as well.[1] However, he tailors incidents to suit his purpose and is evidently more concerned with symbolic effects and poetic justice than with a realistic portrayal of customs and institutions. The poet depicts situations not so much the way he imagines they might actually have occurred in Charlemagne's day but according to the imperatives of the epic universe he has created, a convention suggested by the phrase *Il est escrit en l'anciëne geste* (v. 3742).

Duly impressed by Alda's awesome end, Charles now focuses his attention on the trial. A certain amount of time is needed for the Emperor's messengers to reach his vassals and for the latter to convene at Aix. Meanwhile one image dominates the narrative: the scourging of Ganelon.[2] It appears from v. 3741 (A grant dulur iloec atent sun plait) that Ganelon remains exposed to public ridicule in front of the Emperor's palace (v. 3736) and until he comes before the court. We tend today to recoil at such treatment, not only because it is inhumane but also because we live in a culture that holds that a person, no matter how heinous the crime of which he may be accused, must be presumed innocent until proven otherwise.

Throughout history—and the Middle Ages were no exception—prisoners have been tortured as a punishment or as a means of extorting evidence or a confession. Under the Roman Empire torture was frequently inflicted upon slaves and even upon freemen. Ecclesiastically sanctioned use of torture in heresy trials dates only from the thirteenth century, when it also began to be employed in civil courts. Beginning in the fourteenth century and for the next two hundred years, torture was a common means of judicial examination associated with the Inquisition.

Ganelon's pretrial ordeal is not designed to compel him to confess his crime. Preliminary punishment implies a presumption of guilt, a position Charles publicly adopted when he first had Ganelon beaten by his cooks and chained like a bear (vv. 1816–1827).[3] At the time Charles knew of Ganelon's betrayal only through a dream, although the villain's behavior before and after the mission to Saragossa and upon hearing Roland's oliphant were highly suspicious.

The infliction of bodily pain upon the traitor serves to relieve tension, the audience—in this case the characters in the epic (with the exception of Ganelon and his relatives) and, especially, the persons listening to the poem as it is being declaimed—being impatient to see justice done. The pillorying of the traitor and the beating administered with rods also recalls the Mocking and the Scourging of Christ, in particular the latter, which traditionally involved a pillar.[4] Ganelon at the stake-pillar[5] apes Jesus and poses as innocence persecuted, an attitude designed to arouse sympathy on the part of the unwary.

Charlemagne's vassals assemble on Saint Silvester's Day (v. 3746). It was customary in medieval times to hold court at Pentecost and on other solemn feast days. Consequently the Emperor's choice of date does not at first glance appear to have anything remarkable about it since December 31 falls between Christmas and the Epiphany. In Turoldus's day the year began on the first of March,[6] so Saint Silvester's day did not suggest cyclical culmination or fulfilment the way it does in the Gregorian calendar.[7] Turoldus may have had a different reason for selecting this date, as suggested below.[8]

Ganelon is now haled before Charlemagne (vv. 3749, 3762). One imagines the traitor posturing before the court, at times displaying the old arrogance that typified his behavior in Charles's councils and at Saragossa, at other times affecting the indignant look of a person who has been unjustly wronged.[9] Skillful jongleurs doubtless availed themselves of this great opportunity for miming characteristic gestures and inflections. The knowing audience, cued by the reference to Ganelon *ki traïsun ad faite* (v. 3748), responded with derisive howls.[10]

Charlemagne's complaint is simple: While in Spain, Ganelon betrayed for money the 20,000 men in the rearguard, including Roland, Oliver, and the Twelve Peers, and caused their deaths (vv. 3751–3756). This was, he charges, an act of treason.

The Emperor's accusation (v. 3756: "Les .XII. pers ad traït por aveir") is explicit with regard to Ganelon's motive but lacking in specificity as to the nature of the crime. Is Charles suggesting that when the villain betrayed the Twelve Peers this constituted high treason? There is a difference between disloyalty to the sovereign and betrayal of others. Ganelon will seize upon this distinction.

Charlemagne knows treason was committed because of an angelic visitation. The French barons can only suspect it from the following evidence: the gifts accompanying the villain on his return from Saragossa; the maniacal delight he took in nominating his stepson to the rearguard; and the attempt to mislead the Emperor when the oliphant was heard.[11] The French, gathered for the purpose of trying Ganelon, will now allow themselves to be convinced otherwise. Even Naimes, in whom Charles confided about his prophetic dream (COMMENTARY, 11 and 19), will be strangely silent. Throughout this episode Charlemagne's vassals will symbolize the vanity of worldly wisdom and behave as men of little faith.[12]

Ganelon's defense begins with the claim that Roland wronged him in a matter concerning money (v. 3758: "Rollant me forfist en or e en aveir").[13] He freely admits that he sought his stepson's death. According to Jenkins: "It would seem that Count Roland, in the Spanish wars, had been taking more than his share of the spoils, and had been haughty and overbearing in doing so, and that Count Ganelon, who was covetous, had not been able to forgive this sort of 'desmesure' on the part of the younger man."[14] Jenkins's interpretation is based on the emendation *sorfist* for the hypermetric *me forfist*. A number of other interpretations of Roland's crime in Ganelon's eyes have been proposed, but none seem to have satisfied critics, many of whom are unhappy that a money motive was introduced into the story in the first place.[15] However, if one recognizes that avarice and deceit are the key to Ganelon's psychology, it is evident that the traitor is simply lying here. Ganelon has repeatedly perverted the facts to serve his ends and, notably, to discredit Roland—the apple incident, Charlemagne's message, the drowning of the Caliph and his army, the Noples anecdote[16]—so that lying in this circumstance is merely consistent behavior.[17]

In order to deflect away from himself Charlemagne's accusation of wrongdoing motivated by greed, Ganelon countercharges that Roland committed a criminally grasping act. This is a barefaced lie, which Ganelon attempts to cover up by swearing that he is hiding nothing (v. 3757: "Fel seie se jol ceil!"). The tactic, which consists of prevarication and countercharge, parallels Ganelon's distortion of the meaning of the oliphant blast. When the traitor was on the verge of being unmasked by Naimes (v. 1792: "Cil l'a traït ki vos en roevet feindre"), Ganelon lashed back by accusing his stepson of precisely the same sort of treachery: willfully disobeying the Emperor's orders (v. 1775: "Ja prist il Noples seinz le vostre comant") and trying to hide the traces of his bloody misdeed (v. 1779: "Pur cel le fist ne fust aparissant").[18] Ganelon evidently believes that the best defense is an offense.

The portrait of Ganelon standing before Charlemagne, in Laisse 273, refers to his handsome features, namely, his strong body and the color in his face (v. 3763: Cors ad gaillard, el vis gente color). The poet has given similar descriptions of good characters as well as bad (cf. the virtually identical phrasing for the French in the Emperor's tenth division in v. 3086 [Cors unt gaillarz e fieres cuntenances] and for Charlemagne in vv. 3115–3116 [Gent ad le cors, gaillart e ben seant, / Cler le visage e de bon cuntenant]), but exterior beauty, like that of an outwardly green tree, at times masks a rotten heart.[19]

Turoldus makes this clear in the present passage by adding the qualification *S'il fust leials, ben resemblast barun* (v. 3764). Comparable reservations were made for Saracens in vv. 899 and 3164. Knowing the poet's propensity for breathing new life into formulas by means of contrast, and remembering that the image of the martyred Roland hovers constantly over this passage, it is quite possible, too, that the color in Ganelon's cheek reminds Charlemagne of the grief he experienced while gazing upon the hero's lifeless form:

2894 Guardet a tere, vei gesir sun neüld,
Cors ad gaillard, perdue ad sa culur.

3762 Devant le rei la s'estut Guenelun.
Cors ad gaillard, el vis gente color.

Ganelon now faces the French, who must judge him, and his thirty relatives, who have come to lend him support (vv. 3765–3766). Brazenly invoking the name of God—who will most assuredly punish him for his misdeeds—and referring to loyal services to the Emperor he has shamefully betrayed, the traitor recapitulates the situation alluded to by Charles. Cunningly, however, he focuses the attention of the court on his quarrel with Roland.

The public argument Ganelon had with his stepson is the only bit of hard evidence the French have that offers an apparent motive for the betrayal. At this point the modern reader wonders why Bramimonde, who after all witnessed Ganelon's treason at Saragossa, is not asked to lend her testimony in this trial. To the poet's way of thinking, her status as Charlemagne's prisoner and, above all, as a still unbaptized Saracen, invalidates any support she might lend to the Emperor. Marsile's gifts to Ganelon, suspicious though they may appear, constitute purely circumstantial evidence. To the French they do not appear to differ much from those accepted by the Emperor himself on that occasion.

The traitor's strategy consists in muddying up the waters to such an extent that even those who were present at Galne become confused. At the time Roland's nomination of his stepfather had impressed the French as logical (vv. 278–279: Dient Franceis: "Car il le poet ben faire! / Se lui lessez, n'i trametrez plus saive"). No other reaction on the part of the French to the ensuing quarrel between father and stepson is recorded by Turoldus. They evidently observed the argument in silence, stunned with surprise at the unexpected development. The French who were there listen now to the traitor's claim that Roland volunteered him for a suicidal mission out of hatred, that as a consequence he, Ganelon, formally and publicly challenged Roland and the Twelve Peers, and that he then got his revenge.[20] Their recollection of the fateful quarrel at Galne becomes obscured. Details, which once seemed sharply etched and forever burned into their minds, become hazy and equivocal.

Ganelon insists that Roland instigated the quarrel and, on an earlier occasion, did him wrong. In any event he contends treason was never involved. Ganelon's whole case hinges on what, in Turoldus's day, was a legal question of considerable nicety: How does one define treason?[21] The French are baffled. Obviously Ganelon's strategy is working.

As the Franks withdraw to consider this weighty matter,[22] an important conversation takes place between Ganelon and one of his thirty kinsmen. The relatives can readily be visualized as gathered in a knot, off to one side, nerves tensely strung, determined expressions masking deep concern over the outcome of the deliberation. However, Pinabel of Sorence,[23] a giant of a man, persuasive in speech but, above all, capable of imposing his will by dint of force when necessary (vv. 3784–3785), is openly defiant. The clan is counting heavily on him if things worsen.

Ganelon approaches and throws himself upon his mercy, his desperate words echoing Marsile's plea at the beginning of the poem:

21 "Si me guarisez e de mort e de hunte!"

3787 "Getez mei hoi de mort e de calunje!"

It appears that the traitor is not at all convinced that the judges will return with a favorable decision. Pinabel reassures him, informing him that, if need be, he will personally challenge to a duel anyone bringing in a guilty verdict. It is probable that, as he speaks, Pinabel looks or gestures menacingly over toward the retiring French. The effect is comparable to drawing his sword out two fingers or brandishing it as Ganelon had done at Saragossa (vv. 444, 499). The traitor embraces his loyal kinsman's feet.[24] This extravagant act—and Pinabel's withering glance—are not lost on the French as they gather in council.

In fact, fear of Pinabel does determine the outcome of their deliberations. This is evident from their subdued voices, which, Turoldus informs us, is *pur Pinabel* (v. 3797). The reason offered by one judge for acquitting Ganelon, and the one that will immediately be transmitted to Charlemagne as having prompted the court's decision, is that what is done is done. Roland is dead and all the money in the world will not bring him back (vv. 3802–3803). Fear of Ganelon's giant protector is manifest in the judge's closing observation: "*Mult sereit fols ki . . . se cumbatreit*" (v. 3804).[25] The reference to money (v. 3803: "N'ert recuvret por or ne por aveir"), which produces an ironic echo of Charlemagne's allegation that Ganelon's treason was motivated *por aveir* (v. 3756) and of the traitor's countercharge that "*Rollant me forfist en or e en aveir*" (v. 3758), augments the aura of cravenness emanating from the verdict. Under ordinary circumstances the least that could be expected is the compensation known as wergild.[26] The spinelessness shown by the court is further highlighted by Thierry's lone dissenting vote (vv. 3805–3806) and by the omission, in the verdict as reported to Charlemagne, of the possibility of resolving the matter by means of a judicial combat (v. 3804), or of even the semblance of a warning implied in the recommendation that the prisoner be set free *ceste feiz* (v. 3800).

One pictures the barons reporting their verdict to Charlemagne a little sheepishly perhaps and surely with an eye on Pinabel. Their embarrassment and nervousness afforded the jongleur an opportunity for vocal and gestural mimicry. The angry reaction "*Vos estes mi felun!*" (v. 3814) had similar imitative potential, for the Emperor is in a towering rage when he utters these words. Charlemagne's cry associates the members of the court with the crime committed by Ganelon (v. 1819; see also vv. 674, 844, 1024, 1457, 3735, 3829, 3833, 3973) and hovers between contempt and an accusation of grave malfeasance. In the following verses the mention of Charlemagne's chagrin (v. 3817: doel) is another instance of sorrow mixed with vexation and righteous indignation.

The French have indeed failed the Emperor (v. 3815). First of all, they have made no effort to determine whether or not Ganelon's plea has any merit. By recommending mercy they have dodged the issue entirely. They have also allowed themselves to be intimidated by Pinabel, thus transforming the trial into a mockery, and proving once again the folly of human wisdom.

Charles, who is the plaintiff in this case, is also evidently obliged to carry out the will of his vassals. Scholars have pointed out that what is at stake here is a system of law in which the public weal takes precedence over a private feud.[27] This is no doubt true, but it is also manifest that the recommendation of the court seriously undermines the Emperor's status as an individual enjoying the privilege of revealed truth. Charles learned of Ganelon's treason by means of a celestial vision. Firmly believing he is morally bound to bring Ganelon to speedy justice—Alda's death was a sure sign from God that it was his duty[28]—he now finds that his efforts will seemingly be frustrated.

Faillir (v. 3815: Quant Carles veit que tuz li sunt faillid) is a key concept here. It contrasts with the repeated claims made by the Franks that they will never fail each other or their Emperor (vv. 397, 801, 1048, 1866, 3133, 3344, 3359, 3417), and it threatens to rend the whole fabric of feudal society. *Faillir* is behavior associated with the pagan gods (vv. 2601, 2718), and it is inseparable from the notion of felony expressed in v. 3814 (cf. vv. 2600–2601).[29] Throughout history strong leaders have at times resolutely faced down their counselors, and Charles is clearly about to take such a step. Thierry, moved by the same mysterious promptings that give certain characters in this poem insight as well as exceptional strength,[30] now intervenes in dramatic fashion.

This knight, who was the only one of Charlemagne's judges to dissent from the timorous decision handed down by the court (v. 3806), is unimpressive in appearance, his body skinny, his complexion somber. However, Thierry's mediocre physique, one immediately discovers, contains a heart of oak. Pitting such a puny individual against the giant Pinabel sets the stage for a David and Goliath encounter—Conrad specifically alludes to this[31]—an archetype of Christ's victory over Satan.[32]

The champion's comforting words to the Emperor are uttered *curteisement* (v. 3823). The adverb pairs his speech with Roland's address to his men as the Battle of Roncevaux was about to commence (v. 1164).[33] As noted in the latter instance, the adjective *corteis* encompasses all the qualities felt to be desirable in a knight, including the capacity to give sound advice.[34] The adverb makes it clear that Thierry, faithful to his obligation to give *auxilium et consilium* to his sovereign, is offering loyal aid and counsel in the manner that the court was duty-bound yet failed to do.

Thierry's allusion to his ancestors is a further reminder of Roland's attitude facing the enemy (vv. 1063, 1076 = 3826),[35] as is his instinctive knowledge of Ganelon's betrayal (vv. 1146–1147 = 3829). His reasoning is worthy of note. "Even if Roland had wronged Ganelon" (v. 3827: "Que que Rollant a Guenelun forsfesist")[36] is an allusion to and, perhaps, by implication, a rejection of the alleged misdeed on the hero's part (v. 3758: "Rollant me forfist en or e en aveir"). Let us suppose for argument's sake, says Thierry, that Roland had wronged Ganelon. The fact that Roland was in Charlemagne's service was sufficient to safeguard him (v. 3828: "Vostre servise l'en doüst bien guarir"). According to this interpretation of the law, serving the Emperor renders a person immune from ordinary prosecution, any redress being the sovereign's prerogative. It is difficult to decide whether such was indeed the custom or whether it represents rather the opinion of a political theorist, such as the Norman Anonymous.[37]

The real significance of this passage is that, in Turoldus's view, serving the Emperor—like serving Durendal (v. 2350) or serving God (v. 3666)—is a sacred matter. Anyone enlisted in Charlemagne's service automatically comes under his protection and moreover shares in the mystical body mentioned earlier (v. 3410).[38] Consequently, to pursue Thierry's line of argument, when Ganelon betrayed Roland, he broke his oath of allegiance to Charlemagne (v. 3830), and his body—the words *sun cors* in v. 3832 continue the same corporeal metaphor—was irremediably severed from the Emperor's own and deserves nothing less than death. Thierry now proposes to let God's will become manifest by means of a judicial combat. Acting in belated concert, the Franks give their solemn assent (v. 3837).

Pinabel comes forward, remarkably agile for a man of such size,[39] and confident that he can dispatch with a few blows the upstart who dares affront his family. The ritual that ensues doubtless held as much fascination for Turoldus's contemporaries as it does for us today, but the modalities of its allurement differed in one significant respect. Our interest tends to be almost exclusively commanded by the ceremonial handing over of the gauntlets, symbolizing the surrender of their fiefs should they die (vv. 3845, 3851),[40] the designation of hostages (vv.

3846–3849, 3852),[41] the setting up of four benches—evidently to serve as boundary markers[42]—on which the duelists now seat themselves (vv. 3853–3854), and the formal challenge (v. 3855), with Ogier overseeing all these details (v. 3856). In this as well as in the animal heat, which, in spite of thousands of years of civilization, a duel to the death arouses in us, we are no different from the people of the Middle Ages. A fight always excites brutish instincts, and the commotion of the onlookers mentioned by Pinabel (v. 3842: "Car cumandez que tel noise n'i ait") was doubtless shared by the medieval audience, just as it is felt by us today.

However, for the people of Turoldus's day, the prospect of a manifestation of God's will was far more exciting than it generally is today. To be sure, there was then cynicism and amusement on the part of certain individuals in the matter of celestial interventions. How else can one explain the miraculous cure of Couart the Hare and Isangrin the Wolf after sleeping on the grave of the martyred hen Dame Coupee, a story the court interprets as a lie, in the *Roman de Renart*?[43] But on the whole, supernatural occurrences played a far greater role in people's lives than they do in that of the majority of today's readers of the *Song of Roland.*

Thierry and Pinabel both prepare for the ordeal in identical fashion: They confess their sins and receive absolution (v. 3859), hear mass and take communion (v. 3860), leave substantial donations to churches (v. 3861).[44] Yet it is obvious that, as in the case of Cain and Abel,[45] the Lord is pleased with Thierry and his offerings, but not with Pinabel and his. In Romanesque art God's attitude toward Adam and Eve's children is indicated in one of several ways: by means of the Manus Domini blessing Abel and threatening Cain with a clenched fist, by having the Divinity face one praying figure and turn his back on his brother, or by showing an angel accepting one gift, a devil the other.[46] The fact that the Lord looks favorably upon Thierry but not his adversary is suggested by the 100,000 warriors who are reminded of Roland (v. 3871: Qui pur Rollant de Tierri unt pitiet),[47] and, above all, by the poet's observation that God knows very well how the duel will turn out (v. 3872).

46. *The Judicial Combat*

Laisses 281–287 (verses 3873–3946)

Although the fateful outcome has already been foreshadowed, the duel between Thierry and Pinabel begins with each combatant returning blow for blow. No advantage by either individual is specifically recorded in Laisses 281 or 282.[1] However, there is an indication that Pinabel is faring slightly better in this initial phase of the duel, which, routinely, begins on horseback, then continues on foot. It is in the weeping and lamenting of the 100,000 knights (vv. 3882, 3890), known to favor Thierry (cf. vv. 3870–3871), and in the mention of Pinabel's strength and agility (v. 3885). Charles, however, seems quietly confident as he prays for a sign from heaven.

It is worth noting that the Emperor uses the verb *esclargier* in his invocation (v. 3891: "E! Deus," dist Carles, "le dreit en esclargiez!"). In this poem Old French *esclargier* or *esclargir* (< VL **exclaricare* for CL *exclarare* from *clarus* 'clear, bright') and *esclairier* (< VL *exclariare* also from CL *exclarare*) both allude to the clearing of the choler, that is, the yellow bile, one of the four humors that, according to medieval physiology, determined a person's temperament and disposition; characters also speak of freeing themselves of their anger or chagrin (vv. 301, 3628).[2] However, the same terms are also used for a brightening effect, as, for example, at daybreak (v. 667) or in the full blaze of the afternoon sun (v. 1807). By analogy the expressions refer, in v. 958, to a face lighting up into a smile and, in v. 3302, to the stirring sound of the oliphant. When Charlemagne implores God, then, to "clarify" right, the implication is that justice has been clouded over by Ganelon's deed and by the court's initial decision. The situation parallels Christ's declaration at the Last Supper: "*Nunc clarificatur est Filius hominis*" ("Now has the Son of Man been glorified")[3] and his prayer: "*Pater, venit hora, clarificata Filium tuum, ut Filius tuus clarificet te*" ("Father, the hour has come: glorify your Son so that your Son may glorify you").[4]

The lull in the battle described in Laisses 283 and 284 includes a curious exchange between the two antagonists. Although Pinabel seems to be gaining the upper hand and calls upon his opponent to surrender (v. 3892), he says he will become Thierry's vassal and give him all he owns if only he reconciles Charles with Ganelon.[5] "To the feudal baron," writes Jenkins, "Pinabel's would be a seductive offer."[6]

That may be, but there is a distinct smell of treachery about this proposition, which recalls Marsile's message to Charlemagne:

86 "Serai ses hom par amur e par feid"

3893 "Tes hom serai par amur e par feid"[7]

reinforced by the similar offer of a bribe:

75 "Jo vos durrai or e argent asez,
Teres e fiez tant cum vos en vuldrez."

3894 "A tun plaisir de durrai mun aveir."

It should not be forgotten that Pinabel is a relative of Ganelon[8] and that, to the medieval mind, the entire family was felt to be contaminated with a notorious individual's vice. This view is consistent with the decision to execute Ganelon's thirty kinsmen as being equally guilty of treason once the villain's crime has been proven by the outcome of the judicial combat.[9]

Thierry's reply is immediate and to the point. His observation that he does not even have to think about it (v. 3896: Respunt Tierri: "Ja n'en tendrai cunseill") is perhaps a scornful allusion to the vacillating Francs (v. 3761: Respundent Franc: "Ore en tendrum cunseill"). Echoing Charlemagne's prayer (v. 3891), Thierry maintains that he trusts God will make him the instrument of His justification.

His words to Pinabel, as recorded in Laisse 284, are flattering but uncompromising. After praising his adversary's strength and courage, he agrees to help arrange a reconciliation between Charles and him:

3895 "Mais Guenelun fai acorder al rei!" (Pinabel's condition).

3903 "A Carlemagne te ferai acorder" (Thierry's counterproposal).

As for Ganelon, says the Emperor's champion, such justice shall be done that men will talk about it forever (vv. 3904–3905). The extraordinary punishment to be inflicted upon the traitor is thus foreshadowed in the midst of the judicial combat. Pinabel's desire to sustain his family's honor (v. 3907) apes a similar wish expressed by Roland in vv. 1063 and 1076.[10] Since honor was alluded to by Oliver in the second horn scene, its use in the present context constitutes another instance of triplication.

As the battle commences anew, a formulaic line serves to associate this struggle to the death with the epic encounter between Charlemagne and Baligant:

> 3578 Seinz hume mort ne poet estre achevee.
>
> 3914 Seinz hume mort ne poet estre afinet.

Yet the very mention of *hume mort* also reminds us of the Emperor's chilling words to Alda uttered two hundred verses earlier: "*Soer, cher amie, de hume mort me demandes*" (v. 3713).

Two other images in the same closing lines of Laisse 284 impress the martyred hero's picture on our minds. Pinabel and Thierry locked so tightly in hand-to-hand fighting that *Il ne poet estre qu'il seient desevrez* (v. 3913) recall the closeness of the hero and his slain companion:

> 1977 "A grant dulor ermes hoi desevrez."
>
> 2009 Par tel amur as les vus desevred!

But it is, above all, the sparks flying heavenward (v. 3912: Cuntre le ciel en volet li fous tuz clers) that evoke the figure of the handsome Roland on two earlier occasions and his soul's ascent to its eternal reward:

> 707 Li quens Rollant ad l'enseigne fermee,
> En sum un tertre cuntre le ciel levee.
>
> 1156 Cuntre le ciel vait la mure turnant.
>
> 2396 L'anme del cunte portent en pareïs.

The glimpse of the hero's ghost in a shower of sparks contrasts sharply with another image. Pinabel strikes Thierry a mighty blow and sparks fly from Thierry's helmet. This time the grass is set on fire (v. 3917) and sinister flames beckon Ganelon, his champion, and all his relatives to their everlasting torment.

Pinabel's sword leaves a deep gash in Thierry's cheek, but at this crucial juncture God intervenes and saves the champion (v. 3923).[11] Thierry, reacting with the strength God has just granted him, strikes his adversary a death-dealing blow. The sudden transformation of near defeat into stunning victory is interpreted by the Franks as a sign from above that Ganelon and all his family deserve to be executed forthwith (vv. 3931–3933).[12]

Thierry is congratulated with great ceremony, underscoring the ritualistic aspect of the combat that has just taken place. Charles comes forward accompanied by four of his most trusted barons (v. 3936).

The quadripartite procession parallels the honor guard formed for Alda (v. 3729) and will soon be mirrored in the formal arrangements for Ganelon's execution (vv. 3964, 3967).[13] The Emperor embraces his champion, then wipes the latter's face with his fur cloak (v. 3940) in a gesture recalling Veronica's compassionate act.[14] Instead of retaining his mantle, Charles throws it down and puts on another. According to Jenkins: "The poet would not have Charlemagne appear in public with furs which were soiled."[15] However, one remembers, too, that throwing down a fur cloak is associated with Ganelon in this epic (v. 281; cf. vv. 462–464). Consequently, the gesture may be an ironic allusion to the quarrel that triggered the betrayal of Roland.[16]

The barons disarm Thierry and raise him on the back of a mule (vv. 3942–3943).[17] The joyous return of the saviour to Aix is reminiscent of the celebration after David's victory over the Philistine: "the women came out to meet King Saul from all the towns of Israel, singing and dancing to the sound of tambourine and lyre and cries of joy; and as they danced the women sang:

> 'Saul has killed his thousands,
> and David his tens of thousands'."[18]

David's triumph was believed to prefigure Christ's Entry into Jerusalem,[19] which may account for the mule motif (v. 3943) here.[20] The episode is foreshadowed in earlier passages of this poem involving Ganelon.[21] Even in the midst of this happy celebration, the traitor is on everyone's mind. As in the biblical prototype of the Entry into Jerusalem, joy is only a prelude to an execution. The victorious train has barely arrived in Aix when, Turoldus tells us, *Des ore cumencet l'ocisïun des altres* (v. 3946).

47. The Execution of Ganelon and His Kinsmen

Laisses 288–289 (verses 3947–3974)

God's judgment has been handed down, and there is general agreement that the traitor and his family must be promptly put to death, but the trial must first resume in order that custom be accorded its due.[1] Unanimity is so much in evidence among the judges that Charlemagne receives an instantaneous response. Plainly the Franks are most eager now to bring this matter to an end and, all obstacles in the way of proper sentencing having been removed, they shout their decision. There is, in their cry, an ironic echo of the Ganelon-Roland debate, which culminated in Roncevaux:

196 Il dist al rei: "Ja mar crerez Marsilie!"

220 E dist al rei: "Ja mar crerez bricun!"

3951 Respundent Franc: "Ja mar en vivrat uns!"

The notion that the entire family shares in an individual's honor or guilt—expressed here in proverbial form (v. 3959: Ki hume traïst sei ocit e altroi)[2]—is widespread among primitive peoples. The nomadic law of solidarity, which explains the punishment of Achar's family and that of Dathan and Abiram, sheds light on the origins of these beliefs.[3] It is significant that Dathan and Abiram are specifically mentioned in this poem (v. 1215). However, the execution of Ganelon's relatives is also bound up with the medieval concept of heredity, which held that a person's virtues and vices could be traced back to a remote ancestor and were regularly transmitted to his descendants. The literary manifestations of this view are many: Perceval's progenitor is said to have been Joseph of Arimathea, associated in legend with the grail, to mention but the most familiar instance,[4] and, in Venice IV, the rhymed versions, and the *Rolandslied*, Ganelon is reputed to have descended in direct line from Brutus, Julius Caesar's assassin.[5]

There is in Charlemagne's instructions to Basbrun more than a trace of irritation and contempt: his use of the expression *arbre de mal fust* for the gallows,[6] the oath, the threat to execute the officer himself if he fails in his duty (vv. 3953–3955), and Basbrun's intimidation (v. 3956: Cil li respunt: "Qu'en fereie joe el?").[7] Basbrun, whose humble condition—OFr. *veier* (< Lat. *vicarium*) means a police subaltern; his name also implies inferiority[8]—recalls Charles's earlier decision to turn his prisoner over to his cooks.[9] Surely the harshness of the Emperor's words and of the treatment accorded to Ganelon's thirty relatives is intended to reflect the baseness of the crime.

After the execution of Ganelon's family, Charles's advisers deliberate anew and agree that the traitor must be made to suffer an exceptionally painful death (v. 3963: Que Guenes moerget par merveillus ahan). This concept is repulsive to most civilized people today—for instance, cruel and unusual punishment is explicitly forbidden by the Constitution of the United States—but the call for exemplary chastisement is still heard among the populace whenever a heinous crime is committed.[10] Thierry had vowed that Ganelon's punishment would be a memorable one (vv. 3904–3905), and the council decides that death by quartering rather than by the customary hanging is indicated.

As usual with rituals, externals tend to attract attention—the four horses (v. 3964), the four sergeants (v. 3967), the stream (v. 3968)[11]—and one often neglects the deeper significance of the act. The idea of a dramatic execution to enhance Charlemagne's authority has a precedent in Moses's justification of the putting to death of Dathan and Abiram:

> "By this you will know that Yahweh himself has sent me to perform all these tasks and that this is not my doing. If these people die a natural death such as men commonly die, then Yahweh has not sent me. But if Yahweh does something utterly new, if the earth should open its mouth and swallow them, themselves and all that belongs to them, so that they go down alive to Sheol, then you will know that these men have rejected Yahweh." The moment he finished saying all these words, the ground split open under their feet, the earth opened its mouth and swallowed them, their families too, and all Korah's men and all their belongings. They went down alive to Sheol, they and all their possessions. The earth closed over them and they disappeared from the midst of the assembly.[12]

To be sure, it is the barons, not Charlemagne, who recommend this punishment. However, the plaint against Ganelon was originally lodged by the Emperor and, after the sign from God, his men act on his behalf and are plainly bent on confirming his power.

But why quartering? Jenkins, citing Léon Gautier, maintains that this form of punishment does not appear in the Germanic codes. It is, however, he adds, a shameful mode of execution in the *Roman de Troie* and one that is inflicted upon the traitor Mettus in the *Aeneid.*[13] It is notorious, too, that quartering was inflicted as a punishment in the Middle Ages for attempts on the king's life or on that of princes of the blood.[14] Every French schoolchild knows that Ravaillac, Henri IV's assassin, was put to death in this fashion in 1610.[15] The exemplary and justificatory aspect of Ganelon's punishment is an adequate explanation in itself. Yet the image at the end of the *Psychomachia* of

Discordia being torn limb from limb, the pieces of her body scattered to the breezes and devoured by unclean creatures, may also have exerted an influence here.[16] One cannot help but wonder, too, whether Turoldus's sense of poetic justice affected his decision to have the traitor quartered as a way of underscoring the idea that Roland was an extension of Charlemagne's body. The hero is repeatedly alluded to as the Emperor's right arm.[17] Metaphorically speaking, causing his death was a kind of regicide.[18]

After all that has transpired, the poet concludes that the overriding issue was the possibility that Ganelon, having committed treason, might have lived to brag about it. This, he informs the audience, would have constituted a grave injustice: *Hom ki traïst altre nen est dreiz qu'il s'en vant* (v. 3974). Questions of motivation and of justification fade into insignificance when the central fact of Ganelon's betrayal is accorded its due.

Victorious at Roncevaux, Roland was also posthumously vindicated at Aix. Like Saint Vincent the Martyr, whose corpse miraculously floated back to shore after being thrown into the sea, Roland had a double victory: "Victorious in a cruel death, thou dost then after death in like triumph trample victoriously on the devil merely with thy body."[19]

48. The Baptism of Bramimonde

Laisse 290 (verses 3975–3987)

At the beginning of the *Song of Roland,* the Saracens sought to convince Charlemagne that they desired to embrace Christianity.[1] The Theme of Conversion reaches its culmination in the narrative of Bramimonde's christening.[2] This episode serves to attenuate the harshness of the poem's concluding laisse which contains the disheartening prospect of a new war.

The baptism scene stresses the fact that Charlemagne's victory is not merely a military success but a stunning triumph for the Christian faith.[3] Just as Roland never loses sight of the fact that he is dying for the Church Militant, in the same way, what impels Charles to want Bramimonde's conversion is *amur* (v. 3674), synonymous in this case with generosity.[4] Each act exalts Christian Hope, Roland's deed being an *ars moriendi*, Charles's magnanimity an *ars vivendi*.

There does not appear to be any extant illustration dating from the Middle Ages of Bramimonde's christening.[5] However, there is every chance that Turoldus conceived of the scene in terms of the formula showing the convert standing or squatting in a baptismal font or shoulder-high vat[6] (*Fig. 65*). The illustrator of Conrad's adaptation of the *Roland* depicts Turpin baptizing a bearded pagan in a ciboriumlike receptacle.[7] Lejeune and Stiennon cite similar designs in the Fulda Sacramentary, preserved at Bamberg, the antiphonary of Saint Peter at Salzburg, the *Vitae et Passiones apostolorum* at Munich, and one of the bronze portals of the Cathedral of Gniezno.[8] It is worth noting that the twelfth-century Stuttgart Passionary uses the same formula to depict the baptism of Saint Constantine by Saint Silvester.[9] Since Charlemagne was frequently associated with Constantine in the Middle Ages (e.g., the famous stained-glass window at Chartres),[10] the choice of Saint Silvester's day (v. 3746) may have been determined by Bramimonde's baptism rather than by Ganelon's trial, which immediately precedes it.[11]

The Christian name for Bramimonde (v. 3986: Truvee li unt le num de Juliane) has been the occasion for much debate. Some scholars have endeavored to find a similarly designated notable of the day, reasoning that Turoldus may have been seeking to honor her by using her name and, possibly, other details from her biography.[12] However, the arguments adduced thus far to connect various historical personages named Juliana to the poem are specious and need not even be reviewed here.

Joseph Bédier's explanation is much more sensible:

> Pourquoi ce nom? Sainte Julienne de Cumes (vénérée le 16 février, voir la *Bibliotheca hagiographica latina* n° 4522), vécut parmi les païens, chez son père Africanus. Fiancée à neuf ans à Eleusius, préfet de Nicomédie, grand persécuteur des chrétiens, elle fut livrée au martyre par lui, quand elle eut dix-huit ans. Une telle sainte était assez bien qualifiée pour devenir la patronne céleste d'une sarrasine qui se convertit.[13]

Saint Juliana's popularity in the Middle Ages was due in great measure to an amusing anecdote. According to the legend, during the imprisonment that preceded her martyrdom, the devil appeared in the form of an angel to tempt her. Juliana proceeded to beat him, tied him with the chain that had been used to hold her, and threw him into a latrine.[14] In Romanesque art this energetic saint is usually depicted pulling the devil's hair or holding him by his chain while she strikes him with a rod[15] (*Fig 66*).

The cult of Saint Juliana spread over Europe and, naturally, there were many disputes concerning her relics.[16] It was agreed that this Oriental saint was interred in southern Italy before being transported to a second resting place at Cumae at the end of the sixth century. Later several European cities claimed to be in possession of her remains.[17] However, at the time Turoldus composed the *Song of Roland*, most Frenchmen believed that her relics were preserved in a monastery in northern Spain. The fame of the rich and influential monastery of Santa Juliana, which gave its name to the picturesque village of Santillana del Mar (Santa Juliana = Santa Illana = Santillana) in Asturias, is easy to explain since it was a stop along one of the pilgrimage roads to Santiago de Compostela, the most celebrated shrine of its day.[18]

The following verses from the twelfth-century *Vie de Sainte Julienne* prove that contemporary Frenchmen[19] associated Santillana with the legend of Juliana:

1279 En Esturges en la montangnie
Deza saint Jame, emmi Espanie,
La gist li cors de la pucele
En une fiertre gente et bele.
Trente nonains at el mostier
Ki la servent del Deu mestier.[20]

The great cult of Saint Juliana in the Middle Ages and the fact that she was a convert may be the reasons why the poet chose this name for Bramimonde. Perhaps Juliana had a numerous following among the Christian knights who fought the Muslims in Spain in the eleventh century. This devotion would then have paralleled that shown to Saint Faith because, having been martyred by pagans, she could preserve them from a similar fate.[21] However, the most plausible explanation is that Turoldus was alluding to the tradition connecting the remains of Saint Juliana with the homeland of the Saracen queen.

49. *Epilogue: Charlemagne's Dream*

Laisse 291 (verses 3988–4002)

The *Song of Roland* could quite logically have ended with Ganelon's trial or with Bramimonde's edifying baptism. The two acts of treachery have been resoundingly punished. Spain is now safely in the Christian orbit. However, in a short epilogue Gabriel appears in a vision to the slumbering Charles and summons the Emperor to new battles against the Infidel (vv. 3991–3998).

Menéndez Pidal expressed annoyance at this "final assez mal venu" found in only one supporting version of the legend and in none of the French sources.[1] Others have offered various justifications for the episode.[2] Nevertheless, the conclusion of the *Song of Roland* is best viewed as a transposition[3] with an ingenious switch at the very end. In fact, Turoldus offers not one twist but a unique double twist.

In narrative after narrative throughout Western literary history, a story begins with the motif of the Call to Action by a celestial figure. The story of the Patriarchs in Genesis, for example, begins with Abraham's call: "Yahweh said to Abram, 'Leave your country, your family and your father's house, for the land I will show you'."[4]

The *Pseudo-Turpin Chronicle* begins with such a call.[5] Charles had conquered all the lands he believed were destined to be brought under his sway and had converted all their inhabitants to the Christian faith. In his heart he told himself he would never again wage war but spend the rest of his days in well-earned rest. However, one night Charles looked up at the sky and saw the Milky Way stretching—or so it seemed to him—from the North Sea to Galicia in Spain. What did this signify? wondered Charles. Then Saint James himself appeared to tell him the meaning of the celestial wonder. "The Milky Way signifies that you, Charles, are to lead a great army into Spain to deliver my land and my tomb from the hands of the Infidel." Charles promptly heeded this call.

Turoldus took a tired cliché—the Call to Action by a celestial visitor—and injected new life into it simply by placing it at the end of his poem instead of at the beginning, where it should have come.[6] But reference has been made to a *double* twist.

The poem's last lines state that the Emperor has no desire to set off on his new mission. Charles utters these memorable closing words:

"*Deus!*" *dist li reis,* "*si penuse est ma vie!*" (v. 4000). He pulls his beard, Turoldus says, and tears flow from his eyes.

Throughout the *Song of Roland* the Abraham archetype has served as a fundamental structure (INTRODUCTION, 13, C). Suddenly Charles is no longer Abraham; he is Job in his tribulation.[7]

The poem ends on a plaintive note, showing as do the story of Job and the *Psychomachia*, that man must struggle unceasingly if he is to gain eternal life.[8] For medieval exegetes Job incarnated the Suffering Just and Patience in Adversity. But he was also the symbol of steadfastness in Faith and of the folly of relying on human wisdom. There is therefore metaphorical consistency in the use of a Job figure in connection with the Abraham archetype. For, crushed as Charlemagne may be at the moment by news of the desperate Christians at Imphe, no one doubts what his response will be.[9]

The conclusion of the *Song of Roland* opens up a vista of battles stretching into infinity and thus refers the audience back to the beginning of the poem.[10] This development is not completely unexpected as it was in a sense foretold by Charles in vv. 2921–2925.[11] Thus Roland's presence continues to be strongly felt, for Charles's prophecy was made in the context of his lament for the slain hero (vv. 2887–2943).[12]

Notes to the Introduction

References to the Introduction, Commentary, Manuscript, and Oxford Text, English Translation are in small capitals. References to illustrations in the text are in italics.

1. On the day and month of the battle, see Jenkins, notes to vv. 1002 and 2772 (cf. also his note to v. 2628); André de Mandach, *Naissance et développement de la chanson de geste en Europe*, vol. 1, *La Geste de Charlemagne et de Roland*, Publications romanes et françaises 69 (Geneva: Droz; Paris: Minard, 1961), pp. 50–55; Jules Horrent, "La bataille des Pyrénées de 778," *Le Moyen Age* 78 (1972): 197–227. On the date of the poem, see n. 27 below.

2. *A History of the Crusades*, gen. ed. Kenneth M. Setton, vol 1, *The First Hundred Years*, ed. Marshall W. Baldwin (Madison-Milwaukee-London: University of Wisconsin Press, 1969), pp. 31–34.

3. Ramón Menéndez Pidal, *La Chanson de Roland et la tradition épique des Francs*, trans. Irénée-Marcel Cluzel, 2d ed. (Paris: Picard, 1960), pp. 181–230, provides a detailed account of these events. Cf. Horrent, "La bataille des Pyrénées."

4. *Eginhard, Vie de Charlemagne*, ed. and trans. Louis Halphen, 3d ed. (Paris: Les Belles Lettres, 1947), pp. 28, 30. This work is hereafter referred to as Halphen. English translation mine.

5. Actually, only those in the north of Spain, but not Saragossa. Saracens (Sarraceni) are mentioned by name only once in Einhard's *Vita*, in a passage concerning Charles Martel's victory at Poitiers (Halphen, p. 10). See, however, Charlemagne's close relationship with Harun-al-Rashid (Aaron), Caliph of Bagdad (pp. 46, 48) and his action against the Moorish pirates in the Mediterranean (pp. 52, 54).

6. Gascons, not Basques. Paul Aebischer, *Préhistoire et protohistoire du Roland d'Oxford*, Bibliotheca Romanica, Series prima: Manualia et commentationes (Berne: Francke, 1972), pp. 75–87. Horrent, "La bataille des Pyrénées," pp. 202–3, suggests that the attackers were Pyrenean Gascons, rather than French Gascons (often referred to as Basques).

7. Halphen, pp. 16, 18.

8. Menéndez Pidal, p. 192.

9. Ibid., pp. 194–95; texts on p. 195, nn. 1, 2 (also pp. 528–29); Barton Sholod, *Charlemagne in Spain: The Cultural Legacy of Roncesvalles* (Geneva: Droz, 1966), p. 40 and n. 65.

10. Menéndez Pidal, pp. 204–9; Sholod, p. 41. Horrent, "La bataille des Pyrénées," p. 204, expresses reservations about Saracen complicity in this respect. Aebischer, p. 88: "l'assertion de Menéndez Pidal [à propos d'une] collaboration des Arabes et des Basques à Roncevaux ... ne repose que sur le fait mal interprété par lui de l'enlèvement de Sulaiman par ses fils."

11. In the poem Roland is a *Franc de France*, not a Breton. Bédier, *Commentaires*,

pp. 37–40; Horrent, *La Chanson de Roland*, pp. 305 and 306, n. 2. On the historicity of this personage, see Aebischer, pp. 93–145.

12. In Einhard *perfidia* means 'treachery' and is associated with the Saxons. Halphen, p. 23 and n. 4. In patristic literature *perfidia* often refers to the disbelief of non-Christians and is synonymous with *incredulitas*. Blaise, par. 392; see also COMMENTARY, 2 (vv. 24–26).

13. Originated by Pope Leo III in A.D. 800 and styled the "Empire of the West" and the "Roman Empire," the concept became the "Holy Empire" with Frederick I Barbarossa in 1157 and the "Holy Roman Empire" in 1254. Charlemagne was canonized at Frederick's behest on 29 December 1165.

14. André Burger, "La légende de Roncevaux avant la *Chanson de Roland*," *Romania* 70 (1948–49): 453–73. See, however, Jean Rychner, "A propos de l'article de M. André Burger 'La légende de Roncevaux avant la *Chanson de Roland*'," *Romania* 72 (1951): 239–46, and Burger's reply, "Sur les relations de la *Chanson de Roland* avec le *Récit du faux Turpin* et celui du *Guide du Pèlerin*," *Romania* 73 (1952): 242–47; Horrent, *La Chanson de Roland*, p. 155; Maurice Delbouille, *Sur la Genèse de la Chanson de Roland (Travaux récents—Propositions nouvelles): Essai critique*, Académie royale de langue et de littérature françaises de Belgique (Brussels: Palais des Académies, 1954), p. 100; Menéndez Pidal, pp. 348–49; pp. 417 ff. (speaks of a lost *Cantar de Rodlane*).

15. Horrent, pp. 292–7; Menéndez Pidal, pp. 355–65; Rita Lejeune, "La naissance du couple littéraire 'Roland et Olivier'," *Mélanges Henri Grégoire*, Annuaire de l'Institut de philologie et d'histoire orientales et slaves 10 (Brussels, 1950), 2:371–401; Delbouille, *Genèse*, pp. 98–120. See note 565 below.

16. Horrent, p. 302, n. 1.

17. Ibid., pp. 120–34, 138–40, 242–59; Menéndez Pidal, pp. 123–29; Joseph J. Duggan, *The Song of Roland: Formulaic Style and Poetic Craft* (Berkeley–Los Angeles–London: Center for Medieval and Renaissance Studies, University of California, Los Angeles, 1973), pp. 63–104; John R. Allen, "Du nouveau sur l'authenticité de l'épisode de Baligant," *Société Rencesvals pour l'étude des épopées romanes. VIe Congrès International (Aix-en-Provence, 29 Août–4 Septembre 1973). Actes* (Aix-en-Provence: Imprimerie du Centre d'Aix, 1974), pp. 147–56. For arguments in favor of the authenticity of the Baligant episode, see Paul Aebischer, "Pour la défense et illustration de l'épisode de Baligant," *Mélanges de philologie romane et de littérature médiévale offerts à Ernest Hoepffner* (Paris: Les Belles Lettres, 1949), pp. 173–82; Delbouille, *Genèse*, pp. 32–61. For a more extensive bibliography on this question, consult Marianne Cramer Vos, "Aspects of Biblical Typology in *La Chanson de Roland*," Ph.D. diss., University of Rochester, 1970, pp. 165–66, n. 26; Duggan, p. 69, n. 7; idem, "The Generation of the Episode of Baligant: Charlemagne's Dream and the Normans at Mantzikert," *Romance Philology* 30 (1976): 59–82.

18. For bibliography and discussion relative to this personage, see Jenkins, pp. xlviii–lxv; Bédier, *Commentaires*, pp. 31–40; Horrent, pp. 326–33; Pierre Le Gentil, *La Chanson de Roland*, Connaissance des lettres 43 (Paris: Hatier-Boivin, 1955), pp. 32–35; Martín de Riquer, *Les Chansons de geste françaises*, trans. Irénée-Marcel Cluzel, 2d ed. (Paris: Nizet, 1957), pp. 105–16; Mandach, *Naissance*, 1: 159; Rita Lejeune, "Turold dans la tapisserie de Bayeux," in *Mélanges offerts à René Crozet à l'occasion de son soixante-dixième anniversaire*, eds. Pierre Gallais and Yves-Jean Riou (Poitiers: Société d'études médiévales, 1966), pp. 419–25; Jean Dufournet, *Cours sur la Chanson de Roland*, Les Cours de Sorbonne (Paris: Centre de documentation universitaire, 1972), pp. 16–17. Each of these scholars concludes that Turoldus was the poet or last redactor. For the view that Turoldus was merely a copyist, see Aebischer, *Préhistoire*, pp. 224–28. On the manner in which medieval authors signed their works, see Ernst

Robert Curtius, *La Littérature européenne et le moyen âge latin*, 2d ed., trans. Jean Bréjoux, (Paris: Presses Universitaires de France, 1956), pp. 624–27.

19. On the date, see Jenkins, pp. xliii–xlvi (1099–1120); Bédier, *Commentaires*, pp. 40–59 (c. 1100); Horrent, pp. 287–304 (first half of the eleventh century for "la première *Chanson de Roland*"; c. 1100 for the redaction including the Baligant episode [pp. 315–19]; reign of Henry II [1154–89] for the reworking by Turoldus [p. 330]); Michel de Bouard, "La *Chanson de Roland* et la Normandie," *Annales de Normandie* 2 (1952): 34–38; J. C. Russell, "The *Chanson de Roland*: Written in Spain in 1093?" *Studies in Philology* 49 (1952): 17–24; Delbouille, *Genèse*, pp. 62–73 (c. 1100); Le Gentil, pp. 23–32 (c. 1100); M. Dominica Legge, "Archaism and the Conquest," *Modern Language Review* 51 (1956): 229 (1130–50, but "1150 ... may be on the late side"); Hans Erich Keller, "La conversion de Bramimonde," *Société Rencesvals. VIe Congrès International*, pp. 175–203, and *Olifant* 1, no. 1 (1973): 3–22 (1. "Chanson de Roncevaux," 1086–95; 2. "version capétienne" with Baligant episode, 1147–49 at Saint-Denis; 3. "version angevine" with new version of Bramimonde, third quarter of the twelfth century); see also Keller, "The *Song of Roland*: A Mid-Twelfth-Century Song of Propaganda for the Capetian Kingdom," *Olifant* 3, no. 4 (1976), 242–58. For Menéndez Pidal's dating, see note 22 below. On the place, see Bédier, *Commentaires*, pp. 37–40; Horrent, pp. 304–7; David Douglas, "The *Song of Roland* and the Norman Conquest of England," *French Studies* 14 (1960): 99–116; Keller, "The *Song of Roland*." On the significance of the late-eleventh-century *Nota Emilianense*, see Dámaso Alonso, "La primitiva épica francesa a la luz de una 'Nota Emilianense'," *Rivista de Filología Española* 37 (1953): 1–94; Ronald N. Walpole, "The *Nota Emilianense*: New Light (But How Much?) on the Origins of the Old French Epic," *Romance Philology* 10 (1956/57): 1–18; Le Gentil, pp. 45–47 (including Latin text and Modern French translation); Menéndez Pidal, pp. 384–447 and pls. X, XI; Moignet, pp. 293–94 (Latin text and Le Gentil's translation); Dufournet, *Cours sur Roland*, p. 26.

20. Jean Rychner, *La Chanson de geste: Essai sur l'art épique des jongleurs*, Société de publications romanes et françaises 53 (Geneva: Droz; Lille: Giard, 1955), p. 59.

21. Ibid., pp. 49, 61–62. Cf. Duggan, *Song of Roland*, pp. 63–67.

22. Rychner, p. 36, suggests the exact opposite but concedes that the *Roland* is an exception and involved a "création poétique" of the more conventional type, presumably clerical. See also note 48 below. Menéndez Pidal, p. 342, denies that the original *Song of Roland* was composed by a clerk but allows, pp. 343–76, that later reworkings (e.g., the late-tenth-century version including Oliver and Alda, the eleventh-century version mentioning the Twelve Peers) were produced by individuals with schooling. Joseph J. Duggan, "Virgilian Inspiration in the *Roman d'Enéas* and the *Chanson de Roland*," in *Medieval Epic to the "Epic Theater" of Brecht*, eds. Rosario P. Armato and John M. Spalek, University of Southern California Studies in Comparative Literature 1 (Los Angeles: University of Southern California Press, 1968), pp. 9–23, refuses to see any significant clerical influence in Turoldus's poem. Duggan, *Song of Roland*, pp. 13–14, 16, 36–60, 193, rejects the principle of composite creation: "the *Roland* which we possess must be a very nearly unadulterated product of oral tradition, little changed, except for its orthography, from the form in which it was first taken down from the lips of a singer or written down by a singer who had acquired literacy" (p. 60). My own view bears similarity to that propounded by Le Gentil in the series of articles cited by Duggan, p. 4, n. 7. See also Cecil M. Bowra, *Heroic Poetry* (London: Macmillan, 1952), pp. 247, 250–53, 368; Maurice Delbouille, "Les chansons de geste et le livre," *La Technique littéraire des chansons de geste: Actes du Colloque de Liège (Septembre 1957)*, Bibliothèque de la Faculté de philosophie et lettres de l'Université de Liège 150 (Paris: Les Belles Lettres, 1959), pp. 295–428;

idem, "Le chant héroïque serbo-croate et la genèse de la chanson de geste," *Boletín de la Real Academia de Buenas Letras de Barcelona* 31 (1965/66): 83–98; idem, "Le mythe du jongleur-poète," *Studi in onore di Italo Siciliano* (Florence: Olschki, 1966), pp. 317–27; Jean-Charles Payen, "De la tradition à l'écriture: à propos d'un livre récent," *Le Moyen Age* 75 (1969): 529–39; idem, *Le Moyen Age*, vol. 1, *Des origines à 1300*, Littérature française, ed. Claude Pichois (Paris: Arthaud, 1970), p. 120: "Les plus belles chansons ont été valorisées par l'écriture, et le *Roland* d'Oxford lui-même est un texte trop bien composé pour procéder d'improvisations, même géniales"; Edward A. Heinemann, "La composition stylisée et la transmission écrite des textes rolandiens," *Société Rencesvals. VI*[e] *Congrès International*, pp. 253–72. Robert Scholes and Robert Kellogg, *The Nature of Narrative* (New York: Oxford University Press, 1966), chap. 2, "The Oral Heritage of Written Narrative," pp. 17–56, is a useful introduction to this complex question.

23. William Calin, *The Epic Quest: Studies in Four Old French Chansons de Geste* (Baltimore: Johns Hopkins Press, 1966), pp. 57–117; on the problem of definition in the case of the *Chanson de Guillaume*, see p. 93; for the *Song of Roland, Gormont et Isembart*, and *Girart de Roussillon*, see p. 116. See also Thomas E. Vesce, "Reflections on the Epic Quality of *Ami et Amile: Chanson de Geste*," *Mediaeval Studies* 35 (1973): 129–45, and the critique by S. N. Rosenberg in *Olifant* 3, no. 3 (1976): 221–25.

24. Frederick W. Locke, *The Quest for the Holy Grail: A Literary Study of a Thirteenth-Century French Romance* (Stanford: Stanford University Press, 1960), pp. 18–22.

25. But with important variations; see, for example, the discussion and stemmata in Jenkins, pp. xcv–xcviii; Bédier, *Commentaires*, pp. 83–92; Eyvind Fjeld Halvorsen, *The Norse Version of the Chanson de Roland*, Bibliotheca Arnamagnaeana 19 (Copenhagen: Munksgaard, 1959), pp. 272–73; and Segre, pp. ix–xviii. The medieval texts of the *Roland* are described in Segre, pp. xxxvii–xlvii. Mortier (see ABBREVIATIONS) is a convenient edition of the essential texts.

26. *La Chanson de Roland: Reproduction phototypique du manuscrit Digby 23 de la Bodleian Library d'Oxford*, ed. Comte Alexandre de Laborde, Etude historique et paléographique de M. Ch. Samaran (Paris: Société des anciens textes français, 1933), pp. 28–32. This work is hereafter referred to as Samaran.

27. On the dialect, see Bédier, *Commentaires*, pp. 241–62. Dating of the hand in Digby 23 varies considerably: Bédier, *Commentaires*, p. 66 (c. 1170); Samaran, p. 30 (1130–50); Horrent, pp. 32–42 (second half of the twelfth century); Robert Marichal, *Annuaire 1969–1970 de l'Ecole pratique des hautes études, IV*[e] *section: Sciences historiques et philologiques. Extrait des rapports sur les conférences: Paléographie latine et française* (Paris, 1970), pp. 363–74 ("plus proche de 1125 que de 1150" [p. 367]); Félix Lecoy, reviewing the latter work in *Romania* 92 (1971): 141, accepts its findings; Ian Short, "The Oxford Manuscript of the *Chanson de Roland:* A Paleographical Note," *Romania* 94 (1973): 221–31 (c. 1170); Charles Samaran, "Sur la date approximative du *Roland* d'Oxford," *Romania* 94 (1973): 523–27 (1130–50); Keller, "The *Song of Roland*," pp. 244–45 ("not before 1170"). On the date of the original poem, see note 19 above.

28. Samaran, in *La Chanson de Roland*, ed. Laborde, pp. 33–36, 38.

29. Ibid., pp. 20–22, 39–40. Many, but by no means all, of these are inept changes and give editors of the *Roland* a headache.

30. Ibid., pp. 36–37.

31. Ibid., p. 39, citing the catalogue of the New Palaeographical Society.

32. Ibid., pp. 39–41.

33. See references in note 27 above.

34. Edmond Faral, *Les Jongleurs en France au moyen âge*, 2d ed., Bibliothèque de

l'Ecole des hautes études 187 (1910; rpt. Paris: Champion, 1964); Bowra, *Heroic Poetry*, chap. 1, "The Heroic Poem," pp. 1–90; Rychner, *La Chanson de geste*.

35. Scholes and Kellogg, *Nature of Narrative*, pp. 30–40, discusses the relationship between oral and written versions of the *Roland* and other epics intelligently and objectively but offers no new solutions to this problem.

36. Published, with a slightly different title, as "Les nouvelles tendances de la critique et l'interprétation des épopées médiévales," *Boletín de la Real Academia de Buenas Letras de Barcelona* 31 (1965/66): 131–41; summary in *Bulletin bibliographique de la Société Rencesvals* 4 (1967): 109. Cf. my paper "Quelques nouvelles tendances de la critique et de l'interprétation des chansons de geste," *Société Rencesvals. VIe Congrès International*, pp. 13–26.

37. From summary, p. 109. The phrase was modified in the definitive text.

38. Gaston Paris, *La Poésie du moyen âge, première série*, 4th ed. (Paris: Hachette, 1899), p. 219.

39. Le Gentil, *La Chanson de Roland*, chap. 7.

40. Rosemund Tuve, *Allegorical Imagery: Some Mediaeval Books and Their Posterity* (Princeton: Princeton University Press, 1966), pp. 219–20; Northrop Frye, *Anatomy of Criticism: Four Essays* (New York: Atheneum, 1968), p. 86.

41. W. K. Wimsatt, Jr., and Monroe C. Beardsley, *The Verbal Icon: Studies in the Meaning of Poetry* (Lexington: University of Kentucky Press, 1954), chap. 1.

42. Cf. "The Girl with the Delacroix Face" in James A. Michener, *Kent State: What Happened and Why* (New York: Random House, 1971), pp. 543–54.

43. Horrent, *La Chanson de Roland*, Livre I, pp. 27–418, is an indispensable compendium of considerations of the traditional type.

44. Rychner, p. 7. See also Jules Horrent, *Le Pèlerinage de Charlemagne: Essai d'explication littéraire avec des notes de critique textuelle*, Bibliothèque de la Faculté de philosophie et lettres de l'Université de Liège 158 (Paris: Les Belles Lettres, 1961), pp. 9–15.

45. Rita Lejeune, "Technique formulaire et chansons de geste," *Le Moyen Age* 60 (1954): 311–34; Paul Aebischer, "Halt sunt li pui e li port tenebrus," *Studi Medievali* 18 (1952): 1–22; Maurice Wilmotte, "La *Chanson de Roland* et la *Chançun de Willame*," *Romania* 44 (1915–17): 55–86.

46. Milman Parry, "Studies in the Epic Technique of Oral Verse-Making. I. Homer and Homeric Style," *Harvard Studies in Classical Philology* 41 (1930): 73–147; Francis P. Magoun, Jr., "The Oral-Formulaic Character of Anglo-Saxon Narrative Poetry," *Speculum* 28 (1953): 446–67; Albert B. Lord, *The Singer of Tales*, Harvard Studies in Comparative Literature 24 (Cambridge: Harvard University Press, 1960).

47. Rychner, pp. 154–58, criticized Bédier for having been too categorical in his rejection of the *cantilène* theory. On this theory, generally associated with Gaston Paris, see Joseph Bédier, *Les Légendes épiques: Recherches sur la formation des chansons de geste*, 2d ed., 4 vols. (Paris: Champion, 1921), 3:230–49.

48. Rychner's modified view is found in his article "Observations sur la versification du 'Couronnement de Louis'," *La Technique littéraire des chansons de geste*, pp. 161–82.

49. I have expressed my own indebtedness to Rychner, *La Chanson de geste*, in "Le Thème de la Mort dans la *Chanson de Roland*," *Société Rencesvals. IVe Congrès International. Heidelberg, 28 août—2 septembre 1967. Actes et mémoires*, Studia Romanica 14 (Heidelberg: Winter, 1969), p. 220, n. 1.

50. Delbouille, "Les chansons de geste et le livre"; Duncan McMillan, "A propos de traditions orales," *Cahiers de civilisation médiévale* 3 (1960): 67–71; idem, "A propos d'un travail de M. Delbouille sur les chansons de geste et le livre," *Cahiers de civilisation médiévale* 4 (1961): 47–54; idem, "Notes sur quelques clichés formulaires dans les

chansons de geste de Guillaume d'Orange," *Mélanges de linguistique romane et de philologie médiévale offerts à M. Maurice Delbouille* (Gembloux: Duculot, 1964), 2:477–93.

51. Examples may be found in the works of Mandach, *Naissance*, and Sholod, *Charlemagne in Spain*; Winifred Mary Hackett, "La féodalité dans la *Chanson de Roland* et dans *Girart de Roussillon*," *Société Rencesvals. IVe Congrès International*, pp. 22–27; Hans Erich Keller, "La version dionysienne de la *Chanson de Roland*," *Philologica Romanica. Erhard Lommatzsch gewidmet*, eds. Erich von Richthofen, Manfred Bambeck, and Hans Helmut Christmann (Munich: Fink, 1975), 257–87 (summary in *Olifant* 1, no. 4 [1974]: 64–67); Pierre Jonin, "La 'Clere' Espagne de Blancandrin," *Mosaic* 8 (1975): 85–96 (bibliography, pp. 92–95, and notes). See also COMMENTARY, 2, note 9.

52. Dufournet, *Cours sur Roland*, pp. 75–185.

53. Le Gentil, "Les nouvelles tendances," pp. 134–36.

54. Bédier, *Légendes épiques*, 3:372, 451; Jenkins, p. v; Horrent, p. 307; Le Gentil, *La Chanson de Roland*, pp. 90, 107, 110; Pierre Jonin, "Le climat de croisade des chansons de geste," *Cahiers de civilisation médiévale* 7 (1964): 279–88; Charles A. Knudson, "Quel terrain faut-il céder au néo-traditionalisme? Le cas de la *Chanson de Roland*," *Boletín de la Real Academia de Buenas Letras de Barcelona* 31 (1965/66): 120–23; Moignet, pp. 13–14.

55. Bédier, *Légendes épiques*, 3:368–73; Prosper Boissonnade, *Du Nouveau sur la Chanson de Roland: La genèse historique, le cadre géographique, le milieu, les personnages, la date et l'auteur du poème* (Paris: Champion, 1923), pp. 3–68; Jenkins, pp. lxxvi–lxxvii. On the Spanish campaigns, see *History of the Crusades*, 1:31–39.

56. Léon Gautier, *Les Epopées françaises* (Paris: Palmé, 1865), 1:24–31.

57. George Fenwick Jones, *The Ethos of the Song of Roland* (Baltimore: Johns Hopkins Press, 1963); see also D. D. R. Owen, "The Secular Inspiration of the *Chanson de Roland*," *Speculum* 37 (1962): 390–400; Glyn Sheridan Burgess, *Contribution à l'étude du vocabulaire pré-courtois*, Publications romanes et françaises 110 (Geneva: Droz, 1970).

58. Fighting for Christ is a Pauline metaphor (INTRODUCTION, 15, A); for the evolution of this concept in the eleventh century, see Curtius, pp. 649–50; Hans-Wilhelm Klein, "Der Kreuzzugsgedanke im Rolandslied und die neuere Rolandforschung," *Die Neueren Sprachen*, n.s. 5 (1956), 265–85; Friedrich Heer, *The Medieval World: Europe 1100–1350*, trans. Janet Sondheimer (New York and Toronto: New American Library; London: New English Library, 1961), p. 127; Etienne Delaruelle, "L'idée de croisade dans la littérature clunisienne du XIe siècle et l'abbaye de Moissac," *Annales du Midi* 75 (1963): 419–39; Jean-Charles Payen, *Le Motif du repentir dans la littérature française médiévale (Des origines à 1230)*, Publications romanes et françaises 98 (Geneva: Droz, 1968), p. 448 (bibliography in n. 140). Cf. Menéndez Pidal, pp. 241–44, 261–62.

59. Bédier, *Légendes épiques*, 3:432: "Que pense le poète de leur débat? Il ne le dit pas, il semble les approuver tous les deux." Such a view is diametrically opposed to the theory that a strong didactic element is to be found in all serious medieval literature. D. W. Robertson, Jr., *A Preface to Chaucer: Studies in Medieval Perspectives* (Princeton: Princeton University Press, 1962), p. 67. See INTRODUCTION, 10.

60. For bibliography and discussion, see William W. Kibler, "Roland's Pride," *Symposium* 26 (1972): 147–60; Larry S. Crist, "A propos de la *desmesure* dans la *Chanson de Roland*: quelques propos (démesurés?)," *Olifant* 1, no. 4 (1974): 10–20; Wolfgang G. Van Emden, "'E cil de France le cleiment a guarant': Roland, Vivien et le thème du guarant," *Société Rencesvals. VIe Congrès International*, pp. 31–61, and *Olifant* 1, no. 4 (1974): 21–47; William W. Kibler, "Roland and Tierri," *Olifant* 2, no. 1

(1974): 27–32; Wolfgang G. Van Emden, "Pro Karolo Magno: In Response to William W. Kibler, 'Roland and Tierri'," *Olifant* 2, no. 3 (1975): 175–82.

61. See, notably, Alain Renoir, "Roland's Lament: Its Meaning and Function in the *Chanson de Roland*," *Speculum* 35 (1960): 572–83. Renoir's thesis is sharply criticized by George Fenwick Jones, "Roland's Lament: A Divergent Interpretation," *Romanic Review* 53 (1962): 3–15. Payen, *Le Motif du repentir*, pp. 114–15: "Il n'est nul besoin d'être grand clerc pour déduire de ces quatre vers [vv. 2371–2372, 2387–2388] que Roland y fait une confession générale de tous les péchés qu'il a commis dans son existence, et non la confession particulière de sa toute récente démesure." Cf. the implication, in Charlemagne's third dream, that the Franks are being punished by God for some obscure sin. See COMMENTARY, 28. Frye, *Anatomy of Criticism*, pp. 38–39: "pathos is increased by the inarticulateness of the victim." For Joseph Campbell, *The Hero with a Thousand Faces*, 2d ed., Bollingen Series 17 (Princeton: Princeton University Press, 1973 [c. 1949]), pt 1, chap. 2, 4, "Atonement with the Father" (pp. 126–49) is one stage of the mythological journey.

62. Le Gentil, pp. 118–19. Cf. Julian E. White, "*La Chanson de Roland*: Secular or Religious Inspiration?" *Romania* 84 (1962): 398–408.

63. Jenkins, p. xlii:

> The poet ... makes Roland's rashness (*desmesure*) the cause of the great disaster; but, to our great satisfaction, he makes Roland's dogged obstinacy in the end melt away and yield to compassion, when the paladin views the results of his refusal to listen to the counsels of prudence. The fault is atoned for by suffering and by death. Here is the poet's greatest achievement: he has made a drama of human character and conduct, of human strength and weakness. Roland is not at the end the same person he was at the beginning: he has greatly developed, and we find here the orderly progression within unity which Aristotle demanded of the epic.

See also André Burger, "La question rolandienne, faits et hypothèses," *Cahiers de civilisation médiévale* 4 (1961): 269–91. For a critique of this view, see Payen, *Le Motif du repentir*, p. 121:

> La *Chanson de Roland* n'est pas l'histoire d'une expiation, c'est une oeuvre destinée à galvaniser l'énergie du public chevaleresque pour lequel il est probable qu'elle fut conçue. Epopée chrétienne, elle sauve ses héros en leur ouvrant le Paradis, mais ce n'est là qu'un aspect un peu secondaire des choses. Le véritable sens de la chanson est ailleurs.

Payen's personal interpretation is found on p. 137:

> Pour nous, la *Chanson de Roland* est l'histoire d'un martyre délibérément choisi, après une faute initiale, par un héros trop fier et trop sûr de lui: l'idée de ce martyre est aussitôt acceptée d'enthousiasme par toute une armée subjugée par le prestige de son chef et la promesse du Paradis. Le désastre de Roncevaux est une épreuve providentielle, mais ce n'est pas un châtiment, et l'on ne saurait trop déplorer qu'il soit si vite apparu tel au public du XIIe siècle.

64. Emanuel J. Mickel, Jr., "Parallels in Prudentius' *Psychomachia* and *La Chanson de Roland*," *Studies in Philology* 67 (1970): 447: "Charlemagne is forced to repent of his error and return to his duty." The same notion is in Bernard F. Huppé, "The Concept of the Hero in the Early Middle Ages" in *Concepts of the Hero in the Middle Ages and the Renaissance*, eds. Norman T. Burns and Christopher J. Reagan (Albany: State University of New York Press, 1975), pp. 13–18. For Huppé Roland's heroism is a weakness, but a *felix culpa*. Cf. Sholod, *Charlemagne in Spain*, p. 37: "Was Charles' defeat, together with the loss of Roland (product of incest?), caused by a rare error in 'politico-religious' judgment, looked upon as the 'wages of sin' and considered an expurgation for same? Was *this* the motivating force behind the creation of our epic?"

Cf. the scapegoat (pharmakos) concept; Frye, *Anatomy of Criticism*, pp. 41, 148; Payen, *Le Motif du repentir*, p. 299. Le Gentil, pp. 145–46:

> En se manifestant, Dieu n'y change rien. Mais s'il laisse les personnages maîtres de leur destin, il n'en fait pas moins éclater sa toute-puissance, sa bonté et sa justice. Il donne un sens aux événements et aux actes, parce qu'en même temps qu'il les dirige mystérieusement par sa souveraine Providence, il laisse non moins mystérieusement aux hommes une liberté par laquelle il les grandit sans les priver de son aide. On a pu reconnaître ici le message même de l'Evangile, avec ses promesses d'amour et de rédemption.

Cf. W. J. Brandt, *The Shape of Medieval History: Studies in Modes of Perception* (New Haven: Yale University Press, 1966), p. 61, n. 61: "Providence never illuminates anything in medieval chronicles." See also pp. 62, 64–65.

65. See COMMENTARY, 49.

66. On this concept, see *Job*, The Anchor Bible, vol. 15, trans. Marvin H. Pope (Garden City: Doubleday, 1965), pp. lxviii–lxxviii ("The Purpose and Teaching of the Book"). Cf. v. 1480: *Innocenz* (COMMENTARY, 17, note 15). The notion of innocence here is related to that of martyrdom. See Blaise, par. 109.

67. Bédier, *Légendes épiques*, 3:433–34: "Turold a obtenu que l'intérêt ne sera point dans les épisodes extérieurs, dans les grands coups d'épée; l'intérêt sera tout entier dans le conflit d'Olivier et de Roland, dans la curiosité passionnée qui désormais nous porte à observer Roland"; p. 448:

> Pour que, des éléments légendaires, vagues et amorphes, qui végétaient dans les églises de Roncevaux ou dans les églises de la route de Roncevaux, naquît la *Chanson de Roland*, il est inutile et vain de supposer qu'il y ait fallu des siècles, et que des 'chanteurs' sans nombre se soient succédé. Une minute a suffi, la minute sacrée où le poète, exploitant peut-être quelque frustre roman, ébauche grossière du sujet, a conçu l'idée du conflit de Roland et d'Olivier.

68. Ibid., p. 411. Cf. 3:451–52. In 3:447 and 450, the *Roland* is compared to Racine. Cf. Pierre-Georges Castex and Paul Surer, *Manuel des études littéraires françaises*, vol. 1, *Moyen Age* (Paris: Hachette, 1948), p. 24: "*Tristan* est le roman de la fatalité, comme *Roland* était l'épopée de la volonté: également riches de substance humaine, les deux oeuvres s'opposent et se complètent comme au XVIIe siècle les tragédies de Corneille et celles de Racine"; Albert Gérard, "L'axe Roland-Ganelon: valeurs en conflit dans la *Chanson de Roland*," *Le Moyen Age* 76 (1969): 446: "Le devoir suprême est d'éviter la honte (blâme, 'reproece', 'viltet'), qui est la manifestation de la désapprobation publique, et d'acquérir cette forme d'honneur ('los', 'valur') que les héros cornéliens appelleront plus tard la gloire. En cela, le monde de la *Chanson* ne se distingue nullement des autres sociétés épiques." Eugene Vinaver, "La mort de Roland," *Cahiers de civilisation médiévale* 7 (1964): 133, reproaches Bédier for this view.

69. Jenkins, p. xxxiii. On this concept (hamartia), see Frye, *Anatomy of Criticism*, pp. 38, 210. Vos, "Aspects of Biblical Typology," p. xxi, n. 11, decries Jenkins's assertion.

70. See COMMENTARY, 14 and 18.

71. Curtius, p. 217.

72. Donald Earl, *The Moral and Political Tradition of Rome* (Ithaca: Cornell University Press, 1967), p. 33.

73. Ibid., p. 22.

74. Curtius, p. 216.

75. Leo Spitzer, "Etudes d'anthroponymie française," *PMLA* 58 (1943): 589–93. Riquer, *Chansons de geste*, p. 70, and Menéndez Pidal, pp. 345–46, discount this etymology of Oliver's name. On biblical symbols of Wisdom, see Sister Mary Frances Smith, S.S.N.D., *Wisdom and Personification of Wisdom Occurring in Middle English*

Literature Before 1500 (Washington, D.C.: The Catholic University of America, 1935), pp. 15–17.

76. The olive tree is also associated with Minerva, the goddess of Knowledge and Wisdom. Rita Lejeune, "La naissance du couple littéraire 'Roland et Olivier'," p. 382. For a critique of this view, see Delbouille, *Genèse*, pp. 106–9.

77. Smith, chap. 1, "Wisdom and Personifications of Wisdom in the Bible," pp. 1–18.

78. Curtius, pp. 215–19, notes this topos in Dictys, Dares, Fulgentius, Alcuin, Dante, and in the *Waltharius* and the *Fürstenspiegel*. For the *Chanson de Guillaume*, see Delbouille, *Genèse*, p. 105, n. 1; Jean Frappier, *Les Chansons de geste du cycle de Guillaume d'Orange*, vol. 1 (Paris: Société d'édition d'enseignement supérieur, 1955), pp. 160, 185; Payen, *Le Motif du repentir*, p. 109, n. 2. For examples in English literature, see Robert E. Kaske, "*Sapientia et Fortitudo* as the Controlling Theme of *Beowulf*," *Studies in Philology* 55 (1958): 423–56. Kaske cites several English hagiographic poems as well as the *Disticha Catonis*, the *Eddas*, and the Irish *Instructions of Cormac*. See also *The Works of Geoffrey Chaucer*, ed. F. N. Robinson, 2d ed. (Boston: Houghton Mifflin, 1957), Prologue to the Canterbury Tales, v. 68 ("And though he were worthy, he was wys") and Robinson's note, p. 652. In her contribution "Un lai de Marie de France: Les deux amants," *Mélanges offerts à Rita Lejeune*, 2 vols. (Gembloux: Duculot, 1969), 2:1143–57, Jeanne Wathelet-Willem believes there is an echo of *Roland*, v. 1093, in vv. 81–82 and 237–238 of Marie's poem, and wonders whether the author may have wished to "réunir les qualités des deux héros fameux dans chacun de ses personnages" (p. 1156).

79. Jones, p. 23. For the expression *auxilium et consilium*, see François-Louis Ganshof, *Feudalism*, trans. Philip Grierson, 2d ed. (New York: Harper, 1961), pp. 87–93.

80. *La Chanson de Roland*, ed. William Calin, Series in Medieval French Literature (New York: Appleton-Century-Crofts, 1968), p. 12. For other examples of this topos in the chansons de geste, see William Calin, *The Old French Epic of Revolt: Raoul de Cambrai, Renaud de Montauban, Gormond et Isembard* (Geneva: Droz, 1962), chaps. 3 and 4, especially pp. 148–51.

81. Menéndez Pidal, p. 347.

82. Matthias Waltz, *Rolandslied. Wilhelmslied. Alexiuslied: Zur Struktur und geschichtlichen Bedeutung*, Studia Romanica 9 (Heidelberg: Winter, 1965), pp. 51–56. For further critique, see Eleanor W. Bulatkin, *Structural Arithmetic Metaphor in the Oxford Roland* (Columbus: Ohio State University Press, 1972), pp. 59–68.

83. E.g., Roland's boasting (but see INTRODUCTION, 19, c).

84. According to Le Gentil, pp. 104, 122, Oliver's observation apropos of Roland (vv. 256–57: "Vostre curages est mult pesmes e fiers:/ Jo me crendreie que vos vos meslisez") refers to his companion's *desmesure*. However, Jones, p. 31, points out that: "no insult seems implied when Oliver vetoes Roland as Charlemagne's messenger to Marsilie on the grounds that his heart is too *pesmes* and *fiers* (256). In fact *pesmes* seems almost synonymous with *fiers*, which is generally complimentary" (see also p. 67, n. 79).

85. See COMMENTARY, 6 and 19.

86. The procedure is illustrated by an anecdote in *The Attic Nights of Aulus Gellius*, ed. and trans. John C. Rolfe, The Loeb Classical Library, 3 vols. (1927; rpt. Cambridge: Harvard University Press; London: Heinemann, 1961), 1, 5:10; see also *Diogenes Laertius, Lives of Eminent Philosophers*, ed. and trans. R. D. Hicks, The Loeb Classical Library, 2 vols. (1925; rpt. Cambridge: Harvard University Press; London: Heinemann, 1958), 2:469; *Sextus Empiricus*, ed. and trans. Rev. R. G. Bury, The Loeb Classical Library, 4 vols. (1933; rpt. Cambridge: Harvard University Press; London: Heinemann, 1949), 4:235–36. The anecdote underlines the fallacious aspect

of this refutation technique. See COMMENTARY, 18, note 5. Antistrephon is discussed in a textbook on rhetoric by C. Chirius Fortunatianus (c. A.D. 450), which was widely used in the Middle Ages; *Readings in Medieval Rhetoric*, eds. Joseph M. Miller, Michael H. Prosser, and Thomas W. Benson (Bloomington and London: Indiana University Press, 1973), p. 78. The literary debate enjoyed a great vogue in the Middle Ages; see Paul Zumthor, *Histoire littéraire de la France médiévale* (*VI*[e]*–XIV*[e] *siècle*) (Paris: Presses Universitaires de France, 1954), index, s.v. Altercatio, Débat, Disputatio. For a parallel scene in the *Chanson de Guillaume*, see Frappier, *Chansons de geste*, 1:158–59. Note, finally, Job 24:18–20, 22–25 (placed after 27:23 in *The Jerusalem Bible*), 27:8–23, where the hero, mocked by his three friends, suddenly and derisively switches to their point of view. See *Job*, trans. Pope, p. xxv.

87. See, for example, Alfred Foulet, "Is Roland Guilty of Desmesure?" *Romance Philology* 10 (1957): 145–48; Alfredo del Monte, "Apologia di Orlando," *Filologia Romanza* 4 (1957): 225–34; André Burger, "Les deux scènes du cor dans la *Chanson de Roland*," in *La Technique littéraire des chansons de geste*, pp. 105–26; Robert Guiette, "Les deux scènes du cor dans la *Chanson de Roland* et dans les *Conquestes de Charlemagne*," *Le Moyen Age* 69 (1963): 845–55. On Foulet and Del Monte, see *Olifant* 3, no. 3 (1976), 180–81.

88. Bédier, *Légendes épiques*, 3:444: "Entre le 'preux' et le 'sage' il n'a pas choisi, trop humain pour choisir"; Horrent, p. 277: "Il a senti que l'un et l'autre étaient un aspect de la même vérité contradictoire, et il les a enveloppés chacun d'une même et chaude sympathie."

89. The best general introduction to matters discussed in this section is Marc Bloch, *Feudal Society*, trans. L. A. Manyon, 2 vols. (Chicago: University of Chicago Press, 1961). Another useful survey is J. W. B. Zaal, "*A lei francesa*" (*Sainte Foy, v. 20*): *Etudes sur les chansons de saints gallo-romanes du XI*[e] *siècle* (Leiden: Brill, 1962), chap. 1, "La France géographique et culturelle au XIe siècle," pp. 27–44.

90. Some urban activity is starting up again, but major developments are yet to come. Henri Pirenne, *Economic and Social History of Medieval Europe*, trans. I. E. Clegg (New York: Harcourt Brace, [c. 1956]), chaps. 2 and 3.

91. Bloch, 2:288: "if the concept of nobility as a legal class remained unknown, it is quite permissible from this period [i.e., the first feudal age], by a slight simplification of terminology, to speak of a social class of nobles and especially, perhaps, of a noble way of life." On the role of the clergy, the third element of feudal society, see INTRODUCTION, 5 and 7.

92. Ibid., 1:145–275; Ganshof, *Feudalism*, pp. 65–155.

93. R. C. Smail, *Crusading Warfare* (*1097–1193*) (Cambridge: Cambridge University Press, 1956), pp. 106–7. See also OXFORD TEXT, ENGLISH TRANSLATION, v. 34. The word *chevaler* is used indiscriminately by Turoldus for both Christians and Saracens. That a certain type of behavior was expected of the Christian knight is clearly indicated by the expression *a lei de chevaler* (v. 752).

94. The functions of light-armed horsemen and *pedites* are discussed by Smail, pp. 107–12.

95. On the significance in this regard of "collective" vs. "individual" man about 1150, see Richard William Southern, *The Making of the Middle Ages* (New Haven: Yale University Press, 1961), p. 222; Burgess, *Vocabulaire pré-courtois*, p. 7; Anthony M. Beichman, "Ganelon and Duke Naimon," *Romance Notes* 13 (1971): 358–62. Such a generalization tends to break down upon close scrutiny, as does the familiar dictum that the Middle Ages is an era of participation, the modern period, one of separation.

96. See INTRODUCTION, 15, B. On medieval pilgrimages, see Jacques Le Goff, *La Civilisation de l'occident médiéval* (Paris: Arthaud, 1972), pp. 172–74.

97. On the significance of itineraries, see Stephen G. Nichols, Jr., "The Interaction of Life and Literature in the 'Peregrinationes ad loca sancta' and the 'Chansons de geste'," *Speculum* 44 (1969): 51–77.

98. See, for example, the maps in Jenkins, pp. lxxviii–lxxix, ("after Bédier"), and Menéndez Pidal, pl. IX. Cf. *Le Guide du Pèlerin de Saint-Jacques de Compostelle*, ed. and trans. Jeanne Vielliard, 3d ed. (Macon: Protat, 1963).

99. David Herlihy, "The Generation in Medieval History," *Viator* 5 (1974): 347–64.

100. Léon Gautier observed that *France* occurs 170 times in this poem in the meaning 'Charlemagne's Empire'; see Jenkins, note to v. 36.

101. Jones, p. 130 and n. 97.

102. John F. Benton, "Clio and Venus: An Historical View of Courtly Love," in *The Meaning of Courtly Love*, ed. F. X. Newman (Albany: State University of New York Press, 1968), p. 20. Common sense suggests, however, that the nobleman, who depended for his livelihood on the cooperation of his serfs, realized that harsh treatment would ultimately do more harm than good.

103. Horrent, p. 307; Payen, *Le Moyen Age*, pp. 31–32.

104. *History of the Crusades*, 1:135.

105. Ibid., 1:221.

106. Statistics for the period under consideration are not available, but the percentages were probably not very different from those provided here, which are based on figures for England in Sir Maurice Powicke, *The Thirteenth Century 1216–1307*, 2d ed., The Oxford History of England 4 (Oxford: Clarendon Press, 1962), pp. 445–46 (clerks), and Noel Denholm-Young, *History and Heraldry 1254 to 1310: A Study of the Historical Value of the Rolls of Arms* (Oxford: Clarendon Press, 1965), p. 1 (knights).

107. As early as the end of the fifth century, according to Zumthor, *Histoire littéraire*, p. 19.

108. Bloch, *Feudal Society*, 2:348.

109. Ibid., 2:346–47; Ganshof, *Feudalism*, p. 113.

110. Ganshof, pp. 116–17.

111. Zaal, *A lei francesa*, pp. 42–43.

112. *Bernard de Clairvaux*, Commission d'histoire de l'Ordre de Cîteaux 3 (Paris: Alsatia, 1953), pp. 687–88 ("Bernard et les écolès"). Cf., however, Abbot Guibert of Nogent, writing c. 1115:

> In the time just before my birth and during my childhood there was so great a dearth of teachers that it was practically impossible to find any in the small towns, and scarcely even in the cities. And supposing that by chance they were to be found? Their learning was so meagre that it could not be compared even with that of the little wandering scholars of today.

Text in Bloch, *Feudal Society*, 1:104; see also *Self and Society in Medieval France: The Memoirs of Abbot Guibert of Nogent (1064?–c. 1125)*, trans. C. C. Swinton Bland, revised by John F. Benton (New York and Evanston: Harper & Row, 1970), p. 45. A similar statement is found in Gargantua's letter to his son. François Rabelais, *Pantagruel*, ed. Verdun L. Saulnier, Textes littéraires français (Paris: Droz, 1946), chap. 8, pp. 43–44.

113. Grace Frank, *The Medieval French Drama* (Oxford: Clarendon Press, 1954), chaps. 2–7, pp. 18–73.

114. *Bernard de Clairvaux*, chap. 8, "L'essor économique de Clairvaux," pp. 95–114.

115. Brandt, *Medieval History*.

116. Ibid., p. 169.

117. Ibid., pp. 152–53, 171–72.

118. Paul Archambault, *Seven French Chroniclers: Witnesses to History* (Syracuse: Syracuse University Press, 1974), pp. 1–6, 119.

119. What follows is based upon Hippolyte Delehaye, *Les Légendes hagiographiques*, 4th ed., Subsidia Hagiographica 18a (1927; rpt. Brussels: Société des Bollandistes, 1955), and idem, *Les Passions des martyrs et les genres littéraires*, 2d ed., Subsidia Hagiographica 13 B (1921; rpt. Brussels: Sociéte des Bollandistes, 1966). Father Delehaye's views are accepted by René Aigrain, *L'Hagiographie, ses sources, ses méthodes, son histoire* (Paris: Bloud & Gay, 1953), the best guide available to the Old French scholar for whom Latin saints' lives constitute a terra incognita.

120. Delehaye, *Légendes hagiographiques*, pp. 49, 86–87.

121. Edmond Faral in Joseph Bédier and Paul Hazard, *Histoire de la littérature française illustrée* (Paris: Larousse, 1923), 1:7–8; Horrent, pp. 302–3; Delbouille, *Genèse*, pp. 137–38, 142; Riquer, *Chansons de geste*, p. 109; Zaal, *A lei francesa*, chaps. 2 and 3, pp. 45–136.

122. *Bernard de Clairvaux*, chap. 5, "Le monachisme à l'apparition de Bernard," pp. 45–63. For a list of early Cistercian abbeys, see app. 3, pp. 543–47.

123. This is the traditional figure. On the difficulty of ascertaining the exact number of monks and monasteries at this time, see *Bernard de Clairvaux*, p. 45.

124. For Cluniac establishments in northeastern Spain, the theater of events in most of Turoldus's poem, see Sholod, *Charlemagne in Spain*, p. 65.

125. L. M. Smith, *Cluny in the Eleventh and Twelfth Centuries* (London: Allan, 1930), p. 95, Latin text (Vos estis lux mundi) quoted in n. 2. The phrase, found in a charter granted to Cluny at Abbot Hugh's request by Pope Urban II in 1098, refers to Matthew 5:14.

126. Faral, *Jongleurs*, chap. 2, pp. 25–43.

127. Ibid., pp. 44–47. Faral also studies the relationship between these two genres and pilgrimages. According to Bowra, *Heroic Poetry*, p. 29, the composer of epic poetry "wishes not to instruct but to delight his audience." However, he concedes, p. 30, that the poet with a Christian outlook may also have a didactic purpose.

128. Bloch, *Feudal Society*, 2:412–20.

129. Cited by Bloch, 2:417. Cf. Proverbs 26:11; 2 Peter 2:22.

130. Ibid., 2:312–16.

131. Ibid., 2:316–18.

132. Bruce A. Rosenberg, *Custer and the Epic of Defeat* (University Park and London: Pennsylvania State University Press, 1974).

133. This kind of anecdote is also found in medieval French romances, e.g., *Le Roman de Thèbes*, ed. Guy Raynaud de Lage, Classiques français du moyen âge 96 (Paris: Champion, 1968), 2: vv. 6219–6224, 6241–6244; *Les Romans de Chrétien de Troyes*, vol. 1, *Erec et Enide*, ed. Mario Roques, Classiques français du moyen âge 80 (Paris: Champion, 1952), vv. 2355–2376, 6668–6670 (cf. the more elaborate description of Enide's dress in vv. 6674–6741). This paragraph and the next two are drawn from my article "Ganelon et Roland: Deux anecdotes du traître concernant le héros," *Romania* 92 (1971): 392–94.

134. Cf. Suetonius, an important model for Einhard. Halphen, pp. x–xiii.

135. Alice M. Colby, *The Portrait in Twelfth-Century French Literature: An Example of the Stylistic Originality of Chrétien de Troyes* (Geneva: Droz, 1965), p. 178.

136. Paul Zumthor, "Rhétorique et langage poétique dans le moyen âge roman," *Poetyka* [First International Conference of Work-in-Progress Devoted to Problems of Poetics, Warsaw, August 18–27, 1960] (Warsaw: Państwowe Wydawnictwo Naukowe; The Hague: Mouton, 1961), pp. 745–53; Zaal, *A lei francesa*, pp. 46, 89, 92–116. For useful distinctions between *culture cléricale* and *culture profane*, on the one

hand, and *culture aristocratique* and *culture populaire*, on the other, see Payen, *Le Moyen Age*, pp. 33–42.

137. Jenkins, notes to vv. 1470 and 1490 ff.; Bédier, *Commentaires*, p. 304 (see also Foulet, *Glossaire*, p. 354); Edmond Faral, *La Chanson de Roland: Etude et analyse*, Les chefs-d'oeuvre de la littérature expliqués (Paris: Mellottée, 1934), pp. 198, 199. Duggan, *Song of Roland*, pp. 139–40, treats the verses in question as an elaboration framed between two formulas (v. 1649, Siet el cheval; v. 1657, Beste nen est nule). Jean Györy, in his review of Raimund Rütten, *Symbol und Mythus im altfranzösischen Rolandslied*, Archiv für das Studium der neueren Sprachen und Literaturen 4 (Braunschweig: Westermann, 1970), in *Cahiers de civilisation médiévale* 16 (1974): 345, refers to: "le cheval de Turpin, décrit en ordre inversé, de bas en haut, pour marquer la provenance chtonienne de l'animal et en même temps son élan ascensionnel."

138. Jenkins, p. xxxviii; Menéndez Pidal, p. 375; Zaal, *A lei francesa*, p. 94.

139. Robert L. Politzer, "Synonymic Repetition in Late Latin and Romance," *Language* 37 (1961): 484–87.

140. Jones, *Ethos*, p. 9.

141. Ibid., p. 22.

142. Jones's initial statements relative to this word (pp. 22–23) are judicious enough, but he soon slips into categorical assertions concerning its special meaning and, when discussing semantically related terms, repeatedly suggests that *proz* always refers to courage and physical strength. See my review of Burgess, *Vocabulaire pré-courtois*, in *Speculum* 46 (1971): 363–64.

143. Proverbs are usually considered to be popular in origin and transmission, but many adages are found in classical sources or in collections such as the twenty-nine medieval French compilations analyzed in *Proverbes français antérieurs au XVe siècle*, ed. Joseph Morawski, Classiques français du moyen âge 47 (Paris: Champion, 1925). Maxims such as *Ki tant ne set ne l'ad prod entendut* (v. 2098) and *Mult ad apris ki bien conuist ahan* (v. 2524) have a learned flavor, whereas a phrase like *Plus qu'om ne lancet une verge pelee* (v. 3323) has a decidedly popular aspect.

144. Bloch, *Feudal Society*, 2:345–52. See note 91 above.

145. Horrent, p. 307: "Notre poète était un clerc [n. 2: Mais non un moine (voir O vv. 1880–1881)]," citing Fawtier. Cf., however, Jenkins, note to v. 1881: "Tavernier points out that this judgment necessarily implies no scorn of the monk, as such: each is useful, nay indispensable, in his own field." On clerical self-satire, see Philippe Ménard, *Le Rire et le sourire dans le roman courtois en France au moyen âge (1150–1250)*, Publications romanes et françaises 105 (Geneva: Droz, 1969), pp. 175–78. *Bernard de Clairvaux*, p. 263, n. 1:

> Nous ne confondons pas *clericus* et *canonicus*. Le *clericus* n'est pas nécessairement un *canonicus*. Mais dans le haut Moyen-Age, le terme de *clericus* était singulièrement ambigu. Saint Jérome avait proposé cette définition de l'étymologie du mot *kleros*: 'Les clercs sont appelés de ce mot parce qu'ils sont la part du Seigneur ou bien parce que le Seigneur est leur part' (*ep. ad Nepotianum*, PL. 22, 531). Définition assez imprécise, qui fut reprise par le Décret de Gratien (11[a], *causa* XII, qu. 1, c. 5 et 7) et qui autorise deux acceptions du mot *clericus*, l'une large, l'autre restreinte. Ainsi en matière favorable, c'est-à-dire quand il s'agissait de l'application des privilèges, tous les religieux, même les moniales et les frères convers étaient compris parmi les clercs. Parfois même le terme de *clerici* désignait des laïcs serviteurs de l'Eglise. C'est en ce sens qu'il faut comprendre une décision du concile de Tours en 567, prescrivant à l'archiprêtre de se faire accompagner d'un *canonicus* (clerc) ou au moins d'un *clericus* (serviteur laïc). En un sens plus restreint, en matière pénale, il fut reçu d'exclure du sens du mot clerc, les cardinaux, les évêques, les dignités et les chanoines des églises cathédrales. On n'était pas d'accord sur les chanoines des

églises collégiales. Les clercs qui accomplissaient des fonctions déterminées dans une église (et à cause de ces fonctions percevaient une part des revenus de l'église) portaient le nom de *clerici canonici*, soit qu'ils vécussent selon une règle (*kanón*) soit plutôt parce qu'inscrits sur la table ou liste (*kanón*) d'une église. Un peu plus tard, vers le VIIe siècle, interviendra la notion de vie commune, qui amènera la distinction, classique au XIe siècle, entre *canonici regulares* et *canonici seculares*, les premiers vivant dans des monastères *sub abbate*, les seconds dans des cathédrales ou collégiales (*in domo episcopali*) *sub episcopo*. Sur cette question voir *Dict. Dr. Canon*, éd. Letouzey, t. III (1942) et R. Naz. *Traité de Droit canonique*. Letouzey (1946), t. I. *passim*.

146. Oscar Bloch and Walther von Wartburg, *Dictionnaire étymologique de la langue française*, 4th ed. (Paris: Presses Universitaires de France, 1964), s.v. clerc.

147. Cf. Faral, *Jongleurs*, chap. 3, "Les jongleurs aux cours seigneuriales," pp. 93–102; chap. 4, "Les ménestrels," pp. 103–18; chap. 5, "Les revenus des jongleurs," pp. 119–27.

148. Felix Busigny, *Das Verhältnis der Chansons de geste zur Bible*, Inaugural-Dissertation (Basel: Reinhardt, 1917); Jenkins, pp. xlvi–xlvii; Adolphe J. Dickmann, *Le Rôle du surnaturel dans les chansons de geste* (Paris: Champion, 1926); Faral, *La Chanson de Roland*, pp. 186–95; Jessie Crosland, *The Old French Epic* (Oxford: Blackwell, 1951), p. 74. See also Bédier, *Commentaires*, p. 314; Riquer, *Chansons de geste*, pp. 109–10; Zaal, *A lei francesa*, pp. 130–34; Dufournet, *Cours sur Roland*, p. 28. According to Marie-Madeleine Davy, *Initiation à la symbolique romane (XIIe siècle)* (Paris: Flammarion, 1964), p. 121: "Les moines du XIIe siècle possèdent une parfaite connaissance de la Bible. Ils savent les textes par coeur et leur propre pensée est essentiellement biblique."

149. Jenkins, notes to vv. 3238 and 1215, respectively.

150. For discussion and bibliography, see my paper "Le Thème de la Mort," pp. 229–30, notes 20–23; Zaal, *A lei francesa*, pp. 117–19. See also COMMENTARY, 2 (Marsile's marble couch, and olive branches as a symbol of humility). Bédier, *Commentaires*, p. 314, notes the resemblance between Roland and Judas Maccabaeus. Riquer, *Chansons de geste*, p. 102, believes the image of the stag in vv. 1874–1875 is drawn from the Bible.

151. Faral, *La Chanson de Roland*, pp. 198–201; Jones, pp. 127, 182; Brault, "Le Thème de la Mort," p. 229.

152. Brault, pp. 230–35.

153. Wilhelm Tavernier, "Beiträge zur Rolandsforschung. I. Äneide, Pharsalia und Rolandsepos," *Zeitschrift für französische Sprache und Literatur* 36 (1910): 71–102; Jenkins, pp. xlvii–xlviii; Curtius, pp. 111, 245, 530 (but see, especially, Curtius's article "Zur Literarästhetik des Mittelalters," *Zeitschrift für romanische Philologie* 58 [1938]: 215–32). See also Bédier, *Commentaires*, pp. 316–17; Riquer, *Chansons de geste*, p. 108; Jones, pp. 130–34; Aebischer, *Préhistoire*, pp. 232–34; Dufournet, *Cours sur Roland*, pp. 27–28. Turoldus's contemporary, Saint Bernard, refers in his works to Boethius, Cicero, Horace, Juvenal, Ovid, Persius, Seneca, Statius, Tacitus, Terence, and Virgil. *Bernard de Clairvaux*, p. 479 and app. 4.

154. Virgil is mentioned by name in v. 2616.

155. See note 134 above.

156. See COMMENTARY, 21 and n. 6.

157. See INTRODUCTION 15, A; 19, B. Prudentius is not, strictly speaking, a classical author.

158. Bédier, *Commentaires*, pp. 316–17.

159. Cf. Jones, pp. 134–35, with reference to the *Waltharius*.

160. Delbouille, *Genèse*, p. 121. See COMMENTARY, 6.

161. For Curtius, see note 153 above; Riquer, *Chansons de geste*, pp. 102–5. See also Manfreid Gsteiger, "Note sur les préambules des chansons de geste," *Cahiers de civilisation médiévale* 2 (1959): 213–20; Zaal, *A lei francesa*, pp. 84, 91 Cf. Faral, *La Chanson de Roland*, p. 252: "La rhétorique ne tient ici aucune place."

162. Faral, *Jongleurs*, p. 59, n. 2. Payen, *Le Moyen Age*, p. 125, citing Legge and Duby, suggests that the chansons de geste were primarily intended for *bachelers*. On the latter, see COMMENTARY, 35, note 15.

163. In real life eleventh-century warriors were at times quite satisfied to win campaigns without fighting a single battle. Smail, *Crusading Warfare*, pp. 140–56.

164. Horrent, p. 307. Composing a chanson de geste for different audiences was not unlike preparing a sermon to be preached to the educated at the same time as to the unlettered. On the latter art, see Guibert of Nogent, *Liber quo ordine sermo fieri debeat* (*PL*, 156, cols. 11–21), English translation in *Readings in Medieval Rhetoric*, p. 170.

165. See INTRODUCTION, 5. See also note 127 above.

166. Rychner, p. 14. Payen, *Le Moyen Age*, p. 125, agrees, but cautions against going so far as to term the chansons de geste "popular" literature. See also pp. 38, 126.

167. Smail, *Crusading Warfare*, pp. 166–67, warns historians against using literature as a source of realistic accounts of battles. Poetry, he notes, strives to be vivid and endeavors to make clear what is essentially a confused picture. See also Stephen G. Nichols, Jr., "Historical Illusion and Poetic Reality in the 'Chansons de geste'," *French Review* 43 (1969): 23–33; Payen, *Le Moyen Age*, pp. 61–62. Bowra, *Heroic Poetry*, pp. 476–507, distinguishes three main types of heroic poetry: primitive, proletarian, and aristocratic. The latter two types are characteristic of a society that has a cultured, lettered class. More refined aristocratic poetry exists only where the ruling class shares the interests and outlook of the ruled (pp. 478–79). He considers the *Song of Roland* to be in the latter category (p. 478). Chap. 4, pp. 132–78, is a useful study of "The Realistic Background."

168. Jenkins, p. xxxv, citing Baist, on the organization of Charlemagne's army and trial by combat. For possible verbal archaisms, see Delbouille, *Genèse*, pp. 127–29, 133–34, 149–50. Cf. COMMENTARY, 1, note 2. René Louis, "La grande douleur pour la mort de Roland," *Cahiers de civilisation médiévale* 3 (1960): 67, n. 20, referring to Lot, dismisses the possibility of deliberate archaism in the poet's designation of the boundaries of France. Cf. Guy Raynaud de Lage, "Les romans antiques et la représentation de l'Antiquité," *Le Moyen Age* 68 (1961): 247–91; Raymond J. Cormier, "The Problem of Anachronism: Recent Scholarship on the French Medieval Romances of Antiquity," *Philological Quarterly* 53 (1974): 145–57. On epic distortion of reality, see Eugene Vance, *Reading the Song of Roland*, Landmarks in Literature (Englewood Cliffs, N.J.: Prentice-Hall, 1970), pp. 19–20. Cf. Frye, *Anatomy of Criticism*, p. 127: "it is of the essence of imaginative culture that it transcends the limits both of the naturally possible and of the morally acceptable."

169. *Saint Augustine: On Christian Doctrine*, trans. D. W. Robertson, Jr., Library of Liberal Arts 80 (New York: Liberal Arts Press: 1958), p. 38 (2.6.8); Robertson, *Preface to Chaucer*, pp. 53–54.

170. Le Gentil, p. 120: "Ce serait une erreur de s'appuyer sur une logique trop positive pour contester telle ou telle de ses décisions, pour parler ici ou là d'accidents, de déficiences ou d'interpolations."

171. For discussion and bibliography, see Réau, I, 2: chap. 4; Frye, pp. 141–50 (see also p. 359, note to p. 141, line 21); Robertson, *Preface to Chaucer*, pp. 286–317; Vos, "Aspects of Biblical Typology," chap. 1, pp. 1–25. Working independently of each other, Prof. Vos and I have on occasion used a similar approach but reached different conclusions. See my "Quelques nouvelles tendances," p. 24, n. 29.

172. Réau, II, 1:244.

173. On the Eva-Ave connection, see Pierre Jonin, *Les Personnages féminins dans les romans français de Tristan au XIIe siècle: Etude des influences contemporaines*, Publication des Annales de la Faculté des lettres, Aix-en-Provence, n.s. 22 (Gap: Ophrys, 1958), pp. 444–45. Jonin cites examples in Peter Damian (d. 1072) and Wace, and notes that the association may date back to the eighth century.

174. Percy Ernst Schramm, *Sphaira, Globus, Reichsapfel: Wanderung und Wandlung eines Herrschaftszeichens von Caesar bis zu Elisabeth II; ein Beitrag zum 'Nachleben' der Antike* (Stuttgart: Hiersemann, 1958), pp. 72–73; pls. 28c, 46.

175. Réau, I:197; II, 1:83; II, 2:82.

176. Ibid., I:62; Robertson, *Preface to Chaucer*, p. 293.

177. Réau, I:63.

178. Robertson, *Preface to Chaucer*, p. 315. On these terms, see D. W. Robertson, Jr., "Some Medieval Literary Terminology, with Special Reference to Chrétien de Troyes," *Studies in Philology* 48 (1951): 669–92; F. Douglas Kelly, *Sens and Conjointure in the Chevalier de la Charrette*, Studies in French Litterature 2 (The Hague and Paris: Mouton, 1966). On the importance of exegesis in medieval education, see Payen, *Le Moyen Age*, pp. 44–45.

179. Réau, I:62. Honorius was born c. 1080 and was a native of Regensburg in Bavaria, not Autun, as Réau suggests. Le Goff, *Civilisation*, p. 602. The concept was used metaphorically by Chrétien de Troyes in the *Chevalier de la Charrette* and in *Yvain*; see Gerard J. Brault, "Chrétien de Troyes' *Lancelot*: The Eye and the Heart," *Bibliographical Bulletin of the International Arthurian Society* 24 (1972): 145, n. 4. For Rabelais's satirical use of the notion, see François Rabelais, *Gargantua*, ed. M. A. Screech, Textes littéraires français 163 (Geneva: Droz; Paris: Minard, 1970), Prologue, pp. 12–13.

180. See Morton W. Bloomfield's review of Judson B. Allen, *The Friar as Critic: Literary Attitudes in the Later Middle Ages* (Nashville: Vanderbilt University Press, 1971), in *Speculum* 48 (1973): 329–30, citing Anthony Nemetz, "Literalness and the *Sensus Litteralis*," *Speculum* 34 (1959): 76–89.

181. Curtius, p. 48 (bibliography in n. 1); Robertson, *Preface to Chaucer*, pp. 340–41.

182. Robertson, p. 340.

183. A. Leigh Deneef, "Robertson and His Critics," *Chaucer Review* 2 (1968): 205–34.

184. The expression is Robertson's (*Preface to Chaucer*, p. 92, n. 67), indicating that he has modified certain views he once held.

185. Robertson's interpretation of the *Song of Roland* is in *Preface to Chaucer*, pp. 163–71. For Bernard F. Huppé's views, see note 64 above. At the Fifth International Congress of the Société Rencesvals held at Oxford in 1970, Larry S. Crist and I presented convergent views of the *Song of Roland*. However, my colleague declared himself to be a far more orthodox Robertsonian than I. For Crist's paper, see note 60 above. My paper, "*Sapientia* dans la *Chanson de Roland*," was published in *French Forum* 1 (1976): 99–118. I do not know what prompts Burgess, *Vocabulaire pré-courtois*, p. 13, to assert that "la notion de *sen* était étrangère au poète de la *Chanson de Roland*."

186. Curtius, pp. 248 ff.; Frye, *Anatomy of Criticism*, pp. 89–91; Theodore Silverstein, "Allegory and Literary Form," *PMLA* 82 (1967): 28–32; Paul E. Beichner, "The Allegorical Interpretation of Medieval Literature," *PMLA* 82 (1967): 33–38.

187. Robertson, pp. 297–98.

188. *Historia Karoli Magni et Rotholandi ou Chronique du Pseudo-Turpin*, ed. C. Meredith-Jones (1936; rpt. Geneva: Slatkine, 1972), pp. 71–75 (1130); Horrent, pp. 87–94 (1145–65); Mandach, *Naissance*, 1:56–58, 149 (1125–1130); Frappier, *Chansons de geste*, 2 (1965): 124, note (1125–30). Meredith-Jones, p. 81, does not believe

the author visited Spain. Mandach's elaborate theory concerning the early evolution of the Latin text, presented in *Naissance*, vol. 1, is conveniently summarized in vol. 2, *Chronique de Turpin: Texte anglo-normand de Willem de Briane* (*Arundel 220*), Publications romanes et françaises 77 (Geneva: Droz, 1963), pp. 13–14. The German scholar Adalbert Hämel devoted twenty-three years to the study of the *Pseudo-Turpin*. His edition of that work was published posthumously: *Der Pseudo-Turpin von Compostela*, eds. Adalbert Hämel and André de Mandach, Bayerische Akademie der Wissenschaften, Philosophisch-Historische Klasse, Sitzungsberichte, Jahrgang 1965, Heft 1 (Munich: Beck, 1965).

189. Meredith-Jones, p. 111. On the cult of Saint Facundus (> Sahagún) and Saint Primitivus martyred near this city, see Meredith-Jones, pp. 295–96; Réau, III, 1:485; Vielliard, pp. 6–9, 83, and nn. 1, 2.

190. Meredith-Jones, p. 119 (see also note, p. 300). Cf. the miracle of the red crosses, which appear on the shoulders of the knights in Charles's army who are to die the following day (pp. 146–47; see also note, p. 300).

191. Blaise, par. 484. Cf. the flowering staff associated with Saint Christopher (Réau, III, 1:305, 309) and the attributes of Aaron (Réau, II, 1:188–89) and Saint Joseph (Réau, III, 2:757).

192. See INTRODUCTION, 19, D. Turoldus uses *espiet* 'spear' and *lance* 'lance' interchangeably, although only the former is thrown (Foulet, *Glossaire*, s.v. espiet); cf. *hanste* (< Lat. *hasta* 'lance') 'handle [of the spear]'.

193. Brault, "Le Thème de la Mort," p. 236; see also COMMENTARY, 27, for the observation concerning the relic of the Holy Lance in Joyeuse (vv. 2503–2508).

194. Cf. the further extension constituted by the motif of Marsile's right hand and Ganelon being torn limb from limb, COMMENTARY, 21 (v. 1903) and 47.

195. Meredith-Jones, pp. 111, 113.

196. See also INTRODUCTION, 11, D.

197. Meredith-Jones, p. 113.

198. See also Isaiah 11:5. Blaise, par. 441; *Psychomachia*, v. 52 (*Prudentius*, ed. and trans. H. J. Thomson, The Loeb Classical Library, 2 vols. [1949; rpt. Cambridge: Harvard University Press; London: Heinemann, 1962], 1:274–343); Delehaye, *Les Passions des martyrs*, p. 154; Robertson, *Preface to Chaucer*, p. 175, n. 1, citing Alain de Lille.

199. Rychner, pp. 128, 132–33.

200. Adolf Katzenellenbogen, *Allegories of the Virtues and Vices in Mediaeval Art From Early Christian Times to the Thirteenth Century*, trans. Alan J. P. Crick (1939; rpt. New York: Norton, 1964), chaps. 1 and 2.

201. Meredith-Jones, p. 113.

202. Blaise, par. 462.

203. Meredith-Jones, p. 135. In devotional tracts the enemy of Fortitude is often not Fear, but Sloth (Accidia), the virtue representing not physical strength and force, but a nobler quality. Tuve, *Allegorical Imagery*, pp. 84, 97, 133, et passim.

204. In his Anglo-Norman translation Willem de Briane substitutes another passage from Scripture; see Mandach, *Naissance*, 2:39 (text on p. 64, lines 478–79).

205. Meredith-Jones, p. 143.

206. Ibid., p. 143.

207. Ibid., p. 145.

208. Ibid., p. 145. Cf. the commentary on the Christian warriors who fornicated with Saracen women, p. 185.

209. Ibid., p. 195.

210. Brault, "Le Thème de la Mort," p. 230, n. 21; COMMENTARY, 7, note 36; COMMENTARY, 8.

211. See, for example, INTRODUCTION, 10, B, 1; Robert A. Pratt, "The Old French Sources of the Nonnes Preestes Tale (Part II)," *Speculum* 47 (1972): 653–54, 661–62; Marianne Cramer Vos, "Ganelon's 'Mortal Rage'," *Olifant* 2, no. 1 (1974): 21. It is pointless, therefore, to deny the Ganelon-Judas connection as do, for instance, Tavernier (see Vos, p. 21, n. 20) and John A. Stranges, "The Character and the Trial of Ganelon: A New Appraisal," *Romania* 96 (1975): 354–56.

212. *Das Rolandslied des Pfaffen Konrad*, ed. Carl Wesle, 2d ed., Altdeutsche Textbibliothek 69 (Tübingen: Niemeyer, 1967). On the date, see Lejeune and Stiennon, 1:111–19; André de Mandach, "Encore du nouveau à propos de la date et de la structure de la *Chanson de Roland* allemande," *Société Rencesvals. IVe Congrès International*, pp. 106–16. For a summary of the published findings concerning Conrad's use of the *Pseudo-Turpin*, see Mandach, pp. 108–12, 116.

213. *Fig. 43*. Lejeune and Stiennon, 1:124–25; 2: fig. 96 (the illustration shows a stylized olive tree). Lejeune and Stiennon, 1:124, asserts that the scene in Conrad takes place after the plotters have arrived at Marsile's court. I find no textual basis for situating this daylong stop (v. 1982: Si wonten da allen einen tach) at Saragossa. The arrangement of the figures in this illustration is not without a certain ironic parallel with the formula of Jesus among the Doctors (Réau, II, 2:289–91). One might even consider it to be an extension of the possible parody of the Journey of the Magi in the preceding drawing (Lejeune and Stiennon, 2: fig. 95; discussion in 1:124, with no reference, however, to the Wise Men formula; on the latter, see Gabriel Millet, *Recherches sur l'iconographie de l'évangile aux XIVe et XVIe siècles d'après les monuments de Mistra, de la Macédoine et du Mont-Athos* [1916; rpt. Paris: Boccard, 1960], figs. 36, 37, 38, 39, 67, 85, 86, 87, 95, 100, 101; Gérard Cames, *Byzance et la peinture romane de Germanie: Apports de l'art grec posticonoclaste à l'enluminure et à la fresque ottoniennes et romanes de Germanie dans les thèmes de majesté et les évangiles* [Paris: Picard, 1966], index, p. 319, s.v. Mages (cycle des), se rendent à cheval à Bethléem; idem, *Allégories et symboles dans l'Hortus deliciarum* [Leiden: Brill, 1971], pl. LXXVII).

214. On the concept of "poor" Judas, see Wayland D. Hand, *A Dictionary of Words and Idioms Associated with Judas Iscariot: A Compilation Based Mainly on Material Found in the Germanic Languages*, University of California Publications in Modern Philology 24, no. 3 (Berkeley and Los Angeles: University of California Press, 1942), pp. 303–4.

215. Matthew 7:16–18; cf. 12:33–37. Cf. also the "whited sepulchre" metaphor in Matthew 23:27–28; and the cup, clean outside, but filthy within, in Matthew 23:25. Locke, *Quest*, p. 106, nn. 20, 21. See also COMMENTARY, 12 and 17.

216. On companionage, see William A. Stowell, "Personal Relationships in Medieval France," *PMLA* 28 (1913): 388–416; Bloch, *Feudal Society*, 1:154, 155, 169, 173, 236; Jones, pp. 114, 143.

217. Similarly, in the *Pseudo-Turpin*, Roland fights the giant Ferracutus, who is said to be *de genere Goliath* (Meredith-Jones, p. 147). The David-Goliath aspect of the Pinabel-Thierry duel is noted by Jenkins, p. xxxii.

218. The lines between chronicle, epic, and saint's life are not clearly drawn at this time. See INTRODUCTION, 2.

219. Gerard J. Brault, "Heraldic Terminology and Legendary Material in the *Siege of Caerlaverock* (c. 1300)," in *Romance Studies in Memory of Edward Billings Ham*, ed. Urban T. Holmes, Jr., California State College Publications 2 (Hayward: California State College, 1967), pp. 15–16.

220. See INTRODUCTION, 9. The tendency in the *Pseudo-Turpin* and the *Rolandslied* to explain symbols and clarify mysteries found in Turoldus's poem may be characterized as Gothic. See Eleanor Roach, "Les termes 'roman' et 'gothique' dans le domaine littéraire: Essai de définition," *Les Lettres Romanes* 29 (1975): 63. The *Pseudo-Turpin* and Conrad's adaptation are frequently viewed as distortions of the French

original; see, for example, Helmut A. Hatzfeld, "Le *Rolandslied* allemand: Guide pour la compréhension stylistique de la *Chanson de Roland*," *Cultura Neolatina* 21 (1961): 48–56. The Latin and German versions may well be inferior to the French epic, yet each deserves to be judged on its own terms.

221. See Karl-Heinz Bender, "La genèse de l'image littéraire de Charlemagne élu de Dieu au XIe siècle," *Boletín de la Real Academia de Buenas Letras de Barcelona* 31 (1965/66): 35–39; Dufournet, *Cours sur Roland*, pp. 183–85. See also Campbell, *Hero*, pt. 2, chap. 3, 6, "The Hero as World Redeemer," pp. 349–54.

222. Bédier, *Légendes épiques*, 2d ed. (1921), 4:456; Boissonnade, *Du Nouveau*, pp. 265, 281–85; *History of the Crusades*, 1:241; and, especially, Ernst R. Kantorowicz, *The King's Two Bodies: A Study in Mediaeval Political Theology* (Princeton: Princeton University Press, 1957), chap. 3, "Christ-Centered Kingship," pp. 42–86; chap. 5, par. 3, "Pro patria mori," pp. 232–72. Cf. Menéndez Pidal, pp. 241–62; R. Foreville, "La typologie du roi dans la littérature historiographique anglo-normande aux XIe et XIIe siècles," *Etudes de civilisation médiévale (IXe–XIIe siècles): Mélanges offerts à Edmond-René Labande* (Poitiers: Centre d'études supérieures de civilisation médiévale, 1974), pp. 275–92; Le Goff, *Civilisation*, p. 183.

223. Kantorowicz, p. 48, n. 11 (translation mine); Cames, *Byzance*, p. 40, n. 69.

224. Cames, p. 40. See also Kantorowicz, pp. 61–78.

225. For fuller details, see Eugene F. Rice, *The Renaissance Idea of Wisdom*, Harvard Historical Monographs 37 (Cambridge: Harvard University Press, 1958), chap. 1, "The Medieval Idea of Wisdom," pp. 1–29; Paul Archambault, "Commynes' *saigesse* and the Renaissance Idea of Wisdom," *Bibliothèque d'Humanisme et Renaissance* 29 (1967): 613–32; Morton W. Bloomfield, "Understanding Old English Poetry," *Annuale Medievale (Duquesne Studies)* 9 (1968): 5–25. On the related notion of *contemptus mundi*, see Payen, *Le Moyen Age*, pp. 70–71.

226. *E l'arcevesque, ki fut sages e proz* (v. 3691).

227. Faral, *La Chanson de Roland*, pp. 245–46. INTRODUCTION, 19, E, F, I, K. For the figure of a Carolingian king in the traditional guise of Sapientia enthroned in the New Jerusalem (as in the conclusion of the *Psychomachia*), see Paul Lacroix, *France in the Middle Ages: Customs, Classes and Conditions* (New York: Ungar, 1963), p. 349, fig. 298.

228. Meredith-Jones, pp. 221–29; Réau, I:154–62; Curtius, pp. 47–50; Katzenellenbogen, *Allegories*, index, p. 96, s.v. Arts, the seven liberal. See also INTRODUCTION, 10.

229. See COMMENTARY, 11, 27, and 34. Cf. Bédier, *Légendes épiques* 3:443 (referring to Roland): "comme il convient à un martyr, sa Passion est à la fois toute souffrance et toute joie." The notion of Joy in the Midst of Suffering is found in the Beatitudes; see Matthew 5:11–12. Cf. 1 Colossians 24. Cf. Joy in the Midst of Desolation (COMMENTARY, 3) and vice versa (INTRODUCTION, 16, A, 1). The meaning of *Monjoie* in the *Song of Roland* is a much-debated question; for bibliography, see COMMENTARY, 14, note 75.

230. See INTRODUCTION, 15, E. For a similar view, see Vos, "Aspects of Biblical Typology," p. 89.

231. Brault, "Le Thème de la Mort," pp. 229–35. For Charles as a Christ symbol, see William Wistar Comfort, "The Character Types in the Old French *Chansons de geste*," *PMLA* 21 (1906): 338; Erich Auerbach, *Mimesis: The Representation of Reality in Western Literature*, trans. Willard R. Trask (Princeton: Princeton University Press, 1953), p. 101. The word martyr means 'witness' (in the New Testament, Gr. *martus* 'witness of God'; Bloch and Wartburg, *Dictionnaire*, s.v. martyr), that is, one who confesses his faith. According to Christian belief, this type of confession is superior to merely unburdening one's sins to a priest or to God; Blaise, par. 109.

232. *Guernes de Pont-Sainte-Maxence, La Vie de Saint Thomas Becket*, ed. Emmanuel Walberg, Classiques français du moyen âge 77 (Paris: Champion, 1964), introduction. Cf. Le Gentil, p. 131:

> entre Oliver et Roland il y a toute la différence qui sépare le juste du saint. L'un proportionne ses actes aux simples exigences du devoir et ne voit dans l'excès que folie et orgueil; l'autre se croit toujours en deça de ce que Dieu demande ou espère. Olivier sera sauvé. Mais au ciel, plus encore que parmi les Francs de France, il cédera la première place à Roland. Peut-il même prétendre à la seconde?

233. Meredith-Jones, p. 111. The building metaphor appears in 1 Corinthians 3:9–15. Cf. COMMENTARY, 25 (the construction of churches helps save Charles's soul). In the *Pseudo-Turpin* Roland dies, his arms crossed over his breast in a very explicit *imitatio Christi* (Meredith-Jones, p. 205). For illustrations of the hero in this attitude, see Lejeune and Stiennon, 1: pls. L, LX; 2: figs. 288, 293, 508. See also COMMENTARY, 26, note 11. In the Latin chronicle Saint Denis appears in a vision to Charles and informs him that those who died or are about to die in Spain for the Emperor's edification (Meredith-Jones, p. 219: Illis qui tua ammonitione et exemplo tuae probitatis animati in bellis Sarracenorum in Hyspania mortui et morituri sunt) will be absolved from all sin.

234. Meredith-Jones, p. 183.

235. This passage from John 12:24 is quoted in Conrad, vv. 7885–7888. For the *Pseudo-Turpin*, see INTRODUCTION, 10, A, 2.

236. Delehaye, *Les Passions des martyrs*, pp. 213–18. Cf. also the destruction of the idols in vv. 2585–2591 and Delehaye, pp. 215–16.

237. Matthew 7:13–14. The affection and admiration with which Roland's men view their protector precludes conceiving of him as a kind of Ishmael.

238. Mickel, "Parallels in *Psychomachia* and *Roland*," pp. 451–52. See also INTRODUCTION, 15, A; COMMENTARY, 49.

239. The term formula, as used by art historians, means a conventionalized depiction, and should not be confused with the word referring to a basic element of oral poetic tradition. On the various problems discussed in this section, see F. P. Pickering, *Literature and Art in the Middle Ages* (Coral Gables: University of Miami Press, 1970).

240. Lejeune and Stiennon, 1:405.

241. Jenkins, note to v. 2384. See, however, OXFORD TEXT, ENGLISH TRANSLATION, v. 2384.

242. Cited by Jenkins, note to v. 2384.

243. For other Romanesque examples, see Cames, *Byzance*, figs. 1–9.

244. See Robertson, *Preface to Chaucer*, p. 145; Cames, p. 326, index, s.v. Transposition de schémas. On the use of formulas in Christian iconography, see Réau, I, 1: chap. 2, "L'Héritage de l'Orient, de la Grèce et de Rome," pp. 42–57.

245. Réau, II, 2:364 (Wedding at Cana); 411–12 (Last Supper). For the earliest depictions of the Last Supper, see Millet, *Recherches*, Livre III, chap. 1, "La Cène," pp. 286–309. On the influence of Byzantine formulas in Western Europe, see Otto Demus, *Byzantine Art and the West*, The Wrightsman Lectures 3 (New York: New York University Press, 1970).

246. The council scenes in the *Song of Roland* have been studied in the light of the Bayeux Tapestry by Angela Nuccitelli in an unpublished paper entitled "Structural Devices: The Question of Analogues" read at the Conference on Medieval Studies held at Western Michigan University in 1973 (summary in *Olifant* 1, no. 1, [1973]: 38–39).

247. *Roland*, vv. 2402–2410. COMMENTARY, 27.

248. Faral, *La Chanson de Roland*, pp. 198–201; Jones, pp. 127, 182.

249. For another example of transposition (suffering in God's / the King's name), see COMMENTARY, 13.

250. Lejeune and Stiennon, 2: figs. 102 and 104.

251. On this formula, see Réau, II, 2:418–19. In the Riha Paten the Apostles are crowded together because of the circular frame. On this process, see Réau, I:292–93. The normal alignment is found in the late-sixth-century Rossano Gospels and in an eleventh-century mosaic in the apse of the Cathedral of Hagia Sophia at Kiev. Réau, II, 2:418. In the Rossano Gospels the Communion of the Apostles appears on pages which do not face each other. See my paper "Les dessins du *Ruolantes Liet* et l'interprétation de la *Chanson de Roland*," in the proceedings of the Seventh International Congress of the Société Rencesvals held at Liège in 1976. On synoptic scenes in medieval art, see INTRODUCTION, 18, B.

252. Lejeune and Stiennon, 1:209–14. On the date of the manuscript, see Segre, p. xxxviii.

253. Lejeune and Stiennon, 2: figs. 159 and 160.

254. Richard Offner, *A Critical and Historical Corpus of Florentine Painting*, vol. 5, section 3 (New York: Institute of Fine Arts, New York University, 1947), pp. 243–50; Réau, II, 2:621–26. I am indebted to Mrs. Edith W. Kirsch of the Index of Christian Art, Princeton University, for bibliographical assistance in this respect.

255. See also COMMENTARY, 2 (v. 73), 4 (vv. 196–213), 14 (v. 1163), 23 (v. 2250), 25 (v. 2303), and 46 (v. 3943).

256. Lejeune and Stiennon, 1: pl. II; 2: figs. 344, 368.

257. See COMMENTARY, 22, note 29; 26, note 55.

258. In a discussion of the famous "Communion du chevalier" sculpture at Reims (*see Fig. 28*; Lejeune and Stiennon, 2: fig. 158), Lejeune and Stiennon, 1:203–6, suggests that the armor worn by the personage on the extreme right in the latter composition is "de genre oriental." One might perhaps say the same for the kneeling individual in 2: fig. 159. Cf., however, Roland in 2: fig. 161. The armor in question would appear to be Roman, not Oriental style. See Charles A. Knudson, "La brogne," *Mélanges Rita Lejeune*, 2:1633, citing Schultz:

> Pour ce qui est de la tunique revêtue de lamelles de métal, elle était courante parmi les Romains (*lorica squamata*) et si souvent représentée dans la sculpture que la tradition en est restée dans les arts plastiques du moyen âge jusqu'à une époque où il semble bien qu'elle ne correspondait plus à la réalité. Ainsi, dans les sculptures de la cathédrale de Reims, non loin de chevaliers dont l'armure est représentée de façon à indiquer clairement la cotte de mailles, comme le 'chevalier communiant' bien connu, on trouve un autre chevalier apparemment armé 'à l'antique'.

On the "Communion du chevalier," see note 274 below, and INTRODUCTION, 19, E.

259. This section is based on my article "Structure et sens de la *Chanson de Roland*," *French Review* 45, special issue no. 3 (1971): 1–12.

260. See note 17 above.

261. Rychner, pp. 38–39. For other outlines, see Brault, "Structure et sens," pp. 3–5; see also INTRODUCTION, 18, A and C.

262. Oxford, Bodleian Library, MS. University College 165, fol. 41. Otto Pächt, *The Rise of Pictorial Narrative in Twelfth-Century England* (Oxford: Clarendon Press, 1962), p. 14 and pl. I, fig. 3: "The outstanding characteristic of the Cuthbert illustrations is their dichotomy: each picture comprises, as a rule, two episodes or incidents of the same story." Further discussion, pp. 14–20. Cf. Gaston Paris's observation that each laisse often constitutes "un petit tableau ou une scène à part" cited by Jenkins, p. xxxiv. Similar remarks in Mandach, *Naissance*, 1:155, citing Rychner; Burgess, *Vocabulaire pré-courtois*, p. 15; Eugene Vinaver, *The Rise of Romance* (New York and Oxford: Oxford University Press, 1971), pp. 4–6.

263. Pächt, pp. 14–16:

> in the first episode we may see the Saint making a prophecy and in the second how this prophecy is fulfilled. . . . The miniatures of the Cuthbert Life are not

> composed by setting two consecutive moments merely side by side; they are more closely knit. . . . The figure of the Saint is not repeated, the two moments overlap and merge in him; and because the whole story hinges on him, we feel that it is through him, through his saintliness, that the situation is transformed. . . . The emphasis lies not on gradual transition from one phase of an event to the next, but on abrupt change, revealing the intervention of supernatural powers.

In the *Roland* the same character (Blancandrin, then Ganelon, at the beginning of the epic; and, especially, Charlemagne at Roncevaux and until the end of the poem) appears in consecutive scenes, relating various actions to one another.

264. For another interpretation of this dream, see COMMENTARY, 10.

265. The conclusion refers the audience back to the beginning of the poem, suggesting that a ring structure is also involved here. COMMENTARY, 49.

266. *Roland*, v. 2. The seven-year perspective, which opens the poem, is reiterated in vv. 197, 266, 2610, and 2736, and alluded to in the locution *al premer an*, v. 2613. For a different calculation also resulting in a seven-day chronology, see Roberta A. Kunkle, "Time in the *Song of Roland*," *Romance Notes* 13 (1972): 550–55. On number seven in the *Song of Roland*, see COMMENTARY, 1.

267. An unspecified amount of time elapses between Charles's departure from Saragossa (v. 3682) and his arrival at Aix (vv. 3695–3699, 3705–3706); the summoning of the Emperor's judges (vv. 3700–3703, 3743–3744) supposes further delay. The trial of Ganelon takes place on the 31st of December (v. 3746). See COMMENTARY, 44.

268. The most elaborate study is by Hermann Gräf, *Der Parallelismus im Rolandslied*, Inaugural-Dissertation (Wertheim-am-Main: Bechstein, 1931). Horrent, p. 244 (bibliography, p. 269), refers to: "Le parallélisme, essence même de l'art du poète." Karl D. Uitti, *Story, Myth, and Celebration in Old French Narrative Poetry, 1050–1200* (Princeton: Princeton University Press, 1973), studies the *Song of Roland* in terms of epic binarism. See Larry S. Crist's critique in *Olifant* 1, no. 3 (1974): 23–29. The contrast is usually between Good and Evil (INTRODUCTION, 14, A). However, in the case of Roland and Oliver, this obviously requires qualification. For parallelism in the *Pseudo-Turpin*, see Mandach, *Naissance*, 1:77–78; in Conrad, see note 426 below.

269. Bédier, *Légendes épiques*, 3:412.

270. See, for example, INTRODUCTION, 15, D.

271. Hermann Leisinger, *Romanische Bronzen: Kirchentüren im mittelalterlichen Europa* (Zurich: Europa, 1956), pp. [iv, x] and pls. 12–35. I have deliberately used the neutral terms Plot A and Plot B because it is to no purpose to try to determine which of the two is the main plot. The outline I propose was in part suggested by Eugene Dorfman, *The Narreme in the Medieval Romance Epic: An Introduction to Narrative Structures*, University of Toronto Romance Series 13 (Toronto: University of Toronto Press, 1969). Dorfman's structure (p. 127) is as follows:

I. The Autonomous Core System
- 1/The family quarrel, between Roland and Ganelon.
- 2/The insult, Roland mocks and laughs at Ganelon.
- 3/The act of treachery, Ganelon arranges a Saracen ambush.
- 4/The initial punishment, Ganelon is beaten, chained, and held for trial.

II. Expansion: The Epilogue
- a/The king's council, the assemblage of the peers as judges.
- b/The judicial duel, Roland's champion as proxy.
- c/The final judgment, the execution of the traitor.

See my review of Dorfman's book in *General Linguistics* 10 (1970): 62–67.

272. Marcel Viller, S.J., "Abraham," in *Dictionnaire de spiritualité ascétique et mystique, doctrine et histoire*, ed. Marcel Viller, S.J. (Paris: Beauchesne, 1937–), 1:110; Réau, II, 1:125–38.

273. Genesis 22:10, 12.

274. According to the Preface of Prudentius's *Psychomachia*, the story of Abraham teaches us that when a man would make a sacrifice pleasing to God, he must first overcome "the monsters in the enslaved heart" (v. 14); Isaac was conceived only after the Patriarch had fought and defeated the four great kings and had been blessed by Melchizedek (vv. 15–49); Abraham's example must serve as "a model for our life" and shows that "we must watch in the armour of faithful hearts, and that every part of our body which is in captivity and enslaved to foul desire must be set free by gathering our forces at home" (vv. 50–55); only then will Christ "enter the humble abode of the pure heart" (v. 62). Cf. INTRODUCTION 11, E; 12; 15, A and E; 19, B and E. Early depictions of the meeting of Abraham and Melchizedek show the former still wearing the armor he put on to fight the four kings; *see Fig. 56*; Réau, II, 1:129 (including the "Communion du chevalier" at Reims [*see Fig. 28* and note 258 above]); *Medieval England*, rev. and ed. Austin Lane Poole, 2 vols. (Oxford: Clarendon Press, 1958), 2:501 and pl. 102, fig. a. For Roland as an Abraham figure, see Lejeune and Stiennon, 1:411.

275. A number of isolated themes other than those listed here are mentioned in the Commentary. My purpose here is to discuss those that have special reference to the poem's structure and central meaning.

276. Réau, I:175–84; II, 1:401–6; II, 1:258–59; III, 2:571–79; Robert Will, *Alsace romane*, La nuit des temps 22 (La Pierre-qui-vire: Les Presses monastiques, 1965), pp. 262–63; Lejeune and Stiennon, 1:27, 72.

277. Gérard de Champeaux and Dom Sébastien Sterckx, O.S.B., *Introduction au monde des symboles*, La nuit des temps 3 (La Pierre-qui-vire: Les Presses monastiques, 1966), pp. 276–79, 297; René Crozet, "Le chasseur et le combattant dans la sculpture romane en Saintonge," *Mélanges Rita Lejeune*, 1:669–77.

278. Lejeune and Stiennon, 1:23.

279. Ibid., 1: chaps. 3, 6, 9; p. 401.

280. Réau, II, 1:412.

281. Ibid., II, 1:401–6. On the imagery of the *Ordo commendationis animae*, frequently cited in connection with the dying prayers of the heroes of the *Song of Roland* (Jenkins, note to v. 2384; cf. also "la prière du plus grand péril," Frappier, *Chansons de geste*, 2:131–40), see Réau, II, 1:402, 412.

282. Lejeune and Stiennon, 1:38. See also COMMENTARY, 19, and note 6; COMMENTARY, 21.

283. Ibid., 1:20–22. On the motif depicting the struggle between two old men, see COMMENTARY, 42, n. 1.

284. Lejeune and Stiennon, 1:88; cf. 1:22, 74; COMMENTARY, 12, note 2.

285. Jean Frappier, "Le thème de la lumière de la 'Chanson de Roland' au 'Roman de la Rose'," *Cahiers de l'Association internationale des études françaises* 20 (1968): 101–24. Additional bibliography on this theme in Old French literature in Ménard, *Le Rire*, p. 639, nn. 34, 35. In *Les Romans de Chrétien de Troyes*, vol. 2, *Cligés*, ed. Alexandre Micha, Classiques français du moyen âge 84 (Paris: Champion, 1970), vv. 1672–1696, God, who despises traitors and treachery more than any other villainy (vv. 1683–1684), commands the moon to reflect on the shields and helmets of the enemy soldiers, thus revealing their presence to the sentries.

286. Helmut A. Hatzfeld, "Esthetic Criticism Applied to Medieval Romance Literature," *Romance Philology* 1 (1947/48): 312; idem, *Literature Through Art: A New Approach to French Literature* (New York: Oxford University Press, 1952), pp. 8–9; idem, "Le *Rolandslied* allemand," pp. 54–55; Fern Farnham, "Romanesque Design in the *Chanson de Roland*," *Romance Philology* 18 (1964): 151; Davy, *Symbolique romane*, pp. 160–61; Eugene Vance, "Notes on the Development of Formulaic Language in Romanesque Poetry," in *Mélanges René Crozet*, 1:430.

287. *Psychomachia*, v. 908; Blaise, pp. 69, 75, s.v. lux, nox.

288. Conrad, vv. 43–45. In Turoldus's day the era before the birth of Christ was held to be a time of Darkness. Petrarch appears to have been the first to characterize the period beginning with the Fall of the Roman Empire as the Dark Ages, and antiquity the Light that had to be restored. Theodor E. Mommsen, "Petrarch's Conception of the 'Dark Ages'," *Speculum* 17 (1942): 226–42. See INTRODUCTION, 18, H.

289. Réau, II, 1:5, 35, 62.

290. Marguerite Rumpler, *L'Art roman en Alsace*, Les Cahiers techniques de l'art (Strasbourg: Le Tilleul, 1965), p. 12.

291. Blaise, par. 273. For the meaning attached to the extraordinary radiance emanating from Durendal and Joyeuse, see INTRODUCTION, 19, D.

292. Rumpler, p. 45; pls. XL, XLII.

293. E.g., Réau, II, 1:146–48 (Jacob's Dream at Bethel); II, 2:273–74 (Angelic Warning of Joseph in Slumber); III, 1 (1958): 343 (Constantine's Dream).

294. Lejeune and Stiennon, 1:98–99; 2: figs. 68, 72.

295. Réau, II, 2:732. Cf. Homer's *Iliad* where the battle of the gods is a prelude to the war between the Greeks and the Trojans. COMMENTARY, 1 and note 15.

296. Lejeune and Stiennon, 1:23. For another reference to the Last Judgment, see COMMENTARY, 16 (vv. 1434–1435).

297. COMMENTARY, 26.

298. Stefan Hofer, "Das Verratsmotiv in den Chansons de geste," *Zeitschrift für romanische Philologie* 44 (1924): 594–609; Mark Skidmore, *The Moral Traits of Christians and Saracens as Portrayed by the Chansons de geste*, Colorado College Publication, General series no. 203, Studies series no. 20 (Colorado Springs, 1935), pp. 84, 87; Adalbert Dessau, "L'idée de la trahison au moyen âge et son rôle dans la motivation de quelques chansons de geste," *Cahiers de civilisation médiévale* 3 (1960): 23–26; Calin, *Epic Quest*, p. 78.

299. Marsile's progress from treachery to despair parallels that of Judas and, by implication, that of Ganelon. Deceit may be alluded to in the *malvais saluz* made by Baligant's messengers, v. 2710.

300. Michelle Augier, "A propos de quelques conversions féminines dans l'épopée française," *Mosaic* 8 (1975): 97–105; see COMMENTARY, 3 (v. 102) and 43 (vv. 3669 ff.).

301. In *Erec*, v. 2330, mankind before the Coming of Christ was in prison; cf. v. 3680 (E Bramidonie, qu'il meinet en sa prisun). For other imagery relating to the conversion of the Saracens, see COMMENTARY, 39 (*Fig. 62*). In his adaptation of Turpin's speech offering to go to Saragossa (*Roland*, vv. 265–270), Conrad, vv. 1334–1343, emphasizes the Archbishop's desire to convert the pagan enemy.

302. The Call to Action, which traditionally appears at the beginning of stories such as the *Song of Roland* (see COMMENTARY, 49), frequently cites conversion as one of the chief reasons for undertaking an excursion into pagan lands. Thus in Conrad, vv. 31–46, Charles, having learned of the benighted pagans in Spain, prays to God to save them from darkness and the clutches of the devil. An angel appears and promises that they will be converted (v. 58). In the *Pseudo-Turpin* Saint James pleads with Charles to deliver his remains, buried in Galicia, from Saracen domination. The preliminary matter also makes it clear, however, that converting the pagans, not simply fighting them, is to be one of his main objectives there. Meredith-Jones, pp. 89, 91. Conversion is not explicitly mentioned in the concluding laisse of Turoldus's poem, but such a possibility is doubtless envisaged for the upcoming struggle. According to Menéndez Pidal, pp. 244–48 (see also INTRODUCTION, 1), the conversion motive in the *Song of Roland* has a basis in historical fact. In the *Histoire de Guillaume le Maréchal* the death of King Richard is viewed as an irreparable loss because he would have conquered all lands, Christian and pagan. Brandt, *Medieval History*, p. 112.

303. Frye, *Anatomy of Criticism*, p. 220, considers "the success or completeness of the hero's achievement" to be an essential phase of romance.

304. The first mention of victory in this poem refers to the Emperor's triumphs (v. 3: Tresqu'en la mer cunquist la tere altaigne), but this passage is soon followed by the detailing of Roland's related achievements (vv. 198 ff.). On the hagiographic source of the Theme of Victory, see Brault, "Le Thème de la Mort," pp. 229–35.

305. O. Cullmann, "Death of Christ," in *The Interpreter's Dictionary of the Bible* (New York and Nashville: Abington Press, 1962), 1:807 (Victory over Death). Romanesque crucifixes depict a Christus Victor. Réau, II, 2:476–77.

306. *Vie de Saint Georges*, in *Les Oeuvres de Simund de Freine*, ed. John E. Matzke, Société des anciens textes français (Paris: Didot, 1909), vv. 1639–1641, 1646–1651.

307. *La Vie Seint Edmund le Rei, poème anglo-normand du XIIe siècle par Denis Piramus*, ed. Hilding Kjellman, Göteborgs kungl. vetenskaps- och vitterhets-samhälles handlingar, fol. 5, ser. A, 4, no. 3 (Göteborg: Wettergren and Kerber, 1935), vv. 2511–2513, 2531.

308. *De Saint Laurent, poème anglo-normand du XIIe siècle*, ed. Werner Söderhjelm (Paris: Welter, 1888), vv. 622–626, 772–774.

309. Alfred T. Baker, "Vie anglo-normande de Sainte Foy," *Romania* 66 (1940/41): 69, vv. 510–512.

310. Holger Petersen, "Trois versions inédites de la légende de Saint Eustache en vers français," *Romania* 48 (1922): 399, vv. 2093–2094, 2097–2098.

311. Moral victory, that is, triumph in defeat, is a frequent theme in literature. Cf. Katov's death in André Malraux's *La Condition humaine*. In the *Song of Roland* victory is often indistinguishable from revenge. Jones, pp. 11, 13. However, when Christians are involved, it must be understood that they do not merely seek personal satisfaction for offenses committed against them but wish to punish malefactors. On the identity of divine vengeance and punishment in Ecclesiastical Latin, see Blaise, par. 59, 145, 278.

312. *Prudentius*, ed. and trans. H. J. Thomson, The Loeb Classical Library, 2 vols. (1949; rpt. Cambridge: Harvard University Press; London: Heinemann, 1962), 1: 274–343; Réau, I:175–91; Katzenellenbogen, *Allegories*, especially pt. 1, chap. 1.

313. Mickel, "Parallels in *Psychomachia* and *Roland*," pp. 439–52.

314. Vos, "Aspects of Biblical Typology," p. 70, links the hero with the notion of strife, taken in a spiritual sense.

315. Bédier, *Légendes épiques*, 3:367. On the notion of pilgrimage roads, see INTRODUCTION, 4.

316. For a similar view, see Vos, pp. 349–52 ("The Path"). On the road metaphor, see Frye, *Anatomy of Criticism*, p. 144. In the *Pseudo-Turpin* Charles's Spanish campaign is specifically associated with a *caminus stellarum* (Meredith-Jones, pp. 89, 91), that is, the Milky Way. On this connection, see Meredith-Jones, pp. 262–63; Horrent, p. 360; Réau, III, 2:692–93; Mandach, *Naissance*, 1:38.

317. Blaise, par. 304, 402, 426–28, 451; Locke, *Quest*, chap. 1, "The Grail and the Journey," pp. 1–11; *Introduction au monde des symboles*, p. 68. See also Campbell, *Hero*, pt. 1, chap. 2, 1, "The Road of Trials," pp. 97–109.

318. Lejeune and Stiennon, 1:275; 2: fig. 278.

319. Jean Leclercq, O.S.B., *The Love of Learning and the Desire for God: A Study of Monastic Culture*, trans. Catharine Misrahi (New York: Fordham University Press, 1961), pp. 130–35; Charles Muscatine, "Locus of Action in Medieval Narrative," *Romance Philology* 17 (1963): 115–22; Robertson, *Preface to Chaucer*, pp. 258, 373; F. C. Gardiner, *The Pilgrimage of Desire: A Study of Theme and Genre in Medieval Literature* (Leiden: Brill, 1971); *Voyage, quête, pèlerinage dans la littérature et la civilisation médiévales*, Senefiance n° 2, Cahiers du Cuer Ma (Aix-en-Provence: Cuer Ma [Université de Provence], 1976).

320. Jenkins, note to v. 2397, citing Lanson; Bédier, *Légendes épiques*, 3:442; Le Gentil, pp. 109, 116. See also INTRODUCTION, 18, D.

321. On the mountain symbol, see Davy, *Symbolique romane*, pp. 69, 85, 107, 223; Blaise, par. 166, 207; *Introduction au monde des symboles*, pp. 171–99; Frye, *Anatomy of Criticism*, pp. 203–4; Vos, "Aspects of Biblical Typology," chap. 2, "The Image of the Mountain."

322. For trees as a symbol of Ascent, see *Introduction au monde des symboles*, pp. 331–32; pls. 121, 123.

323. However, Saragossa and the haughty mountain on which it is said to be perched are essentially symbols of arrogance and pride. See COMMENTARY, I.

324. Cf. Psalms 120–134 (Song of the Ascents).

325. Réau, II, 1:147, 281; Katzenellenbogen, *Allegories*, chap. 3, "Man's Arduous Ascent to God (The Ladder of Virtue)," pp. 22–26; Davy, *Symbolique romane*, pp. 223–24; Robertson, *Preface to Chaucer*, p. 26. On the related motif of the children in the tree, see Rose J. Peebles, "The Children in the Tree," in *Medieval Studies in Memory of Gertrude Schoepperle Loomis* (New York: Columbia University Press; Paris: Champion, 1927), pp. 285–99; Ernst Brugger, *The Illuminated Tree in Two Arthurian Romances*, Publications of the Institute of French Studies (New York: Institute of French Studies, 1929); *The Didot-Perceval According to the Manuscripts of Modena and Paris*, ed. William Roach (Philadelphia: University of Pennsylvania Press, 1941), pp. 23–24, 73–76; Robert Will, "Recherches iconographiques sur la sculpture romane en Alsace: Les représentations du Paradis," *Les Cahiers techniques de l'art* 1, no. 3 (1948): 49–53; idem, *Alsace romane*, p. 261; Eleanor Simmons Greenhill, "The Child in the Tree: A Study of the Cosmological Tree in Christian Tradition," *Traditio* 10 (1954): 323–71; *Durmart le Galois: Roman arthurien du treizième siècle*, ed. Joseph Gildea, O.S.A., 2 vols. (Villanova, Pa.: Villanova Press, 1965–66), 2:61, n. 1.

326. Réau, III, 2:723–24. Two illustrations of an eleventh-century *Klimax* manuscript are provided by Katzenellenbogen, *Allegories*, figs. 23, 24.

327. See INTRODUCTION, 3.

328. See INTRODUCTION, 10, A, 5; cf. 19, F (Roland's vision of Paradise).

329. Frye, *Anatomy of Criticism*, pp. 141, 144–45; Calin, *Epic Quest*, pp. 29–31, linking woman and the city.

330. Le Gentil, p. 115, in support of his view that the Baligant episode is an integral part of Turoldus's poem.

331. *Peristephanon*, 4: v. 54 (*Prudentius*, 2: 160). Prudentius appears to have been at Saragossa in A.D. 348. *Prudentius*, 1:vii.

332. Boissonnade, *Du Nouveau*, p. 48.

333. See note 19 above.

334. G. D. West, "The Description of Towns in Old French Verse Romances," *French Studies* 11 (1957): 50–59.

335. See COMMENTARY, I. For a similar view, see Alfred Noyer-Weidner, "Vom biblischen 'Gottesberg' zur Symbolik des 'Heidentals' im *Rolandslied*," *Zeitschrift für französische Sprache und Literatur* 81 (1971): 13–71. Vos, "Aspects of Biblical Typology," vacillates between Jericho (pp. 74, 308, 309, 318) and Babylon (pp. 77, 83, 98, 320) in her identification of Saragossa. In 1 Peter 5:13, Rome is referred to as Babylon.

336. Calin, *Epic Quest*, pp. 194–95.

337. Jenkins, note to v. 2614.

338. Calin, *Epic Quest*, p. 29.

339. For a similar view, see Vos, p. 315.

340. Alonso, "La primitiva épica francesa," pp. 51–52, citing Cirot.

341. Ibid., pp. 51–56; Menéndez Pidal, p. 230, n. 6. The nasalized form *Ronzavalz* begins to appear in Spanish sources between 1101 and 1104 (Bédier, *Légendes épiques*, 3: 315: "entre les années 1100 et 1114"): Alonso, p. 52; Menéndez Pidal, p. 433, n. 1; Mandach, *Naissance*, 1:53–54, 69, 418, n. 93. Alonso, p. 54, citing Gautier, suggests

that the Basque toponym *Ros* or *Arros*, whose meaning is uncertain, may account for the first part of the original name. The proximity of this place-name to CL *ros* 'dew' doubtless suggested the form *roscida*. Note, however, that in a figurative sense Lat. *roscida* could also mean 'bloody' as in *Peristephanon*, 10: v. 705 (*Prudentius*, 2:276). On the transformation of the name, see Jean Frappier, *Etude sur Yvain ou le Chevalier au lion de Chrétien de Troyes* (Paris: Société d'édition d'enseignement supérieur, 1969), pp. 115–16: "les conteurs et les romanciers français . . . ont ajouté parfois à la raison d'euphonie celle d'une 'senefiance', comme tel semble bien être le cas pour Perceval (=celui qui perce le secret du val qui conduit au château du Graal?) dont l'équivalent gallois s'appelle Peredur."

342. Bédier, *Légendes épiques*, 3: 297. There is much debate, however, on the location of the battlefield. For bibliography and discussion, see ibid., pp. 298–327; Boissonnade, *Du Nouveau*, pp. 137–42; Menéndez Pidal, pp. 211, 217–30; Mandach, *Naissance*, 1:53. For a reconstruction of the battle as it happened in reality, see Menéndez Pidal, pp. 209–12.

343. The name appears for the first time in the scene where the Saracens take an oath to destroy Roland and the French rearguard (vv. 892, 901, 912, 923, 934, 944, 963, 985), and is blasphemous in the latter context. The *Pseudo-Turpin* and the *Guide du Pèlerin* everywhere use the nasalized form *Runcia* (or *Ruŋciae*) *vallis*. Jenkins's *Glossary*, p. 362, derives *Rencesvals* from *Runciavallis* but does not discuss the etymology. Medieval Latin *runcia* (see Charles du Fresne, sieur Du Cange, *Glossarium mediae et infimae latinitatis*, 10 vols. revised by Léopold Favre [1883–87; rpt. Paris: Librairie des sciences et des arts, 1938], 7:212, 239, s.v. roncia, runchi, runciae) is akin to *rumicem*, the accusative of CL *rumex*, which yielded Fr. *ronce*. The spelling *en* of *Rencesvals* is unusual. VL close o (CL long o, short u) plus nasal ordinarily gave Anglo-Norman *un*, at times written *on* by the Oxford copyist (e.g., v. 3487: *contre*; elsewhere *cuntre*). Cf., however, the spelling *jesque* (vv. 2538, 2638) for *josque*, *jusque*, noted by Bédier, *Commentaires*, p. 256. Cf. also the form *Rencevals* in Wace's *Roman de Rou* (1160); Moignet, p. 294. Turoldus's poem was often referred to in the Middle Ages by the name of this battle; see Aebischer, *Préhistoire*, pp. 187–203 (summary in Dufournet, *Cours sur Roland*, pp. 4–6). See also INTRODUCTION, 19, D.

344. Blaise, par. 402. Crosland, *Old French Epic*, p. 70, states that the *Roland* symbolizes the Christian's journey through this Vale of Tears, but she makes no specific allusion to Roncevaux in this connection. Vos, "Aspects of Biblical Typology," p. 184, refers in a general way to Roncevaux as a *vallis lachrymarum*, and, p. 287, to the poem as "a journey from the Shadowy Valley to the Height of Sion." Cf. also p. 70 (v. 2461: Val Tenebrus).

345. *La Chanson de Roland*, ed. Gautier, p. 555, mentions in passing Hugo Meyer's suggestion that there is a possible connection between Roncevaux and "'la vallée des épines', dont il est question dans la mythologie du Nord." The iconography of the Crowning with Thorns is discussed in Réau, II, 2:457–59. On the legend of Cain, who after slaying his brother Abel planted thorns, which later became Christ's Crown of Thorns, see Réau, II, 1:98. The relic was purchased by Saint Louis from a Venetian merchant in 1239. Réau, II, 2:458.

346. *Hamartigenia*, vv. 789–801 (*Prudentius*, 1:260).

347. Thorns are the symbol of desolation in Isaiah 7:24–25; 34:13.

348. Bédier, *Légendes épiques*, 3:324–26; Horrent, p. 188; Lejeune and Stiennon, 1:236–37, citing the *Karlamagnús Saga* and Stricker: "l'anecdote est surtout destinée, à notre avis, à fournir une étymologie du nom 'Roncevaux' ou 'Ronsasvals', nom demeuré jusqu'ici inexpliqué."

349. *Peristephanon*, 11: vv. 105–124 (*Prudentius*, 1:312); Delehaye, *Les Passions des martyrs*, p. 204, records several other instances of this torture. Cf. Judges 8:7, 16.

Saint Benedict overcame fleshly temptation by throwing himself nude into thorns and nettles. Réau, III, 1:200; Florence McCulloch, *Mediaeval Latin and French Bestiaries*, University of North Carolina Studies in the Romance Languages and Literatures 33 (Chapel Hill: University of North Carolina Press, 1962), p. 97, n. 36. In the *Speculum Humanae Salvationis* thorns are a prefiguration of Hell. Réau, II, 1:234.

350. Robertson, *Preface to Chaucer*, p. 225, n. 138.

351. Réau, II, 1:135.

352. Writing shortly after Saint Bernard's death in 1153, William of Saint-Thierry suggests that the valley received its name because of its grim aspect and evil repute: "Erat autem Clara-Vallis locus in territorio Linganensi, non longe a fluvio Alba, antiqua spelunca latronum, quae antiquitus dicebatur Vallis absinthialis, seu propter abundantis ibi absinthi copiam, seu propter amaritudinem doloris incidentium ibi in manus latronum" (*PL*, 185, col. 241). On this explanation, which may be nothing more than a pious fiction, see *Bernard de Clairvaux*, pp. 82–83.

353. On the use of landscape in epics, see Bowra, *Heroic Poetry*, pp. 133–49. Vos, "Aspects of Biblical Typology," pp. 58–71, discusses landscape in the *Song of Roland* but treats only mountains, valleys, and trees. Paul Piehler, *The Visionary Landscape: A Study in Medieval Allegory* (London: Arnold, 1971), does not mention Turoldus's epic.

354. For a brief observation concerning lyricism in these verses, see Hatzfeld, *Literature Through Art*, p. 11. Aebischer, "Halt sunt li pui," deals almost exclusively with the meridional provenance of certain terms relative to the landscape in the *Song of Roland.*

355. Le Gentil, p. 154:

> Ces répétitions, on le sent bien, ne sont pas accidentelles; de loin elles se répondent et se font écho. C'est ainsi que le poète associe plus intimement le cadre à l'action, en même temps qu'il entretient et renouvelle l'émotion. Sans doute, le trait reste schématique; mais, plusieurs fois reproduit, il s'accuse et, simplifié à l'extrême, il prend une valeur véritablement essentielle. Une longue description serait à coup sûr moins efficace.

356. On the meaning of *pitet* in the *Song of Roland*, see OXFORD TEXT, ENGLISH TRANSLATION, v. 3871. In *Chanson de Guillaume*, vv. 581–584, Vivien declares that knights wishing to accomplish deeds of valor must banish nostalgic thoughts.

357. See note 229 above.

358. Rychner, p. 72: "Les fameux vers descriptifs du *Roland* claironnent les débuts de laisse [citing vv. 157, 814–815, 1807, 2646, and 3345]. Seuls trois vers de ce type (v. 1002, 1755, et 3991) se trouvent à l'intérieur de la laisse."

359. See COMMENTARY, 24. Mountains figure in the imagery associated with Ascent in the *Song of Roland* (INTRODUCTION, 15, C). For the mountain as a symbol of Pride, see COMMENTARY, 1. In his critique of the *Halt sunt li pui* refrain, Menéndez Pidal, pp. 324–26, cites four passages, omitting v. 1755 and adding vv. 3125–3128. On the latter, see COMMENTARY, 37.

360. Cf. v. 3659: *Clers est la lune e les esteiles flambient.*

361. Henceforth referred to as Marganice in the Oxford manuscript.

362. Discussion and additional references in *The Jerusalem Bible*, p. 101, note *j*.

363. The term was coined by John Ruskin in 1888. See also Frye, *Anatomy of Criticism*, p. 36. On day and night, see INTRODUCTION, 14, A, 4.

364. On the allusion to Christ's death upon the Cross, see COMMENTARY, 16.

365. Cames, *Allégories*, pp. 11–12; pl. 1. See note 476 below.

366. See OXFORD TEXT, ENGLISH TRANSLATION, V. 191.

367. Blaise, par. 331–36.

368. See COMMENTARY, 21 (v. 1874). See also COMMENTARY, 19 (v. 1778), 25 (vv.

2300 ff.), and 27 (v. 2465). Tears constitute a form of water of course. Note, however, that while tears of commiseration are plentiful in this poem, tears of remorse (Payen, *Le Motif du repentir*, index, p. 601, s.v. Larmes) are remarkably absent.

369. See note 45 above. In his inventory of the trees mentioned by Turoldus, Aebischer, "Halt sunt li pui," p. 20, inadvertently omits *eglenter* (v. 114) and *sapide* (v. 993).

370. Frappier, *Chansons de geste*, 1:260; 2:199, n. 1; Delbouille, *Genèse*, pp. 129–33; Jean-Charles Payen, "Encore le problème de la géographie épique," *Société Rencesvals. IVe Congrès International*, p. 266; idem, *Le Moyen Age*, p. 61. For an olive tree in Great Britain, see *Le Haut Livre du Graal: Perlesvaus*, eds. William A. Nitze and collaborators, Modern Philology Monographs of the University of Chicago, 2 vols. (Chicago: University of Chicago Press, 1932–37), 1: line 5815; 2:313, n. Curtius, p. 227, and Delbouille, *Genèse*, p. 152, note a poetic allusion to olive, palm, and cedar trees at Liège. Curtius describes it as a rhetorical convention; Hoepffner, cited by Delbouille, p. 136, n. 1, suggests realism.

371. Curtius, chap. 10, pp. 226–47; Aebischer, "Halt sunt li pui," p. 16: "L'olivier était un accessoire obligé de toute chanson de geste"; Delbouille, *Genèse*, p. 136: "Il s'agit d'une pure convention poétique." Bowra, *Heroic Poetry*, pp. 148–49, considers gardens, like palaces (pp. 147–48), to symbolize power and wealth.

372. Saint Augustine was converted while reading the Epistles of Saint Paul under a tree. Réau, III, 1:153.

373. Moshé Lazar, *Amour courtois et 'fin'amors' dans la littérature du XIIe siècle*, Bibliothèque française et romane, Série C: Etudes littéraires 8 (Paris: Klincksieck, 1964), pp. 123–24.

374. Curtius, p. 245. For a possible rhetorical source, see note 383 below.

375. Joseph J. Duggan, *A Concordance of the Chanson de Roland* (Columbus: Ohio State University Press, 1969), pp. 381, 293, 277, respectively.

376. Conrad, v. 398, substitutes an olive tree for the garden in this passage.

377. Cf. COMMENTARY, 12 (v. 993: sapide).

378. Same observation in H. Perschmann, *Die Stellung von O in der Ueberlieferung des altfranzösischen Rolandsliedes: Eine textskritische Untersuchung*, Ausgaben und Abhandlungen aus dem Gebiete der romanischen Philologie 3 (Marburg: Pfeil, 1880), p. 5.

379. Karl-Josef Steinmeyer, *Untersuchungen zur allegorischen Bedeutung der Träume im altfranzösischen Rolandslied*, Langue et Parole, Sprach- und Literaturstrukturelle Studien 5 (Munich: Hueber, 1963), p. 126; Vos, "Aspects of Biblical Typology," pp. 147–48 (cf. p. 69).

380. *PL*, 112, col. 1029, a connection commented on favorably in Horrent's review of Steinmeyer in *Romance Philology* 23 (1970): 600.

381. Cf. 1 Kings 5:19–20. Harold N. and Alma L. Moldenke, *Plants of the Bible* (Waltham: Chronica Botanica, 1952), pp. 173–77.

382. Moldenke, p. 68.

383. Curtius, p. 245, n. 2.

384. Segre, note to v. 407. See also INTRODUCTION, 10, B, 3.

385. *PL*, 112, col. 1011. Steinmeyer, *Untersuchungen*, p. 126.

386. D. W. Robertson, Jr., "The Doctrine of Charity in Mediaeval Literary Gardens: A Topical Approach Through Symbolism and Allegory," *Speculum* 26 (1951): 24–49; Herman Braet, "Le songe de l'arbre chez Wace, Benoît et Aimon de Varennes," *Romania* 91 (1970): 255–67.

387. INTRODUCTION, 3.

388. In vv. 72, 80, and 93, the olive branches refer to Blancandrin's mission; in v. 203, an earlier episode is involved.

389. See COMMENTARY, 2.

390. Cf. *Apotheosis*, vv. 338–346 (*Prudentius*, 1:144). Cf. also the symbol of the fig tree in Matthew 21:18–22; Mark 11:13–14; Luke 13:6–9. For the illustration in Conrad (*Fig. 43*), see note 213 above.

391. See, for example, Antonius Martyr (c. 570) in *Itinera Hierosolymitana et Descriptionis Terrae Sanctae bellis sacris anteriora et latina lingua exarata*, eds. Titus Tobler and Auguste Molinier, Publications de la Société de l'Orient latin, Série géographique 1 (Geneva, 1879), pp. 100–101. Cf. Payen, *Le Motif du repentir*, p. 175. In the *Morgante Maggiore*, Canto XXV, st. 77, Ganelon's treachery is planned in the shade of a wild carob or false Saint John's bread, the same species of tree, Pulci affirms, as the one from which Judas hanged himself. Archer Taylor, "The Gallows of Judas Iscariot," *Washington University Studies, Humanistic Series* 9, no. 2 (1922): 153. On the figure of Despair in medieval thought, see Robertson, *Preface to Chaucer*, pp. 388, 483; Payen, index, s.v. Désespoir, Impénitence, Suicide.

392. Frye, *Anatomy of Criticism*, p. 43: "The close association with animal and vegetable nature that we noted in the elegiac recurs in the sheep and pleasant pastures (or the cattle and ranches) of the idyllic, and the same easy connection with myth recurs in the fact that such imagery is often used, as in the Bible, for the theme of salvation."

393. Leclercq, *Love of Learning*, p. 166; Cames, *Allégories*, p. 14. *Flores martyrum* 'Holy Innocents' occurs in *Liber Cathemerinon*, 12: v. 125 (*Prudentius*, 1:110); *floriferas sedes* in Cassiodorus, *Expositio in Psalmos* (*PL*, 70, col. 9) and Caelius Sedulius, *Carmen paschalis* (*PL*, 19, col. 593).

394. G. D. Huck, "Flowers, Symbolism of," *New Catholic Encyclopedia* (New York: McGraw-Hill, 1967), 5:982.

395. In v. 2573, Marsile falls, mortally wounded, *sur la verte herbe*. Foulet, *Glossaire*, notes that the fourteen uses of the adjective *verte* in Turoldus's poem all refer to grass.

396. See Nichols, "The Interaction of Life and Literature." For very different conceptions of tone, see Rychner, pp. 69–70 ("la laisse avait une réalité musicale. . . . Le dessin musical de la laisse était marqué par un timbre d'intonation et par un timbre de conclusion; dans le corps de la laisse, le timbre d'intonation, répété, pouvait alterner avec un timbre de développement. . . . Timbre conclusif peut-être que le AOI du *Roland* d'Oxford") and Ménard, *Le Rire*, pp. 122–42 ("Les tons," i.e., L'humour et l'ironie, les apostrophes et les injures).

397. Jenkins, p. xxxvii. On the poem's lyrical passages, see Rychner, pp. 118–24; on its elegiac tone, see Duggan, *Song of Roland*, pp. 167, 175–76, 179, 181, 182–83. On omens, see Rychner, pp. 73–74. Frye, *Anatomy of Criticism*, p. 139: "The introduction of an omen or portent, or the device of making a whole story the fulfilment of a prophecy given at the beginning . . . suggests, in its existential projection, a conception of ineluctable fate or hidden omnipotent will." I doubt, however, that the mood was meant to be as lugubrious as that suggested by Jean Deschamps's oral interpretation of *La Chanson de Roland*, L'Encyclopédie sonore, Collection "Les Grands Textes," Librairie Hachette, disque 270 E 047.

398. Jenkins, p. xcix. There are some problems, however, many of them due to obvious scribal errors.

399. Ibid., p. cxliii–cxliv. The latter, p. c, notes that close *o* here was like the *u* in English *full*. Vos, "Aspects of Biblical Typology," p. 60, refers to these "desperate, rising" long -*u* sounds.

400. *Annales monastici*, ed. Henry Richards Luard, vol. 4, Rerum britannicarum medii aevi scriptores; or Chronicles and Memorials of Great Britain and Ireland during the Middle Ages 36 (London: Longman, Green, Longman, Roberts, and Green, 1869), p. 19; Louis F. Salzman, *Building in England, Down to 1540: A Documentary*

History (Oxford: Clarendon Press, 1952), p. 366; Otto Georg von Simson, *The Gothic Cathedral: The Origins of Gothic Architecture and the Medieval Concept of Order* (London: Routledge and Paul, 1956), p. 2. Cf. Suger's emotional reaction to the remodeling of the abbey church of Saint-Denis c. 1144, *A Documentary History of Art*, vol. 1, *The Middle Ages and the Renaissance*, ed. Elizabeth G. Holt (Garden City: Doubleday, 1957), pp. 22–48. On the concept of *tremendum*, see Hatzfeld, *Literature Through Art*, pp. 4, 14; cf. Blaise, par. 96, 379; 473 (timor Dei). See also COMMENTARY, 34. According to Campbell, *Hero*, p. 77, beyond the first threshold which the mythological hero must cross in his journey lie "darkness, the unknown, and danger." This region may be a "desert, jungle, deep sea, alien land, etc." (p. 79).

401. Bédier, *Commentaires*, pp. 313–14. Add 1 Peter 5:8.

402. Cf. Corsablix (v. 1236: Barbarins est, d'un estrange païs), earlier identified as one who practices the black art (v. 886).

403. Foulet, *Glossaire*, gives the meaning 'étranger' for all uses of the word *estrange* in the *Song of Roland* except in Alda's phrase (v. 3717), where he renders it as 'étrange'. Similarly, *mar* often suggests a good deal more than 'in an evil hour' or 'in vain' (see Jenkins, note to v. 350). Also, whenever blasphemy or sacrilege is involved, the poem's tone is obviously affected.

404. Louis-Fernand Flutre, *Table des noms propres avec toutes leurs variantes figurant dans les romans du moyen âge écrits en français ou en provençal et actuellement publiés ou analysés*, Publications du Centre d'études supérieures de civilisation médiévale 2 (Poitiers: Centre d'études supérieures de civilisation médiévale, 1962), p. 236. On this imaginary universe, see Ménard, *Le Rire*, pp. 94–98 and, especially, chap. 5, "L'étrange et le merveilleux," pp. 376–416.

405. *Chrétien de Troyes, Le Roman de Perceval ou le Conte du Graal*, ed. William Roach, 2d ed., Textes littéraires français 71 (Geneva: Droz; Paris: Minard, 1959); *Perlesvaus*, 2:247–49, note to line 1717.

406. Blaise, par. 402. Cf. Exodus 2:22: "I am a stranger in a foreign land" (see also 18:3).

407. Rychner, chap. 4, "La structure strophique des chansons," pp. 68–125. Rychner's four-part division of Turoldus's poem (pp. 38–39) is accepted by Duggan, *Song of Roland*, pp. 63–68. On the geometric view of nature in the Middle Ages, see Brandt, *Medieval History*, pp. 33–42; Robertson, *Preface to Chaucer*, pp. 148–50. Geometricism is not necessarily a learned trait. See Leonhard Adam, *Primitive Art*, 3d ed., Pelican Books (Melbourne-London-Baltimore: Penguin, 1954), pp. 38–41.

408. Rychner, pp. 119, 122, 124. Rychner's patterns remind one of *technopaignon*, a popular device in Carolingian times consisting of writing words so as to form an image. See David M. Robb, *The Art of the Illuminated Manuscript* (South Brunswick and New York: Barnes; London: Yoseloff, 1973), p. 108.

409. Rychner, p. 98.

410. Farnham, "Romanesque Design," pp. 156–57. Joseph I. Donohoe, "Ambivalence and Anger, the Human Center of the *Chanson de Roland*," *Romanic Review* 62 (1971): 251–61, focuses on the hero's question in v. 2000: "*Sire cumpain, faites le vos de gred?*"

411. Hatzfeld, *Literature Through Art*, pp. 3–4; see also idem, "Les études de style et la littérature médiévale," *Mélanges Rita Lejeune*, 2:1609–10.

412. Hatzfeld, *Literature Through Art*, pp. 8–13. Guy R. Mermier, "More About Unity in the *Song of Roland*," *Olifant* 2, no. 2 (1974): 91–108, compares the poem to the tympanum at Conques (*see Fig. 19*).

413. Mandach, *Naissance*, 1:164–66.

414. Per Nykrog, "La composition du *Roland* d'Oxford," *Romania* 88 (1967): 509–26. Cf. Vos, "Aspects of Biblical Typology," pp. 183–84, 228.

415. Bulatkin, *Structural Arithmetic Metaphor.*

416. Jenkins, p. xxxviii, considers them to be a rhetorical device; cf. Rychner, pp. 93–107; Duggan, *Song of Roland,* pp. 101–2. The technique makes its appearance in the Hague Fragment and experienced a decline in the twelfth century. Jenkins, p. xxxviii, n. 1; Menéndez Pidal, pp. 374–75, 380; Payen, *Le Moyen Age,* pp. 78–79. Jenkins, note to vv. 24–61, lists several examples, adding that vv. 1796–1850 constitute a possible case of four laisses similaires. Parallel laisses are a distinct phenomenon. Rychner, pp. 83–93; Duggan, pp. 98, 144–47. In an unpublished paper, "The Laisses Similaires in the *Song of Roland,*" read at the Kentucky Foreign Language Conference in 1968, Barbara N. Sargent argued that since the strophes at times relate to a single action, at other times to a repeated occurrence, laisses similaires is an inadequate designation (summary in *Bulletin bibliographique de la Société Rencesvals* 5 [1970]: 46, item 90).

417. Eugene Vinaver, "La mort de Roland," *Cahiers de civilisation médiévale* 7 (1964): 133–43. Cf. Rychner, pp. 99, 124–25; Payen, *Le Motif du repentir,* pp. 111–20; Duggan, *Song of Roland,* pp. 184–88.

418. Lejeune and Stiennon, 1:195–96 (correct marginal reference to read pl. XIV [transposed with reference to pl. XV]).

419. See OXFORD TEXT, ENGLISH TRANSLATION, V. 9.

420. Jenkins, p. xxxviii.

421. The Romanesque church at Ottmarsheim in Alsace is a replica of this chapel. Will, *Alsace romane,* pp. 54–55. For other examples, see p. 58; W. Eugene Kleinbauer, "Charlemagne's Palace Chapel at Aachen and its Copies," *Gesta* 4 (1965): 2–11. Cloisters provide a similar opportunity for viewing in the round. The corridor following the curve of the apse in medieval churches (for Romanesque examples, see Henri Focillon, *Art d'Occident,* vol. 1, *Le Moyen Age roman,* Le Livre de Poche, Série Art [Paris: Colin, 1971], 136–37) was originally intended to afford the pilgrim a view into the radiating chapels, thus produces a centrifugal effect, if the main altar is considered to be the focal point.

422. Réau, II, 2:747.

423. *Introduction au monde des symboles,* p. 394.

424. Ibid., p. 395.

425. Ibid., p. 395; COMMENTARY, 24.

426. Philipp August Becker, "Der distichisch-tristichische Rhythmus im Rolandslied," *Philologische Studien aus dem romanisch-germanischen Kulturkreise. Karl Voretzsch zum 60. Geburtstag und zum Gedenken an seine erste akademische Berufung vor 35 Jahren* (Halle: Niemeyer, 1927), pp. 539–43. Cf. William S. Woods, "The Symbolic Structure of *La Chanson de Roland,*" *PMLA* 65 (1950): 1247–62; Rychner, p. 124. See also note 268 above. Hans Erich Keller, "La place du *Ruolantes Liet* dans la tradition rolandienne," *Le Moyen Age* 71 (1965): 215–46, 401–21, notes that Conrad tends to repeat two or three times episodes found in his French source.

427. Réau, I:68; Curtius, pp. 607–23; Guy Beaujouan, "Le symbolisme des nombres à l'époque romane," *Cahiers de civilisation médiévale* 4 (1961): 159–69; Bulatkin, *Structural Arithmetic Metaphor,* chap. 1, "The Meaning of Numbers in the Middle Ages," pp. 3–22. See also INTRODUCTION, 18, A.

428. The illusory aspect of number symbolism is scored by Le Gentil, p. 120. When using Duggan's *Concordance* for such investigations, one should not fail to tally Roman numerals (e.g., ii, iii, iiii, xx, xxx, c) together with the numbers that happen to have been spelled out by the scribe.

429. See INTRODUCTION, 18, H.

430. Meredith-Jones, p. 127: "Ut enim Dominus noster Ihesus Christus una cum duodecim apostolis et discipulis suis mundum adquisivit, sic Karolus rex Galliorum

et imperator Romanorum cum his pugnatoribus Yspaniam adquisivit ad decus nominis Dei." See Meredith-Jones, pp. 302–3, n. On the Twelve Peers, see COMMENTARY, 3, note 7.

431. On the delimitation of the Baligant episode, see Horrent, pp. 255–59. For the average duration of performances, see Rychner, pp. 48–49; Duggan, *Song of Roland*, pp. 63–68, 74.

432. Joachim E. Gaehde, "The Painters of the Carolingian Bible Manuscript of San Paolo Fuori le Mura in Rome [with] Appendix," Ph.D. diss., New York University, 1963, pt. 2, pl. 79 (Conversion of Saint Paul). For discussion of this illustration, see pt. 1, pp. 426–42. On the manuscript, see also idem, "The Turonian Sources of the Bible of San Paolo Fuori le Mura in Rome," *Frühmittelalterliche Studien*, Jahrbuch des Instituts für Frühmittelalterforschung der Universität Münster 5 (1971): 386–92. Cf. the highlighting of Judas receiving the Thirty Pieces of Silver in a ninth-century ivory diptych preserved in the Cathedral of Milan. John Beckwith, *Early Medieval Art*, Praeger World of Art (New York and Washington, D.C.: Praeger, 1965), figs. 113, 114.

433. *Perlesvaus*, 2:165.

434. But see Nitze in *Perlesvaus*, 2:165–69.

435. See, however, Jenkins, p. cxliv and n. 1.

436. See also COMMENTARY, 11.

437. Irony here is not to be confused with sarcasm. On the use of the term irony by Aristotle, see Frye, *Anatomy of Criticism*, p. 41 et passim.

438. Richard A. Lanham, *A Handlist of Rhetorical Terms: A Guide for Students of English Literature* (Berkeley and Los Angeles: University of California Press, 1969), pp. 61–62: "From the literary critic's point of view, irony and allegory ought to bear some relation, since irony is clearly a particular, 180-degree-reversed, instance of allegory's double meaning. That is, the ironist depends on an allegorical habit of mind in his reader, a habit that will juxtapose surface and real meanings."

439. Jenkins, note to v. 2678.

440. Jones, p. 36.

441. Cf. INTRODUCTION, 18, F.

442. Dorfman, *Narreme*, p. 112.

443. The Franks at times epitomize the reverse of Charles's Sapientia. See INTRODUCTION, 19, K.

444. *Introduction au monde des symboles*, p. 275; pl. 107. Cf. also the figure of Christ with right hand raised in a heavenward gesture of truth contrasted with Satan whose left hand is extended downward, on the west façade of the Romanesque church at Conques (*see Fig. 19*). *The Song of Roland*, trans. Harrison, p. 21.

445. Frye, p. 156.

446. H. W. Janson, *Apes and Ape Lore in the Middle Ages and the Renaissance*, Studies of the Warburg Institute 20 (London: Warburg Institute, 1952), pp. 16–20. In Revelation 13:3 the risen dragon is a grotesque representation of the risen Christ (*The Jerusalem Bible*, p. 441, n. *b*; see also n. *c*).

447. Janson, p. 29.

448. Ibid., p. 34. In the *Psychomachia* Discordia masquerades as Concordia. Katzenellenbogen, *Allegories*, p. 3.

449. Janson, pp. 36–37. On the figure of Avaritia simulating Thrift in the *Psychomachia*, see Katzenellenbogen, p. 3; Cames, *Allégories*, p. 63.

450. Janson, p. 110.

451. Ibid., pp. 165–69.

452. There is possible aping of Roland's praise of Durendal in the apostrophe addressed by Ganelon to Murglais in vv. 445–449. See INTRODUCTION, 19, D.

453. Eugene Vance, "Spatial Structure in the *Chanson de Roland*," *MLN* 82 (1967): 604–23; idem, *Reading the Song of Roland*, pp. 16–18. Le Goff, *Civilisation*, chap. 6, "Structures spatiales et temporelles," pp. 169–248, is an excellent general introduction to the matter at hand.

454. For examples of narrative economy, see COMMENTARY, 9, 29, and 30. On the Seven-Day Chronology in Turoldus's poem, see INTRODUCTION, 13. For signals beyond space and time, see COMMENTARY, 22 (ritual alignment), 26 (v. 2363), and 34 (v. 2867).

455. Flashback: COMMENTARY, 9, 29 (vv. 2570 ff., 2616 ff.), and 49 (circle concept); flashforward: COMMENTARY, 44 (vv. 3698–3703), all dreams, and the poet's announcements in vv. 844 and 1408–1410.

456. See COMMENTARY, 1.

457. See COMMENTARY, 9. On the more elaborate narrative technique known as *entrelacement*, see Payen, *Le Moyen Age*, pp. 79–80, and, especially, Vinaver, *Rise of Romance*, chap. 5, "The Poetry of Interlace," pp. 68–98.

458. See COMMENTARY, 20–27.

459. See INTRODUCTION, 13.

460. Réau, I: 302; II, 2:245, 439. For Herod, see Otto Pächt, C. R. Dodwell, and Francis Wormald, *The St. Albans Psalter* (*Albani Psalter*), Studies of the Warburg Institute 25 (London: Warburg Institute, 1960), p. 83 and pl. 17b. For the crenelated wall, see Lejeune and Stiennon, 2: fig. 146.

461. Lejeune and Stiennon, 2: figs. 85, 86, 91, etc.

462. Ibid., 1:215; 2: fig. 172.

463. Jenkins, citing Clark, observes apropos of v. 668 (Guenes li quens est venuz as herberges): "The author of *Rol.* is a skillful raconteur: he passes over the details of Ganelon's return journey which would only make his audience impatient." Cf. the condensation device in vv. 2630–2644 (COMMENTARY, 29).

464. Réau, I: 292–93.

465. Cola Minis, "Über Rolands Horn, Burgers Passio Rotolandi und Konrads Roland," *Mélanges de linguistique et de littérature romanes à la mémoire d'István Frank, offerts par ses anciens maîtres, ses amis et ses collègues de France et de l'étranger*, Annales Universitatis Saraviensis 6 (Saarbrücken: Universität des Saarlandes, 1957), pp. 439–53; Stephen G. Nichols, Jr., "Roland's Echoing Horn," *Romance Notes* 5 (1963): 78–84; Brault, "Le Thème de la Mort," p. 236; Emilie P. Kostoroski, "Further Echoes from Roland's Horn," *Romance Notes* 13 (1972): 541–44.

466. On the notion of time in medieval French literature, see Payen, *Le Moyen Age*, pp. 77–91. Epic time conventions are discussed by Calin, *Old French Epic*, pp. 189–96; idem, *Epic Quest*, p. 105.

467. See note 168 above.

468. See Payen, *Le Moyen Age*, pp. 82–83 ("La 'laudatio temporis acti'"); Le Goff, *Civilisation*, pp. 213–14. Cf. the Golden Age or Paradise Lost topos. Curtius, *Littérature européenne*, pp. 102, 149, 326–27.

469. *The Life of Saint Alexis: An Old French Poem of the Eleventh Century*, ed. V. L. Dedeck-Héry, Publications of the Institute of French Studies (New York: Institute of French Studies, 1931), vv. 1–5. Cf. Le Goff, pp. 213–14.

470. Paul Archambault, "The Ages of Man and the Ages of the World," *Revue des études augustiniennes* 11 (1966): 193–202; Le Goff, p. 212. Medieval writers referred to the world before the Birth of Christ, whether Jewish, Saracen, or pagan, as the Old Law. Payen, *Le Motif du repentir*, p. 429. Cf. Réau, II, 1: viii; Payen, *Le Moyen Age*, pp. 84–85. See also note 288 above.

471. As for the future, the single most important fact to bear in mind, as Romanesque portals almost invariably impressed upon Turoldus's contemporaries (see Focillon, *Art d'Occident*, 1: 225), was the Last Judgment.

472. William Wistar Comfort, "The Character Types in the Old French *Chansons de geste*," *PMLA* 21 (1906): 279–434 (the King, pp. 282–306; the Hero, pp. 307–35; the Traitor, pp. 336–58; see also: Woman, pp. 359–84; Bourgeois and Vilain, pp. 384–404; the Saracens, pp. 404–31); Brandt, *Medieval History*, pp. 131, n. 68, 172; Cf. the technique of primitive artists. Adam, *Primitive Art*, pp. 37 ff. On the development of character portrayal in Western literature, consult Scholes and Kellogg, *Nature of Narrative*, chap. 5, "Character in Narrative," pp. 160–206. Cf. Frappier, *Etude sur Yvain*, pp. 160–76.

473. Frye, *Anatomy of Criticism*, p. 210: "It is true that the great majority of tragic heroes do possess hybris, a proud, passionate, obsessed or soaring mind which brings about a morally intelligible downfall."

474. Ibid., p. 38:

> Aristotle's hamartia or 'flaw', therefore, is not necessarily wrongdoing, much less moral weakness: it may be simply a matter of being a strong character in an exposed position, like Cordelia. The exposed position is usually the place of leadership, in which a character is exceptional and isolated at the same time, giving us that curious blend of the inevitable and the incongruous which is peculiar to tragedy.

Cf. essentially evil natures (see below), a concept implied in v. 899: *Fust chrestïens, asez oüst barnet.*

475. Ibid., p. 212:

> The discovery or *anagnorisis* which comes at the end of the tragic plot is not simply the knowledge by the hero of what has happened to him—*Oedipus Tyrannus*, despite its reputation as a typical tragedy, is rather a special case in that regard—but the recognition of the determined shape of the life he has created for himself, with an implicit comparison with the uncreated potential life he has forsaken.

476. Colby, *Twelfth-Century French Literature*, pp. 47–48. Payen, *Le Moyen Age*, p. 62:

> il existe une correspondance secrète entre le macrocosme et le microcosme, entre l'univers et la personne. Il ne s'agit pas seulement d'influences astrologiques qui font qu'un homme est *bon* ou *mal eüré*, né sous une bonne ou une mauvaise étoile; plus profondément, aux quatre éléments: feu, air, terre et eau, correspondent les quatre humeurs: sang, lymphe, bile et mélancolie, qui définissent les quatre tempéraments. La cosmologie et la physiologie s'unissent dans une même science, conformément à un enseignement très ancien, puisqu'il remonte à la plus haute philosophie antique.

On the Microcosm, see note 365 above.

477. A character may of course play more than one role; see INTRODUCTION, 19, E.

478. Marsile is plainly oblivious to the significance of the marble couch (v. 12). Cf., however, the Saracens' deliberate use of the Entry into Jerusalem image later in the same passage (COMMENTARY, 2). Charles senses the mountains' moodiness or is at least in tune with it (INTRODUCTION, 16, A, 1), and Roland may understand why he is dying near three trees and four marble objects (INTRODUCTION, 16, F), but others seem unaware of the symbolic landscape and even, on occasion, misinterpret its manifestations (vv. 1434–1437).

479. Brandt, *Medieval History*, pp. 130–31, 154–56, 160, 162; Payen, *Le Moyen Age*, p. 63. Cf. INTRODUCTION, 15, A.

480. Bloch, *Feudal Society*, 2: chaps. 21–23; Curtius, *Littérature européenne*, pp. 628–50; Robertson, *Preface to Chaucer*, p. 174; Brandt, pp. 108–10, 117.

481. Jones, pp. 32–34, 56. On the concept of honor, see Jones, pp. 46–47; Brandt, pp. 111–14.

482. Bloch, 1: chap. 4.

483. Meredith-Jones, p. 307, note to p. 152, lines v ff.; Horrent, pp. 95–100. Cf. the courtly ideal epitomized in *Conte del graal*, vv. 7594–7596. Smail, *Crusading*

Warfare, p. 45, relates the following anecdote for the year 1108: "After the fighting the opposing leaders exchanged friendly messages, and Tancred requested the gift of a horse belonging to a member of the Munqidhite household. It was dispatched to him, ridden by a young Kurd named Hasanun. Tancred admired the physique and bearing of the youth, and promised him that if ever he became Tancred's prisoner, he would be set free."

484. See COMMENTARY, 6 and 19. Cf. Ganelon's allusion to Charlemagne's *grant orguill* in v. 578. On point of view, consult Scholes and Kellogg, *Nature of Narrative*, chap. 7, pp. 240–82.

485. See COMMENTARY, 5.

486. On this notion, see Bowra, *Heroic Poetry*, p. 51; Charles A. Knudson, "Serments téméraires et gabs: notes sur un thème littéraire," *Société Rencesvals. IVe Congrès International*, pp. 254–60. Cf. the emphatic language of the martyrs. Delehaye, *Les Passions des martyrs*, pp. 191–92; Réau, III, 2:787. Jenkins, note to vv. 867 ff., points to the frequency of *vantances* in the chansons de geste; Brandt, *Medieval History*, pp. 124–25, discusses boasting as an aristocratic stance; Duggan, *Song of Roland*, pp. 118–25, 161, details its formulaic aspect. In the *Psychomachia*, vv. 161–168, Job "thought of his healed sores and, by the number of his scars, recounted his thousands of hard-won fights, his own glory and his foes' dishonour." This passage is cited by Mickel, "Parallels in *Psychomachia* and *Roland*," pp. 442–43, but with reference to Turpin.

487. Past: COMMENTARY, 4 (vv. 198–200) and 25 (Roland's praise of Durendal); future: COMMENTARY, 34 (Roland's prophetic words at Aix). On this function of speeches, see Bowra, *Heroic Poetry*, p. 31.

488. INTRODUCTION, 19, C; COMMENTARY, 34. Cf. Durendal = Roland's soul (COMMENTARY, 24, n. 66). In *Chanson de Guillaume*, vv. 328–329 and 333–334, the noble warriors who decide to stay with Vivien are compared to gold that has been separated from an alloy. Jeanne Wathelet-Willem, *Recherches sur la Chanson de Guillaume: Etudes accompagnées d'une édition*, 2 vols., Bibliothèque de la Faculté de Philosophie et Lettres de l'Université de Liège 210 (Paris: Les Belles Lettres, 1975), 1:297, n. 79.

489. Hanns Swarzenski, *Monuments of Romanesque Art: The Art of Church Treasures in North-Western Europe* (Chicago: University of Chicago Press, 1954), p. 27; Cames, *Byzance*, index, p. 314, s.v. Coloris, fond d'or. Cf. COMMENTARY, 25. Certain characters in the *Song of Roland* give off emanations of a different sort. Petit de Julleville, cited by Jenkins, note to v. 866, observes apropos of the Saracens' prebattle *vantances:* "Roland n'assiste pas à là scène qui suit, et pourtant il la remplit. Tous les principaux chefs sarrasins s'avancent tour à tour, et jurent de tuer Roland. Dans toute l'armée chrétienne ils ne voient que Roland; et cette haine universelle de l'ennemi contre un seul homme rehausse singulièrement le héros. Il y a là un art incontestable et délicat." Burger, "Les deux scènes du cor," p. 114, writes of the "présence invisible" of Ganelon in the first debate between Roland and Oliver. In the discussion that followed this paper at the Liège Colloquium in 1957, Pierre Le Gentil pointed out that, in similar fashion, Roland's presence could be felt in the discussion between Ganelon and Marsile at Saragossa (*La Technique littéraire des chansons de geste*, p. 125). Additionally, the spectres of Basan and Basile hover over the first French council; several characters, veiled and unveiled, appear in Charlemagne's dreams; the image of the dying hero beckons insistently to the French as they hasten to his rescue (vv. 1804 ff.); Saint Giles figures mysteriously at Roncevaux (COMMENTARY, 22); and the spirit of Roland and Oliver inhabits Rabel and Guinemant in the battle against Baligant (v. 3016). But it is after the hero's death that a ghost looms largest in this poem. Roland's ethereal presence is sensed by the French on the banks of the Ebro (v. 2475), and his memory guides the Emperor as he searches for his nephew's body (vv. 2402, 2855–2876).

Above all, Roland's form rises before French minds at Aix, when Alda falls dead, when the color of Ganelon's cheeks is noted (COMMENTARY, 45, vv. 3762–3763), when sparks fly heavenward during the judicial combat (COMMENTARY, 46, v. 3912), and when the hero is ultimately vindicated by Thierry (COMMENTARY, 47). Ghostly appearances, good and bad (Fr. *revenant*), are frequent in folklore, but Roland's posthumous returns are more in the tradition of the supernatural occurrences following the death of martyrs (Delehaye, *Les Passions des martyrs*, pp. 213–18).

490. On Ganelon's apostrophe to his sword (vv. 445–449), see INTRODUCTION, 18, G. For another evil reflection, see COMMENTARY, 2 (Marsile's marble couch).

491. Cf. Vance, *Reading the Song of Roland*, p. 68: "Roland and Charlemagne are supreme in the warrior's ethos and share in a single identity, except that one is young and bold, the other old and wise." On the notion that Charlemagne and Roland share the same mystical body, see Thierry's speech at the trial of Ganelon (COMMENTARY, 45). In Roland's apostrophe to Durendal in the *Pseudo-Turpin*, the hero refers to his weapon as a sword of justice (Meredith-Jones, p. 191: "Per te Dei iusticia adimpletur") and Charles later links this image to that of the right arm when alluding to his nephew (Meredith-Jones, p. 205: "O brachium dextrum corporis mei . . . spata iusticiae, asta inflexibilis"). The sword of justice is one of the attributes of the Messiah as an eschatological judge (Revelation 1:16) and symbolizes the power of the Word of God, which strikes down pagans (Revelation 19:15; cf. Isaiah 11:4 [a rod]). The iconography of Roland as Charles's sword-bearer, that is, as the incarnation of the Emperor's justice, has been studied by Lejeune and Stiennon, 1:120, 140–42, 359, and pl. III; 2: fig. 85. In v. 1195 Charlemagne's right arm seems to encompass all the Franks; in v. 2935, Roland is synonymous with France. Cf. COMMENTARY, 11, n. 17.

492. Cf. Albert Pauphilet, "Sur la *Chanson de Roland*," *Romania* 59 (1933): 161–98; idem, *Le Legs du moyen âge* (Melun: Librairie d'Argences, 1950), pp. 77–90; see also the discussion in *Olifant* 1, no. 3 (1974): 8; no. 4, p. 75. On the related debate concerning the effects of Charles's victory over Baligant, which supposedly tarnishes that of Roland, see Menéndez Pidal, pp. 124–25, cited by Moignet, p. 257.

493. On Roland and Oliver as reflections of each other, see INTRODUCTION, 19, C and H.

494. Gaston Paris, *Histoire poétique de Charlemagne* (1865; rpt. Paris: Bouillon, 1905); Bédier, *Légendes épiques*, 4:437–69; Robert Folz, *Le Souvenir et la légende de Charlemagne dans l'Empire germanique médiéval* (Paris: Les Belles Lettres, 1950).

495. Adam, *Primitive Art*, pp. 48–49.

496. Baudouin de Gaiffier, S.J., "La légende de Charlemagne: Le péché de l'empereur et son pardon," in *Recueil de travaux offert à M. Clovis Brunel par ses amis, collègues et élèves*, Ecole des Chartes, Mémoires et documents 12 (Paris: Société de l'Ecole des Chartes, 1955), 1:490–503; Rita Lejeune, "Le péché de Charlemagne et la *Chanson de Roland*," in *Studia philologica: Homenaje ofrecido a Dámaso Alonso por sus amigos y discípulos con ocasión de su 60.° aniversario* (Madrid: Gredos, 1961), 2:339–71; Gerard J. Brault, "The Legend of Charlemagne's Sin in Girart d'Amiens," *Romance Notes* 4 (1962): 72–75; Auguste Demoulin, "Charlemagne, la légende de son péché et le choix de Ganelon pour l'ambassade," *Marche romane* 25 (1975): 105–26. Is there perhaps a parallel in Moses's sin, the exact nature of which is left in doubt in Numbers 20:12, and which means he cannot lead the sons of Israel into the Promised Land? In Deuteronomy 1:37 the Hebrew liberator's sin is said to be his abandonment of the campaign against Canaan. See *The Jerusalem Bible*, note to Numbers 20:12. Cf. note 64 above.

497. Bédier, *Légendes épiques*, 4:443; Réau, III, 1:342; Menéndez Pidal, pp. 245, 310. Charles is associated with David in the *Pseudo-Turpin* (Meredith-Jones, p. 223), as is Roland (Meredith-Jones, p. 205). Katzenellenbogen, *Allegories*, p. 15:

in a miniature of the Bamberg Apocalypse (executed 1001–2) Abraham is associated with God-fearing Obedience, Moses with Purity, David with Penitence and Job with Patience [n. 3: 'The inscription: "Jussa Dei complens. Mundo sis corpore splendens. Poeniteat culpae. Quid sit patientia disce" defines virtuous conduct as that which the Emperor Otto III, possessor of the manuscript, seeks to realise and which is represented by the four virtues and their Old Testament counterparts'].

On Charles's largesse, see COMMENTARY, 43.

498. Bédier, *Légendes épiques*, 3:448; 4:440; Jenkins, notes to vv. 339–40, 1931, 3066; Kantorowicz, *King's Two Bodies*, pp. 46 ff. The idea can be traced back to Hebrews 4:14–7:28. Vos, "Aspects of Biblical Typology," p. 115, suggests that Charles is more *rex* than *sacerdos*.

499. *The Jerusalem Bible*, p. 31, note *g*; Locke, *Quest*, pp. 62–63.

500. Réau, II, 1:128–29. See notes 258 and 274 above.

501. Lejeune and Stiennon, 1:203–6.

502. Ibid., 2: fig. 102. The communion scene does not appear in Turoldus's poem. On a related tradition (Roland's lay communion), see Gerard J. Brault, "Girart d'Amiens and the *Pseudo-Turpin Chronicle*," *Zeitschrift für romanische Philologie* 76 (1960): 88–90; Payen, *Le Motif du repentir*, p. 119 and n. 27.

503. *The Song of Roland*, trans. Dorothy L. Sayers, The Penguin Classics (Baltimore: Penguin, 1963), p. 14.

504. See INTRODUCTION, 3. *La Chanson de Roland*, ed. Calin, p. 10: "C'est l'archétype du Père qui domine chez lui, un Père puissant mais tendre, désolé de la perte du Fils mais qui continue la lutte, à la tête de son peuple, afin que la société survive. Il est homme et surhomme à la fois." See also idem, *Epic Quest*, p. 209.

505. Erich Köhler, "'Conseil des barons' und 'jugement des barons': Epische Fatalität und Feudalrecht im altfranzösischen Rolandslied," *Sitzungsberichte der Heidelberger Akademie der Wissenschaften*, Philosophisch-historische Klasse (Heidelberg: Winter, 1968), p. 28; Herman Braet, "Fonction et importance du songe dans la chanson de geste," *Le Moyen Age* 77 (1971): 409–10.

506. Matthew 26:20–25; Mark 14:18–21; Luke 22:21–23; John 13:21–30. Cf. COMMENTARY, 11 (v. 840).

507. Frye, *Anatomy of Criticism*, pp. 174–75, on the theme of withdrawal and return. Cf. the death and rebirth archetype; Calin, *Epic Quest*, pp. 113–15. See also note 504 above.

508. Meredith-Jones, pp. 195, 199, 201, 229, 231.

509. Jenkins, pp. xxiv–xxvi, xl-xliii; Faral, *La Chanson de Roland*, pp. 227–41.

510. Jenkins, p. xxv.

511. See, for example, Le Gentil, p. 124.

512. See INTRODUCTION, 19, C.

513. Jones, pp. 66–68. Cf. Glyn S. Burgess, "*Orgueil* and *Fierté* in Twelfth-Century French," *Zeitschrift für romanische Philologie* 89 (1973): 103–22.

514. Jones, p. 67.

515. INTRODUCTION, 19, C and D; COMMENTARY, 25; Burgess, *Vocabulaire précourtois*, p. 105, n. 8.

516. INTRODUCTION, 19, A.

517. Jenkins, p. xlii: "Roland is not at the end the same person he was at the beginning: he has greatly developed." Cf. Lanson, cited by Jenkins, note to v. 2397.

518. Blaise, par. 494. On Cluny's role in the formulation of the chivalric ideal, see Paul Rousset, "L'idéal chevaleresque dans deux *Vitae* clunisiennes," *Mélanges Edmond-René Labande*, pp. 623–33, especially pp. 630–32. Heer, *Medieval World*, p. 108: "[According to Saint Bernard,] man was made in the image of God, and had a

'great soul', *anima magna*. A good man could stand upright and erect before God. But man was bowed low by sin: the bent soul, *anima curva*, turned away from God in rebellion. The source of all sin was wilfulness, *proprium consilium*: man thought he knew better than God." For further discussion of Roland as a Humility figure, see INTRODUCTION, 12, and notes 255 and 519.

519. For a comparison of the figure of Faith in the *Psychomachia*, a personage endowed with a stout heart and a burning desire to fight new battles, with Roland, see Mickel, "Parallels in *Psychomachia* and *Roland*," pp. 440–41. According to Renoir, "Roland's Lament," p. 575, the tone of the passage where the hero recognizes that the French rearguard is dying for his sake (Laisse 140) is "consistently one of profound humility." However, Renoir believes that Roland was initially proud. See INTRODUCTION, 3 and note 61; COMMENTARY, 21 and notes 5 and 9. Cf. Le Gentil, p. 107: "[Roland] se dépouille peu à peu de tout égoïsme . . . il consent un bel acte d'humilité."

520. Jenkins, p. liv. This Turoldus is Jenkins's candidate for authorship of the *Song of Roland*.

521. Meredith-Jones, pp. 201, 203. In this lament the author states that Roland protected the widow, the orphan, and the poor. A few lines later, Charlemagne lauds the same traits in his nephew's character: "*baculus orfanorum et viduarum cibus, refectio tam pauperum quam divitum*" (p. 205). On the evolution of these obligations of the king and, later, the knight, see Bloch, *Feudal Society*, 2:316–19, and, especially, Jean Larmat, "La veuve, le pauvre et l'orphelin: Un aspect politique de Charlemagne dans le *Couronnement de Louis*," Proceedings of the Seventh International Congress of the Société Rencesvals held at Liège in 1976. The concept stems from Isaiah 1:17.

522. Meredith-Jones, p. 243. Before the Franks set out for Spain, Conrad, v. 216, has Charles urge them to be humble.

523. Anna Granville Hatcher, "Eulalie, lines 15–17," *Romanic Review* 40 (1949): 241–49.

524. F. J. Barnett, "Virginity in the Old French Sequence of Saint Eulalia," *French Studies* 13 (1959): 252–56; idem, "Some Notes to the Sequence of Saint Eulalia," in *Studies in Medieval French Presented to Alfred Ewert in Honour of His Seventieth Birthday* (Oxford: Clarendon Press, 1961), pp. 1–25.

525. *The Jerusalem Bible*, p. 121, note *i*.

526. Meredith-Jones, p. 199.

527. Paul's vision is never depicted in medieval art. Réau, III, 3:1044.

528. Blaise, p. 110, s.v. virginalis, virgineus, virginitas, virgo, and Virgo. In the Middle Ages male virginity was admired in such exemplars as Saint Benedict, Saint John the Evangelist, and Saint Joseph. Frye, *Anatomy of Criticism*, p. 201: "The central theme of [the fourth phase of the hero's life] is that of the maintaining of the integrity of the innocent world against the assault of experience. . . . The integrated body to be defended may be individual or social, or both. . . . The theme of invincible innocence or virginity is associated with similar images in literature." On the motif of the chaste knight, see *Perlesvaus*, 2:181–82. In *La Queste del saint graal: Roman du XIIIe siècle*, ed. Albert Pauphilet, Classiques français du moyen âge 33 (Paris: Champion, 1949), pp. 123–25, a hermit explains to Lancelot that the supreme virtues are Virginity and Humility which he ranks higher than Patience, Justice, or even Charity. The problem of Perceval's virginity in the *Conte del graal* is far more complex. See Jean Frappier, *Chrétien de Troyes et le mythe du graal: Etude sur Perceval ou le Conte du Graal* (Paris: Société d'édition d'enseignement supérieur, 1972), pp. 94–108.

529. Blaise, pp. 63–65, s.v. intactus, integer, integritas, inviolabilis, inviolatus. These, and the related epithets *immaculata*, *innocentia*, and *purissima*, are most frequently found in hymns, litanies, and prayers to the Virgin. On the concept of integrity, see *The Jerusalem Bible*, p. 1145, note *q*.

530. Cf. martyrs who suffer no wounds in spite of being tortured. Delehaye, *Les Passions des martyrs*, p. 209. On the aureole surrounding the entire body as a sign of divine protection, see COMMENTARY, 22. In the *Pseudo-Turpin* Roland is pierced by four Saracen lances and also grievously wounded by enemy spears and stones (Meredith-Jones, p. 187).

531. See COMMENTARY, 25. The cult of the Virgin in the *Pseudo-Turpin* is discussed by Meredith-Jones, pp. 52, 318, note to p. 198, line v.

532. Conrad, v. 3291.

533. Ibid., vv. 3297–3298.

534. In v. 89, Conrad states that the Franks must have pure hearts to serve God; in v. 266, Turpin tells his men to purify their hearts; and in v. 6187, the poet refers to Roland as being 'whiter than snow'.

535. In the second horn scene Oliver angrily swears that if they survive the battle he will see to it that Roland never lies in Alda's embrace (COMMENTARY, 18, vv. 1719–1721). Frye, *Anatomy of Criticism*, p. 200: "The archetype of erotic innocence is less commonly marriage than the kind of 'chaste' love that precedes marriage; the love of brother for sister, or of two boys for each other."

536. Conrad dwells on Alda's virginity in vv. 8717–8719.

537. However, in the *Karlamagnús Saga*, Roland is seduced by Geluviz, Ganelon's wife. *Karlamagnús Saga: The Saga of Charlemagne and His Heroes*, trans. Constance B. Hieatt, vol. 1 (Toronto: The Pontifical Institute of Mediaeval Studies, 1975), pp. 152–53 (see also p. 154). Boiardo's *Orlando innamorato* and Ariosto's *Orlando furioso* are works of the Italian Renaissance. Lejeune and Stiennon, 1:340, 390, and 393, n. 29. There is no medieval source for the wedding referred to in Victor Hugo's poem "Le Mariage de Roland," a work ultimately derived from *Girart de Vienne*.

538. Lejeune and Stiennon, 1:320–23, 349, n. 11, 354, 387–88; pl. LV; 2: figs. 372–75, 431, 472, 474.

539. Bibliography in Gérard, "L'axe Roland-Ganelon," p. 452, n. 10; Stranges, "The Character and the Trial of Ganelon," pp. 333–67. See also note 542 below and COMMENTARY, 7, note 4.

540. T. Atkinson Jenkins, "Why Did Ganelon Hate Roland?" *PMLA* 36 (1921): 119–33. For a review of scholarship on Ganelon, see Menéndez Pidal, pp. 323–24, 425–27; Mandach, *Naissance*, 1:67–69, 154; Vos, "Aspects of Biblical Typology," pp. 146–54 (see also idem, "Ganelon's 'Mortal Rage'," pp. 15–26). Add the motivation provided by the *Karlamagnús Saga* (Ganelon's wife seduced Roland). See n. 537 above.

541. Meredith-Jones, p. 181. In this version Marsile also sends forty horses laden with excellent wine and a thousand beautiful Saracen women so that the Christians will become inebriated and fornicate, angering God, who will let them die (Meredith-Jones, pp. 181, 183, 185; see also p. 316, n.). Gaston Paris believed that greed was the original motivation for Ganelon's treachery and that Turoldus added the further complication of the quarrel. This was one of the arguments he used to prove that the *Pseudo-Turpin* antedated the *Roland*. Since then scholars have generally considered the matter of the traitor's greed within the framework of this discussion, usually concluding with Bédier, *Légendes épiques*, 3:405, n. 1, that the argument is reversible and therefore not very convincing. Horrent, p. 119, n. 3.

542. Leslie C. Brook, "Le 'forfait' de Roland dans le procès de Ganelon: Encore sur un vers obscur de la *Chanson de Roland*," *Société Rencesvals. IVe Congrès International*, pp. 120–28. In note to vv. 342ff., *La Chanson de Roland*, ed. Jenkins, refers to "the human side of Count Ganelon" and suggests that Turoldus "draws the opposite of an ignoble personage." For a list of scholars who have endeavored to "rehabilitate" Ganelon, see bibliography referred to in note 539 above. Bowra, *Heroic Poetry*, pp.

306–8, analyzes Ganelon's character as "a series of psychological states," which the poet presents piecemeal.

543. Petit de Julleville, cited by Jenkins, note to v. 217, observes: "Il est clair que Ganelon hait Roland avant que le poème commence." Cf. Bédier, *Légendes épiques*, 3:413: "une haine obscure, ancienne, dont lui-même ne sait pas encore toute l'intensité, l'anime contre son fillâtre." Lejeune, "Le péché de Charlemagne," suggests that awareness of Roland's incestuous birth explains Ganelon's hypersensitivity to insult in the scene where a messenger must be chosen to deliver the Emperor's message to Saragossa.

544. See, for example, Moignet, pp. 45, 49, 262, note to v. 3758. I no longer feel, as I stated apropos of v. 3756, in "Le Thème de la Mort," p. 230, n. 21, that: "Sans doute Charles simplifie un peu trop la chose quand il qualifie le mobile de Ganelon de cupidité." I now agree with Jenkins, p. xxix: "Greed for riches and display, and envy of the wealth of others, is the cause of the proud Count's downfall." The greed motive is mentioned in a passage of Venice IV, which many critics believe was part of the original material missing in the Oxford copy. Segre, after v. 813 (discussion, pp. 159–60).

545. P. K. Meagher, "Avarice," in *New Catholic Encyclopedia*, 1:1122–23.

546. Réau, I:165. Similarly, in the *Chanson de Guillaume*, the traitor Tiébaut is guilty of greed. Wathelet-Willem, 1:298–99 and n. 87. For passages in Old French romances concerning this vice, see Ménard, *Le Rire*, pp. 161, 174–75.

547. Lester K. Little, "Pride Goes Before Avarice: Social Change and the Vices in Latin Christendom," *American Historical Review* 76 (1971): 16–49.

548. Job 31:24; Psalms 52:7; Proverbs 11:28; John 12:6; *Psychomachia*, v. 530; Little, p. 37; Cames, *Allégories*, pp. 98–99.

549. Blaise, par. 46–47, 150, 472.

550. Cames, *Allégories*, p. 61, states that the list was derived in part from the *Psychomachia* and in part from a treatise ascribed to Hugh of Saint Victor; see, however, *PL*, 76, col. 621.

551. The second part of this quotation is drawn from Saint Paul's admonition to the deacons in 1 Timothy 3:8.

552. Katzenellenbogen, *Allegories*, fig. 60; Cames, *Allégories*, fig. 60.

553. Katzenellenbogen, *Allegories*, p. 2; Cames, *Allégories*, pp. 63–64. The image of the murderous and treacherous fox in association with Judas and Ganelon occurs in Chaucer, "The Nun's Priest's Tale," vv. 3227, 3286. Cf. the image of Herod the fox in Luke 13:32. For Ganelon as a Herod figure, see Vos, "Aspects of Biblical Typology," pp. 150–51.

554. Mickel, "Parallels in *Psychomachia* and *Roland*," pp. 448–49, cites this passage in the *Psychomachia* and observes: "Although Ganelon's betrayal certainly appears to have been motivated by a desire for vengeance, considerable emphasis is placed in the bribes he accepts from the Saracens."

555. Brault, "Le Thème de la Mort," p. 230; idem, "Ganelon et Roland," p. 404. On the diabolical implications of lying, see note 563 below.

556. Cames, *Allégories*, p. 64.

557. Ibid., pp. 64–66.

558. Ibid., p. 65. In the *Charroi de Nîmes*, vv. 678 ff., Aymon le Vieil also preaches prudence at the wrong time. Payen, *Le Motif du repentir*, p. 158 and n. 2.

559. Cf. also Ganelon's relatives, vv. 2558, 2564. Brault, "Le Thème de la Mort," p. 235.

560. Cames, *Allégories*, p. 64.

561. The dog and the pig are also mentioned in *Roland*, vv. 1751, 2591. Cf. also vv. 30, 1874, 3223, 3527. Brault, "Le Thème de la Mort," p. 235. In the apocryphal

gospel known as the *Acta Thomae*, Judas is associated with the serpent who enticed Eve, Cain, and Pharaoh. Hand, *Dictionary*, p. 289.

562. INTRODUCTION, 10, A, 8; B, 1. Modern critics have not been unaware of the connection; see, for example, Comfort, "Character Types," pp. 336, 338, 344; Jenkins, note to v. 178. For bibliography and discussion, see Vos, "Aspects of Biblical Typology," p. 149 and nn. 80–82 (see also p. 68). Medieval exegetes viewed Judas and his prototype Cain as symbols of Felony. Réau, II, 1:96. On this typology, see *Queste*, pp. 217–18. For Ganelon's ancestry in the rhymed versions of the *Roland*, see Bédier, *Commentaires*, pp. 120–22; Horrent, pp. 180–81, 345; Segre, pp. 353–55.

563. Robertson, *Preface to Chaucer*, p. 164. For Baligant as an Envy figure, see COMMENTARY, 40. Ganelon's diabolism is clearly indicated by Charlemagne in v. 746 (COMMENTARY, 11). The traitor's demonic aspect is further underscored when he plays the role of accuser (see INTRODUCTION, 10, B, 3; COMMENTARY, 4, n. 11; COMMENTARY, 6; Blaise, par. 325 [adversarius]) and, through the process of inversion, when he suggests that Roland is a seducer (COMMENTARY, 4; Blaise, par. 325 [tentator]). On Ganelon as a liar (cf. the devil in Job 16:8), see note 555 above. Finally, the following description in Proverbs 6:16–19 suits Ganelon to a T: "There are six things that Yahweh hates, seven that his soul abhors: a haughty look, a lying tongue, hands that shed innocent blood, a heart that weaves wicked plots, feet that hurry to do evil, a false witness who lies with every breath, a man who sows dissension among brothers."

564. *La Chanson de Roland: A Modern French Translation*, trans. J. Geddes (1906; rpt. New York: Macmillan, 1926), p. xxxii. On Oliver's role in the *Song of Roland*, see Menéndez Pidal, pp. 336–65; Dufournet, *Cours sur Roland*, pp. 215–23.

565. Jenkins, pp. xxvi–xxix. Aebischer, *Préhistoire*, p. 280, points out that Oliver needs to be studied as part of an inseparable pair of companions. Aebischer implies, however, that this may not always have been so, since no special relationship is indicated in the *Pseudo-Turpin*. Cf., however, the testimony of the brothers Roland and Oliver in documents dating back to the beginning of the eleventh century. INTRODUCTION, 2, and n. 15.

566. Faral, *La Chanson de Roland*, pp. 215–21.

567. *FEW*, 11:203.

568. Cf. Manassas of Reims in 1080. Bloch, *Feudal Society*, 2:347. Other historical parallels include Odo, Bishop of Bayeux and brother of William the Conqueror, who was at the Battle of Hastings (Jenkins, p. xxxi); Adhémar, Bishop of Le Puy, who commanded a division of Bohémond's army during the First Crusade in 1098 (Jenkins, p. xxxii); and Turoldus, another brother, or perhaps a nephew of William the Conqueror (Rita Lejeune, "Le caractère de l'archevêque Turpin et les événements contemporains de la *Chanson de Roland* [version d'Oxford]," *Société Rencesvals. IVe Congrès International*, pp. 19–21). On the historical and spiritual background, see C. A. Robson, "The Character of Turpin in the *Chanson de Roland*," *Medium Aevum* 10 (1941): 97–100; Edmond Faral, "A propos de la *Chanson de Roland:* Genèse et signification du personnage de Turpin," *La Technique littéraire des chansons de geste*, pp. 271–80; Maurice Delbouille, "D'où venait la chanson de geste? A propos du livre d'Italo Siciliano, *Les Chansons de geste et l'épopée*," *Cahiers de civilisation médiévale* 15 (1972): 216–18. In Old French the noun *turpin*, of uncertain origin, means a kind of soldier. Barthélemy, the Recluse of Molliens, in his *Roman de Carité*, dated 1204, observes that *Cloistriers ont lor robe escourtee; / Escuiier sanlent et turpin* (Greimas, *Dictionnaire*, p. 648).

569. Faral, *La Chanson de Roland*, p. 221; Lejeune, "Le caractère de l'archevêque Turpin," p. 11.

570. Bédier, *Commentaires*, p. 307.

571. *The Jerusalem Bible*, p. 37, n. *b*.

572. Ibid., p. 1116: "The prophet is the bearer and interpreter of the word of God. This is succinctly expressed in two parallel passages: in Ex 4: 15–16, Aaron is the interpreter of Moses, Aaron the 'mouth' of Moses, Moses 'the god who inspired him'; in Ex 7:1, Moses is to be 'a god for Pharaoh', and Aaron his 'prophet' (*nabi*). We are reminded of the words of Yahweh to Jeremiah: 'I am putting my words into your mouth', Jr 1:9."

573. The prophetic role of women in heroic poetry is discussed by Bowra, *Heroic Poetry*, pp. 480–81, 489. Frye, *Anatomy of Criticism*, pp. 38–39: "Pathos presents its hero as isolated by a weakness which appeals to our sympathy because it is on our own level of experience. I speak of a hero, but the central figure of pathos is often a woman or a child . . . pathos is increased by the inarticulateness of the victim." Alda's role has been analyzed by Menéndez Pidal, pp. 366–67 and by Aebischer, *Préhistoire*, p. 279. On the name, see Delbouille, *Genèse*, pp. 110–11. Roland's prediction at Aix of the manner of his own passing and Charlemagne's anticipation of the arrival of *hume estrange* (vv. 2911, 2918) show the latter in more conventional prophetic roles. On Naimes, see INTRODUCTION, 19, K.

574. Frye, *Anatomy of Criticism*, p. 149: "The demonic erotic relation becomes a fierce destructive passion that works against loyalty or frustrates the one who possesses it. It is generally symbolized by a harlot, witch, siren, or other tantalizing female, a physical object of desire which is sought as a possession and therefore can never be possessed," Cf. Augier, "Conversions féminines," pp. 101–2; COMMENTARY, 8 (Bramimonde).

575. In medieval French literature, a king's counselors often give him bad advice; e.g., the Tristan romances and *Cligés*, vv. 1059–1071. Cf. the Pharaoh's wicked advisers in the Old Testament (COMMENTARY, 4). The Franks at times also incarnate the Theme of War-Weariness. Le Gentil, p. 151. Such *recreantise* runs counter to the chivalric ideal. Brandt, *Medieval History*, p. 111.

576. For bibliography on weeping, see COMMENTARY, 11, note 10. On the Franks as assessors, see COMMENTARY, 3 (vv. 110–113). The Franks are "functional onlookers," an audience within the poem. On this notion see Robert M. Lumiansky, "Dramatic Audience in *Beowulf*," *Journal of English and Germanic Philology* 51 (1952): 545–50. Cf. Alexandre Micha, "Le discours collectif dans l'épopée et dans le roman," *Mélanges de langue et de littérature du moyen âge et de la Renaissance offerts à Jean Frappier par ses collègues, ses élèves et ses amis*, Textes littéraires français 112 (Geneva: Droz, 1970), pp. 811–21.

577. Jonin, "La 'Clere' Espagne de Blancandrin," pp. 92–95, suggests that Christian communities in Spain, such as the important colony at Córdoba, communicated information about the Saracens to the outside world. Turoldus's view of the Saracens at times involves a curious confusion of Jews and pagan enemies of the Jews in the Bible. See, for example, the identification Ganelon-Judas-Jew in INTRODUCTION, 16, D (v. 366), and COMMENTARY, 2 (Marsile's hardness of heart) and 43 (the destruction of the idols found in synagogues and mosques). See also Bédier, *Commentaires*, pp. 51 (Caneliu) and 44–48 (Butentrot). In his apostrophe to Durendal in the *Pseudo-Turpin* Roland claims that he has often avenged the death of Christ by slaying Saracens and Jews (Meredith-Jones, p. 191).

578. Skidmore, *Moral Traits of Christians and Saracens*; William Wistar Comfort, "The Literary Role of the Saracens in the French Epic," *PMLA* 55 (1940): 628–59; C. Meredith-Jones, "The Conventional Saracen of the Songs of Geste," *Speculum* 17 (1942): 201–25; Frappier, *Chansons de geste*, 2:122–24; Payen, *Le Moyen Age*, pp. 105–7; Barbara D. Edmonds, "Le portrait des Sarrasins dans la *Chanson de Roland*," *French Review* 44 (1971): 870–80.

579. Bédier, *Commentaires*, p. 50; Horrent, p. 291. Cf. *Historia Karoli Magni et*

Rotholandi, ed. Meredith-Jones, pp. 288–89, note to p. 99, line x; pp. 296–99, note to p. 114, lines i–vi.

580. *Perlesvaus*, 1: lines 2172–2173; 2:231–32. For a similar use in the *Waltharius*, see Curtius, p. 245. On T-O (three-part world) maps, consult G. R. Crone, *Maps and Their Makers: An Introduction to the History of Cartography* (New York: Capricorn Books, 1966), p. 25. See also Le Goff, *Civilisation*, p. 178 and fig. 47.

581. Ménard, *Le Rire*, pp. 78–80.

582. Jenkins, note to v. 3662; Janson, *Apes and Ape Lore*, p. 17. See vv. 886 (males arz), 1392 (artimal), 3665 (sorz, falserie).

583. Halphen, p. 22.

584. Impurity is perhaps implicit in the name Bramimonde (COMMENTARY, 33, note 5). Conrad, v. 33, refers to the impure life of the Saracens in Spain (Wie unkuscli-chen si lebeten). On the moral significance of Saracen swarthiness and ugliness, see Colby, *Twelfth-Century French Literature*, pp. 72–88; Ménard, *Le Rire*, pp. 542–48. I do not know what prompts Payen, *Le Motif du repentir*, pp. 429–30, to assert: "Dans la chanson de geste, le païen n'est pas une figure de Satan." According to Hugh of Saint Victor, the contemplation of ugliness should turn men to sainthood and eternal beauty. Fritz Peter Knapp, "Die hässliche Gralsbotin und die victorinische Ästhetik," *Sprachkunst* 3 (1972): 1–10. According to Jonin, "La 'Clere' Espagne de Blancandrin," p. 90, Turoldus's contemporaries associated the Orient with opulence: "on a l'impression que les jongleurs dès qu'il s'agit d'Espagne ou d'Afrique traînent cet or comme une obsession." See also COMMENTARY, 4, note 21. Cf., however, OXFORD TEXT, ENGLISH TRANSLATION, v. 59, and COMMENTARY, 8, n. 10. On the notion of Oriental indolence, see COMMENTARY, 2, note 7.

585. See INTRODUCTION, 13, B; 14, B.

586. Brandt, *Medieval History*, pp. 138–39, cites examples of Christian knights being spared by Muslim warriors because of their valor, generous acts suggesting an appreciation of Saracen nobility. One is reminded, too, of Saint Louis's high opinion of Saladin. See COMMENTARY, 39 and note 9.

587. See INTRODUCTION, 14, B; 16, D; 19, G.

588. Cf. Einhard's designation of the Saracens, who sought to invade France but were halted by Charles Martel: *Nam pater ejus Karolus, qui tyrannos per totam Franciam dominatum sibi vindicantes obpressit et Sarracenos Galliam occupare temptantes duobus magnis proeliis* (Halphen, p. 10; see also p. 11, n. 2). Rare as an insult in Old French romances (Ménard, *Le Rire*, p. 723), the word often refers to frightful beasts in these works (Ménard, p. 132 and n. 334). Frye, *Anatomy of Criticism*, p. 148: "In the sinister human world one individual pole is the tyrant-leader, inscrutable, ruthless, melancholy, and with an insatiable will, who commands loyalty only if he is egocentric enough to represent the collective ego of his followers."

589. Peter Brieger, *English Art 1216–1307*, The Oxford History of English Art, 4 (Oxford: Clarendon Press, 1957), pp. 142, 145; Paul Deschamps and Marc Thibout, *La Peinture murale en France: Le haut moyen âge et l'époque romane*, Collection Ars et Historia (Paris: Plon, 1951), pls. XLIX, 2; LXII, 1; Cames, *Byzance*, pp. 148–49, pl. 44, figs. 176–77 (Herod and the Massacre of the Innocents); Lejeune and Stiennon, 2: figs. 86, 100, 122 (Marsile; cf., however, Charles in 2: figs. 103, 124). In medieval art a seated figure with crossed legs was the formula for a judge (*The Year 1200: A Centennial Exhibition at the Metropolitan Museum of Art*, vol. 1, Konrad Hoffmann, *The Exhibition*, The Cloisters Studies in Medieval Art 1 [New York: The Metropolitan Museum of Art, 1970], pp. 58, 98, 278), but it could also represent an Oriental despot. Brieger, pp. 149–50 (pls. 50–51). However, a leg crossed over the knee is not to be confused with the crossed-leg posture associated with tailors. See COMMENTARY, 2, note 7.

590. Reto R. Bezzola, *Les Origines et la formation de la littérature courtoise en Occident (500–1200)*, Bibliothèque de l'Ecole des hautes études 319 (Paris: Champion, 1963), vol. 3, pt. 1: 79–80, especially p. 79, n. 4. For *tyrannus*, a synonym for the devil, see Blaise, par. 314.

591. *Les Chétifs* in *La Chanson du Chevalier au cygne et de Godefroid de Bouillon*, ed. C. Hippeau, Collection des poètes français du moyen âge, 2 vols. (Paris: Aubry, 1877), 2:206. See also *Huon de Bordeaux*, ed. Pierre Ruelle, Université Libre de Bruxelles, Travaux de la Faculté de philosophie et lettres 20 (Brussels: Presses Universitaires de Bruxelles; Paris: Presses Universitaires de France, 1960), v. 5737.

592. Delehaye, *Les Passions des martyrs*, pp. 177–218. For Marsile as a Herod figure, see Vos, "Aspects of Biblical Typology," p. 145. On the association of Baligant with Superbia, see COMMENTARY, 30.

593. Auerbach, *Mimesis*, chap. 5, "Roland Against Ganelon," pp. 96–122, especially, pp. 116 ff.

594. Delbouille, "Les chansons de geste et le livre," p. 338, n. 30.

595. *Recueil général et complet des fabliaux des XIIIe et XIVe siècles imprimés ou inédits, publiés d'après les manuscrits*, eds. Anatole de Montaiglon and Gaston Raynaud, 6 vols. (Paris: Librairie des bibliophiles, 1872), 1:1–12. See also Faral, *Jongleurs*, pp. 81–82; Delbouille, p. 338.

596. Rychner, pp. 18–19 (p. 18: "Non seulement, donc, les chansons de geste étaient chantées, mais leur mélodie leur était propre: on pouvait parler de la musique du *Roland* comme de ses paroles"); Jacques Chailley, "Etudes musicales sur la chanson de geste et ses origines," *Revue de musicologie* 27 (1948): 1–27; idem, *L'Ecole musicale de Saint-Martial de Limoges jusqu'à la fin du XIe siècle* (Paris: Les Livres essentiels, 1960), Livre IV. See also G. Vecchi's unpublished paper, "La récitation chantée des chansons de geste," read at the Second International Congress of the Société Rencesvals, Venice, 1961 (summary in *Bulletin bibliographique de la Société Rencesvals* 3 [1963]: 108, item 280); Marilyn Feller Somville, "L'art du chanteur au moyen âge," *Société Rencesvals. VIe Congrès International*, pp. 287–302.

597. Faral, *Jongleurs*, p. 77; Rychner, p. 17. Cf. Bowra, *Heroic Poetry*, p. 39.

598. See the painting at Cressac (Charente) dated 1170–80 in Deschamps and Thibout, *Peinture murale*, p. 133; pl. LXVI, 1. Cf. Bowra, p. 38. On jongleur dress, see Faral, pp. 64–65; Lejeune, "Turold dans la tapisserie de Bayeux," pp. 419–25.

599. Rychner, p. 17.

600. Jeanne Wathelet-Willem, "L'épée dans les plus anciennes chansons de geste: Etude de vocabulaire," *Mélanges René Crozet* 1:435–49.

601. Foulet, *Glossaire*, p. 336: "La locution comporte toujours un pronom personnel—régime indirect,—par où se marque l'intérêt que prend à l'action annoncée soit un des personnages du poème . . . soit . . . le lecteur ou l'auditeur." See also Dufournet, *Cours sur Roland*, pp. 179–81.

602. Perhaps there were at times symbolic sides in this respect as in medieval art and drama, the jongleur looking or stepping to the right to highlight a good action or statement, to the left an evil equivalent.

603. Bowra, *Heroic Poetry*, p. 34; Wathelet-Willem, "L'épée," p. 448. Cf. also *The Vulgate Version of the Arthurian Romances*, ed. H. Oskar Sommer, Carnegie Institution of Washington, Publication no. 74 (Washington, D. C.: Carnegie Institution, 1911), 3, pt. 2:88.

604. The list of epics studied is provided by Rychner, pp. 7–8.

605. For bibliographical references, see Gerard J. Brault, "Kinesics and the Classroom: Some Typical French Gestures," *French Review* 36 (1963): 374–82, especially p. 374, n. 1.

606. Carl Sittl, *Die Gebärden der Griechen und Römer* (Leipzig: Teubner, 1890);

Barthélemy A. Taladoire, *Commentaires sur la mimique et l'expression corporelle du comédien romain*, Collection de la Faculté des lettres de l'Université de Montpellier 1 (Montpellier: Déhan, 1951), especially pt. 4, "Le Témoignage des rhéteurs"; Richard Brilliant, *Gesture and Rank in Roman Art: The Use of Gestures to Denote Status in Roman Sculpture and Coinage*, Memoirs of the Connecticut Academy of Arts and Sciences 14 (New Haven: The Academy, 1963). See also Faral, *Jongleurs*, pp. 233–36, "Caractère mimique de la littérature du moyen âge"; pp. 236–37, "Le monologue dramatique."

607. Erhard Lommatzsch, "Deiktische Elemente im Altfranzösischen," in his *Kleinere Schriften zur romanischen Philologie* (Berlin: Akademie, 1954), pp. 3–56.

608. Ganshof, *Feudalism*, p. 126.

609. *The Bayeux Tapestry: A Comprehensive Survey*, gen. ed. Sir Frank Stenton (London and New York: Phaidon, 1957), fig. 29.

610. Lejeune and Stiennon, 1:125–26; 2: fig. 98.

611. Philippe Ménard, "*Tenir le chief embronc, crosler le chief, tenir la main a la maissele*: trois attitudes de l'ennui dans les chansons de geste du XIIe siècle," *Société Rencesvals. IVe Congrès International*, pp. 145–55.

612. Yvonne Labande-Mailfert, "La douleur et la mort dans l'art des XIIe et XIIIe siècles," *Atti del V Convegno di Studi sulla spiritualità medievale* (Todi: Presso L'Accademia Tudertina, 1967), pp. 295–332. See also Erhard Lommatzsch, "Darstellung von Trauer und Schmerz in der altfranzösischen Literatur," *Zeitschrift für romanische Philologie* 43 (1923): 20–67.

613. Mary Laura Heuser, "Gestures and Their Meaning in Early Christian Art," Ph.D. diss., Radcliffe College, 1954.

614. Karl von Amira, "Die Handgebärden in den Bilderhandschriften des Sachsenspiegels," *Akademie der Wissenschaften* [Munich], Abhandlungen der philosophisch-philologischen Klasse 23 (1909): 163–263.

615. Cf. (1) absolution: *Roland*, v. 340; Lejeune and Stiennon, 2: fig. 28.

(2) blessing: *Roland*, vv. 2194, 2848, 3066; *Le Voyage de Charlemagne à Jérusalem et à Constantinople*, ed. Paul Aebischer, Textes littéraires français 115 (Geneva: Droz; Paris: Minard, 1965), v. 87; *Raoul de Cambrai, chanson de geste*, eds. Paul Meyer and Auguste Longnon, Société des anciens textes français (Paris: Didot, 1882), v. 73; Amira, "Die Handgebärden," p. 202; Lejeune and Stiennon, 2: figs. 30, 104, 114, 118.

(3) commendation: *Roland*, vv. 223, 696; *Le Couronnement de Louis, chanson de geste du XIIe siècle*, ed. Ernest Langlois, 2d ed., Classiques français du moyen âge 22 (Paris: Champion, 1925), v. 1902; Amira, "Die Handgebärden," p. 242.

(4) embrace: *Roland*, vv. 2174, 2202, 3939; *Couronnement de Louis*, v. 1742; *Le Charroi de Nîmes, chanson de geste du XIIe siècle*, ed. J.-L. Perrier, Classiques français du moyen âge 66 (Paris: Champion, 1931), v. 723; Amira, "Die Handgebärden," p. 246; Lejeune and Stiennon, 2: figs. 95, 113, 148.

(5) orant attitude of prayer: *Roland*, v. 419; *Couronnement de Louis*, v. 58; Labande-Mailfert, "La douleur et la mort," p. 323; Lejeune and Stiennon, 2: figs. 146, 147, 149.

See also note 611 above. On gestures in Turoldus's poem, see Ruth Hoppe, *Die romanische Geste im Rolandslied*, Schriften der Albertus-Universität 10 (Königsberg and Berlin: Ost-Europa, 1937).

Notes to the Commentary

References to the Introduction, Commentary, Manuscript, and Oxford Text, English Translation are in small capitals. References to illustrations in the text are in italics.

COMMENTARY 1

1. Paul John Jones, *Prologue and Epilogue in Old French Lives of Saints Before 1400*, Series in Romanic Languages and Literatures 24 (Philadelphia: University of Pennsylvania Press, 1933).

2. Manfreid Gsteiger, "Note sur les préambules des chansons de geste," *Cahiers de civilisation médiévale* 2 (1959): 213–20. Payen, *Le Moyen Age*, p. 38, cautions against taking the injunctions to silence in these prologues too literally: "il faut bien se garder d'être dupe, puisque les 'Oyez seigneurs' et les 'Faites paix' se rencontrent surtout dans l'épopée décadente, à une époque où la chanson de geste est indubitablement lue et non plus récitée, dans les salles des châteaux et non plus en plein air." On this archaistic device, see INTRODUCTION, n. 166. On formulas in prologues, see Pierre Gallais, "Recherches sur la mentalité des romanciers français du moyen âge," *Cahiers de civilisation médiévale* 7 (1964): 479–93.

3. Gsteiger, p. 213.

4. Venice IV, vv. 1–11. Cf. Conrad, vv. 1–16.

5. Gsteiger, p. 213, n. 6, citing Ernst R. Curtius, "Ueber die altfranzösische Epik," *Zeitschrift für romanische Philologie* 54 (1944): 280–82 (who states that the *Roland*'s beginning *in medias res* is a reminiscence of the *Aeneid*), suggests that this procedure may be evidence of clerical influence. On *ordo artificialis* vs. *ordo naturalis* in medieval rhetorical treatises, see Kelly, *Sens and Conjointure*, pp. 86 ff. Karl D. Uitti, "Chrétien de Troyes' *Yvain*: Fiction and Sense," *Romance Philology* 22 (1969): 471–83, discusses the opening scenes of the *Vie de Saint Alexis*, the *Roland*, and Chrétien's *Yvain*.

6. The expression recurs in vv. 197, 266, 2610, and 2736. On epic seven, see Vos, "Aspects of Biblical Typology," chap. 4, pp. 178–228 (reference, p. 186, to fullness of time).

7. Seven years is a commonplace in Old French literature and has classical antecedents; Jenkins, note to v. 2. Cf. seven days, seven years, and seven times twenty years in *Yvain*, v. 173; *Conte del graal*, vv. 6176, 8029–8030, 8851–8852. In the *Enéas* seven years is the length of time Venus has not slept with Vulcan because of a quarrel (*Enéas, roman du XIIe siècle*, ed. J.-J. Salverda de Grave, vol. 1, Classiques français du moyen âge 44 [1925; rpt. Paris: Champion, 1964], v. 4349. During the Middle Ages the end of the world was expected in 7,000 years, a period of time equated to the seven days of Genesis. Locke, *Quest*, p. 49. Vance, "Notes on the Development of Formulaic Language," p. 430, relates the verse to the archetype of the Descent into Hell, or the Underworld. See also INTRODUCTION, 13, and n. 266.

8. Jenkins, caption for Laisse 1; Le Gentil, p. 91; Rychner, p. 38, Cf. Le Gentil,

p. 112, where the entire first part of the poem is referred to as prologue to "l'épisode central," that is, Roncevaux.

9. Lejeune and Stiennon, 2: fig. 266.

10. Ibid., 1:51–58.

11. Ibid., 1:271. Cf. the concept of the preamble in Stricker as an "image liminaire" in Lejeune and Stiennon, 1:230, and the opening passages of Revelation (Réau, II, 2:685–86) and the *Psychomachia*. The dueling knights ornamenting Psalm 1 in the Saint Albans Psalter do not relate to the initial hymn but constitute "a kind of pictorial motto for the whole Psalter" (*The St. Albans Psalter*, p. 151; for the text of the great marginal gloss that explicates the Book of Psalms as a metaphor of spiritual warfare, see pp. 163–64).

12. Charles is actually at Cordres when Marsile holds his council (v. 71) and this is where the Saracen emissaries find him (v. 97). By the time Ganelon returns from his mission, however, Charles will have reached Galne (v. 662) which, Turoldus informs us, is nearer his homeland and was destroyed by Roland. On anatopism, see INTRODUCTION, 16, D.

13. Ménard, *Le Rire*, p. 111: "Par définition, le conteur sait d'avance le sort finalement réservé aux méchants. A l'égard de ses personnages le romancier a la même prescience que Dieu devant sa création. Voilà qui lui permet d'ironiser. Ainsi dans le *Roland* l'annonce d'un malheur inexorable pour Marsile est faite dès les premiers vers." See also pp. 472–78, 484–85. The line in question (v. 9) is referred to as an illustration of a classical rhetorical procedure (Exclamatio ex persona poetae) by Curtius, *Littérature européenne*, p. 545, and as being part of the jongleur's oral technique by Rychner, p. 73.

14. The title Magnus was first given to Charles by Nithardus. Bédier, *Légendes épiques*, 4: 442. It is not a Latinism here. Curtius, p. 40. Proper names are a formulaic way of beginning a laisse. Rychner, pp. 71–72. On the significance of being named first in the *Song of Roland*, see Pauphilet, *Le Legs du moyen âge*, p. 77: "Il est le signe évident de l'unité du poème." On the affective quality of the term *nostre*, see Frappier, *Chansons de geste*, 2:68, n. 2.

15. Gräf, *Parallelismus im Rolandslied*, p. 10, notes the Charles-Marsile, God-pagan divinities opposition here. Zaal, *A lei francesa*, p. 91, mentions antithesis. As in Job 1:6–22 (see also Revelation 12:7; Réau, II, 1:56), a war in heaven parallels the struggle on earth. INTRODUCTION, 14, A, 5, and n. 295.

16. Cf. the notion of Carthage as a seaside fortress in *Enéas*, vv. 407–548. See Raymond J. Cormier, "The Present Status of Studies on the *Roman d'Enéas*," *Cultura Neolatina* 31 (1971): 7, n. 1; 12. The city of Saragossa was never captured by Charlemagne. Menéndez Pidal, pp. 263–64, believes it may reflect a tradition present in certain early chronicles.

17. Jenkins, note to v. 6.

18. Aurelio Roncaglia, "Sarraguce, ki est en une muntaigne," *Studi in onore di Angelo Monteverdi* (Modena: Società tip. editrice modenese, 1959), 2:629–40. Cf. Menéndez Pidal's explanation of *El Cid*, v. 2698 (los montes son altos), where *monte* = forest. Curtius, p. 246, n. 1.

19. Mandach, *Naissance*, 1:154. A comparable symbolic elevation occurs in connection with Jerusalem in the series of psalms known as the Song of Ascents. The city itself is actually located between two valleys. INTRODUCTION, 15, C.

20. Isaiah 14:13–14; cf. 2:14–15; Jeremiah 50:29; Ezekiel 28:14. Proceeding in analogous fashion, Noyer-Weidner, "Vom biblischen 'Gottesberg'," notes the Saragossa-Babylon connection. Vos, "Aspects of Biblical Typology," pp. 71–84, 98, identifies Saragossa with Jericho and the biblical "mountain of evil," but also, pp. 318–20, with Babylon (Babylon-New Jerusalem archetype).

21. Cf. the eagle, the tall ship, and the cedar of Lebanon in Psalms 37:35; Ezekiel 17; 27:3; 31:3.

22. Jeremiah 51:53.

COMMENTARY 2

1. In Venice IV Marsile also weeps (si plure). The Saracen king is again in the shade of a tree in vv. 407 and 2571; cf., however, v. 383 (Charles). *Verger* (v. 11) becomes an olive tree in other versions of the poem, including Conrad and the Norse *Saga*. Paul Aebischer, *Rolandiana Borealia: La Saga af Runzivals bardaga et ses dérivés scandinaves comparés à la Chanson de Roland. Essai de restauration du manuscrit français utilisé par le traducteur norrois*, Publications de la Faculté des lettres de l'Université de Lausanne 11 (Lausanne: Rouge, 1954), pp. 33, 89, asserts that the Norse translator did not know the meaning of *verger* (or of *pin* in v. 168 [p. 31]). Segre, note to v. 11, suggests that a different word was used to distinguish Marsile from Charles. See INTRODUCTION, 16, D. For the shade of a tree as a reminiscence of Adam and Eve (attempted concealment and, consequently, a symbol of Despair or paganism), see Robertson, "The Doctrine of Charity," p. 26. Cf. the shade of the juniper tree in 1 Kings 19:4–5 (Réau, II, 1:353–54).

2. Greimas, *Dictionnaire*, p. 255: *esmarbre* 'froid comme le marbre, glacé par la terreur'.

3. Curtius, pp. 240–45; Hatzfeld, *Literature Through Art*, p. 13; Stephen G. Nichols, Jr., *Formulaic Diction and Thematic Composition in the Chanson de Roland*, University of North Carolina Studies in the Romance Languages and Literatures 36 (Chapel Hill: University of North Carolina Press, 1961), pp. 29–35; Duggan, *Song of Roland*, pp. 42–48.

4. Bédier, *Légendes épiques*, 3:411–12. See also Gräf, *Parallelismus im Rolandslied*, p. 12; Horrent, p. 248. On the apparent contradiction between vv. 18 and 564, see Horrent, p. 237; Paul Zumthor, *Langue et techniques poétiques à l'époque romane (XI*e*–XIII*e *siècles)*, Bibliothèque française et romane, Série C: Etudes littéraires 4 (Paris: Klincksieck, 1963), p. 76. Marsile's desperate appeal in this scene will later be echoed by Ganelon's words during his trial (v. 21: "Si me guarisez e de mort e de hunte!" = v. 3787: "Getez mei hoi de mort e de calunje!"). Note also the ironic contrast between Saracen confusion here (v. 22: N'i ad paien ki un sul mot respundet) and French determination in the battle against Baligant (v. 3540: N'i ad icel ki un sul mot respundet).

5. Horrent, pp. 265–66. Foulet, *Glossaire*, referring also to v. 2556, defines the *perrun* in question as follows: "Bloc de pierre ou de marbre, qui se trouve à proximité d'un palais, où le roi peut siéger." On v. 2556, see COMMENTARY, 28. The technique here is evidently one of triplication: (1) Marsile on a marble slab (v. 12); (2) Charles on a throne (v. 115); (3) Marsile on a throne (v. 407). See Gräf, *Parallelismus im Rolandslied*, p. 11 and n. 9; see also, however, Baligant in v. 2804 (Horrent pp. 247–48, draws a parallel between Charles and Baligant only). Cf. also v. 21 ("Si me guarisez e de mort e de hunte!") and v. 3513 ("Morz estes, Baligant!").

6. Faral, La *Chanson de Roland*, p. 59. Cf. Horrent, p. 265: "Marsile étendu à l'oriental"; *The Song of Roland*, trans. Sayers, p. 20: "Oriental manner."

7. Clarence D. Rouillard, *The Turk in French History, Thought and Literature (1520–1660)* (Paris: Boivin, [1941]), p. 17 (Froissart, in 1396, reports a sultan seated in his tent on a silk rug), p. 21 (Jean de Wavrin, in 1442, refers to the seated Grand Turk), p. 39 (Gilles le Bouvier, early in the fifteenth century, mentions eating seated). Lying on an ivory bed or sprawling on a divan are symbols of self-indulgence and a false

sense of security in Amos 6:4. In the *Psychomachia*, v. 317, Luxuria is said to be lying down at a banquet table, but Prudentius specifies that this vice comes from the West, not the Orient. *Prudence, Psychomachie*, ed. and trans. Maurice Lavarenne (Paris: Les Belles Lettres, 1948), p. 61, note: "On s'étonne que Prudence fasse venir la Sensualité de l'Occident, plutôt que de l'Orient, pays du luxe et de la mollesse pour les anciens." Thomson in *Prudentius*, 1:300, note: "Many tentative explanations have been offered, one of them (with which Mr. T. R. Glover agrees) that Rome is meant." In 968 the Bishop of Cremona, returning from a visit to Constantinople, referred to the Greeks as soft and effeminate. Le Goff, *Civilisation*, p. 183. On Saracen opulence, see INTRODUCTION, n. 584. The Turkish custom of sitting cross-legged, like tailors, is attested in French sources beginning in 1519 (Rouillard, p. 178; for later citations, see pp. 194, 201, 235, n. 1, 274, 279). This posture is not to be confused with that of crossing a leg over the knee. See INTRODUCTION, n. 589. On the habit of reclining at meals, see pp. 205 (Thevet), 364 (Montaigne). Eastern mystery and lasciviousness are mentioned in passing, p. 173. For medieval illustrations of Arabs wearing turbans, see Lejeune and Stiennon, 1:246 (2: fig. 237), 281 (pl. XXXVIII), 288 (2: fig. 292A), 289 (2: figs. 297, 298), 304 (2: figs. 333, 354). See also Le Goff, *Civilisation*, pp. 54–56. In one of the sketches illustrating Conrad's version, one of the figures wears what appears to be a burnoose. Lejeune and Stiennon, 1:123 (2: fig. 94).

8. See INTRODUCTION, 19.

9. Horrent, *Pèlerinage*, pp. 32–63. See INTRODUCTION, note 51.

10. See INTRODUCTION, 12. The reclining figure of the Fisher King in the *Conte del graal*, vv. 3085 ff., is not Byzantinism, for he is *mehaingné*. In a lyrical passage not found in its Ovidian source, the hero of *Piramus et Tisbé* throws himself down on the ground, lamenting his inability to be with his true love (*Piramus et Tisbé, poème du XIIe siècle*, ed. C. de Boer, Classiques français du moyen âge 26 [Paris: Champion, 1921], vv. 209–215). Assuming a prone position or throwing oneself on a bed are conventional ways of expressing the torment of love as a sickness in the Old French romances. Ménard, *Le Rire*, pp. 193–201 (see especially *degieter soi*, pp. 195–96). Add to Ménard's examples: *Béroul, Le Roman de Tristan, poème du XIIe siècle*, ed. Ernest Muret, 4th ed. revised by L. M. Defourques, Classiques français du moyen âge 12 (Paris: Champion, 1967), vv. 235–237; *Le Roman de Tristan par Thomas, poème du XIIe siècle*, ed. Joseph Bédier, Société des anciens textes français, 2 vols. (Paris: Didot, 1902), 1: vv. 1876–1877 (see 1: 368, note). In other Old French texts, marble is usually associated with caskets, horse-blocks, temples, or walls. Cf. *Roland*, vv. 2268, 2272, 2966. For other beds made of hard material, see *Erec*, v. 5830 (silver), and *Conte del graal*, vv. 7692 ff. (gold with silver cords).

11. *Les Romans de Chrétien de Troyes*, vol. 3, *Le Chevalier de la Charrete*, ed. Mario Roques, Classiques français du moyen âge 86 (Paris: Champion, 1958), vv. 1856–1936. On this espisode, see Tom Peete Cross and William A. Nitze, *Lancelot and Guenevere: A Study of the Origins of Courtly Love*, Modern Philology Monographs (Chicago: University of Chicago Press, 1930), pp. 8–9, Episode 11; *Perlesvaus*, 2:220–21, note to line 469; Roger Sherman Loomis and Gertrude Schoepperle Loomis, *Arthurian Legends in Medieval Art* (London: Oxford University Press; New York: Modern Language Association of America, 1938), fig. 250; Alexandre Micha, "L'épreuve de l'épée," *Romania* 70 (1948): 37–41; *Arthurian Literature in the Middle Ages*, ed. Roger Sherman Loomis (Oxford: Clarendon Press, 1961), p. 298; Moshé Lazar, "Lancelot et la 'mulier mediatrix': La Quête de soi à travers la femme," *L'Esprit créateur* 9 (1969): 248–49 and notes 6–7. Cf. also Lancelot's lament over the tomb of Guenevere in the *Perlesvaus* (Payen, *Le Motif du repentir*, pp. 432–33) and the Knight of the Tomb episode in the *Didot-Perceval*, pp. 172 ff. (Roach, p. 52, derives it from the *First Continuation*). See also Ménard, *Le Rire*, p. 412 and n. 114. On Arthurian tombstones generally,

see Régine Colliot, "Les épitaphes arthuriennes," *Bibliographical Bulletin of the International Arthurian Society* 25 (1973): 155–75.

12. *L'Atre périlleux*, ed. Brian Woledge, Classiques français du moyen âge 76 (Paris: Champion, 1936), vv. 1131 ff.; Loomis, *Arthurian Literature*, p. 368.

13. Loomis, *Arthurian Literature*, p. 368.

14. *Cligés*, vv. 6025–6030:

Et Jehanz maintenant s'an torne,
La sepolture bien atorne
Et de ce fist que bien apris:
Un lit de plume a dedanz mis
Por la pierre qui estoit dure,
Et plus encor por la froidure.

15. In *Le Roman de Renart: Première branche*, ed. Mario Roques, Classiques français du moyen âge 78 (Paris: Champion, 1948), vv. 468–486, Couart the Hare, who is suffering from fever, is cured after sleeping on the tomb (vv. 475 [la tonbe], 478 [le martir], 483 [la tombe]) of Dame Coupee (v. 475). The stone over her grave is referred to as *un maubre* (v. 440) and *la lame* (v. 442). Ysangrain's earache is healed by the same treatment. On the satiric aspect of this scene, see Alfred Foulet's review of Ménard, *Le Rire*, in *Romance Philology* 26 (1972): 188; COMMENTARY, 45.

16. *Ovid, Metamorphoses*, ed. and trans. Frank Justin Miller, The Loeb Classical Library, 2 vols. (1916; rpt. Cambridge: Harvard University Press; London: Heinemann, 1960), I, 4: vv. 88–89.

17. Simone Viarre, *L'Image et la pensée dans les 'Métamorphoses' d'Ovide*, Publications de la Faculté des lettres et sciences humaines de Paris, Série "Recherches" 22 (Paris: Presses Universitaires de France, 1964), p. 203: "un cadre approprié à la cérémonie magique [that is, the metamorphosis of the berries of the mulberry tree, stained with Pyramus's blood, from white to red]." In n. 70 Viarre specifies that she is referring to "La nuit, l'arbre et surtout le tombeau." Cf. Shakespeare's *Romeo and Juliet*, which was inspired by this scene.

18. *Piramus et Tisbé*, vv. 652–654. Cf. vv. 587–589:

A la fontaine me querez,
Sous le morier enmi les prez,
La ou Ninus fu enterrez.

19. Paris, Bibliothèque nationale, lat. 15158 (also contains Prudentius's *Psychomachia*), fol. 47. Erwin Panofsky and Fritz Saxl, "Classical Mythology in Medieval Art," *Metropolitan Museum Studies* 4 (1933): 268, fig. 56; Erwin Panofsky, *Renaissance and Renascences in Western Art*, Harper Torchbooks (New York and Evanston: Harper & Row, 1969), p. 86 and fig. 54.

20. On self-burial, practiced by many hermits during the Middle Ages, consult Réau, III, 2:709, 718–19; III, 3:1209. For the figure of Death pointing to an open grave, see Réau, II, 2:654.

21. On legal impurity, contracted by touching a grave, see *The Jerusalem Bible*, p. 113, note *l*.

22. Delehaye, *Les Passions des martyrs*, p. 191.

23. Luke 11:44; Matthew 23:27. The throats of the wicked are "yawning graves" in Psalms 5:9 and Romans 3:13.

24. INTRODUCTION, 10, B, 2; 19, L.

25. See also Hebrews 3:7–19.

26. Payen, *Le Motif du repentir*, pp. 55, 60, n. 22; 68. On the iconography of the Raising of Lazarus (John 11:38–44), see Millet, *Recherches*, pp. 232–54; Réau, II, 2:388–90; Cames, *Byzance*, index, p. 321, s.v. Résurrection: Lazare. The earliest tradition shows Lazarus standing at the mouth of a cave; in Byzantine and Romanesque

art, Lazarus is often shown in a sarcophagus. The figure also appears in the Mystery plays.

27. *Queste*, pp. 37, 39, 67–68, 178. Locke, *Quest*, pp. 34, 36.

28. On the possible historical basis for the Saracen gifts, see Menéndez Pidal, pp. 152–54, 265–67, 295–302. In the *Pseudo-Turpin* Aigolandus offers Charles sixty loads of gold and silver (Meredith-Jones, p. 115). Cf. God's gift of 14,000 sheep, 6,000 camels, 1,000 yoke of oxen, and 1,000 she-donkeys in Job 42:12.

29. Le Gentil, p. 151. Cf. Halphen, pp. 18, 20 (see also p. 20, n. 1) and Ganelon's speech in vv. 220 ff.

30. Turoldus may have been thinking here of the perfidy of Charlemagne's Saxon enemies, who, according to Einhard, swore an oath, gave hostages, and expressed a desire to become converts to Christianity (Halphen, pp. 22, 24). In v. 2620 conversion becomes a threat used against Baligant.

31. In addition to bringing out Saracen cruelty, hostages also lend plausibility to Charles's decision to accept the pagan offer and figure in the Haltille incident involving Basan and Basile (vv. 208, 330, 490), in the judicial combat, and in the punishment ultimately meted out to Ganelon. Early commentators of the *Song of Roland* made much of the fact that Turoldus fails to dispose of the hostages after they are turned over to Charles. See Bédier, *Légendes épiques*, 3:407, 408, n. 6; Menéndez Pidal, pp. 210, 212, 265–67; Sholod, *Charlemagne in Spain*, p. 35.

32. Jones, *Ethos*, p. 47 (see also p. 44); Burgess, *Vocabulaire pré-courtois*, pp. 78–80, 86, 89. According to Jonin, "La 'Clere' Espagne de Blancandrin," p. 91, the Saracens are strongly motivated by fear of losing their riches.

33. In the *Enfances Vivien* the hero is sent as a hostage for his father. Skidmore, *Moral Traits of Christians and Saracens*, p. 47: "Here the intention is perhaps not to show the weakness of the father relation, but rather to exalt filial piety and duty among the Christians."

34. Jenkins, note to vv. 30–31. On camels, see Dufournet, *Cours sur Roland*, pp. 93, 94, n. 1; on mules, pp. 84–85. The relevance of camels to the dating of the poem is commented on by Le Gentil, p. 31; Riquer, *Chansons de geste*, p. 75. Jonin, "La 'Clere' Espagne de Blancandrin," p. 90, emphasizes the notion of Saracen opulence in this passage.

35. Brault, "Le Thème de la Mort," p. 235. See also INTRODUCTION, 19, G.

36. Dogs are also diabolical figures. Sommer, *Vulgate Version of Arthurian Romances* (1913), 7:127; Réau, I:128. Cf. Max Prinet, "Le langage héraldique dans le *Tournoiement Antechrist*," *Bibliothèque de l'Ecole des Chartes* 83 (1922): 49 (Felonie).

37. See COMMENTARY, 27.

38. Davy, *Symbolique romane*, p. 104.

39. Jenkins, note to vv. 72, 80; Dufournet, *Cours sur Roland*, pp. 27, 28, 33, 211–13. See also the discussions concerning the name Oliver; INTRODUCTION, 3. In a sculpture of the portal of the church of Saint-Faron of Meaux (c. 1200), Charlemagne carries an olive branch. Lejeune and Stiennon, 1:163.

40. Jenkins gives no examples; see, however, *La Chanson d'Aspremont*, ed. Louis Brandin, 2d ed., Classiques français du moyen âge 25 (Paris: Champion, 1924), vv. 7780–7781:

> En sa main porte un rainscel d'olivier:
> Ce senefie que il est messagier.

41. Conrad, vv. 995–999. For other biblical meanings, see Moldenke, *Plants of the Bible*, p. 159. In *Peristephanon*, 4: v. 55 (*Prudentius*, 2:160), a wreath of olive leaves is a sign of peace. In medieval art several virtues are depicted with this attribute. Katzenellenbogen, *Allegories*, pp. 30, n. 2 (Misericordia), 48 and n. 2, 49 (Pax, Spes), 56 (Spes), 76 (Concordia). Cf. palm branches: Katzenellenbogen, pp. 12 (Humilitas),

13, n. 1 (Misericordia), 31, n. 2 (Virtues in general), 43 (Amor coelestis), 52, n. 1 (Cardinal Virtues), 64, n. 3 (Justitia), 83, n. 1 (Castitas).

42. Jones, pp. 68–69; cf. p. 174: "[Turoldus] lacked a word for 'humility' and used the word *humilitet* only in the sense of homage, which suggests humiliation rather than humility." See, however, INTRODUCTION, 19, F, and n. 513 (Burgess, *Vocabulaire pré-courtois*).

43. Lat. *humus* 'soil' > *humilis* 'physically low, base'. The Church Fathers made a virtue out of a concept that was generally held in contempt by the Romans.

44. Charles Foulon, "Les deux humiliations de Lancelot," *Bibliographical Bulletin of the International Arthurian Society* 8 (1956): 79–90; Brault, "Chrétien de Troyes' *Lancelot*," pp. 147, 153.

45. On the iconography of the Entry into Jerusalem, see Millet, *Recherches*, pp. 255–84; Réau, II, 2:396–401; Cames, *Byzance*, index, p. 318, s.v. Entrée du Christ à Jérusalem. The use of this motif in Arthurian literature is discussed in *Perlesvaus*, 2:285, 317. In early depictions of the scene, Christ either holds nothing at all in his left hand, or a scroll or book. However, in the stained-glass windows of the cathedrals of Chartres and Bourges, the Savior bears a palm branch. The *Reallexikon zur deutschen Kunstgeschichte*, ed. Otto Schmitt et al. (Stuttgart: Druckenmüller, 1958), 4:1044, 1048, lists a window at Erfurt (c. 1230), a fresco at Cologne (c. 1250), and another window at Strasbourg (first third of the fourteenth century), all showing Christ holding a palm.

46. Matthew 21:1–5, citing Zechariah 9:9. See also Frye, *Anatomy of Criticism*, p. 152.

47. Réau, II, 2:398. In folk art the animal is associated with Balaam's ass. Réau, II, 2:397.

48. John 12:13. Waving branches was a traditional sign of acclamation. *The Jerusalem Bible*, p. 903, n. *k*.

49. Matthew 21:8; Blaise, par. 342.

50. Possibly influenced by the tradition that the branches thrown before the Savior were cut from olive trees. See note 49 above.

51. Ernst H. Kantorowicz, "The 'King's Advent' and the Enigmatic Panels in the Doors of Santa Sabina," *Art Bulletin* 26 (1944): 207–31, points out that two of the panels of the sixth-century doors of Santa Sabina in Rome are typological, representing, on the one hand, the historical Adventus, or Coming (that is, the Entry into Jerusalem), and, on the other, the eschatological Adventus, or Second Coming.

COMMENTARY 3

1. Bédier, *Légendes épiques*, 3: 411–12.

2. See also Le Gentil, p. 153.

3. In the earliest depictions Charlemagne is consistently shown beardless. Mandach, *Naissance*, 1:54–55, 158. On the Emperor's age, see Julian Harris, "How Old Was Charlemagne in the *Chanson de Roland?*" *Romance Philology* 25 (1971): 183–88.

4. Conrad dwells on Charles's terrifying aspect, especially his eyes, which emit blinding rays like the sun (vv. 686 ff.). On the latter attribute, see Frye, *Anatomy of Criticism*, p. 153; Robertson, *Preface to Chaucer*, p. 256, n. 189; Jones, p. 66. The notion of a king whose majesty is so great one need not point him out is discussed by Bédier, *Légendes épiques*, 3:412; see also INTRODUCTION, 19, D. Cf. Roland in vv. 1596 ff.; *Enéas*, vv. 712–716 (2:131, note). Cf. also the irony of Perceval, who must ask who Arthur is. D. D. R. Owen, "Two More Romances by Chrétien de Troyes," *Romania* 92 (1971): 256. Naturally, in iconography and in the poet's imagination, the king

always wears a crown and carries a scepter (cf. COMMENTARY, 17, v. 1670). The devil may be helping the Saracens here too. The latter possibility occurred to Charles VII's advisers when, at Chinon, in 1429, Joan of Arc went straight to the king who was hiding in the crowd.

5. On the symbolism of the pine tree, see INTRODUCTION, 16, D. The figure of Charles seated in majesty in the *Pèlerinage de Charlemagne* is discussed by Cäcilie Gaenssle-Pfeuffer, "'Majestez' und 'vertut' in der *Karlsreise:* Zur Problematik der Deutung der Dichtung," *Zeitschrift für romanische Philologie* 83 (1967): 257–67. Cf. Sedes Sapientiae (Réau, II, 1:293–94).

6. Dancing, music, and singing are traditionally associated with religious ceremonies (Blaise, par. 9–12), and choirs of angels are thought of as singing hymns to God (Blaise, par. 112, 312). The saints in heaven are also conceived of as dancing carols and playing musical instruments (Blaise, par. 312; for dancing, see the dream in a fourteenth-century French translation of a late-thirteenth-century poem by Mahieu le Bigame in Charles-Victor Langlois, *La Vie en France au moyen âge de la fin du XIIe au milieu du XIVe siècle d'après les moralistes du temps* [Paris: Hachette, 1925], 2:284–85). However, medieval exegetes also considered frolicsome amusement and sport, notably dancing, to be vain and symbolic of man enslaved by his lower instincts. John V. Fleming, *The Roman de la Rose: A Study in Allegory and Iconography* (Princeton: Princeton University Press, 1969), pp. 86ff. In the mid-thirteenth-century *Bible moralisée*, worldly life is often represented as a youth holding a chessboard. Comte A. de Laborde, *Etude sur la Bible moralisée illustrée* (Paris, 1927), 5:165. Cf. the image of Solomon contemplating marionettes in Cames, *Allégories*, pp. 83–85; fig. 76. The notion stems from Matthew 24:37–39, where Christ, counseling alertness and referring to eating and drinking, says: "As it was in Noah's day, so it will be when the Son of Man comes" (cf. Luke 17:26–27; comparable stricture in Romans 13:13). The Last Judgment aspect of the passage under consideration here suits this eschatological motif. Conrad describes at length the joyful activities of the scene at Cordres, adding several new details, including the presence of elegantly dressed ladies (vv. 666–670). Although he makes no adverse comment in this passage, the German translator earlier depicted Saracens cavorting, dancing, and sounding trumpets, actions that he condemns in scathing fashion (v. 285: Haiden die tumbi). One is tempted, therefore, to conclude that, for Conrad, gamboling about borders on illicit carousing and fornicating. On the eve of Roncevaux, according to the *Pseudo-Turpin* (Meredith-Jones, p. 181), certain French knights succumbed to temptation—wine and women were provided by the Saracens for this purpose—to their eternal sorrow. Cf. INTRODUCTION, 19, K. The knights' games in the *Song of Roland* may, consequently, also portend their deaths. Finally, with reference to the Assessors motif, Conrad, v. 234, alludes to the victims of Roncevaux as being in heaven, where they serve as God's advisers (Da sint si rat geben) and, in v. 702, Charles is characterized as a judge (Er was recht richtere).

7. Jenkins, note to vv. 104ff., and Bédier, *Commentaires*, pp. 140–41, discuss the presence here of Geoffrey of Anjou, who is not one of the Twelve Peers (cf. vv. 2402–2410), but reject various proposals for emending the text to include a complete list of Roland's companions in this passage. The identification of Geoffrey as "one of the Twelve Peers" by Jenkins, p. 329, is an error. Gräf, *Parallelismus im Rolandslied*, pp. 11–12, notes the parallel with the short list of Saracen leaders in vv. 503–505. For a summary of what is known about the Twelve Peers in Turoldus's day, see Jenkins, notes to vv. 793ff., 794, 795, 797; Menéndez Pidal, pp. 370–72; Bulatkin, *Structural Arithmetic Metaphor*, pp. 72–76; Dufournet, *Cours sur Roland*, pp. 177–78. The author of the *Pseudo-Turpin* compares the Twelve Peers to the Twelve Apostles (Meredith-Jones, p. 127; see INTRODUCTION, 18, c). In the *Pèlerinage de Charlemagne*, vv. 120–121, the

Emperor and his Peers visit Jerusalem and sit in the seats occupied by Christ and the Twelve at the Last Supper. The parallel is underscored when a Jew mistakes them for Christ and his Apostles (vv. 129–139). Horrent, *Pèlerinage*, pp. 34–38; Ménard, *Le Rire*, p. 108. On the Twelve Peers–Twelve Apostles connection, see Comfort, "Character Types," pp. 338–39. Listing individuals present at a council or at court is a familiar device in the Bible (e.g., Acts 1:13) and in Old French epics and romances (e.g., *Erec*, vv. 311 ff., 1504, 1671 ff., 1884 ff.). Margaret M. Pelan, *L'Influence du Brut de Wace sur les romanciers français de son temps* (Paris: Droz, 1931), pp. 21–28, characterizes it as an epic tradition but also notes a similar use in the *Brut*.

8. The Last Judgment is one of the most frequent scenes depicted in medieval portals. The visions of the Apocalypse relate a series of events said to *precede* the Last Judgment, but the two are often fused in medieval art. The notion of assessors, that is, of individuals assisting Christ in his judging (see note 6 above), derives from that of the Twenty-Four Elders before the throne of Christ in Majesty (Revelation 4:5–11). Réau, II, 2:688–93. See the tympanum at Moissac (*Fig. 21*). The Twelve were substituted for the Old Men partly because the latter were believed to represent the twelve Old Testament Prophets plus the New Testament Apostles. Réau, II, 2:690. At times, not all the Twelve Apostles were depicted (Réau, II, 2:740), and, as in the *Song of Roland*, an arbitrary number is provided. Early examples of Christ the Judge with the Assessors are found on the lintel of the abbey church of Saint-Genis-des-Fontaines (Pyrénées-Orientales), c. 1020 (*Fig. 37*), the west porch of the church of Saint-Gilles at Argenton-Château (Deux-Sèvres), c. 1135 (Katzenellenbogen, *Allegories*, pp. 17–18; fig. 18), and Carennac (Emile Mâle, *L'Art religieux du XII*[e] *siècle en France: Etude sur les origines de l'iconographie du moyen âge* [Paris: Colin, 1922], fig. 218). See also Cames, *Byzance*, figs. 204, 206. At Chartres, the Apostles appear in the lower register, the Elders in the voussures (Mâle, fig. 219). See also Le Mans, Saint-Loup-de-Naud, Bourges, and Saint-Trophime of Arles (Mâle, figs. 220–23). At Beaulieu, Christ has his arm outstretched and shows his wounds and the Cross (Mâle, fig. 137); cf. the much-restored tympanum at Saint-Denis (Mâle, fig. 136). The Saved and the Damned appear on other tympana, e.g., Conques and Autun (Mâle, figs. 235, 238).

9. *Roland*, vv. 3660 ff. The Theme of Conversion is present in both scenes too (cf. vv. 3668, 3673–3674). The mention of six of the Twelve Peers also foreshadows Roncevaux, for all will die in this battle.

10. See v. 420. Cf. Faral, *La Chanson de Roland*, p. 62. This is the archaic orant gesture found in early Christian art; INTRODUCTION, note 615. For Charles's attitude in v. 139, see Ménard, "*Tenir le chief embronc*," p. 148. Cf. James 1:19 ("Be quick to listen but slow to speak and slow to rouse your temper"). Beard-pulling expresses pensiveness in v. 215, but controlled anger in v. 2982 (COMMENTARY, 35).

11. Christian history is full of dramatic conversions by former persecutors, for instance Saints Paul and Constantine, and similar miraculous occurrences abound in hagiography. Delehaye, *Les Passions des martyrs*, p. 218.

COMMENTARY 4

1. Charles's hopes are at their zenith at this point, as symbolized by the bright sun. Hatzfeld, "Le *Rolandslied* allemand," p. 54: "Quand il y a encore de l'espoir de paix avec les païens, le climat favorable se décèle dans le vers: Bels fut li vespres e li soleilz fut cler." Baligant's optimism is similarly represented by the sun's brilliance in v. 2646. Charles's hospitality to the Saracen emissaries is a sign of his nobility. On this epic virtue, consult Bowra, *Heroic poetry*, pp. 179–81.

2. Rychner, p. 59.

3. Cf. the triplication in vv. 196, 220, and 791. Verse 196 also marks the beginning of the *mar* leitmotif. INTRODUCTION, 17.

4. Twenty thousand persons, and even a thousand, constitute very large councils indeed. As in the battle scenes, however, Turoldus focuses on a few individuals only, and their deliberations are to be visualized as in Conrad's illustrations (*Figs. 40 and 41*; Lejeune and Stiennon, 2: figs. 86, 96). See COMMENTARY, 5, note 4 below. On the council formula in medieval art (the monarch surrounded by his counselors), see Karl Künstle, *Ikonographie der christlichen Kunst* (Freiburg im Breisgau: Herder, 1928), 1:33 and fig. 8; Raimond Van Marle, *Iconographie de l'art profane au moyen-âge et à la Renaissance* (The Hague: Nijhoff, 1931), 1:1–3; André Grabar, *L'Empereur dans l'art byzantin: Recherches sur l'art officiel de l'empire d'Orient*, Publications de la Faculté des lettres de l'Université de Strasbourg 75 (Paris: Les Belles Lettres, 1936), pp. 90–92, 207–9. In Conrad, Turpin, in what corresponds to the French Council, Part 2, is said to be seated on a chair (v. 1359) and the protagonists in a related scene are all envisioned thus by the illustrator (*Fig. 40*). In the French original, however, Turpin is seated on a white silk cloth (v. 272; cf. vv. 110, 251). In the part of the council under discussion, the French rise to their feet one by one (vv. 195, 218), come before Charlemagne (v. 218; cf. vv. 195, 230), and address him directly (vv. 196, 220, 232). The counselors are seated in rows or in a circle (v. 264: renc). On the latter term, see COMMENTARY, 22 (v. 2192: en reng).

5. British Museum, Cotton MS. Claudius B iv, fol. 65v; Monte Casino, Rabanus Maurus, MS. Katzenellenbogen, *Allegories*, p. 12, fig. 10.

6. Paris, Bibliothèque Nationale, MS. lat. 2077, fol. 164v. Katzenellenbogen, p. 12, fig. 11.

7. Conrad, v. 1154.

8. Lejeune and Stiennon, 2: fig. 90 (cf. fig. 91). A certain Bishop John, said to be a holy man, offers to preach the word of God to the Saracens in their city (vv. 1055–1089; see COMMENTARY, 5, note 6). This individual, who does not appear in the French original, is also designated as the spokesman for the Franks following their council. In view of his prominence in this passage, there is a possibility that he may be the mitred figure, traditionally assumed to be Turpin, in the Conrad drawing.

9. Lejeune and Stiennon, 2: fig. 92.

10. On Ganelon's attitude, see Lejeune and Stiennon, 1:122; see also 2: figs. 100, 103.

11. Cf. the court of justice, presided over by the angel of the Lord, where a malevolent angel called the Accuser (Heb. *satan*) plays the role of the enemy of man. Job 1:6; Psalms 109:6; Zechariah 3:1; Revelation 12:10. Cf. INTRODUCTION, 19, G and note 563; COMMENTARY, 6 (vv. 366 ff.: image of the Seducer).

12. On Roland's boasting, see below.

13. The parallelism between vv. 194 ff. and 217 ff. is noted by Gräf, *Parallelismus im Rolandslied*, pp. 26–27. On this passage, see André Burger, "Le rire de Roland," *Cahiers de civilisation médiévale* 3 (1960): 8; Jones, p. 59, n. 61 a.

14. Roland does not, however, suggest taking revenge for Basan and Basile on the Saracen ambassadors. Baligant's messengers are also spared (vv. 2976–2981). On the other hand, Ganelon at Saragossa will twice be within an ace of suffering the French messengers' fate (vv. 438–440, 496–498). On the concept of revenge in the *Song of Roland*, see COMMENTARY, 27 (v. 2428). The hero's concern for revenge is a variation on the Theme of Victory. INTRODUCTION, 14, D. Roland's phrase is prophetic too: it is what he will want Charles to do after he dies (destroy Marsile) and at the trial (punish Ganelon).

15. In a typical characterization, Renoir, "Roland's Lament," p. 576, refers to

Roland's speech as an "outburst," "utterly uncouth," and "an embarrassing display of the most outrageous pride."

16. Cf. the use of *sempres* in the saints' lives. Burgess, *Vocabulaire pré-courtois*, p. 104, n. 1.

17. On *captatio benevolentiae*, see Curtius, pp. 86, n. 3, 507–11. Ganelon's self-deprecatory use of the phrase *Ne mei ne altre* (v. 221) may be a *mea parvitas* formula. Jones, p. 59 and n. 61 a. Cf. COMMENTARY, 25 (Roland's praise of Durendal) and 34 (Roland's boast at Aix). In the present passage Roland refers to the cities he has vanquished; in v. 2322, the provinces and countries. Cf. vv. 371–373 (Charles's conquests).

18. Cf. the triplication in vv. 206, 300, 513. On the fourth use, by Oliver, see COMMENTARY, 18 (v. 1726). Blancandrin, evidently aware of Ganelon's sore spot, will deftly reopen the wound. COMMENTARY, 6 (vv. 378–379). The notion of bad advice is related to the Theme of Sapientia. INTRODUCTION, 11, C; cf. Calin, *Epic Quest*, p. 108 (Hardré in *Ami et Amile*).

19. See INTRODUCTION, 11, E.

20. Menéndez Pidal, p. 165: "Cette impétuosité guerrière est un trait essentiel du caractère héroïque; elle fait la gloire du héros. Mais c'est également un conseil clairvoyant, comme l'événement devait le montrer."

21. Jonin, "La 'Clere' Espagne de Blancandrin," p. 90: gold is "l'évocation même de l'Orient." See INTRODUCTION, note 584. On Ganelon's envy of Roland, see Jenkins, p. xxix; Burger, "Le rire de Roland," pp. 7–8; Jones, p. 60. Is Ganelon cowardly, too? His behavior at Saragossa seems to belie this possibility. See, however, OXFORD TEXT, ENGLISH TRANSLATION, v. 280, and COMMENTARY, 7. Craven Aymon le Vieil in the *Charroi de Nîmes* also counsels prudence at the wrong time. See INTRODUCTION, note 558 above. Frye, *Anatomy of Criticism*, p. 197, concerning the dwarf in Spenser: "he is 'fearful', and urges retreat when the going is difficult." For possible father-son rivalry, see COMMENTARY, 5.

22. Jenkins, note to v. 178, citing Tavernier: "Note the skill with which the name of Ganelon is first introduced here: eleven heroes are enumerated, the twelfth and last is 'he who did the treason'. May this not be a souvenir of Luke vi:16, where, in the list of the twelve Apostles, the last named is Judas, 'qui fuit traditor'?"

23. Strictly speaking, the Saracen king offers to hold Spain as a *fief de reprise*. Ganshof, *Feudalism*, p. 123.

24. *Prod* is also associated with Ganelon in vv. 507 and 699. Cf. v. 1407 (vendre). On the Judas-Avarice association, see INTRODUCTION, 19, G.

25. Verse 227. Ganelon again slanderously refers to Roland's fascination with *thanatos* in v. 390. Cf. Bramimonde's evident admiration for the Franks, who *n'unt cure de lur vies* (v. 2604). Ganelon obviously confuses fighting with abandon, a much-vaunted virtue on the aristocratic scale of values of Turoldus's day (Jones, p. 34), and plain recklessness. On the meaning of *sages* in v. 229, see COMMENTARY, 5.

26. See, for example, v. 1163 (E vers Franceis humeles e dulcement), his reaction on seeing the mortally wounded Oliver (vv. 1982–1988), his laments over his dead companion-in-arms (vv. 2027–2030, 2207–2214), his gathering up of the bodies of the slain French victims (vv. 2184–2192), and his lament for Turpin (vv. 2252–2258). On the proximity of solicitude to the notion of *guarant*, see COMMENTARY, 14 (vv. 1161, 1163). For a different interpretation, see Van Emden, "'E cil de France'."

27. Cf. Mickel, "Parallels in *Psychomachia* and *Roland*," p. 447, who affirms that Naimes's speech shows: "The extent to which the Christian will has been weakened." For a view closer to my own, see E. C. Schweitzer, Jr., "'Mais qu'il seit entendut': Ganelon's and Naimon's Speeches at the Council of the French in the *Chanson de Roland*," *Romance Notes* 12 (1971): 428–34.

28. Cf. Jones, p. 31: 'disadvantageous'.

29. On the meaning of *orguill* in this line, see OXFORD TEXT, ENGLISH TRANSLATION, v. 28.

30. See OXFORD TEXT, ENGLISH TRANSLATION, v. 400.

COMMENTARY 5

1. The parallel with the scene in which Roland is nominated to command the rearguard is noted by Bédier, *Légendes épiques*, 3:421; Gräf, *Parallelismus im Rolandslied*, pp. 8, 27–30; Horrent, *La Chanson de Roland*, p. 266. The passage is analyzed by William S. Woods, "The Choice of Ganelon as a Messenger to the Pagans (*La Chanson de Roland*, Lines 274–336)," *Studies in Philology* 48 (1952): 707–16.

2. Silvio Pellegrini, "L'ira di Gano," *Cultura Neolatina* 3 (1943): 157–66. Roland's nomination of Ganelon and his scornful laughter (v. 302; see note 21 below) are small incidents leading to enormous consequences. Medieval chroniclers usually treated such incommensurability as an ironic reflection on man's inability to understand the strange workings of God's will. Brandt, *Medieval History*, pp. 65–66 and n. 69. On medieval dislike for "disturbances" like quarrels, see Brandt, pp. 70–76, 80.

3. Jenkins, note to v. 287. See also OXFORD TEXT, ENGLISH TRANSLATION, v. 283.

4. Gräf, *Parallelismus im Rolandslied*, p. 4, compares this passage and the presentation of gifts to Ganelon at Saragossa in vv. 617 ff. The council is attended by a throng but the poet presents dialogues, thus focusing attention upon only two persons at a time. On this narrative technique, see COMMENTARY, 4, note 4.

5. Jones, p. 83.

6. On the possibly comic aspect of Turpin's offer, see Horrent, p. 277; idem, *Pèlerinage*, p. 76; Lejeune, "Le caractère de l'archevêque Turpin," p. 10. Humor is doubted by Jenkins, notes to vv. 251, 272. On looks as a key to intentions, see OXFORD TEXT, ENGLISH TRANSLATION, v. 283; but cf. INTRODUCTION, 10, B, 2. Conrad, vv. 1332–1353, has Turpin volunteering to try to convert the Saracens. Cf. Bishop John's similar offer (COMMENTARY, 4, note 8).

7. Le Gentil, p. 104: "Préparé par une courte phrase d'Olivier, dès la délibération sur l'ambassade, il marque le terme d'une gradation qui porte à son comble la démesure de Roland, cette démesure qui explique le drame, et en fonction de laquelle tout à l'heure le héros sera jugé"; p. 122: "C'est aussi révéler un tempérament. Un mot d'Olivier ne tarde pas à le confirmer, qui trouvera plus tard un écho puissamment amplifié dans le débat que l'on sait."

8. Jones, pp. 31, 67. Hostility generally characterizes the attitude of messengers in Old French epics and offers one reason why Basan and Basile may have been executed.

9. Cf. *meslisez* (v. 257) and *mellee* (v. 450).

10. OXFORD TEXT, ENGLISH TRANSLATION, v. 280. It is not clear whether Charles prompts Roland or how, but Ganelon may infer that the Emperor considers him to be expendable, as opposed to the others who have volunteered and been refused. For various interpretations, see Robert A. Hall, Jr., "On Individual Authorship in the *Roland*," *Symposium* 15 (1961): 298; Jones, p. 69; Köhler, "'Conseil des barons'," pp. 28–31; Demoulin, "Charlemagne"; see also OXFORD TEXT, ENGLISH TRANSLATION, v. 275.

11. Le Gentil, p. 95. Cf. rending one's garments, the biblical gesture of anger and frustration. Cames, *Byzance*, figs. 131–33. See also MANUSCRIPT, v. 2412.

12. *Psychomachia*, vv. 439–440: "Ostentation, that paradox of empty grandeur, is stripped bare of her vain flowing robe." See also Matthew 23:5: glorying in clothes is a form of vainglory. Robertson, *Preface to Chaucer*, p. 385. On expensive furs as a sign of wealth and nobility, see Jenkins, note to vv. 281 ff. Ganelon's chief vice is

avarice, which often produces a tendency to hide one's wealth. In his frustration, however, the villain may be unconsciously divesting himself of his evil proclivity, which seems to be strangling him. For another possible association of greed with fur cloaks, see COMMENTARY, 7 (vv. 462–464, 515).

13. The removal of a cloak here and in v. 3941 frames the entire epic and relates to the Theme of Revenge. Cf. vv. 301 and 3989: the "purging" of anger alluded to by Ganelon will be reserved for Charlemagne. On *esclairer* vs. *esclargier* in the latter passages, see Mario Roques, "Pour le commentaire d'*Aucassin et Nicolette* 'esclairier le cuer'," *Mélanges d'histoire du moyen âge offerts à M. Ferdinand Lot par ses amis et ses élèves* (Paris: Champion, 1925), pp. 729, 733; Foulet, *Glossaire*; Dufournet, *Cours sur Roland*, pp. 42–44.

14. Ménard, *Le Rire*, p. 160, shows that throwing a cloak on the ground is a gesture of defiance: "Dans le *Lancelot en prose*, lorsque Lancelot dénonce son allégeance à Arthur, il jette son *mantel* à terre en pleine cour [Sommer, *Vulgate Version of Arthurian Romances*, 4:59]. Geste de défi qui vise à faire scandale!" Ménard cites several examples to which one may add the note by Lucien Foulet, *Glossary of the First Continuation* in *The Continuations of the Old French Perceval of Chrétien de Troyes*, ed. William Roach, vol. 3, pt. 2 (Philadelphia: American Philosophical Society, 1955), pp. 178–79, s.v. mantel; *Les Romans de Chrétien de Troyes*, vol. 4, *Le Chevalier au Lion (Yvain)*, ed. Mario Roques, Classiques français du moyen âge 89 (Paris: Champion, 1971), vv. 2714–2715; and *Joufroi de Poitiers: Roman d'aventures du XIIIe siècle*, eds. Percival B. Fay and John L. Grigsby, Textes littéraires français 183 (Geneva: Droz; Paris: Minard, 1972), vv. 275–276 (see p. 213, note). Cf. Jones, pp. 36–38; Menéndez Pidal, pp. 94, 96.

15. Bédier, *Légendes épiques*, 3:413; Jenkins, note to v. 277. Lejeune, "Le péché de Charlemagne," pp. 339–71, believes that the importance given to the terms *parastre* in this scene (vv. 277, 287; cf. vv. 753, 762, 1027) and *fillastre* in v. 743 constitutes a thinly veiled allusion to Roland's incestuous birth, a legend with which Turoldus may have been acquainted. See also Lejeune and Stiennon, 1:145–49, and Rita Lejeune, "La signification du nom 'marche' dans la *Chanson de Roland*," *Boletim de Filologia* 18 (1961): 269–72.

16. Cf. the meaning of *saive* in v. 20 (COMMENTARY, 2).

17. See COMMENTARY, 4, note 21.

18. Foulet, *Glossaire*, p. 341: "le mot *baron* en vient naturellement à exprimer toutes les qualités qui conviennent à un homme noble, et particulièrement le courage." Cf. Jones, p. 26: "a man must be loyal to be *ber*, [but] the word is most frequently associated with strength and courage, whether or not they are connected with moral integrity." See COMMENTARY, 7 (v. 531).

19. Jenkins, note to v. 292: "[*orgoill* and *folage*] were the very accusations brought by Ganelon against Roland in the assembly (vv. 228, 229), and the younger man has by no means forgotten them." See also Jones, p. 67; Ménard, *Le Rire*, p. 125. Cf. the parallel reactions to threats in vv. 293 and 1232.

20. Jenkins, note to vv. 274–330; Bédier, *Commentaires*, pp. 93–101; Horrent, *La Chanson de Roland*, pp. 213–18; Delbouille, *Genèse*, pp. 4–9; Menéndez Pidal, pp. 89–104; Burger, "Le rire de Roland," pp. 9ff.; Payen, *Le Motif du repentir*, p. 111, n. 6; Ménard, *Le Rire*, p. 34; Segre, pp. 50–52.

21. Burger, "Le rire de Roland," attaches far too much importance to Roland's laughter as the incident that triggers the ultimate catastrophe. Roncevaux was caused by the fortuitous encounter of two vicious individuals, Marsile and Ganelon, neither of whom, acting alone, could have brought Roland down. On the rhetorical convention of calm before the storm, see COMMENTARY, 11, note 5. See also note 2 above.

22. See OXFORD TEXT, ENGLISH TRANSLATION, v. 283.

23. Ganelon's defiance of the Twelve Peers is discussed by Bédier, *Commentaires*,

p. 99; Köhler, "'Conseil des barons'," pp. 14–17. Conrad, v. 1418, says Ganelon has the look of a she-wolf as he utters these words. Cf. v. 8260. Originally, *desfier* meant 'to renounce faith, to break a feudal engagement', but by the end of the eleventh century it had also come to signify 'to issue a challenge, to declare hostilities against'. Ganshof, *Feudalism*, pp. 98–99. The sense of *desfier* here and in vv. 2002 and 3775 seems clear, especially in view of the accompanying gesture. The tragedy which ensues stems in part from the failure of Roland, Oliver, and the Twelve Peers to take Ganelon at his word, but the word, in this instance, may be ambiguous.

24. The witnesses to this scene may be visualized as assuming attitudes of distress: (1) both hands chest high, palms outwards (Lejeune and Stiennon, 1: pls. XXV, XXVII; 2: figs. 287, 290); or (2) both hands holding head (Labande-Mailfert, "La douleur et la mort," figs. 311, 328). The manner in which contemporaries viewed omens is detailed by Brandt, *Medieval History*, pp. 59–65. On the gauntlet and staff, see Jenkins, note to v. 247; Horrent, p. 157, n. 5. For the other versions of this passage, see Horrent, pp. 157–59.

25. Conrad, v. 1440, states it is a bad omen for Ganelon.

26. Ganelon's relatives grasp the implications for Roland (vv. 353–356).

27. Cf. Luke 23:34: "Father forgive them; they do not know what they are doing." Other religious in the *Song of Roland* also give absolution (v. 2957; cf. v. 3859). Jenkins, note to vv. 339–340, considers the request for the *congié* to be a matter of etiquette; Alwin H. Schutz, "*Roland*, v. 337," *MLN*, 62 (1937): 456–61, refers to the abbot's benediction for departing missionaries. In v. 3066 Charles blesses his men preparing to join battle with Baligant.

28. Matthew 5:39.

29. The traitor is already bent on sinful revenge, and death is in his soul. For the moment of actual possession by the devil, see COMMENTARY, 5 (v. 602) and 11 (vv. 746–747). In spite of his lying assertions to the contrary, Ganelon's refusal to be accompanied by anyone (vv. 357–359) is not an act of courage or concern for his men but a way of masking his shameful betrayal. Cf. Roland's leave-taking (COMMENTARY, 11). On the departure motif in epic poetry, see Bowra, *Heroic Poetry*, pp. 183–86.

COMMENTARY 6

1. Discussion in Horrent, p. 160. On the olive tree symbol, see INTRODUCTION, 16, D. For the illustration in Conrad (*Fig. 43*), see INTRODUCTION, note 213.

2. Horrent, p. 270.

3. This passage usually figures in discussions of the date of Turoldus's poem. Horrent, p. 290; Dufournet, *Cours sur Roland*, p. 32.

4. Jenkins, note to v. 386. Same observations relative to the royal orb in Emile Mireaux, *La Chanson de Roland et l'Histoire de France*, Les chefs-d'oeuvre et l'histoire (Paris: Michel, 1943), pp. 178–79, and Delbouille, *Genèse*, p. 121, n. 2. For an impressive list of examples of this symbol of sovereignty, see Schramm, *Sphaira*. Concerning the alleged humor in this episode, see Curtius, p. 530, contradicted by Frederick W. Locke, "Ganelon and the Cooks," *Symposium* 20 (1966): 141–42. The views that follow were first presented in my article "Ganelon et Roland," pp. 395–98. For a critique by Gerald Bertin and my reply, see *Olifant* 3, no. 2 (1975): 129–33. Another interpretation has been given by Kathleen M. Capels, "The Apple Incident in Laisse XXIX of the *Song of Roland*," *Romance Notes* 14 (1973): 599–605.

5. Riquer, *Chansons de geste*, p. 95. Lejeune, "La naissance du couple épique 'Roland et Oliver'," p. 391, considers this passage to contain a "scène mutilée"; Delbouille, *Genèse*, pp. 109–10, 121, opposes this view.

6. OXFORD TEXT, ENGLISH TRANSLATION, V. 28.

7. See also INTRODUCTION, 19, G.

8. Cf. COMMENTARY, 4 (vv. 220ff.) and 11 (v. 746). Cf. also Faral, *La Chanson de Roland*, p. 229: "Est-ce médisance intéressée du traître en quête de moyens pour éveiller la haine de son compagnon? Pourtant, l'anecdote s'accorde assez bien avec la physionomie du héros." For another anecdote, see COMMENTARY, 19.

9. Not an apple in Genesis 3, but an unspecified fruit of the Tree of the knowledge of good and evil. For an early variant use of this symbol, see INTRODUCTION, 12 (Essen Madonna). Many later examples are listed by Lilian M. C. Randall, *Images in the Margins of Gothic Manuscripts*, California Studies in the History of Art 4 (Berkeley and Los Angeles: University of California Press, 1966), p. 65, s.v. apple.

10. Réau, II, 2:747.

11. On the original, see Victor Bayer, *La Sculpture médiévale du Musée de l'oeuvre Notre-Dame, Catalogue*, 2d ed. (Strasbourg: Edition des Musées de la Ville, 1968), p. 30, item 137. To the bibliography provided here, add Gustav Münzel, *Der Skulpturenzyklus in der Vorhalle des Freiburger Münsters* (Freiburg im Breisgau: Rombach, [1959]), pp, 105–27. For early examples of the handsome devil, see the temptations of Saints Benedict (Réau, III, 1:200), Bernard (Réau, III, 1:209), and Juliana (Réau, III, 2:772–73). To the medieval mind, beauty was a *magica quaedam persuasis* used by the devil. Panofsky and Saxl, "Classical Mythology," p. 270. On the early depictions of Lucifer, see Robert Hughes, *Heaven and Hell in Western Art* (New York: Stein and Day, 1968), pp. 243, 247–52.

12. 2 Corinthians 11:14. In an illumination of the Old English Junius manuscript (c. 1000), Satan appears to Eve not as a serpent but as an angel of light. Henry Ansgar Kelly, "The Metamorphoses of the Eden Serpent During the Middle Ages and Renaissance," *Viator* 2 (1971): 304.

13. Matthew 4:1–11. Robertson, *Preface to Chaucer*, p. 13, n. 16: "The temptation involving the kingdoms of the world is that of avarice" (see also pp. 144, 243, 307, 333, 382–86). On the latter, cf. INTRODUCTION, 19, G. The iconography of the Three Temptations is discussed in Réau, II, 2:304–10. A crown figures in the third Temptation in the *St. Albans Psalter*, pl. 23, b; see also Francis Wormald, *The Winchester Psalter with 134 Illustrations* (London: Miller and Medcalf, 1973), fig. 21.

14. Above all, of course, Roland counts on God to assist him. See COMMENTARY, 43.

COMMENTARY 7

1. Cf. vv. 2689, 2818, 2842, 3697. Bowra, *Heroic Poetry*, pp. 210–14, characterizes the ride motif as a marker of great events and an occasion for display. On the indirect way in which the plotting is narrated, consult Bédier, *Légendes épiques*, 3:415–16; Horrent, p. 270. Cf. Matthew 26:16, which describes how Judas betrayed Jesus.

2. Horrent, pp. 238–39; Menéndez Pidal, p. 133.

3. Horrent, p. 266, contrasts the tension in the first part of this scene with the cold-blooded betrayal in the second part.

4. Robert A. Eisner, "In Search of the Real Theme of the *Song of Roland*," *Romance Notes* 14 (1972): 182–83. Cf. Faral, *La Chanson de Roland*, p. 211: "Qui fait pareille figure n'attire pas le mépris; la haine qui conduit à cette sorte d'héroïsme ne manque pas de grandeur"; Horrent, pp. 271–72:

> Ganelon y est-il odieux? Non. Le poète ne veut point de personnage tout d'une pièce, tout à fait sympathique ou tout à fait antipathique. Ganelon n'est pas odieux quand il se venge, parce que sa vengeance lui fait courir les pires dangers. Lui qui

redoutait tant de perdre la vie, qui craignait pour cette raison de voir se prolonger la guerre, qui avait misérablement tenté d'influencer Charlemagne, ce peureux aime mieux maintenant perdre la vie que renoncer à sa vengeance. Une telle attitude n'est pas sans grandeur.

See INTRODUCTION, 19, G and note 539.

5. On messengers, see Wilhelm Fischer, *Der Bote im altfranzösischen Epos*, Inaugural-Dissertation (Marburg, 1887).

6. Hand-holding is frequently depicted in medieval art and literature. Occurrences fall into two basic types: (1) *Hand-holding as a functional act.* Saint Paul, blinded by the vision on the road to Damascus, is led into the city by a companion (Acts 9:8 [*see Fig. 25*]; Prüm, 1026–68 [Swarzenski, *Monuments of Romanesque Art*, fig. 177]; twelfth-century mosaics at Monreale and Palermo). In *Chanson de Guillaume*, v. 33, Estourmi supports his drunken uncle Tiébaut by holding his hand. In the *Tristan de Béroul* the hero is dragged away in disgrace by guards (v. 899), King Mark gives Isolt over to the lepers (v. 1220), Governal rescues Isolt from her captors (v. 1264). In *Yvain* the hero is led away (vv. 1945, 3304). (2) *Hand-holding as a sign of friendship, love, or regard.* For Patience with Job, see Helen Woodruff, "The Illustrated Manuscripts of Prudentius," *Art Studies* (1929): 63, figs. 93–95, 97. In the *Aspremont* Saint George takes Roland by the hand (Lejeune and Stiennon, 1:203). By far the largest number of examples of this practice are found in the romances where it is often a sign of courtliness and good breeding, or a conversation gesture. *Enéas*, v. 1393; *Cligés*, vv. 1546–1547, 3935, 5535; *Erec*, vv. 474, 677, 1530, 1533, 1658, 1717, 4521, 5258–5260, 5510, 5520, 6535, 6540; *Charrette*, vv. 188, 1192, 3938; *Yvain*, vv. 1930–1931; *Conte del graal*, vv. 1550, 4042, 4545, 5252, 5718, 5790, 8102; *Tristan de Béroul*, vv. 1125, 3324; "Lanval," vv. 251–252, in *Les Lais de Marie de France*, ed. Jean Rychner, Classiques français du moyen âge 93 (Paris: Champion, 1966), p. 80; *Tristan de Thomas*, 1:57, 58, 301, 331; *La Folie Tristan d'Oxford*, ed. Ernest Hoepffner, 2d ed., Publications de la Faculté des lettres de l'Université de Strasbourg, Textes d'étude 8 (Rodez: Carrère, 1943), v. 861; Amira, "Die Handgebärden," p. 254. In "La Disputoison de Charlot et du Barbier," vv. 5–8, in *Oeuvres complètes de Rutebeuf*, eds. Edmond Faral and Julia Bastin, Fondation Singer-Polignac (Paris: Picard, 1960), 2:261, Charlot is holding the Barber by the hand. As he approaches them, the poet erroneously assumes they are engaged in a friendly conversation, but it turns out that they are arguing vehemently. To grasp an adversary in debate is apparently symbolic of the effort to "hold" his attention. Perhaps, however, Charlot is interrupting his adversary or even manhandling him. The gesture being discussed in the *Song of Roland* conveys the same meaning as the hand on the shoulder in v. 647 (COMMENTARY, 8, note 5).

7. Bédier, *Légendes épiques*, 3:417. Ganelon evidently later corrects this impression, for no further reference is made to it by the poet, and Charles gives the order for the French to depart as soon as his envoy returns.

8. 1 Samuel 19:10. Jones, p. 17. Biblical exegetes believed Saul's gesture foreshadowed Judas's betrayal of Christ. Réau, I:204; II, 1:264. An identical pose is found in an illustration of the slaying of the hero by King Mark in a manuscript dated c. 1300 of the *Prose Tristan* (Loomis, *Arthurian Legends in Medieval Art*, p. 117 and fig. 320). Threatening to strike a messenger bearing bad tidings became a literary commonplace. See *Huon de Bordeaux*, Introduction, p. 79, where reference is made to thirty-two medieval examples. On the weapon itself (algier), see Henning Keller, "Einige afr. Bezeichnungen für 'Lanze' und 'Speer': Ein Beitrag zur Etymologie von afr. *javelot*, *a(l)gier* und *guivre*," *Zeitschrift für romanische Philologie* 83 (1967): 268–79.

9. The gesture that consists of drawing the sword partially out of its sheath is discussed in INTRODUCTION, 20.

10. Ganelon expressed the same idea as he prepared to leave the French camp for Saragossa (v. 359). The thought also obsesses other Franks; see vv. 839, 2864.

11. Bédier, *Légendes épiques*, 3:418; Le Gentil, p. 101. See also Bédier's additional comment, pp. 418–19: "qui sait même s'il n'aimerait pas mieux être frappé là, mourir là, pourvu que la nouvelle de sa mort parvienne à Charles, à Roland, et que Roland en porte longuement le remords et la honte?"

12. See note 22 below.

13. This passage is discussed by Horrent, pp. 115–16.

14. Bédier, *Commentaires*, pp. 145–46; Julian Harris, "*Chanson de Roland*, Line 485: A Disputed Reading," *Romanic Review* 27 (1936): 22–27; Robert Fawtier, "Notes pour le commentaire des vers 1877–1881 et 485–487 de la *Chanson de Roland*," *Studies in French Language and Mediaeval Literature Presented to Professor Mildred K. Pope by Pupils, Colleagues and Friends*, Publications of the University of Manchester 268 (Manchester: Manchester University Press, 1939), pp. 99–102; Horrent, pp. 238, 307; Segre; Dufournet, *Cours sur Roland*, p. 37.

15. Letters customarily began with the name of the sender. Leclercq, *Love of Learning*, p. 19. Cf. *Charrette*, v. 5258.

16. For discussion of the versions that incorporate all the information presented orally by Ganelon in Charles's letter, see Bédier, *Commentaires*, pp. 132–34; Horrent, pp. 157–59; Segre, pp. 60–63.

17. Jones, p. 37: "Marsilie means that Charlemagne will continue hostilities." Nevertheless the expression is tactful.

18. See INTRODUCTION, note 489.

19. Leaning against a tree is a literary commonplace (*Tristan de Béroul*, v. 1694) and may be compared with the defensive action taken by Count Angrés, who, in *Cligés*, v. 2000, leans against a stake, or by the Archbishop of Canterbury, who, in *La Vie de Saint Thomas Becket*, v. 5527, backs up to a pillar. This is not to be confused with the resting attitude: in *Yvain*, v. 306, a seated rustic, watching some bulls fighting among themselves, leans idly upon his club and in *Conte del graal*, v. 4197 (cf. vv. 4329, 4423), Perceval leans upon his lance as he contemplates drops of blood on the snow. See also *Fig. 18*.

20. A different explanation is provided by Jenkins, note to v. 507: "One wonders why Blancandrin has not revealed this important fact before, and thus protected his accomplice from danger. Had Ganelon told him to keep 'hands off' until the message of Charles was formally delivered?" Cf. Horrent, p. 238; Moignet, p. 59.

21. See OXFORD TEXT, ENGLISH TRANSLATION, v. 509.

22. Jenkins, note to v. 518: "Marsile has hit upon Ganelon's weak spot: the French noble is covetous, and a gift of costly furs is exactly what will please him most; cf. vv. 281, 462. Ganelon accepts with polite words, but the gleam of avarice is in his eye." See text at note 12 above.

23. Ménard, *Le Rire*, p. 96, believes Marsile is mocking Charles here. Cf. Horrent, pp. 160–61; Harris, "How Old Was Charlemagne in the *Chanson de Roland*?" p. 185: "all that can be gleaned from the passages featuring the famous line is that the pagan M[arsile] has uttered the preposterous statement three times"; p. 186: "numerous bits of evidence, conversely, suggest that [Charlemagne] was actually in the prime of life."

24. Moignet, p. 61: "les réponses de Ganelon marquent chaque fois quelque progrès; ce n'est pas, à vrai dire, un progrès narratif, mais un progrès psychologique et dramatique, dévoilant peu à peu ses pensées secrètes, suggérant, insinuant la trahison."

25. Brault, "Le Thème de la Mort," p. 225, n. 11.

26. Jenkins, note to vv. 425 ff.; Le Gentil, p. 99; Moignet, p. 59.

27. Ganelon's admiration for Charles is also that of the devil who hates God but must recognize his power.

28. See COMMENTARY, 5, note 18, and cf. OXFORD TEXT, ENGLISH TRANSLATION, VV. 25, 176, 231, 533, and 576.

29. Cf. Jones, p. 54: 'God has distinguished him with such courage that he would rather die than abandon his barons'.

30. Réau, I:423; Lejeune and Stiennon, 1:140, 193 ff. (Chartres windows); 2: figs. 278, 293.

31. Réau, II, 1:12; II, 2:185, 226–27, 302, 595; Blaise, par. 273; Cames, *Byzance*, figs. 87, 138, 144, 186, 226, 302. Cf. Jones, p. 32: "The word *vertut* should be understood in the sense in which it is used in the Gospel of St. Mark (5:25–34) when Jesus feels His virtue go out of Himself into the woman with the issue of blood." Cf. Psalms 27:1: *Deus illuminatio mea.* For traditional illustrations of this psalm, see Brieger, *English Art*, p. 84.

32. The Turks were in the habit of attacking the rearguard of an army on the march. Smail, *Crusading Warfare*, p. 80. The lead and rear elements were usually appointed on a daily basis. Smail, p. 157.

33. The narrative of the Battle of Roncevaux is defective in the Oxford copy and is often emended on the basis of Ganelon's scenario. Horrent, p. 226.

34. The notion of entering into a pact with the devil was popularized during the Middle Ages by the legends of Saints Basil and Theophilus. Frank, *Medieval French Drama*, pp. 106–12; Réau, II, 2:628–30. See also Payen, *Le Motif du repentir*, p. 170 (Robert le Diable).

35. Cf. also v. 648: "*Mult par ies ber e sage.*"

36. On the traitor's kiss, see George Fenwick Jones, "El papel del beso en el cantar de gesta," *Boletín de la Real Academia de Buenas Letras de Barcelona* 31 (1965/66): 105–18. Jones emphasizes the feudal aspect of the gesture; the kiss seals a contract. See also Jenkins, note to v. 626; Moignet, p. 67. On the ceremonial kiss, see Ganshof, *Feudalism*, pp. 78–79; Ménard, *Le Rire*, p. 254. However, kissing in this instance is clearly related to Judas's betrayal of Jesus. Brault, "Le Thème de la Mort," pp. 229–30. See also INTRODUCTION, 19, G. On the Judas kiss, see Pratt, "Noones Preestes Tale," pp. 653–54. Also, Saracens were viewed as diabolical, so kissing resulted in contamination. Meredith-Jones, "The Conventional Saracen," pp. 221–22; Ménard, pp. 91, n. 210, 92, 273–75. See COMMENTARY, 8. In the thirteenth-century Chertsey Tiles, the barons who treacherously kiss Tristan can also be associated with Judas's act. Loomis, *Arthurian Legends in Medieval Art*, p. 47.

COMMENTARY 8

1. On the association with Judas, see INTRODUCTION, 10, A, 8; 10, B, 1; COMMENTARY, 7, note 36. Martín de Riquer, "Un problema en la *Chanson de Roland*," *Revista de Literatura* [Madrid] 5 (1954): 9–20, suggests that the term *traditio* in a presumed Latin source for Turoldus's poem was mistakenly taken to be synonymous with *proditio*, thus explaining Ganelon's role here. See also Riquer, *Chansons de geste*, p. 109.

2. Réau, II, 2:413. For a devil, see Millet, *Recherches*, p. 291.

3. See also the Garden of Olives association in v. 366. INTRODUCTION, 16, D.

4. Cf. COMMENTARY, 17 (v. 1645: herite), 18 (v. 1721, Alda's embrace), and 30 (v. 2664, phallic oath).

5. See COMMENTARY, 7, note 6. The hand on the shoulder in v. 647 is reminiscent of a gesture made by Judas as he betrays Jesus in certain depictions of this scene (Millet, *Recherches*, figs. 341–45) and thus may be a sign of false friendship. An identical gesture occurs in portraits of donors presenting a model of a church to Christ in Early Christian and Ottonian art. Cames, *Byzance*, pp. 43–44 and n. 112.

6. John 13:2: "They were at supper, and the devil had already put it into the mind of Judas Iscariot son of Simon, to betray him"; 21–27:

> Having said this, Jesus was troubled in spirit and declared, "I tell you most solemnly, one of you will betray me". The disciples looked at one another, wondering which he meant. The disciple Jesus loved was reclining next to Jesus; Simon Peter signed to him and said, "Ask who it is he means", so leaning back on Jesus' breast he said, "Who is it, Lord?" "It is the one" replied Jesus "to whom I give the piece of bread that I shall dip in the dish." He dipped the piece of bread and gave it to Judas son of Simon Iscariot. At that instant, after Judas had taken the bread, Satan entered him.

Vos, "Aspects of Biblical Typology," p. 150, cites this gospel passage, but suggests that the moment of diabolic possession occurs at vv. 746–747. However, the parallel sacrileges (Judas's communion [on the latter, see Réau, II, 2:413; *The Jerusalem Bible*, p. 177, n. *n*] and Ganelon's kiss) pinpoint the moment of entry in the present scene. The Stuttgart Psalter shows a little blackbird entering Judas's mouth with the bread; the Saint Albans Psalter has a tiny devil (*The St. Albans Psalter*, pp. 59, 89–90).

7. See *Fig. 32*; Lejeune and Stiennon, 2: fig. 98.

8. Le Gentil, p. 100: "Ganelon ose jurer sur la croix de son épée, et, poussant jusqu'au bout l'ignominie, reçoit le prix de la trahison." In the *Pseudo-Turpin* (Meredith-Jones, p. 189), Durendal is *cruce aurea splendidissimus*.

9. Jenkins points out that the term *Alcoran* does not appear in French until the fourteenth century and suggests that *la lei* clearly implies sacrilegious writings. The problem of finding Roland at Roncevaux is discussed in COMMENTARY, 12.

10. Vance, *Reading the Song of Roland*, p. 77: "The Saracen world satisfies all the direst criteria for evil but seems to satisfy, as well, a taste for the exotic and for sensuous delight. One wonders, indeed, if the *Roland* does not betray a certain ambivalence of motive which the crusaders shared—those of them who came back from the East. For the Saracens are most damnably worldly. They love gold, jewelry, fine silk, and gorgeous colors." There is perhaps a touch of Orientalism in the present passage, but Turoldus was doubtless more interested in conveying the lure of evil than that of the fabled riches of the East. See OXFORD TEXT, ENGLISH TRANSLATION, v. 59. Accepting a gift of jewelry can cost a person dearly. Langlois, *La Vie en France*, 2:197. Robert de Blois (late thirteenth century) claims that women's brooches were invented to discourage indecent hands from touching the bosom. Langlois, 2:196. Another erotic association with a brooch is found in Guillaume de Lorris's *Roman de la Rose*, vv. 1166ff. (Largesse gives away her brooch, baring her breast in the process). Hatzfeld, *Literature Through Art*, pp. 34–35. Bramimonde's gift is discussed in note 12 below. On the royal gift of a golden brooch, see 1 Maccabees 10:89; wearing a golden brooch is a sign of royalty in 1 Maccabees 11:58.

11. See OXFORD TEXT, ENGLISH TRANSLATION, v. 29.

12. H. A. Smith, "La femme dans les chansons de geste," *Colorado College Studies* 9 (1901): 6–24; 10 (1903): 24–40; F. W. Warren, "The Enamoured Moslem Princess in Orderic Vital and the French Epic," *PMLA* 29 (1914): 341–58; Skidmore, *Moral Traits of Christians and Saracens*, p. 42; Meredith-Jones, "The Conventional Saracen," pp. 220–21; Charles A. Knudson, "Le thème de la princesse sarrasine dans la *Prise d'Orange*," *Romance Philology* 22 (1969): 449–62; Ménard, *Le Rire*, pp. 89–94 (bibliography, p. 88, n. 199); cf. pp. 86–88, 193, 214–17 ("hardiesse féminine"), 234; Augier, "Conversions féminines," pp. 102–4. For the figure of Luxuria, see Réau, I: 166–68; *Psychomachia*, vv. 311–331. In Saint Paul's Epistles, Lechery is associated with Avarice (e.g., 1 Corinthians 5:10–11; Colossians 3:5). See also INTRODUCTION, 19, G, note 541. Other prototypes of Bramimonde may be found in the lady of the Song of Songs, and the Queen of Sheba. On the Queen's triumph over Luxuria, see Janson,

Apes and Ape Lore, pp. 51–52. In the chansons de geste, Saracen women were often associated with magic. Dickmann, *Le Rôle du surnaturel*, p. 96; Augier, "Conversions féminines," p. 102. Rather than brooches, then (see note 10 above), one might expect Bramimonde to offer a charm or potion capable of healing or casting a spell. Consequently, sorcery, and not only eroticism, may be muted in this passage and for the same reasons (see note 13 below). This is of course a clerical view of Saracen women. In real life Crusaders did not hesitate to use them to indulge their passions. Boissonnade, *Du Nouveau*, p. 278; Meredith-Jones, pp. 314–15. Intermarriage between Christians and Saracens was rare in Turoldus's day. However, see Smail, *Crusading Warfare*, p. 45, for an instance of a Frankish girl wedded to a Muslim.

13. Horrent, pp. 97–98, apropos of the major role played by Bramimonde in the thirteenth-century *Carmen de prodicione Guenonis:*

> Dans le *Galien* de Cheltenham (ms. du XVe s.) . . . elle s'offre à lui en récompense de sa trahison (éd. Stengel, p. 96). Dans le *Viaggio di Carlo Magno in Ispagna* (2e moitié du XIVe s.), elle est plus insistante et plus séductrice. Mais où le rôle de la reine ressemble le mieux à celui qu'on lui fait jouer dans le *Carmen*, c'est chez David Aubert (XVe s.). Marsile s'emporte contre Ganelon 'et l'eust Marcille occis, quant la royne sa femme l'en destourna, mal de la faulte. Ce fu grant dommage pour la crestienté que Marcille ne oultra son vouloir sur ce desleal traittre, mais il n'eust mie failly, n'eust esté la royne que l'en garda; laquelle s'estoit enamouree de lui, et dist a Marcille: . . .'

On the name Bramimonde, see COMMENTARY, 33, note 5.

14. Payen, *Le Motif du repentir*, pp. 217–19, 222; Augier, "Conversions féminines," pp. 102–4.

COMMENTARY 9

1. See also COMMENTARY, 6, where Ganelon's apparent triumph contrasts with Roland's true victory near Carcasoine (vv. 385, 662–663). Horrent, p. 239, n. 6. Charles's mention of *prod* in v. 699 also reminds us of earlier associations of this word with Ganelon. See COMMENTARY, 4 (v. 221) and 7 (v. 507).

2. The motif of rising in the morning (including prayers) is said by Bowra, *Heroic Poetry*, p. 186, to show that the hero is like other men.

3. See COMMENTARY, 7 (v. 535).

4. On the notion of not seeing anyone ever again (v. 690), see Brault, "Le Thème de la Mort," p. 225, n. 11.

5. Storms were viewed as instruments of God's vengeance in the Middle Ages. *Tristan de Thomas*, 1:38, n. 1; *Queste*, p. 244; Le Goff, *Civilisation*, p. 176. But the tempest and drowning here also anticipate the baptism of the Saracens. On this symbolism, see M. S. Luria, "The Storm-Making Spring and the Meaning of Chrétien's *Yvain*," *Studies in Philology* 64 (1967): 564–85.

6. Brault, "Le Thème de la Mort," p. 236 (cf. v. 1156). According to Lejeune and Stiennon, 1:34, 194, this scene is alluded to on a sculpture of the Cathedral of Angoulême and in one of the medallions of the Charlemagne Window at Chartres. On the lance symbol, see INTRODUCTION, 19, D.

7. On the sinister forest, see Frye, *Anatomy of Criticism*, p. 149; Calin, *Epic Quest*, pp. 192–93. Cf. v. 2549. Payen, *Le Moyen Age*, pp. 57–58, notes that the forest in medieval French literature is also a place of exile and of sanctuary.

8. Cf. also COMMENTARY, 29 (vv. 2613, 2645).

9. See INTRODUCTION, 18, H.

10. Jenkins, note to v. 668.

11. See INTRODUCTION, 18, H.

12. Bédier translates v. 813 (Une bataille lur livrat le jour pesme) as 'Ce jour-là même [le roi Almaris, du pays de Belferne,] leur livra une bataille dure'. Jones, *Ethos*, p. 31: "[either] the pagan prince fought a fierce battle on that day or . . . he fought a battle on that evil day. Since the S[ong of] R[oland] most often uses *pesme* in the sense of fierce, the former interpretation is perhaps the better, despite Jenkins' contrary explanation." See also n. 71.

COMMENTARY 10

1. A. H. Krappe, "The Dreams of Charlemagne in the *Chanson de Roland*," *PMLA* 36 (1921): 134–41; Bédier, *Commentaires*, pp. 149–50; Faral, *La Chanson de Roland*, pp. 194–95. Jenkins, note to vv. 725 ff., discusses the two divergent interpretations of the second dream. More recent studies include Horrent, pp. 245–46; Herman Braet, "Le second rêve de Charlemagne dans la *Chanson de Roland*," *Etudes de philologie romane*, Romanica Gandensia 12 (Ghent: Rijksuniversiteit te Gent, 1969), pp. 5–19; idem, "Fonction et importance du songe"; idem, *Le Songe dans la chanson de geste au XIIe siècle*, Romanica Gandensia 15 (Ghent: Rijksuniversiteit te Gent, 1975); Steinmeyer, *Untersuchungen* (see also Horrent's review in *Romance Philology* 23 [1970]: 595–600); Dufournet, *Cours sur Roland*, pp. 109–15; Wolfgang Van Emden, "Another Look at Charlemagne's Dreams in the *Chanson de Roland*," *French Studies* 28 (1974): 257–71; Tony Hunt, "Träume und die Überlieferungsgeschichte des altfranzösischen *Rolandslied*," *Zeitschrift für romanische Philologie* 90 (1974): 241–46; and Frederick Whitehead, "Charlemagne's Second Dream," *Olifant* 3, no. 3 (1976): 189–95. The dream motif in epic poetry is discussed by Bowra, *Heroic Poetry*, pp. 291–98. On the *visio* as a literary genre, see Carl Fritzsche, "Die lateinischen Visionen des Mittelalters bis zur Mitte des 12. Jahrhunderts: Ein Beitrag zur Culturgeschichte," *Romanische Forschungen* 2 (1886): 246–79; 3 (1887): 337–69. A double vision occurs before a battle in 2 Maccabees 15:12–16. On prophetic dreams as opposed to private delusions, see *The Jerusalem Bible*, p. 1293, note *m*. D. D. R. Owen, "Charlemagne's Dreams, Baligant and Turoldus," *Zeitschrift für romanische Philologie* 87 (1971): 197–208, believes that the laisse beginning with v. 2555 belongs before v. 737. Cf. André Burger, "Remarques sur la composition de l'épisode de Baligant," *Mélanges Maurice Delbouille*, 2:59–69.

2. Braet, "Fonction et importance du songe," p. 412, suggests that the dream is ambiguous: "le rêveur, qui ignore la trahison, ne conçoit qu'un obscur pressentiment." Cf. INTRODUCTION, 13, C. Medieval chroniclers generally explained dreams in the light of what transpired later. See, however, Brandt, *Medieval History*, p. 60. Also, in the *Pseudo-Turpin*, the Archbishop's vision (Meredith-Jones, p. 203) concerns an event that has just occurred. Individuals usually turned to religious to interpret their dreams (Jonin, *Personnages féminins*, p. 358 and n. 3). The fact that Charles relies on his own lights tells us a good deal about his role in this poem.

3. Walter C. Curry, *Chaucer and the Mediaeval Sciences* (New York and London: Oxford University Press, 1926), pp. 220 ff. Cf. Steinmeyer, *Untersuchungen*, pp. 11–22; Braet, *Le Songe dans la chanson de geste*, chap. 1. Much of medieval scientific lore concerning dreams is derived from Macrobius's *Commentary on the Somnium Scipionis* (c. 400).

4. Cf. the roman *hasta* of authority. Brilliant, *Roman Art*, p. 42.

5. Whitehead, "Charlemagne's Second Dream," p. 191: "Whatever interpretation we adopt, the symbolism of the dream will remain confused, irrational, and enigmatic, perhaps designedly so."

6. Marsile appears in a later dream and it seems unlikely that the poet would have referred to him in two separate ways. For the opposite view, see Steinmeyer, *Untersuchungen*, chap. 2; Owen, "Charlemagne's Dreams," p. 200.

7. Bédier, *Commentaires*, pp. 107–8; Segre.

8. Charles dreams while the Saracens go about perpetrating evil here and in vv. 2630 ff. See COMMENTARY, 12 and 28.

COMMENTARY 11

1. By repeating the word *parastre* in v. 1753, Roland indicates that he did not miss Ganelon's dig here. See also COMMENTARY, 5.

2. See INTRODUCTION, 13, C.

3. Cames, *Allégories*, p. 63.

4. For various proposals as to the correct order of the laisses here, see Segre, pp. 143–44.

5. On the apparent contradiction in the hero's anger and self-control in this passage, see Horrent, pp. 161–64; Vinaver, "La mort de Roland," p. 142; Segre, pp. 143–44. The same calm before the storm, here hinging on v. 760, may be seen in Ganelon's reactions in Laisses 20–21 before and after Roland's laughter (v. 302). A rhetorical convention may be involved here. See COMMENTARY, 5, note 21.

6. Bédier, *Légendes épiques*, 3:420–24. According to the latter, Ganelon is able to predict that Roland will accept this assignment because he knows his stepson will be too proud to refuse it.

7. The *impedimenta* mentioned in vv. 756–758 propertly belonged in the rearguard and probably included the Saracen hostages. Nothing more is heard of either the baggage train or the prisoners. Menéndez Pidal, pp. 204, 210.

8. Roland's reply is "chivalrous" (v. 752: a lei de chevaler), but eleventh-century notions in this respect are not to be confused with the gentlemanly ideal with which one tends to associate that term today. Cf. vv. 1162–1164 and see note 5 above.

9. Jenkins, note to v. 760: "the traitor can afford to be polite and ironically concede this trifling matter to Roland's pride." Cf. Bédier, *Légendes épiques*, 3:426; Burger, "Le rire de Roland," p. 6: 'Je compte là-dessus pour tenir ma vengeance'; Moignet, p. 75: "un sarcasme féroce."

10. See INTRODUCTION, 19, K. On weeping, see Jenkins, note to v. 349 (includes bibliography); Jones, pp. 143–46; Leclercq, *Love of Learning*, pp. 72–73; Payen, *Le Motif du repentir*, pp. 18, 23, 32–33 (bibliography, p. 32, n. 59), 37–38.

11. Charles's adviser is introduced in precisely the same manner and makes an identical declaration in vv. 230–232.

12. Horrent, p. 261; Jones, p. 18; Segre, p. 146.

13. Gräf, *Parallelismus im Rolandslied*, pp. 14–16, notes a possible parallel between Roland and Aelroth, notably in vv. 791 and 872. However, for similar echoes, see vv. 196 and 220. Horrent, p. 266, contrasts the dignity and enthusiasm of Roland's men with the vain boasting of the Saracen Peers in vv. 860 ff. For a similar refusal of assistance, see *Erec*, vv. 2688 ff. Roland's pledge not to lose a single palfrey, war-horse, mule, jenny, packhorse or sumpter entrusted to him is reminiscent of John 18:9: "Not one of those you gave me have I lost" (see also 6:39, 10:28, 17:12; cf. *The Jerusalem Bible*, p. 153, n. *r*, and *Vie de Saint Thomas Becket*, vv. 5540–5545). Mickel, "Parallels in *Psychomachia* and *Roland*," pp. 440–41, points out that Roland, like Faith in the *Psychomachia*, relies on a stout heart. In Venice IV Roland carries *un escu de Sanson* (Segre, p. 152). For a discussion of the way in which this passage is treated in the other versions, see Horrent, pp. 164–65.

14. In a variant of this motif, the Lord counsels Gideon to take only a few men with him (Judges 7:1–7). For illustrations of this scene, see Réau, II, 1:233.

15. Ganelon has treachery in his heart, Roland courage. See COMMENTARY, 5, note 29 (vv. 357–359).

16. On Gautier, see Horrent, pp. 140–43, 172–77, 305, n. 2. The marching formation was normally simply a column, but flank guards were sometimes deployed. Smail, *Crusading Warfare*, p. 157; Paul Bancourt, "'Sen' et 'chevalerie': Réflexions sur la tactique des chevaliers dans plusieurs chansons de geste des XIIe et XIIIe siècles," *Société Rencesvals. VIe Congrès International*, p. 628. Roland says nothing to the rearguard about staying close to the main body of the army, but this was a basic tactic in Turoldus's day. Smail, p. 157.

17. Similarly, in v. 835, France = Roland. See below.

18. Cf. Menéndez Pidal, p. 326: "Les quatre descriptions avec *Halt sunt li pui* manquent poétiquement d'à propos." For brief appreciations, see Jenkins, p. xxxix; Le Gentil, p. 154.

19. See INTRODUCTION, 17.

20. See INTRODUCTION, 15, C.

21. On the meaning of *pitet* in v. 822, see INTRODUCTION, 16, A.

22. The plight of women in the eleventh century was pitiable, their living and working conditions often incredibly poor. They also had to contend with the hostility of clerks and with feudal economics, which regarded them as mere chattels. Francis Lee Utley, *The Crooked Rib: An Analytical Index to the Argument About Women in English and Scots Literature to the End of the Year 1568* (Columbus: Ohio State University Press, 1944), pp. 3–38; Margaret Adlum Gist, *Love and War in the Middle English Romances* (Philadelphia: University of Pennsylvania Press; London: Oxford University Press, 1947); Andrée Lehmann, *Le Rôle de la femme dans l'histoire de France au moyen âge* (Paris: Berger-Levrault, 1952); Doris Mary Stenton, *The English Woman in History* (London: Allen and Unwin; New York: Macmillan, 1957), chaps. 1, 2, 3, and 5; Heer, *Medieval World*, pp. 317–23; Katherine M. Rogers, *The Troublesome Helpmate: A History of Misogyny in Literature* (Seattle and London: University of Washington Press, 1966), pp. 3–22; W. B. Faherty, "Woman," in *New Catholic Encyclopedia*, 14: 993–95.

23. Braet, "Fonction et importance du songe," p. 409, states that Charles is incapacitated because of incomplete information.

24. Matthew 26:39; virtually identical phrasing in Luke 22:42. Cf. Mark 14:36.

25. Rychner, *La Chanson de geste*, p. 38.

26. On the length of sessions, see Rychner, pp. 48–54.

27. Ibid., p. 49.

28. See INTRODUCTION, 19, K.

29. Lejeune and Stiennon, 1:35–36 (2: fig. 18), 200–202 (2: fig. 154 B), 240 (2: fig. 211). For a heathen sacrifice to Apollo, see *Illustrations to the Life of St. Alban in Trinity College Dublin MS. E. i. 40*, eds. W. R. L. Lowe and E. F. Jacob, with a description of the illustrations by M. R. James (Oxford: Clarendon Press, 1924), pl. 9.

30. Réau, II, 1:205–6.

31. Lejeune and Stiennon, 1:125–26; 2: fig. 98. According to the latter, the illustration is modeled on a sketch found in a copy of the *Vitae et passiones apostolorum*.

32. Ibid., 1:236; 2: fig. 205.

33. This possibility is mentioned in passing by Duggan, "The Generation of the Episode of Baligant," p. 78.

34. Jenkins, note to v. 1188, mentions the Libyan king Aillrous as the possible source of this name. Samaran, p. 34, n. 1, believing that the form was only attested in the Oxford copy, characterized it as Anglo-Saxon. Cf., however, *Adalroth* in two

manuscripts of the Old Norse translation (Segre, note to v. 1188). Wathelet-Willem, *Recherches*, 1:596, n. 413, identifies *le veil Astarut*, a male pagan god in *Chanson de Guillaume*, v. 2139, with Astaroth/Astarte. On Aelroth, see COMMENTARY, 15, note 19.

35. See INTRODUCTION, 18, D. Cf. also raising an idol (v. 853) and tumbling an idol (v. 2587).

36. Brault, "Chrétien de Troyes' *Lancelot*," pp. 148–50. Add to bibliography: Delbouille, *Genèse*, pp. 146–47; Rychner, p. 130. See also COMMENTARY, 13, note 4.

COMMENTARY 12

1. I found Annette Laming and Monique Roussel, *La Grotte de Lascaux* (Paris: Caisse nationale des monuments historiques, 1950) quite helpful in refreshing my memory about this cave, which I was privileged to visit in 1952, before it was closed to the general public. Anthropologists view the rites of any people as a series of acts fixed by tradition and usually involving religion or magic, and, consequently, would not see any significant difference between what the Franks and Saracens do here. A medieval Christian audience would not have viewed such matters in this light. The formulaic aspect of the Saracen oaths is commented upon by Rychner, pp. 90–91, and Michael Holland, "Rolandus resurrectus," *Mélanges René Crozet*, 1:398–400.

2. The Saracens in this passage are contrasted with the French and pagan leaders in the Baligant episode (Gräf, *Parallelismus im Rolandslied*, p. 3) and with the Franks at Galne (p. 16); see also the Roland-Aelroth opposition (p. 16). The similarity of Saracen and French equipment has some basis in historical fact and at times made identification in combat difficult. Smail, *Crusading Warfare*, p. 85 and n. 3. The elongated Christian kite-shaped shields as opposed to the small, round Saracen bucklers did provide one distinguishing feature (Smail, p. 78) and this contrast is carried over in contemporary iconography. INTRODUCTION, 14, A, 3.

3. See COMMENTARY, 10, note 8. On nighttime as the occasion for evil, see Le Goff, *Civilisation*, p. 226. The darkness of the cave at Lascaux is said by Laming and Roussel, pp. 4, 30, to offer an appropriate environment for such rites.

4. See v. 1000. I do not understand why Moignet, p. 84, asserts, apropos of *poignant* in v. 889: "ici 'rapidement', et non, comme ailleurs, 'en éperonnant', puisque Malprimis est à pied." Cf. Turpin in v. 1124.

5. See INTRODUCTION, 19, F.

6. OXFORD TEXT, ENGLISH TRANSLATION, v. 886.

7. On the terminology of killing, see Brault, "Le Thème de la Mort," p. 225, n. 11; Timothy D. Hemming, "La mort dans la *Chanson de Roland:* étude lexico-syntactique," *Société Rencesvals. IVe Congrès International*, pp. 90–94.

8. It is significant that the name Roncevaux appears for the first time in a passage noted for its sinister overtones. INTRODUCTION, 15, E.

9. How will the Saracens know the hero? See INTRODUCTION, 19, A; COMMENTARY, 15.

10. They will be called the Twelve [Saracen] Peers by Turoldus in v. 990, if the emendation is correct. To medieval exegetes the Twelve Saracen Peers may have suggested *les Juïs de la Viez Loi*, compared in the *Perlesvaus*, 1:257–58, to twelve yelping dogs. The verb *glatir* used in the latter connection (line 5985) is the same as Turoldus employs to characterize the voices of the Saracens in v. 3527.

11. See INTRODUCTION, 18, G.

12. Blood is not just a grisly detail here: It is associated with making a pact with the devil. See "Le miracle de Théophile," v. 653, in *Oeuvres complètes de Rutebeuf*, 2:202, referring to Strohmayer's review of Sepet's edition of that work in *Romania* 23

(1894): 605, n. 1. Two Saracens wish to pit their swords against Durendal (vv. 925–927, 988). Cf. the Rash Saracen who tries to steal Roland's sword (COMMENTARY, 24).

13. See OXFORD TEXT, ENGLISH TRANSLATION, v. 862.

14. Horrent, p. 305: "le centre même de la 'France'." Cf. Jenkins, note to v. 973, apropos of a similar remark by Petit de Julleville: "this is forcing the meaning."

15. On these portraits, see Ménard, *Le Rire*, pp. 48, 98, n. 229, 549; Frappier, *Chansons de geste*, 2:83–84. The expression *Il est juget* (v. 884) sounds like Muslim fatalism, but the resemblance is doubtless purely accidental. Cf. COMMENTARY, 40 (vv. 3273–3274). On the meaning of the verb, see OXFORD TEXT, ENGLISH TRANSLATION, v. 262.

16. A similar technique is often used in the romances, the most celebrated instance being, perhaps, the naming of the hero in Chrétien's *Charrette*.

17. See COMMENTARY, 11. An exotic female name (Semiramis) is used for a man in *Charrette*, v. 5796. The opposite occurs in the name Archipiades, doubtless for Alcibiade, one of the "dames du temps jadis" (*François Villon, Oeuvres*, ed. Auguste Longnon, 4th ed. revised by Lucien Foulet, Classiques français du moyen âge 2 [Paris: Champion, 1932], p. 22, "Testament," v. 331). Astaroth is mentioned as a pagan deity by Rabelais in *Pantagruel*, ed. Saulnier, chap. 10, p. 78.

18. Noted by many scholars, e.g., Ménard, *Le Rire*, p. 46.

19. Jenkins, note to v. 955; Menéndez Pidal, pp. 104–12; Horrent, p. 220, n. 4; Henry and Renée Kahane, "Die Margariten," *Zeitschrift für romanische Philologie* 76 (1960): 185–204; Ménard, *Le Rire*, p. 46 (bibliography in notes 101 and 102).

20. See INTRODUCTION, 6.

21. In view of the generally sinister aspect of this scene, Aelroth's appearance on a mule is not comic but related to the packhorse motif (vv. 481, 1748, 1828).

22. Identical features appear in descriptions of Charles (vv. 118, 3115–3116), Ganelon (vv. 283–285, 3762–3764), and Roland (vv. 1159, 1597).

23. Horrent, p. 220, refers to this description as containing "de teintes à la fois pittoresques et souriantes." According to Bloch, *Feudal Society*, 2:307: "'We shall yet talk of this day in ladies' chambers,' said the count of Soissons, at the battle of Mansurah. This remark, the equivalent of which it would be impossible to find in the *chansons de geste*, but which might be heard on the lips of more than one hero of courtly romance as early as the twelfth century, is characteristic of a society in which sophistication has made its appearance and, with it, the influence of women."

24. See INTRODUCTION, 10, B, 2. Cf. COMMENTARY, 17, note 31.

25. Similar expressions are used in *Roland*, vv. 3164 and 3764; cf. vv. 1485, 1760. For occurrences in other works, see Boissonnade, *Du Nouveau*, p. 253; Skidmore, *Moral Traits of Christians and Saracens*, p. 60; Delbouille, *Genèse* pp. 147–48; Riquer, *Chansons de geste*, p. 97, n. 125; Jones, p. 27; Lewis A. M. Sumberg, *La Chanson d'Antioche: étude historique et littéraire. Une chronique en vers français de la première Croisade par le Pèlerin Richard* (Paris: Picard, 1968), pp. 348–49. Add *Charrette*, v. 2615; *Anonymous Chronicle of the First Crusade* (1097–1099) in *The Portable Medieval Reader*, eds. James Bruce Ross and Mary Martin McLaughlin (New York: Viking Press, 1949), p. 440. Cf. Petrarch's observation: "it seems certain to me that Cicero himself would have been a Christian if he had been able to see Christ or to know the teaching of Christ." Robertson, *Preface to Chaucer*. p. 344.

COMMENTARY 13

1. Bowra, *Heroic Poetry*, pp. 191–94; Rychner, pp. 128, 132–33. See also COMMENTARY, 35, note 5.

2. In the *Pseudo-Turpin* the noise frightens the French knights' horses, but the Christians solve this problem by stopping up their mounts' ears (Meredith-Jones, p. 165).

3. Ronald N. Walpole, "Humor and People in Twelfth-Century France," *Romance Philology* 11 (1958): 215, finds this statement amusing.

4. Hatzfeld, "Le *Rolandslied* allemand," p. 55: "la teichoscopie de l'armée ennemie inspire Olivier encore d'un courage haussé par une ivresse de lumière en vue du camp des païens." See also idem, *Literature Through Art*, pp. 8–9. Vance, *Reading the Song of Roland*, p. 42, suggests that the hill that Oliver climbs symbolizes his moral pre-eminence. Frappier, *Chansons de geste*, 1: 158–59, using Hoepffner's term, refers to this passage as the "scène du guet," and notes a similar occurrence in the *Chanson de Guillaume*. On the motif of the knight gazing from afar, see COMMENTARY, 11, note 36. The scene parallels the beginning of the Battle of Roncevaux, Part 2. See COMMENTARY, 17.

5. See OXFORD TEXT, ENGLISH TRANSLATION, v. 1036.

6. Jones, p. 46. Cf. v. 1098. The they-are-many-we-are-few leitmotif running through Oliver's words in this passage (vv. 1021, 1040, 1049–1050, 1084–1087) echoes the words of the Israelites to Judas Maccabaeus in 1 Maccabees 3:17. Cf. COMMENTARY, 40, note 17, and note 18 below.

7. Jenkins, note to vv. 1026–1027.

8. Menéndez Pidal, p. 243, cited by Moignet, p. 101.

9. George Fenwick Jones, "La complainte de Roland—une interprétation divergente," *Cultura Neolatina* 21 (1961): 41. Cf. Edmond Faral, "Sur trois vers de la *Chanson de Roland* (vers 1016, 1465, 1517)," *Modern Philology* 38 (1940/41): 235–42.

10. See INTRODUCTION, 11, B.

11. Cf. vv. 1117–1119. Robertson, *Preface to Chaucer*, p. 165; *Introduction au monde des symboles*, pp. 376–89. Jenkins, note to vv. 1009 ff., cites analogues in Lucan and Tacitus. Jones, *Ethos*, p. 109: "When Roland declares that a follower must be ready to lose hide and hair (*perdre e del quir e del peil*, 1012), his choice of words may reflect the old Germanic legal term *hût und hâr*; for loss of hide and hair was a common form of punishment."

12. See INTRODUCTION, 11, B.

13. Note the specific mention of God in v. 1008.

14. Cited by Jean Györy, *Etude sur la Chanson de Roland* (Paris: Droz, 1936), p. 85. On the same page Györy also quotes Robert the Monk:

Concito vitalis calor ossa reliquit eorum,
Frigidus atque pavor possedit corda reorum.

See also COMMENTARY, 14 (Laisses 83 ff., and 89).

15. Meredith-Jones, pp. 195, 197.

16. 2 Corinthians 11:27. Cf. 1 Corinthians 4:11–13.

17. Blaise, par. 442–45.

18. The French scorn for the enemy army in spite of its great size (vv. 1049–1050, 1084–1087) will be echoed by Charles in v. 3339. It is clear that in both instances their courage comes not from their own physical strength, but from the superiority of their religion (v. 1015 = v. 3338). INTRODUCTION, 11, A. Jenkins, note to v. 1050, points out a possible reminiscence of 1 Maccabees 9:9. See note 6 above.

19. Cf., however, vv. 899, 918.

COMMENTARY 14

1. See INTRODUCTION, 3. For a discussion of four textual problems in this passage, see Horrent, pp. 165–71.

2. Bédier, *Légendes épiques*, 3:448. In typical assessments in Bédier's wake, Pauphilet, "Sur la *Chanson de Roland*," p. 176, terms the horn scene "son essence même," and Burger, "Les deux scènes du cor," p. 105, "le point central de toute la conception du poème."

3. See INTRODUCTION, 3.

4. Viewed in purely human terms, Roland's decision to stand and fight is a typical reaction for a knight of Turoldus's day. Smail, *Crusading Warfare*, p. 146. Cf., however, the Crusaders' successful march to and from Bosra in 1147, during which discipline was maintained despite many provocations to fight. Smail, pp. 158–59. Other similar incidents in 1150 and 1190 are cited by Smail, pp. 159–61, 161–62.

5. Bédier, *Légendes épiques*, 3:439. Such a view runs counter to the didacticism of the *Roland*. See INTRODUCTION, 10. Cf. Bédier's roughly similar view in 3:432: "Que pense le poète de leur débat? Il ne le dit pas, il semble les approuver tous les deux." Roland experiences neither embarrassment nor guilt. Were he to speak bluntly, he would tell his friend what Christ said to Peter when the latter remonstrated with him for announcing his imminent death: "Get behind me, Satan! You are an obstacle in my path, because the way you think is not God's way but man's" (Matthew 16:21–23). For another parallel involving Peter, see note 33 below.

6. See INTRODUCTION, 3.

7. 1 Corinthians 12:4–31. Blaise, par. 271.

8. See COMMENTARY, 18.

9. On the oliphant symbol, see COMMENTARY, 19.

10. Bédier, *Légendes épiques*, 3:438; Gräf, *Parallelismus im Rolandslied*, p. 31; Le Gentil, p. 104. Dorfman, *Narreme*, p. 112, notes the parallel in the debate between Roland and Oliver, on the one hand, and Charles and Ganelon, on the other.

11. Scholes and Kellogg, *Nature of Narrative*, p. 185 (the debate, in Homer, between Ajax and Ulysses over Achilles's shield was used as a rhetorical drill); INTRODUCTION, note 86.

12. Between Christians and pagans, see Payen, *Le Motif du repentir*, p. 436, n. 92. On the debate between Saint Augustine and Faustus, see Réau, III, 1:156; between Saint Catherine of Alexandria and the fifty philosophers, Réau, III, 1:269–70. On forensic encounters between Christians and Jews, see Györy, *Etude sur Roland*, pp. 102–3; add the debate between Chilperic and Priscus the Jew (W. P. Ker, *The Dark Ages*, Mentor Book [New York: New American Library, 1958], p. 88), and, especially, Saint Paul confounding the Jewish colony at Damascus (Acts 9:22; Beckwith, *Early Medieval Art*, p. 198 [illustration p. 201, fig. 190]; Lejeune and Stiennon, 1:136). Cf. the debate between God and Satan in Job 1 and 2 (cf. Réau, II, 2:656), between angels and devils (Payen, pp. 420, 517, n. 4, 518, n. 8), and *De Altercatione Ecclesiae et Synagogae Dialogus*, attributed in the Middle Ages to Saint Augustine (*PL*, 42, cols. 1131–40; Réau, II, 2:744). See also COMMENTARY, 18, note 3. Medieval dispute pictures are discussed by J. J. G. Alexander, *Norman Illumination at Mont-Saint-Michel 966–1100* (Oxford: Clarendon Press, 1970), pp. 100–102. For illustrations, see pls. 22, 24 a.

13. Delehaye, *Les Passions des martyrs*, pp. 189–95, especially p. 194; Jones, *Prologue and Epilogue*, p. 11.

14. Meredith-Jones, chaps. 13 and 17; Mandach, *Naissance*, 1:89, 142–43 and n. 377, 290–93; Lejeune and Stiennon, 1:73; 2: figs. 244, 283, 284, 305, 306, 348 B, 351, 480, 485, 505. See also COMMENTARY, 18, note 3. After his debate with Ferracutus, Roland slays the giant with a sword thrust through the navel, which may be where Saint Louis got his idea for the proper way to answer a Jew's argument. On the latter, see Frappier, *Chansons de geste*, 2:128; Archambault, *Seven French Chroniclers*, pp. 47–48. On theological debates in epic literature, see Meredith-Jones, p. 305; Frappier, 2:124–30.

15. *PL*, 40, cols. 1091–1106.

16. Zumthor, *Histoire littéraire*, pp. 183, 255.

17. Charles Oulmont, *Les Débats du clerc et du chevalier dans la littérature poétique du moyen-âge, étude historique et littéraire suivie de l'édition critique des textes* (Paris: Champion, 1911); Paul Rémy, "Jeu parti et roman breton," in *Mélanges Maurice Delbouille*, 2:545–61. Francis Sheeran's unpublished paper, "The Demise of a Genre: The Medieval Debate and *Dives and Pauper*," read at the Seventh Conference on Medieval Studies at Western Michigan University in 1972, offers a survey of this type of poetry. I quote from the author's abstract:

> While the debate as genre was popular and useful in structuring medieval ideas of a more whimsical nature, it had built within it a weakness which was to be its death as a vital literary form by the year 1400. St. Augustine had permitted two apparent truths to have equal weight. Both could be amplified and allegorized. As long as topics of later centuries were of a morally and politically neutral sort, such as the priority of night and day, the ways of the owl versus the ways of the nightingale, or the superiority of night and day, the genre challenged the mind of the author into invention of appropriate things to say. But by 1350 these sorts of composition were in marked decline. The rediscovery of Aristotle had led to a marshalling of authorities to prove one side right and vanquish the other as untrue. When the subjects of debate entered the realms of politics and religion, one side almost always had to be right and the other wrong. Thus balanced debate, so necessary to artistic form in the genre, became impossible. The devil could not be given all the good lines.

18. Etienne Gilson, quoted in *Larousse du XXe siècle* (Paris: Larousse, 1928), 1:13, s.v. Abélard: "Quant à l'intention qui a déterminé la composition de l'ouvrage, rien ne permet d'y voir le désir de ruiner le principe d'autorité en opposant les Pères de l'Eglise les uns aux autres. . . . La méthode du *Sic et non* passera tout entière dans la *Somme théologique* de saint Thomas, où chaque question oppose les autorités pour aux autorités contre, mais dénoue cette opposition en choisissant, déterminant et prouvant la solution." See also Györy, *Etude sur Roland*, pp. 99–102; Payen, *Le Moyen Age*, p. 86. On this technique in the romances, see Ménard, *Le Rire*, p. 200 (see also pp. 557–59, 563–65); Charles Muscatine, *Chaucer and the French Tradition: A Study in Style and Meaning* (Berkeley: University of California Press, 1957), pp. 24–29. The notion of two conflicting duties is referred to by Ménard, p. 564 and n. 170 as a "situation cornélienne."

19. Cf. vv. 2028, 2066–2069. The identical worthiness of Roland and Oliver is underscored in Bertrand de Bar-sur-Aube's *Girart de Vienne*, where a lengthy duel between the two heroes ends in a draw. The expression 'to give a Roland for an Oliver' attests to the fact that this appraisal was commonplace. According to Bowra, *Heroic Poetry*, p. 65, the friendship companions share is "based on mutual respect and . . . founded on an identity of ideals and interests." The junior partner may criticize his comrade, but "in the end agreement is reached, even if one partner doubts its wisdom."

20. As in v. 1212. Cf., however, v. 1015.

21. See Tobler and Lommatzsch, 7:1916–30, s.v. pro. Guiette, "Les deux scènes du cor," p. 850: "Sur le sens du mot *preux*, aucune hésitation." In fact, most critics consider *proz* in this passage as the equivalent of MFr. *preux*, that is, 'brave, courageous'. See Théo Venkeleer, *Rollant li proz: Contribution à l'histoire de quelques qualifications laudatives en français du moyen âge* (Paris: Champion, 1975). The meaning 'excessive courage' has even been ascribed to this term; see Monika Beinhauer, *Ritterliche Tapferkeitsbegriffe in den altfranzösischen Chansons de geste des 12. Jahrhunderts* (Cologne, 1958), p. 100; Hans Krings, *Die Geschichte des Wortschatzes der Höflichkeit im Französischen*, Romanistische Versuche und Vorarbeiten 11 (Bonn: Romanisches Seminar

der Universität Bonn, 1961), p. 32, n. 2. The best study is still the Münster dissertation by Agnka L. Boysen, *Ueber den Begriff preu im Französischen (preux, prou, prouesse, prud'homme, prud'homie, prude, pruderie)* (Lengerich, 1941).

22. Foulet, *Glossaire*, s.v. prod.

23. *FEW*, 9:417–23, s.v. prode.

24. Ibid., p. 420; Burgess, *Vocabulaire pré-courtois*, pp. 91–103. See my review of the latter in *Speculum*.

25. Jenkins, note to v. 26: "The *prozdome* at this time is brave, loyal to his lord, and faithful to his word. His merits also include religious devotion, even if, as here, he be an infidel." Cf. Foulet, *Glossaire*, s.v. ber, chevaler, prozdom; Jones, *Ethos*, pp. 22–24; Burgess, *Vocabulaire pré-courtois*, p. 93.

26. *E Oliver, li proz e li curteis* (v. 576); "*Se jo ai parenz, n'en i ad nul si proz*" (v. 2905); *Dist Baligant: "Oïl, car mult est proz"* (v. 3180); *E Oliver, li proz e li vaillanz* (v. 3186). Jones, pp. 22, 61, 62, and Burgess, pp. 21–22, 93, assert that, in these sentences, *proz* refers to courage and that, consequently, that is the meaning of *curteis* and *vaillanz*. However, the premise is false.

27. *Dist l'arcevesque: "Nostre hume sunt mult proz"* (v. 1441); *Mult par est proz danz Ogers li Daneis* (v. 3546); *Mult par est proz Pinabel de Sorence* (v. 3915).

28. Cf. also v. 604 (Cunseill n'est proz dunt hume ...); v. 1209 ("Il fist que proz qu'il nus laisad as porz"); v. 2423 (Naimes li dux d'iço ad fait que proz). Note the striking resemblance between vv. 1209 and 2423. Bédier translates *proz* in the first verse as 'preux', in the second as 'sage', yet, in v. 1209, Roland is contradicting the antonym *folz* in v. 1193 ("Folz est li reis ki vos laissat as porz"). On intelligence as a characteristic of the hero, consult Bowra, *Heroic Poetry*, pp. 100–102.

29. One of the procedures used to elucidate the precise meaning of a term as vague as *prod* consists in taking into consideration the word that is linked to it by a conjunction (e.g., E Oliver, li proz e li gentilz). More often than not, such formulas were made up of synonyms, and the poet sought to reinforce the idea rather than suggest a shading of meaning. See Politzer, "Synonymic Repetition." Thus, in a phrase such as *X est proz e sage*, *proz* refers to the character's wisdom, while the same term alludes to his courage in *X est proz e hardi*.

30. Cf. vv. 24–26:

> Blancandrins fut des plus saives paiens,
> De vasselage fut asez chevaler:
> Prozdom i out pur sun seignur aider.

Verse 1093 is not unlike *Aspremont*, v. 9362: *Rollans est jovenes et Ogiers est prodon.* On the chivalric ideal expressed by OFr. *jovens*, see Burgess, *Vocabulaire pré-courtois*, p. 118 (bibliography in n. 10). Jenkins, note to vv. 1093–1096, cites *Aeneid*, XI:291, where Virgil compares Hector to Aeneas. Similarly, in vv. 2066–2068, the trio of warriors, Roland, Gautier de l'Hum, and Turpin, are said to be equal in merit:

> Li quens Rollant fut noble guerrer,
> Gualter de Hums est bien bon chevaler,
> Li arcevesque prozdom e essaiet.

See COMMENTARY, 21. Such comparisons are not uncommon in Old French literature. Cf. *Erec*, vv. 1484 ff. Referring to the preliminaries to the Battle of Roncevaux, which include the laisse under consideration here, Horrent, p. 165, underscores the fact that: "Nulle part peut-être, la tradition rolandienne ne ressemble plus à un hallier inextricable." As for v. 1093, the only manuscripts that contain this line reproduce it very closely:

> Châteauroux, v. 1465: *Rollant est proz et Oliver est sage.*
> Venice IV, v. 1037: *Rollant est proç, Oliver est saçe.*

However, in a number of manuscripts, including Châteauroux, a new laisse in *-er*, occurring a little later but corresponding very closely to Laisse 87, offers an interesting variant:

Châteauroux, v. 1939: *Rollant fu prouz et Oliver fu ber.*
Paris, v. 396: *Rollans fu preus et Oliviers li bers.*
Venice VII, Laisse 113: *Rollanz fu proz & Oliver fu ber.*

In the verse in question, *ber* may be a make-rhyme. It appears far more likely, however, that the author of this version of Turoldus's poem wished, by means of this substitution, to remove any uncertainty as to the equal merit of the two companions-in-arms.

31. The double-truth theory favored by exegetes to resolve similar dilemmas offers another viable approach to the Roland-Oliver debate, the point being that each view is valid in itself. See note 17 above. One may also say that according to the pagan ethos, Oliver is right, Roland wrong, but that a Christian perspective reverses the situation completely. Finally, one may consider the circularity of Oliver's argumentation to be an inverted image of Sapientia. INTRODUCTION, 11, C.

32. *Charrette*, vv. 365–377. On the classical background of the interior debate to depict the shift from fear to courage or the throes of love, consult Scholes and Kellogg, *Nature of Narrative*, pp. 179–83.

33. COMMENTARY, 7. Roland's disagreement with Oliver can be compared to the controversy at Antioch: When Peter suggested that the only true Christians were converted Jews who observed the Law, Paul was adamant: "I opposed him to his face, since he was manifestly in the wrong" (Galatians 2:11). Roland turns a deaf ear to Oliver's entreaties, yet his flat refusal, like Paul's, has a decidedly situational aspect. As *The Jerusalem Bible*, p. 325, n. *h*, observes: "Peter's conduct was not in itself blameworthy, and in different circumstances Paul was to do the same." Cf. Peter, the unwitting tool of Satan, in Matthew 16:21–23. See note 5 above.

34. Conrad, vv. 3891–3892, affirms that Roland will not sound the oliphant because the Saracens will think the Franks are afraid. Cf. *Chanson de Guillaume*, v. 204.

35. On Roland's integrity, see INTRODUCTION, 19, F.

36. Horrent, pp. 168, 218–20, suggests that a better progression would be Laisses 83–85–84, as in Venice IV and Châteauroux. See also Delbouille, *Genèse*, p. 10; Menéndez Pidal, p. 337, n. 1. Cf., however, Segre, p. 197.

37. See COMMENTARY, 13, note 6.

38. Jones, pp. 47, 89. Cf. Bowra, *Heroic Poetry*, pp. 102–7; D. W. Robertson, Jr., "The Idea of Fame in Chrétien's *Cligés*," *Studies in Philology* 69 (1972): 414–33. It is not certain, either, that *mun los* is the first argument made by Roland. See note 36 above.

39. See INTRODUCTION, 11, B; COMMENTARY, 13.

40. *Psychomachia*, vv. 381–383; Mickel, "Parallels in *Psychomachia* and *Roland*," pp. 445–46. In v. 1194 Aelroth, alluding to the deaths of Roland and the Franks, says France will forfeit its *los*. Cf. the hero's rebuttal, v. 1210. Bédier, *Commentaires*, pp. 39–40: "ce que le poète célèbre sous le nom de 'douce France', ou de '*Terre majur*' (v. 600, etc.), qui est *terra majorum*, qui est 'patrie', ce n'est ni le vague empire des Carolingiens, ni l'étroit domaine des premiers Capétiens, ce n'est pas un territoire délimité; c'est une personne morale, celle qui se révèle à ses yeux, aux jours de la Croisade de Terre Sainte, tandis que s'exécutent les *gesta Dei per Francos:* par les 'Francs de France'." Bédier was chided for this view by Ferdinand Lot, "Etudes sur les légendes épiques françaises. V. La *Chanson de Roland.* A propos d'un livre récent," *Romania* 54 (1928): 374, n. 1: "Voilà qui est délicieux, juste même—à certains égards—et, tout de même, dérisoire." For Lot's interpretation, see COMMENTARY, 16, note 12. One is reminded, however, of the concept of *gimu*, "which embodies all of a Japanese citizen's sense of obligation to his family, his associates, the organization or

institution to which he belongs, and ultimately to the Emperor and the nation itself" (Richard Halloran, "Soldier's Return from 30 Years in Jungle Stirs Japanese Deeply," *New York Times*, 13 March 1974, p. 12, relative to the return of Lt. Hiroo Onoda from the Philippines; on *gimu*, see Ruth Benedict, *The Chrysanthemum and the Sword: Patterns of Japanese Culture* [Boston: Houghton Mifflin, 1946], pp. 115–34, 198–99, 205–7, 210–11, 312).

41. Concern for the family's honor is ultimately related to ancestor worship. E. O. James, *Comparative Religion: An Introductory and Historical Study*, University Paperbacks (London: Methuen; New York: Barnes & Noble, 1961), pp. 37–38. There is triplication in the references to family in this passage (vv. 1063, 1076), v. 1706 (second horn scene) and v. 3907 (Pinabel).

42. Menéndez Pidal, p. 210, estimates that, in 778, the 5,000 men of Charles's army, moving by twos and threes, together with the rearguard and its *impedimenta*, probably stretched out over nine or ten kilometers. Turoldus speaks of 350,000 men in the Emperor's army!

43. See COMMENTARY, 43. Cf. Christ weeping over Jerusalem (COMMENTARY, 29, note 14).

44. Cf. the custom of reciting acclamations to the ruler as a symbol of exaltation of the Lord. In the absence of the sovereign, the bishop received the praises. Ernst H. Kantorowicz, *Laudes regiae: A Study in Liturgical Acclamations and Mediaeval Ruler Worship* (Berkeley and Los Angeles: University of California Press, 1946), p. 88. One also associates Turpin and Charles in the blessing and absolution rites (vv. 340, 1133, 1137). For Turpin as a Charles surrogate, see COMMENTARY, 22.

45. On Turpin's role as a preacher, see INTRODUCTION, 19, I; COMMENTARY, 23. Turpin can also be viewed as a reflection of Roland. INTRODUCTION, 19, D.

46. Cf. vv. 1443–1444.

47. On confession and communion before battle, see Meredith-Jones, p. 318; Payen, *Le Motif du repentir*, p. 119, n. 28. In the German translation the Franks have time to hear mass. On the communion scene in the Conrad drawings, see INTRODUCTION, 12.

48. On martyrdom, see Payen, p. 46. The notion of seats in Heaven derives from that of Christ seated at the right hand of God (Hebrews 1:3; Colossians 3:1), popularized by a phrase in the Nicene Creed: *sedet ad dexteram Patris*. Blaise, par. 201. In v. 1111 Turoldus says Roland assumes an attitude fiercer than a lion or leopard. Dufournet, *Cours sur Roland*, p. 95, refers to the leopard as a symbol of Antichrist. See also Helmut Hatzfeld, "Style 'roman' dans les littératures romanes: Essai de synthèse," *Studi in onore di Italo Siciliano*, p. 535. One need not, however, turn to Scripture for the source of this image which is a folk commonplace. One thinks, too, of the lion as a symbol of protection. See Jozsef Deér, *The Dynastic Porphyry Tombs of the Norman Period in Sicily*, trans. G. A. Gillhoff, Dumbarton Oaks Studies 5 (Cambridge: Harvard University Press, 1959), pp. 66ff.; *The Year 1200*, 1:81.

49. On confession and contrition, see Payen, *Le Motif du repentir*, pp. 25–31; on absolution, pp. 49, 109, n. 1.

50. Menéndez Pidal, pp. 257–59 (indulgentia); *History of the Crusades*, 1:245–46.

51. According to Fulcher, at any rate. *History of the Crusades*, 1:242, 244, 245.

52. Blaise, par. 110.

53. *History of the Crusades*, 1:248.

54. Ibid., 1:245.

55. In the *Chanson de Guillaume*, Vivien also carries a white banner. Frappier, *Chansons de geste*, 1:120–21, 163. On the lance symbol, see INTRODUCTION, 19, D.

56. Jones, pp. 68, 174. Like a shepherd, Roland gazes fondly on his flock and looks fiercely toward the wolves. For another shepherd image, see COMMENTARY, 22. Cf.

v. 2984, where Charles looks at his own men *fierement*. See also Siegfried Heinimann, "'Dulcis': Ein Beitrag zur lateinisch-romanischen Stilgeschichte des Mittelalters," in *Studia philologica: Homenaje ofrecido a Dámaso Alonso*, 2:215–32. Lejeune and Stiennon, 1:61, refers to Christ as lion and lamb.

57. Foulet, *Glossaire*. On Roland's humility, see INTRODUCTION, 19, F; COMMENTARY, 4.

58. Greimas, *Dictionnaire*, p. 651, s.v. umele. See also Burgess, "*Orgueil* and *Fierté*," p. 105.

59. Jenkins, note to v. 1164: 'quietly, privately'. The first serious study of the term is by Jean Frappier, "Vues sur les conceptions courtoises dans les littératures d'oc et d'oïl au XIIe siècle," *Cahiers de civilisation médiévale* 2 (1959): 135–56. See also Lazar, *Amour courtois et 'fin'amors'*, pp. 21–46; Burgess, *Vocabulaire pré-courtois*, pp. 20–34. In certain instances, including here in v. 1164, *corteis* may have been influenced by OFr. *cort* 'short, brief'. Cf. *Thèbes*, vv. 993–994:

Mout parolent cortoisement
Et ne font pas lonc parlement.

Le Roman de Troie par Benoît de Sainte-Maure, ed. Léopold Constans, Société des anciens textes français (Paris: Didot: 1906), 2:vv. 13853–13854:

Corteisement e a briés moz
E sagement respont a toz.

60. Jones, p. 62.

61. For another use of *corteisement*, see COMMENTARY, 45 (v. 3823).

62. See also Jones, p. 76.

63. Booty is approved of under certain conditions in Numbers 31:25–30, and 1 Maccabees 4:18. In Psalms 76:5, "mountains of spoil" are awe-inspiring proof of the power and majesty of God in battle. According to Einhard, Charlemagne's men took booty (Halphen, p. 38).

64. Jenkins, p. lxxxiii; Smail, *Crusading Warfare*, pp. 92, 123, 185. For rules governing the division of spoils, see 2 Maccabees 8:27–28; Smail, p. 103, n. 3.

65. In *Psychomachia*, vv. 388–389, 454 ff., 536–541, spoils are associated with Avarice (for illustrations, see Katzenellenbogen, *Allegories*, p. 2; Cames, *Allégories*, pp. 61, 62) and reference is made to Achar (= Achan, in Joshua 7), Samuel (1 Samuel 15), and Judas. See also Sobrietas's strictures against this practice in vv. 450–453. According to Einhard, the Gascons attacked Charles's rearguard for spoils; this act is characterized as perfidy (Halphen, pp. 28, 30). See also the other chronicles relating this event cited by Menéndez Pidal, pp. 204, 212, 295–97. For Alain de Lille's condemnation of spoils, see Robertson, *Preface to Chaucer*, p. 174. According to the author of the *Itinerarium peregrinorum et gesta regis Ricardi*, the Crusaders were punished by God on one occasion in 1187 for searching for booty rather than continuing the battle. Smail, *Crusading Warfare*, p. 188. See also INTRODUCTION, 10, A, 7. On clerical attitudes toward riches in general, see Burgess, *Vocabulaire pré-courtois*, p. 77, n. 28. In short, Roland, the warrior, is keenly interested in spoils, but Roland, as idealized by the clerk Turoldus, has his mind on other things.

66. On the identical phrase in v. 2478, see COMMENTARY, 27. The taking of booty was mentioned earlier in v. 99; cf. also Charles's promise to his men in vv. 3409–3410.

67. OFr. *cembel* derives from Lat. *cymbalum* 'bell', associated with 'alarm' and ultimately with 'battle'.

68. Jones, p. 63. Segre emends *gent* to *grant*, a reading supported by all other copies (see his note, p. 213).

69. Conrad, vv. 3991–3993.

70. Jones, p. 25.

71. Cf. Moignet: 'jamais roi de France n'en eut un [i.e., butin] de telle valeur'; *The*

Song of Roland, trans. Owen: 'More precious [booty] than French king has ever won'.

72. On the lengthy interpolation here in the rhymed versions, see Horrent, pp. 165–71.

73. The testing of friendship is a frequent motif in the chansons de geste. Calin, *Epic Quest*, pp. 69–71.

74. Blaise, par. 62, 239.

75. Julian Harris, "'Munjoie' and 'Reconuisance' in *Chanson de Roland*, l. 3620," *Romance Philology* 10 (1957): 169 (see also Dufournet, *Cours sur Roland*, p. 31), terms *Monjoie* here and in vv. 3092, 3300, and 3565, a call for divine assistance. On the etymology of *Monjoie*, see Jenkins, note to v. 1181; Vos, "Aspects of Biblical Typology," pp. 84–97 (bibliography); and Wathelet-Willem, *Recherches*, 1:578 and n. 301 (bibliography). The sacred nature of battle cries in Scripture is discussed in *The Jerusalem Bible*, p. 815, n. *a*.

76. Crusaders usually charged not in a single body, as suggested here, but in squadrons of 100 to 150 horsemen, attacking in line or in echelon. Smail, *Crusading Warfare*, pp. 200–201. Lynn White, Jr., *Medieval Technology and Social Change* (Oxford: Oxford University Press, 1964), p. 32, n. 4, speaks of knights charging in *conrois* of twelve to forty horsemen. Considered to be the most powerful Crusader tactic, the charge was often rendered ineffective simply by not offering a stable line for the mounted knights to collide against. Smail, pp. 86–87, 114–15.

77. This locution is referred to as an *addubitatio* by Curtius, p. 545.

78. Joseph E. Gillett, "The Autonomous Character in Spanish and European Literature," *Hispanic Review* 24 (1959): 179–90.

79. Lejeune and Stiennon, 1:27, 72; 2: fig. 46.

80. Once the charge was effected, the idea was to form up again as soon as possible for a second onslaught. However, Turoldus details individual duels next. Calin, *Epic Quest*, p. 41: "epic melees admit little or no question of tactics or strategy. Pincer movements, flank attacks, surprise sorties, an opportune withdrawal to a better position—these are inconceivable in the world of Roncevaux and L'Archamp. Epic action hinges on the fact that it is considered dishonorable for Roland to call for reinforcements, even when ambushed, and for Vivien to retreat, even when betrayed by his allies." Similar observation relative to medieval chronicles in Brandt, *Medieval History*, pp. 120–22. Cf., however, Bancourt, "'Sen' et 'chevalerie'," pp. 628–30.

COMMENTARY 15

1. Bédier, *Légendes épiques*, 3:434, was the first to distinguish the first three phases listed here as well as the progression from gravity and joy to Roland's victorious death. Moignet begins Part 2 at v. 1396; I start it at v. 1438. See also Gräf, *Parallelismus im Rolandslied*, p. 8, n. 3; Horrent, p. 266. On the first two phases of the battle, see note 31 below.

2. Actually, not an exact match-up, for Turpin is not a Peer, and Roland and Oliver have two duels each. On this series of combats, see Holland, "Rolandus resurrectus," pp. 403–5; June H. Martin, "The Divisions of the *Chanson de Roland*," *Romance Notes* 6 (1965): 191–92.

3. Rychner, p. 141. Gräf, p. 2, had earlier cited this passage as an instance of the "true" repetition characteristic of oral composition.

4. On contemporary lance tactics, see D. J. A. Ross, "L'originalité de 'Turoldus': le maniement de la lance," *Cahiers de civilisation médiévale* 6 (1963), 127–38; Smail, *Crusading Warfare*, pp. 112–13. Edward A. Heinemann, "La place de l'élément 'brandir la lance' dans la structure du motif de l'attaque à la lance," *Romania* 95 (1974): 105–17,

points out that, in the *Song of Roland*, knights do not brandish their lances before dueling.

5. See INTRODUCTION, 15, A; 19, B.

6. Cf. the illustration of the battle scene in Conrad (*see Fig. 48*). In my paper "Les dessins du *Ruolantes Liet* et l'interprétation de la *Chanson de Roland*," I suggested that this sketch was based on a *Psychomachia* formula (cf. Lejeune and Stiennon, 2: fig. 8). I note the same view in M. Alison Stones, "Sacred and Profane Art: Secular and Liturgical Book-Illumination in the Thirteenth Century," in *The Epic in Medieval Society: Aesthetic and Moral Values*, ed. Harald Scholler (Tübingen: Niemeyer, 1977), p. 101. Lejeune and Stiennon, 1:23, suggests that some of the earliest representations of Good versus Evil, and Christian versus Saracen were later interpreted as depictions of Roland in combat.

7. Cf. Tuve, *Allegorical Imagery*, p. 120.

8. Réau, I:189; Cames, *Allégories*, fig. 125. Cf. Réau, I:175, 189; *Introduction au monde des symboles*, pls. 129–31, 137; Cames, figs, 123, 124.

9. Cf. *Psychomachia*, vv. 285–304, referring to Goliath's vain taunts.

10. See INTRODUCTION, 6.

11. Katzenellenbogen, *Allegories*, pp. 1, n. 3; 6. Cf. Réau, III, 3:1041–42: the earliest iconography of Saint Paul struck down on the road to Damascus shows him on foot; influenced by Pride's Fall in the *Psychomachia*, depictions, beginning in the fourteenth century, have him tumbling from a horse.

12. See COMMENTARY, 12, note 9.

13. Meredith-Jones, p. 187. The *Song of Roland* was composed before the beginning of heraldry in the second quarter of the twelfth century. Jenkins, note to v. 3090; Bédier, *Commentaires*, p. 315; Gerard J. Brault, *Early Blazon: Heraldic Terminology in the Twelfth and Thirteenth Centuries With Special Reference to Arthurian Literature* (Oxford: Clarendon Press, 1972), pp. 3, 18.

14. See *Fig. 7*; Lejeune and Stiennon, 2: figs. 68–70, 102, 104, 114, 116, 203, 204. Turpin's crozier is mentioned indirectly in v. 1670 (see COMMENTARY, 17).

15. Jenkins, note to v. 767.

16. On Roland's banner, see INTRODUCTION, 19, F. The *oriflamme* is discussed in COMMENTARY, 35. The term suggests a connection with OFr. *orie* 'golden' (Jenkins, *Glossary*, p. 351, derives the word from Lat. *aurea flammula* [cf. Bloch and Wartburg, *Dictionnaire*, s.v. flamme: Lat. *aurea flamma*]) but Burger (see COMMENTARY, 35, note 28) proposes Lat. *aurita flammula* 'eared (i.e., swallowtail) pennant'. At Chartres, Roland may be the bearer of this banner. Lejeune and Stiennon, 1:194.

17. The Saracens doubtless expect the French Peers to make an appropriate response to their taunts, thus identifying themselves. Ménard, *Le Rire*, p. 124: "Les Français se gardent d'une telle jactance. . . . Dès l'origine du genre épique, alors que les païens font figure de fanfarons sûrs de leur force, les héros chrétiens restent pénétrés de prudence et de réserve. Leur silence s'oppose à la jactance des païens. Contraste significatif! Toutefois, nos héros soulignent railleusement leur victoire une fois l'ennemi déconfit." Cf., however, Roland in vv. 1548–1549, and Turpin in vv. 1645–1647. See also COMMENTARY, 5 and 17, note 20. Ménard, p. 329, suggests that the place where the slain adversary is thrown (vv. 1273, 1287, 1334, 1375, 1385) may be comical.

18. Marsile is a king, too, of course, and his son is Jurfaleu (v. 1904); Malquiant, v. 1551, is the son of King Malcud; and Grandoine, v. 1570, is the son of the King of Cappadocia. For a clear case of identification, see COMMENTARY, 17 (vv. 1596–1599).

19. Le Gentil, p. 106, cited by Moignet, p. 105. On Aelroth, see Samaran, p. 34; Horrent, p. 324; Dufournet, *Cours sur Roland*, p. 32. On the name, see COMMENTARY, 11, note 34.

20. Charles's right arm may mean the Franks in general here. COMMENTARY, 14.

21. Dorfman, *Narreme*, p. 111.

22. See also Lyon, vv. 55–59; Paris, v. 573; Cambridge, vv. 439–440.

23. See also v. 2847 (Gabriel has Charles in his keeping).

24. On the meaning of *fol*, see Ménard, *Le Rire*, p. 129 and n. 319; pp. 178–83.

25. Jones, p. 91: "the *mals moz* (1190) spoken by Aelroth against the Franks ... serve as both calumny and malediction."

26. See MANUSCRIPT, v. 1215.

27. Colby, *Twelfth-Century French Literature*, pp. 37–39.

28. Ibid., p. 75.

29. See INTRODUCTION, 19, D.

30. *Gargantua*, ed. Screech, chap. 49. Cf. vv. 1541–1546, 1601–1606. See Jenkins, note to v. 1327; Meredith-Jones, pp. 306–7, note to p. 150, line vii; Menéndez Pidal, pp. 376–78, 380, 512; Ménard, *Le Rire*, pp. 54–55. Add Charlemagne's gab, *Pèlerinage de Charlemagne*, vv. 454–64. On medieval insensitivity to cruelty, see Brandt, *Medieval History*, pp. 134–35. Cf. Bowra, *Heroic Poetry*, pp. 70–72, 75.

31. See v. 1320. Bowra, *Heroic Poetry*, p. 53: "heroic narrative ... concentrates on the happy few and neglects the others."

32. At the Battle of Hastings, an English soldier is said to have cut off the head of a Norman horse, making a profound impression on all (*Le Roman de Rou de Wace*, ed. A. J. Holden, Société des anciens textes français [Paris: Picard, 1971], 2:vv. 8253–8280). On charging tactics, see COMMENTARY, 14, note 76.

33. David Talbot Rice, *A Concise History of Painting From Prehistory to the Thirteenth Century*, Praeger World of Art (New York and Washington, D.C.: Praeger, 1968), figs. 105, 106, 132.

34. Deschamps and Thibout, *Peinture murale*, pp. 71–86.

35. Lejeune and Stiennon, 2: figs. 105, 107, 110. Cf. also the technique of the Aachen Casket; Lejeune and Stiennon, 2: figs. 146, 150.

36. See INTRODUCTION, 18, H.

37. Bédier, *Commentaires*, p. 183, suggests that Turoldus has Margariz fight the second last duel in order to allow him time to reach Marsile before the next phase of the battle begins.

38. The episode appears in the other versions of the poem. Bibliography and discussion in Horrent, pp. 220–22; Segre, pp. 266–68.

39. Bédier, *Commentaires*, p. 191.

40. Cf. the following *diabolical* interventions: (1) the devil takes possession of Ganelon (COMMENTARY, 8); (2) Satan carries the soul of Malprimes away (v. 1268). See also vv. 1510, 3647. The mention of any Saracen automatically suggests demonic presence—the connection is specifically made in vv. 983, 1663, 2543—but the Rash Saracen and the ugly pagans, especially those who practice sorcery, are particularly suggestive of the devil. INTRODUCTION, 19, L.

41. On the term martyr, see INTRODUCTION, note 231.

COMMENTARY 16

1. Durendal was mentioned earlier by the Saracens and by the hero (vv. 1055, 1065, 1079; see also v. 1120).

2. See also v. 1399.

3. Oliver's reactions in this passage have been analyzed by Horrent, p. 172. On the name *Malun*, possibly an error for *Malsaron*, see Segre; Dufournet, *Cours sur Roland*, p. 33.

4. Frappier, *Chansons de geste*, 1:267; Walpole, "Humor and People," p. 215; Panofsky, *Renaissance and Renascences*, p. 95; Katzenellenbogen, *Allegories*, p. 83, n. 1; Jeanne Wathelet-Willem, "Quelle est l'origine du tinel de Rainouart?" *Boletín de la*

Real Academia de Buenas Letras de Barcelona 31 (1965/66): 355–64; Ménard, *Le Rire*, p. 99; Gerald Herman, "Unconventional Arms as a Comic Device in Some *Chansons de Geste*," *Modern Language Quarterly* 30 (1969): 328–29. Cf. Goliath's sarcastic observation in 1 Samuel 17:43: "Am I a dog for you to come against me with sticks?" In *Conte del graal*, v. 5116, a knight is scoffed at for carrying *un tros de lance*.

5. Cf. vv. 720–723.

6. Réau, II, 2:745–47; Beyer, *La Sculpture médiévale*, pp. 20–21, item 70.

7. Saracen enchanters are a commonplace in the chansons de geste. Skidmore, *Moral Traits of Christians and Saracens*, p. 37; Ménard, *Le Rire*, p. 97 (for the romances, see pp. 397–403, 413). Hell was often depicted in medieval art as an open mouth. See *Fig. 50*; COMMENTARY, 27, note 30.

8. Cf. v. 2916.

9. This passage marks the first occurrence of the expression *De ço qui calt*? Cf. vv. 1806, 1840, 1913, 2411, 3339. See also v. 227. On the ironic use of OFr. *caleir*, consult Ménard, *Le Rire*, p. 470.

10. The entire passage, which begins with a large initial in this copy, is considered suspect by many scholars. Segre, p. 249.

11. See, for example, Rychner, p. 54.

12. Lot, "Etudes," pp. 374–76, suggested the geography reflects a tenth-century view of France. See also Horrent, pp. 177–79; Menéndez Pidal, pp. 334–36. The passage in question has been studied by Louis, "La grande douleur pour la mort de Roland." For bibliography and discussion relative to the various toponyms in this laisse, consult Jenkins, notes to vv. 152, 1428, 1429; Horrent, pp. 300–301; Rita Lejeune, "Le Mont-Saint-Michel-au-péril-de-la-mer, la 'Chanson de Roland' et le Pèlerinage de Compostelle," *Millénaire monastique du Mont-Saint-Michel*, Bibliothèque d'Histoire et d'Archéologie chrétiennes (Paris: Lethielleux, 1967), 2:415; Segre, notes to vv. 1428–1429; Dufournet, *Cours sur Roland*, pp. 163–65. On the significance of thunderstorms in Scripture, see *The Jerusalem Bible*, p. 101, n. *j*; Blaise, par. 442. See also Maxwell S. Luria, "The Christian Tempest: A Symbolic Motif in Medieval Literature," Ph.D. diss., Princeton University, 1965.

13. Cf. Hatzfeld, "Le *Rolandslied* allemand," p. 55: "Des éclairs fendent les nuages noirs comme seule lumière à l'approche de la défaite."

14. Dufournet, *Cours sur Roland*, pp. 166–67, studies various literary manifestations of the signs announcing the end of the world. Bédier, *Commentaires*, p. 314, recognized the allusion to the Apocalypse, but also suggested a possible reminiscence of the portents announcing the death of Julius Caesar in the *Aeneid*. Matthew Paris's *Chronica majora* records the fact that in the year 1244, many people interpreted a storm as a sign of the imminence of the Last Judgment. Brandt, *Medieval History*, p. 60, n. 59. Cf. Jenkins, note to v. 1436. On the tempest as a sign of celestial displeasure, see Payen, *Le Motif du repentir*, pp. 34–35; as a prognostication, see Brandt, pp. 52–62.

15. Jenkins, note to v. 1436, alluding to Matthew 27:45 ff.; Luke 23:44 ff.; Revelation 8:5; 16:18, 21. Conrad adds that a great light appeared in the sky, a further reference to the account in Revelation.

16. All other copies preserve this laisse. Segre, pp. 254–55.

17. Réau, II, 2:486–87.

COMMENTARY 17

1. Jenkins, notes to vv. 1444, 3262; Foulet, *Glossaire*; Segre.

2. Bédier, *Commentaires*, p. 215; Zumthor, *Langue et techniques poétiques*, pp. 30, 53, n. 1; Segre. Jenkins, note to v. 1444, translates: 'That our Emperor's men are heroes'. On the latter interpretation (*li* = *celui de*), see *Perlesvaus*, 2:239.

3. Bédier, *Commentaires*, p. 214; Moignet, p. 120: "Ce vers est particulièrement plat; il est peut-être altéré"; Dufournet, *Cours sur Roland*, p. 146.

4. Foulet, *Glossaire*.

5. Segre: "[Foulet] cita la possibilità di attribuire l'agg. *vassal* a Carlo, ma non serve qui."

6. See INTRODUCTION, 18, H.

7. In medieval thought the contemplation of cadavers inspired conversion. Payen, *Le Motif du repentir*, p. 38. For another commentary on this passage, see Menéndez Pidal, pp. 105, 108–9, 111–12.

8. Charles A. Knudson, "Etudes sur la composition de la *Chanson de Roland*," *Romania* 63 (1937): 48–92; André Burger, "Sur la transposition des vers 1467 à 1509 du ms. O de la *Chanson de Roland*," *Essais de philologie moderne (1951)*, Bibliothèque de la Faculté de philosophie et lettres de l'Université de Liège 129 (Paris: Les Belles Lettres, 1953), pp. 155–60; Horrent, pp. 222–28; Michael Holland, "Gautier et Margarit: deux épisodes de la *Chanson de Roland*," *Cahiers de civilisation médiévale* 3 (1960): 339–49.

9. Delbouille, *Genèse*, pp. 111–30.

10. Jenkins, note to v. 1454, relative to *la menee*: "Originally, this was the way along which a hunted animal led the hunters and the dogs."

11. Jones, p. 184; Dorfman, *Narreme*, p. 111: "At this point, Roland announces the next great phase of the poem [= revenge]." Cf., too, the concern about *male chançun* (v. 1466; see also v. 1014). On the latter, see Jenkins, note to v. 1466; Jones, p. 89. Cf. *parole* in *Erec*, v. 2476. Zaal, *A lei francesa*, pp. 7–10, recognizes this as an epic cliché but points out an instance in the hagiographic poem *Sainte Foy*.

12. On vengeance, see Blaise, par. 145; INTRODUCTION, 14, D. See also note 18 below.

13. For an inverted image, see below, observation relative to v. 1617.

14. Venice IV's *maltallant* 'anger' alters the meaning completely.

15. See INTRODUCTION, note 66. For a similar association with the Holy Innocents, see *Couronnement de Louis*, v. 734. In medieval iconography the Massacre of the Innocents is depicted as soldiers dashing infants or piercing them with swords or spears. Réau, II, 2:269; Robb, *Illuminated Manuscript*, p. 74.

16. See INTRODUCTION, 3.

17. Three Peers plus two other knights. Jenkins, note to v. 1639. The procedure here, involving initial victories followed by the gradual elimination of every single French knight, is the exact reverse of the situation encountered in one episode of the *Pseudo-Turpin*, where the Christians lose at first but ultimately vanquish their Saracen enemies (Meredith-Jones, pp. 133, 135).

18. Revenge is specified in v. 1505 and alluded to indirectly in v. 1590. See note 12 above.

19. Their exultation, v. 1609, does mask the growing gloom expressed in v. 1585.

20. See COMMENTARY, 15, note 17. On Climborin's boast, reported indirectly in v. 1490, see INTRODUCTION, 18, G.

21. The importance attached to maintaining a united front in battle formations is discussed by Smail, *Crusading Warfare*, pp. 78, 127–28; Bancourt, "'Sen' et 'chevalerie'," pp. 625–27.

22. Rychner, p. 54. See COMMENTARY, 16, note 11.

23. The allusion to Valdabron's violation of the Temple of Jerusalem and assassination of the Patriarch in vv. 1524–1525 has often been held to be a historical allusion (Jenkins, note to v. 1566; Horrent, p. 290), thus useful when it comes to determining a terminus a quo. However, the anecdote may be modeled on the profanation of the Temple by Heliodorus in 2 Maccabees 3:7–23. At any rate, the story serves to give

the pagans a sacrilegious background consonant with Ganelon's behavior at Saragossa. See COMMENTARY, 8.

24. Cf. also the allusion to devils in v. 1510.

25. According to Jenkins, *Glossary*, p. 341, the name is properly *Malquidant* and may mean 'presumptuous' (*mal* + *cuidant*).

26. Falsaron is Marsile's brother.

27. On sister-son relationships, see William O. Farnsworth, *Uncle and Nephew in the Old French Chansons de Geste: A Study in the Survival of Matriarchy*, Columbia University Studies in Romance Philology and Literature (New York: Columbia University Press, 1913); Jones, pp. 110–14.

28. On the importance of family ties in the *Song of Roland*, see INTRODUCTION, 19, D.

29. Jones, p. 24.

30. Text in Segre, pp. 273–77; discussion in Bédier, *Commentaires*, pp. 115–18; Horrent, pp. 229–30; Segre, pp. 277–78.

31. See INTRODUCTION, 10, B, 2; COMMENTARY, 12.

32. See COMMENTARY, 12 and 15.

33. Charles is, to be sure, seated upon a golden throne (v. 115).

34. Colby, *Twelfth-Century French Literature*, pp. 69–71.

35. See INTRODUCTION, 19, D.

36. Bédier, *Commentaires*, p. 303, citing Tavernier.

37. See MANUSCRIPT, v. 1488.

38. Jenkins, p. cxxix.

39. See above, discussion of the word *guarant* in vv. 1470 and 1478.

40. Elsewhere in the *Song of Roland*, *gesir* usually suggests an attitude of repose. Cf., however, vv. 1230 and 1251.

41. Rice, *Painting from Prehistory to Thirteenth Century*, figs. 135, 190; *Introduction au monde des symboles*, p. 361.

42. Lejeune and Stiennon, 1:130; 2: fig. 110.

43. See COMMENTARY, 22.

44. Blaise, par. 318. Cf. also the depths of the sea (COMMENTARY, 27, n. 30). For the various meanings of the term, see Gerard J. Brault, "'Ung abysme de science': On the Interpretation of Gargantua's Letter to Pantagruel," *Bibliothèque d'Humanisme et Renaissance* 28 (1966): 627, n. 1.

45. Jenkins, note to v. 1470; Faral, *La Chanson de Roland*, pp. 221–22; Lejeune and Stiennon, 1:32–33, 39, n. 12. See also Ruggero M. Ruggieri's unpublished paper "L'épisode d'Abisme dans la *Chanson de Roland*," read at the Fifth International Congress of the Société Rencesvals held at Oxford in 1970 (summary in the *Bulletin bibliographique de la Société Rencesvals* 6 [1971]: 151–52, item 474).

46. On the association of pitch and Hell, see Tobler and Lommatzsch, 7:1365, s.v. poiz. For skin black as molten pitch, see Colby, *Twelfth-Century French Literature*, pp. 85–86. Ménard, *Le Rire*, p. 38: "le rire, c'est-à-dire l'enjouement, semble déjà tenu pour un des charmes de l'existence. En faisant le portrait du païen Abisme, l'auteur, comme pour ajouter une noirceur supplémentaire au Sarrasin, observe: *unches nuls homs nel vit juer ne rire* (1477 [= 1638]). C'est là un trait chargé de réprobation. Il implique que le rire a sa place dans la civilisation médiévale." On Val Metas, see OXFORD TEXT, ENGLISH TRANSLATION, v. 1663.

47. Blaise, par. 321, 328; Brault, *Early Blazon*, pp. 171–72.

48. See OXFORD TEXT, ENGLISH TRANSLATION, v. 1660.

49. Bloch and Wartburg, *Dictionnaire*, s.v. felon; Jones, pp. 28–30.

50. Jones, p. 34; Dufournet, *Cours sur Roland*, p. 153: "Nous ne sommes pas sûr qu'il faille les traduire de la même manière, l'un s'appliquant à un vassal, l'autre à

un suzerain." See also p. 154. Cf., however, Foulet, *Glossaire*, s.v. vasselage: "Ensemble des qualités du bon vassal et en particulier 'bravoure'."

51. Moignet, note to v. 1486.

52. Bloch and Wartburg, *Dictionnaire*, s.v. hérétique; Greimas, *Dictionnaire*, p. 236, s.v. erege, irese. On the vice of sodomy, see Ménard, *Le Rire*, p. 695 and n. 123. Cf. Robert A. Hall, Jr.'s, etymology of *felon*, cited by Jones, p. 29. In the *Psychomachia*, vv. 709–710, Haeresis is another name for Discordia.

53. See COMMENTARY, 8. In v. 2922 *Bugre* means 'Bulgars', but the medieval audience doubtless associated this term with the notion conveyed by MFr. *bougre*, E. *bugger*. The thirteenth-century translation of the *Pseudo-Turpin* in the *Grandes Chroniques* renders *fidem contra haereticam pravitatem* (Meredith-Jones, p. 113) as *foi contre l'eresie des Bogres* (Mortier, p. 19; the corresponding passage in the Latin version cited by Mortier, p. 18, was badly garbled by the editor).

54. Cf. the Old Norse translation where reference is made to Turpin's function rather than to his sign of office. Aebischer, *Rolandiana Borealia*, p. 188: 'Il est bien en rapport avec la charge qu'occupe l'archevêque!' Segre, note to v. 1670. On Turpin's horse, see INTRODUCTION, 7, and note 137.

55. If one accepts the interpretation of the Angoulême sculpture in Lejeune and Stiennon, 1:32–33, the Archbishop slays Abisme with a spear. However, there is not much to identify Turpin in this illustration (2: fig. 16).

56. COMMENTARY, 15, note 14.

57. Réau, II, 2:531 (Anastasis). See also COMMENTARY, 27, note 30. The Harrowing of Hell motif appears in several Old French grail romances. For discussion, see *Perlesvaus*, 2:233–34. Croziers are utilized as spears in the iconography of Saints Athanasius and Augustine. Alexander, *Norman Illumination*, p. 102, n. 1. In an illustration of *Aspremont*, Turpin is depicted riding into battle bearing a huge cross. Lejeune and Stiennon, 1:210; 2: fig. 168 B.

COMMENTARY 18

1. See COMMENTARY, 14.

2. See INTRODUCTION, 3.

3. No medieval illustration of the Roland-Oliver debate survives, an indication of the fact that commentators attached far less importance to the event than do modern critics. Lejeune and Stiennon, 1:97–98, suggests that the Brindisi mosaic depicts the incident (2: fig. 69), but even if one accepts this view, it is significant that Oliver is missing from the scene. Efforts to visualize the second phase of the debate the way Turoldus imagined it can be aided if one bears in mind that argumentation was frequently indicated by showing one of the debaters ticking off his points on the fingers of his hand. O. Chomentovskaja, "Le comput digital: Histoire d'un geste dans l'art de la Renaissance italienne," *Gazette des Beaux-Arts* 20 (1938): 157–72. To the illustrations referred to above in COMMENTARY, 14, note 12, add John the Baptist preaching in the Wilderness (Réau, II, 1:448) and Jesus arguing with the Doctors (Réau, II, 2:290). The gesture occurs in the iconography of Roland's debate with Ferracutus. Lejeune and Stiennon, 2: figs. 305, 348 B. Cf. COMMENTARY, 14, note 14.

4. COMMENTARY, 14.

5. INTRODUCTION, 3 and note 86. On turning the tables as a refutation technique, see *Argumentation and Debate: Principles and Practices. Prepared under the Auspices of Tau Kappa Alpha*, ed. David Potter (New York: Dryden Press, 1954), pp. 154–55. "The best defense against a turning-the-tables refutation is to question the frame of reference of the opponent's conclusion and to point out that the opponent is in effect not only

admitting the proponent's argument but also shifting around" (p. 179). Turning the tables is not unlike Ganelon's ironic use of *fillastre* in v. 743. Cf. the "chiasme psychologique" in the *Chanson de Guillaume* alluded to by Frappier, *Chansons de geste*, 1:158, n. 1, 159.

6. Bédier, *Légendes épiques*, 3:439.

7. See INTRODUCTION, 3.

8. Vance, *Reading the Song of Roland*, pp. 43–44, 47, 51.

9. The detailing of motivation is often one of the features that distinguishes modern from medieval literary technique, and, in his character portrayal, Turoldus simply did not provide the sort of telltale clues one generally looks for today. INTRODUCTION, 19. For examples of sudden and unmotivated changes in behavior in Old French romances, see Ménard, *Le Rire*, pp. 563–65. The latter, p. 563, remarks apropos of the *Prose Lancelot:*

> Le dessein de l'auteur est surtout de multiplier les rebondissements afin de donner une teinte dramatique à cet ample épisode. Mais si le lecteur moderne regarde avec un certain détachement le comportement de Pharien ou de Lambègue, il est enclin à sourire de leurs brusques changements d'attitude. Nous demandons inconsciemment aux personnages d'avoir une certaine unité, une certaine stabilité psychologique. Or, les volte-face ne manquent pas. . . . Nulle hésitation, nul débat intérieur chez nos personnages. Ils donnent l'impression de se lancer à corps perdu dans l'action. Ensuite, un soudain et secret repentir s'empare d'eux: ils font marche arrière. En fait, nos personnages se trouvent devant une alternative dont aucun des deux termes ne les satisfait pleinement. Bien que leurs réactions paraissent impulsives, ils sont en quelque sorte enfermés dans une situation cornélienne. Deux devoirs contraires—peut-être successivement, plus que simultanément—les sollicitent et les tirent en sens inverse.

10. Nichols, *Formulaic Diction*, p. 36: "nowhere does the poet mention Roland as 'thinking' about this problem."

11. Blaise, par. 145.

12. Ibid., par. 276, 456, 458. Bramimonde's conversion may also be viewed as a fruit of Roland's sacrifice. See COMMENTARY, 48, note 3.

13. On *legerie*, see OXFORD TEXT, ENGLISH TRANSLATION, v. 113, and COMMENTARY, 4. For conjectures relative to Oliver's initial statement (v. 1723: "Cumpainz, vos le feïstes"), see Jenkins; William A. Nitze, "Two *Roland* Passages: Verses 147 and 1723," *Romance Philology* 2 (1948/49): 234–37; Segre. Verses 1724–1725 have an aphoristic quality suggesting clerical influence. *Erec*, v. 231 (Folie n'est pas vaselages) echoes v. 1724 here. See also Philippe de Novare, *Les Quatre Ages de l'homme*, cited by Langlois, *La Vie en France*, 2:229.

14. Bédier, *Légendes épiques*, 3:438, terms Oliver's arguments here ironic and cruel but concedes, p. 439, that there is also much tenderness in his words. Riquer, *Chansons de geste*, p. 96, writes of an "amicale plaisanterie." For a divergent view, see Burger, "Les deux scènes du cor," pp. 118 ff.; Payen, *Le Motif du repentir*, p. 110 ("ironie très amère"). The verbs *cuntrarïer* (v. 1737) and *cuntralïez* (v. 1741) indicate a heated argument. The conventional nature of the debate in no way lessens the emotional impact upon the audience (see COMMENTARY, 14). Turpin's kindly reproof (v. 1739: castïer) does, however, pour oil on the troubled waters. On *deignastes* in v. 1716, see COMMENTARY, 14.

15. Cf. *astysmos* 'sarcasm without bitterness', one of the seven forms of *alieniloquium* mentioned by Isidore of Seville. Robertson, *Preface to Chaucer*, p. 288.

16. 1 Corinthians 1:18; Blaise, par. 192.

17. See COMMENTARY, 8. Horrent, *Pèlerinage*, p. 76: "Dans la pure *Chanson de Roland* . . . surgit, l'éclair d'un instant, l'évocation précise d'amours passionnées et

charnelles (v. 1720–21)." For other brief mentions, see idem, *La Chanson de Roland*, p. 241; Bowra, *Heroic Poetry*, p. 345; Menéndez Pidal, p. 366. In *La Chanson de Guillaume*, ed. Duncan McMillan, Société des anciens textes français (Paris: Picard, 1949), 1: v. 1036, Guibourc's meaning is clear when she threatens her spouse: "*Si nel me renz, ne girras mes entre mes braz*." The expression *gesir entra sa brace* may thus be a euphemism (see also Ménard, *Le Rire*, pp. 684, 686). In the romances lovers' bliss is frequently compared to heaven (Ménard, pp. 643–49). However, Roland clearly has another paradise in mind. INTRODUCTION, 19, F and I.

18. Cf. Bédier, *Légendes épiques*, 3:438: "comme s'il s'attendrissait malgré lui"; Jenkins, note to v. 1711: "Oliver, who disagrees with Roland most unwillingly, softens his emphatic objections with a compliment" (referring also to his note to v. 1723: "Oliver's attitude towards Roland is ever one of deep respect"). In his edition Bédier translates v. 1711 as: 'Mais comme vos deux bras sont sanglants!' Burger, "Les deux scènes du cor," p. 120, objects: "Il n'y a rien dans le texte qui justifie le 'mais', le 'comme', ni la tournure exclamative." For 'mais', see Foulet, *Glossaire*, p. 408. Burger links the phrase to v. 1710 and suggests that it is a continuation of Oliver's argument. However, the phrase is also clearly reminiscent of Roland's promise in v. 1056: "*Sanglant en ert li branz entresqu'a l'or*": Durendal is merely an extension of his arm.

19. The Old Norse translation makes this connection even more apparent. Aebischer, *Rolandiana Borealia*, p. 192: "mais maintenant tu as les deux mains sanglantes!" For another reference to Lady Macbeth's hands, see COMMENTARY, 19.

20. The expression *mult ert gref la departie* (v. 1736) is close to being that of lovers. Cf. Roland's dying thoughts in Châteauroux, vv. 3805–3808:

> Lors li remenbre d'Aude qui fu s'amie,
> Si la regrete o parole serie:
> "Amie douce, con dure departie,
> Mais ne serez de tel home servie."

On the portrayal of Alda in the rhymed versions, see Horrent, pp. 134–38. For a similar use of *departie* 'lovers' parting' in the *Tristan de Thomas*, see Lazar, *Amour courtois et 'fin'amors'*, p. 162. On the terminology of companionage, see Georges Gougenheim, "'Compagnon' dans la *Chanson de Roland*," *Mélanges Pierre Le Gentil*, pp. 325–28.

21. For a discussion of the various versions of this passage, see Horrent, p. 179.

22. In his caption, p. 132, Jenkins says Turpin would recall Charles, "but for a different reason"! The author of the *Pseudo-Turpin* has Roland sound his oliphant so that his remaining companions, or at least Charles and his men, may witness his last moments, save his sword and his horse, and pursue the fleeing Saracens (Meredith-Jones, p. 193; cf. p. 187). The phrase *vel si illi qui portus iam transierant* is missing in many copies (Meredith-Jones, p. 192; Mandach, *Naissance*, 2:78); cf., however, the French translation of the *Pseudo-Turpin* in the *Grandes Chroniques* (Mortier, p. 69).

23. Bédier, *Commentaires*, p. 313. In Matthew 7:6, dogs and pigs are symbols of the devil; in 15:26, pagans are associated with dogs. Being devoured by pigs also suggests the legendary fate of Mohammed; see COMMENTARY, 29 and note 20. For an illustration of the legend, see Montague Rhodes James, "The Drawings of Matthew Paris," *Walpole Society* 14 (1925/26): 4 and pl. 2. James, *Comparative Religion*, p. 92, explains that the wandering souls of the unburied dead "are a continual source of danger and discomfort to the survivors. Therefore, every effort is made to dispose of the body in a decent manner calculated to secure rebirth and renewal beyond the grave." In the Old Testament earth must cover the body or its blood will cry to heaven for vengeance. *The Jerusalem Bible*, p. 747, n. *h*. In Christian belief, the remains must be accorded proper respect because they were once the temple of the Holy Spirit and will someday resurrect. Blaise, par. 394, 398. In *Peristephanon*, 5: vv. 397–400

(*Prudentius*, 2:192), Saint Vincent the Martyr's body is delivered to wild beasts and dogs, but no animal dares "pollute the memorial of glorious victory with its unclean touch." See also Deschamps and Thibout, *Peinture murale*, fig. 14; Réau, II, 2:415; INTRODUCTION, 19, F (integrity).

24. Foulet, *Glossaire*; Moignet, p. 138, note.

25. Jenkins, note to v. 1750.

26. James, *Comparative Religion*, p. 281.

27. Psalms 92:13.

28. Robertson, *Preface to Chaucer*, p. 225 and n. 138; Blaise, par. 109; INTRODUCTION, 16, E.

29. INTRODUCTION, 10, A, 1.

30. Lejeune and Stiennon, 1:171–74 (pl. VI; 2: fig. 148), 194–95 (pl. X), 320–21 (pl. LV), 395 (2: fig. 502).

31. Ibid., 1:98; 2: figs. 68, 70.

32. James, *Comparative Religion*, chap. 12.

33. Cited by Bédier, *Commentaires*, p. 305.

34. Blaise, par. 198, 410.

COMMENTARY 19

1. Jenkins, note to vv. 1753 ff. In the *Pseudo-Turpin* Roland is referred to as the 'trumpeter' (Meredith-Jones, p. 203: *tubicem* [all other copies *tubicinem*] *virum*). MFr. *oliphant, olifant* rarely fails to evoke Roland. Bloch and Wartburg, *Dictionnaire*, s.v. éléphant. According to Lejeune and Stiennon, 1:195, Charlemagne is depicted listening to Roland's horn in a medallion of a stained-glass window at Chartres (pl. XV).

2. Jenkins, note to v. 1769; Auerbach, *Mimesis*, p. 107.

3. *La Chanson de Roland*, ed. Calin, p. 12.

4. Bédier, *Légendes épiques*, 3:439; Jenkins, note to v. 1762; Le Gentil, pp. 106–8, cited by Moignet, pp. 139, 141. Cf. Ezekiel 33:6: "If, however, the sentry has seen the sword coming but has not blown his horn, and so the people are not alerted and the sword overtakes them and destroys one of them, the latter shall indeed die for his sin, but I will hold the sentry responsible for his death."

5. For a description of the sound of the hunting horn, see *Tristan de Thomas*, 1:48 (also Bédier's note, 1:49, n. 1).

6. Will, *Alsace romane*, p. 261 and fig. 114. See also INTRODUCTION, 14, A, 2; COMMENTARY, 21.

7. And may even have given the mysterious adventure its name. Loomis, *Arthurian Literature in the Middle Ages*, p. 168.

8. Ibid., pp. 113–16.

9. Mireaux, *Chanson de Roland*, pp. 237–39; *Le Guide du pèlerin de Saint-Jacques de Compostelle*, p. 79; Georges Costa, *Trésors des Eglises de France*, I, *Epoques pré-romane et romane*, Grandes expositions (Paris: Publications filmées d'art et d'histoire, 1966): 134–36. The Saint-Seurin oliphant is ornamented with a lion devouring a harpy, another preying on a dog, and a dromedary. These motifs were drawn from Oriental tapestries.

10. Loomis, *Arthurian Literature*, p. 114.

11. For these and other points of similarity, see *Huon de Bordeaux*, p. 74.

12. It matters little whether the leagues be fifteen, as in Venice IV (see Segre), or eight, as in the *Pseudo-Turpin* (Meredith-Jones, p. 193): The feat is just as miraculous. Cf. the anecdote concerning the jongleur who, granted all the land reached by the sound of his horn, in 773, climbed to a mountaintop to give the blast. Faral, *Jongleurs*, p. 18. The Saracen bugles and trumpets (vv. 1319, 1629) do not have mana, for their

sound does not reach Charles's ears. On this notion, see COMMENTARY, 25, note 18. Durendal is of divine origin (vv. 2318–2320) and it required no great stretch of the imagination for the medieval audience to assume that Roland's horn was similarly brought forth.

13. Meredith-Jones, p. 193.

14. Hanns Swarzenski, "Two Oliphants in the Museum," *Bulletin of the Museum of Fine Arts, Boston* 60 (1962): 27–45, is an excellent study of the ornamentation and provenance of several eleventh-century carved oliphants. Add John R. Allen, "The Saversnake Horn," *Olifant* 3, no. 3 (1976): 200–202; Ian Short, "A Note on Our Eponymous Horn," *Olifant* 3, no. 4 (1976): 259–61; idem, "Postscript to the Savernake Horn," *Olifant* 4, no. 2 (1976): 87–88 (notes the correct spelling Savernake).

15. It is worth noting that oliphants of the day bore religious as well as profane motifs. Swarzenski, "Two Oliphants," p. 34.

16. Minis, "Über Rolands Horn," believes that, primitively, Roland's oliphant was a *buisine* 'trumpet (for rallying)', not a hunting horn.

17. Cf. Jenkins, note to v. 1436.

18. On the confusion of the signs announcing Christ's death with those foreshadowing the Last Judgment, see Réau, II, 2:486. See also COMMENTARY, 27 (v. 2459). In the Old Testament the horn is often a symbol of power and strength. Blaise, par. 165. It is also a signal and an instrument with which to praise the Lord.

19. Rychner, pp. 94–95.

20. The lie is of course Ganelon's. Jenkins, note to v. 1772: "such latitude of speech may be quite in character for the French kings and nobles of the XIth century. At this moment, the traitor is tasting whatever sweetness there may be in the success of his elaborately-plotted revenge." Charles is in doubt as to the sound of the oliphant. Cf. the "uncertain" trumpet sound in 1 Corinthians 14:8. Naturally, repetition of the Emperor's query is also a literary technique comparable to Oliver's thrice-reiterated appeal to sound the horn.

21. Vance, *Reading the Song of Roland*, p. 33, refers to Ganelon's use of language "differently from other men in the poem" as a tool of subversion. The same can be said, however, of Saracens such as Blancandrin. The mention, in v. 1781, of Roland's boasting may be an allusion to the event at Aix referred to in vv. 2860 ff. Cf. also v. 1075. A knight fleeing from a hare is the symbol of Ignavia in a thirteenth-century sculpture at Notre-Dame de Paris. Katzenellenbogen, *Allegories*, p. 76. See also Brault, *Early Blazon*, p. 227, s.v. lievre rampant. Ganelon thus implies that Roland is a coward, which is actually his problem (see INTRODUCTION, 19, C; COMMENTARY, 6). Cf. Roland's stance in vv. 1074–1075. For other interpretations of this passage, see Horrent, pp. 179–84; Jones, pp. 69–70; Ménard, *Le Rire*, p. 21. On the corresponding passage in the *Pseudo-Turpin*, see Mandach, *Naissance*, 1:57.

22. Paris, *Histoire poétique de Charlemagne*, p. 263; Jenkins, p. xciv and notes to vv. 198. 1775–1779; Paul Aebischer, *Textes norrois et littérature française du moyen âge*, I, *Recherches sur les traditions épiques antérieures à la Chanson de Roland d'après les données de la première branche de la Karlamagnús saga*, Publications romanes et françaises 44 (Geneva: Droz; Lille: Giard, 1954): 9–49; Robert Guiette, "Notes sur la Prise de Nobles," in *Etudes de philologie romane*, Romanica Gandensia 4 (Ghent: Rijksuniversiteit te Gent, 1955), pp. 67–80; Menéndez Pidal, p. 160; Lejeune and Stiennon, 1:194, 252–55, 335–36; Paul Aebischer, "Sur le vers 1776 du *Roland* d'Oxford," *Mélanges de philologie offerts à Alf Lombard à l'occasion de son soixante-cinquième anniversaire par ses collègues et ses amis*, Etudes romanes de Lund 18 (Lund: Gleerup, 1969), pp. 17–21; Gustave A. Beckman, "L'identification Nobles = Dax," *Le Moyen Age* 79 (1973): 5–24; *Karlamagnús Saga: The Saga of Charlemagne and His Heroes*, trans. Constance B. Hieatt, 1:48–49. The views that follow were first presented in my article entitled

"Ganelon et Roland," pp. 399–404. For a critique by Gerald Bertin and my reply, see *Olifant* 3, no. 2 (1975): 129–33.

23. The version closest to that preserved in the Oxford copy seems to be the *Saga af Runzivals bardaga* [= *Rolandiana Borealia*], or Branch VIII of the *Karlamagnús Saga*, a thirteenth-century Norse prose work. Halvorsen, *The Norse Version of the Chanson de Roland*, has proved, after Aebischer, that the original (*n*) of the Norse *Roland* followed a French version (*k*), which is very close to the Oxford text. In the passage relative to the Capture of Nobles, the Norse version reproduces quite faithfully the Bodleian version except, in fact, vv. 1778–1779, where the washing of the battlefield is omitted and a phrase explaining how Roland "fit aveugler les uns et pendre les autres, qu'il mena les autres à la décapitation" is substituted (Aebischer, *Rolandiana Borealia*, p. 195; Halvorsen, pp. 153–56). Halvorsen concludes quite plausibly that this substitution can be explained by the fact that the Norse translator could not understand the verse in question in his French model ("could make neither head nor tail of the O verse *Puis od les ewes lavat les prez del sanc*," p. 156). However, Branch I of the same *Karlamagnús Saga* also contains an allusion to the Capture of Nobles. This branch is made up of several epic elements, including a summary of a primitive version of the *Entrée d'Espagne*. It so happens that in the only extant copy of this poem, that narrative of the Capture of Nobles takes up more than 2,000 verses, but does not mention flooding the battlefield. On the other hand, the summary of the *Entrée d'Espagne* in Branch I makes it clear that "Les Français lavent et sèchent le champ de bataille, afin que Charles ne voie pas le sang" (Aebischer, *Textes norrois*, p. 17). Aebischer believes this detail reflects a primitive version of the *Entrée d'Espagne*, which contained this theme. I prefer to align myself with Halvorsen, p. 155, n. 17, who opines that the detail concerning the flooding of the battlefield in Branch I derives from *k*.

24. Jenkins, note to v. 1777. However, the construction appears to me to be of the *apo koinou* type. For another example, see v. 509. On the use of this word order, see Yves Lefèvre, *Manuel d'ancien français*, vol. 3, Philippe Ménard, *Syntaxe* (Bordeaux: Société bordelaise de diffusion de travaux des lettres et sciences humaines, 1968), p. 85, par. 99.

25. For conjectures relative to vv. 1778–1779, see Segre.

26. See MANUSCRIPT, V. 1779.

27. Tobler and Lommatzsch, 5:244. *Lever* = *laver*. In Paris (ed. Mortier, p. 37, note), the city of Nobles is not mentioned in this passage and the incident is narrated as if it had occurred at Roncevaux.

28. The confusion of *les prez* and *s'espee* may have been due to the similarity of *l* and *s* in this copy. On this type of error, see Samaran, p. 34. Note also the resemblance between *la spee* and *la pree*, forms attested in vv. 1375, 3145 (see the note in Bédier's edition), and 3873. Reading *s'espee* instead of *les prez* does add a syllable, which seems to produce a hypermetric verse. However, final mute *e*, even when not followed by a word beginning with a vowel, was at times omitted in the scansion. Bédier, *Commentaires*, p. 265; M. K. Pope, *From Latin to Modern French with Especial Consideration of Anglo-Norman: Phonology and Morphology*, 2d ed. (Manchester: Manchester University Press, 1952), par. 1133 (iii).

29. The connection with the biblical symbol of the meadows as evildoers (Psalms 37:20) is very remote here.

30. Motif C 913 (Bloody key as a sign of disobedience). In *Aliscans*, is Rainouart's rinsing of his *tinel* in a stream a parody of Roland's sword-washing? On the episode in question, see Frappier, *Chansons de geste*, 1:271. In a thirteenth-century stained-glass window at Chartres, Saint Julian the Hospitaler wipes the blood from his sword after mistakenly slaying his own parents. Réau, III, 2:767, 768. Bloody hands are mentioned above, COMMENTARY, 18, note 19.

31. *Psychomachia*, vv. 98–104. For medieval illustrations of the scene, see Woodruff, "Illustrated Manuscripts of Prudentius," figs. 82, 89, 99, 101, 102, 107.

32. *Psychomachia*, trans. Thomson, p. 287.

33. In the *Tournoiement Antecrit* Patience's banner is washed in tears of compunction (vv. 1570–1574); cf. Fornication's in the river of Vileness (vv. 1033), Peace and Mercy's in Pity's tears (vv. 1965–1969). On the washing away of sins, see Réau, II, 2:30–31; Payen, *Le Motif du repentir*, app., p. 601, s.v. Laver (le péché). For a similar allegation, accusing Charlemagne of excessive killings, see Brault, "The Legend of Charlemagne's Sin," p. 74. According to Chrétien de Troyes, washing honor in shame soils rather than cleanses it (*Charrette*, vv. 4386–4387).

34. See v. 227.

35. See INTRODUCTION, 19, C; COMMENTARY, 6.

36. *Yvain*, vv. 2602–2615 (see Roger S. Loomis, *Arthurian Tradition and Chrétien de Troyes* [New York: Columbia University Press, 1949], pp. 239, 296–97, 301, 304–5); *Erec*, vv. 5765–5766.

37. See INTRODUCTION, 19, F.

38. OFr. *temple* < VL **tempula* < CL *tempora*, plural of the neuter noun *tempus*. The rivalry between this term and CL *templum* was reinforced by the Pauline notion that *membra vestra templum sunt Spiritus Sancti* (1 Corinthians 6:19). Blaise, par. 398. There is a possible suggestion here of the Crown of Thorns, blood also flowing from a wound in Christ's head.

COMMENTARY 20

1. See COMMENTARY, 14.

2. Rychner, pp. 128, 132–37. On the significance of arming, see INTRODUCTION, 10, A, 3.

3. Cf. v. 2548: *il ad desturber*.

4. Jenkins, note to v. 3814.

5. Frederick W. Locke, "Ganelon and the Cooks," *Symposium* 20 (1966): 141–48. Since Petit de Julleville, this passage has been said to provoke barbarous laughter. Jenkins, note to vv. 1816ff.; Curtius, p. 530; Frappier, *Chansons de geste*, 1:200; Herman, "Unconventional Arms," pp. 320–21 (bibliography, p. 321, n. 5); Peter Noble, "Attitudes to Social Class as Revealed by Some of the Older Chansons de Geste," *Romania* 94 (1973): 362–63. A similar punishment is related in the *Vengement Alixandre*. Ménard, *Le Rire*, p. 324. For related cruelties, consult Ménard, pp. 72, 75–78 (reference is made here to the saints' lives; for bibliography, see p. 78, n. 174). In the rhymed versions, Ganelon escapes. Horrent, pp. 194–98.

6. It is often said that vv. 1874–1875 contain the only comparison in Turoldus's poem. Jenkins, p. xxxvi; Crosland, *The Old French Epic*, p. 85; Hatzfeld, "Le *Rolandslied* allemand," p. 53; Lejeune and Stiennon, 1:38. In addition to the usage in v. 1827, see vv. 3153, 3162, 3173, 3319, 3503, 3521. Horrent, p. 254, notes that comparisons are more frequent in the Baligant episode than in the rest of the poem. Turoldus's similes are discussed by Bowra, *Heroic Poetry*, pp. 269, 275.

7. It is also condign punishment, for Ganelon is a diabolical figure (cf. Satan the Fowler). Blaise, par. 323 (laqueator). In *Yvain*, vv. 625–627:

> Home qu'an ne puet chastïer
> Devroit en au mostier lïer
> Come desvé, devant les prones.

The reference is to possession by the devil. Chains are associated with the damned and sin. Réau, II, 2:743; Blaise, p. 110, s.v. vinculum. In Revelation 20:1–3, an angel chains the devil and throws him into a well, whose cover is sealed for a thousand years. For illustrations, see Réau, II, 2:720–21. Other symbolic aspects of the bear are listed by Réau, I:110–11, 130; Dufournet, *Cours sur Roland*, pp. 94–95. See also INTRODUCTION, 19, G; OXFORD TEXT, ENGLISH TRANSLATION, V. 727.

8. In *Couronnement de Louis*, v. 2186, a traitor, forced to ride bound on a horse, is derisively compared to a *cofre en somier*. Ménard, *Le Rire*, p. 118. On humiliating mounts, see Réau, I:125–26, 127, 128, 171; II, 1:217; II, 2:488; Ruth Mellinkoff, "Riding Backwards: Theme of Humiliation and Symbol of Evil," *Viator* 4 (1973): 153–76 (add Ménard, p. 77 and n. 173).

9. See also vv. 2320, 2912, 3709. In vv. 2320 and 2912 the term is preceded by the word *cunte*. In v. 3085 *cataignes* refers to the French barons in general. In *Ami et Amile, chanson de geste*, ed. Peter F. Dembowski, Classiques français du moyen âge 97 (Paris: Champion, 1969), the term means 'captain', but also, at times, 'worthy'. Cf.:

517 Iluec trouva Amile le chatainne.
2042 Va s'en Amiles, li prouz et li chatainnes.

10. Boissonnade, *Du Nouveau*, p. 269.

11. Cf. *caecus* 'blind' and its relationship to the legend of Saint Caecilia. Réau, III, 1:278.

12. In the *Song of Roland caitive* always refers to Bramimonde (vv. 2596, 2722, 3673, 3978). In the latter two instances it has the literal meaning 'captive'. When the hero of Chrétien's *Conte del graal* discovers for the first time what his name is (Perchevax li Galois), he is told by a damsel that he is rather *Perchevax li chaitis* (v. 3582). On the latter episode, see Ménard, *Le Rire*, p. 507; Frappier, *Chrétien de Troyes et le mythe du graal*, pp. 118–26.

13. Philipp Haerle, *Captivus, cattivo, chétif: Zur Einwirkung des Christentums auf die Terminologie der Moralbegriffe*, Romanica Helvetica 55 (Berne: Francke, 1955); Jones, p. 52; Payen, *Le Motif du repentir*, pp. 98 and n. 5, 217, 270, 304, 436, 520, 526, 556.

14. Cf. Zumthor's observation relative to *nevold*, cited below, COMMENTARY, 34, note 13. A further association with OFr. *cadeir, caeir, caïr* 'to fall' is also possible. The term captain seems to retain its pathetic connotation to this day in English as well as in French. In the last scene of Shakespeare's *Hamlet*, the dead hero is borne off the stage by four captains; cf. also Walt Whitman's poem (1865) on the death of Abraham Lincoln, "O Captain! My Captain!," and this verse from Baudelaire's "Le Voyage": "O mort, vieux capitaine, il est temps! levons l'ancre!" Erich von Richthofen, "El lugar de la batalla en la Canción de Roldán, la leyenda de Otger Catalò y el nombre de Cataluña," *Revista de Filología Española* 38 (1954): 282–88, suggests a connection between *cataigne* and *Catalò, Cataluña*.

15. Hatzfeld, *Literature Through Art*, p. 12, sees a sign of peace in the sea of light that bathes Charlemagne's army in this passage. Cf. idem, "Le *Rolandslied* allemand," p. 55: "Mais quand Roland a sonné le cor comme signe de désastre, le paysage sans soleil apparaît de nouveau, les vallées à parcourir semblent plus profondes encore, les échos si lointains avec l'étincelle d'espoir de la réponse des cors de l'armée de Charlemagne."

16. Roland sounds his oliphant one more time (v. 2104) and it is heard by Charles (v. 2105). The Saracens hear Charles's bugles (vv. 2113, 2115–2116, 2150), but there is no indication that the rearguard does.

COMMENTARY 21

1. Vance, *Reading the Song of Roland*, p. 55.
2. Cf. also vv. 1018, 2185. A similar expression is found in *Thèbes*, vv. 3497–3498.
3. Paul Zumthor, "Etude typologique des planctus contenus dans la *Chanson de*

Roland," in *La Technique littéraire des chansons de geste*, pp. 219–35. Cf. idem, "Les *planctus* épiques," *Romania* 84 (1963): 61–69.

4. Payen, *Le Motif du repentir*, p. 137.

5. Renoir, "Roland's Lament," believes that the hero exhibits humility and repentance in this passage. See INTRODUCTION, note 519. Jones, "La complainte de Roland," finds no Christian sentiments whatsoever.

6. Burgess, *Vocabulaire pré-courtois*, pp. 105, 159.

7. The expression is repeated in v. 2384.

8. Read *en vain* rather than *pour son malheur*. Payen, *Le Motif du repentir*, pp. 122–23. Renoir's article ("Roland's Lament") is based on Jenkins's interpretation. See also Menéndez Pidal, p. 339; Vance, *Reading the Song of Roland*, p. 55, citing Renoir.

9. Sorrow because he can no longer protect (v. 1864: tenser) his men. Dufournet, *Cours sur Roland*, p. 31. Jenkins, note to v. 1863:

> *por mei* 'because of me' 'thru my fault'; not 'for my sake' (as Tavernier, Chamard, Moncrieff). Cf. vv. 1090, 2937. Like Hector before Troy, Roland bitterly reproaches himself, because, 'by trusting his own might, he undid the host'. Oliver's charge (v. 1726) is then true, and Roland, stung intolerably by the realization of its truth, can find relief only in violent action, and in the hope that he may yet be of use to his brother-in-arms. The poet's psychology rings true.

Cf. Foulet, *Glossaire*, p. 452: 'dans l'intérêt de', not 'à cause de'; Jones, "La complainte de Roland," pp. 36–37: 'par égard pour moi'; see also Waltz, *Rolandslied*, p. 52. However, see Payen, *Le Motif du repentir*, p. 123: "il n'est pas certain qu'il faille interpréter: 'Barons franceis, pur mei vos vei murir' (v. 1863), par: 'Seigneurs barons, c'est par ma faute que je vous vois mourir' (sens défendu entre autres par Henri Chamard et Léon Gautier)."

10. It is often referred to as the only formal comparison in the *Song of Roland*. See, however, COMMENTARY, 20, note 6.

11. Delbouille, *Genèse*, p. 146, adds a reference to Fulcher of Chartres. Cf. *Ovid, The Art of Love, and Other Poems*, ed. and trans. J. H. Mozley, The Loeb Classical Library, (1929; rpt. Cambridge: Harvard University Press; London: Heinemann, 1969), 1: vv. 117–119; *Yvain*, vv. 882–889, 3199–3200.

12. Lejeune and Stiennon, 1:38, 87, 88.

13. Ibid., 1:87. For a further connection with a helpful stag in a later version of the legend, see 1:38.

14. Ibid. Cf. the image of the *piscatores hominum* in Matthew 4:19; Mark 1:17. Réau, II, 2:31; Blaise, par. 172. Crozet, "Le chasseur et le combattant dans la sculpture romane en Saintonge," p. 670, states that this church imagery may also be pure fantasy and a reflection of the contemporary passion for hunting.

15. Robertson, *Preface to Chaucer*, p. 263.

16. For other symbolism concerning the stag, see McCulloch, *Mediaeval Latin and French Bestiaries*, pp. 172–74; Katzenellenbogen, *Allegories*, p. 44, n. 1; Johannes Rathofer, "Der 'wunderbare Hirsch' der Minnegrotte," *Zeitschrift für deutsches Altertum* 95 (1966): 27–42; Robertson, *Preface to Chaucer*, pp. 193, 253, 255, 263–64, 394, 425, 464, 465; *The Year 1200*, 1:69.

17. Cf. also Isaiah 13:14: "Then like a startled gazelle, like sheep that no one shepherds, each man will return to his people, each take flight to his native land." Riquer, *Chansons de geste*, p. 102: "C'est une comparaison d'origine biblique, et prise également à l'exercice de la chasse." He opines that it is somewhat surprising to find such a rhetorical device in an otherwise arid text.

18. Horrent, p. 307, n. 2, citing Fawtier. However, the opposition between the active life of the soldier and the contemplative life of the monk was a commonplace of medieval satirical literature.

19. Jenkins, note to v. 1881.

20. Lejeune, "Le caractère de l'archevêque Turpin," p. 18.

21. See INTRODUCTION, note 568.

22. Ecclesiastes 3:1–8.

23. *Huon de Bordeaux*, p. 79. On the feudal punishment, see Payen, *Le Motif du repentir*, p. 197; *The Song of Roland*, trans. Harrison, pp. 15–16. Jenkins, note to v. 2574, refers to "a similar happening at the battle of Zalaca (1086)," but the King of Seville was only wounded in the hand (Jenkins, p. lxxxiii). For the legend of Belzeray, the Jew who tried to spill the coffin of the Virgin and had his hand cut off by Saint Michael, see Réau, II, 2:611–12, citing other examples. Cf. the legend of Saint John of Damascus; Réau, III, 2:725–26. Cf. also COMMENTARY, 47, note 17.

24. Jones, *Ethos*, p. 45, states that this mutilation "was an especially great shame for a Mohammedan."

25. Ménard, *Le Rire*, p. 327; see also pp. 158–59.

26. Robert S. Picciotto, "Marsile's Right Hand," *Romance Notes* 7 (1966): 207–8. Cf. Ganelon's punishment (COMMENTARY, 47).

27. The scene is illustrated by the Master of the Apocrypha Drawings. Walter F. Oakeshott, *The Artists of the Winchester Bible* (London: Faber & Faber, 1945), pl. XIII. In a similar historical example, the murderer of Charles the Good, Count of Flanders in 1127, asked that his hand be cut off before his execution. Payen, *Le Motif du repentir*, p. 42, n. 112.

28. Jenkins, note to vv. 725 ff.

29. Lejeune and Stiennon, 1:33–35.

30. On the different phases of the battle here, see Horrent, p. 226, n. 3.

31. Hatzfeld, *Literature Through Art*, p. 9. Ménard, *Le Rire*, p. 49, notes that the contrasting whiteness of the Saracens' teeth is also mentioned in the *Bataille Loquifer*. See also *Blancandin et l'Orgueilleuse d'amour: Roman d'aventure du XIIIe siècle*, ed. Franklin P. Sweetser, Textes littéraires français 112 (Geneva: Droz, 1964), vv. 3060, 3750 (and note to v. 3060). In *Psychomachia*, v. 654, Egyptians are referred to as "the dark-skinned people of the Nile."

32. A line added after v. 1936 in the rhymed versions makes this clear. See Segre.

33. Jenkins, note to v. 1931: "If Charles, the priest-king, does not blame them but gives them his blessing, all will be well." In my view, it never enters Roland's mind that the Emperor will blame them, nor does the hero doubt for a minute that his uncle will grasp the significance of what has happened.

34. According to Jenkins, note to vv. 680–691, the copyist, taking Ganelon's false report about the Caliph's death (Laisse 54) in earnest, "thought it wrong to make any further mention of the Algalife as alive: hereafter he regularly replaced his name with *Marganice*, or *le Marganice*, but he is not supported by the other versions." See Segre, citing Knudson. Granting that the Caliph and Marganice are one and the same person, could not the copyist simply be giving him a new name? Cf. Bramimonde/Bramidonie.

35. Owen: 'for your bane'.

36. Moignet, p. 151: "C'est d'un coup déloyal, dans le dos, que Marganice frappe Olivier à mort, et son cri haineux (v. 1951): *Kar de vos sul ai ben venget les noz* constitue en réalité le plus beau des éloges."

37. Cf. the Count of Soisson's remark at the Battle of Mansurah. COMMENTARY, 12, note 23.

38. Murray A. Potter, *Sohrab and Rustem, the Epic Theme of a Combat Between Father and Son: A Study of its Genesis and Use in Literature and Popular Tradition* (London: Nutt, 1902), pp. 207–9. The Roland-Oliver encounter is cited p. 209. See also Loomis, *Arthurian Tradition*, p. 326, n. 1.

39. Ménard, *Le Rire*, p. 337. Loomis, pp. 328–31, believes that the latter two

examples may derive from the *Cattle Raid of Cooley* in the Irish *Cuchulainn Saga*. Ménard, p. 339.

40. *Erec*, vv. 4960 ff.; *Yvain*, vv. 5985–6454; *Prose Lancelot*, ed. Sommer, 3:398; 5:287.

41. Ménard, p. 337.

42. Thus Ménard, p. 338, is technically correct in asserting that the motif is not found in the Old French epic. On the fight between Roland and Oliver in *Girart de Vienne*, consult Lejeune and Stiennon, 1:214–15.

43. Payen, *Le Motif du repentir*, pp. 494–95. For a portrait of Sudden Death, see *Herrade de Landsberg, Hortus deliciarum*, eds. A. Straub and G. Keller, Société pour la conservation des monuments historiques d'Alsace (Strasbourg: Imprimerie Strasbourgeoise, 1879–1899), fol. 112.

44. Payen, pp. 41, 52, 116. See also index, p. 602, s.v. Mort subite, and idem, *Le Moyen Age*, pp. 65–66.

45. Saint Christopher (Réau, III, 1:305–6); Saints Barbara and Veronica (Réau, III, 3:1315; Payen, *Le Moyen Age*, p. 66).

46. Jeremiah 5:21; Ezekiel 12:2; Mark 8:18; Blaise, p. 59, s.v. illumino; Payen, *Le Motif du repentir*, p. 103 and n. 16.

47. Faral, *La Chanson de Roland*, p. 118; Jones, p. 42; Vance, *Reading the Song of Roland*, pp. 57–58; Donohoe, "Ambivalence and Anger." Varying interpretations of this passage are provided by these scholars, but all accept the premise that Roland is brave, Oliver is wise.

48. Mario Roques, "L'attitude du héros mourant dans la *Chanson de Roland*," *Romania* 66 (1940): 355–66.

49. Payen, *Le Motif du repentir*, p. 112, believes it may be accidental: the hero has probably knelt, then fallen forward. However, there is no mention of kneeling in the text; on the contrary, the poet tells us explicitly that Oliver lies down (v. 2013: al tere se culchet). Turning from a supine to a prone position would definitely require willpower and physical exertion. On the expression *adenz*, see Gerard J. Brault, "Old French *adenz*, *endenz*, Latin *ad dentes*, *in dentes*," *Romania* 85 (1964): 323–35. In the Brindisi mosaic, dated 1178, Oliver lies supine. Lejeune and Stiennon, 1:98–99. In the *Pseudo-Turpin* he is tortured and dies in a kind of crucifixion with his arms staked to the ground. Meredith-Jones, p. 207.

50. Payen, *Le Motif du repentir*, p. 53: "à cette époque . . . le repentir le plus fréquent est celui de l'agonie"; p. 112: "la *coulpe* est un aveu de condition pécheresse . . . aveu très général."

51. Segre, note to v. 2014, argues in favor of emending *Durement en halt* to *D'ures en altres*.

52. In *Peristephanon*, 3: v. 166 (*Prudentius*, 2:152), the head droops as the soul departs. Jenkins, *Glossary*, p. 336, defines *joster* in v. 2020 as 'to come together, crumple up (?)'; Foulet, *Glossaire:* 'ne fait plus qu'un avec la terre'.

53. Cf. the bonds of affection and feudal loyalty between Roland and Alda; INTRODUCTION, 19, 1. Friends identical in appearance is folk motif F 577.1. On the use of this notion in *Ami et Amile*, see Calin, *Epic Quest*, p. 60. Roland's lament over Oliver's body is depicted in the Brindisi mosaic. See *Fig. 18*; Lejeune and Stiennon, 1:98–99.

54. On the theme of identity in worthiness, see COMMENTARY, 14 (vv. 1093 ff.), and below, vv. 2066–2069.

55. Cf. Alda's death wish, vv. 3718–3719.

56. On this episode in Chrétien de Troyes, see Frappier, *Chrétien de Troyes et le mythe du graal*, pp. 130–41; to his bibliography, add Ménard, *Le Rire*, pp. 243–44.

57. Horrent, pp. 140–43, 173–77; Paul Aebischer, "Un problème d'exégèse

rolandienne: *Maelgut*, la conquête de Gautier de l'Hum (*Chanson de Roland*, ms. Digby, v. 2047)," *Cultura Neolatina* 23 (1963): 146–52; Rita Lejeune, "La composition du personnage de Gautier del Hum dans la *Chanson de Roland*," in *La Technique littéraire des chansons de geste*, pp. 237–69; D. J. A. Ross, "Gautier del Hum: an Historical Element in the *Chanson de Roland*?" *Modern Language Review* 61 (1966): 409–15.

58. Text in Segre, pp. 389–90, discussion, pp. 391–92.

59. For bibliography and discussion, see Segre, p. 391.

60. Bédier, *Commentaires*, pp. 189–92; Lejeune, "La composition," pp. 252–53; Segre, p. 391. Payen, *Le Motif du repentir*, p. 129, n. 68, does not see any allusion to Suetonius here. See INTRODUCTION, 7.

61. Holland, "Gautier et Margarit," pp. 339–44; Segre, p. 391.

62. Lejeune, "La composition," p. 255. Bédier, *Commentaires*, p. 190, believes that Gautier: "a quelque chose à lui dire ou à se faire dire par lui" and feels, consequently, that something is missing in this passage. However, Holland and Segre argue that Gautier is merely seeking help to fight the Saracens who are pursuing him and whom they jointly attack in the next laisse.

63. To the references in this connection provided in Brault, *Early Blazon*, pp. 34–35 (White Knights), add Saint James the Moor-Slayer (Santiago Matamoros) at the Battle of Clavijo in 844, henceforth patron saint of the Reconquista. Réau, III, 2:693, 696–97.

64. See note 54 above.

65. Jenkins, note to v. 2073; Jones, pp. 16–17. Turoldus is writing before one of the great tactical lessons of the Crusades was assimilated, namely that the role of the Saracen archers was to provoke the enemy into breaking formation. The Franks had to learn to resist the temptation to charge too soon. Smail, *Crusading Warfare*, pp. 82–83, 146. The poet seems to ignore the main purpose of archery here and is intent upon contrasting the brave Franks and the cowardly Saracens who dare not approach (v. 2073).

66. Horrent, pp. 266–68, notes the progression from the simple description of Oliver's death to the more detailed exposition of Turpin's passing and to Roland's theatrical yet noble and triumphant departure from this world.

67. Blaise, par. 348, 452 (aedificatio).

68. Meredith-Jones, pp. 103, 105. On this concrete meaning, see Blaise, par. 452, n. 1.

69. Meredith-Jones, pp. 229, 231 (see also pp. 335–36, note). Cf. COMMENTARY, 25 (Roland's laud of Durendal). For another vision by Turpin, see below.

70. On *adtestatio rei visae*, see Curtius, pp. 205, 545.

71. Cf. the opening verses in Venice IV:

> Chi voil oïr vere significance?
> A San Donis ert une geste, in France.

72. *La Vie de Saint Gilles par Guillaume de Berneville, poème du XIIe siècle*, eds. Gaston Paris and Alphonse Bos, Société des anciens textes français (Paris: Didot, 1881), pp. lxxii–lxxxix.

73. Lejeune and Stiennon, 1:145. De Gaiffier, "La légende de Charlemagne," believes that the legend is based upon the Emperor's flagrant disregard for the Church's teaching concerning chastity. Charlemagne had several mistresses who presented him with numerous illegitimate children.

74. According to Lejeune and Stiennon, 1:145–50. However, the earliest specific allusion is in the *Karlamagnús Saga* (1230–50). Paris, *Histoire poétique de Charlemagne*, pp. 378–82.

75. Lejeune, "Le péché de Charlemagne et la *Chanson de Roland*," argues that Turoldus was familiar with the tradition; see also Lejeune and Stiennon, 1:146.

76. Lejeune and Stiennon, 1:145–50.

77. Ibid., 1:172, 196–97.

78. Jenkins, note to vv. 2095–2098; Bédier, *Commentaires*, pp. 26–27; Meredith-Jones, pp. 315–16; Aebischer, *Textes norrois*, p. 41; Menéndez Pidal, p. 332; Riquer, *Chansons de geste*, pp. 29–31; Sholod, *Charlemagne in Spain*, pp. 22, n. 36, 24, n. 49; Dufournet, *Cours sur Roland*, p. 73. Jean Györy, "Réflexions sur le jongleur guerrier," *Annales universitatis Budapestinensis, Sectio philologica* 3 (1961): 47–60, compares Saint Giles to the jongleurs who claim to have witnessed the battle they relate in their poems. George F. Jones, "St. Giles at Roncevaux," *French Review* 54 (1971): 881–88, believes Turoldus may have mistaken the name Eginhardus (Einhard) for Aegidius (Giles). On *Loüm* in v. 2097, see Sholod, p. 38; Lejeune and Stiennon, 1:149, 152, n. 14 (= Lyon).

79. For another vision by Turpin, see note 69 above. For yet another vision (by Charles), see Meredith-Jones, p. 219. See INTRODUCTION, note 233.

80. Meredith-Jones, p. 195.

81. Ibid., p. 203.

82. Lejeune and Stiennon, 1: pl. II; see also 2: fig. 368. Cf. 2: figs. 293, 294, 317, 318, 344.

83. Stricker says Saint Giles, not Turpin, had the vision concerning Roncevaux, further confusing the authenticating mechanism. Lejeune and Stiennon, 1:234.

84. On this motif in medieval art and thought, see Mâle, *L'Art religieux*, pp. 339–40; Joan Evans, *Cluniac Art of the Romanesque Period* (Cambridge: University Press, 1950), p. 78 and n. 7; Helen Adolf, "The Ass and the Harp," *Speculum* 25 (1950): 49–57.

COMMENTARY 22

1. *Erec*, vv. 5689–5695. A similar wall of air occurs in the *Vulgate Merlin Sequel*, ed. Sommer, 2:461. See Loomis, *Arthurian Literature*, p. 168, n. 6.

2. Blaise, par. 203.

3. Segre emends *asez* to *sez*, altering the meaning of this verse in the process.

4. Jones, p. 36.

5. On the tactics of Saracen archers who usually fought on foot, see Smail, *Crusading Warfare*, pp. 81, 85.

6. Muslim archers deliberately sought to slay the Crusaders' horses with their arrows. Ibid., p, 81.

7. Similar occurrences are reported by contemporary chroniclers, the harmless arrows dangling from the knights' armor being said to resemble a porcupine's quills. Ibid.

8. The bubble is a stylized cloud of divine protection. Otto Brendel, "Origin and Meaning of the Word Mandorla," *Gazette des Beaux-Arts* 25 (1944): 5–24; Réau, I:423–25. Cf. the concept of Virginitas (INTRODUCTION, 19, F).

9. Réau, II, 2:39.

10. On the tactical value of horses, see Smail, p. 81.

11. Cf. the Franks' reaction to Thierry's victorious blow in v. 3931: "*Deus i ad fait vertut!*"

12. Also 2 Kings 4:34. For illustrations, see Réau, II, 1:352–53. Medieval exegetes viewed this episode as a prefiguration of Christ's resurrection of Lazarus. Réau, II, 1:349.

13. Cf. Death's embrace (COMMENTARY, 41). On the various notions concerning immortality among primitive peoples, see James, *Comparative Religion*, pp. 275–81.

14. Cf. Labande-Mailfert, "La douleur et la mort," fig. 32.

15. The theme of inseparability in companionage is discussed in COMMENTARY, 18.

16. Jenkins, note to v. 2177.

17. Riquer, *Chansons de geste*, p. 100: "Dans cette phrase est condensé tout l'esprit militaire de ce singulier archevêque."

18. In the *Karlamagnús Saga* and the rhymed versions of the *Roland*, only a miracle allows Charles to distinguish the Christian from the Saracen bodies. Horrent, p. 188 and n. 3; INTRODUCTION, 15, E.

19. The scene is illustrated in the Brindisi mosaic (*see Fig.* 54). Lejeune and Stiennon, 1:98; 2: fig. 70.

20. See COMMENTARY, 5. One thinks, too, of the sixty champions around the litter of Solomon, "the flower of the warriors of Israel" (Song of Songs 3:7–8), which, for medieval exegetes, represented the mystical union of Christ and his Church. For the illustration in Herrad of Landsberg, see Cames, *Allégories*, pp. 74–77. Crosland, *Old French Epic*, p. 88, compares the alignment of the bodies by Roland to "the reverent act of Walther of Aquitaine in the Waltharius, where the hero places the appropriate heads to the trunks of the twelve knights whom he has killed in a single combat."

21. Autun, Bibliothèque municipale, MS. 19, folio 173. Katzenellenbogen, *Allegories*, p. 33; Beckwith, *Early Medieval Art*, p. 61, fig. 51. The Sacramentary is dated 844–845. Raganaldus holds a crozier in his left hand. See note 27 below. Cf. the chaotic arrangement of the Saracen cadavers. COMMENTARY, 15.

22. INTRODUCTION, 10, B, 4.

23. Réau, II, 2:690; COMMENTARY, 3, note 8.

24. Ibid. The Apostles are mentioned later in this passage (v. 2255).

25. Ibid., II, 2:692. See also the discussion relative to the Apocalypse of Saint-Sever in Mâle, *L'Art religieux*, pp. 4 ff. Cf. Conrad, vv. 7005–7006 (the Angel of the Lord comforts Charles after he finds the bodies of Roland, Oliver, and Turpin):

Din baitent alle rechte
Da zedem oberisten trone.

(All the Just await you
Next to the sublime throne).

26. Cf. portraits depicting homage to the Emperor; Cames, *Byzance*, pp. 68–69.

27. Réau, II, 2:45. The pastoral symbolism is enhanced if Turpin is visualized with crozier in hand. See note 21 above. In this scene Turpin is a Charlemagne surrogate.

28. Réau, II, 2:44.

29. Cf. the flowers in the Brindisi mosaic (*see Fig.* 54). One is reminded, too, of representations of Abraham's bosom (*see Fig.* 13). Will, "Les représentations du Paradis," p. 71; Réau, II, 1:138; Cames, *Allégories*, pp. 124–26. Additional bibliography in COMMENTARY, 26, note 55. Cf. Lejeune and Stiennon, 1:pl. II. For depictions of the Saved arranged in a semicircle in Heaven, see Will, pp. 77–79 ("Le cortège des Elus").

30. Roland's comrade is not dead yet in Conrad's narration of this scene. Lejeune and Stiennon, 1:131.

31. Ibid., 1:98; 2: fig. 70. The Good Shepherd association is not made by the Belgian scholars.

32. The formula dates back to the art of the Catacombs. Réau, II, 2:33–34. In an interesting transposition, Abel is depicted in this characteristic pose in the Roda Bible. Réau, II, 1:93; *Introduction au monde des symboles*, pl. 24 (for a parody, see p. 333 and pl. 128).

33. Réau, II, 2:32. The ritual alignment may indeed represent a symbolic fold.

34. In the same way, the four spears that pierce Turpin's body (vv. 2080–2084) may have suggested the image of sin entering the soul like a poisoned arrow (*Hamartigenia*, vv. 533–544, [*Prudentius*, 1:242]) without necessarily implying that the Archbishop is guilty of any transgression.

COMMENTARY 23

1. The Archbishop crosses his own hands, for no change of subject is indicated.
2. See INTRODUCTION, 16, C. Cf. the bitter stream in the death scene of the *Chanson de Guillaume*. Frappier, *Chansons de geste*, 1:121, 124, 132, 211–12, and, especially, 194; Brault, "Le Thème de la Mort," pp. 230–31.
3. Jenkins, note to v. 2225.
4. See COMMENTARY, 21 (v. 1874). See also Blaise, p. 54, s.v. fons. Water is a metaphor for sorrow and trouble in Psalms 124:4–5.
5. Jenkins, note to v. 2226; Brault, "Le Thème de la Mort," p. 230. In the rhymed versions Roland actually dies of thirst. Horrent, p. 360.
6. Cf. COMMENTARY, 22 and note 34.
7. Blaise, par. 281 ff. Turpin takes Roland's oliphant in a vain effort to secure life-giving water for the expiring hero (vv. 2224–2232). The split in the horn (v. 2295) suggests, then, that Roland's life is ebbing away. Baptismal imagery also involves water. Mark 1:4–5; Blaise, par. 331. Medieval exegetes viewed the crossing of the Red Sea as a prefiguration of Baptism, a notion already present in 1 Corinthians 10:2.
8. Tripping is involved in the etymology of the term scandal and, consequently, is associated with the notion of sin. Blaise, par. 454. Cf. the concept of falling into sin and, with special reference to *cancelant* in v. 2227, *lubricum* 'that which causes to waver, to stagger'. Blaise, par. 421. Stumbling is also an image of sorrow in Psalms 66:9.
9. Cf. the image of man driven from home by war, looking up and down and finding only distress and darkness, in Isaiah 8:21–23. On the notion of the inaccessible sky, stressing the futility of the character's acts and his remoteness, see Frye, *Anatomy of Criticism*, p. 147. But, in the present context, looking heavenward is essentially a gesture of hope. In medieval thought only man is capable of raising his face toward the source of his salvation. Janson, *Apes and Ape Lore*, p. 81 (cf. Lactantius's etymology of Gr. *anthropos* 'he who looks upward [to God]', Janson, p. 103, n. 31).
10. On the notion of raising "pure" hands to heaven, see Blaise, par. 84.
11. Bloch and Wartburg, *Dictionnaire*, s.v. champion. For the ideal of serving God willingly, see Burgess, *Vocabulaire pré-courtois*, p. 109, n. 24.
12. See COMMENTARY, 14 and 18.
13. Blaise, par. 271.
14. Cf. the titles of many medieval sermons containing the word *contra*, e.g., Saint Augustine's *Contra Faustum*, *De Baptisma contra Donatistas*, *De Genesi contra Manichaeos*, Finda's *Contra paganos*. In Conrad, vv. 1333–1353, Turpin volunteers to go to Saragossa to try to convert Marsile.
15. Foulet, *Glossaire:* "'prophète', ou plutôt 'homme de Dieu'"; Faral, *La Chanson de Roland*, p. 190.
16. Blaise, p. 416, n. 1; INTRODUCTION, 19, I.
17. On the literary uses of gore, see COMMENTARY, 15 and 24 (vv. 2275–2276). The detailing of Turpin's wounds in vv. 2247–2248 inspires horror but also pity. Matthias Grünewald's *Crucifixion* at Colmar is the supreme example of the use of bleeding wounds for this purpose.
18. Cf. *Fig. 18*.
19. Jenkins, *Glossary*, p. 369: 'lack, want, privation'.

20. The words *doel ne*, found in Venice IV before *sufraite*, are inserted by many editors. On this emendation, see Segre's note to v. 2257.

21. Bédier, *Commentaires*, p. 305, note to v. 1856.

22. On ecclesiastical terminology relative to Purgatory, see Blaise, par. 93; Payen, *Le Motif du repentir*, index, p. 603, s.v. Purgatoire.

COMMENTARY 24

1. At Roland's death, vv. 2393–2395.

2. Gabriel is the unnamed angel in v. 836 and doubtless also the one in vv. 2319 and 2452. On this archangel's role in the *Song of Roland*, see Faral, *La Chanson de Roland*, pp. 190–94.

3. In the Annunciation, for example. Réau, II, 1:52.

4. Réau, II, 1:44 (Michael); COMMENTARY, 42, note 6 (Gabriel).

5. Will, *Alsace romane*, pp. 74–77; Réau, II, 1:49–50. See also note 64 below. Thus, in the *Pseudo-Turpin*, he alone takes Roland's soul to heaven (Meredith-Jones, p. 203).

6. I am indebted to my daughter Suzanne, who was twelve years old at the time, for this suggestion.

7. See COMMENTARY, 34 (vv. 2847–2848) and 42 (v. 3612). This notion is distinct from the guardian-angel concept, attested about this time in Honorius Augustodunensis. Le Goff, *Civilisation*, p. 209. The popular devotion, associated with Raphael, dates from the sixteenth century only. Réau, II, 1:53.

8. Réau, II, 1:52; Focillon, *Art d'Occident*, fig. 91; *The Year 1200*, 1:81. Cf. the cherubim with flaming swords posted at the entrance to the Garden of Eden to fend off evildoers. Genesis 3:24; Réau, II, 1:89–90. On this scene in Genesis, see note 61 below.

9. Lejeune and Stiennon, 1:61–69.

10. Ibid., 1:61, 69.

11. See vv. 2361–2363, 2863–2867. Cf. also vv. 2265–2267, 2868–2869.

12. Cf. Vivien's "step" in the *Chanson de Guillaume*. COMMENTARY, 34, note 7.

13. See COMMENTARY, 34.

14. See MANUSCRIPT, v. 2267.

15. Bédier, *Commentaires*, p. 308, asserts that the stone is one of the four marble objects. See also Jenkins, note to vv. 2874–2875. However, Turoldus specifies that the stone in question is a *perre byse* (v. 2300), a *perrun de sardonie* (v. 2312), and a *perre bise* (v. 2338). The fact that one and the same stone is involved in all three laisses similaires is clear from Turoldus's use of *une* in vv. 2300 and 2338, and the enclitic *el* in v. 2312. See also OXFORD TEXT, ENGLISH TRANSLATION, vv. 2300, 2312; cf. also v. 2875 (COMMENTARY, 34, note 11). This rock is in its natural state, whereas the marble has been shaped (v. 2268: faiz).

16. On the significance of the split in Roland's oliphant, see COMMENTARY, 23, n. 7. Eyes also pop out from a sharp blow to the head in *Liber Cathemerinon*, 12: v. 120 (*Prudentius*, 1:108 [Massacre of the Innocents]): *Oculosque per vulnus vomit.*

17. See OXFORD TEXT, ENGLISH TRANSLATION, v. 2857, and COMMENTARY, 34.

18. Some of the comments that follow first appeared in my paper "Le Thème de la Mort," pp. 229–30.

19. See INTRODUCTION, 13, C.

20. At Aix (vv. 2863–2867). See COMMENTARY, 34.

21. COMMENTARY, 16 (vv. 1423–1437).

22. Frappier, *Chansons de geste*, 1:193–94. See also p. 193, n. 2 (association with the *lama sabachthani*).

23. Ibid., 1:193. The differences between Roland's agony and that of Vivien are underlined by Frappier, pp. 195–96.

24. Rychner, p. 126, apropos of *Raoul de Cambrai*: "La mort du héros sera traitée à l'aide de motifs comme 'derniers coups reçus', chute du héros, prière, 'battre sa coulpe', 'l'âme s'en va', découverte du corps, regrets prononcés sur le cadavre." The conventional aspects of the epic death scene were already recognized in the nineteenth century: Johannes Altona, *Gebete und Anrufungen in den altfranzösischen Chansons de geste*, Ausgaben und Abhandlungen aus dem Gebiete der romanischen Philologie 9 (Marburg: Elwert, 1883); Gustav Albrecht, *Vorbereitung auf den Tod, Totengebräuche und Totenbestattung in der altfranzösischen Dichtung* (Halle: Kaemmerer, 1892). Further bibliography in Brault, "Le Thème de la Mort," p. 231, n. 27.

25. Delehaye, *Les Passions des martyrs*, p. 19; Aigrain, *L'Hagiographie*, p. 209.

26. Delehaye, p. 21 (bibliography in n. 5). Further discussion in Brault, "Le Thème de la Mort," p. 233, n. 32.

27. Burger, "La légende de Roncevaux avant la *Chanson de Roland*," pp. 438, 447. It is unnecessary to postulate, as does Burger, the existence of a *Passio Beati Rotolandi martyris*.

28. Bédier, *Commentaires*, p. 308.

29. Were the Pyrenees considered to be the border? At the time Turoldus was composing his epic, Christian dominion extended over the Spanish March.

30. Bédier, *Commentaires*, p. 309.

31. See, for example, Whitehead, *Glossary*, p. 156; Jones, p. 187: "he seeks out a hill on which stand four large blocks of marble, as if these were a fitting monument to commemorate his heroic death"; Lejeune and Stiennon, 1:396 (apropos of 2: fig. 508: "un perron monumental, analogue à ceux qui marquaient l'emplacement des frontières"; on this illustration, see note 44 below); Moignet, p. 170, note to v. 2268.

32. In the *Pseudo-Turpin* no mention is made of four marble objects, but Roland strikes a marble stone (Meredith-Jones, p. 192: lapidem marmoreum; variant, p. 193: petronum marmoreum) with his sword. For the view that the description in v. 2271 is "fort mal amenée," see Menéndez Pidal, p. 325. Cf. Hatzfeld, *Literature Through Art*, p. 11; Rychner, pp. 72 ff.; Zumthor, *Langue et techniques poétiques*, p. 185.

33. The *pui agut* referred to in vv. 2367 and 2869 is identical with the *tertre* in v. 2267.

34. For bibliography and discussion, see Segre's note to v. 2875.

35. Aebischer, *Rolandiana Borealia*, p. 230; Conrad, vv. 7487–7489; Segre, notes to vv. 2874, 2875. Jean Györy, "Les prières de Guillaume d'Orange dans le *Couronnement de Louis*," in *Mélanges Rita Lejeune*, 2:772, n. 1: "A propos des trois perrons de marbre où monte Roland à Roncevaux, il est difficile de ne pas penser à un modèle figuratif."

36. Bédier, *Commentaires*, p. 309.

37. Ibid., p. 308. For another square, formed by benches set up as a boundary, see Jenkins, note to v. 3853.

38. *FEW*, 8:315–16.

39. For the meaning of *perrun* in v. 2556, see below.

40. Godefroy, 6:110; *FEW*, 8:316.

41. Godefroy, 6:110; *FEW*, 8:316, and 322, n. 10.

42. Bédier, *Commentaires*, p. 309; Tobler and Lommatzsch, 1:1056.

43. Tobler and Lommatzsch, 3:1330 (including a reference to the *Chronique rimée de Philippe Mouskés*, where *coulonbe* and *estace* are synonyms).

44. Lejeune and Stiennon, 1:132: "Au milieu des pierres de marbre (v. 6793) auxquelles l'artiste a donné l'apparence de frustres colonnes rectangulaires fichées en terre, Roland se redresse, tenant dans sa main gauche un énorme olifant avec lequel il assène un coup formidable sur le heaume du païen qui s'élançait pour lui ravir son

épée"; 2: fig. 117. In the passages corresponding to *Roland*, vv. 2268 and 2272, Conrad, vv. 6782 and 6793, uses the words *stainen* and *marmil stainen*, respectively. In the *Pseudo-Turpin* a solitary marble object has been erected in a meadow near a tree (Meredith-Jones, p. 188: sub arbore quadam iuxta lapidem [variant, p. 189: petronum] marmoreum qui ibi erectus erat [variant, p. 189: erigebatur] in prato optimo; cf. the French translations [ed. Mortier, p. 67: drechiez; Mandach, *Naissance*, 2:77: dressé]) and Roland dies *iuxta lapidem* (Meredith-Jones, p. 202; variant, p. 203: *petronum*). On this passage in the *Song of Roland*, see Menéndez Pidal, pp. 325–26, 330. Turoldus distinguishes between the four marble objects and the rock that Roland strikes in this passage, but illustrators of the *Pseudo-Turpin* at times conceived of the latter stone as a monument. Lejeune and Stiennon, 2: figs. 267, 508 (see note 31 above). Cf. also 1: pl. L. Natural stones are depicted in 1: pls. XIV, XXV; 2: fig. 54 (if, as the Belgian scholars suggest in 1:87, the figure in this sculpture is in fact striking a stone). Medieval artists frequently portray a fountain in similar fashion, even when a natural spring is intended.

45. Kantorowicz, *King's Two Bodies*, p. 67. For illustrations of the Temple columns and veil, see *Introduction au monde des symboles*, pls. 25, 137; Cames, *Byzance*, pl. 30; idem, *Allégories*, pl. 8. Stylized depictions of the Temple of Jerusalem are not to be confused with early medieval illustrations of the Fountain of Life, an enigmatic pillared structure surmounted by a conical roof. According to P. Underwood, "The Fountain of Life in Manuscripts of the Gospels," *Dunbarton Oaks Papers* 5 (1950): 43–138, the latter is ultimately a reference to the Holy Sepulchre.

46. Kantorowicz, p. 67.

47. See COMMENTARY, 26 (v. 2396).

48. Kantorowicz, p. 68.

49. Ibid., pp. 68–69; *Introduction au monde des symboles*, fig. 183.

50. André Grabar and Carl Nordenfalk, *Romanesque Painting From the Eleventh to the Thirteenth Century*, trans. Stuart Gilbert, The Great Centuries of Painting (Lausanne: Skira, 1958), p. 60; *Introduction au monde des symboles*, p. 151 and fig. 65; cf. fig. 138.

51. The square symbol, a "centre cosmique," representing a Passageway to the Next World, or a Door to Heaven, is discussed by Davy, *Symbolique romane*, pp. 185–90; see also *Introduction au monde des symboles*, p. 205; Hughes, *Heaven and Hell in Western Art*, pp. 88–91; Campbell, *Hero*, pt. 1, Prologue, "The World Navel," pp. 40–46. Cf. Réau, III, 3:1094 (legend of Saint Peter's struggle with Simon the Magician). Woods, "The Symbolic Structure of *La Chanson de Roland*," p. 1260, suggests that the four stones represent "the material plane" (the three blows, "the spiritual plane"); cf. *La Chanson de Roland*, ed. Calin, p. 13: "sur le point d'expirer, Roland se trouve sous un pin, entre quatre blocs de pierre, étendu sur l'herbe: un *locus amoenus* (Curtius), image du paradis terrestre et qui annonce le paradis céleste"; Rütten, *Symbol und Mythus*, pp. 46ff. For representations of the Bridge to the Other World, see Réau, II, 2:729–30. Cf. the *verger aventureux* in the *Châtelaine de Vergy* (Burgess, *Vocabulaire pré-courtois*, p. 48, citing Frappier).

52. Cf. the notion of Agnus Dei (Will, "Recherches iconographiques," pp. 34–35; Réau, II, 2:30–31, 476) and the embalming of the body of Jesus on a slab (Réau, II, 2:522).

53. Will, "Recherches iconographiques," pp. 36–39; Katzenellenbogen, *Allegories*, pp. 63–68; Robertson, "The Doctrine of Charity in Mediaeval Literary Gardens," pp. 25–28; Davy, *Symbolique romane*, pp. 221, 263; *Introduction au monde des symboles*, pp. 297–326.

54. Genesis 2:9.

55. Réau, II, 2:483.

56. Will, "Recherches iconographiques," p. 40; *Introduction au monde des symboles*,

pp. 308–10, pl. 117, figs. 135, 136; Robb, *Illuminated Manuscript*, pp. 154, 156, fig. 96.

57. In the *Hortus Deliciarum* the image of *Paradisus Voluptatis* is paired with that of the Expulsion from the Garden of Eden.

58. The heads which appear on the Tree of Life are discussed by Will, "Recherches iconographiques," pp. 44–48.

59. Ibid., fig. 11. On the sources of this miniature, see pp. 44–49 (cf., especially, figs. 12 and 13).

60. *Introduction au monde des symboles*, p. 308. Cf. the image of Christ in Majesty seated between two trees within a walled enclosure representing Paradise (San Pietro al Monte, Civate, Italy; *Introduction au monde des symboles*, p. 214, fig. 94).

61. Gaston Paris believed the episode was invented to explain how the oliphant was split (see Jenkins, note to vv. 2271–2296). Horrent, p. 269, characterizes this passage as "le seul épisode imprévu," and adds, p. 278:

> [Le poète] veut créer un climat d'inquiétude autour du moribond, climat qui justifie à la fois les conseils passés de Turpin et les gestes prochains de Charles enterrant ses morts. Il veut aussi justifier à l'avance le sacrifice audacieux de Durendal, la bonne épée, auquel se résout Roland. Les fameuses scènes de Durendal frisent en effet le sacrilège: alors qu'il sait Charles sur le chemin du retour, Roland a-t-il le droit de briser sa bonne épée, qui est elle-même comme un personnage héroïque? Il faut légitimer ce geste, 'autoriser' les grandes scènes de l'épée. La péripétie du Sarrasin n'a pas d'autre rôle. Elle ne crée pas de l'imprévu: elle prépare la suite du récit.

James C. Atkinson, "Laisses 169–170 of the *Chanson de Roland*," *MLN* 82 (1967): 271–84, views Roland's destruction of the oliphant as a repudiation of his prideful decision not to call for help. Cf. Donohoe, "Ambivalence and Anger," p. 261, note 6. See, however, the final paragraph in this section for a different interpretation of the split in the oliphant. For Vos, "Aspects of Biblical Typology," pp. 152–54, the Rash Saracen is a *Guenes alter*. According to Lejeune and Stiennon, 1:99, the scene is depicted in the Brindisi mosaic. A parallel episode in the *Chanson de Guillaume* is discussed by Wilmotte, "La *Chanson de Roland* et la *Chanson de Willame*," pp. 68–69.

62. For other literary uses of gore, see COMMENTARY, 15 and 23 (note 17). Looting is discussed in INTRODUCTION, 10, A, 7, and COMMENTARY, 14 (v. 1167).

63. The epithet *immundus* is frequently applied to the devil. Blaise, par. 323, 325, 327; Cames, *Allégories*, p. 16 (cf. Réau, III, 1:341 [legend of Constantine's leprosy]). According to medieval thought, man has three mortal enemies: Spiritus immundus (Satan), Caro (the Flesh), and Mundus (the World); Zumthor, *Histoire littéraire*, p. 246; Langlois, *La Vie en France*, 2:114. See also COMMENTARY, 33, note 5 (Bramimonde). The Rash Saracen may be aping Roland, who is also covered with blood (v. 1343).

64. Blaise, par. 325; Le Goff, *Civilisation*, p. 207. In medieval iconography, the last-minute struggle is often depicted as a contest between Satan and Saint Michael, a tradition originally associated with the death of Moses. Réau, II, 1:50, 212; Cames, *Allégories*, pp. 44–45. Saint Michael appears in v. 2394. See also text above at note 5. The Saracen (Satan) tries to steal Roland's most precious possession, his sword (soul). For Durendal as a reflection of Roland, see INTRODUCTION, 19, D. Is the dying hero merely under a hallucination? The line between such aberrations and diabolic visitations was blurred in the Middle Ages. Cf. Roland's apostrophe to his sword in the *Pseudo-Turpin*: "*Qui te possidebit non erit victus, . . . non ullis fantasiis formidatus*" (Meredith-Jones, p. 191), and the exorcising power of the crucifix: "*fugiant phantasmata cuncta*" (Blaise, par. 347; Le Goff, *Civilisation*, p. 207).

65. Skidmore, *Moral Traits of Christians and Saracens*, pp. 45 and 68, n. 5.

66. *Tristan de Thomas*, 1:117 ff. The Seneschal cuts off the dragon's head, but Tristan produces its tongue and is vindicated. Folk motif K 1932 (Imposter claims reward

earned by hero). Calin, *Epic Quest*, pp. 61, 63 (apropos of *Ami et Amile*); Payen, *Le Motif du repentir*, p. 429, n. 69. Cf. Conrad, vv. 6784–6790, where the Saracen plans to boast he has slain Roland. The Rash Saracen's false claim also echoes Psalms 13:4–5; "Give my eyes light, or I shall sleep in death, and my enemy will say, 'I have beaten him'." Cf. also the Amelekite who slays Saul at his request, then takes the crown from his head and the bracelet from his arm back to King David after the Battle of Gilboa (2 Samuel 1:10). For an illustration of the latter scene, see Oakeshott, *Artists of Winchester Bible*, pl. 24. Another version of Saul's end is recounted in 1 Samuel 31:4. Boasting in ladies' chambers is mentioned in COMMENTARY, 12, note 23.

67. The notion of the lying exterior is discussed in INTRODUCTION, 10, B, 2. For *mortel rage*, see OXFORD TEXT, ENGLISH TRANSLATION, v. 2279. The Saracen falls at Roland's feet (v. 2291). On the image of crushing an enemy in the dust, see COMMENTARY, 30, note 9.

68. *Psychomachia*, vv. 470–479. Smiting the skull is mentioned in v. 472 (cf. *Roland*, v. 2289).

69. On the later history of the oliphant, see COMMENTARY, 25, note 3; COMMENTARY, 35 and note 11.

COMMENTARY 25

1. Jenkins, note to vv. 3685–3687; Horrent, pp. 144–45.

2. Horrent, p. 145, n. 4; Halvorsen, *Norse Version of Roland*, p. 233; Mendéndez Pidal, pp. 174–78; Aebischer, *Rolandiana Borealia*, p. 232. Cf. Joël H. Grisward, "Le motif de l'épée jetée au lac: la mort d'Arthur et la mort de Batradz," *Romania* 90 (1969): 289–340, 473–514. On the disposition of Durendal in other versions of the poem, see Horrent, pp. 143–49 (summary in Dufournet, *Cours sur Roland*, pp. 50–52). Jones, p. 96: "he tries to avoid reproach to himself by destroying his sword so it will not fall into the enemy's hands." For an illustration of Ignavia throwing away her sword, see Katzenellenbogen, *Allegories*, p. 80, n. 1.

3. Jenkins, note to v. 3017; Horrent, p. 144 and n. 3; COMMENTARY, 35 and note 11. The verse in question may mean that Rabel carries Oliver's sword, Halteclere. Moignet, p. 218. On the split in the oliphant, see COMMENTARY, 24, final paragraph.

4. Mandach, *Naissance*, 1:106–13, compares the hero's apostrophe to his sword in the *Roland* with that found in the *Pseudo-Turpin*. For a literary analysis of the passage in Turoldus's poem, see Vinaver, "La mort de Roland," pp. 136–37. On the various mentions of the name Durendal in Turoldus's poem, see Dufournet, *Cours sur Roland*, pp. 52–59.

5. For the countries mentioned here by Roland, see Menéndez Pidal, pp. 158–61; Segre's notes, pp. 438–40; Dufournet, p. 32. On the rhetorical procedure, see COMMENTARY, 4 (vv. 197–200) and 6 (vv. 370–373).

6. Cf. Ganelon's apostrophe to his sword in vv. 445–449; INTRODUCTION, 19, D.

7. On the ritual consecration of swords, see Bloch, *Feudal Society*, 2:314; Zumthor, *Histoire littéraire*, p. 63.

8. INTRODUCTION, 19, C; COMMENTARY, 4, note 17.

9. Breast-beating represents striking the fault itself. Brother Leo Charles Yedlicka, *Expressions of the Linguistic Area of Repentance and Remorse in Old French*, Catholic University Studies in Romance Languages and Literatures, (27 [*sic*, for 28]), Washington, D.C.: Catholic University of America Press, 1945), p. 383.

10. See COMMENTARY, 21 and note 69.

11. Blaise, par. 98, 110.

12. Cf. the golden sword given by the prophet Jeremiah to Judas Maccabaeus in

2 Maccabees 15:15–16. In 1 Maccabees 3:12, the hero takes the sword of his enemy Apollonius and keeps it as his own. On the connection between Judas Maccabaeus and Perceval's Espee as Estranges Renges, see Nitze's notes in *Perlesvaus*, 2:234, 248. On the mystical provenance of another sword, see *Queste*, pp. 207 ff. In the Old Testament the sword symbolizes power, especially divine power, and the Word of God. In the Song of the Sword (Ezekiel 21:13–22), it represents imminent disaster. For Christian symbolism (the spiritual struggle, justice, sorrow), see Blaise, par. 440, 441. For uses in profane literature (law and order, righteousness, virtue), see Anthime Fourrier, *Le Courant realiste dans le roman courtois en France au moyen âge*, vol. 1, *Les débuts* (*XII*[e] *siècle*) (Paris: Nizet, 1960), p. 86, n. 342. *La Chanson de Roland*, ed. Calin, p. 12 (apropos of Durendal and Joyeuse): "Ce sont des *gladii Dei*, créés et employés pour la Croisade. . . . [Durendal] incarne la *fortitudo* du guerrier."

13. Dufournet, *Cours sur Roland*, p. 56, n. 1, terms this a "magnifique expression."

14. Foulet, *Glossaire*, s.v. servir (apropos of v. 2350): "Roland parle à Durendal avec une sorte de ferveur religieuse."

15. On the rhetorical procedure, see Curtius, p. 545. In v. 2321 Roland switches from the second to the third person singular, first speaking to, then about, his sword.

16. Cf. the anecdote relative to Margariz's sword, v. 967. The scene in which an angel brings Durendal down from heaven to Charles is depicted in a manuscript of Stricker's *Karl der Grosse* (c. 1300). Lejeune and Stiennon, 1:230, pl. XXIV.

17. In v. 2297 Turoldus notes Roland's failing vision. However, the hero is evidently still able to see his sword or at least to discern its brilliance.

18. Hatzfeld, *Literature Through Art*, p. 12; INTRODUCTION, 19, D. In classical Greek statuary, the right hand shading the eyes (aposkopein) is an expression of wonder before the deity's radiance. Brilliant, *Roman Art*, p. 11. Anthropologists would say that Durendal has mana (Cf. COMMENTARY, 19, note 12), that an object with such power is a fetish, and that Charles is a shaman. Adam, *Primitive Art*, p. 51 (in note: "A *shaman* is supposed to be endowed with supernatural gifts, acting as a mediator between man and the supernatural world").

19. Cf. INTRODUCTION, 19, D, and note 489.

20. On the term *seintisme*, see Zumthor, *Langue et techniques poétiques*, p. 76. Turoldus makes no mention of the etymology of Durendal, but the *Pseudo-Turpin* (Meredith-Jones, p. 189) and Conrad, vv. 3301–3318, both allude to its hardness (cf. Lat. *durus*, OFr. *dur*). On this and other names for weapons in Turoldus's epic, consult Rita Lejeune, "Les noms d'épée dans la *Chanson de Roland*," *Mélanges de linguistique et de littérature romanes offerts à Mario Roques par ses amis, ses collègues et ses anciens élèves de France et de l'étranger* (Baden: Editions Art et Science, 1951), 1:149–66; Gerhard Rohlfs, "Ci conte de Durendal l'espee," *Mélanges Rita Lejeune*, 2:859–69; Dufournet, *Cours sur Roland*, pp. 47–50. Noting that the custom of naming swords is not found in classical literature but only in Germanic and Scandinavian sources, Lejeune, p. 151, argues that the tradition may be ascribed to Norman and ultimately Scandinavian influence. However, the practice is also attested in Tatar epic poems (Bowra, *Heroic Poetry*, p. 152), which suggests the possibility of a spontaneous development on French soil. The broken-sword motif is discussed by Frappier, *Chrétien de Troyes et le mythe du graal*, pp. 109–113.

21. Blaise, par. 464, 465.

22. See INTRODUCTION, 19, F.

23. On this relic, see Jenkins, note to v. 2348; Réau, II, 2:61–63; Brault, *Early Blazon*, p. 141. The Virgin is the traditional advocate to whom the Christian prays for intercession in the hour of his death (John 19:26–27). Delbouille, *Genèse*, p. 147; Payen, *Le Moyen Age*, p. 66. On Roland's devotion to Mary in the *Pseudo-Turpin*, see Meredith-Jones, p. 318. See also note 24 below.

24. Réau, II, 1:200–202. Moses's rock is mentioned in the *Queste*, p. 69. In the same work, p. 101, a hard rock is identified as the Church. A dark stone also symbolizes the Blessed Virgin. Davy, *Symbolique romane*, p. 219.

COMMENTARY 26

1. Roland's dying prayers are discussed in Bédier, *Commentaires*, pp. 310–13; Sister Marianna Gildea, R.S.M., *Expressions of Religious Thought and Feeling in the Chansons de Geste* (Washington, D.C.: Catholic University of America Press, 1943), pp. 163–73; Frappier, *Chansons de geste*, 2:131–40; and Jacques De Caluwé, "La 'prière épique' dans les plus anciennes chansons de geste françaises," *Olifant* 4, no. 1 (1976): 7–9. Edelgard Dubruck, *The Theme of Death in French Poetry of the Middle Ages and the Renaissance*, Studies in French Literature 1 (The Hague: Mouton, 1964), p. 37, refers to Roland's "prayer of so-called precedence," that is, a plea alluding to others who have been saved before him. Cf. the argumentation used in "Du vilain qui conquist Paradis par plait" (*Recueil*, eds. Montaiglon and Raynaud, 3 [1878]: 209–14): in both cases the plea is based on the concept of *Deus verax* 'God who keeps His promises' (Blaise, par. 164). Roland reminds God of his promise that sinners who repent shall be saved (Blaise, par. 303). Contrary to what Frappier suggests, Roland is not asking to be rescued from physical danger, but to be pardoned and saved for all eternity. The contrast between Roland's death and those of Marsile and the Saracens is noted by Gräf, *Parallelismus im Rolandslied*, pp. 16–18. On this entire passage, see Vinaver, "La mort de Roland."

2. On the heart as the seat of life, see Brault, "Chrétien de Troyes' *Lancelot*," p. 143.

3. Jones, p. 32.

4. Jenkins, note to v. 2369; Foulet, *Glossaire*, pp. 355, 498; Albert Henry, *Chrestomathie de la littérature en ancien français*, 5th ed., Bibliotheca Romanica, Series altera: Scripta Romanica Selecta 3–4, 2 pts. in 1 vol. (Berne: Francke, 1970), pt. 2, p. 18: 'mon repentir monte vers ta puissance'; Vinaver, "La mort de Roland," p. 140: 'mon cri de *mea culpa* monte vers ta haute puissance'.

5. An attitude of humility (cf. v. 3097). Roques, "L'attitude du héros mourant," pp. 355–66; Blaise, par. 83.

6. In the *Pseudo-Turpin*, Roland leaves the field at the end of the battle and rides *usque ad pedem portuum Ciserae* to a meadow *super Runciamvallem* (Meredith-Jones, p. 189). Since the Valley of the Cize lies on the north slope of the Pyrenees, Menéndez Pidal, p. 329, n. 1, concludes that in the Latin chronicle the hero dies facing France. On the Valley of the Cize, see Menéndez Pidal, pp. 228–30. In Châteauroux, vv. 3974 and 3986, the dying hero initially looks *vers (douce) France*, but then, in vv. 4131 and 4140, *vers Espe(i)gne la grant*. In Turoldus's poem Roland's attitude is much more than an aristocratic stance of the type Brandt, *Medieval History*, p. 114, characterizes as "pursued for their sake, with no other end in view beyond the public posture they permitted."

7. Cf. Vivien's *covent* in the *Chanson de Guillaume*. See COMMENTARY, 34, note 7.

8. Some critics (e.g., Burger, "Les deux scènes du cor," p. 125) believe that Roland is alluding here to the sin of pride he has committed but has now expiated. However, this is merely a general confession. See INTRODUCTION, note 61 (Payen). It is more typical of epic heroes to regret the many men they have slain. Skidmore, *Moral Traits of Christians and Saracens*, p. 44, n. 14 (*Moniage Guillaume*, *Charroi de Nîmes*); Payen, *Le Motif du repentir*, p. 169 (*Gerbert de Metz*); Brault, "The Legend of Charlemagne's Sin in Girart d'Amiens," p. 74.

9. Foulet, *Glossaire*, p. 423; Payen, *Le Motif du repentir*, p. 114.

10. Pauphilet, *Le Legs du moyen âge*, p. 75, terms this "le geste le plus sublime de toute la littérature française." Roland reaches skyward and may even be said to touch heaven. Bédier, *Légendes épiques*, 3: 322. Cf. the early iconography of the Ascension, where Christ's extended arm is grasped by the Hand of God. Réau, II, 2: 584, 588; *The Year 1200*, 1:50–51 (includes bibliography).

11. Ménard, "*Tenir le chief embronc*," p. 146, states: "Cette posture symbolise l'épuisement physique, mais peut-être aussi l'accablement moral." However, this attitude is also one of rest, frequent, for example, in depictions of dreams, e.g., Réau, II, 2: 206–8. Resting the head in this fashion is a posture of prayer, too. Blaise, par. 83. This gesture could easily have been mimed by the jongleur. Cf. COMMENTARY, 23 (v. 2227). In the *Pseudo-Turpin* Roland dies, his arms folded in a cross over his breast (cf. Oliver's "crucifixion"; Meredith-Jones, p. 207; COMMENTARY, 21, note 49). Meredith-Jones, p. 205. On the iconography of Roland's attitude in death, see INTRODUCTION, note 233.

12. Blaise, p. 546, n. 4; COMMENTARY, 18 and 44.

13. Menéndez Pidal, pp. 366–67, notes the absence of Alda in Roland's dying thoughts. Cf. Châteauroux, vv. 3805–3811. See COMMENTARY, 18, note 20.

14. Daniel in the lions' den was believed to prefigure Christ in the Sepulchre. Réau, II, 1: 391. Much of the imagery in Roland's dying prayers derives ultimately from the ancient *Ordo commendationis animae*. Jenkins, note to v. 2384; Bédier, *Commentaires*, pp. 311–12, citing Tavernier. The same associations appear in the art of the Catacombs. *La Chanson de Roland: Texte critique, traduction et commentaire, grammaire et glossaire*, ed. and trans. Léon Gautier, Edition classique, 20th ed. (Tours: Mame, 1892), p. 222, note to v. 2384. Lazarus's sepulchre was a symbol of stubbornness in sin. COMMENTARY, 2, note 26. On the Raising of Lazarus as a *pignus resurrectionis*, see Réau, II, 2:388.

15. The prayer here is one of faith and hope. Cf. Charlemagne's "prière du plus grand péril" (COMMENTARY, 36).

16. *La Chanson de Roland*, ed. Guillaume Picot, Nouveaux Classiques Larousse, 2 vols. (Paris: Larousse, 1965), 2: 34.

17. Gaston Paris, *Extraits de la Chanson de Roland*, 3d ed. (Paris: Hachette, 1891), p. 104, n. 105. On the concept of offering up one's own person as a sacrificial victim, see Blaise, par. 246.

18. Jenkins, note to v. 2365.

19. Ganshof, *Feudalism*, pp. 70–78.

20. Ibid., pp. 78–79.

21. Ibid., p. 74.

22. Ibid., pp. 73–74. It has often been claimed that the custom of joining hands over the breast to pray derives from the gesture of homage. This view has been challenged by Gerhart B. Ladner, "The Gestures of Prayer in Papal Iconography of the Thirteenth and Early Fourteenth Centuries," in *Didascaliae: Studies in Honor of Anselm M. Albareda, Prefect of the Vatican Library, Presented by a Group of American Scholars* (New York: Rosenthal, 1961), pp. 246–75, who argues that the gesture is a Franciscan devotional practice symbolizing the elevation of the heart during mass.

23. Ganshof, *Feudalism*, pp. 73–74.

24. The latter ceremony is discussed by Ganshof, pp. 125–27.

25. Ibid., p. 126.

26. Thus in the *Chanson de Guillaume*, vv. 2533–2537, William throws his gauntlet down before the king and says: "*Ci vus rend voz feez*."

27. Bédier, *Commentaires*, pp. 312–13.

28. Ibid., p. 312.

29. Ibid., pp. 312–13.

30. Jenkins, note to v. 2365, cites *Gormont et Isembart* (ed. Alphonse Bayot, Classiques français du moyen âge 14 [Paris: Champion, 1921]), vv. 374–377, where the expression *tenir quite son fieu* is used is used in this sense:

Ber saint Denise, or m'an aidiez!
Jeo tenc de vus quite mun fieu
De nul autre n'en conois ren
Fors sul Deu, le veir del ciel.

In Conrad, vv. 91–96, Charlemagne reminds his men that God has granted them a rich and full life but requires service in return. He then goes on to say, vv. 97–100:

Da der Keiser allir Hiemele
Uorderet hin widere,
Daz Er iu uirlihin hat,
Frolichen ir uor Im stat.

(Since the Lord of all the Heavens
Now claims back again
That which He granted to you in fief,
Appear before Him joyfully).

On the pledge (pignus) of Heaven, see 2 Corinthians 1:22; Ephesians 1:14; Blaise, par. 259. If Turoldus implies that Roland is responsible for a fief of some sort, he is evidently thinking of the biblical notion of stewardship or of the parable of the talents. Matthew 24:45–51; 25:14–30.

31. *The Song of Roland*, trans. Sayers, note to vv. 2390–2391. Cf. the gift of faith viewed as a *bonum depositum custodi* (2 Timothy 1:14; Blaise, p. 598, n. 1).

32. Vinaver, "La mort de Roland," p. 140.

33. Faral, *La Chanson de Roland*, pp. 239–40.

34. Ibid., p. 240.

35. Ibid.

36. See vv. 1268, 1510, 3647.

37. Jones, p. 73.

38. Complete summary of Faith Lyons's unpublished paper, "More About Roland's Glove," read before the Fifth International Congress of the Société Rencesvals held at Oxford in 1970, in the *Bulletin bibliographique de la Société Rencesvals* 6 (1971): 148, item 469. The article referred to by Dr. Lyons is W. M. Hackett, "Le gant de Roland," *Romania* 89 (1968): 253–56.

39. On the notion of expiatory homage, see Bloch, *Feudal Society*, 2:334. For other propitiatory offerings, see Blaise, par. 234. A gauntlet is proffered to Saint Michael in Avranches MS. 210, fol. 25. See Alexander, *Norman Illumination*, p. 99 and pl. 19, h. I am indebted to M. François Avril, Keeper of Manuscripts at the Bibliothèque Nationale in Paris, for specifying, in a private communication to me dated 2 April 1969, that the manuscript in question is a cartulary of Mont-Saint-Michel compiled during the abbacy of Robert of Torigni (1154–86). The drawing illustrates a charter recording a donation by Duke Robert the Magnificent to the Abbey. For bibliography on this cartulary, see Alexander, p. 19, n. 2.

40. On these signs of remorse, see Yedlicka, *Repentance and Remorse in Old French*, pp. 352–84.

41. Blaise, par. 83.

42. Yedlicka, pp. 381–84. In the *Pseudo-Turpin* Roland presses his breasts and offers his flesh in expiation for his sins; in the rhymed versions he partakes of lay communion. Brault, "Girart d'Amiens and the *Pseudo-Turpin Chronicle*," pp. 88–90; Payen, *Le Motif du repentir*, p. 119. The five senses, avenues of temptation, were often

alluded to in confessions. Janson, *Apes and Ape Lore*, p. 240; *Vie de Saint Thomas Becket*, vv. 1175–1177; *Ronsasvals*, ed. Mortier, pp. 141–42.

43. *Aliscans, chanson de geste*, eds. François Guessard and Anatole de Montaiglon, Les Anciens Poètes de la France 10 (Paris: Franck, 1870), Laisse 4, cited by Tobler and Lommatzsch, 4: 31.

44. Yedlicka, *Repentance and Remorse in Old French*, p. 186.

45. Ibid.

46. Ibid.; Blaise, p. 392, n. 4.

47. Cf. the hero's gesture in returning his ring to Isolt as a sign that he has fulfilled a pledge. *Tristan de Thomas*, 1:401.

48. E.g., *Roland*, v. 1140: *Ben sunt asols e quites de lur pecchez.*

49. Cf. *Erec*, vv. 2687, 3269. For other legal terms in the *Roland*, see Jones, p. 45. Ecclesiastical Latin *proferre* refers to the symbolical offering of a gift. Blaise, par. 237.

50. Bédier's translation here is accepted by Jones, p. 50.

51. Blaise, par. 61, 67, 80.

52. Will, "Recherches iconographiques," p. 76 (fig. 39) and n. 125.

53. Lejeune and Stiennon, 1: pl. II; 2: figs. 293, 344, 368.

54. COMMENTARY, 24.

55. Twelfth-century console from Alspach, now in the Musée d'Unterlinden at Colmar. Will, "Recherches iconographiques," p. 71; Rumpler, *L'Art roman en Alsace*, pl. XXXIX. See also INTRODUCTION, 12 and 14, A, 5; COMMENTARY, 22, note 29.

COMMENTARY 27

1. The dramatic contrast in these two scenes is noted by Horrent, p. 268.

2. Faral, *La Chanson de Roland*, pp. 198–201; Jones, pp. 127, 182; Vance, *Reading the Song of Roland*, pp. 64–65. The reasons why, historically, Roncevaux was not avenged are discussed by Menéndez Pidal, pp. 212–13.

3. For another dusty pursuit, see COMMENTARY, 43 (vv. 3633–3635).

4. Cf. Genesis 4:10. On the iconography of the *vox sanguinis*, see Réau, II, 1:97.

5. Jones, pp. 83–84, explains that not only must the French deaths be avenged, but that the insult (Marsile gave his word to Charles) must be wiped out.

6. Ibid., pp. 44–45: "Before pursuing the fleeting Saracens to avenge Roland, Charlemagne asks his vassals to grant him his feudal rights (*e dreiture e honur*, 2430), which probably designates the military service the vassals owe him as their feudal lord." However, the Emperor is clearly addressing God (v. 2429). On divine justice, see Paul Rousset, "La croyance en la justice immanente à l'époque féodale," *Le Moyen Age* 54 (1948): 225–48; Calin, *Epic Quest*, p. 85.

7. Bibliography in Bédier's n. 1.

8. Bédier, *Commentaires*, p. 313. Curtius, pp. 227–28, considers such references to be epic clichés ultimately derived from classical sources. On medieval lion symbolism, see Dufournet, *Cours sur Roland*, pp. 95–97.

9. Jenkins, note to vv. 2436 ff.

10. John 20:17. Modern commentators explain that Christ's words may contain an indirect allusion to the Ascension, but they are mainly a way of urging Mary Magdalene not to delay "but go, tell my brethren." See also Réau, II, 2:557. However, medieval exegetes believed the scene was prefigured by Moses when he interdicted the Israelites from approaching Mount Sinai (Exodus 19:12–13). Réau, II, 1:204; II, 2:557. Numbers 19:11–22 states that touching a corpse causes a person to become unclean for seven days.

11. See COMMENTARY, 20.

12. The problem of distinguishing the Franks from the Saracens occasions a miracle in the *Karlamagnús Saga* and the rhymed versions. Horrent, p. 188.

13. See INTRODUCTION, II, D; COMMENTARY, 34.

14. On the pursuit itself, see OXFORD TEXT, ENGLISH TRANSLATION, v. 2445.

15. Locke, *Quest*, p. 41, suggests that the lateness of the day also relates to the ninth hour, the time of Christ's death. Menéndez Pidal, pp. 284–85, sees a historical reminiscence here derived from the account in Einhard.

16. Jenkins, note to v. 2450.

17. Menéndez Pidal, pp. 305–11, 317–18; Lejeune and Stiennon, 1:48; Brault, "Le Thème de la Mort," p. 229, n. 19; Dufournet, *Cours sur Roland*, pp. 182–85. Cf. the Chronicle of Moissac (c. 1050), cited by Jenkins, note to v. 2450, who also mentions a comparable phenomenon at the Battle of Ascalon (1099).

18. The miracle of the lengthening day is repeated in Conrad, in the battle against Paligan (= Baligant), vv. 8431–8435, with reference (vv. 8421–8422) to the stratagem employed by Gideon in Judges 7:16.

19. Meredith-Jones, chap. 2. The miracle is repeated by Charles at Lucerna (Meredith-Jones, chap. 3, p. 99) and, by Roland, at Gratianapolis (variant: Granapolis; Meredith-Jones, chap. 33, pp. 237, 239, with specific references to Jericho [Joshua 6], p. 237).

20. Réau, II, 1:225.

21. Ibid., II, 1:223.

22. See COMMENTARY, 19.

23. Joshua 5:14. The spiritual visitor appears first in the form of an angel, then is identified as Yahweh in Joshua 6:2 ff. Cf. Genesis 16:7, 13; 21:17; Exodus 23:20–23; 33:2; Judges 2:1–4; 6:11–24.

24. A clear allusion to its mystical power. Cf. Durendal's brilliance, COMMENTARY, 25 (vv. 2316–2317).

25. Cf. the opening scene of the *Conte del graal.* On the latter, see Mario Roques, "Les anges exterminateurs de Perceval," in *Fin du moyen âge et Renaissance: Mélanges de philologie française offerts à M. Robert Guiette* (Antwerp: De Nederlandsche Boeckhandel, 1961), pp. 1–4; Brault, *Early Blazon*, p. 183.

26. Blaise, par. 315, 316, 318, 322. Cf. the Valley of Jehoshaphat (Joel 4:2, 12), where the Last Judgment will be held, popularly associated with the Valley of Kidron in Jerusalem. In *Erec*, v. 2359, the *Val Perilleus* is said to be the place where Morgan la Fée lives. See also *Les Oeuvres d'Adenet le Roi*, vol. 3, *Les Enfances Ogier*, ed. Albert Henry, Rijksuniversiteit te Gent, Werken uitgegeven door de Faculteit van de wijsbegeerte en letteren 121 (Bruges: De Tempel, 1956), p. 347, note to v. 1730.

27. Blaise, par. 392.

28. There is a contrast here, too, between the Saracens meeting their end in the *Val Tenebrus* and Roland dying in *Rencesvals.*

29. The expression *par merveillus ahan* (v. 2474) will echo in v. 3963, when Ganelon's punishment is decided. See COMMENTARY, 47.

30. 1 Peter 3:21. The medieval audience may have visualized the drowning of the Saracens in the *Song of Roland* as evildoers being swallowed up by Leviathan, the gaping mouth of Hell. This is the association made by Conrad in vv. 7067–7069. On this image, referring to Job 40:25–32; 41:1–26, see Réau, II, 2:751–52; A. Caiger-Smith, *English Medieval Mural Painting* (Oxford: Clarendon Press, 1963), p. 36; Ménard, *Le Rire*, p. 547. For the iconography of the Drowning of Pharaoh's Host, see Réau, II, 1:192–96. The scene is represented allegorically in the tenth-century Paris Psalter (Bibliothèque Nationale, MS. gr. 139): a naked man (= Abyss) seizes Pharaoh by the hair and drags him down to the deep. Charles Diehl, *Manuel d'art byzantin*, 2d ed., 2 vols. (Paris: Picard, 1926), 2:610, fig. 288 (cf. also p. 617, fig. 293);

Robb, *Illuminated Manuscript*, p. 48. On Abyss (Abisme), see COMMENTARY, 17, note 44. On the folk motif of the sea that becomes angry when evil deeds are committed, see *Tristan de Thomas*, 1:38, note; Jonin, *Personnages féminins*, p. 448; Robertson, *Preface to Chaucer*, pp. 400, 413.

31. Cf. Psalms 114:3.

32. Plunging straight down to the bottom or perhaps descending in a spinning or tumbling motion (v. 2471: s'en turnerent). Cf. OFr. *gorge* 'whirlpool'. Brault, *Early Blazon*, p. 270.

33. See COMMENTARY, 29 (vv. 2587, 2590). On the possible humor here, see Ménard, *Le Rire*, p. 59.

34. See OXFORD TEXT, ENGLISH TRANSLATION, v. 2475.

35. According to Horrent, p. 250, n. 1, the destruction of the Saracen army in this passage is not a true battle.

36. See COMMENTARY, 14.

37. In fact, except for a single letter, vv. 99 and 2478 are identical in every respect. The possibility that v. 2478 may be out of place here (cf. v. 2242) is remote, for it occurs in this passage in other copies. However, Jenkins notes that Venice IV substitutes *joie*, "which seems preferable," for *eschec*.

38. Prostration (vv. 2449, 2480) is an attitude of prayer found in the Bible. Blaise, par. 83. For illustrations of this posture in Prudentius, see Woodruff, "Illustrated Manuscripts of Prudentius," figs. 18, 70, 73–76.

39. Some scholars believe the Saracens have now been fittingly punished and use this as an argument against the authenticity of the Baligant episode. Horrent, pp. 249–50.

40. Cf. Isaiah 11:6–9, where repose is a reflection of the eternal rest of Paradise. Blaise, par. 94, 307 and n. 25 (refrigerii locus). Hatzfeld, "Le *Rolandslied* allemand," p. 55: "Après la vengeance de Charles la nature semble prendre part à la victoire, mais pas—hélas—à la douleur de l'empereur pour la perte de son neveu." The elegiac quality of this scene is commented on by Vance, *Reading the Song of Roland*, pp. 66–67. Jenkins interprets *la tere deserte* in v. 2489 as a 'wilderness', but 'deserted land' is doubtless more accurate, for an eerie peace and calm is suggested rather than uncultivated land. Cf. v. 3127, *tere guaste*. On the concept of the Waste Land, consult Vinaver, *Rise of Romance*, chap. 4, pp. 53–67.

41. Psalms 32:9; Robertson, *Preface to Chaucer*, pp. 253–54. The horse is also a symbol of devotion (Frye, *Anatomy of Criticism*, p. 152), majesty (Davy, *Symbolique romane*, p. 225; Segre, note to v. 45, citing Robert de Blois's *Ensoignement des princes*, vv. 236–238: *Par le cheval entendre puet / Chascons saiges qu'i senefie / Et digneté et seignorie*), and nobility (Dufournet, *Cours sur Roland*, p. 88). For other uses of the horse in epic poetry, see Bowra, *Heroic Poetry*, pp. 157–70.

42. The Four Horsemen of the Apocalypse, today often associated with divine retribution, were Christ symbols of another sort to medieval exegetes. See Réau, II, 2:696. *Ronsasvals*, p. 143, refers to animals being still out of respect for the dead. Cf. the legend of the animals on Christmas eve (Réau, II, 2:228–29), a possible allusion to Isaiah 1:3. The tradition is mentioned in Shakespeare's *Hamlet*.

43. Psalms 23:2.

44. On the cock symbol, see Blaise, p. 128, n. 2. For references to Christian vigilance, see Réau, II, 2:429, 439, 747. Cf. the monachal custom of rising for prayer in the middle of the night (vigil). Blaise, par. 13.

45. See COMMENTARY, 16.

46. In 1 Samuel 26:7 David finds Saul asleep inside his camp, his spear stuck in the ground beside his head.

47. See *Perlesvaus*, 2:256–57. The relic was discovered at Antioch in 1098. Jenkins,

note to vv. 2503–2511; Horrent, p. 291; Menéndez Pidal, p. 243; Frappier, *Chrétien de Troyes et le mythe du graal*, pp. 171–74. Charlemagne's sword, preserved at Saint-Denis, was part of the regalia used in the crowning ceremony. Costa, *Trésors des Eglises de France*, p. 50.

48. Blaise, par. 9. On the notion of God's bounty in this connection (v. 2507), see Jones, p. 54; Burgess, *Vocabulaire pré-courtois*, pp. 110–11.

49. For a similar interpretation, see Pauphilet, *Le Legs du moyen âge*, pp. 88–89; Hatzfeld, *Literature Through Art*, p. 12; and Vos, "Aspects of Biblical Typology," pp. 84–97, with special reference to earlier studies by Heisig. Bowra, *Heroic Poetry*, p. 188, suggests that Charles is "full of fears about Roland," but the Emperor already knows his nephew is dead (vv. 2513, 2516).

50. Horrent, p. 360, n. 5, explains that Charles does not yet know that Roland's soul has been saved, although the audience is well aware of this. Vance, *Reading the Song of Roland*, pp. 70–71, suggests that the figure of Charlemagne in this passage "provides a context of wisdom and maturity in which the consequences of Roland's ordeal and passion take on their full meaning. Although with the unfolding of time the psychological outline of neither Roland nor Charlemagne has changed, we of the audience have experienced a profound reversal of perspective, which carries us beyond the arrogant pride of a young knight to the tragic wisdom of supreme old age." For a possible parody of the alternation between Charles's joy and grief in this passage, see COMMENTARY, 33 (v. 2789).

COMMENTARY 28

1. At this point—or thereabouts (Horrent, pp. 255–56)—begins the Baligant episode. For bibliography, see INTRODUCTION, note 17.

2. See COMMENTARY, 24 (v. 2262).

3. See vv. 2529–2530:

> Par avisiun li ad anunciet
> D'une bataille ki encuntre lui ert.

4. Jenkins, note to vv. 2555 ff.; Horrent, p. 245, n. 2. Faral, *La Chanson de Roland*, p. 185; Braet, "Fonction et importance du songe," p. 414; and Dufournet, *Cours sur Roland*, pp. 27–28, see an allusion to Lucan.

5. On the significance of the Ardennes in these passages, see Bédier, *Commentaires*, pp. 107–8. Calin, *Epic Quest*, p. 13, considers the woods in this passage to be a symbol of anarchy.

6. Horrent, p. 256. On meteorological disturbances in Turoldus's poem, see INTRODUCTION, 16, B.

7. Réau, II, 1:115–16. Medieval chroniclers characteristically viewed such afflictions as divine retribution. Smail, *Crusading Warfare*, p. 100. Conrad, vv. 7454–7457, has Charles say that whatever God sends him will be considered a punishment for his sins and those of his ancestors.

8. Cf. Ami's leprosy in *Ami et Amile*. Calin, *Epic Quest*, p. 88.

9. *Hamartigenia*, v. 735 (*Prudentius*, 1:256); Réau, II, 1:116; Calin, *Epic Quest*, p. 13.

10. Horrent, p. 245, n. 3, observes that this dream foreshadows the same events as those in the second vision, vv. 724 ff. Owen inserts the passage in question after v. 737. See COMMENTARY, 10, note 1.

11. See OXFORD TEXT, ENGLISH TRANSLATION, vv. 2556, 2557, and COMMENTARY, 24 (vv. 2268, 2272, 2556) and 45 (v. 3736).

12. Vance, *Reading the Song of Roland*, p. 33.

13. INTRODUCTION, 19, G.

COMMENTARY 29

1. See INTRODUCTION, 18, H.

2. To be sure, if there were moonlight, the shadows could be cast by the olive tree, but see vv. 2632–2637. The stopping of the sun by Charlemagne plainly has no bearing on the matter at hand.

3. See COMMENTARY, 12.

4. See INTRODUCTION, 16, D; COMMENTARY, 6 (v. 366). Cf. v. 2705 (arrival of Saracen messengers).

5. The contrast between Marsile's powerlessness and despair, and Roland's hope is noted by Gräf, *Parallelismus im Rolandslied*, p. 17.

6. Lejeune and Stiennon, 1:35.

7. Ibid., 1:35.

8. It is a painted chamber (v. 2594), often, in the romances, associated with magic (Loomis, *Arthurian Tradition and Chrétien de Troyes*, p. 304, n. 15); cf., however, *Tristan de Thomas*, 1:309–10 (see Bédier's note 1, p. 309), and Charlemagne's painted palace at Aachen (Meredith-Jones, pp. 221, 223, 225, 227, 229; but see p. 333, note to p. 220, lines xii–xiv).

9. The Saracen queen's observation concerning the Franks in v. 2604 ("Ki si sunt fiers n'unt cure de lur vies") is reminiscent of Ganelon's complaint about Roland in v. 227 ("Ne li chalt, sire, de quel mort nus murjuns").

10. Bramimonde's religion is contrasted with that of Charlemagne and Roland by Gräf, *Parallelismus im Rolandslied*, p. 17 (Saracen treatment of idols is contrasted with Christian reverence and hope, pp. 17–18). See also Skidmore, *Moral Traits of Christians and Saracens*, p. 24. On the importance of Bramimonde's despair in the debate over the authenticity of the Baligant episode, consult Horrent, pp. 244–45. Lejeune and Stiennon, 1:35–36, identify a statue in the Angoulême sculpture as the idol of Apollo (v. 2580).

11. On this epic motif, see Skidmore, *Moral Traits of Christians and Saracens*, p. 34, n. 40; *Huon de Bordeaux*, p. 79; Frappier, *Chansons de geste*, 2:129; Ménard, *Le Rire*, pp. 62, 192 and n. 38. In Conrad, vv. 4177–4216, Roland demolishes a pagan temple on the battlefield of Roncevaux. His men wish to keep the gold they find there, but Roland forbids it. Lejeune and Stiennon, 1:128; 2: fig. 105. For similar episodes in the Roland legend, consult Lejeune and Stiennon, 1:216 (2: fig. 181), 240 (2: fig. 211), 328 (2: figs. 385, 386). In the *Pseudo-Turpin* Charles says that the Saracens adore the devil in the form of idols (Meredith-Jones, p. 131). According to Le Goff, *Civilisation*, p. 158, the destruction of idols was a preoccupation of the early Middle Ages. It was also an important motif in the saints' lives. Delehaye, *Les Passions des martyrs*, pp. 190, 215–16. In *Apotheosis*, vv. 402–403 (*Prudentius*, 1:150), Apollo writhes when Christ's name is uttered.

12. Faral, *La Chanson de Roland*, p. 242, n. 1: "le rôle attribué à la reine Bramimonde dans cet épisode est nécessaire pour expliquer sa conversion à la fin du poème; . . . il est impossible, sans ce chaînon, d'établir une liaison satisfaisante entre les événements qui précèdent et ceux de l'épilogue." Cf. Horrent, pp. 244–45. Among the arguments developed by the latter, pp. 249–54, against the authenticity of the Baligant episode, there is one that calls for brief comment here. Horrent underscores "La manière gauche de présenter pour la première fois l'amiral de Babylone" and the fact that "jusqu'à présent, personne n'a soufflé mot de l'aide hypothétique de l'allié d'outre-mer" (p. 251). However, the transition between the destruction of the idols by Bramimonde and the recollection of Marsile's threat to deny his gods is executed with considerable skill. The procedure is the same as the poet used in the ride to Saragossa, where the word *cunseill* in v. 379 prompts Ganelon to tell the story concerning the red apple, an anecdote designed to show that his stepson is a bad counselor (COMMENTARY, 6).

13. For the parallel between Bramimonde and Guibourc, see Frappier, *Chansons de geste*, 1:176–79.

14. Bramimonde's cries over Saragossa (vv. 2598–2599) are reminiscent of biblical laments over Jerusalem: Jeremiah 15:5–9; Lamentations 1:1–22; Matthew 23:37–39. Cf. COMMENTARY, 14, note 43.

15. Some editors emend *.XX.* in v. 2578 to *.XXX.* For this and other conjectures, see Segre.

16. For contemporary illustrations, see Diehl, *Manuel d'art byzantin*, 2: figs. 303, 304; OXFORD TEXT, ENGLISH TRANSLATION, v. 8. On pagan idols, see Janson, *Apes and Ape Lore*, p. 21; Panofsky and Saxl, "Classical Mythology," p. 248, n. 26; Réau, II, 1:205 (Golden Calf); II, 2:280–81 (Fall of the Idols [monkey = idol]).

17. There is perhaps an ironic reference here to Climborin's vaunt that he would remove the Emperor's crown (v. 1490).

18. On carbuncles, see note 35 below.

19. The incident also foreshadows the beating of Ganelon in vv. 3737–3739, which involves aping of the Scourging of Christ. COMMENTARY, 45. Taking away scepter and crown is an inversion of the conferring of these objects on Christ.

20. Jenkins, note to v. 2582, citing Comfort; Frappier, *Chansons de geste*, 2:124–26; Ménard, *Le Rire* p. 79. Cf. also vv. 1751, 3223. In the *Psychomachia*, vv. 721–725, the body of Discord is torn asunder, then parceled out to unclean animals. See also COMMENTARY, 18, note 23.

21. Meredith-Jones, chap. 4, pp. 101, 103 (see note, pp. 291–92).

22. See INTRODUCTION, 18, H.

23. Cf. v. 2.

24. See COMMENTARY, 28, note 1.

25. Györy, *Etude sur Roland*, pp. 25, 97–98; *La Chanson de Roland*, ed. Calin, p. 11. Vos, "Aspects of Biblical Typology," pp. 142–43, views Marsile as an Antichrist figure. It was believed that Antichrist would be born of the tribe of Dan in Babylon or Antioch. Steven Runciman, *A History of the Crusades*, 3 vols. (Cambridge: University Press, 1954), 3:41–42.

26. See, for example, Horrent, p. 254.

27. There are numerous examples of lengthy continuations in Old French literature, often changing the spirit of the original (e.g., *Conte del graal*, *Roman de la Rose*), but also of the work of one author being finished by another, but in accordance with the former's wishes (*Charrette*).

28. See, for example, Jenkins, note to v. 2614; Bédier, *Commentaires*, p. 53; Duggan, "The Generation of the Episode of Baligant," p. 71. Cf. Wathelet-Willem, *Recherches*, 1:622.

29. This identification is reinforced by mention of Alexandria in v. 2626.

30. Hatzfeld, *Literature Through Art*, pp. 7–8; Vos, "Aspects of Biblical Typology," p. 77; INTRODUCTION, 15, D.

31. Daniel 7:9; Revelation 1:9–16.

32. Homer was known through the *Ilias latina*. Curtius, p. 59; Davy, *Symbolique romane*, p. 142.

33. Faral, *Jongleurs*, pp. 20, 272; Davy, *Symbolique romane*, p. 144; Le Goff, *Civilisation*, p. 217. Cf. the image of Socrates and Plato in Herrad of Landsberg; Cames, *Allégories*, pp. 15–16, and fig. 5 (blackbirds, representing Satan, whisper in their ear).

34. Domenico Comparetti, *Virgilio nel medio evo*, 3d ed., 2 vols. (Florence: La Nuova Italia, 1943–46); John W. Spargo, *Virgil the Necromancer*, Harvard Studies in Comparative Literature 10 (Cambridge: Harvard University Press, 1934); Davy, *Symbolique romane*, p. 145. The revolving castle in *Perlesvaus*, line 5788, was made by Virgil and is associated with Hell (2:316).

35. According to Bowra, *Heroic Poetry*, pp. 206–7, the ships in this passage underscore the wealth and brilliance of the Saracens. However, in reality, the illuminated vessels cast evil reflections on their owners. See INTRODUCTION, 19, D. In the Bible a tall ship is a symbol of pride (COMMENTARY, 1, note 21). To the bibliography on carbuncles in Brault, *Early Blazon*, pp. 139–40, add *Perlesvaus*, 2:315; Calin, *Epic Quest*, pp. 29, 39, 40; Tuve, *Allegorical Imagery*, p. 16, n. 7. In v. 2589 it is an attribute of Tervagant. The lanterns (vv. 2633, 2643) suggest a moonless night (cf. vv. 2570 ff.). The moon rises the night following Baligant's arrival (v. 3659). Cf. INTRODUCTION, note 285.

36. Cf. *Yvain*, v. 861: "s'an fu la bataille plus bele." On medieval attitudes toward sirens, see McCulloch, *Mediaeval Latin and French Bestiaries*, pp. 166–69. It is late evening or night, after the scenes described in vv. 2570–2608 when the news of Baligant's arrival has not yet reached Marsile.

37. Jenkins, note to v. 2772. In Turoldus's day ships did not generally sail in the Mediterranean from early December to the middle of March. Le Goff, *Civilisation*, p. 231.

38. For a comparable condensation, see COMMENTARY, 9 (Roland gives the signal to the French army to halt for the night).

COMMENTARY 30

1. Blaise, p. 473, n. 13; par. 405 (pompa). The passage in question figures in discussions relative to the authenticity of the Baligant episode. Horrent, pp. 182, 247, 253.

2. Katzenellenbogen, *Allegories*, pp. 2, 10, 64; Blaise, par. 494. The number of major vices varied throughout the Middle Ages but, by convention, was often seven. Accompanying someone, like holding his stirrup, is a sign of *reverentia*. COMMENTARY, 5 (v. 348).

3. Horrent, p. 248, notes that Baligant's men must remain standing (v. 2655), whereas Charles's men are seated (v. 110).

4. The laurel tree in v. 2651 is commented upon by Curtius, p. 245 and n. 2. INTRODUCTION, 16, D. See also Hatzfeld, *Literature Through Art*, p. 13.

5. The parallelism with feudal customs and institutions associated with the Franks is noted by Gräf, *Parallelismus im Rolandslied*, p. 39.

6. Ezekiel 21:18.

7. In Genesis 24:2, Abraham says to Eliezer: "Place your hand under my thigh" (cf. 24:9). *The Jerusalem Bible*, p. 41, n. *b*: "The same gesture as in 47:29; contact with the genital organs is intended to make the oath inviolable." For an eleventh-century illustration of the *manum sub femore*, see Réau, II, 1:140: "Par fémur, il faut entendre, selon les Pères de l'Eglise, *genus, generatio*, le membre d'où sort la descendance du patriarche. Ce serment phallique était considéré comme particulièrement sacré parce que, dans les organes de la génération, source de vie, résidaient des forces divines."

8. See COMMENTARY, 8 (Bramimonde), 12 (Margariz), 17 (Abisme).

9. On this attitude, see Katzenellenbogen, *Allegories*, p. 14; Cames, *Byzance*, p. 62 and fig. 77. Cf. COMMENTARY, 24, note 67; 35, note 7. Horrent, p. 313, notes the grotesqueness of certain details in this scene.

10. Baligant's threat echoes that found in the message delivered by Ganelon to Marsile in vv. 430 ff.

11. Mention of the sun in v. 2646 enhances this impression. Cf. vv. 157, 3345, 3675. For illustrations of the Wheel of Fortune, see Réau, II, 2:639–41; Payen, *Le Moyen Age*, p. 82. The image was popularized by Boethius's *Consolation of Philosophy*. See *Boethius, The Theological Tractates*, eds. and trans. H. F. Stewart, E. K. Rand, and

S. J. Tester; and *The Consolation of Philosophy*, ed. and trans. S. J. Tester, The Loeb Classical Library (1918; rpt. Cambridge: Harvard University Press; London: Heinemann, 1973), 2, 1: vv. 1–9.

12. Jenkins, note to v. 2678.

13. The difference was doubtless underscored by intonation, the jongleur affecting haughty airs when delivering lines spoken by Baligant. For further observations on Baligant's precipitateness, see COMMENTARY, 33 and 40.

14. *Caritas* is sometimes opposed to *paupertas*, which obviously has a pejorative meaning in this instance. Katzenellenbogen, *Allegories*, pp. 19, n. 3; 21, n. 2 (fig. 20). Cf. *paupertas*, pp. 37, n. 2; 72.

COMMENTARY 31

1. Jenkins notes that v. 2691 contains the first attestation of "this fateful word." Skidmore, *Moral Traits of Christians and Saracens*, p. 33, points out the anachronism of ascribing this feudal institution to Saracens.

2. See INTRODUCTION, 15, D; COMMENTARY, 32.

3. Perhaps some of the more than one hundred thousand new converts are not inhabitants of Saragossa but the remnants of Baligant's army.

4. For comparative figures relative to the population of medieval cities, see Pirenne, *Economic and Social History of Medieval Europe*, pp. 170–71. Note, however: "We possess no statistical data until the fifteenth century, and even those which have come down to us for that period are inadequate and far from clear" (p. 170).

5. Boissonnade, *Du Nouveau*, p. 84, cited by Jenkins, note to v. 2690.

6. Pierre Lavedan, *Représentation des villes dans l'art du moyen âge*, Art médiéval, Bibliothèque de documentation (Paris: Vanoest, 1954), p. 33. For the illustration of *Corderes* (= *Roland*, vv. 71, 97: *Cordres*) in Conrad, see Lejeune and Stiennon, 1:120–22; 2:fig. 88.

7. Lavedan, p. 32. Cf. the Heavenly Jerusalem, Réau, II, 2:721–23; Davy, *Symbolique romane*, p. 185; *Introduction au monde des symboles*, pp. 73–74.

8. Lavedan, pp. 33–34.

9. Ibid., pl. VII; figs. 1, 3, 4.

10. Ibid., p. 34.

11. *Le Guide du Pèlerin*, pp. 86, 88, 90, 92.

12. Horrent, *Pèlerinage*, p. 51. The description of Cairo in *Huon de Bordeaux* is said to be derived from that of Constantinople in the *Pèlerinage de Charlemagne*. *Huon de Bordeaux*, pp. 76, 86; Horrent, pp. 51–54; Calin, *Epic Quest*, p. 188.

13. See COMMENTARY, 19.

14. On the use of the term *confusion* in vv. 2699 and 3276, see Horrent, *La Chanson de Roland*, p. 254.

COMMENTARY 32

1. Moignet: 'les messagers se tenaient par leurs manteaux'; Owen: 'each holding the other by the cloak'. Foulet, *Glossaire*, p. 484: "'Tenir'. Avec *se* indiquant réciprocité 2707."

2. Jenkins, note to v. 2707.

3. On mantel etiquette, see COMMENTARY, 5, note 14 (Foulet). Cf. COMMENTARY, 7, note 6.

4. Thus Owen is able to interpret this verse exactly opposite the manner it is rendered in the present translation as: 'with friendly greetings couched in sorry terms'. Jones, p. 20: "When the Emir's messengers report to Marsilie and Bramimunde, they give

a bad salutation (*malvais saluz*, 2710), which is an invocation to their heathen gods" (cf. also p. 22).

5. Jenkins, note to v. 2709 *a*; Ker, *Dark Ages*, p. 226.

6. Conrad, vv. 7271–7272:

Siê gruzten den chüninc undare,
Daz taten sie ime zeuare.

7. Bédier, *Commentaires*, p. 227.

8. Ibid., n. 1: "Ce vers est une refonte de deux vers de *P* (p. 155): *Le roi trouverent enz en son lit gisant, Et la roïnne fu devant lui plorans.*"

9. See Segre, pp. 491–92: "Tuttavia il *li*, così sospeso, lascia qualche dubbio, tanto più che il saluto è rivolto anche alla regina. E quanto alla fine del verso, è probabile che *γ* terminasse con *dïent*, col vantaggio di evitare ripetizione di *firent* rispetto a 2716."

10. Pope, *From Latin to Modern French*, par 1251: "In Later Anglo-Norman ... *le* and *la* functioned sometimes as *li*, and the northern use of *les* as a dative pronoun (N. [read N.E.] par. xv) led to a confusion between *les* and *lur* in the fourteenth century." See OXFORD TEXT, ENGLISH TRANSLATION, v. 820.

11. The Bramimonde-Charlemagne connection is mentioned by Gräf, *Parallelismus im Rolandslied*, p. 32.

12. See COMMENTARY, 7, note 5.

13. Foulet, *Glossaire*, p. 338.

14. Isaiah 2:16.

15. Charles's decision not to attack Saragossa immediately is termed a serious tactical error by Horrent, p. 250.

16. Psalms 22:17. An equivalent expression today would be: "I can count all my ribs."

COMMENTARY 33

1. Cf. Rychner, p. 59.

2. See COMMENTARY, 27. Gräf, *Parallelismus im Rolandslied*, p. 38, compares Baligant's attitude here with that of Charles in vv. 771 ff.

3. Cf. also the ape, *sicut et diabulus, non habet finem bonum*. Janson, *Apes and Ape Lore*, p. 16 (also p. 24, n. 24).

4. The vocabulary relative to conversion is quite extensive in the *Song of Roland*. See Gerard J. Brault, "'Truvet li unt le num de Juliane': sur le rôle de Bramimonde dans la *Chanson de Roland*," *Mélanges Pierre Le Gentil*, p. 145, n. 16.

5. The name Bramimonde has a Germanic sound: cf. Raimund, Rosamund, Sigismund, etc., where the suffix (-mund) means 'protection'. The stem, on the other hand, suggests a connection with Germ. **brammôn* 'to roar' (*FEW*, 1:495–96; 15:240–42; cf. OFr. *brame*, MFr. *bramer*; Tobler and Lommatzsch, 1:1117). However, the substantive *brame* is rare in Old French, and, as Keller, "La conversion de Bramimonde," p. 8, proposes, the stem may have been intended to suggest OFr. *braire* 'to shout'. On the latter, see COMMENTARY, 41, note 23. Beginning at v. 2822, the Oxford manuscript always provides the variant form *Bramidonie*. For the sake of convenience, I shall continue to refer to the Saracen queen as Bramimonde. Is there a connection between Bramimonde and OFr. *immonde* (*FEW*, 4:574, s.v. immundus; see also INTRODUCTION, note 584, and COMMENTARY, 24, note 63), between Bramidonie and OFr. *idoine* (*FEW*, 4:540–41, s.v. idoneus)? For further discussion of the etymology of this name and its variants, and the suggestion that the suffix *-monde* may be related to Germ. *munt* (Modern German *Mund*) 'mouth', see Keller, pp. 6–9 (accepting my explanation of the suffix of Bramidonie [p. 9]). *The Jerusalem Bible*, p. 33, n. *d*: "For

the ancients a name did not merely indicate, rather it made a thing what it was, and a change of name meant a change of destiny." Cf. Genesis 17:5 (Abram/Abraham); 17:15 (Sarai / Sarah); 35:10 (Jacob / Israel); Luke 6:14 (Simon / Peter); Acts 13:9 (Saul/Paul). At her baptism Bramimonde / Bramidonie will be given the Christian name Juliane. COMMENTARY, 48, note 12.

6. Bramimonde mentions her spouse in v. 2824. Her fall in vv. 2825–2826 also parallels that of Alda in vv. 3720, 3726. COMMENTARY, 44, note 8.

7. COMMENTARY, 24.

COMMENTARY 34

1. Blaise, p. 469, n. 12; *Queste*, p. 103. See COMMENTARY, 24.
2. Blaise, par. 342.
3. This is the morning of Day 7. See COMMENTARY, 9.
4. On this search in other versions of the poem, see Horrent, pp. 184–88.
5. Jenkins, note to v. 2854.
6. Knudson, "Serments téméraires et gabs: notes sur un thème littéraire." On the feast motif in epic poems, see Bowra, *Heroic Poetry*, pp. 197–202, 280–82.
7. Comparable boasts are to be found in *Conte del graal*, vv. 4718 ff. The practice is satirized in *Pèlerinage de Charlemagne*, vv. 445 ff. In *Yvain*, vv. 594–595, Kay scornfully observes:

> Aprés mangier, sanz remüer,
> Vet chascuns Loradin tüer.

The closest parallel with Roland's vow is in the *Chanson de Guillaume*. See Jenkins, note to v. 2361; Frappier, *Chansons de geste*, 1:187–91; Payen, *Le Motif du repentir*, pp. 140–45. Frappier contrasts Roland's public oath with what he suggests was Vivien's private promise to God. See also Wathelet-Willem, *Recherches*, 1:295, n. 69. However appealing such *intériorité* may be to modern critics, it is more likely that the medieval poet imagined Vivien, like Roland, making a public vow. It needs to be emphasized that the author of the *Covenant Vivien* has Vivien take his oath during a knighting ceremony (see Frappier, *Chansons de geste*, 1:23).

8. See INTRODUCTION, 14, D.
9. Bédier, *Commentaires*, p. 315. Add *Liber Cathemerinon*, 12: v. 125 (*Prudentius*, 1:110); *Peristephanon*, 11: vv. 120–124 (*Prudentius*, 2:312); *Vie de Saint Thomas Becket*, vv. 1126–1128 (see also Blaise, par. 111: purpuratus, purpureus). White (Lat. *candidus*), signifying purity (Blaise, par. 334; INTRODUCTION, 19, F), was also associated with the martyr's innocence (Blaise, par. 110).
10. See INTRODUCTION, 16, D; COMMENTARY, 24.
11. Jenkins, note to vv. 2874–2875, identifies the three *perruns* in v. 2875 with the four marble objects in vv. 2300, 2312, 2338. See, however, COMMENTARY, 24. In the present passage the number of *perruns* varies with each source. See Segre. On paleographical grounds, it is easy to explain how *un* could have been confused by the scribe with *.iii.* It can also be argued that the three mentions of blows (vv. 2300 ff., 2312 ff., and 2338 ff.; the *Pseudo-Turpin* [Meredith-Jones, p. 193] and *Le Guide du Pèlerin*, pp. 26, 78, also speak of a stone being split in half by three blows [trino ictu]) suggested the existence of three different stones. Jenkins, note to vv. 2874–2875; Segre, note to v. 2875. The same sort of faulty reasoning on the part of the scribe led to invention of the new character Marganice (vv. 1914 ff.) to replace the Caliph, who is falsely reported dead by Ganelon. Jenkins, note to vv. 680–691. Note, however, that the poet refers in v. 2301 to *.X. colps*.

12. See also INTRODUCTION, note 400.

13. Zumthor, "Etude typologique des planctus contenus dans la *Chanson de Roland*," p. 221: "tout au long du *Roland*, le mot *nevold*, dans la bouche de Charles, exprime par rapport à Roland, non seulement la parenté familiale, mais, conformément au sentiment féodal du clan, l'affection du seigneur pour son vassal." Cf. COMMENTARY, 20, note 14 (v. 1846), and note 17 below.

14. Jones, pp. 46, 86.

15. In Conrad, v. 7565, and other sources, Charles sits on a stone. On this tradition in the *Kaiserchronik* (c. 1150), see Lejeune and Stiennon, 1:47–48.

16. Cf. Charles's behavior at the death of his children in the *Vita Karoli Magni* (Halphen, p. 60). The passage in Einhard is based on Suetonius. In the *Pseudo-Turpin* Charles's lament is compared to those of David (Meredith-Jones, p. 205). Another possible source of influence in the *Roland* may be found in the Threnos, or Lamentation for Christ, an incident that does not occur in the gospels but is widely attested in medieval art. Réau, II, 2:519–21; Cames, *Byzance*, pl. 63. Cf. Lejeune and Stiennon, 2: figs. 207, 288.

17. Horrent, p. 241, notes that the Emperor's lament will be echoed by Alda in vv. 3709–3710. Cf. note 27 below. On the conventional aspect of this planctus, see Delbouille, *Genèse*, p. 147. Analyses are made by Zumthor, "Etude typologique des planctus contenus dans la *Chanson de Roland*," pp. 220–23, and Eugene Vinaver, "The Historical Method in the Study of Literature," in *The Future of the Modern Humanities: The Papers Delivered at the Jubilee Congress of the Modern Humanities Research Association in August 1968*, Publications of the Modern Humanities Research Association 1 ([Cambridge?]: Modern Humanities Research Association, 1969), 1:86–105 (summary in *Bulletin bibliographique de la Société Rencesvals* 6 [1971]: 87, item 339).

18. On the meaning of *onur* in v. 2903, see Jones, p. 47; Burgess, *Vocabulaire pré-courtois*, pp. 80, 83.

19. Jones, pp. 44, 46–48.

20. Bédier translates *gaillard* as 'beau', but see Foulet, *Glossaire*: 'qui respire la force'.

21. Vance, *Reading the Song of Roland*, p. 69: "Roland in death expresses something he could never express in life: his body retains both the beauty of his youth and the tragic darkness of death. Shadows in the *Song of Roland* have repeatedly suggested death, and now shadows are located in Roland's very eyes."

22. Cf. vv. 124, 429, 2196, 2253. On this concept in the Middle Ages, see Antonius J. Vermeulen, *The Semantic Development of Gloria in Early-Christian Latin* (Nijmegen: Dekker & Van de Vegt, 1956); María Rosa Lida de Malkiel, *L'Idée de la gloire dans la tradition occidentale: Antiquité, Moyen-âge occidental, Castille*, trans. Sylvia Roubaud, Bibliothèque française et romane, Série C: Etudes littéraires 15 (Paris: Klincksieck, 1968); Burgess, *Vocabulaire pré-courtois*, p. 68, n. 3.

23. Cf. COMMENTARY, 20 (v. 1846).

24. See COMMENTARY, 24.

25. See INTRODUCTION, 17. Bédier translates *li hume estrange* (v. 2911) and *li hume* (v. 2918) as 'les vassaux étrangers' and 'les vassaux', respectively. After pointing out that *hum* is used in the meaning 'vassal' and 'soldier' in the *Song of Roland*, Foulet, *Glossaire*, p. 403, goes on to say: "Voici maintenant des cas où le sens de *hum*, au lieu de se restreindre, se généralise: *li hume* 2918 'les gens'; *li hume estrange* 2911 'les étrangers'."

26. Matthew 2:1–2. According to Einhard, Charlemagne liked foreign visitors (Halphen, p. 64: peregrinos) and greeted them warmly. At receptions for foreign

ambassadors (Halphen, p. 70: exterarum gentium legati), he would gird on a jeweled sword. On hospitality for strangers, see Payen, *Le Moyen Age*, pp. 100–102.

27. 1 Kings 10:1; cf. Ezekiel 23:40. The Queen of Sheba was also viewed as a symbol of the Church of the Gentiles hastening to hear the word of the Lord. Réau, II, 1:294. In *Ronsasvals*, p. 145, the visitors are ladies who ask a question reminiscent of Alda's query in v. 3709. Cf. note 17 above.

28. Cf. the notion of Roland's youth, v. 2916: "*juvente bele*" (see also v. 1401). Frye, *Anatomy of Criticism*, p. 220: "The second phase [of tragedy] corresponds to the youth of the romantic hero, and is in one way or another the tragedy of innocence in the sense of inexperience, usually involving young people." See also Vance, *Reading the Song of Roland*, p. 68. On the medieval ideal of youth, see Burgess, *Vocabulaire pré-courtois*, pp. 118–19.

29. See COMMENTARY, 49 (vv. 3994–3998). Cf. also COMMENTARY, 25 (vv. 2321–2332). Menéndez Pidal, p. 129, believes the original *Song of Roland* ended here (cf. p. 334).

30. In v. 2935 Charles implies that Roland was slain by a Saracen, which is not accurate, for the hero died from the strain of sounding his oliphant. The evidence of Roland's wound should have made it clear how the hero died.

31. On the death wish, see Vance, *Reading the Song of Roland*, p. 70; INTRODUCTION, 7.

32. Blaise, par. 235; Burgess, *Vocabulaire pré-courtois*, pp. 88–89. Labande-Mailfert, "La douleur et la mort," p. 328: "Les soins donnés au corps après la mort reflètent l'attente de la résurrection."

33. Brieger, *English Art*, pp. 103, 196, 208; *Larousse du XXe siècle*, 2:326, s.v. coeur. On the symbolism of whiteness, see INTRODUCTION, 19, F; see also note 9 above.

34. Segre, note to v. 2965 bis.

35. In the *Pseudo-Turpin* bonfires burn all night long (Meredith-Jones, p. 207). According to Lejeune and Stiennon, 1:149 (2: fig. 127), a capital dated before 1150 in the church of San Gil at Luna, Spain, shows the French slain in their leather sacks. However, the four draped figures on the right look to me suspiciously like the Holy Women at the Sepulchre, the round object each holds, perfume (Réau, II, 2:541–43; the number of Holy Women varies from two to four in early iconography [Réau, II, 2:559]), and the "slain," sleeping Roman soldiers (Réau, II, 2:549–50). The scene on the left, which Lejeune and Stiennon identify as the Mass of Saint Giles, is very badly damaged but may be the Meal at Emmaus, with which it is often associated in art (Réau, II, 2:563–66).

36. On the custom of repatriating slain combatants, see Menéndez Pidal, pp. 213–16 (cf. also pp. 114 ff., 124).

COMMENTARY 35

1. Many translators indicate that Charles is setting out for France. This interpretation is supported by Châteauroux, Cambridge, and Conrad's German version. Julian Harris, "*Nen est fins que t'en alges* (*Roland* 2978) and its Context," *Romance Philology* 29 (1976): 511: "the context makes it plain that he was simply about to turn away from the distressing scene of the burial, needing as he did a brief respite."

2. This formal challenge is cited by Horrent, p. 254, as proof that the Baligant episode is extraneous material.

3. On the Charles-Baligant parallel, see Gräf, *Parallelismus im Rolandslied*, p. 19. For beard-pulling as a sign of anger, not pensiveness, see James, "The Drawings of Matthew Paris," pl. XIII.

4. Cf. Roland gazing *fierement* toward the enemy, but *humeles e dulcement* toward his own men (vv. 1162–1163).

5. For the arming motif, see COMMENTARY, 13, note 1. The parallel with the arming in vv. 3140ff. is noted by Gräf, *Parallelismus im Rolandslied*, pp. 19–21; Holland, "Rolandus resurrectus," p. 411. In the Baligant episode the word *targe* is used for 'shield', vv. 3361 and 3569. Elsewhere Turoldus utilizes *escut*. Horrent, p. 254. In v. 2991, the word *escut* (and not *targe*, as Horrent suggests) is employed.

6. See INTRODUCTION, 6.

7. Cames, *Byzance*, fig. 77. See COMMENTARY, 30, note 9.

8. On the *eslais* motif, see Rychner, pp. 128, 135.

9. Jenkins, note to v. 2998, identifies the *apostle* as Saint Peter. Aurelio Roncaglia suggests this may be a Gregorian concept. See his observation following Paul Imbs's paper "Quelques aspects du vocabulaire des plus anciennes chansons de geste," *La Technique littéraire des chansons de geste*, p. 73.

10. On mana, see COMMENTARY, 25, note 18.

11. Bédier, *Légendes épiques*, 3:388, n. 1; Jenkins, note to v. 3017; Horrent, pp. 144, 252; Menéndez Pidal, pp. 124, 175; COMMENTARY, 25, note 3. On the Death and Rebirth archetype, see Calin, *Epic Quest*, pp. 113–15 (Ami), 119 (Huon), 209–10; Vos, "Aspects of Biblical Typology," p. 134 (Rabel and Guinemant as symbols of Christ's Resurrection). See also Campbell, *Hero*, pp. 90–94, 358. On the kindred rejuvenation of Charles, see COMMENTARY, 37 (v. 3122). The oliphant reminds Charles's men of Roland, but it also corresponds to the *hasta* of command. Guinemant thus becomes a marked man (v. 3193) and will be slain by Baligant (v. 3464). Sounding the horn in battle may have been associated with blowing the death in a boar hunt. See Thiébaux, "Mouth of the Boar," p. 290. In v. 3194 Rabel sounds a *graisle* echoing his companion's oliphant call.

12. See COMMENTARY, 14.

13. Holland, "Rolandus resurrectus," pp. 413–18.

14. Such detailing was doubtless considered to be a tour de force on the part of the jongleur declaiming the poem. Calin, *Epic Quest*, p. 47.

15. The term *bacheler* also referred to knights who had not yet received a benefice. Ganshof, *Feudalism*, p. 96.

16. Jenkins, note to v. 3024; Segre, note to v. 3029.

17. The Emperor's 100,000 men are also mentioned in vv. 842, 2907, 2932, etc. For the number of men Charles is believed to have actually taken with him into Spain (5,000 heavy cavalry plus an equal number of infantrymen), see Menéndez Pidal, p. 209 and note 2. On the Emperor's guard in the *Song of Roland*, see Pauphilet, *Le Legs du moyen âge*, p. 88.

18. The role of marshals is discussed by Denholm-Young, *History and Heraldry*, chap. 8, pp. 120–24. The subdivision of the army into smaller units is required for better control in battle. Smail, *Crusading Warfare*, pp. 124, 125. The formation will be maintained until the decisive charge. Smail, p. 126.

19. This parallelism is noted by Gräf, *Parallelismus im Rolandslied*, pp. 21–22.

20. Jenkins, notes to vv. 3014, 3031, 3032, 3038, 3042, 3049, 3050, 3056, 3057, 3067, 3073, 3083, referring frequently to Baist, Boissonnade, and Tavernier.

21. Jenkins, notes to vv. 3093–3095 ("it was here and now, the poet adds, that its name was changed from 'Romaine' to 'Monjoie'"). On the term *Romaine*, see Mandach, *Naissance*, 1:424, n. 412. Bédier does not translate *iloec*, but see Foulet, *Glossaire*.

22. Jenkins, note to v. 3094; Richard Krautheimer, "The Carolingian Revival of Early Christian Architecture," *Art Bulletin* 24 (1942): 36: "The apse of the building contained a mosaic with the Mission of the Apostles, the triumphal arch a group of three figures on either side. In its original state the group to the right represented

Saint Peter giving the pallium to Leo III and a standard to Charlemagne; in the group to the left Christ conferred the keys on a pope, probably Sylvester, and the labarum on Constantine." The entire mosaic is illustrated in Krautheimer, fig. 25; the group to the right (Peter, Leo, and Charlemagne) in Menéndez Pidal, pl. VI, and in *La Chanson de Roland*, ed. Picot, 2:78. For Charles as the "New Constantine," see COMMENTARY, 48, note 10.

23. This may explain the stylized stars on the oriflamme in the Lateran triclinium. On this device in heraldry, see Brault, *Early Blazon*, pp. 197–98, s.v. estencelé. In Conrad, v. 7896, the oriflamme has a portrait of Our Lord with golden flames. The image reminds Conrad, vv. 7898–7900, of the Majestas Domini of the Apocalypse (Revelation 4:5) with its flashes of lightning. Instead of the Twenty-Four Elders, however, Conrad mentions Saint Peter at Christ's feet and the Traditio legis (vv. 7901–7902). See note 26 below. Lejeune and Stiennon 1:133 (2: fig. 121).

24. See INTRODUCTION, 6.

25. The iconographic theme is sometimes referred to as the Donatio. Rumpler, *L'Art roman en Alsace*, pp. 48–51.

26. The formula is modeled on the image of Liberalitas Augusti. Réau, II, 2:315–16. Five Romanesque representations of this theme have been identified in Alsace alone. Rumpler, *L'Art roman en Alsace*, p. 47. Cf. Jenkins, note to v. 3094, and see note 23 above.

27. Curtius, p. 34. Cf. the kindred notion of *translatio studii* to indicate that the center of learning had been shifted from Athens to Rome, then to Paris (earliest attestation in a letter from Eric of Auxerre to Charles the Bald; Curtius, p. 34, n. 1; Zumthor, *Histoire littéraire*, p. 70). The notion, which stems from a passage in Horace's *Epistles*, is found in *Cligés*, vv. 27 ff., as a transfer of *chevalerie* and *clergie* from Greece, to Rome, then to France. Curtius, p. 475.

28. See note 23 above. Cf. Laura Hibbard Loomis, "L'oriflamme de France et le cri 'Munjoie' au XIIe siècle," *Le Moyen Age* 65 (1959): 469–99; Sholod, *Charlemagne in Spain*, pp. 20–21; A. Burger, "Oriflamme," *Festschrift: Walther von Wartburg zum 80. Geburtstag, 18. Mai 1968*, ed. Kurt Baldinger (Tübingen: Niemeyer, 1968), 2:357–62; Henri Diament, "Une interprétation hagio-toponymique de l'ancien cri de guerre des Français *Montjoie Saint-Denis*!" *Romance Notes* 12 (1971): 447–57; idem, "La légende dionysienne et la juxtaposition des toponymes *Montjoie* et *Saint-Denis* dans la formation du cri de guerre," *Romance Notes* 13 (1971): 177–80; Keller, "The *Song of Roland*," pp. 247–48.

COMMENTARY 36

1. The most recent studies of this type of prayer, termed "la prière du plus grand péril" by Frappier, *Chansons de geste*, 2:135 and n. 2, are by Jacques De Caluwé, "Les prières de 'Berte aus grans piés' dans l'oeuvre d'Adenet le Roi," *Mélanges Pierre Le Gentil*, pp. 151–60; J. Garel, "La prière du plus grand péril," in the same homage study, pp. 311–18; and Jacques De Caluwé, "La 'prière épique' dans les plus anciennes chansons de geste françaises," *Olifant* 4, No. 1 (1976): 4–20.

2. *Webster's Seventh New Collegiate Dictionary* (Springfield: G. & C. Merriam Company, 1972), s.v. mercy. Cf. Foulet, *Glossaire*: 'pitié, miséricorde'.

3. The expression is derived from the Memento recited by the priest in the Canon of the mass. Blaise, par. 95, 329.

4. Evidently the split in the oliphant does not impair its sound. Jenkins, note to v. 3119; Horrent, p. 253; COMMENTARY, 24, final paragraph.

5. On the Death and Rebirth archetype, see COMMENTARY, 35, note 11; 37 (v. 3122).

COMMENTARY 37

1. Menéndez Pidal, p. 326; Moignet, p. 225. The slip, if it is one, cannot be ascribed to the so-called Baligant author only, for a similar lapse is found at v. 2271.

2. See COMMENTARY, 20. On the association of the wilderness motif (v. 3127) with tragic destiny, see Frye, *Anatomy of Criticism*, p. 149.

3. Jenkins, note to v. 3123.

4. See COMMENTARY, 35, note 11.

5. Jenkins, note to v. 2976; Bédier, *Commentaires*, pp. 52–53; Moignet, p. 229; Smail, *Crusading Warfare*, pp. 48 ff. On the phrasing, see Bédier, *Commentaires*, pp. 200–201.

COMMENTARY 38

1. The order is also the same in vv. 2499–2501.

2. Gräf, *Parallelismus im Rolandslied*, pp. 36–37.

3. Jenkins, note to v. 3164: "The poet enhances the greatness of Charles by magnifying his opponent."

4. For similar expressions designating Hell, see Blaise, par. 314, and cf. Abisme (COMMENTARY, 17).

5. See OXFORD TEXT, ENGLISH TRANSLATION, v. 3146. On the parallel, see Gräf, *Parallelismus im Rolandslied*, pp. 20–21.

6. See COMMENTARY, 27.

7. Baligant, v. 3235, will echo his son's very thought: "*Bataille i ert, se il ne s'en destolt.*" Cf. v. 3179: "*Mult me merveill se ja verrum Carlun.*"

8. *Charrette*, vv. 1634–1814.

9. See COMMENTARY, 29.

10. Baligant scorns all the others (v. 3189).

11. See COMMENTARY, 36.

12. In Venice IV and other copies, the victory must be over the one who sounds the oliphant, that is, Rabel, Roland's surrogate.

13. Ganshof, *Feudalism*, pp. 118–19; COMMENTARY, 27 (v. 2478).

14. See COMMENTARY, 41 (vv. 3409–3410). Cf. Baligant's offer in vv. 3398–3399.

15. Ganshof, p. 126.

16. Ibid., pp. 125–26.

17. Jenkins, *Glossary*, p. 352, s.v. pan; OXFORD TEXT, ENGLISH TRANSLATION, v. 3141.

18. Amira, "Die Handgebärden," p. 236.

19. Venice IV reads: *envestì*. On this passage, see Segre's notes to vv. 3212 and 3213.

COMMENTARY 39

1. Jenkins's notes provide identifications for many of the peoples listed here. See also A. Prioult, "Au sujet des notions géographiques de Turold," *Les Lettres Romanes* 2 (1948): 287–95 (summary in *Bulletin bibliographique de la Société Rencesvals* 1 [1958]: 35–38); Moignet, pp. 231, 233; Ménard, *Le Rire*, pp. 46–47. Gräf, *Parallelismus im Rolandslied*, p. 22, notes the parallel between Torleu and Dapamort, on the one hand, and Naimes and Jozeran, on the other.

2. Jenkins, *Glossary*, p. 290, s.v. Arabie; Foulet, *Glossaire*, s.v. Arabe.

3. Boissonnade, *Du Nouveau*, pp. 194–95; Jenkins, note to v. 1556: "Latin historians call them *Moabitae* = Moabites, the Biblical enemies of the chosen people"; Foulet, *Glossaire*, s.v. Arrabit.

4. *History of the Crusades*, 1:256.

5. On this subject, see Montague Rhodes James, *Marvels of the East: A Full Reproduction of the Three Known Copies* (Oxford: University Press, 1929). The letter of Prester John, ruler of the East, to Manuel Comnenus contains a list of fabulous races, but is generally dated 1164. Cf. the illustration of the Monstrous Races of the Far Ends of the Earth in a manuscript from Arnstein (Middle Rhine), second half of the twelfth century, now in the British Museum. Swarzenski, *Monuments of Romanesque Art*, pl. 189, fig. 431. On the Cananaens (v. 3238), see Jenkins's note; Skidmore, *Moral Traits of Christians and Saracens*, p. 28; COMMENTARY, 41, note 25.

6. Hatzfeld, *Literature Through Art*, pp. 8–10 and fig. 2, but referring to vv. 1017–1040 and 1932–1934 (Marsile's army). To Hatzfeld's bibliography on Vézelay, p. 225, n. 8, add Mâle, *L'Art religieux*, pp. 326–32; Adolf Katzenellenbogen, "The Central Tympanum at Vézelay, Its Encyclopedic Meaning and Its Relation to the First Crusade," *Art Bulletin* 26 (1944): 141–51; Evans, *Cluniac Art*, p. 71; Réau, II, 2:592. Mâle believed the scene depicted the Pentecost, when in reality it illustrates the Mission of the Apostles (Matthew 28:19). *Sainte Foy* provides a similar list of pagan tribes; C. A. Robson, "Aux origines de la poésie romane: art narratif et mnémotechnique," *Le Moyen Age* 67 (1961): 55.

7. See COMMENTARY, 18 (v. 1751) and 29 (v. 2591). Richard Bernheimer, *Wild Men in the Middle Ages: A Study in Art, Sentiment, and Demonology* (Cambridge: Harvard University Press, 1952), fig. 20, is an eleventh-century illustration of a giant with bristles on his spine and arms. See also Jones, p. 131; Ménard, *Le Rire*, p. 51, n. 117.

8. In Romanesque art the enemies of the Lord are sometimes shown as apes or other monsters. Janson, *Apes and Ape Lore*, p. 180. On the hideous (that is, diabolic) aspect of pagans in the Old French epics, see Ménard, *Le Rire*, pp. 48–49.

9. *History of the Crusades*, 1:568. For Albert of Aix's praise of the Emir Suleiman, see Jenkins, note to v. 3164. On the evolution of attitudes toward the Saracens in the twelfth-century chansons de geste, see Le Goff, *Civilisation*, p. 190; INTRODUCTION, n. 586.

10. Leprosy was generally viewed as a sign of celestial displeasure. However, it was also held to be a source of purification. Jonin, *Personnages féminins*, pp. 360–65; Saul N. Brody, *The Disease of the Soul: Leprosy in Medieval Literature* (Ithaca: Cornell University Press, 1974).

COMMENTARY 40

1. See COMMENTARY, 33.

2. Desmond Stewart, *Early Islam*, Great Ages of Man (New York: Time, 1967), pp. 35–36. On pagan attitudes and postures, see Meredith-Jones, "The Conventional Saracen," pp. 212–13.

3. The dragon symbol is discussed in COMMENTARY, 41.

4. Jenkins, note to v. 3238.

5. See INTRODUCTION, II, C.

6. On this practice in contemporary tactics, see Smail, *Crusading Warfare*, p. 170.

7. Horrent, p. 253, n. 1. Cf. OXFORD TEXT, ENGLISH TRANSLATION, v. 3294.

8. See OXFORD TEXT, ENGLISH TRANSLATION, v. 3294.

9. In vv. 3502 ff., it would appear from Gemalfin's words that Baligant has not actually been able to discern Charlemagne on this occasion and needs a physical description of his adversary. Cf. the Emperor's recognizability in v. 119.

10. As indicated by the many aping actions of the Saracen leader. In the fourteenth-century *Pèlerinage de la vie humaine* by Guillaume de Deguileville, two spears shoot

forth from Envy's eyes. According to Tuve, *Allegorical Imagery*, p. 182, they represent the two forms of this vice's malice: "resentment at others' joy, delight at their adversity." For an illustration of Envy, see Tuve, pp. 188–89 (fig. 55). On Envy's shifty eyes in Guillaume de Lorris's *Roman de la Rose*, see Robertson, *Preface to Chaucer*, pp. 207–8 (figs. 68, 70); Fleming, *Roman de la Rose*, pp. 33–34.

11. See COMMENTARY, 34 (v. 2865). The allusion is an argument against emending v. 3324 to read *passees*, as suggested by many editors on the basis of Venice IV, in order to shorten the hypermetric line.

12. Harden, "Depreciatory Comparison," pp. 71–73 (branches), 67–68 (*pelé*). For a similar interpretation of the apple anecdote in Turoldus's poem, see Capels, "Apple Incident."

13. *Verge pelee* 'penis' is attested in the *Roman de Renart*. *FEW*, 14:499.

14. See COMMENTARY, 9 and 14.

15. For a similar observation in the *Anonymous Chronicle*, see *The Portable Medieval Reader*, pp. 438–39.

16. Bédier's translation of *bons vassals* in this verse as 'bons vassaux' (see also Dufournet, *Cours sur Roland*, p. 148: "parce que dévoués et fidèles, endurants et courageux") is incorrect. Foulet, *Glossaire*, p. 495: "Le 'vassal', c'est proprement celui qui relève d'un suzerain, mais il ne semble pas que le mot soit employé une seule fois dans notre poème en ce sens." Turoldus everywhere uses *hum* in this meaning.

17. His observation in v. 3339 echoes Judas Maccabaeus's assertion that: "victory in war does not depend on the size of the fighting force; it is from heaven that strength comes" (1 Maccabees 3:19). Cf. also Roland's reaction to Oliver's observation that they are many, we are few, in vv. 1039 ff. COMMENTARY, 14.

COMMENTARY 41

1. The word *noit* in this verse is merely a conjecture. See MANUSCRIPT, v. 3395. Cf., however, vv. 3478, 3560, 3658.

2. On the phases of the Battle of Roncevaux, see COMMENTARY, 15 and note 1.

3. On the meaning of *justees* in vv. 3347 and 3384, see COMMENTARY, 14 (vv. 1169, 1187).

4. Malprimes rides a white horse (v. 3369), often a symbol of victory (Revelation 19:11–16; Réau, II, 2: 718–19) but plainly a case of aping here.

5. Revelation 16:16.

6. The offer of fiefs is discussed in COMMENTARY, 38.

7. Gräf, *Parallelismus im Rolandslied*, p. 24, notes the parallel between Baligant's offer and the one made by Charles in vv. 3405 ff.

8. Meredith-Jones, "The Conventional Saracen," p. 216. On Saracen women, see COMMENTARY, 8.

9. On the image of Lechery in medieval art and thought, see Katzenellenbogen, *Allegories*, index, p. 100, s.v. Luxuria; Réau, I: 166–68; Robertson, *Preface to Chaucer*, index, p. 513, s.v. luxuria; Fleming, *Roman de la Rose*, pp. 51, 73 ff. (Oiseuse).

10. On the mutuality of feudal obligations, see Ganshof, *Feudalism*, pp. 83–97.

11. According to Jenkins, note to v. 613, citing Tobler, the expression is a periphrastic locution for 'a person'.

12. See, for example, Ganshof, *Feudalism*, pp. 76–77, 85.

13. Matthew 26:26; Mark 14:22; Luke 22:19; 1 Corinthians 10:16–17. For an ironic use (Mohammed's body), see v. 3233. In the *Policratus* the king's body represents his people; D. W. Robertson, Jr., *The Literature of Medieval England* (New York: McGraw-Hill, 1970), p. 218.

14. Blaise, par. 236.

15. Ibid., par. 234, 236.

16. Ibid., par. 236.

17. Ibid., par. 348. See also Frye, *Anatomy of Criticism*, pp. 142–43.

18. After the duke is wounded, Charles, seeking to protect him, tells him: "Ride by my side now!" (v. 3455). Naimes is referred to in v. 3500 as a *Franceis*. Later tradition will associate him with Bavaria. Jenkins, note to v. 230; Adalbert Hämel, "Vom Herzog Naimes 'von Bayern', dem Pfaffen Konrad von Regensberg und dem Pseudo-Turpin," *Sitzungsberichte der Bayerischen Akademie der Wissenschaften*, Philosophisch-historische Klasse, Jahrgang 1955, Heft 1.

19. In the Bayeux Tapestry Harold is depicted lying dead over the neck of his horse. Illustration in Moignet, p. 260. This is doubtless similar to the swoon attitude in vv. 1988–1989. In vv. 2031–2034 it is clear that Roland's stirrups help him to keep his seat.

20. Alison Moore Smith, "The Iconography of the Sacrifice of Isaac in Early Christian Art," *American Journal of Archaeology* 26 (1922): 159–73; Réau, II, 1:134–37.

21. COMMENTARY, 21 (v. 2010, death's embrace) and 22 (v. 2202, life-giving hug). Cf. vv. 280: *anguisables* 'vexed, frustrated'; 3634: *anguissent* 'pursue'; 823, 2880: *anguissus* 'anguished'.

22. Cf. COMMENTARY, 21 (v. 2009).

23. Bédier translates this term as 'hurler' and Foulet, *Glossaire*, as "'crier', en parlant des blessés qui meurent sur le champ de bataille." Bloch and Wartburg, *Dictionnaire*, dates the modern meaning 1640 only. See Ménard, *Le Rire*, p. 585 and n. 38, citing Raynaud de Lage. Cf. COMMENTARY, 33, note 5 (Bramimonde).

24. In *Roman de Rou*, 2:vv. 8068–8069, Wace observes that the Normans say the English make barking sounds (abaient) because they cannot understand their words. Same remark, vv. 8231–8232 (glatisseient). On the Muslims' battle cries, see Smail, *Crusading Warfare*, p. 76.

25. Jenkins, note to v. 3526. Conrad, v. 2656, describes the King of Funde as having the head of a dog, and in *Perlesvaus*, 1:257, twelve yelping dogs signify the Jews of the Old Law. On dog-headed people (cynocephali), see Janson, *Apes and Ape Lore*, pp. 74–75; Colby, *Twelfth-Century French Literature*, p. 73 (bibliography in n. 2). For a twelfth-century illustration (Arnstein Bible), see COMMENTARY, 39, note 5. The association of Lat. *canis* 'dog' and *Canelius* 'Cananaens' (vv. 3238, 3269) cannot be ruled out. Cf. the depiction of Saint Christopher with a dog's head (Réau, III, 1:308) and the legend connected with Saint Dominic (Domini canis; Réau, III, 1:391). The monastic gesture that consists of touching a finger to the ear to ask for a book by a pagan author is a related instance of clerical humor. Leclercq, *Love of Learning*, p. 157.

26. Cf. vv. 7, 3247. On service to God, see Burgess, *Vocabulaire pré-courtois*, p. 105.

27. Joel T. Rosenthal, *The Purchase of Paradise: Gift Giving and the Aristocracy, 1307–1485*, Studies in Social History (London: Routledge and Paul; Toronto: University of Toronto Press, 1972). Cf. Jones, pp. 116, 138.

28. Exodus 32:1–6, 21, 30, 31. The cult of graven images is forbidden by the Second Commandment (Exodus 34:17). For a bovine idol, see *Fig. 32*.

29. Gräf, *Parallelismus im Rolandslied*, p. 38, notes the parallel with Charles in vv. 2873 ff.

30. The Emperor is immediately recognizable because of his majestic and terrifying appearance (v. 119).

31. Cf. v. 482: "*Par jugement iloec perdrez le chef.*" Cf. also v. 21: "*Si me guarisez e de mort e de hunte!*"

32. Reiterated in vv. 470–471.

33. Cf. vv. 2468–2469:

Paiens recleiment un lur deu, Tervagant,
Puis saillent enz, mais il n'i unt guarant.

34. Reiterated in vv. 558–562.

35. For another interpretation of this passage, see COMMENTARY, 7.

36. Cf. Pilate's answer to the Jews who were urging him to change the inscription placed upon the Cross: "'What I have written, I have written.'" (John 19:22).

37. Jenkins, note to v. 3526.

38. On the importance of not breaking formation, see Smail, *Crusading Warfare*, pp. 129–30.

39. The legends associated with Ogier are discussed by Bédier, *Légendes épiques*, 2:297–304; Boissonnade, *Du Nouveau*, pp. 351–55.

40. Menéndez Pidal, pp. 416–19.

41. Jenkins, note to v. 3534.

42. See INTRODUCTION, 19, 1.

43. *The Jerusalem Bible*, p. 1246.

44. See COMMENTARY, 21.

45. The title is also used for Oliver (v. 1367) and Geoffrey (v. 3806). The line is a nearly verbatim repetition of v. 546 and will occur again in v. 3915. Jenkins transposes verses 3545 and 3546, thus attributing the action to Geoffrey, not Ogier. See next note.

46. Jenkins, note to vv. 3545 ff.: "How many pagans fall before Jeffrey is not clear: does Amborrés hold the dragon, as well as the ensign?"

47. On vv. 3549–3550, see Bédier, *Commentaires*, p. 238.

48. Jenkins, note to vv. 3545 ff.; Mireaux, *Chanson de Roland*, pp. 47–48. See, however, *History of the Crusades*, 1:341, where the vizir's banner is captured in his tent by Robert's bodyguard and, more prosaically, bought by the Count for twenty silver marks and presented to the Patriarch.

49. Revelation 12:1–8.

50. Réau, II, 2:708–12.

51. Modern exegetes tend to interpret the personage more loosely as a prophecy of the Church of the Old and New Covenants.

52. *Queste*, pp. 96–97.

53. Ibid., p. 101.

54. Ibid., p. 103.

55. A dragon banner is ascribed to Pharoah in *Liber Cathemerinon*, 5:56 (*Prudentius*, 1:40), but a similar ensign is borne by the Christians in *Contra Orationem Symmachi*, v. 713, and *Peristephanon*, 1:36 (*Prudentius*, 2:62, 100). Such a device is associated with the Roman imperial armies. *Prudentius*, 1:41, n. *b*; Brault, *Early Blazon*, p. 172, s.v. dragon. A dragon emblem appears on Saracens' shields in illustrations of the *Pseudo-Turpin*. Lejeune and Stiennon, 1: pl. XXVI; 2: fig. 240. The serpent represents prudence in Matthew 10:16.

56. Cf. the Saint George motif in medieval iconography. Réau, III, 2:571–79.

57. *Larousse du XXe siècle*, 1:424, s.v. Attila.

COMMENTARY 42

1. Jenkins, note to v. 3562: "a supreme conflict of Truth against Error." On the iconographic motif of two old men fighting, forehead against forehead, while a woman looks on, see Mâle, *L'Art religieux*, pp. 15–16. Cf. INTRODUCTION, 14, A, 3.

2. André Burger, "Remarques sur la composition de l'épisode de Baligant."

Cf. also the fire from the sparks caused by sword blows in vv. 3586, 3912, 3917. For other parallels, see Gräf, *Parallelismus im Rolandslied*, p. 25.

3. See COMMENTARY, 28.

4. Baligant's proposal is in the tradition of the magistrate's offer in the saints' lives. Delehaye, *Les Passions des martyrs*, pp. 186–89. Cf. John Halverson, "Ganelon's Trial," *Speculum* 42 (1967): 665, n. 10: "Much has been made of this latter combat between the two colossal old men as a kind of archetypal clash of Cross and Crescent. The crusading spirit, though undoubtedly present, is easily exaggerated. Neither, after all, has religious motives; they fight for property, conquest, and revenge. The Emir shouts, 'Preciuse!' not 'Allah Akbar!' Charles cries, 'Mountjoy!' not 'Deus vult!'" On the significance of the phrase in v. 3609 (Deus ne volt) reminiscent of Pope Urban II's cry, see COMMENTARY, 43, note 1.

5. Similarly, in *Psychomachia*, vv. 691–692, Discord strikes Concord, "Yet she was not permitted to pierce the vital parts of thy sacred body."

6. Matthew 8:26. Jenkins, note to vv. 3610 ff., suggests a connection with the legend of a bird who called out to Charles in the wilderness with similar words. Another parallel is to be found in Saint James's query to Charlemagne in the *Pseudo-Turpin*: "*Quid agis, fili mi?*" (Meredith-Jones, p. 91; for variants, see Mandach, *Naissance*, 2:25). Faral, *La Chanson de Roland*, pp. 192–93, suggests that Turoldus was familiar with a tradition stemming from Saint Jerome's commentary on the Book of Daniel that Gabriel's major role was to preside over battles.

7. Including Basan and Basile (v. 489).

8. See COMMENTARY, 27 and cf. Harris, "'Munjoie' and 'Reconuisance' in *Chanson de Roland*, l. 3620," p. 173: "'He shouts "Munjoie" because of his gratitude (or to acknowledge his subservience [to God])'." Harris's interpretation is accepted by Dufournet, *Cours sur Roland*, p. 31.

9. On the *digitus Dei*, see Blaise, par. 133.

10. Cf. Jenkins, *Glossary*, p. 334: "*ad icel que* 'in accord with, on the same scale as'." For discussion see Segre.

11. Blaise, par. 48.

12. Ibid., par. 311; *Charrette*, v. 3852.

COMMENTARY 43

1. Jenkins, note to v. 3609; Mireaux, *Chanson de Roland*, p. 51; Rachel P. Rindone, "An Observation on the Dating of the Baligant Episode in the *Chanson de Roland*," *Romance Notes* 11 (1969): 181–85. See also COMMENTARY, 42, note 4.

2. See COMMENTARY, 27.

3. On the notion of purging the soul from sin, see Blaise, par. 281.

4. Cf. v. 2426. For dust as a symbol of vanity, see Blaise, par. 224, 400. Smoke has a similar connotation in Psalms 37:20; 68:2.

5. The pursuit of the Saracens is discussed in Horrent, p. 256.

6. Viewing from a tower may be a classical reminiscence. Edmond Faral, *Recherches sur les sources latines des contes et romans courtois du moyen âge* (Paris: Champion, 1913), p. 130, citing Ovid. Cf. Petrarch viewing the ruins of Ancient Rome from the roof of the Baths of Diocletian. Mommsen, "Petrarch's Conception of the Dark Ages," p. 232. The Lady in the Tower motif tends to be associated with impending disaster. In addition to Hero and Leander, cf. the Knight's wife in Marie de France's "Laostic," Melibea in *La Celestina*, Anne in Perrault's "Barbe-bleue." Cf. also the Watchman in the tower announcing the fall of Babylon (Isaiah 21:8–9). In *Psychomachia*, v. 183, Superbia wears her hair piled on her head in the form of a tower. In Hildegard

of Bingen's *Liber Scivias*, a tower symbolizes "the divine will preparing salvation." Katzenellenbogen, *Allegories*, p. 42 (figs. 46–47). On the use of the viewing motif in early French epics, see Rychner, pp. 130–31; in twelfth-century romances, see Brault, "Chrétien de Troyes' *Lancelot*," p. 149; Cormier, "The Present State of Studies on the *Roman d'Enéas*," p. 26. A tower marked the spot of Christ's baptism in the Jordan as early as the sixth century and recurs in the iconography of that scene. Woodruff, "Illustrated Manuscripts of Prudentius," p. 61, n. 1. For sepulchral associations, see *The Year 1200*, 1:63–65. The tower is also a "point of epiphany" and a "place of confrontation between the human and the supernatural." Frye, *Anatomy of Criticism*, p. 203; Calin, *Epic Quest*, p. 195.

7. Bramimonde does not fall from her tower; symbolically, it is Marsile who does. The iconography of King Ahaziah's death parallels that of the Saracen king's demise. Ahaziah, having fallen from a balcony, was informed by the prophet Elijah that he would die in his bed (2 Kings 1:1–18). However, medieval artists consistently depicted Ahaziah plunging to his death, a symbol of Pride's Fall. Réau, II, 1:355–56; Tuve, *Allegorical Imagery*, p. 120. Cf. the defenestration of Jezabel in 2 Kings 9:30–37. Réau, II, 1:301. In *Prose Lancelot*, 3:426, the hero threatens to throw Camille down from a tower unless she surrenders.

8. In Conrad, vv. 8595 ff., Marsile sees the flight of the Saracens and dies. Bramimonde throws herself over him, vainly offers anything to save him from the fires of Hell, then mounts the tower. The poet may have visualized Marsile's soul as a blackbird leaving his mouth at the moment of death. Cf. the death of Saladin in James, "The Drawings of Matthew Paris," pls. VII, XX. On a similar mission, devils form a cortege in the *Pseudo-Turpin* (Meredith-Jones, p. 229) and a procession in *Conte del graal*, v. 6968.

9. For iconographic parallels, see Réau, II, 2:663–757. Should this event occur after v. 2759? See Horrent, pp. 250–51. For similar events in the epics, see Skidmore, *Moral Traits of Christians and Saracens*, p. 42, who also cites, pp. 67–70, many contemporary French and Latin chronicles detailing such sieges.

10. Cf. the Ancient of Days in Daniel's vision and, especially, the Son of Man in Revelation 1:14: "His head and his hair were white as white wool or as snow"; Réau, II, 2:686. Christ the Reaper appears in Revelation 14:14 (Réau, II, 2:713–14).

11. Augier, "Conversions féminines," pp. 99–100.

12. According to Einhard, Charles steadfastly demonstrated *magnanimitas* and *perpetua constantia* despite repeated betrayals (Halphen, p. 24; cf. also pp. 64, 66). On the virtue itself, consult Marian P. Whitney, "Queen of Mediaeval Virtues: Largesse," *Vassar Mediaeval Studies by Members of the Faculty of Vassar College*, ed. Christabel Forsyth Fiske (New Haven: Yale University Press, 1923), pp. 183–215; *Cligés*, p. xvii. For divergent interpretations of Charles's motivation, see Menéndez Pidal, pp. 126–27; Jones, p. 137: "Even the mercy shown to Bramimunde does not necessarily depend upon Christian tradition, since the pagan Greeks and Romans had also advised showing mercy to the suppliant" (see also p. 170); Vance, *Reading the Song of Roland*, pp. 90–91: "[Bramimonde] is the only person in the *Song of Roland* who has experienced a personal tragedy equivalent to Charlemagne's own ... so Charlemagne is perhaps drawn to his enemy precisely because she is the only figure in the poem who has suffered in life as much as he." The Saracen converts Guibourc (*Chanson de Guillaume*) and Bramimonde are compared by Skidmore, *Moral Traits of Christians and Saracens*, p. 48, and Frappier, *Chansons de geste*, 1:176–79.

13. Lejeune and Stiennon, 1:133–34.

14. Ibid., 2: fig. 126; Cames, *Byzance*, p. 62 and fig. 84.

15. See, however, Crozet, "Le chasseur et le combattant."

16. Lejeune and Stiennon, 1:134–35.

17. See INTRODUCTION, 14, C. Skidmore, *Moral Traits of Christians and Saracens*, p. 109, n. 12, cites eight chansons de geste, in addition to the *Roland*, where special clemency is shown to a captured Saracen princess. In v. 3680 *prisun* refers to benign captivity rather than harsh incarceration. Cf. INTRODUCTION, note 301.

18. Jenkins, note to v. 3657: "An idea often expressed by the historians of the Crusades: 'pro nobis pugnat Deus!'" Note that Saragossa's mountain (v. 6) has been flattened, as it were, by the fury of Charles's onslaught.

19. Cf. this fury with the night of peaceful watching over the body of Alda (v. 3731).

20. See COMMENTARY, 29.

21. Cf. the destruction of Babylon in Jeremiah 51:20 ff., where a mace or hammer is specifically mentioned. See also the city in ruins in Isaiah 24:12.

22. E.g., Moses and Aaron before Pharaoh (Exodus 7:8–13).

23. Burning may be considered to be condign punishment for the diabolic sorcerers. On whether v. 3670 should read *prendre* or *pendre*, see Jenkins; *La Chanson de Roland*, ed. Whitehead, p. 129; Segre.

24. Matthew 3:10. For two eleventh-century illustrations, see Réau, II, 1:450.

25. Réau, II, 2:299.

26. Ibid., III, 1:238.

27. Jeremiah 50:2. Delehaye, *Les Passions des martyrs*, pp. 215–16; Ménard, *Le Rire*, p. 79 and n. 178. Cf. INTRODUCTION, 19, L, and OXFORD TEXT, ENGLISH TRANSLATION, v. 8.

28. Réau, II, 2:281–82. Cf. the legend of Saint Aphrodisius (Réau, III, 1:125).

29. For a discussion of the various textual problems in this passage, consult Horrent, pp. 148–49; Segre, pp. 640–41.

30. According to *Liber Cathemerinon*, 1: vv. 37–40, 45–48 (*Prudentius*, 1:8), the evil spirits of night flee in fear at dawn, awakening being the symbol of hope.

31. White is associated with martyrdom. See COMMENTARY, 34, note 9.

32. On these traditions, see Jenkins, notes to vv. 3685–3687, 3687, 3689–3694. In the rhymed versions Ganelon escapes, only to be recaptured. Horrent, pp. 194–98, 351–52. Charles's sense of urgency (v. 3696) is chiefly due to his burning desire to bring Ganelon to justice.

33. Delbouille, *Genèse*, pp. 124–25, discusses the possibility of a pilgrimage by the poet to the places mentioned in this passage. Cf. also Meredith-Jones, pp. 321–22; Horrent, pp. 189–94.

34. Horrent, pp. 147–50.

35. Jenkins, note to vv. 3685–3687; Horrent, p. 143.

36. Cf. the arrival of Charles at Aix and that of Baligant at Saragossa, vv. 2812–2826. Both rulers are confronted by female personages.

COMMENTARY 44

1. On this theme, consult Ernst H. Kantorowicz, "The King's Advent," *Art Bulletin* 26 (1944): 207–31; E. Baldwin Smith, *The Architectural Symbolism of Imperial Rome and the Middle Ages* (Princeton: Princeton University Press, 1956), p. 152.

2. Blaise, par. 178.

3. Ibid., par. 202–3.

4. Cf. INTRODUCTION, 13 and 18, H.

5. For a similar view, see Vance, *Reading the Song of Roland*, p. 46. The authenticity of the Alda episode is discussed by Horrent, pp. 134–40; Menéndez Pidal, pp. 366–67. On the variant versions, see Horrent, pp. 198–202; Nichols, "The Interaction of Life and Literature," pp. 70–76.

6. See note 8 below.

7. Cf. vv. 2709 and 3698.

8. The only surviving illustration of this scene is in a fourteenth-century manuscript of Stricker's *Karl der Grosse*. Lejeune and Stiennon, 1:238 and pl. XXVII. Prince Louis's presence is an error on the part of the miniaturist, for Charles's son is merely mentioned in the imperial offer to Alda. On the Bramimonde-Alda parallel, see Riquer, *Chansons de geste*, pp. 92–93; Vos, "Aspects of Biblical Typology," p. 155; COMMENTARY, 33. Riquer, p. 93, also notes opposition between Marsile and Bramimonde, on the one hand, and Roland and Alda, on the other.

9. On Alda as a prophetic figure, see INTRODUCTION, 19, 1. In a sense, Alda's role is also to inject sorrow where joy reigns (v. 3682). On the latter verse, see Segre.

10. Riquer, *Chansons de geste*, p. 92, writes of the "profond amour de la belle Aude, qui n'a pas eu besoin de breuvage, comme Yseut la blonde, pour être conduite au trépas." See Nichols's critique of the latter view in "The Interaction of Life and Literature," p. 69. Cf. the late-fifteenth-century Cambridge copy, where *Morte sera belle Aude pour l'amour de Roullant* (v. 4237). Horrent, p. 372. Cf. COMMENTARY, 26, note 13. On contemporary marriage contracts, see Benton, "Clio and Venus," p. 20.

11. Cf. v. 840: "*Deus! se jol pert, ja n'en avrai escange.*" Jones, p. 43.

12. Horrent, p. 136; Aebischer, *Préhistoire*, p. 277. Cf. Skidmore, *Moral Traits of Christians and Saracens*, p. 108: "The most famous expression of profound love between the sexes in the chansons de geste."

13. Alda is referred to as *gente* (v. 1720) and *bel(e)* (vv. 3708, 3723). No details are provided, but the poet doubtless had in mind ideal features such as those discussed by Colby, *Twelfth-Century French Literature*, pp. 25–72.

14. See COMMENTARY, 20. Alda's question echoes that of the mysterious visitors in v. 2912. Horrent, p. 241. There is perhaps, in Oliver's mention of Alda's embrace (v. 1721), a suggestion that his sister will perform her wifely duties with enthusiasm.

15. Note also vv. 1089 = 3718; 2030 = 3719. Rita Lejeune, *Recherches sur le thème: les chansons de geste et l'histoire*, Bibliothèque de la Faculté de philosophie et lettres de l'Université de Liège, 108 (Liège: Faculté de philosophie et lettres, 1948), pp. 241 ff.; Horrent, p. 257, n. 2; Brault, "Le Thème de la Mort," p. 224.

16. Faral, *La Chanson de Roland*, p. 167: "La mort d'Aude, c'est le souvenir de Roland qui revient, plus émouvant que jamais. Le preux a été vengé de la perfidie sarrasine: le sera-t-il de la félonie de Ganelon?" Horrent, p. 242: "[L'épisode d'Aude] m'apparaît comme le véritable achèvement de la bataille de Roncevaux, le couronnement de l'action funeste de Ganelon. Aude est la dernière victime de Roncevaux." Aebischer, *Préhistoire*, p. 277: "elle incarne à mes yeux le seul sentiment que n'anime pas Roland, l'amour absolu. Elle représente ce sentiment à l'état idéal, de même que son fiancé représente l'idéal du sacrifice suprême à la cause féodale et chrétienne. . . . de tous les homages qui vont à la gloire de Roland, celui d'Aude est le plus émouvant. C'est là la raison de l'épisode, et la seule, la raison pour laquelle l'amour paraît et meurt, si étranger que soit ce sentiment à cette chanson essentiellement guerrière." Calin, *Epic Quest*, p. 10: "One of Roland's greatest claims to glory was that this beautiful girl loved him so much that she could not survive him."

17. On this custom, see Jenkins, note to v. 1750.

18. Réau, II, 2:604–11; Cames, *Byzance*, pp. 88–90 and pl. 42. Cf. the Entombment of the Virgin (Réau, II, 2:613).

19. Réau, II, 2:616. Cf. COMMENTARY, 18 and 26.

20. Zaal, *A lei francesa*, pp. 119–20: "Le motif de la virginité apparaît peut-être une fois dans le *Roland*. Après avoir appris la mort de Roland, la belle Aude refuse d'accepter comme mari le fils de l'empereur (v. 3714–3719). La situation est quelque peu analogue au passage du *Saint Alexis* où l'épouse, après la mort d'Alexis, déclinera tout offre de mariage (v. 492–493). C'est là une sorte de transposition littéraire de la

tradition de veuvage consacré: ici la 'veuve' est vierge." In Conrad, vv. 8717–8722, Alda prays to the Virgin's Son and for the grace of dying immaculate so that she may reside with the virgins in heaven. Cf. INTRODUCTION, 19, F.

21. The formula in question was the object of numerous transpositions in Romanesque art. Cf. the Master of the Apocrypha Drawing's rendering of the Burial of Judas Maccabaeus (*Fig. 33*) and the Death of Saint Aubin (Beckwith, *Early Medieval Art*, fig. 175). In Gothic art Hecuba is shown embracing the dead body of Troilus in similar fashion (Panofsky and Saxl, "Classical Mythology," p. 363, fig. 50). The formula also influenced El Greco's *Burial of the Conde de Orgaz* at Toledo.

COMMENTARY 45

1. On the trial, consult Jenkins, note to v. 3741; Bédier, *Commentaires*, pp. 317–20; Ruggero M. Ruggieri, *Il processo di Gano nella "Chanson de Roland"* (Florence: Sansoni, 1936); Halverson, "Ganelon's Trial"; Gérard, "L'axe Roland-Ganelon"; Stranges, "The Character and Trial of Ganelon." The manner in which this episode is related in the other versions of the poem is discussed by Horrent, pp. 150–54, 203.

2. The scene is anticipated by the scourging of the idol of Apollo, vv. 2586–2588.

3. See COMMENTARY, 20.

4. No pillar is mentioned in the accounts found in Matthew 27:26, Mark 15:15, Luke 23:16, or John 19:1. However, a column invariably appears in early depictions of the scene because of the relic shown in Jerusalem and Rome. The column is mentioned in *Tituli historiarum*, 41 (*Prudentius*, 2:364, 366; for Saint Jerome's mention of this relic, see ibid., p. 366, n. *a*). Millet, *Recherches*, pp. 652–53; Réau, II, 2:452–53. Typologically, the scene was said to have been prefigured by the beating administered to Lamech by his two wives, by that to Job by his spouse, and by Achior tied to a tree. Réau, II, 2:446–48. On the narrative technique, cf. below (v. 3762).

5. The term *estache* is regularly used in reference to the Scourging. See Tobler and Lommatzsch, 3:1330. In *Pèlerinage de Charlemagne*, v. 349, the revolving palace spins on an *estache*. Ogier's gab in this respect (vv. 521, 524), is compared to Samson tearing down the temple pillars. Horrent, *Pèlerinage*, p. 70. Cf. *The Medieval French Roman d'Alexandre*, vol. 2, *Version of Alexandre de Paris*, eds. E. C. Armstrong, D. L. Buffum, B. Edwards, and L. F. H. Lowe, Elliott Monographs in the Romance Languages and Literatures 37 (Princeton: Princeton University Press, 1937), p. 219, v. 3390: "Les estaches du pont sont de marbre votis." On the identity of *estache* in v. 3737 and *perrun* in v. 2556, see COMMENTARY, 24. The meaning of *perrun* in v. 2268 is also discussed in the same commentary. Cf. the pillar (culumbe) to which the pagans tie the idol of Apollo (v. 2586).

6. "The month in which the world began" and "when God created Man," according to "The Nun's Priest's Tale" in Chaucer's *Canterbury Tales*. March corresponds roughly to Nisan, the first month of the ecclesiastical year in the Jewish calendar. Exodus 12:1. *The Jerusalem Bible*, p. 91, n. *b*. Cf. Le Goff, *Civilisation*, p. 224; Payen, *Le Moyen Age*, p. 77: "L'année commence à des dates variables, souvent à Pâques, parfois à la Sainte-Marie-Madeleine, le 22 juillet."

7. As suggested by John A. Stranges, "The Significance of Bramimonde's Conversion in the *Song of Roland*," *Romance Notes*, 16 (1974), 193. Cf. INTRODUCTION, 18, H.

8. See COMMENTARY, 48.

9. In the latter pose, he reminds us of the formula of the Arraignment Before Pilate (Réau, II, 2:449–50), this attitude, like the scourging, being a grotesquely inverted image of the Suffering Christ. Cf. Lejeune and Stiennon, 2: fig. 124.

10. Cf. Frye, *Anatomy of Criticism*, p. 158 (the hated father figure as demonic modulation of the just wrath of God).

11. Jenkins, notes to vv. 740–744, 3756. Oliver and Roland's deduction that Ganelon betrayed them (vv. 1024–1025; in 1145–1148, Roland specifies it was for money) was merely a shrewd guess.

12. See INTRODUCTION, 19, K.

13. After reviewing earlier interpretations of this verse, Brook, "Le 'forfait' de Roland dans le procès de Ganelon," suggests that *en or e en aveir* means 'valeur, honneur, réputation' and translates this verse as: 'Roland a nui à ma réputation, à ma valeur'. Cf. Hackett, "La féodalité dans la *Chanson de Roland* et dans *Girart de Roussillon*," pp. 21–24; Köhler, "'Conseil des barons'," p. 22, n. 47; Moignet, p. 262; Dufournet, *Cours sur Roland*, p. 39.

14. Jenkins, note to v. 3758.

15. See INTRODUCTION, 19, G.

16. See COMMENTARY, 6, 7, 9, 19.

17. See INTRODUCTION, 19, G.

18. He also implies cowardice (v. 1780: "Pur un sul levre vat tute jur cornant") and empty boasting (v. 1781: "Devant ses pers vait il ore gabant"), characteristics properly associated with the traitor. INTRODUCTION, 19, G, and COMMENTARY, 19. Similarly, in the apple anecdote, the diabolic Ganelon insinuates that Roland is the Seducer. COMMENTARY, 6. Ganelon's behavior parallels that of Judas in this respect. When Mary Magdalene anoints Jesus at Bethany, Judas protests that the ointment could have been sold and the money distributed to the poor. But, according to John 12:6: "He said this, not because he cared about the poor, but because he was a thief; he was in charge of the common fund and used to help himself to the contributions."

19. See INTRODUCTION, 10, B, 2.

20. In Conrad Charles views Ganelon's public avowal as adequate grounds for conviction (vv. 8747–8751). He is about to sentence the traitor when Ganelon's kinsmen intervene, begging him for mercy (vv. 8752–8770). The *Karlamagnús Saga* abridges the narrative of the trial, adding simply that Naimes was instrumental in persuading the council to convict Ganelon. Aebischer, *Rolandiana Borealia*, pp. 237–38. On the meaning of *desfier* in v. 3775, see COMMENTARY, 5, note 23.

21. On the revival of interest in written laws c. 1100, see Bloch, *Feudal Society*, 1:116–17. Jenkins, note to v. 3741, points out that the court is not supposed to "try to get at the truth of the charge" but merely to rule on "the logic of the plea and the validity of the proofs."

22. Jenkins, note to v. 3741, suggests that the Franks withdraw twice. However, it seems more logical to assume that they listen to Ganelon's complete defense, then retire to deliberate. Jenkins asserts that the Auvergnats are "the most inclined to clemency" and persuade the other judges to excuse Ganelon. He also places a colon at the end of v. 3796, linking fear of Pinabel in the next line to the Auvergnats. These character traits are pure speculation on Jenkins's part. In my view, the actions and words detailed in vv. 3797 ff. refer to all the barons involved in the deliberation and not to any particular group. On the meaning of *curteis*, see OXFORD TEXT, ENGLISH TRANSLATION, v. 3796.

23. He is mentioned in passing in v. 362.

24. For Jenkins's interpretation, see OXFORD TEXT, ENGLISH TRANSLATION, v. 3792.

25. Cf. also OXFORD TEXT, ENGLISH TRANSLATION, v. 3812.

26. Jones, p. 110; Benton, "Clio and Venus," p. 24.

27. Jenkins, note to v. 3741; Karl-Heinz Bender, "Les métamorphoses de la royauté de Charlemagne dans les premières épopées franco-italiennes," *Cultura Neolatina* 21 (1961): 164–74; Gérard, "L'axe Roland-Ganelon," p. 456.

28. See COMMENTARY, 44.

29. According to Dessau, "L'idée de la trahison," p. 23, *fel* in v. 3829 characterizes an individual who broke the contract of vassalage.

30. In the *Pseudo-Turpin* Thierry is present at Roland's death (Meredith-Jones, p. 195). The thirteenth-century French translation in the *Grandes Chroniques* says that he knew about Ganelon's plot (ed. Mortier, p. 81: et savoit tout le covine), but no such mention appears in the Latin original (Meredith-Jones, p. 209).

31. See INTRODUCTION, 10, B, 5.

32. Réau, II, 1:254. The Thierry-Pinabel encounter is analyzed in terms of a suspense device by Menéndez Pidal, pp. 138–39; Vance, *Reading the Song of Roland*, p. 85. For possible comic effects, cf. Ménard, *Le Rire*, pp. 59–61.

33. See COMMENTARY, 14. Kibler, "Roland and Tierri," p. 32: "It is the scene with Tierri which enables us to appreciate the wisdom and insight of Roland. Like Roland, Tierri defends an unpopular position, and like him he is proven to be right. . . . the poet seems clearly to intend us to recognize God's approval of both the victory and the methods of Roland through His approval and intervention in that of Tierri."

34. Note that v. 3755 (E Oliver, li proz e li curteis) is identical to v. 576. Cf. also v. 176 (E Oliver, li proz e li gentilz) and OXFORD TEXT, ENGLISH TRANSLATION, V. 3796.

35. Thierry explains that he must pass judgement *par anceisurs* (v. 3826). In the *Song of Roland* words like *anceissor* represent everything a knight holds dear, above all his Maker. COMMENTARY, 14. Turoldus makes it clear that the champion is Geoffrey of Anjou's brother (vv. 3806, 3819) but does not specify that he is any relation to Roland. Jones, p. 71; Gérard, "L'axe Roland-Ganelon," pp. 457–58.

36. The locution *que que*, akin to MFr. *quoique*, occurs only once in the *Song of Roland* but is common in Old French. Jenkins translates this phrase as follows: 'Whatever wrong Roland may have done to Ganelon'.

37. See INTRODUCTION, 11, B.

38. See COMMENTARY, 41.

39. Jones, p. 28, translates *isnel* (v. 3839) as 'courageous'. Cf., however, vv. 1312 and 3885 (isnels e legers).

40. Jenkins, note to v. 3741; COMMENTARY, 26.

41. On this custom, see Bédier, *Commentaires*, pp. 318–20; Menéndez Pidal, p. 138; Jones, pp. 55–56. *The Song of Roland*, trans. Harrison, suggests that v. 3852 should be interpreted to mean that Charles offers himself as surety for Thierry.

42. Jenkins, note to v. 3853. Cf. Bédier's explanation of the four marble slabs in v. 2272 (COMMENTARY, 24).

43. *Le Roman de Renart: Première branche*, vv. 468–486. See COMMENTARY, 2, note 15.

44. On the meaning of arming (vv. 3863–3868), see INTRODUCTION, 10, A, 3.

45. Genesis 4:5. It would appear from the Bible narrative that God prefers Abel's unstinted offering to Cain's minimal contribution. *Genesis*, trans. E. A. Speiser, The Anchor Bible 1 (Garden City: Doubleday, 1964), p. 30.

46. Réau, II, 1:95.

47. Cf. the meaning of *pitet* in vv. 822 and 825 (INTRODUCTION, 16, A.).

COMMENTARY 46

1. On the legal and spiritual aspects of this duel, consult Menéndez Pidal, pp. 137–38; Le Gentil, pp. 116–17; Holland, "Rolandus resurrectus," pp. 405–6.

2. Roques, "Pour le commentaire *d'Aucassin et Nicolette* 'esclarier le cuer'," pp. 729, 733.

3. John 13:31.

4. John 17:1. Blaise, par. 170, 196. Bloch and Wartburg, *Dictionnaire*, s.v. clarifier:

"Emprunté du latin ecclésiastique *clarificare* 'glorifier'; n'a que ce sens avant le XVIe siècle." See also observation concerning v. 3989.

5. Jones, p. 53: "Bédier translates *car te recreiz* as 'reconnais-toi vaincu', but it is unlikely that Pinabel would offer homage to a man who has just surrendered to him. He is not asking Thierry to surrender, but merely to cease fighting. Nevertheless, Thierry cannot do so for fear of risking reproach."

6. Jenkins, note to v. 3893.

7. Cf. also Baligant's offer to Charles (v. 3593: "Deven mes hom, en fiet le te voeill rendre"). On the formula *par amur e par feid*, see Jones, p. 44, n. 17.

8. Jenkins, note to v. 3783.

9. See COMMENTARY, 47.

10. Jenkins, note to v. 3907: "Pinabel's code of family honor is exactly that of Roland and of Oliver." See also COMMENTARY, 45.

11. This celestial intervention may be visualized as a Hand of God. Cf. the tenth-century Corbie Psalter showing the Manus Dei protecting David while a devil is perched on Goliath's helmet. Réau, II, 1:261.

12. Hanging (v. 3932) still appears to be the punishment in store for Ganelon. Cf. OXFORD TEXT, ENGLISH TRANSLATION, v. 1409.

13. Cf. also vv. 2817 (Baligant accompanied by four dukes) and 2820 (four counts hold his stirrup).

14. There is no mention of Veronica in the gospels, but the legend of the woman who wiped Christ's face with a cloth as he made his way to Calvary—an impression of his features remains on the cloth, whence her name, perhaps (*vera icona* 'true image') —has a long and curious history. The purported relic has been at Saint Peter's in Rome since the beginning of the eighth century. Donald Attwater, *The Penguin Dictionary of the Saints*, Penguin Reference Books (Baltimore: Penguin, 1965), p. 334. The cult of Veronica became very popular in the latter part of the Middle Ages. Réau, II, 2:19, 465; III, 3:1314–17. In 1 Samuel 18:4, Jonathan gives his cloak to David, as a sign of his devotion, after the latter has slain Goliath. Vos, "Aspects of Biblical Typology," p. 138. However, Charles does not present the cloak to Thierry. Note, finally, the custom of investing with a robe (Isaiah 22:21) and the mantle of integrity (Isaiah 61:10; Baruch 5:2).

15. Jenkins, note to v. 3941.

16. See COMMENTARY, 5.

17. Jean Frappier, "Les destriers et leurs épithètes," *La Technique littéraire des chansons de geste*, p. 93, n. 15, is uncertain as to whether a historical allusion or irony is involved here.

18. 1 Samuel 18:6–7. Vos, "Aspects of Biblical Typology," p. 141, believes this scene is patterned on Christ's Entry into Jerusalem. See note 20 below.

19. Réau, II, 1:262; II, 2:398.

20. See COMMENTARY, 2 (aping of the Entry into Jerusalem). Since the ass is a symbol of humility (Frye, *Anatomy of Criticism*, p. 152), its use here suggests that Thierry is again imitating Roland. Cf. INTRODUCTION, 19, F.

21. See COMMENTARY, 7 (Ganelon threatens Marsile) and 20 (Ganelon's preliminary punishment).

COMMENTARY 47

1. Jenkins, note to v. 3741. However, nothing is said of the Saracen hostages. Menéndez Pidal, pp. 266–67. On the behavior of the Franks, who act with dispatch once they have seen a sign from Heaven, see INTRODUCTION, 19, K.

2. On the meaning of *altroi*, see OXFORD TEXT, ENGLISH TRANSLATION, v. 1963. Cf. *Perlesvaus*, line 5270: *Salomons nos dit que li pechieres qui autrui maudit, maudit soi meïsmes.*

3. Numbers 16:31–35; Joshua 7:24–26.

4. Bibliography in G. D. West, *An Index of Proper Names in French Arthurian Romances, 1150–1300*, University of Toronto Romance Series 15 (Toronto: University of Toronto Press, 1969), pp. 130–31.

5. Bibliography and discussion in Bédier, *Commentaires*, pp. 120–22; Horrent, pp. 180, 182, 345–46; Segre, p. 355 (passage cited, pp. 353–54). See also OXFORD TEXT, ENGLISH TRANSLATION, v. 763. Venice VII adds that Alexander's assassins are also to be numbered among Ganelon's ancestors. Horrent, pp. 180, 182.

6. Jenkins, note to v. 3953. One is reminded, too, of the rich lore surrounding the Judas tree—often, in French sources, an elder. On this and other traditions, see Taylor, "The Gallows of Judas Iscariot." Cf. Brault, "Girart d'Amiens and the *Pseudo-Turpin Chronicle*," pp. 76–78. On the association of the hanging of Ganelon's relatives and Judas's suicide, see Vos, "Aspects of Biblical Typology," p. 140.

7. See OXFORD TEXT, ENGLISH TRANSLATION, v. 3956.

8. Jenkins, *Glossary*, p. 294, suggests the translation 'Short-and-dark'.

9. See COMMENTARY, 20 (vv. 1817–1829).

10. Ménard, *Le Rire*, p. 75, notes that a cruel execution would have pleased a medieval audience. The punishment of Ganelon is alluded to in a document dated 1131. Horrent, p. 292, citing Rajna.

11. See OXFORD TEXT, ENGLISH TRANSLATION, v. 3968.

12. Numbers 16:28–34.

13. Jenkins, note to v. 3963. Add *Thèbes*, vv. 6746 ff. and cf. *Cligés*, vv. 1482–1485 (dragging to death). On quartering and other means of execution in the chansons de geste, see Skidmore, *Moral Traits of Christians and Saracens*, pp. 43, 86–87, 94–95; Ménard, *Le Rire*, p. 78 (bibliography in n. 174).

14. Bédier, *Commentaires*, pp. 319–20.

15. Robert-François Damiens was also quartered in 1757 for daring to cut Louis XV with a penknife to "warn" him and to remind him of his duties. Before he was executed, Damiens was systematically tortured. The hand that held the knife was burned, and molten lead and boiling oil were poured over his wounds.

16. *Psychomachia*, vv. 718–725; Mickel, "Parallels in *Psychomachia* and *Roland*," pp. 450–51. For illustrations, see Katzenellenbogen, *Allegories*, p. 3. Cf. *Roland*, v. 3971.

17. Katzenellenbogen, p. 58, n. 3, citing Gregory the Great and listing several examples in medieval art: "The theologians are agreed that sinners are punished through the organs of their lust." Add the fourth-century *Visio sancti Pauli*. Réau, II, 2:730. Cf. the tariff system of penances, where an appropriate act must be performed to show repentance for each sin. Payen, *Le Motif du repentir*, pp. 27 ff. For another possible instance of condign punishment in Turoldus's poem, see COMMENTARY, 21 (v. 1903) and note 23. See also following note. In the rhymed versions several tortures are proposed for Ganelon, among them the condign punishment of dying of thirst. Horrent, p. 354.

18. On another plane, quartering may also be a demonic parody of ritual killing involving *sparagmos*, or the tearing apart of the sacrificial body. On this concept, see Frye, *Anatomy of Criticism*, p. 148.

19. *Peristephanon*, 5: vv. 537–544 (*Prudentius*, 2:200).

COMMENTARY 48

1. This commentary constitutes a revised and expanded version of views first put forth in my article "'Truvet li unt le num de Juliane': sur le rôle de Bramimonde dans la *Chanson de Roland*." Vos, "Aspects of Biblical Typology," pp. 159–60, inter-

prets Bramimonde as a *sponsa coelestis*, a view rejected by Keller, "La conversion de Bramimonde," p. 5. On pp. 156–59, Vos also suggests a connection with Rahab. Keller, p. 22, believes that the entire episode was interpolated in the Anglo-Norman version of the poem, which he dates in the third quarter of the twelfth century. For a summary and critique of Ann Tukey Harrison's unpublished paper, "A Feminist Look at the *Chanson de Roland*," read at the Tenth Conference on Medieval Studies at Western Michigan University in 1975, which deals in a large measure with Bramimonde, see Sara Sturm's review in *Olifant* 3, no. 3 (1976): 228–29. For another interpretation, see Stranges, "Significance of Bramimonde's Conversion." On the historical background of conversion in the chansons de geste, see C. Meredith-Jones, "Vis baptizari?" *Culture* 24 (1963): 250–73.

2. On the variant versions, consult Horrent, pp. 203–6; Keller, pp. 11–18.

3. In v. 154 Marsile promised Charles to come to Aix to be baptized *Enz en voz bainz que Deus pur vos i fist*. This was of course treachery on his part. On the other hand, Bramimonde's conversion is *par veire conoisance* (v. 3987), a change of heart brought about, at least in part, no doubt by the martyrdom of the French at Roncevaux. See COMMENTARY, 18, note 12.

4. Vance, *Reading the Song of Roland*, pp. 90–91, suggests that what prompts Charlemagne is not magnanimity but compassion and sympathy born of shared misfortune.

5. Not, at any rate, in Lejeune and Stiennon.

6. Beckwith, *Early Medieval Art*, p. 178, fig. 167; Lejeune and Stiennon, 1:218 (2: fig. 186); Cames, *Allégories*, figs. 46, 108–10 (discussion, pp. 107, 114–15). In medieval iconography widow's weeds usually included a veil.

7. Lejeune and Stiennon, 1:119; 2: fig. 84. The scene was interpolated by Conrad. For depictions of the Baptism of Christ, see Réau, II, 2:295–304.

8. Lejeune and Stiennon, 1:119–20.

9. Louis Réau, *Histoire de la peinture au moyen âge: La miniature* (Melun: Librairie d'Argences, 1946), p. 103; idem, *Iconographie de l'art chrétien*, III, 3:1220.

10. Frontispiece of Jenkins's edition. The caption reads: "Charlemagne, invincible champion of Christianity, is revealed by an angel to the Emperor Constantine in a dream. Charlemagne Window, Cathedral of Chartres, 13th century." Réau, III, 1:292: "L'empereur Constantin voit apparaître en songe Charlemagne qui, après avoir délivré Jérusalem, arrive aux portes de Constantinople." In a note Réau explains: "Charlemagne vivait cinq siècles après Constantin. Mais la légende n'a cure des anachronismes." On Charles as the New Constantine, see Bédier, *Légendes épiques*, 4:443; Réau, III, 1:342. See also above, COMMENTARY, 35, note 22.

11. COMMENTARY, 45.

12. Brault, "'Truvet li unt le num de Juliane'," p. 145, n. 18. Adopting a different name at baptism symbolizes the fact that the convert has assumed a new personality. On this tradition in the epics, see Frappier, *Chansons de geste*, 2:317, and n. 1, and see COMMENTARY, 33, note 5.

13. Bédier, *Commentaires*, p. 320. The same suggestion had earlier been made by Jenkins, note to v. 3986: "Is there special fitness in the choice of this name for the former Queen Bramimonde? St. Juliana, the martyr, was of noble blood and beautiful; she was the daughter of Africanus, a persecutor of Christians; her mother had inclined to neither Christians nor pagans." For further references and discussion, see Brault, "'Truvet li unt le num de Juliane'," p. 146, n. 19.

14. According to a Latin version preserved in Oxford, Bodleian MS. 285: *in loco stercoris*. *The Liflade ant te passiun of Seinte Iuliene*, ed. S. R. T. O. d'Ardenne, Early English Text Society 248 (London and New York: Oxford University Press, 1961), p. 46. Another Latin version cited by Réau, III, 2:772, reads: *in latrinam*.

15. For iconographic references, see Brault, "'Truvet li unt le num de Juliane',"

p. 146, n. 21. Keller, "La conversion de Bramimonde," p. 22, adds a thirteenth-century illustration produced at Saint Albans. Another portrait of Saint Juliana is to be found in the Stuttgart Psalter (1180). Réau, *Histoire de la peinture au moyen âge*, p. 104. I am indebted to C. W. Kruyter of the Department of Manuscripts, Koninklijke Bibliotheek, The Hague, for confirming the existence of yet another illustration in the Bible of Saint Bertin, that is, MS. 76 F 5, fol. 32, pl. 4, of that library.

16. *Seinte Iuliene*, ed. d'Ardenne, p. xviii.

17. Especially Naples, beginning with the year 1207. *Seinte Iuliene*, ed. d'Ardenne, p. xviii (for Brussels, see pp. xviii–xix).

18. Dom Abundio Rodriguez, O.S.B., and Dom Luis-Maria de Lojendio, O.S.B., *Castille romane*, trans. Dom Norbert Vaillant, O.S.B., La nuit des temps 23 (La Pierre-qui-vire: Les Presses monastiques, 1966), 1:54: "Par Santillana passait un des chemins secondaires du pèlerinage à Saint-Jacques de Compostelle: le chemin de la côte qui, sans être le traditionnel *camino francés* (chemin français), n'en était pas moins très fréquenté; il eut ses hospices pour les indigents et les pèlerins." This is the birthplace of the hero of Lesage's *Gil Blas de Santillane*. Keller, "La conversion de Bramimonde," p. 19, turns my argument around: Conceding that Santillana was one of the famous pilgrimage centers of the day associated with Juliana, he points out that the saint was also venerated in several other localities in Europe. Keller's contention, pp. 19–20, based on the provenance of several manuscripts containing saints' lives including that of Juliana, that England was a more important center of the saint's cult than the Spanish monastery, is unconvincing. See Paul Barrette, "La légende de Sainte Julienne et ses rapports avec la *Chanson de Roland*," in the proceedings of the Seventh International Congress of the Société Rencesvals held at Liège, 1976.

19. And, pace Keller, the author of the Anglo-Norman *Song of Roland*.

20. *Li Ver del jüise*, ed. Hugo von Feilitzen (Upsala: Berling, 1883), app. On the date (after 1150), see *Seinte Iuliene*, ed. d'Ardenne, p. xxi.

21. On Saint Faith, see Bédier, *Légendes épiques*, 3:312–16; Réau, III, 1:513–16.

COMMENTARY 49

1. Menéndez Pidal, pp. 127–29. On the transitional laisse theory, consult Horrent, pp. 203–4. The possibility of a fragmentary conclusion was dismissed by Horrent, p. 204, but has been revived by Aebischer, *Préhistoire*, pp. 205–22 (see, however, Segre, p. 675). Horrent, pp. 204–5, considers that the Emperor's dream may continue in the reader's musing, but suggests that this view is "peut-être trop moderne." In the *Pseudo-Turpin* Saint Denis appears to Charles at the end of the chronicle to inform him that all his soldiers killed in Spain went to heaven (Meredith-Jones, p. 219). On the conclusion in the other versions of Turoldus's poem, see Horrent, pp. 205–6; Aebischer, pp. 203–22; Dufournet, *Cours sur Roland*, pp. 7–9.

2. Bowra, *Heroic Poetry*, pp. 328–29; Le Gentil, p. 114; Dufournet, *Cours sur Roland*, pp. 7–8.

3. See INTRODUCTION, 12.

4. Genesis 12:1. Similar calls to action are found in Genesis 6:14 ff.; Exodus 3:4 ff.; Joshua 1:2–9; Judges 6; 1 Samuel 3; 1 Kings 19; Isaiah 1:2; Jeremiah 1:5 ff.; Ezekiel 1:1; Zechariah 1:1. One is reminded, too, of Joan of Arc's voices and of the youthful Joseph Smith's visions. See also Campbell, *Hero*, pt. 1, chap. 1, 1, "The Call to Adventure," pp. 49–58.

5. Meredith-Jones, pp. 89–93 (on the conclusion of the *Pseudo-Turpin*, see note 1 above). The possible sources of the vision of Saint James are discussed by Meredith-Jones, pp. 262–63; Mandach, *Naissance*, 1:38. Add Abraham's vision in Genesis

15:3–5: "Then Abram said, 'See, you have given me no descendants; some man of my household will be my heir.' And then this word of Yahweh was spoken to him, 'He shall not be your heir; your heir shall be of your own flesh and blood.' Then taking him outside he said, 'Look up to heaven and count the stars if you can. Such will be your descendants' he told him." For depictions of this scene, see Réau, II, 1:129–30.

6. Cf. Conrad, vv. 47–64, 1798–1800. On Stricker, see Lejeune and Stiennon, 1:229–30. In *Chanson de Guillaume*, v. 3491, Rainouart is baptized in a *grant cuve*.

7. Note that the figure of Job does not merely symbolize resignation but, above all, courage in adversity. Blaise, par. 489. Mickel, "Parallels in *Psychomachia* and *Roland*," pp. 445–46, sees a parallel between Charles and David. According to *Psychomachia*, vv. 386–387, David "never rested from the troubles of war." Mickel, pp. 442–43, mentions Job in connection with the image of Roland and Turpin in battle. On Sorrow in the Midst of Joy, see INTRODUCTION, 11, C. Riquer, *Chansons de geste*, p. 94, n. 124, observes that Charles's weeping at the close of the poem recalls a similar image in the *Cantar del Cid*. Sholod, *Charlemagne in Spain*, p. 21, suggests that the conclusion is a call to arms against the Muslims.

8. See INTRODUCTION, 15, A. That the poem's conclusion "nous fait bien naïvement, bien naturellement comprendre que la vie est une lutte perpétuelle" was recognized by Léon Gautier as early as 1880 (cited by Aebischer, *Préhistoire*, p. 206). See also Mickel, "Parallels in *Psychomachia* and *Roland*," pp. 451–52, and cf. Payen, *Le Motif du repentir*, p. 513. The beginning of the concluding laisse makes it clear that conversion is an ever-present concern as well.

9. Le Gentil, p. 118, comparing Charles to Vigny's Moses.

10. On this circular structure, see INTRODUCTION, 13, and COMMENTARY, 1. Cf. Payen, *Le Moyen Age*, p. 82: "La Roue de Fortune ne permet que la résignation." The device that consists of ending a work by suggesting a new beginning is frequently used in quest stories. See, for example, the conclusion of Rabelais's Fifth Book. Thomas M. Greene, *Rabelais: A Study in Comic Courage*, Landmarks in Literature (Englewood Cliffs, N.J.: Prentice-Hall, 1970), p. 113.

11. Not the specific appeal for help detailed in vv. 3995–3998, but the prospect of never-ending warfare.

12. Verse 4001 is an exact duplicate of the line that concludes the Emperor's planctus (v. 2943). Horrent, p. 205, relates the conclusion to Roland but emphasizes Charles's chagrin and disappointment (cf. the concept of the patience of Job, note 7 above).

Bibliography of Works Cited

Adam, Leonhard. *Primitive Art*. 3d ed. Pelican Books. Melbourne-London-Baltimore: Penguin, 1954.

A Documentary History of Art. Vol. 1. *The Middle Ages and the Renaissance*. Ed. Elizabeth G. Holt. Garden City: Doubleday, 1957.

Adolf, Helen. "The Ass and the Harp." *Speculum* 25 (1950): 49–57.

Aebischer, Paul. "Halt sunt li pui e li port tenebrus." *Studi Medievali* 18 (1952): 1–22.

———. "Les graphies toponymiques 'Sebre' et 'Balaguet' de la 'Chanson de Roland', Ms. Digby." *Boletín de la Real Academia de Buenas Letras de Barcelona* 28 (1959/60): 185–209.

———. "Pour la défense et illustration de l'épisode de Baligant." *Mélanges Ernest Hoepffner*. Pp. 173–82.

———. *Préhistoire et protohistoire du Roland d'Oxford*. Bibliotheca Romanica. Series prima: Manualia et commentationes. Berne: Francke, 1972.

———. *Rolandiana Borealia: La Saga af Runzivals bardaga et ses dérivés scandinaves comparés à la Chanson de Roland. Essai de restauration du manuscrit français utilisé par le traducteur norrois*. Publications de la Faculté des lettres de l'Université de Lausanne 11. Lausanne: Rouge, 1954.

———. *Rolandiana et Oliveriana: Recueil d'études sur les chansons de geste*. Publications romanes et françaises 92. Geneva: Droz, 1967.

———. "Sur le vers 1776 du *Roland* d'Oxford." *Mélanges de philologie offerts à Alf Lombard à l'occasion de son soixante-cinquième anniversaire par ses collègues et ses amis*. Etudes romanes de Lund 18. Lund: Gleerup, 1969. Pp. 17–21.

———. *Textes norrois et littérature française du moyen âge*. Vol. 1. *Recherches sur les traditions épiques antérieures à la Chanson de Roland d'après les données de la première branche de la Karlamagnús saga*. Publications romanes et françaises 44. Geneva: Droz; Lille: Giard, 1954.

———. "Un problème d'exégèse rolandienne: *Maelgut*, la conquête de Gautier de l'Hum (*Chanson de Roland*, ms. Digby, v. 2047)." *Cultura Neolatina* 23 (1963): 146–52.

A History of the Crusades. Gen ed. Kenneth M. Setton. Vol. 1. *The First Hundred Years*. Ed. Marshall W. Baldwin. Madison-Milwaukee-London: University of Wisconsin Press, 1969.

Aigrain, René. *L'Hagiographie, ses sources, ses méthodes, son histoire*. Paris: Bloud & Gay, 1953.

Albrecht, Gustav. *Vorbereitung auf den Tod, Totengebräuche und Totenbestattung in der altfranzösischen Dichtung*. Halle: Kaemmerer, 1892.

Alexander, J. J. G. *Norman Illumination at Mont-Saint-Michel 966–1100*. Oxford: Clarendon Press, 1970.

Aliscans, chanson de geste. Eds. François Guessard and Anatole de Montaiglon. Les Anciens Poètes de la France 10. Paris: Franck, 1870.

Allen, John R. "Du nouveau sur l'authenticité de l'épisode de Baligant." *Société Rencesvals. VIe Congrès International.* Pp. 147–56.

———. "The Saversnake Horn." *Olifant* 3, no. 3 (1976): 200–202.

Allen, Judson B. *The Friar as Critic: Literary Attitudes in the Later Middle Ages.* Nashville: Vanderbilt University Press, 1971.

Alonso, Dámaso. "La primitiva épica francesa a la luz de una 'Nota Emilianense'." *Revista de Filología Española* 37 (1953): 1–94.

Altona, Johannes. *Gebete und Anrufungen in den altfranzösischen Chansons de geste.* Ausgaben und Abhandlungen aus dem Gebiete der romanischen Philologie 9. Marburg: Elwert, 1883.

Ami et Amile, chanson de geste. Ed. Peter F. Dembowski. Classiques français du moyen âge 97. Paris: Champion, 1969.

Amira, Karl von. "Die Handgebärden in den Bilderhandschriften des Sachsenspiegels." *Akademie der Wissenschaften* [Munich]. Abhandlungen der philosophisch-philologischen Klasse 23 (1909): 163–263.

Annales monastici. Ed. Henry Richards Luard. Vol. 4. Rerum britannicarum medii aevi scriptores; or Chronicles and Memorials of Great Britain and Ireland during the Middle Ages 36. London: Longman, Green, Longman, Roberts, and Green, 1869.

Archambault, Paul. "Commynes' *saigesse* and the Renaissance Idea of Wisdom." *Bibliothèque d'Humanisme et Renaissance* 29 (1967): 613–32.

———. *Seven French Chroniclers: Witnesses to History.* Syracuse: Syracuse University Press, 1974.

———. "The Ages of Man and the Ages of the World." *Revue des études augustiniennes* 11 (1966): 193–202.

Argumentation and Debate: Principles and Practices. Prepared Under the Auspices of Tau Kappa Alpha. Ed. David Potter. New York: Dryden Press, 1954.

Arteta, Antonio Ubieto. "Una nota para la cronología de la 'Chanson de Roland'." Unpublished paper read at the Third International Congress of the Société Rencesvals, Barcelona, 1964. Summary in *Bulletin bibliographique de la Société Rencesvals* 4 (1967): 100.

Arthurian Literature in the Middle Ages. Ed. Roger S. Loomis. Oxford: Clarendon Press, 1961.

Atkinson, James C. "Laisses 169–170 of the *Chanson de Roland.*" *MLN* 82 (1967): 271–84.

Attwater, Donald. *The Penguin Dictionary of the Saints.* Penguin Reference Books. Baltimore: Penguin, 1965.

Auerbach, Erich. *Mimesis: The Representation of Reality in Western Literature.* Trans. Willard R. Trask. Princeton: Princeton University Press, 1953.

Augier, Michelle. "A propos de quelques conversions féminines dans l'épopée française." *Mosaic* 8 (1975): 97–105.

Baker, Alfred T. "Vie anglo-normande de Sainte Foy." *Romania* 66 (1940/41): 49–84.

Bancourt, Paul. "'Sen' et 'chevalerie': Réflexions sur la tactique des chevaliers dans plusieurs chansons de geste des XIIe et XIIIe siècles." *Société Rencesvals. VIe Congrès International.* Pp. 621–37.

Barnett, F. J. "Some Notes to the Sequence of Saint Eulalia." *Studies in Medieval French Presented to Alfred Ewert in Honour of His Seventieth Birthday.* Oxford: Clarendon Press, 1961. Pp. 1–25.

———. "Virginity in the Old French Sequence of Saint Eulalia." *French Studies* 13 (1959): 252–56.

Barrette, Paul. "La légende de Sainte Julienne et ses rapports avec la *Chanson de Roland.*" Proceedings of the Seventh International Congress of the Société Rencesvals, Liège, 1976.

Bayer, Victor. *La Sculpture médiévale du Musée de l'oeuvre Notre-Dame. Catalogue.* 2d ed. Strasbourg: Edition des Musées de la Ville, 1968.

Beaujouan, Guy. "Le symbolisme des nombres à l'époque romane." *Cahiers de civilisation médiévale* 4 (1961): 159–69.

Becker, Philipp August. "Der distichisch-tristichische Rhythmus im Rolandslied." *Philologische Studien aus dem romanisch-germanischen Kulturkreise. Karl Voretzsch zum 60. Geburtstag und zum Gedenken an seine erste akademische Berufung vor 35 Jahren.* Halle: Niemeyer, 1927. Pp. 539–43.

Beckman, Gustave A. "L'identification Nobles = Dax." *Le Moyen Age* 79 (1973): 5–24.

Beckwith, John. *Early Medieval Art.* Praeger World of Art. New York and Washington, D.C.: Praeger, 1965.

Bédier, Joseph. "De l'édition princeps de la *Chanson de Roland* aux éditions les plus récentes: Nouvelles remarques sur l'art d'établir les anciens textes." *Romania* 63 (1937): 433–69; 64 (1938): 145–244, 489–521.

———. *La Chanson de Roland commentée.* 1927; rpt. Paris: Piazza, 1968.

———. *Les Légendes épiques: Recherches sur la formation des chansons de geste.* 2d ed. 4 vols. Paris: Champion, 1914–21.

———. "Remarques sur vingt passages difficiles de la *Chanson de Roland.*" *Mélanges Ferdinand Lot.* Pp. 38–40.

Bédier, Joseph, and Paul Hazard. *Histoire de la littérature française illustrée.* 2 vols. Paris: Larousse, 1923–24.

Beichman, Anthony M. "Ganelon and Duke Naimes." *Romance Notes* 13 (1971): 358–62.

Beichner, Paul E. "The Allegorical Interpretation of Medieval Literature." *PMLA* 82 (1967): 33–38.

Beinhauer, Monika. *Ritterliche Tapferkeitsbegriffe in den altfranzösischen Chansons de geste des 12. Jahrhunderts.* Cologne, 1958.

Bender, Karl-Heinz. "La genèse de l'image littéraire de Charlemagne élu de Dieu au XIe siècle." *Boletín de la Real Academia de Buenas Letras de Barcelona* 31 (1965/66): 35–39.

———. "Les métamorphoses de la royauté de Charlemagne dans les premières épopées franco-italiennes." *Cultura Neolatina* 21 (1961): 164–74.

Benedict, Ruth. *The Chrysanthemum and the Sword: Patterns of Japanese Culture.* Boston: Houghton Mifflin, 1946.

Benton, John F. "Clio and Venus: An Historical View of Courtly Love." *The Meaning of Courtly Love.* Ed. F. X. Newman. Albany: State University of New York Press, 1968. Pp. 19–42.

Bernard de Clairvaux. Commission d'histoire de l'Ordre de Cîteaux 3. Paris: Alsatia, 1953.

Bernheimer, Richard. *Wild Men in the Middle Ages: A Study in Art, Sentiment, and Demonology.* Cambridge: Harvard University Press, 1952.

Béroul. Le Roman de Tristan, poème du XIIe siècle. Ed. Ernest Muret. 4th ed. Revised by L. M. Defourques. Classiques français du moyen âge 12. Paris: Champion, 1967.

Bertin, Gerald. Review of Brault, "Ganelon et Roland." *Olifant* 3, no. 2 (1975): 129–32.

Bezzola, Reto R. *Les Origines et la formation de la littérature courtoise en Occident (500–1200).* Bibliothèque de l'Ecole des hautes études 319. Vol. 3, Pt. 1. Paris: Champion, 1963.

Blaise, Albert. *Le Vocabulaire latin des principaux thèmes liturgiques.* Turnhout: Brepols, 1966.

Blancandin et l'Orgueilleuse d'amour: Roman d'aventure du XIIIe siècle. Ed. Franklin P. Sweetser. Textes littéraires français 112. Geneva: Droz, 1964.

Bloch, Marc. *Feudal Society*. Trans. L. A. Manyon. 2 vols. Chicago: University of Chicago Press, 1961.

Bloch, Oscar, and Walther von Wartburg. *Dictionnaire étymologique de la langue française*. 4th ed. Paris: Presses Universitaires de France, 1964.

Bloomfield, Morton W. Review of Allen, *The Friar as Critic*. *Speculum* 48 (1973): 329–30.

———. "Understanding Old English Poetry." *Annuale Medievale (Duquesne Studies)* 9 (1968): 5–25.

Boethius. The Theological Treatises. Eds. and trans. H. F. Stewart, E. K. Rand, and S. J. Tester. *The Consolation of Philosophy*. Ed. and trans. S. J. Tester. The Loeb Classical Library. 1918; rpt. Cambridge: Harvard University Press; London: Heinemann, 1973.

Boissonnade, Prosper. *Du Nouveau sur la Chanson de Roland: La genèse historique, le cadre géographique, le milieu, les personnages, la date et l'auteur du poème*. Paris: Champion, 1923.

Bossuat, Robert. *Manuel bibliographique de la littérature française du moyen âge*. Melun: Librairie d'Argences, 1951. *Supplément (1949–53)*. Paris: Librairie d'Argences, 1955. *Second Supplément (1954–60)*. Paris: Librairie d'Argences, 1961.

Bouard, Michel de. "La *Chanson de Roland* et la Normandie." *Annales de Normandie* 2 (1952): 34–38.

Bowra, Cecil M. *Heroic Poetry*. London: Macmillan, 1952.

Boysen, Agnka L. *Ueber den Begriff preu im Französischen (preux, prou, prouesse, prud'-homme, prud'homie, prude, pruderie)*. Lengerich, 1941.

Braet, Herman. "Fonction et importance du songe dans la chanson de geste." *Le Moyen Age* 77 (1971): 405–16.

———. "Le *brohun* dans la *Chanson de Roland*." *Zeitschrift für romanische Philologie* 89 (1973): 97–102.

———. "Le second rêve de Charlemagne dans la *Chanson de Roland*." *Etudes de philologie romane*. Romanica Gandensia 12. Ghent: Rijksuniversiteit te Gent, 1969. Pp. 5–19.

———. *Le Songe dans la chanson de geste au XIIe siècle*. Romanica Gandensia 15. Ghent: Rijksuniversiteit te Gent, 1975.

———. "Le songe de l'arbre chez Wace, Benoît et Aimon de Varennes." *Romania* 91 (1970): 255–67.

Brandt, W. J. *The Shape of Medieval History: Studies in Modes of Perception*. New Haven: Yale University Press, 1966.

Brault, Gerard J. "Chrétien de Troyes' *Lancelot*: The Eye and the Heart." *Bibliographical Bulletin of the International Arthurian Society* 24 (1972): 142–53.

———. *Early Blazon: Heraldic Terminology in the Twelfth and Thirteenth Centuries With Special Reference to Arthurian Literature*. Oxford: Clarendon Press, 1972.

———. "Ganelon et Roland: Deux anecdotes du traître concernant le héros." *Romania* 92 (1971): 392–405.

———. "Girart d'Amiens and the *Pseudo-Turpin Chronicle*." *Zeitschrift für romanische Philologie* 76 (1960): 64–93.

———. "Heraldic Terminology and Legendary Material in the *Siege of Caerlaverock* (c. 1300)." *Romance Studies in Memory of Edward Billings Ham*. Ed. Urban T. Holmes, Jr. California State College Publications 2. Hayward: California State College, 1967. Pp. 15–20.

———. "Kinesics and the Classroom: Some Typical French Gestures." *French Review* 36 (1963): 374–82.

———. "Le Coffret de Vannes et la légende de Tristan au XIIe siècle." *Mélanges Rita Lejeune*. Vol. 1. Pp. 652–68.

———. "Les dessins du *Ruolantes Liet* et l'interprétation de la *Chanson de Roland*." Proceedings of the Seventh International Congress of the Société Rencesvals, Liège, 1976.

———. "Le Thème de la Mort dans la *Chanson de Roland*." *Société Rencesvals. IVe Congrès International*. Pp. 220–37.

———. 'Old French *adenz, endenz*, Latin *ad dentes, in dentes*." *Romania* 85 (1964): 323–35.

———. "Quelques nouvelles tendances de la critique et de l'interprétation des chansons de geste." *Société Rencesvals. VIe Congrès International*. Pp. 13–26.

———. Reply to Bertin's review of Brault, "Ganelon et Roland." *Olifant* 3, no. 2 (1975): 132–33.

———. Review of Burgess, *Contribution à l'étude du vocabulaire pré-courtois. Speculum* 46 (1971): 362–64.

———. Review of Dorfman, *The Narreme in the Medieval Romance Epic. General Linguistics* 10 (1970): 62–67.

———. "*Sapientia* dans la *Chanson de Roland*." *French Forum* 1 (1976): 99–118.

———. "Structure et sens de la *Chanson de Roland*." *French Review* 45, special issue no. 3 (1971): 1–12.

———. "The Legend of Charlemagne's Sin in Girart d'Amiens." *Romance Notes* 4 (1962): 72–75.

———. " 'Truvet li unt le num de Juliane': sur le rôle de Bramimonde dans la *Chanson de Roland*." *Mélanges Pierre Le Gentil*. Pp. 134–149.

———. " 'Ung abysme de science': On the Interpretation of Gargantua's Letter to Pantagruel." *Bibliothèque d'Humanisme et Renaissance* 28 (1966): 615–32.

Brendel, Otto. "Origin and Meaning of the Word Mandorla." *Gazette des Beaux-Arts* 25 (1944): 5–24.

Brieger, Peter. *English Art 1216–1307*. The Oxford History of English Art 4. Oxford: Clarendon Press, 1957.

Brilliant, Richard. *Gesture and Rank in Roman Art: The Use of Gestures to Denote Status in Roman Sculpture and Coinage*. Memoirs of the Connecticut Academy of Arts and Sciences 14. New Haven: The Academy, 1963.

Brody, Saul N. *The Disease of the Soul: Leprosy in Medieval Literature*. Ithaca: Cornell University Press, 1974.

Brook, Leslie C. "Le 'forfait' de Roland dans le procès de Ganelon: Encore sur un vers obscur de la *Chanson de Roland*." *Société Rencesvals. IVe Congrès International*. Pp. 120–28.

Brugger, Ernst. *The Illuminated Tree in Two Arthurian Romances*. Publications of the Institute of French Studies. New York: Institute of French Studies, 1929.

Bulatkin, Eleanor W. *Structural Arithmetic Metaphor in the Oxford Roland*. Columbus: Ohio State University Press, 1962.

Burger, André. "La légende de Roncevaux avant la *Chanson de Roland*." *Romania* 70 (1948/49): 433–73.

———. "La question rolandienne, faits et hypothèses." *Cahiers de civilisation médiévale* 4 (1961): 269–91.

———. "Le rire de Roland." *Cahiers de civilisation médiévale* 3 (1960): 2–11.

———. "Les deux scènes du cor dans la *Chanson de Roland*." *La Technique littéraire des chansons de geste*. Pp. 105–26.

———. "Oriflamme." *Festschrift: Walther von Wartburg zum 80. Geburtstag, 18. Mai 1968*. Ed. Kurt Baldinger. Tübingen: Niemeyer, 1968. Vol. 2. Pp. 357–62.

———. "Remarques sur la composition de l'épisode de Baligant." *Mélanges Maurice Delbouille*. Vol. 2. Pp. 59–69.

———. "Sur la transposition des vers 1467 à 1509 du ms. O de la *Chanson de Roland*."

Essais de philologie moderne (1951). Bibliothèque de la Faculté de philosophie et lettres de l'Université de Liège 129. Paris: Les Belles Lettres, 1953. Pp. 155–60.

———. "Sur les relations de la *Chanson de Roland* avec le *Récit du faux Turpin* et celui du *Guide du Pèlerin*." *Romania* 73 (1952): 242–47.

Burgess, Glyn S. *Contribution à l'étude du vocabulaire pré-courtois.* Publications romanes et françaises 110. Geneva: Droz, 1970.

———. "La *Chanson de Roland*, Line 400." *Romance Notes* 13 (1971): 165–67.

———. "*Orgueil* and *Fierté* in Twelfth-Century French." *Zeitschrift für romanische Philologie* 89 (1973): 103–22.

———. "Remarques sur deux vers de la *Chanson de Roland* (v. 3796–7)." *Société Rencesvals. VIe Congrès International.* Pp. 63–78.

———. "*Talent* in Early Old French (to 1150)." *Romania* 95 (1974): 443–66.

Busigny, Felix. *Das Verhältnis der Chansons de geste zur Bible.* Inaugural-Dissertation. Basel: Reinhardt, 1917.

Caiger-Smith, A. *English Medieval Mural Painting.* Oxford: Clarendon Press, 1963.

Calin, William. *The Epic Quest: Studies in Four Old French Chansons de Geste.* Baltimore: Johns Hopkins Press, 1966.

———. *The Old French Epic of Revolt: Raoul de Cambrai, Renaud de Montauban, Gormond et Isembard.* Geneva: Droz, 1962.

Cames, Gérard. *Allégories et symboles dans l'Hortus deliciarum.* Leiden: Brill, 1971.

———. *Byzance et la peinture romane de Germanie: Apports de l'art grec posticonoclaste à l'enluminure et à la fresque ottoniennes et romanes de Germanie dans les thèmes de majesté et les évangiles.* Paris: Picard, 1966.

Campbell, Joseph. *The Hero With a Thousand Faces.* 2nd ed. Bollingen Series 17. Princeton: Princeton University Press, 1973 [c. 1949].

Capels, Kathleen M. "The Apple Incident in Laisse XXIX of the *Song of Roland*." *Romance Notes* 14 (1973): 599–605.

Castex, Pierre-Georges, and Paul Surer. *Manuel des études littéraires françaises.* Vol. 1. *Moyen Age.* Paris: Hachette, 1948.

Chailley, Jacques. "Etudes musicales sur la chanson de geste et ses origines." *Revue de musicologie* 27 (1948): 1–27.

———. *L'Ecole musicale de Saint-Martial de Limoges jusqu'à la fin du XIe siècle.* Paris: Les Livres essentiels, 1960.

Champeaux, Gérard de, and Dom Sébastien Sterckx, O.S.B. *Introduction au monde des symboles.* La nuit des temps 3. La Pierre-qui-vire: Les Presses monastiques, 1966.

Chomentovskaja, O. "Le comput digital: Histoire d'un geste dans l'art de la Renaissance italienne." *Gazette des Beaux-Arts* 20 (1938): 157–72.

Chrétien de Troyes. Le Roman de Perceval ou le Conte du Graal. Ed. William Roach. 2d ed. Textes littéraires français 71. Geneva: Droz; Paris: Minard, 1959.

Colby, Alice M. *The Portrait in Twelfth-Century French Literature: An Example of the Stylistic Originality of Chrétien de Troyes.* Geneva: Droz, 1965.

Colliot, Régine. "Les épitaphes arthuriennes." *Bibliographical Bulletin of the International Arthurian Society* 25 (1973): 155–75.

Comfort, William Wistar. "The Character Types in the Old French *Chansons de geste*." *PMLA* 21 (1906): 278–434.

———. "The Literary Role of the Saracens in the French Epic." *PMLA* 55 (1940): 628–59.

Comment on Foulet, "Is Roland Guilty of Desmesure?" and Del Monte, "Apologia di Orlando." *Olifant* 3, no. 3 (1976): 180–1.

Comparetti, Domenico. *Virgilio nel medio evo.* 3d ed. 2 vols. Florence: La Nuova Italia, 1943–46.

Corbett, Noel L. "Encore une fois *pleine sa hanste.*" *Revue de linguistique romane* 33 (1969): 349–52.

Cormier, Raymond J. "The Present Status of Studies on the *Roman d'Enéas.*" *Cultura Neolatina* 31 (1971): 7–39.

———. "The Problem of Anachronism: Recent Scholarship on the French Medieval Romances of Antiquity." *Philological Quarterly* 53 (1974): 145–57.

Cornu, Jules. "Trois passages de la *Chanson de Roland* corrigés à tort." *Romania* 9 (1880): 118.

Costa, Georges. *Trésors des Eglises de France.* Vol. 1. *Epoques pré-romane et romane.* Grandes Expositions. Paris: Publications filmées d'art et d'histoire, 1966.

Crist, Larry S. "A propos de la desmesure dans la *Chanson de Roland:* quelques propos (démesurés?)." *Olifant* 1, no. 4 (1974): 10–20.

———. Review of Uitti, *Story, Myth, and Celebration in Old French Narrative Poetry, 1050–1200. Olifant* 1, no. 3 (1974): 23–29.

Crone, G. R. *Maps and Their Makers: An Introduction to the History of Cartography.* New York: Capricorn Books, 1966.

Crosland, Jessie. *The Old French Epic.* Oxford: Blackwell, 1951.

Cross, Tom Peete, and William A. Nitze. *Lancelot and Guenevere: A Study of the Origins of Courtly Love.* Modern Philology Monographs. Chicago: University of Chicago Press, 1930.

Crowley, Frances and Cornelius. "Le problème de l'étymologie de AOI dans la *Chanson de Roland.*" *Cahiers de civilisation médiévale* 3 (1960): 12–13.

Crozet, René. "Le chasseur et le combattant dans la sculpture romane en Saintonge." *Mélanges Rita Lejeune.* Vol. 1. Pp. 669–77.

Cullmann, O. "Death of Christ." *The Interpreter's Dictionary of the Bible.* New York and Nashville: Abington Press, 1962. Vol. 1. Pp. 804–8.

Curry, Walter C. *Chaucer and the Mediaeval Sciences.* New York and London: Oxford University Press, 1926.

Curtius, Ernst R. *La Littérature européenne et le moyen âge latin.* 2d ed. Trans. Jean Bréjoux. Paris: Presses Universitaires de France, 1956.

———. "Ueber die altfranzösische Epik." *Zeitschrift für romanische Philologie* 64 (1944): 233–320.

———. "Zur Literarästhetik des Mittelalters." *Zeitschrift für romanische Philologie* 58 (1938): 215–32.

Das Rolandslied des Pfaffen Konrad. Ed. Carl Wesle. 2d ed. Altdeutsche Textbibliothek 69. Tübingen: Niemeyer, 1967.

Davy, Marie-Madeleine. *Initiation à la symbolique romane (XIIe siècle).* Paris: Flammarion, 1964.

De Caluwé, Jacques. "La 'prière épique' dans les plus anciennes chansons de geste françaises." *Olifant* 4, no. 1 (1976): 4–20.

———. "Les prières de 'Berte aus grans piés' dans l'oeuvre d'Adenet le Roi." *Mélanges Pierre Le Gentil.* Pp. 151–60.

Deér, Jozsef. *The Dynastic Porphyry Tombs of the Norman Period in Sicily.* Trans. G. A. Gillhoff. Dunbarton Oaks Studies 5. Cambridge: Harvard University Press, 1959.

Delaruelle, Etienne. "L'idée de croisade dans la littérature clunisienne du XIe siècle et l'abbaye de Moissac." *Annales du Midi* 75 (1963): 419–39.

Delbouille, Maurice. "D'où venait la chanson de geste? A propos du livre d'Italo Siciliano, *Les Chansons de geste et l'épopée.*" *Cahiers de civilisation médiévale* 15 (1972): 205–21.

———. "Le chant héroïque serbo-croate et la genèse de la chanson de geste." *Boletín de la Real Academia de Buenas Letras de Barcelona* 31 (1965/66), 83–98.

———. "Le mythe du jongleur-poète." *Studi in onore di Italo Siciliano.* Pp. 317–27.

———. "Les chansons de geste et le livre." *La Technique littéraire des chansons de geste.* Pp. 295–428.

———. *Sur la Genèse de la Chanson de Roland (Travaux récents—Propositions nouvelles): Essai critique.* Académie royale de langue et de littérature françaises de Belgique. Brussels: Palais des Académies, 1954.

Delehaye, Hippolyte. *Les Légendes hagiographiques.* 4th ed. Subsidia Hagiographica, 18a. 1927; rpt. Brussels: Société des Bollandistes, 1955.

———. *Les Passions des martyrs et les genres littéraires.* 2d ed. Subsidia Hagiographica, 13 B. 1921; rpt. Brussels: Société des Bollandistes, 1966.

Del Monte, Alfredo. "Apologia di Orlando." *Filologia Romanza* 4 (1957): 225–34.

Demoulin, Auguste. "Charlemagne, la légende de son péché et le choix de Ganelon pour l'ambassade." *Marche romane* 25 (1975): 105–26.

Demus, Otto. *Byzantine Art and the West.* The Wrightsman Lectures 3. New York: New York University Press, 1970.

Deneef, A. Leigh. "Robertson and His Critics." *Chaucer Review* 2 (1968): 205–34.

Denholm-Young, Noel. *History and Heraldry 1254 to 1310: A Study of the Historical Value of the Rolls of Arms.* Oxford: Clarendon Press, 1965.

Der Pseudo-Turpin von Compostela. Eds. Adalbert Hämel and André de Mandach. Bayerische Akademie der Wissenschaften. Philosophisch-Historische Klasse. Sitzungsberichte, Jahrgang 1965. Heft 1. Munich: Beck, 1965.

De Saint Laurent, poème anglo-normand du XIIe siècle. Ed. Werner Söderhjelm. Paris: Welter, 1888.

Deschamps, Paul, and Marc Thibout. *La Peinture murale en France: Le haut moyen âge et l'époque romane.* Collection Ars et Historia. Paris: Plon, 1951.

Dessau, Adalbert. "L'idée de la trahison au moyen âge et son rôle dans la motivation de quelques chansons de geste." *Cahiers de civilisation médiévale* 3 (1960): 23–26.

Devoto, Daniel. "L'AOI dans la *Chanson de Roland.*" Unpublished paper read at the Second International Congress of the Société Rencesvals, Venice, 1961. Summary in *Bulletin bibliographique de la Société Rencesvals* 3 (1963): 92, item 260.

Diament, Henri. "La légende dionysienne et la juxtaposition des toponymes *Montjoie* et *Saint-Denis* dans la formation du cri de guerre." *Romance Notes* 13 (1971): 177–80.

———. "Une interprétation hagio-toponymique de l'ancien cri de guerre des Français *Montjoie Saint-Denis!*" *Romance Notes* 12 (1971): 447–57.

Dickmann, Adolphe J. *Le Rôle du surnaturel dans les chansons de geste.* Paris: Champion, 1926.

Diehl, Charles. *Manuel d'art byzantin.* 2d ed. 2 vols. Paris: Picard, 1925–26.

Diogenes Laertius. Lives of Eminent Philosophers. Ed. and trans. R. D. Hicks. The Loeb Classical Library. 2 vols. 1925; rpt. Cambridge: Harvard University Press; London: Heinemann, 1958–59.

Discussion concerning the central hero in the *Song of Roland. Olifant* 1, no. 3 (1974): 8; no. 4, p. 75.

Donohoe, Joseph I. "Ambivalence and Anger, the Human Center of the *Chanson de Roland.*" *Romanic Review* 62 (1971): 251–61.

Dorfman, Eugene F. *The Narreme in the Medieval Romance Epic: An Introduction to Narrative Structures.* University of Toronto Romance Series 13. Toronto: University of Toronto Press, 1969.

Douglas, David. "The *Song of Roland* and the Norman Conquest of England." *French Studies* 14 (1960): 99–116.

Dubois, Jean. *Etude sur la dérivation suffixale en français moderne et contemporain.* Paris: Larousse, 1962.

Dubruck, Edelgard. *The Theme of Death in French Poetry of the Middle Ages and the Renaissance.* Studies in French Literature 1. The Hague: Mouton, 1964.

Du Cange, Charles du Fresne, sieur. *Glossarium mediae et infimae latinitatis.* Revised by Léopold Favre. 10 vols. 1883–87; rpt. Paris: Librairie des sciences et des arts, 1937–38.

Dufournet, Jean. *Cours sur la Chanson de Roland.* Les Cours de Sorbonne. Paris: Centre de documentation universitaire, 1972.

Duggan, Joseph J. *A Concordance of the Chanson de Roland.* Columbus: Ohio State University Press, 1969.

———. "The Generation of the Episode of Baligant: Charlemagne's Dream and the Normans at Mantzikert." *Romance Philology* 30 (1976): 59–82.

———. *The Song of Roland: Formulaic Style and Poetic Craft.* Berkeley and Los Angeles: Center for Medieval and Renaissance Studies, University of California, Los Angeles, 1973.

———. "Virgilian Inspiration in the *Roman d'Enéas* and the *Chanson de Roland.*" *Medieval Epic to the "Epic Theater" of Brecht.* Eds. Rosario P. Armato and John M. Spalek. University of Southern California Studies in Comparative Literature 1. Los Angeles: University of Southern California Press, 1968. Pp. 9–23.

Durmart le Galois: Roman arthurien du treizième siècle. Ed. Joseph Gildea, O.S.A. 2 vols. Villanova, Pa.: Villanova Press, 1965–66.

Earl, Donald. *The Moral and Political Tradition of Rome.* Ithaca: Cornell University Press, 1963.

Edmonds, Barbara D. "Le portrait des Sarrasins dans la *Chanson de Roland.*" *French Review* 44 (1971): 870–80.

Eginhard. Vie de Charlemagne. Ed. and trans. Louis Halphen. 3d ed. Paris: Les Belles Lettres, 1947.

Eisner, Robert A. "In Search of the Real Theme of the *Song of Roland.*" *Romance Notes* 14 (1972): 179–83.

Elcock, W. D. "Pleine sa hanste." *French Studies* 7 (1953): 35–47.

Eneas, roman du XIIe siècle. Ed. J.-J. Salverda de Grave. Classiques français du moyen âge 44 and 62. 2 vols. 1925–29; rpt. Paris: Champion, 1964.

Etudes de civilisation médiévale (IXe–XIIe siècles): Mélanges offerts à Edmond-René Labande. Poitiers: Centre d'études supérieures de civilisation médiévale, 1974.

Evans, Joan. *Cluniac Art of the Romanesque Period.* Cambridge: University Press, 1950.

Ewert, Alfred, and Mario Roques. "L'accident du vers 2242 de la *Chanson de Roland.*" *Romania* 59 (1933): 81–83.

Faherty, W. B. "Woman." *New Catholic Encyclopedia.* New York: McGraw-Hill, 1967. Vol. 14. Pp. 993–95.

Faral, Edmond. "A propos de la *Chanson de Roland:* Genèse et signification du personnage de Turpin." *La Technique littéraire des chansons de geste.* Pp. 271–80.

———. *La Chanson de Roland: Etude et analyse.* Les Chefs-d'oeuvre de la littérature expliqués. Paris: Mellottée, 1934.

———. *Les Jongleurs en France au moyen âge.* 2d ed. Bibliothèque de l'Ecole des hautes études 187. 1910; rpt. Paris: Champion, 1964.

———. *Recherches sur les sources latines des contes et romans courtois du moyen âge.* Paris: Champion, 1913.

———. "Sur trois vers de la *Chanson de Roland* (vers 1016, 1465, 1517)." *Modern Philology* 38 (1940/41): 235–42.

Farnham, Fern. "Romanesque Design in the *Chanson de Roland.*" *Romance Philology* 18 (1964): 143–64.

Farnsworth, William O. *Uncle and Nephew in the Old French Chansons de Geste: A*

Study in the Survival of Matriarchy. Columbia University Studies in Romance Philology and Literature. New York: Columbia University Press, 1913.

Fawtier, Robert. "Notes pour le commentaire des vers 1877–1881 et 485–487 de la *Chanson de Roland*." *Studies in French Language and Mediaeval Literature Presented to Professor Mildred K. Pope by Pupils, Colleagues and Friends*. Publications of the University of Manchester 268. Manchester: Manchester University Press, 1939. Pp. 99–102.

Fischer, Wilhelm. *Der Bote im altfranzösischen Epos*. Inaugural-Dissertation. Marburg, 1887.

Fleming, John W. *The Roman de la Rose: A Study in Allegory and Iconography*. Princeton: Princeton University Press, 1969.

Flutre, Louis-Fernand. *Table des noms propres avec toutes leurs variantes figurant dans les romans du moyen âge écrits en français ou en provençal et actuellement publiés ou analysés*. Publications du Centre d'études supérieures de civilisation médiévale 2. Poitiers: Centre d'études supérieures de civilisation médiévale, 1962.

Focillon, Henri. *Art d'Occident*. Vol. 1. *Le Moyen Age roman*. Le Livre de Poche. Série Art. Paris: Les Belles Lettres, 1950.

Folz, Robert. *Le Souvenir et la légende de Charlemagne dans l'Empire germanique médiéval*. Paris: Les Belles Lettres, 1950.

Foreville, R. "La typologie du roi dans la littérature historiographique anglo-normande aux XIe et XIIe siècles." *Mélanges Edmond-René Labande*. Pp. 275–92.

Foulet, Alfred. "Is Roland Guilty of Desmesure?" *Romance Philology* 10 (1957): 145–48.

———. Review of Ménard, *Le Rire et le sourire dans le roman courtois au moyen âge (1150–1250)*. *Romance Philology* 26 (1972): 187–92.

Foulet, Lucien. *Petite Syntaxe de l'ancien français*. 3d ed. Classiques français du moyen âge. 2e série: Manuels. Paris: Champion, 1930.

Foulon, Charles. "Les deux humiliations de Lancelot." *Bibliographical Bulletin of the International Arthurian Society* 8 (1956): 79–90.

Fourrier, Anthime. *Le Courant réaliste dans le roman courtois en France au moyen âge*. Vol. 1. *Les débuts (XIIe siècle)*. Paris: Nizet, 1960.

François, Charles. "'Pleine sa hanste': remises en question." *Marche romane* 25 (1975): 11–29.

François Villon. Oeuvres. Ed. Auguste Longnon. 4th ed. Revised by Lucien Foulet. Classiques français du moyen âge 2. Paris: Champion, 1932.

Frank, Grace. *The Medieval French Drama*. Oxford: Clarendon Press, 1954.

Frappier, Jean. *Chrétien de Troyes et le mythe du graal: Etude sur Perceval ou le Conte du Graal*. Paris: Société d'édition d'enseignement supérieur, 1972.

———. *Etude sur Yvain ou le Chevalier au lion de Chrétien de Troyes*. Paris: Société d'édition d'enseignement supérieur, 1969.

———. *Les Chansons de geste du cycle de Guillaume d'Orange*. 2 vols. Paris: Société d'édition d'enseignement supérieur, 1955–65.

———. "Les destriers et leurs épithètes." *La Technique littéraire des chansons de geste*. Pp. 85–104.

———. "Le thème de la lumière de la 'Chanson de Roland' au 'Roman de la Rose'." *Cahiers de l'Association internationale des études françaises* 20 (1968): 101–24.

———. "Vues sur les conceptions courtoises dans les littératures d'oc et d'oïl au XIIe siècle." *Cahiers de civilisation médiévale* 2 (1959): 135–56.

Fritzche, Carl. "Die lateinischen Visionen des Mittelalters bis zur Mitte des 12. Jahrhunderts: Ein Beitrag zur Culturgeschichte." *Romanische Forschungen* 2 (1886): 246–79; 3 (1887): 337–69.

Frye, Northrop. *Anatomy of Criticism: Four Essays*. New York: Atheneum, 1968.

Gaehde, Joachim E. "The Painters of the Carolingian Bible Manuscript of San Paolo Fuori le Mura in Rome [with] Appendix." Ph.D. dissertation, New York University, 1963.

———. "The Turonian Sources of the Bible of San Paolo Fuori le Mura in Rome." *Frühmittelalterliche Studien*. Jahrbuch des Instituts für Frühmittelalterforschung der Universität Munster 5 (1971): 386–92.

Gaenssle-Pfeuffer, Cäcilie. "'Majestez' und 'vertut' in der *Karlsreise*: Zur Problematik der Deutung der Dichtung." *Zeitschrift für romanische Philologie* 83 (1967): 257–67.

Gaiffier, Baudouin de, S.J. "La légende de Charlemagne: Le péché de l'empereur et son pardon." *Recueil de travaux offert à M. Clovis Brunel par ses amis, collègues et élèves*. Ecole des chartes. Mémoires et documents 12. Vol. 1. Paris: Société de l'Ecole des Chartes, 1955. Pp. 490–503.

Gallais, Pierre. "Recherches sur la mentalité des romanciers français du moyen âge." *Cahiers de civilisation médiévale* 7 (1964): 479–93.

Ganshof, François-Louis. *Feudalism*. Trans. Philip Grierson. 2d ed. New York: Harper, 1961.

Gardiner, F. C. *The Pilgrimage of Desire: A Study of Theme and Genre in Medieval Literature*. Leiden: Brill, 1971.

Garel, J. "La prière du plus grand péril." *Mélanges Pierre Le Gentil*. Pp. 311–18.

Gautier, Léon. *Les Epopées françaises*. 3 vols. Paris: Palmé, 1865–68.

Genesis. Trans. E. A. Speiser. The Anchor Bible 1. Garden City: Doubleday, 1964.

Gérard, Albert. "L'axe Roland-Ganelon: valeurs en conflit dans la *Chanson de Roland*." *Le Moyen Age* 76 (1969): 445–66.

Gildea, Sister Marianna, R.S.M. *Expressions of Religious Thought and Feeling in the Chansons de Geste*. Washington, D.C.: Catholic University of America Press, 1943.

Gillett, Joseph E. "The Autonomous Character in Spanish and European Literature." *Hispanic Review* 24 (1959): 179–90.

Ginette, Robert. "Notes sur la Prise de Nobles." *Etudes de philologie romane*. Romanica Gandensia 4. Ghent: Rijksuniversiteit te Gent, 1955. Pp. 67–80.

Gist, Margaret Adlum. *Love and War in the Middle English Romances*. Philadelphia: University of Pennsylvania Press; London: Oxford University Press, 1947.

Glossaire du Parler Français au Canada. Quebec City: L'Action Sociale, 1930.

Godefroy, Frédéric. *Dictionnaire de l'ancienne langue française et de tous ses dialectes, du IXe au XVe siècle*. 10 vols. 1881–1902; rpt. Paris: Librairie des sciences et des arts, 1937–38.

Gormont et Isembart. Ed. Alphonse Bayot. Classiques français du moyen âge 14. Paris: Champion, 1921.

Gougenheim, Georges. "'Compagnon' dans la *Chanson de Roland*." *Mélanges Pierre Le Gentil*. Pp. 325–28.

———. "De 'chevalier' à 'cavalier'." *Mélanges Ernest Hoepffner*. Pp. 117–26.

———. "*Orgueil* et *fierté* dans la *Chanson de Roland*." *Mélanges Jean Frappier*. Vol. 1. Pp. 365–73.

———. "*Place* dans la *Chanson de Roland*: Recherche d'un contenu sémantique." *Bulletin des Jeunes Romanistes* 9 (1964): 1–4.

Grabar, André. *L'Empereur dans l'art byzantin: Recherches sur l'art officiel de l'empire d'Orient*. Publications de la Faculté des lettres de l'Université de Strasbourg 75. Paris: Les Belles Lettres, 1936.

Grabar, André, and Carl Nordenfalk. *Romanesque Painting From the Eleventh to the Thirteenth Century*. Trans. Stuart Gilbert. The Great Centuries of Painting. Lausanne: Skira, 1958.

Gräf, Hermann. *Der Parallelismus im Rolandslied*. Inaugural-Dissertation. Wertheim-am-Main: Bechstein, 1931.

Green, H. J. "The Etymology of AOI and AE." *MLN*, 85 (1970): 593–98.
Greene, Thomas M. *Rabelais: A Study in Comic Courage*. Landmarks in Literature. Englewood Cliffs, N. J.: Prentice-Hall, 1970.
Greenhill, Eleanor Simmons. "The Child in the Tree: A Study of the Cosmological Tree in Christian Tradition." *Traditio* 10 (1954): 323–71.
Greimas, A. J. *Dictionnaire de l'ancien français jusqu'au milieu du XVI*[e] *siècle*. Paris: Larousse, 1969.
Grisward, Joël H. "Le motif de l'épée jetée au lac: la mort d'Arthur et la mort de Batradz." *Romania* 90 (1969): 289–340, 473–514.
Gsteiger, Manfreid. "Note sur les préambules des chansons de geste." *Cahiers de civilisation médiévale* 2 (1959): 213–20.
Guernes de Pont-Sainte-Maxence. La Vie de Saint Thomas Becket. Ed. Emmanuel Walberg. Classiques français du moyen âge 77. Paris: Champion, 1964.
Guiette, Robert. "Les deux scènes du cor dans la *Chanson de Roland* et dans les *Conquestes de Charlemagne*." *Le Moyen Age* 69 (1963): 845–55.
Györy, Jean. *Etude sur la Chanson de Roland*. Paris: Droz, 1936.
———. "Les prières de Guillaume d'Orange dans le *Couronnement de Louis*." *Mélanges Rita Lejeune*. Vol. 2. Pp. 769–77.
———. "Réflexions sur le guerrier jongleur." *Annales Universitatis Budapestinensis, Sectio philologica* 3 (1961): 47–60.
———. Review of Rütten, *Symbol und Mythus im altfranzösischen Rolandslied*. *Cahiers de civilisation médiévale* 16 (1974): 344–45.
Hackett, Winifred Mary. "La féodalité dans la *Chanson de Roland* et dans *Girart de Roussillon*." *Société Rencesvals. IV*[e] *Congrès International*. Pp. 22–27.
———. "Le gant de Roland." *Romania* 89 (1968): 253–56.
Haerle, Philipp. *Captivus, cattivo, chétif: Zur Einwirkung des Christentums auf die Terminologie der Moralbegriffe*. Romanica Helvetica 55. Berne: Francke, 1955.
Hall, Robert A., Jr. "On Individual Authorship in the *Roland*." *Symposium* 15 (1961): 297–301.
Halloran, Richard. "Soldier's Return from 30 Years in Jungle Stirs Japanese Deeply." *New York Times*, 13 March 1974, pp. 1, 12.
Halverson, John. "Ganelon's Trial." *Speculum* 42 (1967): 661–69.
Halvorsen, Eyvind Fjeld. *The Norse Version of the Chanson de Roland*. Bibliotheca Arnamagnaeana 19. Copenhagen: Munksgaard, 1959.
Hämel, Adalbert. "Vom Herzog Naimes 'von Bayern', dem Pfaffen Konrad von Regensberg und dem Pseudo-Turpin." *Sitzungsberichte der Bayerischen Akademie der Wissenschaften*. Philosophisch-historische Klasse. Jahrgang 1955. Heft 1.
Hand, Wayland D. *A Dictionary of Words and Idioms Associated with Judas Iscariot: A Compilation Based Mainly on Material Found in the Germanic Languages*. University of California Publications in Modern Philology 24, no. 3. Berkeley and Los Angeles: University of California Press, 1942.
Harden, A. Robert. "The Depreciatory Comparison: A Literary Device of the Medieval French Epic." *Mediaeval Studies in Honor of Urban Tigner Holmes, Jr.* Eds. John Mahoney and John Esten Keller. University of North Carolina Studies in the Romance Languages and Literatures 56. Chapel Hill: University of North Carolina Press, 1965. Pp. 63–78.
Harris, Julian. "*Chanson de Roland*, Line 485: A Disputed Reading." *Romanic Review* 27 (1936): 22–27.
———. "How Old Was Charlemagne in the *Chanson de Roland*?" *Romance Philology* 25 (1971): 183–88.
———. "'Munjoie' and 'Reconuisance' in *Chanson de Roland*, l. 3620." *Romance Philology* 10 (1957): 168–73.

———. "*Nen est fins que t'en alges* (*Roland* 2978) and its Context." *Romance Philology* 29 (1976): 507–14.

———. "*Pleine sa hanste* in the *Chanson de Roland*." *French and Provençal Lexicography: Essays Presented to Honor Alexander Herman Schutz*. Eds. Urban T. Holmes and Kenneth R. Scholberg. Columbus: Ohio State University Press, 1964. Pp. 100–17.

Harrison, Ann Tukey. "A Feminist Look at the *Chanson de Roland*." Unpublished paper read at the Tenth Conference on Medieval Studies, Western Michigan University, 1975. See review by Sara Sturm.

Hatcher, Anna Granville. "Eulalie, lines 15–17." *Romanic Review* 40 (1949): 241–49.

———. "The Old French Poem St. Alexis: A Mathematical Demonstration." *Traditio* 8 (1952): 111–58.

Hatzfeld, Helmut A. "Esthetic Criticism Applied to Medieval Romance Literature." *Romance Philology* 1 (1947/48): 305–27.

———. "Le *Rolandslied* allemand: Guide pour la compréhension stylistique de la *Chanson de Roland*." *Cultura Neolatina* 21 (1961): 48–56.

———. "Les études de style et la littérature médiévale." *Mélanges Rita Lejeune*. Vol. 2. Pp. 1601–11.

———. *Literature Through Art: A New Approach to French Literature*. New York: Oxford University Press, 1952.

———. "Style 'roman' dans les littératures romanes: Essai de synthèse." *Studi in onore di Italo Siciliano*. Pp. 525–40.

Heer, Friedrich. *The Medieval World: Europe 1100–1350*. Trans. Janet Sondheimer. New York and Toronto: New American Library; London: New English Library, 1961.

Heinemann, Edward A. "La composition stylisée et la transmission écrite des textes rolandiens." *Société Rencesvals. VIe Congrès International*. Pp. 253–72.

———. "La place de l'élément 'brandir la lance' dans la structure du motif de l'attaque à la lance." *Romania* 95 (1974): 105–13.

Heinimann, Siegfried. "'Dulcis': Ein Beitrag zur lateinisch-romanischen Stilgeschichte des Mittelalters." *Studia philologica: Homenaje ofrecido a Dámaso Alonso por sus amigos y discípulos con ocasión de su 60.° aniversario*. Madrid: Gredos, 1961. Vol. 2. Pp. 215–32.

Hemming, Timothy D. "La mort dans la *Chanson de Roland*: étude lexico-syntactique." *Société Rencesvals. IVe Congrès International*. Pp. 90–94.

———. "Restrictions lexicales dans la chanson de geste." *Romania* 89 (1968): 96–105.

Henry, Albert. *Chrestomathie de la littérature en ancien français*. 5th ed. 2 parts in 1 vol. Bibliotheca Romanica. Series altera: Scripta Romanica Selecta 3–4. Berne: Francke, 1970.

Herlihy, David. "The Generation in Medieval History." *Viator* 5 (1974): 347–64.

Herman, Gerald. "Unconventional Arms as a Comic Device in Some *Chansons de Geste*." *Modern Language Quarterly* 30 (1969): 319–30.

Herrade de Landsberg. Hortus deliciarum. Eds. A. Straub and G. Keller. Société pour la conservation des monuments historiques d'Alsace. Strasbourg: Imprimerie Strasbourgeoise, 1879–89.

Heuser, Mary Laura. "Gestures and Their Meaning in Early Christian Art." Ph.D. dissertation, Radcliffe College, 1954.

Historia Karoli Magni et Rotholandi ou Chronique du Pseudo-Turpin. Textes revus et publiés d'après 49 manuscrits. Ed. C. Meredith-Jones. 1936; rpt. Geneva: Slatkine, 1972.

Hoepffner, Ernest. "Les rapports littéraires entre les premières chansons de geste." *Studi Medievali*, n.s. 4 (1931): 233–58; 6 (1933): 45–81.

Hofer, Stefan. "Das Verratsmotiv in den Chansons de geste." *Zeitschrift für romanische Philologie* 44 (1924): 594–609.

Holland, Michael. "Gautier et Margarit: deux épisodes de la *Chanson de Roland.*" *Cahiers de civilisation médiévale* 3 (1960): 339–49.

———. "Rolandus resurrectus." *Mélanges René Crozet.* Vol. 1. Pp. 397–418.

Hoppe, Ruth. *Die romanische Geste im Rolandslied.* Schriften der Albertus-Universität 10. Königsberg and Berlin: Ost-Europa, 1937.

Horrent, Jules. "La bataille des Pyrénées de 778." *Le Moyen Age* 78 (1972): 197–227.

———. *La Chanson de Roland dans les littératures française et espagnole au moyen âge.* Bibliothèque de la Faculté de philosophie et lettres de l'Université de Liège 120. Paris: Les Belles Lettres, 1951.

———. *Le Pèlerinage de Charlemagne: Essai d'explication littéraire avec des notes de critique textuelle.* Bibliothèque de la Faculté de philosophie et lettres de l'Université de Liège 158. Paris: Les Belles Lettres, 1961.

———. Review of Steinmeyer, *Untersuchungen zur allegorischen Bedeutung der Träume im altfranzösischen Rolandslied. Romance Philology* 23 (1970): 595–600.

Huck, G. D. "Flowers, Symbolism of." *New Catholic Encyclopedia.* New York: McGraw-Hill, 1967. Vol. 5. Pp. 981–82.

Hughes, Robert. *Heaven and Hell in Western Art.* New York: Stein and Day, 1968.

Hunt, Tony. "Träume und die Überlieferungsgeschichte des altfranzösischen *Rolandslied.*" *Zeitschrift für romanische Philologie* 90 (1974): 241–46.

Huon de Bordeaux. Ed. Pierre Ruelle. Université Libre de Bruxelles. Travaux de la Faculté de philosophie et lettres 20. Brussels: Presses Universitaires de Bruxelles; Paris: Presses Universitaires de France, 1960.

Huppé, Bernard F. "The Concept of the Hero in the Early Middle Ages." *Concepts of the Hero in the Middle Ages and the Renaissance.* Eds. Norman T. Burns and Christopher J. Reagan. Albany: State University of New York Press, 1975. Pp. 1–26.

Illustrations of the Life of St. Albans in Trinity College Dublin MS. *E. i. 40.* Eds. W. R. L. Lowe and E. F. Jacob, with a description of the illustrations by M. R. James. Oxford: Clarendon Press, 1924.

Imbs, Paul. "Quelques aspects du vocabulaire des plus anciennes chansons de geste." *La Technique littéraire des chansons de geste.* Pp. 71–72 (discussion, pp. 72–74).

Itinera Hierosolymitana et Descriptionis Terrae Sanctae bellis sacris anteriora et latina lingua exarata. Eds. Titus Tobler and Auguste Molinier. Publications de la Société de l'Orient latin. Série géographique 1. Geneva, 1879.

Jackson, W. T. H. Review of Steinmeyer, *Untersuchungen zur allegorischen Bedeutung der Träume im altfranzösischen Rolandslied. Romanic Review* 57 (1966): 56.

James, E. O. *Comparative Religion: An Introductory and Historical Study.* University Paperbacks. London: Methuen; New York: Barnes & Noble, 1961.

James, Montague Rhodes. *Marvels of the East: A Full Reproduction of the Three Known Copies.* Oxford: University Press, 1929.

———. "The Drawings of Matthew Paris." *Walpole Society* 14 (1925/26): 1–26.

Janson, H. W. *Apes and Ape Lore in the Middle Ages and the Renaissance.* Studies of the Warburg Institute 20. London: Warburg Institute, 1952.

Jenkins, T. Atkinson. "Why Did Ganelon Hate Roland?" *PMLA* 36 (1921): 119–33.

Job. Trans. Marvin H. Pope. The Anchor Bible 15. Garden City: Doubleday, 1965.

Johnson, Ronald C. "*Hoese* 'Boot' in the *Chanson de Roland,* Line 641." *Modern Language Review* 58 (1963): 391–92.

Jones, George Fenwick. "El papel del beso en el cantar de gesta." *Boletín de la Real Academia de Buenas Letras de Barcelona* 31 (1965/66): 105–18.

———. "La complainte de Roland—une interprétation divergente." *Cultura Neolatina* 21 (1961): 34–47.

———. "Roland's Lament: A Divergent Interpretation." *Romanic Review* 53 (1962): 3–15.

———. "St. Giles at Roncevaux." *French Review* 54 (1971): 881–88.

———. *The Ethos of the Song of Roland.* Baltimore: Johns Hopkins Press, 1963.

Jones, Paul John. *Prologue and Epilogue in Old French Lives of Saints Before 1400.* Series in Romanic Languages and Literature 24. Philadelphia: University of Pennsylvania Press, 1933.

Jonin, Pierre. "La 'Clere' Espagne de Blancandrin." *Mosaic* 8 (1975): 85–96.

———. "Le climat des croisades des chansons de geste." *Cahiers de civilisation médiévale* 7 (1964): 279–88.

———. *Les Personnages féminins dans les romans français de Tristan au XIIe siècle: Etude des influences contemporaines.* Publication des Annales de la Faculté des lettres, Aix-en-Provence, n.s. 22. Gap: Ophrys, 1958.

Joufroi de Poitiers: Roman d'aventures du XIIIe siècle. Eds. Percival B. Fay and John L. Grigsby. Textes littéraires français 183. Geneva: Droz; Paris: Minard, 1972.

Kahane, Henry and Renée. "Die Margariten." *Zeitschrift für romanische Philologie* 76 (1960): 185–204.

———. "Magic and Gnosticism in the 'Chanson de Roland'." *Romance Philology* 12 (1958/59): 216–31.

Kantorowicz, Ernst H. *Laudes regiae: A Study in Liturgical Acclamations and Mediaeval Ruler Worship.* Berkeley and Los Angeles: University of California Press, 1946.

———. "The King's Advent." *Art Bulletin* 2 (1944): 207–31.

———. "The 'King's Advent' and the Enigmatic Panels in the Doors of Santa Sabina." *Art Bulletin* 26 (1944): 207–31.

———. *The King's Two Bodies: A Study in Mediaeval Political Theology.* Princeton: Princeton University Press, 1957.

Karlamagnús Saga: The Saga of Charlemagne and His Heroes. Trans. Constance B. Hieatt. Vol. 1. Toronto: The Pontifical Institute of Mediaeval Studies, 1975.

Kaske, Robert E. "*Sapientia et Fortitudo* as the Controlling Theme of *Beowulf.*" *Studies in Philology* 55 (1958): 423–56.

Katzenellenbogen, Adolf. *Allegories of the Virtues and Vices in Mediaeval Art From Early Christian Times to the Thirteenth Century.* Trans. Alan J. P. Crick. 1939; rpt. New York: Norton, 1964.

———. "The Central Tympanum at Vézelay: Its Encyclopedic Meaning and Its Relation to the First Crusade." *Art Bulletin* 26 (1944): 141–51.

Keller, Hans Erich. "La conversion de Bramimonde." *Société Rencesvals. VIe Congrès International.* Pp. 175–203. Also in *Olifant* 1, no. 1 (1973): 3–22.

———. "La place du *Ruolantes Liet* dans la tradition rolandienne." *Le Moyen Age* 71 (1965): 215–46, 401–21.

———. "La version dionysienne de la *Chanson de Roland.*" *Philologica Romanica. Erhard Lommatzsch gewidmet.* Eds. Erich von Richthofen, Manfred Bambeck, and Hans Helmut Christmann. Munich: Fink, 1975. Pp. 257–87.

Keller, Henning. "Einige afr. Bezeichnungen für 'Lanze' und 'Speer': Ein Beitrag zur Etymologie von afr. *javelot, a(l)gier,* und *guivre.*" *Zeitschrift für romanische Philologie* 83 (1967): 268–79.

Kelly, F. Douglas. *Sens and Conjointure in the Chevalier de la Charrette.* Studies in French Literature 2. The Hague: Mouton, 1966.

Kelly, Henry Ansgar. "The Metamorphoses of the Eden Serpent During the Middle Ages and Renaissance." *Viator* 2 (1971): 301–27.

Ker, W. P. *The Dark Ages.* Mentor Book. New York: The New American Library, 1958.

Kibler, William W. "Again *La Chanson de Roland,* Verse 400." *Romance Notes* 14 (1972): 621–23.

———. "Roland and Tierri." *Olifant* 2, no. 1 (1974): 27–32.

———. "Roland's Pride." *Symposium* 26 (1972): 147–60.

Kirschbaum, E. "L'angelo rosso e l'angelo turchino." *Revista di archeologia cristiana* 17 (1940): 209–27.

Klein, Hans-Wilhelm. "Der Kreuzzugsgedanke im Rolandslied und die neuere Rolandforschung." *Die Neueren Sprachen*, n.s. 5 (1956): 265–85.

Kleinbauer, W. Eugene. "Charlemagne's Palace Chapel at Aachen and its Copies." *Gesta* 4 (1965): 2–11.

Knapp, Fritz Peter. "Die hässliche Gralsbotin und die victorinische Ästhetik." *Sprachkunst* 3 (1972): 1–10.

Knudson, Charles A. "Etudes sur la composition de la *Chanson de Roland*." *Romania* 63 (1937): 48–92.

———. "La brogne." *Mélanges Rita Lejeune*. Vol. 2. Pp. 1625–35.

———. "Le thème de la princesse sarrasine dans la *Prise d'Orange*." *Romance Philology* 22 (1969): 449–62.

———. "Quel terrain faut-il céder au néo-traditionalisme? Le cas de la *Chanson de Roland*." *Boletín de la Real Academia de Buenas Letras de Barcelona* 31 (1965/66): 120–23.

———. "Serments téméraires et gabs: notes sur un thème littéraire." *Société Rencesvals. IVe Congrès International*. Pp. 254–64.

Köhler, Erich. "'Conseil des barons' und 'jugement des barons': Epische Fatalität und Feudalrecht im altfranzösischen Rolandslied." *Sitzungsberichte der Heidelberger Akademie der Wissenschaften*. Philosophisch-historische Klasse. Heidelberg: Winter, 1968. Pp. 5–42.

Kostoroski, Emilie P. "Further Echoes from Roland's Horn." *Romance Notes* 13 (1972): 541–44.

Krappe, A. H. "The Dreams of Charlemagne in the *Chanson de Roland*." *PMLA* 36 (1921): 134–41.

Krautheimer, Richard. "The Carolingian Revival of Early Christian Architecture." *Art Bulletin* 24 (1942): 1–38.

Krings, Hans. *Geschichte des Wortschatzes der Höflichkeit im Französischen*. Romanistische Versuche und Vorarbeiten 11. Bonn: Romanisches Seminar der Universität Bonn, 1961.

Kunkle, Roberta A. "Time in the *Song of Roland*." *Romance Notes* 13 (1972): 550–55.

Künstle, Karl. *Ikonographie der christlichen Kunst*. 2 vols. Freiburg im Breisgau: Herder, 1926–28.

Labande-Mailfert, Yvonne. "La douleur et la mort dans l'art des XIIe et XIIIe siècles." *Atti del V Convegno di Studi sulla spiritualità medievale*. Todi: Presso L'Accademia Tudertina, 1967. Pp. 295–332.

Laborde, Comte Alexandre de. *Etude sur la Bible moralisée illustrée*. 5 vols. Paris, 1911–27.

La Chanson d'Aspremont. Ed. Louis Brandin. 2d ed. Classiques français du moyen âge 25. Paris: Champion, 1924.

La Chanson de Guillaume. Ed. Duncan McMillan. Société des anciens textes français. 2 vols. Paris: Picard, 1949–50.

La Chanson de Roland: A Modern French Translation. Trans. J. Geddes. 1906; rpt. New York: Macmillan, 1926.

La Chanson de Roland: Oxford Version. Ed. T. Atkinson Jenkins. Rev. ed. Heath's Modern Language Series. Boston–New York–Chicago–London: Heath, 1929.

La Chanson de Roland. Reproduction phototypique du Manuscrit Digby 23 de la Bodleian Library d'Oxford. Ed. Comte Alexandre de Laborde. Paris: Société des anciens textes français, 1933.

La Chanson de Roland: Texte critique, traduction et commentaire, grammaire et glossaire. Ed. and trans. Léon Gautier. Edition classique. 20th ed. Tours: Mame, 1892.

La Chanson de Roland. Ed. F. Whitehead. Blackwell's French Texts. 1946; rpt. Oxford: Blackwell, 1965.

La Chanson de Roland. Ed. and trans. Gérard Moignet. Bibliothèque Bordas. Paris: Bordas, 1969.

La Chanson de Roland. Ed. and trans. J. Bédier. Paris: Piazza, 1921.

La Chanson de Roland. Ed. Cesare Segre. Documenti di filologia, 16. Milan and Naples: Ricciardi, 1971.

La Chanson de Roland. Ed. Guillaume Picot. Nouveaux Classiques Larousse. 2 vols. Paris: Larousse, 1965.

La Chanson de Roland. Ed. William Calin. Series in Medieval French Literature. New York: Appleton-Century-Crofts, 1968.

La Chanson de Roland. L'Encyclopédie Sonore. Collection "Les Grands Textes." Librairie Hachette. Disque 270 E 047.

La Chanson du Chevalier au cygne et de Godefroid de Bouillon. Ed. C. Hippeau. Collection des poètes français du moyen âge. 2 vols. Paris: Aubry, 1874–77.

Lacroix, Paul. *France in the Middle Ages: Customs, Classes and Conditions.* New York: Ungar, 1963.

Ladner, Gerhart B. "The Gestures of Prayer in Papal Iconography of the Thirteenth and Early Fourteenth Centuries." *Didascaliae: Studies in Honor of Anselm M. Albareda, Prefect of the Vatican Library, Presented by a Group of American Scholars.* New York: Rosenthal, 1961. Pp. 246–75.

La Folie Tristan de Berne. Ed. Ernest Hoepffner. 2d ed. Publications de la Faculté des lettres de l'Université de Strasbourg. Textes d'étude 3. Paris: Les Belles Lettres, 1949.

La Folie Tristan d'Oxford. Ed. Ernest Hoepffner. 2d ed. Publications de la Faculté des lettres de l'Université de Strasbourg. Textes d'étude 8. Rodez: Carrère, 1943.

Laming, Annette, and Monique Roussel. *La Grotte de Lascaux.* Paris: Caisse nationale des monuments historiques, 1950.

Lang, H. R. "*Seignor* as a Vocative Singular." *Romanic Review* 3 (1912): 309–10.

Langlois, Charles-Victor. *La Vie en France au moyen âge de la fin du XIIe au milieu du XIVe siècle d'après les moralistes du temps.* Vol. 2. Paris: Hachette, 1925.

Lanham, Richard A. *A Handlist of Rhetorical Terms: A Guide for Students of English Literature.* Berkeley and Los Angeles: University of California Press, 1969.

La Queste del saint graal: Roman du XIIIe siècle. Ed. Albert Pauphilet. Classiques français du moyen âge 33. Paris: Champion, 1949.

Larmat, Jean. "La veuve, le pauvre et l'orphelin: Un aspect poétique de Charlemagne dans le *Couronnement de Louis.*" Proceedings of the Seventh International Congress of the Société Rencesvals, Liège, 1976.

Larousse du XXe siècle. 6 vols. Paris: Larousse, 1928.

La Technique littéraire des chansons de geste: Actes du Colloque de Liège (Septembre 1957). Bibliothèque de la Faculté de philosophie et lettres de l'Université de Liège 150. Paris: Les Belles Lettres, 1959.

L'Atre périlleux. Ed. Brian Woledge. Classiques français du moyen âge 76. Paris: Champion, 1936.

Lavedan, Pierre. *Représentation des villes dans l'art du moyen âge.* Art médiéval. Bibliothèque de documentation. Paris: Vansest, 1954.

La Vie de Saint Gilles par Guillaume de Berneville, poème du XIIe siècle. Eds. Gaston Paris and Alphonse Bos. Société des anciens textes français. Paris: Didot, 1881.

La Vie de Seint Edmund le rei, poème anglo-normand du XIIe siècle par Denis Piramus. Ed. Hilding Kjellman. Göteborgs kungl. vetenskaps- och vitterhets-samhälles handlingar, fol. 5, ser. A, 4, no. 3. Göteborg: Wettergren and Kerber, 1935.

Lazar, Moshé. *Amour courtois et 'fin'amors' dans la littérature du XIIe siècle.* Bibliothèque française et romane. Série C: Etudes littéraires 8. Paris: Klincksieck, 1964.

———. "Lancelot et la 'mulier mediatrix': La Quête de soi à travers la femme." *L'Esprit Créateur* 9 (1969): 243–56.

Leblond, B. "Ci falt la geste que Turoldus declinet." *Annales de Normandie* 7 (1957): 159–63.

Le Charroi de Nîmes, chanson de geste du XIIe siècle. Ed. J.-L. Perrier. Classiques français du moyen âge 66. Paris: Champion, 1931.

Leclercq, Jean, O.S.B. *The Love of Learning and the Desire for God: A Study of Monastic Culture.* Trans. Catharine Misrahi. New York: Fordham University Press, 1961.

Le Couronnement de Louis, chanson de geste du XIIe siècle. Ed. Ernest Langlois. 2d ed. Classiques français du moyen âge 22. Paris: Champion, 1925.

Lecoy, Félix. "Notules sur le texte du *Roland* d'Oxford." *Mélanges Rita Lejeune.* Vol. 2. Pp. 793–800.

———. Review of Marichal, *Annuaire 1969–1970 ... Paléographie latine et française. Romania* 92 (1971): 141.

Lefèvre, Yves. *Manuel d'ancien français.* Vol. 3. Philippe Ménard. *Syntaxe.* Bordeaux: Société bordelaise de diffusion de travaux des lettres et sciences humaines, 1968.

Le Gentil, Pierre. Comment on Burger, "Les deux scènes du cor dans la *Chanson de Roland.*" *La Technique littéraire des chansons de geste.* P. 125.

———. *La Chanson de Roland.* Connaissance des lettres 43. Paris: Hatier-Boivin, 1955.

———. "Les nouvelles tendances de la critique et de l'interprétation des épopées médiévales." *Boletín de la Real Academia de Buenas Letras de Barcelona* 31 (1965/66): 131–41. Summary in *Bulletin bibliographique de la Société Rencesvals* 4 (1967): 109.

Legge, M. Dominica. "Archaism and the Conquest." *Modern Language Review* 51 (1956): 227–29.

Le Goff, Jacques. *La Civilisation de l'occident médiéval.* Paris: Arthaud, 1972.

Le Guide du Pèlerin de Saint-Jacques de Compostelle. Ed. and trans. Jeanne Vielliard. 3d ed. Macon: Protat, 1963.

Le Haut Livre du Graal: Perlesvaus. Eds. William A. Nitze and collaborators. Modern Philology Monographs of the University of Chicago. 2 vols. Chicago: University of Chicago Press, 1932–37.

Lehmann, Andrée. *Le Rôle de la femme dans l'histoire de France au moyen âge.* Paris: Berger-Levrault, 1952.

Leisinger, Hermann. *Romanische Bronzen: Kirchentüren im mittelalterlichen Europa.* Zurich: Europa, 1956.

Lejeune, Rita. "La composition du personnage de Gautier del Hum dans la *Chanson de Roland.*" *La Technique littéraire des chansons de geste.* Pp. 237–69.

———. "La naissance du couple littéraire 'Roland et Olivier'." *Mélanges Henri Grégoire.* Annuaire de l'Institut de philologie et d'histoire orientales et slaves 10. Brussels, 1950. Vol. 2. Pp. 371–401.

———. "La signification du nom 'marche' dans la *Chanson de Roland.*" *Boletim de Filologia* 18 (1961): 263–74.

———. "Le caractère de l'archevêque Turpin et les événements contemporains de la *Chanson de Roland* (version d'Oxford)." *Société Rencesvals. IVe Congrès International.* Pp. 9–21.

———. "Le Mont-Saint-Michel-au-Péril-de-la-Mer, la 'Chanson de Roland' et le Pèlerinage de Compostelle." *Millénaire monastique du Mont-Saint-Michel.* Bibliothèque d'Histoire et d'Archéologie chrétiennes. Paris: Lethielleux, 1967. Vol. 2. Pp. 411–33.

———. "Le péché de Charlemagne et la *Chanson de Roland.*" *Studia Philologica:*

Homenaje ofrecido a Dámaso Alonso por sus amigos y discípulos con ocasión de su 60.° aniversario. Madrid: Gredos, 1961. Vol. 2. Pp. 339–70.

———. "Les noms d'épée dans la *Chanson de Roland.*" *Mélanges de linguistique et de littérature romanes offerts à Mario Roques par ses amis, ses collègues et ses anciens élèves de France et de l'étranger*. Baden: Editions Art et Science, 1951. Vol. 1. Pp. 149–66.

———. *Recherches sur le thème: les chansons de geste et l'histoire*. Bibliothèque de la Faculté de philosophie et lettres de l'Université de Liège 108. Liège: Faculté de philosophie et lettres, 1948.

———. "Technique formulaire et chansons de geste." *Le Moyen Age* 60 (1954): 311–34.

———. "Turold dans la tapisserie de Bayeux." *Mélanges René Crozet*. Vol. 1. Pp. 419–425.

Lejeune, Rita, and Jacques Stiennon. *La Légende de Roland dans l'art du moyen âge*. 2d ed. 2 vols. Brussels: Arcade, 1967.

Lerch, E. "Le 'verrat' dans la *Chanson de Roland:* une correction inutile." *Romania* 64 (1938): 398–405.

Le Roman de Renart: Première branche. Ed. Mario Roques. Classiques français du moyen âge 78. Paris: Champion, 1948.

Le Roman de Rou. Ed. A. J. Holden. Société des anciens textes français. 2 vols. Paris: Picard, 1971.

Le Roman de Thèbes. Ed. Guy Raynaud de Lage. Classiques français du moyen âge 94 and 96. 2 vols. Paris: Champion, 1968.

Le Roman de Tristan par Thomas, poème du XIIe siècle. Ed. Joseph Bédier. Société des anciens textes français. 2 vols. Paris: Didot, 1902–05.

Le Roman de Troie par Benoît de Sainte-Maure. Ed. Léopold Constans. Société des anciens textes français. 6 vols. Paris: Didot, 1904–12.

Les Lais de Marie de France. Ed. Jean Rychner. Classiques français du moyen âge 93. Paris: Champion, 1966.

Les Oeuvres d'Adenet le Roi. Vol. 3. *Les Enfances Ogier*. Ed. Albert Henry. Rijksuniversiteit te Gent. Werken uitgegeven door de Faculteit van de wijsbegeerte en letteren 121. Bruges: De Tempel, 1956.

Les Oeuvres de Simund de Freine. Ed. John E. Matzke. Société des anciens textes français. Paris: Didot, 1909.

Les Romans de Chrétien de Troyes. Vol. 1. *Erec et Enide*. Ed. Mario Roques. Vol. 2. *Cligés*. Ed. Alexandre Micha. Vol. 3. *Le Chevalier de la Charrete*. Ed. Mario Roques. Vol. 4. *Le Chevalier au Lion (Yvain)*. Ed. Mario Roques. Classiques français du moyen âge 80, 84, 86, 89. Paris: Champion, 1952, 1970, 1958, 1971.

Les Textes de la Chanson de Roland. Ed. Raoul Mortier. 10 vols. Paris: La Geste Francor, 1940–44.

Le Voyage de Charlemagne à Jérusalem et à Constantinople. Ed. Paul Aebischer. Textes littéraires français 115. Geneva: Droz; Paris: Minard, 1965.

Levy, Raphael. "Interpretations of *venir* in *Roland* 602 and *Perceval* 6428." *Zeitschrift für romanische Philologie* 75 (1961): 342–45.

Leyerle, John. "The Heart and the Chain." *Harvard English Studies* 5 (1974): 113–45. (*The Learned and the Lewed: Studies in Chaucer and Medieval Literature*. Ed. Larry D. Benson.)

Li Tournoiemenz Antecrit von Huon de Mery. Ed. Georg Wimmer. Ausgaben und Abhandlungen aus dem Gebiete der romanischen Philologie 76. Marburg: Friedrich, 1888.

Little, Lester K. "Pride Goes Before Avarice: Social Change and the Vices in Latin Christendom." *American Historical Review* 76 (1971): 16–49.

Li Ver del juïse. Ed. Hugo von Feilitzen. Upsala: Berling, 1883.

Locke, Frederick W. "Ganelon and the Cooks." *Symposium* 20 (1966): 141–49.

———. *The Quest for the Holy Grail: A Literary Study of a Thirteenth-Century French Romance*. Stanford: Stanford University Press, 1960.

Lommatzsch, Erhard. "Darstellung von Trauer und Schmerz in der altfranzösischen Literatur." *Zeitschrift für romanische Philologie* 43 (1923): 20–67.

———. *Kleinere Schriften zur romanischen Philologie*. Berlin: Akademie, 1954.

Loomis, Laura Hibbard. "L'oriflamme de France et le cri 'Monjoie' au XIIe siècle." *Le Moyen Age* 65 (1959): 469–99.

Loomis, Roger S. *Arthurian Tradition and Chrétien de Troyes*. New York: Columbia University Press, 1949.

Loomis, Roger S., and Gertrude Schoepperle Loomis. *Arthurian Legends in Medieval Art*. London: Oxford University Press; New York: Modern Language Association of America, 1938.

Lord, Albert B. *The Singer of Tales*. Harvard Studies in Comparative Literature 24. Cambridge: Harvard University Press, 1960.

Lot, Ferdinand. "Etudes sur les légendes épiques françaises. V. La *Chanson de Roland*. A propos d'un livre récent." *Romania* 54 (1928): 357–80.

Louis, René. "La grande douleur pour la mort de Roland." *Cahiers de civilisation médiévale* 3 (1960): 62–67.

Lumiansky, Robert M. "Dramatic Audience in *Beowulf*." *Journal of English and Germanic Philology* 51 (1952): 545–50.

Luria, Maxwell S. "The Christian Tempest: A Symbolic Motif in Medieval Literature." Ph. D. dissertation, Princeton University, 1965.

———. "The Storm-Making Spring and the Meaning of Chrétien's *Yvain*." *Studies in Philology* 64 (1967): 564–85.

Lyons, Faith. "More About Roland's Glove." Unpublished paper read at the Fifth International Congress of the Société Rencesvals, Oxford, 1970. Summary in *Bulletin bibliographique de la Société Rencesvals* 6 (1971): 148, item 469.

Magoun, Francis P., Jr. "The Oral-Formulaic Character of Anglo-Saxon Poetic Narrative Poetry." *Speculum* 28 (1953): 446–67.

Mâle, Emile. *L'Art religieux du XIIe siècle en France: Etude sur les origines de l'iconographie du moyen âge*. Paris: Colin, 1922.

Malkiel, María Rosa Lida de. *L'Idée de la gloire dans la tradition occidentale: Antiquité, Moyen-âge occidental, Castille*. Trans. Sylvia Roubaud. Bibliothèque française et romane. Série C: Etudes littéraires 15. Paris: Klincksieck, 1968.

Mandach, André de. "Encore du nouveau à propos de la date et de la structure de la *Chanson de Roland* allemande." *Société Rencesvals. IVe Congrès International*. Pp. 106–16.

———. *Naissance et développement de la chanson de geste en Europe*. Vol. 1. *La Geste de Charlemagne et de Roland*. Vol. 2. *Chronique de Turpin: Texte anglo-normand de Willem de Briane (Arundel 220)*. Publications romanes et françaises 69 and 77. Geneva: Droz; Paris: Minard, 1961–63.

———. "The So-Called AOI in the *Chanson de Roland*." *Symposium* 11 (1957): 303–15.

Marichal, Robert. Report in *Annuaire 1969–1970 de l'Ecole pratique des hautes études. IVe section: Sciences historiques et philologiques. Extrait des rapports sur les conférences: Paléographie latine et française*. Paris, 1970. Pp. 363–74.

Martin, June H. "The Divisions of the *Chanson de Roland*." *Romance Notes* 6 (1965): 182–95.

McCulloch, Florence. *Mediaeval Latin and French Bestiaries*. University of North Carolina Studies in the Romance Languages and Literatures 33. Chapel Hill: University of North Carolina Press, 1962.

McMillan, Duncan. "A propos de traditions orales." *Cahiers de civilisation médiévale* 3 (1960): 61–71.

———. "A propos d'un travail de M. Delbouille sur les chansons de geste et le livre." *Cahiers de civilisation médiévale* 4 (1961): 47–54.

———. "Notes sur quelques clichés formulaires dans les chansons de geste." *Mélanges Maurice Delbouille*. Vol. 2. Pp. 477–93.

Meagher, P. K. "Avarice." *New Catholic Encyclopedia*. New York: McGraw-Hill, 1967. Vol. 1. Pp. 1122–23.

Medieval England. Revised and edited by Austin Lane Poole. 2 vols. Oxford: Clarendon Press, 1958.

Mélanges de langue et de littérature du moyen âge et de la Renaissance offerts à Jean Frappier par ses collègues, ses élèves et ses amis. Textes littéraires français 112. 2 vols. Geneva: Droz, 1970.

Mélanges de langue et de littératures médiévales offerts à Pierre Le Gentil par ses collègues, ses élèves et ses amis. Paris: Société d'édition d'enseignement supérieur, 1973.

Mélanges de linguistique romane et de philologie médiévale offerts à M. Maurice Delbouille. 2 vols. Gembloux: Duculot, 1964.

Mélanges de philologie romane et de littérature médiévale offerts à Ernest Hoepffner. Paris: Les Belles Lettres, 1949.

Mélanges d'histoire du moyen âge offerts à M. Ferdinand Lot par ses amis et ses élèves. Paris: Champion, 1925.

Mélanges Edmond-René Labande. See *Etudes de civilisation médiévale*.

Mélanges offerts à René Crozet à l'occasion de son soixante-dixième anniversaire. Eds. Pierre Gallais and Yves-Jean Riou. 2 vols. Poitiers: Société d'études médiévales, 1966.

Mélanges offerts à Rita Lejeune. 2 vols. Gembloux: Duculot, 1969.

Mellinkoff, Ruth. "Riding Backwards: Theme of Humiliation and Symbol of Evil." *Viator* 4 (1973): 153–76.

Mellor, Geoffrey. "*Roland* 602 (O: Puis si cumencet a venir ses tresors)." *MLN* 72 (1957): 111–13.

Ménard, Philippe. *Le Rire et le sourire dans le roman courtois au moyen âge (1150–1250)*. Publications romanes et françaises 105. Geneva: Droz, 1969.

———: "*Tenir le chief embronc, crosler le chief, tenir la main a la maissele:* trois attitudes de l'ennui dans les chansons de geste du XIIe siècle." *Société Rencesvals. IVe Congrès International*. Pp. 145–55.

Menéndez Pidal, Ramón. "El *aoi* del manuscrito Rolandiano de Oxford." *Revista de Filología Española* 46 (1963): 173–77.

———. *La Chanson de Roland et la tradition épique des Francs*. Trans. Irénée-Marcel Cluzel. 2d ed. Paris: Picard, 1960.

Meredith-Jones, C. "The Conventional Saracen of the Songs of Geste." *Speculum* 17 (1942): 201–25.

———. "Vis baptizari?" *Culture* 24 (1963): 250–73.

Mériz, Diana Teresa. "Encore une fois *pleine sa hanste*." *Romania* 94 (1973): 549–54.

Mermier, Guy R. "More About the Unity of the *Song of Roland*." *Olifant* 2, no. 2 (1974): 91–108.

———. "The *Chanson de Roland*'s Mysterious AOI." *The Michigan Academician* 5 (1973): 481–91.

Micha, Alexandre. "Le discours collectif dans l'épopée et dans le roman." *Mélanges Jean Frappier*. Vol. 2. Pp. 811–21.

———. "L'épreuve de l'épée." *Romania* 70 (1948): 37–50.

Michener, James A. *Kent State: What Happened and Why*. New York: Random House, 1971.

Mickel, Emanuel J., Jr. "Parallels in Prudentius' *Psychomachia* and *La Chanson de Roland*." *Studies in Philology* 67 (1970): 439–52.

Migne, Jacques-Paul. *Patrologiae cursus completus.... Series latina*. 221 vols. Paris: Migne, 1884–91.

Millet, Gabriel. *Recherches sur l'iconographie de l'évangile au XIVe et XVe siècles d'après les monuments de Mistra, de la Macédoine et du Mont-Athos*. 1916; rpt. Paris: Boccard, 1960.

Minis, Cola. "Über Rolands Horn, Burgers Passio Rotolandi und Konrads Roland." *Mélanges de linguistique et de littérature romanes à la mémoire d'István Frank, offerts par ses anciens maîtres, ses amis et ses collègues de France et de l'étranger*. Annales Universitatis Saravienses 6. Saarbrücken: Universität des Saarlandes, 1957. Pp. 439–53.

Mireaux, Emile. *La Chanson de Roland et l'Histoire de France*. Les chefs-d'oeuvre et l'histoire. Paris: Michel, 1943.

Moldenke, Harold N. and Alma L. *Plants of the Bible*. Waltham: Chronica Botanica, 1952.

Mommsen, Theodor E. "Petrarch's Conception of the 'Dark Ages'." *Speculum* 17 (1942): 226–42.

Münzel, Gustav. *Der Skulpturenzyklus in der Vorhalle des Freiburger Münsters*. Freiburg im Breisgau: Rombach, 1959.

Muscatine, Charles. *Chaucer and the French Tradition: A Study in Style and Meaning*. Berkeley and Los Angeles: University of California Press, 1957.

———. "Locus of Action in Medieval Narrative." *Romance Philology* 17 (1963): 115–22.

Nemetz, Anthony. "Literalness and *Sensus Litteralis*." *Speculum* 34 (1959): 76–89.

Nichols, Stephen G., Jr. *Formulaic Diction and Thematic Composition in the Chanson de Roland*. University of North Carolina Studies in the Romance Languages and Literatures 36. Chapel Hill: University of North Carolina Press, 1961.

———. "Historical Illusion and Poetic Reality in the 'Chansons de geste'." *French Review* 43 (1969): 23–33.

———. "Roland's Echoing Horn." *Romance Notes* 5 (1963): 78–84.

———. "The Interaction of Life and Literature in the 'Peregrinationes ad loca sancta' and the 'Chansons de geste'." *Speculum* 44 (1969): 51–77.

Nitze, William A. "Two Roland Passages: Verses 147 and 1723." *Romance Philology* 2 (1948/49): 233–37.

Noble, Peter. "Attitudes to Social Class as Revealed by Some of the Older Chansons de Geste." *Romania* 94 (1973): 359–85.

Noyer-Weidner, Alfred. "Vom biblischen 'Gottesberg' zur Symbolik des 'Heidentals' im *Rolandslied*." *Zeitschrift für französische Sprache und Literatur* 81 (1971): 13–71.

Nuccitelli, Angela. "Structural Devices: The Question of Analogues." Unpublished paper read at the Eighth Conference on Medieval Studies, Western Michigan University, 1973. Summary in *Olifant* 1, no. 1 (1973): 38–39.

Nykrog, Per. "La composition du *Roland* d'Oxford." *Romania* 88 (1967): 509–26.

Oakeshott, Walter F. *The Artists of the Winchester Bible*. London: Faber & Faber, 1945.

Oeuvres complètes de Rutebeuf. Eds. Edmond Faral and Julia Bastin. Fondation Singer-Polignac. 2 vols. Paris: Picard, 1959–60.

Offner, Richard. *A Critical and Historical Corpus of Florentine Painting*. 13 vols. New York: Institute of Fine Arts, New York University, 1930–69.

Oulmont, Charles. *Les Débats du clerc et du chevalier dans la littérature poétique du moyen-âge, étude historique et littéraire suivie de l'édition critique des textes*. Paris: Champion, 1911.

Ovid. Metamorphoses. Ed. and trans. Frank Justin Miller. The Loeb Classical Library. 2 vols. 1916; rpt. Cambridge: Harvard University Press; London: Heinemann, 1960.

Ovid. The Art of Love, and Other Poems. Ed. and trans. J. H. Mozley. The Loeb Classical Library. 1929; rpt. Cambridge: Harvard University Press; London: Heinemann, 1969.

Owen, D. D. R. "Charlemagne's Dreams, Baligant and Turoldus." *Zeitschrift für romanische Philologie* 87 (1971): 197–208.

———. "The Secular Inspiration of the *Chanson de Roland.*" *Speculum* 37 (1962): 390–400.

———. "Two More Romances by Chrétien de Troyes." *Romania* 92 (1971): 246–60.

Pächt, Otto. *The Rise of Pictorial Narrative in Twelfth-Century England.* Oxford: Clarendon Press, 1962.

Pächt, Otto, C. R. Dodwell, and Francis Wormald. *The St. Albans Psalter (Albani Psalter).* Studies of the Warburg Institute 25. London: Warburg Institute, 1960.

Panofsky, Erwin. *Renaissance and Renascences in Western Art.* Harper Torchbooks. New York and Evanston: Harper & Row, 1969.

———. *Tomb Sculpture.* New York: Abrams, 1964.

Panofsky, Erwin, and Fritz Saxl. "Classical Mythology in Medieval Art." *Metropolitan Museum Studies* 4 (1933): 228–80.

Paris, Gaston. *Extraits de la Chanson de Roland.* 3d ed. Paris: Hachette, 1891.

———. *Histoire poétique de Charlemagne.* 1865; rpt. Paris: Bouillon, 1905.

———. *La Poésie du moyen âge, première série.* 4th ed. Paris: Hachette, 1899.

Parry, Milman. "Studies in the Epic Technique of Oral Verse-Making. I. Homer and Homeric Style." *Harvard Studies in Classical Philology* 41 (1930): 73–147.

Pauphilet, Albert. *Le Legs du moyen âge.* Melun: Librairie d'Argences, 1950.

———. "Sur la *Chanson de Roland.*" *Romania* 59 (1933): 161–98.

Payen, Jean-Charles. "De la tradition à l'écriture: à propos d'un livre récent." *Le Moyen Age* 75 (1969): 529–39.

———. "Encore le problème de la géographie épique." *Société Rencesvals. IVe Congrès International.* Pp. 261–66.

———. *Le Motif du repentir dans la littérature française médiévale (Des origines à 1230).* Publications romanes et françaises 98. Geneva: Droz, 1968.

———. *Le Moyen Age.* Vol. 1. *Des origines à 1300.* Littérature française. Gen. ed. Claude Pichois. Paris: Arthaud, 1970.

Peebles, Rose J. "The Children in the Tree." *Medieval Studies in Memory of Gertrude Schoepperle Loomis.* New York: Columbia University Press; Paris: Champion, 1927. Pp. 285–99.

Pelan, Margaret M. *L'Influence du Brut de Wace sur les romanciers français de son temps.* Paris: Droz, 1931.

Pellegrini, Silvio. "Iterazioni sinonimiche nella *Canzone di Rolando.*" *Studi mediolatini e volgari* 1 (1953): 155–65.

———. "L'ira di Gano." *Cultura Neolatina* 3 (1943): 157–66.

Perschmann, H. *Die Stellung von O in der Ueberlieferung des altfranzösischen Rolandsliedes: Eine textkritische Untersuchung.* Ausgaben und Abhandlungen aus dem Gebiete der romanischen Philologie 3. Marburg: Pfeil, 1880.

Petersen, Holger. "Trois versions inédites de la légende de Saint Eustache en vers français." *Romania* 48 (1922): 365–402.

Picciotto, Robert S. "Marsile's Right Hand." *Romance Notes* 7 (1966): 207–8.

Pickering, F. P. *Literature and Art in the Middle Ages.* Coral Gables: University of Miami Press, 1970.

Piehler, Paul. *The Visionary Landscape: A Study in Medieval Allegory.* London: Arnold, 1971.

Piramus et Tisbé, poème du XIIe siècle. Ed. C. de Boer. Classiques français du moyen âge 26. Paris: Champion, 1921.

Pirenne, Henri. *Economic and Social History of Medieval Europe.* Trans. I. E. Clegg. New York: Harcourt Brace, [c. 1956].

Politzer, Robert L. "Synonymic Repetition in Late Latin and Romance." *Language* 37 (1961): 484–87.

Pope, Mildred K. *From Latin to Modern French with Especial Consideration of Anglo-Norman: Phonology and Morphology.* 2d ed. Manchester: Manchester University Press, 1952.

Potter, Murray A. *Sohrab and Rustem, the Epic Theme of a Combat Between Father and Son: A Study of its Genesis and Use in Literature and Popular Tradition.* London: Nutt, 1902.

Powicke, Sir Maurice. *The Thirteenth Century 1216–1307.* 2d ed. The Oxford History of England 4. Oxford: Clarendon Press, 1962.

Pratt, Robert A. "The Old French Sources of the Nonnes Preestes Tale." *Speculum* 47 (1972): 422–44, 648–68.

Prinet, Max. "Le langage héraldique dans le *Tournoiement Antechrist.*" *Bibliothèque de l'Ecole des Chartes* 83 (1922): 43–53.

Prioult, A. "Au sujet des notions géographiques de Turold." *Les Lettres Romanes* 2 (1948): 287–95.

Proverbes français antérieurs au XVe siècle. Ed. Joseph Morawski. Classiques français du moyen âge 47. Paris: Champion, 1925.

Prudence. Psychomachie. Ed. and trans. Maurice Lavarenne. Paris: Les Belles Lettres, 1948.

Prudentius. Ed. and trans. H. J. Thomson. The Loeb Classical Library. 2 vols. 1949; rpt. Cambridge: Harvard University Press; London: Heinemann, 1962.

Rabelais, François. *Gargantua.* Ed. M. A. Screech. Textes littéraires français 163. Geneva: Droz; Paris: Minard, 1970.

———. *Pantagruel.* Ed. Verdun L. Saulnier. Textes littéraires français. Paris: Droz, 1946.

Randall, Lilian M. C. *Images in the Margins of Gothic Manuscripts.* California Studies in the History of Art 4. Berkeley and Los Angeles: University of California Press, 1966.

Raoul de Cambrai, chanson de geste. Eds. Paul Meyer and Auguste Longnon. Société des anciens textes français. Paris: Didot, 1882.

Rathofer, Johannes. "Der 'wunderbare Hirsch' der Minnegrotte." *Zeitschrift für deutsches Altertum* 95 (1966): 27–42.

Raynaud de Lage, Guy. "Les romans antiques et la représentation de l'Antiquité." *Le Moyen Age* 68 (1961): 247–91.

Readings in Medieval Rhetoric. Eds. Joseph M. Miller, Michael H. Prosser, and Thomas W. Benson. Bloomington and London: Indiana University Press, 1973.

Reallexicon zur deutschen Kunstgeschichte. Eds. Otto Schmitt et al. Stuttgart: Metzler (also Druckenmüller); Munich: Druckenmüller, 1937–

Réau, Louis. *Histoire de la peinture au moyen âge: La miniature.* Melun: Librairie d'Argences, 1946.

———. *Iconographie de l'art chrétien.* 3 parts in 6 vols. Paris: Presses Universitaires de France, 1955–59.

Recueil général et complet des fabliaux des XIIIe et XIVe siècles imprimés ou inédits, publiés d'après les manuscrits. Eds. Anatole de Montaiglon and Gaston Raynaud. 6 vols. Paris: Librairie des bibliophiles, 1872–90.

Rémy, Paul. "Jeu parti et roman breton." *Mélanges Maurice Delbouille.* Vol. 2. Pp. 545–61.

Renoir, Alain. "Roland's Lament: Its Meaning and Function in the *Song of Roland.*" *Speculum* 35 (1960): 572–83.

Rice, David Talbot. *A Concise History of Painting From Prehistory to the Thirteenth*

Century. Praeger World of Art. New York and Washington, D.C.: Praeger, 1968.
Rice, Eugene F. *The Renaissance Idea of Wisdom*. Harvard Historical Monographs 37. Cambridge: Harvard University Press, 1958.
Richthofen, Erich von. "El lugar de la batalla en la Canción de Roldán, la leyenda de Otger Catalò y el nombre de Cataluña." *Revista de Filología Española* 38 (1954): 282–88.
———. "Style and Chronology of the Early Romance Epic." *Saggi e ricerche in memoria di Ettore Li Gotti*. Palermo: Centro di studi filologici e linguistici siciliani, 1962.
Rindone, Rachel P. "An Observation on the Dating of the Baligant Episode in the *Chanson de Roland*." *Romance Notes* 11 (1969): 181–85.
Riquer, Martín de. *Les Chansons de geste françaises*. Trans. Irénée-Marcel Cluzel. 2d ed. Paris: Nizet, 1957.
———. "Un problema en la *Chanson de Roland*." *Revista de Literatura* [Madrid] 5 (1954): 9–20.
Roach, Eleanor. "Les termes 'roman' et 'gothique' dans le domaine littéraire: Essai de définition." *Les Lettres Romanes* 29 (1975): 59–65.
Robb, Daniel M. *The Art of the Illuminated Manuscript*. South Berwick and New York: Barnes; London: Yoseloff, 1973.
Robertson, D. W., Jr. *A Preface to Chaucer: Studies in Medieval Perspectives*. Princeton: Princeton University Press, 1962.
———. "Some Medieval Literary Terminology with Special Reference to Chrétien de Troyes." *Studies in Philology* 48 (1951): 669–92.
———. "The Doctrine of Charity in Mediaeval Literary Gardens: A Topical Approach Through Symbolism and Allegory." *Speculum* 26 (1951): 24–49.
———. "The Idea of Fame in Chrétien's *Cligés*." *Studies in Philology* 69 (1972): 414–33.
———. *The Literature of Medieval England*. New York: McGraw-Hill, 1970.
Robson, C. A. "Aux origines de la poésie romane: art narratif et mnémotechnique." *Le Moyen Age* 67 (1961): 41–84.
———. "The Character of Turpin in the *Chanson de Roland*." *Medium Aevum* 10 (1941): 97–100.
Rodriguez, Dom Abundio, O.S.B., and Dom Luis-Maria de Lojendio, O.S.B. *Castille romane*. Trans. Norbert Vaillant, O.S.B. La nuit des temps 23. 2 vols. La Pierre-qui-vire: Les Presses monastiques, 1966.
Rogers, Katherine M. *The Troublesome Helpmate: A History of Misogyny in Literature*. Seattle and London: University of Washington Press, 1966.
Rohlfs, Gerhard. "Ci conte de Durendal l'espee." *Mélanges Rita Lejeune*. Vol. 2. Pp. 859–69.
Roncaglia, Aurelio. Comment on Imbs, "Quelques aspects du vocabulaire des plus anciennes chansons de geste." *La Technique littéraire des chansons de geste*. P. 73.
———. "Les quatre eschielles de Rollant." *Cultura Neolatina* 21 (1961): 191–205.
———. "Sarraguce, ki est en une muntaigne." *Studi in onore di Angelo Monteverdi*. Modena: Società tip. editrice modenese, 1959. Vol. 2. Pp. 629–40.
Roques, Mario. "*Entre les dous furceles (Roland*, vv. 1294 et 2249)." *Studies in French Language and Mediaeval Literature Presented to Professor Mildred K. Pope by Pupils, Colleagues, and Friends*. Manchester: University Press, 1939. Pp. 321–28.
———. "L'attitude du héros mourant dans la *Chanson de Roland*." *Romania* 66 (1940): 355–66.
———. "Les anges exterminateurs de Perceval." *Fin du moyen âge et Renaissance: Mélanges de philologie française offerts à M. Robert Guiette*. Antwerp: De Nederlandsche Boeckhandel, 1961. Pp. 1–4.
———. "Pour le commentaire d'*Aucassin et Nicolette* 'esclairier le cuer'." *Mélanges Ferdinand Lot*. Pp. 723–36.

Rosenberg, Bruce A. *Custer and the Epic of Defeat.* University Park and London: Pennsylvania State University Press, 1974.

Rosenberg, S. N. Critique of Vesce, "Reflections on the Epic Quality of *Ami et Amile: Chanson de Geste.*" *Olifant* 3, no. 3 (1976): 221–25.

Rosenthal, Joel T. *The Purchase of Paradise: Gift-Giving and the Aristocracy 1307–1485.* Studies in Social History. London: Routledge and Paul; Toronto: University of Toronto Press, 1972.

Ross, D. J. A. "Gautier del Hum: an Historical Element in the *Chanson de Roland?*" *Modern Language Review* 61 (1966): 409–15.

———. "L'originalité de 'Turoldus': le maniement de la lance." *Cahiers de civilisation médiévale* 6 (1963): 127–38.

———. "Pleine sa hanste." *Medium Aevum* 20 (1951): 1–10.

Rouillard, Clarence D. *The Turk in French History, Thought and Literature (1520–1660).* Paris: Boivin, [1941].

Rousset, Paul. "La croyance en la justice immanente à l'époque féodale." *Le Moyen Age* 54 (1948): 225–48.

———. "L'idéal chevaleresque dans deux *Vitae* clunisiennes." *Mélanges Edmond-René Labande.* Pp. 623–33.

Ruggieri, Ruggero M. *Il processo di Gano nella "Chanson de Roland."* Florence: Sansoni, 1936.

———. "L'épisode d'Abisme dans la *Chanson de Roland.*" Unpublished paper read at the Fifth International Congress of the Société Rencesvals, Oxford, 1970. Summary in *Bulletin bibliographique de la Société Rencesvals* 6 (1971): 151–52, item 474.

Rumpler, Marguerite. *L'Art roman en Alsace.* Les Cahiers techniques de l'art. Strasbourg: Le Tilleul, 1965.

Runciman, Steven. *A History of the Crusades.* 3 vols. Cambridge: University Press, 1951–54.

Russell, J. C. "The *Chanson de Roland:* Written in Spain in 1093?" *Studies in Philology* 49 (1952): 17–24.

Rütten, Raimund. *Symbol und Mythus im altfranzösischen Rolandslied.* Archiv für das Studium der neueren Sprachen und Literaturen 4. Braunschweig: Westermann, 1970.

Rychner, Jean. "A propos de l'article de M. André Burger 'La légende de Roncevaux avant la *Chanson de Roland*'." *Romania* 72 (1951): 239–46.

———. *La Chanson de geste: Essai sur l'art épique des jongleurs.* Société de publications romanes et françaises 53. Geneva: Droz; Lille: Giard, 1955.

———. "Observations sur la versification du 'Couronnement de Louis'." *La Technique littéraire des chansons de geste.* Pp. 161–82.

Saint Augustine: On Christian Doctrine. Trans. D. W. Robertson, Jr. Library of Liberal Arts 80. New York: Liberal Arts Press, 1958.

Saltzman, Louis F. *Building in England, Down to 1540: A Documentary History.* Oxford: Clarendon Press, 1952.

Samaran, Charles. "Sur la date approximative du *Roland* d'Oxford." *Romania* 94 (1973): 523–27.

Sargent, Barbara N. "The Laisses Similaires in the *Song of Roland.*" Unpublished paper read at the Kentucky Foreign Language Conference, 1968. Summary in *Bulletin bibliographique de la Société Rencesvals* 5 (1970): 46, item 90.

Scholes, Robert, and Robert Kellogg. *The Nature of Narrative.* New York: Oxford University Press, 1966.

Schramm, Percy Ernst. *Sphaira, Globus, Reichsapfel: Wanderung und Wandlung eines Herrschaftszeichens von Caesar bis zu Elisabeth II; ein Beitrag zum 'Nachleben' der Antike.* Stuttgart: Hiersemann, 1958.

Schultz, Alvin H. "*Roland,* v. 337." *MLN* 62 (1937): 456–61.

Schweitzer, E. C., Jr. "'Mais qu'il seit entendut': Ganelon's and Naimon's Speeches at the Council of the French in the *Chanson de Roland*." *Romance Notes* 12 (1971): 428–34.

Self and Society in Medieval France: The Memoirs of Abbot Guibert of Nogent (1064?–c. 1125). Trans. C. C. Swinton Bland. Revised by John F. Benton. New York and Evanston: Harper & Row, 1970.

Sepet, Marius. *Un Drame religieux au moyen âge: Le Miracle de Théophile.* Paris: Retaux-Bray, 1894.

Sextus Empiricus. Ed. and trans. Rev. R. G. Bury. The Loeb Classical Library. 4 vols. 1933; rpt. Cambridge: Harvard University Press; London: Heinemann, 1949.

Sheeran, Francis. "The Demise of a Genre: The Medieval Debate and *Dives and Pauper*." Unpublished paper read at the Seventh Conference on Medieval Studies, Western Michigan University, 1972.

Sholod, Barton. *Charlemagne in Spain: The Cultural Legacy of Roncesvalles.* Geneva: Droz, 1966.

Short, Ian. "A Note on Our Eponymous Horn." *Olifant* 3, no. 4 (1976): 259–61.

———. "Postscript to the Savernake Horn." *Olifant* 4, no. 2 (1976): 87–88.

———. "Roland's Final Combat." *Cultura Neolatina* 30 (1970): 135–55.

———. "The Oxford Manuscript of the *Chanson de Roland*: A Paleographical Note." *Romania* 94 (1973): 221–31.

Silverstein, Theodore. "Allegory and Literary Form." *PMLA* 82 (1967): 28–32.

Simson, Otto Georg von. *The Gothic Cathedral: The Origins of Gothic Architecture and the Medieval Concept of Order.* London: Routledge and Paul, 1956.

Sittl, Carl. *Die Gebärden der Griechen und Römer.* Leipzig: Teubner, 1890.

Skidmore, Mark. *The Moral Traits of Christians and Saracens as Portrayed by the Chansons de geste.* Colorado College Publication. General series no. 203. Studies series no. 20. Colorado Springs, 1935.

Smail, R. C. *Crusading Warfare (1097–1193).* Cambridge: Cambridge University Press, 1956.

Smith, Alison Moore. "The Iconography of the Sacrifice of Isaac in Early Christian Art." *American Journal of Archeology* 26 (1922): 159–73.

Smith, E. Baldwin. *The Architectural Symbolism of Imperial Rome and the Middle Ages.* Princeton: Princeton University Press, 1956.

Smith, H. A. "La femme dans les chansons de geste." *Colorado College Studies* 9 (1901): 6–24; 10 (1903): 24–40.

Smith, L. M. *Cluny in the Eleventh and Twelfth Centuries.* London: Allan, 1930.

Smith, Sister Mary Frances, S.S.N.D. *Wisdom and Personification of Wisdom Occurring in Middle English Literature Before 1500.* Washington, D.C.: The Catholic University of America, 1935.

Société Rencesvals. IVe Congrès International. Heidelberg, 28 août–2 septembre 1967. Actes et Mémoires. Studia Romanica 14. Heidelberg: Winter, 1969.

Société Rencesvals pour l'étude des épopées romanes. VIe Congrès International (Aix-en-Provence, 29 août–4 septembre 1973). Actes. Aix-en-Provence: Imprimerie du Centre d'Aix, 1974.

Somville, Marilyn Feller. "L'art du chanteur au moyen âge." *Société Rencesvals. VIe Congrès International.* Pp. 287–302.

Southern, Richard William. *The Making of the Middle Ages.* New Haven: Yale University Press, 1961.

Spargo, John W. *Virgil the Necromancer.* Harvard Studies in Comparative Literature 10. Cambridge: Harvard University Press, 1934.

Spitzer, Leo. "Etudes d'anthroponymie française." *PMLA* 58 (1943): 589–93.

———. "Le vers 830 du *Roland*." *Romania* 68 (1944/45): 471–77.

———. "Pucelle." *Romania* 72 (1951): 100–7.

Steinmeyer, Karl-Josef. *Untersuchungen zur allegorischen Bedeutung der Träume im altfranzösischen Rolandslied.* Langue et Parole. Sprach- und Literaturstrukturelle Studien 5. Munich: Hueber, 1963.

Stenton, Doris Mary. *The English Woman in History.* London: Allen and Unwin; New York: Macmillan, 1957.

Stewart, Desmond. *Early Islam.* Great Ages of Man. New York: Time, 1967.

Stones, M. Alison. "Sacred and Profane Art: Secular and Liturgical Book-Illumination in the Thirteenth Century." *The Epic in Medieval Society: Aesthetic and Moral Values.* Ed. Harald Scholler. Tübingen: Niemeyer, 1977. Pp. 100–12.

Storey, C. "AOI in the *Chanson de Roland.*" *Essays Presented to C. M. Girdlestone.* Newcastle upon Tyne: University of Durham, 1960. Pp. 311–17.

Stowell, William A. "Personal Relationships in Medieval France." *PMLA* 28 (1913): 388–416.

Stranges, John A. "The Character and the Trial of Ganelon: A New Appraisal." *Romania* 96 (1975): 333–67.

———. "The Significance of Bramimonde's Conversion in the *Song of Roland.*" *Romance Notes* 16 (1974): 189–95.

Strohmayer, Henri. Review of Sepet, *Un Drame religieux au moyen âge. Romania* 23 (1894): 601–7.

Studi in onore di Italo Siciliano. Florence: Olschki, 1966.

Sturm, Sara. Review of Harrison, "A Feminist Look at the *Chanson de Roland.*" *Olifant* 3, no. 3 (1976): 228–9.

Sumberg, Lewis A. *La Chanson d'Antioche: étude historique et littéraire. Une chronique en vers français de la première Croisade par le Pèlerin Richard.* Paris: Picard, 1968.

Swarzenski, Hanns. *Monuments of Romanesque Art: The Art of Church Treasures in North-Western Europe.* Chicago: University of Chicago Press, 1954.

———. "Two Oliphants in the Museum." *Bulletin of the Museum of Fine Arts, Boston* 60 (1962): 27–45.

Taladoire, Barthélemy A. *Commentaires sur la mimique et l'expression corporelle du comédien romain.* Collection de la Faculté des lettres de l'Université de Montpellier 1. Montpellier: Déhan, 1951.

Tanquerey, F. J. "Ancien français *por les membres trenchier.*" *Romania* 64 (1938): 1–17.

Tavernier, Wilhelm. "Beiträge zur Rolandsforschung. I. Äneide, Pharsalia und Rolandsepos." *Zeitschrift für französische Sprache und Literatur* 36 (1910): 71–102.

Taylor, Archer. "The Gallows of Judas Iscariot." *Washington University Studies, Humanistic Series* 9, no. 2 (1922): 135–56.

The Attic Nights of Aulus Gellius. Ed. and trans. John C. Rolfe. The Loeb Classical Library. 3 vols. 1927; rpt. Cambridge: Harvard University Press; London: Heinemann, 1960–61.

The Bayeux Tapestry: A Comprehensive Survey. Gen. ed. Sir Frank Stenton. New York: Phaidon, 1957.

The Continuations of the Old French Perceval of Chrétien de Troyes. Ed. William Roach. Vol. 3, Pt. 2. Lucien Foulet. *Glossary of the First Continuation.* Philadelphia: American Philosophical Society, 1955.

The Didot-Perceval According to the Manuscripts of Modena and Paris. Ed. William Roach. Philadelphia: University of Pennsylvania Press, 1941.

The Jerusalem Bible. Gen. ed. Alexander Jones. Garden City: Doubleday, 1966.

The Life of Saint Alexis: An Old French Poem of the Eleventh Century. Ed. V. L. Dedeck-Héry. Publications of the Institute of French Studies. New York: Institute of French Studies, 1931.

The Liflade ant te passiun of Seinte Iuliene. Ed. S. R. T. O. d'Ardenne. Early English Text Society 248. London and New York: Oxford University Press, 1961.

The Medieval French Roman d'Alexandre. Vol. 2. *Version of Alexandre de Paris*. Eds. E. C. Armstrong, D. L. Buffum, B. Edwards, and L. F. H. Lowe. Elliott Monographs in the Romance Languages and Literatures 37. Princeton: Princeton University Press, 1937.

The Medieval French Roman d'Alexandre. Vol. 3. *Version of Alexandre de Paris. Variants and Notes to Branch I*. Ed. Alfred Foulet. Elliott Monographs in the Romance Languages and Literatures 38. Princeton: Princeton University Press; Paris: Presses Universitaires de France, 1949.

The Portable Medieval Reader. Eds. James Bruce Ross and Mary Martin McLaughlin. New York: Viking Press, 1949.

The Song of Roland: The Oxford Text. Trans. D. D. R. Owen. Unwin Books Classics 3. London: Unwin, 1972.

The Song of Roland. Trans. Dorothy L. Sayers. The Penguin Classics. Baltimore: Penguin, 1963.

The Song of Roland. Trans. Robert Harrison. Mentor Book. New York and Toronto: New American Library; London: New English Library, 1970.

The Vulgate Version of the Arthurian Romances. Ed. H. Oskar Sommer. Carnegie Institution of Washington 74. 8 vols. Washington, D.C.: Carnegie Institution, 1908–16.

The Works of Geoffrey Chaucer. Ed. F. N. Robinson. 2d ed. Boston: Houghton Mifflin, 1957.

The Year 1200: A Centennial Exhibition at the Metropolitan Museum of Art. Vol. 1. Konrad Hoffmann. *The Exhibition*. Vol. 2. *A Background Survey*. Ed. Florens Deuchler. The Cloisters Studies in Medieval Art 1 and 2. New York: The Metropolitan Museum of Art, 1970.

Thiébaux, Marcelle. "The Mouth of the Boar in Medieval Literature." *Romance Philology* 22 (1969): 281–99.

Thompson, Stith. *Motif Index of Folk Literature: A Classification of Narrative Elements in Folktales, Ballads, Myths, Fables, Mediaeval Romances, Exempla, Fabliaux, Jest-Books and Local Legends*. Revised and enlarged ed. 6 vols. Bloomington: Indiana University Press, 1955–58.

Tobler, Adolf, and Erhard Lommatzsch. *Altfranzösisches Wörterbuch*. Berlin: Weidmann; Wiesbaden: Steiner, 1925– .

Tuve, Rosemund. *Allegorical Imagery: Some Mediaeval Books and Their Posterity*. Princeton: Princeton University Press, 1966.

Uitti, Karl D. "Chrétien de Troyes' *Yvain*: Fiction and Sense." *Romance Philology* 22 (1969): 471–83.

———. *Story, Myth, and Celebration in Old French Narrative Poetry, 1050–1200*. Princeton: Princeton University Press, 1973.

Underwood, P. "The Fountain of Life in Manuscripts of the Gospel." *Dunbarton Oaks Papers* 5 (1950): 43–138.

Utley, Francis Lee. *The Crooked Rib: An Analytical Index to the Argument About Women in English and Scots Literature to the End of the Year 1568*. Columbus: Ohio State University Press, 1944.

Vance, Eugene. "Notes on the Development of Formulaic Language in Romance Poetry." *Mélanges René Crozet*. Vol. 1. Pp. 427–34.

———. *Reading the Song of Roland*. Landmarks in Literature. Englewood Cliffs, N.J.: Prentice-Hall, 1970.

———. "Spatial Structure in the *Chanson de Roland*." *MLN* 82 (1967): 604–23.

Van Emden, Wolfgang G. "Another Look at Charlemagne's Dreams in the *Chanson de Roland*." *French Studies* 28 (1974): 257–71.

———. "'E cil de France le cleiment a guarant': Roland, Vivien et le thème du guarant." *Société Rencesvals. VIe Congrès International*. Pp. 31–61. Also in *Olifant* 1, no. 4 (1974): 21–47.

Van Marle, Raimond. *Iconographie de l'art profane au moyen-âge et à la Renaissance*. 2 vols. The Hague: Nijhoff, 1931–32.

Vecchi, G. "La récitation chantée des chansons de geste." Unpublished paper read at the Second International Congress of the Société Rencesvals, Venice, 1961. Summary in *Bulletin bibliographique de la Société Rencesvals* 3 (1963): 108, item 280.

Venkeleer, Théo. *Rollant li proz: Contribution à l'histoire de quelques qualifications laudatives en français du moyen âge*. Paris: Champion, 1975.

Vermulen, Antonius J. *The Semantic Development of Gloria in Early-Christian Latin*. Nijmegen: Dekker & Van de Vegt, 1956.

Vesce, Thomas E. "Reflections on the Epic Quality of *Ami et Amile: Chanson de Geste*." *Mediaeval Studies* 35 (1973): 129–45.

Viarre, Simone. *L'Image et la pensée dans les 'Métamorphoses' d'Ovide*. Publications de la Faculté des lettres et sciences humaines de Paris. Série "Recherches" 22. Paris: Presses Universitaires de France, 1964.

Viller, Marcel, S.J. "Abraham." *Dictionnaire de spiritualité ascétique et mystique, doctrine et histoire*. Ed. Marcel Viller, S.J. Paris: Beauchesne, 1937– . Vol. 1. P. 110.

Vinaver, Eugene. *A la recherche d'une poétique médiévale*. Paris: Nizet, 1970.

———. "La mort de Roland." *Cahiers de civilisation médiévale* 7 (1964): 133–43.

———. "Note sur le vers 2900 de la *Chanson de Roland*." *Mélanges Rita Lejeune*. Vol. 2. Pp. 929–34.

———. "The Historical Method in the Study of Literature." *The Future of the Modern Humanities: The Papers Delivered at the Jubilee Congress of the Modern Humanities Research Association in August 1968*. Publications of the Modern Humanities Research Association 1. [Cambridge?]: Modern Humanities Research Association, 1969. Vol. 1. Pp. 86–105. Summary in *Bulletin bibliographique de la Société Rencesvals* 6 (1971): 87, item 339.

———. *The Rise of Romance*. New York and Oxford: Oxford University Press, 1971.

Vos, Marianne Cramer. "Aspects of Biblical Typology in *La Chanson de Roland*." Ph. D. dissertation, University of Rochester, 1970.

———. "Ganelon's 'Mortal Rage'." *Olifant* 2, no. 1 (1974): 15–26.

Voyage, quête, pèlerinage dans la littérature et la civilisation médiévales. Senefiance, no. 2. Cahiers du Cuer Ma. Aix-en-Provence: Cuer Ma [Université de Provence], 1976.

Wagner, Robert-Léon. *Les phrases hypothétiques commençant par 'si' dans la langue française, des origines à la fin du XVIe siècle*. Paris: Droz, 1939.

Walpole, Ronald N. "Humor and People in Twelfth-Century France." *Romance Philology* 11 (1958): 210–25.

———. "The *Nota Emilianense*: New Light (But How Much?) on the Origins of the Old French Epic." *Romance Philology* 10 (1956/57): 1–18.

Waltz, Matthias. *Rolandslied. Wilhelmslied. Alexiuslied: Zur Struktur und geschichtlichen Bedeutung*. Studia Romanica 9. Heidelberg: Winter, 1965.

Warren, F. W. "The Enamoured Moslem Princess in Orderic Vital and the French Epic." *PMLA* 29 (1914): 341–58.

Wartburg, Walther von. *Französisches etymologisches Wörterbuch*. Basel, Bonn, Leipzig, Tübingen (the latter only: Mohr), 1922– .

Waters, E. G. R. "Gleanings from MS. Digby 23." *Modern Language Review* 25 (1930): 95–99.

Wathelet-Willem, Jeanne. "L'épée dans les plus anciennes chansons de geste: Etude de vocabulaire." *Mélanges René Crozet*. Vol. 1. Pp. 435–49.

———. "Quelle est l'origine du tinel de Rainouart?" *Boletín de la Real Academia de Buenas Letras de Barcelona* 31 (1965/66): 355–64.

———. *Recherches sur la Chanson de Guillaume: Etudes accompagnées d'une édition.* Bibliothèque de la Faculté de philosophie et lettres de l'Université de Liège 210. 2 vols. Paris: Les Belles Lettres, 1975.

———. "Un lai de Marie de France: Les deux amants." *Mélanges Rita Lejeune.* Vol. 2. Pp. 1143–57.

Webster's Seventh New Collegiate Dictionary. Springfield, Mass.: G. & C. Merriam Company, 1972.

West, G. D. *An Index of Proper Names in French Arthurian Romances, 1150–1300.* University of Toronto Romance Series 15. Toronto: University of Toronto Press, 1969.

———. "The Description of Towns in Old French Verse Romances." *French Studies* 11 (1957): 50–59.

White, Julian E. "*La Chanson de Roland:* Secular or Religious Inspiration?" *Romania* 84 (1962): 398–408.

White, Lynn, Jr. *Medieval Technology and Social Change.* Oxford: Oxford University Press, 1964.

Whitehead, Frederick. "Charlemagne's Second Dream." *Olifant* 3, no. 3 (1976): 189–95.

Whitney, Marian P. "Queen of Mediaeval Virtues: Largesse." *Vassar Mediaeval Studies by Members of the Faculty of Vassar College.* Ed. Christabel Forsyth Fiske. New Haven: Yale University Press, 1923. Pp. 183–215.

Will, Robert. *Alsace romane.* La nuit des temps 22. La Pierre-qui-vire: Les Presses monastiques, 1965.

———. "Recherches iconographiques sur la sculpture romane en Alsace: Les représentations du Paradis." *Les Cahiers techniques de l'art* 1, no. 3 (1948): 29–80.

Wilmotte, Maurice. "La *Chanson de Roland* et la *Chançun de Willame.*" *Romania* 44 (1915/17): 55–86.

Wimsatt, W. K., Jr., and Monroe C. Beardsley. *The Verbal Icon: Studies in the Meaning of Poetry.* Lexington: University of Kentucky Press, 1954.

Woledge, Brian, J. Beard, C. H. M. Horton, and Ian Short. "La déclinaison des substantifs dans la *Chanson de Roland* (Recherches mécanographiques)." *Romania* 88 (1967): 145–74.

Woodruff, Helen. "The Illustrated Manuscripts of Prudentius." *Art Studies* (1929): 33–79.

Woods, William S. "*La Chanson de Roland,* Line 147." *Romance Philology* 5 (1951/52): 35–38.

———. "*Sarrazins Espans* in the *Roland,* vv. 269, 612, 2828." *Romance Studies Presented to W. Morton Dey.* Chapel Hill: University of North Carolina Press, 1950. Pp. 193–96.

———. "The Choice of Ganelon as a Messenger to the Pagans (*La Chanson de Roland,* Lines 274–336)." *Studies in Philology* 48 (1952): 707–16.

———. "The Symbolic Structure of *La Chanson de Roland.*" *PMLA* 65 (1950): 1247–62.

Wormald, Francis. *The Winchester Psalter with 134 Illustrations.* London: Miller and Medcalf, 1973.

Yedlicka, Brother Leo Charles. *Expressions of the Linguistic Area of Repentance and Remorse in Old French.* Catholic University Studies in Romance Languages and Literatures 27 [*sic,* for 28]. Washington, D.C.: Catholic University of America Press, 1945.

Zaal, J. W. B. "*A lei francesa*" *(Sainte Foy, v. 20): Etudes sur les chansons de saints gallo-romanes du XI*[e] *siècle*. Leiden: Brill, 1962.

Zumthor, Paul. "Etude typologique des planctus contenus dans la *Chanson de Roland*." *La Technique littéraire des chansons de geste*. Pp. 219–35.

———. *Histoire littéraire de la France médiévale (VI*[e]*–XIV*[e] *siècle)*. Paris: Presses Universitaires de France, 1954.

———. *Langue et techniques poétiques à l'époque romane (XI*[e]*–XIII*[e] *siècles)*. Bibliothèque française et romane. Série C: Etudes littéraires 4. Paris: Klincksieck, 1963.

———. "Les *planctus* épiques." *Romania* 84 (1963): 61–69.

———. "Rhétorique et langage poétique dans le moyen âge roman." *Poetyka* [First International Conference on Work-in-Progress Devoted to Problems of Poetics, Warsaw, 18–27 August 1960]. Warsaw: Państwowe Wydawnictwo Naukowe; The Hague: Mouton, 1961. Pp. 745–54.

Picture Credits

Alinari: 11; Anderson-Giraudon: 60; Archives Photographiques, Paris/S.P.A.D.E.M.: 3, 4 (Martin-Sabon), 5, 16 (Gudiol), 19, 21, 22, 24 (Gudiol), 28 (Martin-Sabon), 30 (Gudiol), 31, 37, 47 (Gudiol), 49, 52, 62; Bayerische Staatsbibliothek, Munich: 20, 34; Bibliothek der Rijksuniversiteit, Utrecht: 45; Bibliothèque de l'Arsenal, Paris: 35 (Lalance); Bibliothèque Municipale, Autun: 53 (Varlez); Bibliothèque Nationale, Paris: 12, 39; Bildarchiv Foto Marburg: 1, 2, 15, 23; Bodleian Library, Oxford: 14; British Library Board: 27, 38, 46, 50, 57; The Dean and Chapter, Winchester: 33 (Sollars); Dumbarton Oaks Collection, Washington, D.C.: 8; Foto Toso, Venice: 9, 10; Herzog August Bibliothek, Wolfenbüttel: 64; Joachim E. Gaehde: 25; Landesbibliothek, Karlsruhe: 36; Musée de Strasbourg: 17, 42 (Franz); Musée d'Unterlinden, Colmar: 13; Musées Nationaux, Paris: 59; The Pennsylvania State University: 29, 44, 58, 65; Skira: 56; Universitätsbibliothek, Heidelberg: 6, 7, 18, 32, 40, 41, 43, 48, 51, 54, 55, 63; Zodiaque: 26 (Simonin), 61, 66

Index

Page numbers preceded by 2: refer to Volume II; all other references are to Volume I.

1. Virgin and Child. Embossed gold, filigree, precious stones, enamel, and gilded copper, c. 1100. Essen Minster.

2. Otto II Christomimetes. Gospel Book of Otto II, c. 973. Cathedral of Aachen.

3. Christ in Glory. Wall painting covering the apse, c. 1100. Monastic chapel, Berzé-la-Ville.

4. The Last Supper. Tympanum, c. 1140. Church of Saint-Fortunat, Charlieu.

5. Bishop Odo saying grace. Detail of the Bayeux Tapestry, late eleventh century. Former Bishop's Palace facing the cathedral of Notre-Dame, Bayeux.

6. Archbishop Turpin administering holy communion to the Twelve Peers. Pen-and-ink drawing, *Rolandslied*, c. 1180–90. Heidelberg, Universitätsbibliothek, Pal. germ. 112, fol. 47.

7. Archbishop Turpin blessing the Twelve Peers. Pen-and-ink drawing, *Rolandslied*, c. 1180–90. Heidelberg, Universitätsbibliothek, Pal. germ. 112, fol. 53.

8. The Communion of the Apostles. Silver patten from Riha, 565–78. Dumbarton Oaks Collection, Washington.

9. Scene from the *Song of Roland*. Historiated initial, early fourteenth century. Venice, Biblioteca Marciana, MS. 225 (= Venice IV), fol. 69.

10. King Agolant crowning his son Eaumont. Historiated initial, early fourteenth century. Venice, Biblioteca Marciana, MS. 225 (= *Aspremont*), fol. 1.

11. The Coronation of the Virgin by Turone. Detail of a polyptych, 1360. Museum, Verona.

12. The Death of Roland. Miniature, French translation of the *Pseudo-Turpin Chronicle* in *Les Grandes Chroniques de France*, 1375–79. Paris, Bibliothèque Nationale, f. fr. 2813, fol. 122.

13. Abraham's Bosom. Console from the abbey church of Alspach, twelfth century. Musée d'Unterlinden, Colmar.

14. Cuthbert prophesying. Durham Life of Saint Cuthbert, early twelfth century. Oxford, Bodleian Library, University College MS. 165, fol. 41.

15. *Left:* Scenes from Genesis; *right:* Scenes from the Life of Christ. Bronze doors of the chapel of Saint Anne, 1015. Cathedral of Hildesheim.

16. Stag hunt. Detail of the lintel of the second blind portal to the right of the main portal, c. 1120. Cathedral of Angoulême.

17. The Annunciation to the Shepherds. Architrave from the cloister of the abbey church of Eschau, c. 1130. Musée de l'Oeuvre Notre-Dame, Strasbourg.

18. Roland lamenting over the slain Oliver. Detail of a mosaic from the cathedral of Brindisi, 1178. Destroyed, 1858. Copy by Schultz.

19. The Last Judgment. Tympanum, c. 1130. Church of Sainte-Foy, Conques.

20. The Microcosm. *Glossarium Salomonis*, 1158–65. Munich, Bayerische Staatsbibliothek, Clm. 13002, fol. 7.

21. Christ in Glory between the Four Living Creatures with the Twenty-Four Elders. Tympanum, c. 1115. Church of Saint-Pierre, Moissac.

22. *Left:* Roland attempting to break Durendal; *right:* Roland sounding the oliphant. Detail of the Charlemagne Window, early thirteenth century. Cathedral of Notre-Dame, Chartres.

23. View of the interior. Palace chapel of Charlemagne, late eighth century. Aachen.

24. Christ in Majesty. Tympanum and voussures, twelfth century. Church of Saint-Nicolas, Civray.

25. Scenes from the Life of Saint Paul. Bible of San Paolo Fuori le Mura, c. 870. Benedictine monastery of San Paolo fuori le mura, near Rome.

26. *Left:* Daniel in the Lions' Den; *right:* The Original Sin; *upper register:* The Angel carrying Habakkuk by the Hair to feed Daniel. Tympanum, twelfth century. Church of Saint-Gabriel.

27. Oliver riding to meet Charlemagne and Roland before Vienne. Miniature, *Girart de Vienne*, first half of the fourteenth century. London, British Museum, Royal MS. 20 D. XI, fol. 53.

28. La Communion du chevalier. Statues within an arcade, interior of the west portal, second half of the thirteenth century. Cathedral of Notre-Dame, Reims.

29. Avaritia's Chariot. *Hortus Deliciarum*, 1159–1205. Formerly in the Bibliothèque Municipale, Strasbourg. Destroyed, 1870. Straub and Keller, Supplément, pl. LI bis.

30. Scene from the Life of Saints Savinus and Cyprianus. Wall painting, early twelfth century. Abbey church of Saint-Savin-sur-Gartempe.

31. Harold's oath. Detail of the Bayeux Tapestry, late eleventh century. Former Bishop's Palace facing the cathedral of Notre-Dame, Bayeux.

32. Ganelon's oath. Pen-and-ink drawing, *Rolandslied*, c. 1180–90. Heidelberg, Universitätsbibliothek, Pal. germ. 112, fol. 32.

33. The Burial of Judas Maccabaeus. Winchester Bible, c. 1150–60. Winchester, Cathedral Library, Vol. 4, fol. 351.

34. Pagan gods. Remigius of Auxerre's *Commentary on Martianus Capella*, c. 1100. Munich, Bayerische Staatsbibliothek, Clm. 14271, fol. 11.

35. Charlemagne besieging a Saracen city. Historiated initial, French translation of the *Pseudo-Turpin Chronicle*, second half of the thirteenth century. Paris, Bibliothèque de l'Arsenal, Réserve, MS. 5201, fol. 189.

36. The Entry into Jerusalem. Gospel Book of Speyer, c. 1200. Karlsruhe, Landesbibliothek, Bruchsal 1, fol. 17.

37. Christ the Judge with the Assessors. Lintel, 1020. Church of Saint-Genis-des-Fontaines.

38. Joseph before Pharaoh. *Paraphrases of Aelfric*, first half of the eleventh century. London, British Museum, Cotton MS. Claudius B IV, fol. 65.

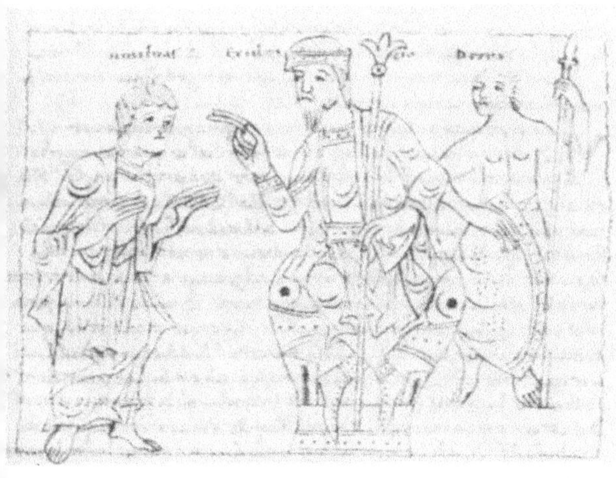

39. Humilitas before Exultatio. *Conflictus Virtutum et Vitiorum*, late eleventh century. Paris, Bibliothèque Nationale, MS. lat. 2077, fol. 164.

40. French council. Pen-and-ink drawing, *Rolandslied*, c. 1180–90. Heidelberg, Universitätsbibliothek, Pal. germ. 112, fol. 15.

41. Charlemagne appointing Ganelon as messenger to King Marsile. Pen-and-ink drawing, *Rolandslied*, c. 1180–90. Heidelberg, Universitätsbibliothek, Pal. germ. 112, fol. 19.

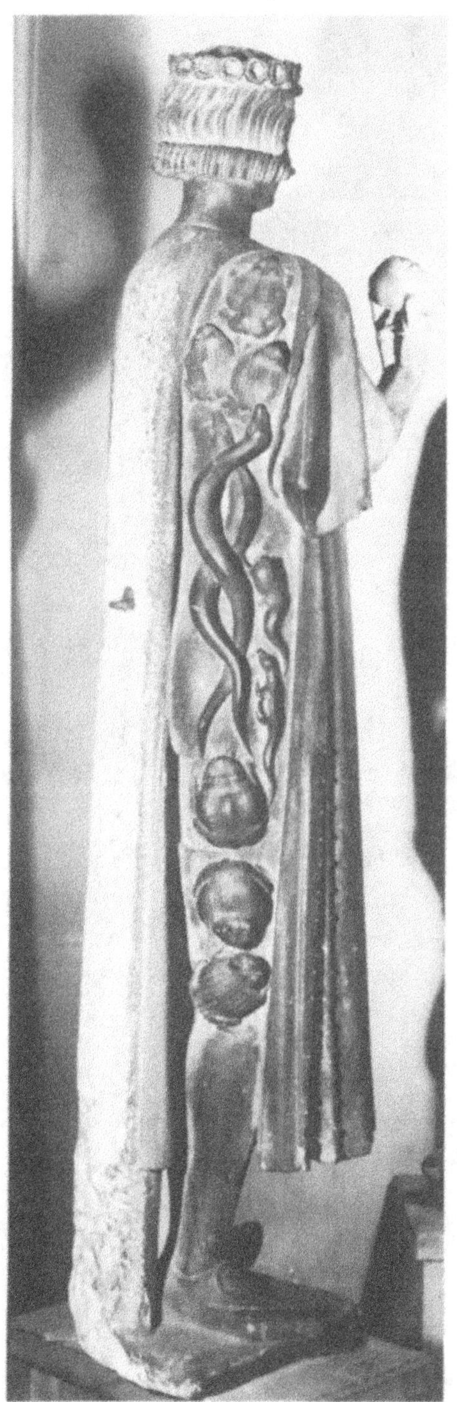

42. Satan the Tempter. Statue from the south portal of the cathedral of Notre-Dame, Strasbourg, 1280–85. Musée de l'Oeuvre Notre-Dame, Strasbourg.

gesellen. mit genelunes uol leiste. wande in sine
oge geiste. was ne heim truwe. uon ime chom
michel ruwe. er eruolte daz altsprochene wort.
ia ist gescrieben dort. under sconem schade

43. Der Pinrat. Pen-and-ink drawing, *Rolandslied*, c. 1180–90. Heidelberg, Universitätsbibliothek, Pal. germ. 112, fol. 26.

44. *Left:* Pride's Fall; *right:* Humility decapitating Pride. Illustration of the *Psychomachia* in the *Hortus Deliciarum*, 1159–1205. Formerly in the Bibliothèque Municipale, Strasbourg. Destroyed, 1870. Straub and Keller, pl. XLIII.

45. Illustration of Psalm 27. Utrecht Psalter, c. 832. Utrecht, Bibliothek der Rijksuniversiteit, MS. 32, fol. 15.

46. Illustration of Psalm 17. Canterbury Psalter, c. 1000. London, British Museum, Harley MS. 603, fol. 8.

47. View of the interior. Wall painting covering the barrel-vault of the nave, early twelfth century. Abbey church of Saint-Savin-sur-Gartempe.

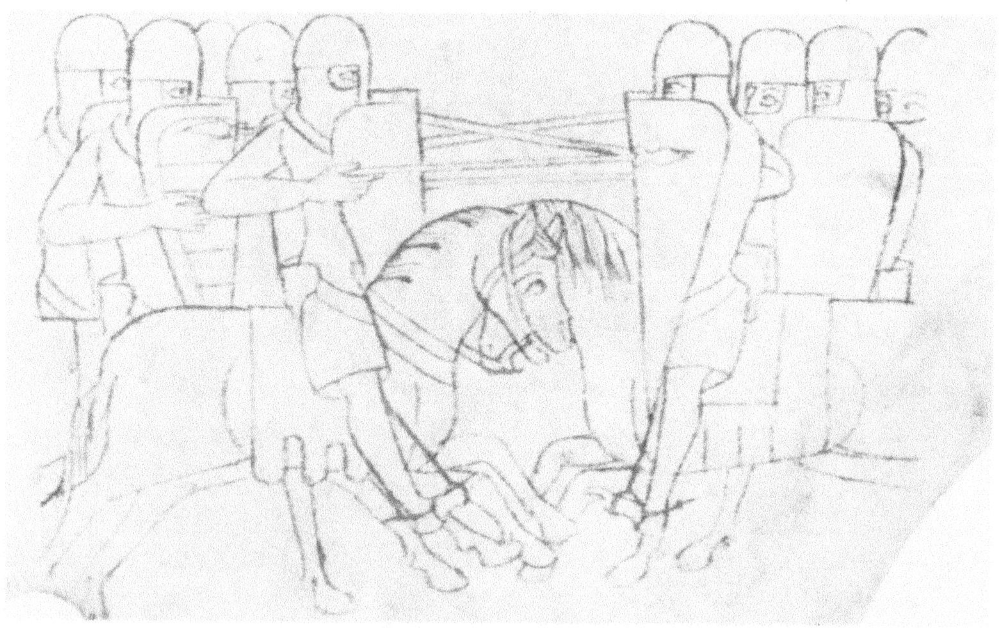

48. Battle scene. Pen-and-ink drawing, *Rolandslied*, c. 1180–90. Heidelberg, Universitätsbibliothek, Pal. germ. 112, fol. 63.

49. Border showing slain warriors. Detail of the Bayeux Tapestry, late eleventh century. Former Bishop's Palace facing the cathedral of Notre-Dame, Bayeux.

50. The Mouth of Hell. Psalter of Henry of Blois, c. 1150. London, British Museum, Cotton MS. Nero C. IV, fol. 39.

wertten. si uielen sam daz uihe zetal. si slugen

si uon dem wal. rechte sam di hunte si riefen

51. Roland in combat. Pen-and-ink drawing, *Rolandslied*, c. 1180–90. Heidelberg, Universitätsbibliothek, Pal. germ. 112, fol. 74.

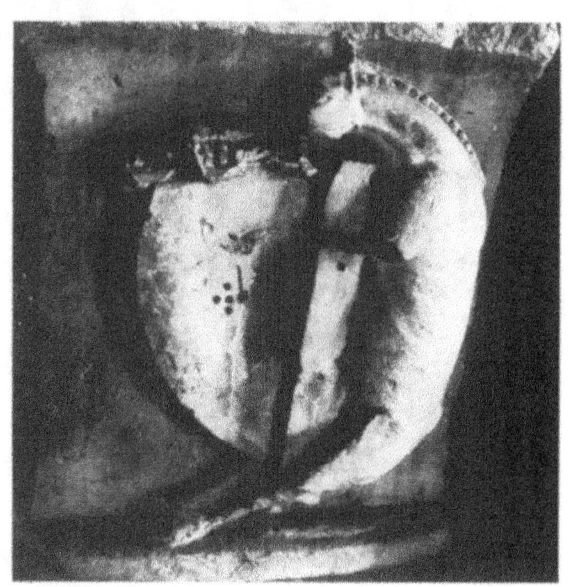

52. Donkey harper. Capital from the church of Saint-Sauveur, Nevers, early twelfth century. Musée de la Porte de Croux, Nevers.

53. Bishop Raganaldus blessing the people. Marmoutier Sacramentary, 844–45.
Autun, Bibliothèque Municipale, MS. 19 bis, fol. 173.

54. Roland carrying the slain Oliver. Detail of a mosaic from the cathedral of Brindisi, 1178. Destroyed, 1858. Copy by Schultz.

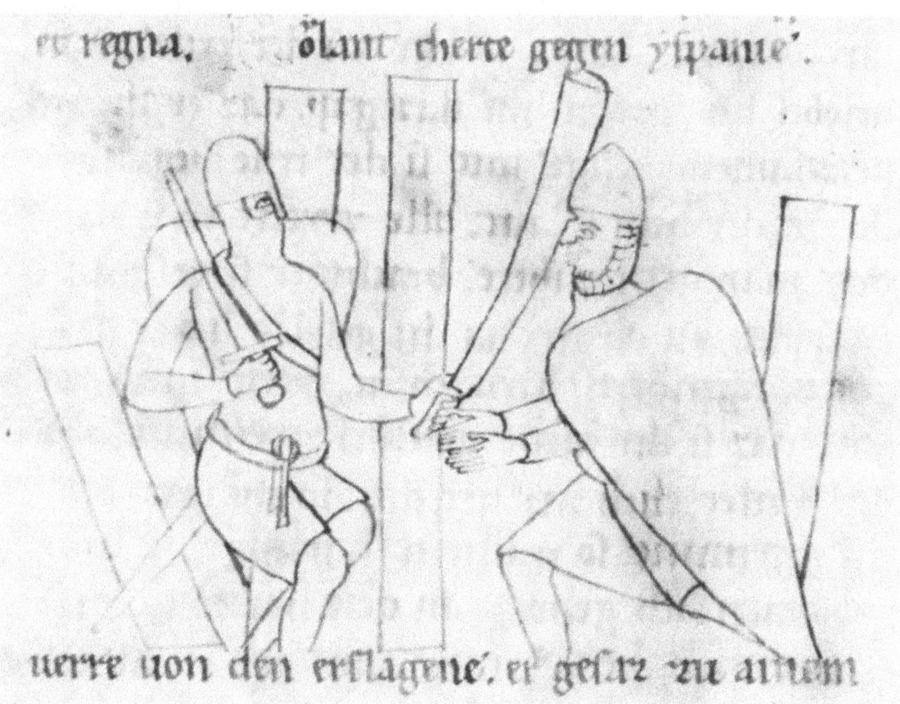

55. Roland slaying the Rash Saracen. Pen-and-ink drawing, *Rolandslied*, c. 1180–90. Heidelberg, Universitätsbibliothek, Pal. germ. 112, fol. 93.

56. Melchizedek and Abraham. Wall painting, c. 1255. Cathedral of Anagni.

57. The Crucifixion. New Minster of Winchester Psalter, c. 1060. London, British Museum, Arundel MS. 60, fol. 52.

58. Paradisus Voluptatis. *Hortus Deliciarum*, 1159–1205. Formerly in the Bibliothèque Municipale, Strasbourg. Destroyed, 1870. Straub and Keller, Supplément, pl. VIII bis.

59. Homage to the Emperor. Barberini Ivory, sixth century. Paris, Musée du Louvre.

60. *Center:* The Mission of the Apostles; *left:* Christ conferring the keys on a pope (Silvester?) and the labarum on Constantine; *right:* St. Peter conferring the oriflamme on Charlemagne and the pallium on Pope Leo III. Mosaic of the Lateran triclinium, c. 800, Rome. Restored, mid-eighteenth century.

61. Traditio Legis. Tympanum, twelfth century. Abbey church of Andlau.

62. The various peoples who are the object of the Mission of the Apostles. Detail of the central tympanum in the narthex, c. 1120–32. Abbey church of Sainte-Madeleine, Vézelay.

63. Bramimonde surrendering Saragossa to Charlemagne. Pen-and-ink drawing, *Rolandslied*, c. 1180–90. Heidelberg, Universitätsbibliothek, Pal. germ. 112, fol. 117.

64. The Death of the Virgin. Reichenau Lectionary, late tenth century. Wolfenbüttel, Herzog August Bibliothek, Cod. 84, 5 Aug., fol. 2.

65. Saint Paul baptizing the Ethiopian. *Hortus Deliciarum*, 1159–1205. Formerly in the Bibliothèque Municipale, Strasbourg. Destroyed, 1870. Straub and Keller, pl. XLII.

66. Saint Juliana pulling the devil by the hair. Bas-relief of the transept, twelfth century. Church of Santa Maria, Siones, near Burgos.

www.ingramcontent.com/pod-product-compliance
Lightning Source LLC
Chambersburg PA
CBHW070148120726
47909CB00001B/21
9780271024554